PROFESSIONAL
ANDROID™ 4 APPLICATION DEVEL

D0131622

PROFESSIONAL

Android™ 4 Application Development

PROFESSIONAL

Android™ 4 Application Development

Reto Meier

WILEY

John Wiley & Sons, Inc.

Professional Android™ 4 Application Development

Published by
John Wiley & Sons, Inc.
10475 Crosspoint Boulevard
Indianapolis, IN 46256
www.wiley.com

Copyright © 2012 by John Wiley & Sons, Inc., Indianapolis, Indiana

Published simultaneously in Canada

ISBN: 978-1-118-10227-5
ISBN: 978-1-118-22385-7 (ebk)
ISBN: 978-1-118-23722-9 (ebk)
ISBN: 978-1-118-26215-3 (ebk)

Manufactured in the United States of America

10 9 8 7 6 5 4

For general information on our other products and services please contact our Customer Care Department within the United States at (877) 762-2974, outside the United States at (317) 572-3993 or fax (317) 572-4002.

Wiley publishes in a variety of print and electronic formats and by print-on-demand. Some material included with standard print versions of this book may not be included in e-books or in print-on-demand. If this book refers to media such as a CD or DVD that is not included in the version you purchased, you may download this material at http://booksupport.wiley.com. For more information about Wiley products, visit www.wiley.com.

Library of Congress Control Number: 2011945019

To Kris

ABOUT THE AUTHOR

RETO MEIER grew up in Perth, Western Australia, and then lived in London for 6 years before moving to the San Francisco Bay Area in 2011.

Reto currently works as a Developer Advocate on the Android team at Google, helping Android developers create the best applications possible. Reto is an experienced software developer with more than 10 years of experience in GUI application development. Before coming to Google, he worked in various industries, including offshore oil and gas and finance.

Always interested in emerging technologies, Reto has been involved in Android since the initial release in 2007.

You can find out entirely too much about Reto's interests and hobbies on his web site, The Radioactive Yak (`http://blog.radioactiveyak.com`), or on Google+ (`http://profiles.google.com/reto.meier`) or Twitter (`www.twitter.com/retomeier`), where he shares more than he probably should.

ABOUT THE TECHNICAL EDITOR

DAN ULERY is a software engineer with experience in .NET, Java, and PHP development, as well as in deployment engineering. He graduated from the University of Idaho with a Bachelor of Science degree in computer science and a minor in mathematics.

CREDITS

ACKNOWLEDGMENTS

FIRST, I'D LIKE TO THANK KRISTY, whose love, patience, and understanding are pushed to new limits every time I forget what's involved in writing a book and agree to do another one. Your support makes everything I do possible.

A big thank you to my friends and colleagues at Google, particularly the Android engineers and my colleagues in developer relations. The pace at which Android grows makes life difficult for those of us who choose to write books, but the opportunities it creates for developers makes the stress and rewrites easy to bear.

I also thank Dan Ulery for his sharp eye and valuable insights; Robert Elliot and John Sleeva for their patience in waiting for me to get this book finished; San Dee Phillips; and the whole team at Wrox for helping to get it done.

A special shout-out goes out to the entire Android developer community. Your passion, hard work, and excellent applications have helped make Android the huge success that it is. Thank you.

CONTENTS

INTRODUCTION

THIS IS AN EXCITING TIME FOR ANDROID DEVELOPERS. Mobile phones have never been more popular; powerful smartphones are now a regular choice for consumers; and the Android ecosystem has expanded to include tablet and TV devices to further expand the audience of your Android applications.

Hundreds of stylish and versatile devices — packing hardware features such as GPS, accelerometers, NFC, and touch screens, combined with reasonably priced data plans — provide an enticing platform upon which to create innovative applications for all Android devices.

Android offers an open alternative for mobile application development. Without artificial barriers, Android developers are free to write applications that take full advantage of increasingly powerful mobile hardware and distribute them in an open market. As a result, developer interest in Android devices has exploded as handset sales have continued to grow. As of 2012, there are hundreds of handset and tablet OEMs, including HTC, Motorola, LG, Samsung, ASUS, and Sony Ericsson. More than 300 million Android devices have been activated, and that number is growing at a rate of over 850,000 activations every day.

Using Google Play for distribution, developers can take advantage of an open marketplace, with no review process, for distributing free and paid applications to all compatible Android devices. Built on an open-source framework, and featuring powerful SDK libraries, Android has enabled more than 450,000 applications to be launched in Google Play.

This book is a hands-on guide to building mobile applications using version 4 of the Android SDK. Chapter by chapter, it takes you through a series of sample projects, each introducing new features and techniques to get the most out of Android. It covers all the basic functionality to get started, as well as the information for experienced mobile developers to leverage the unique features of Android to enhance existing products or create innovative new ones.

Google's philosophy is to release early and iterate often. Since Android's first full release in December 2008, there have been 19 platform and SDK releases. With such a rapid release cycle, there are likely to be regular changes and improvements to the software and development libraries. While the Android engineering team works hard to ensure backward compatibility, future releases are likely to date some of the information provided in this book. Similarly, not all active Android devices will be running the latest platform release.

Wherever possible, I have included details on which platform releases support the functionality described, and which alternatives may exist to provide support for users of older devices. Further, the explanations and examples included will give you the grounding and knowledge needed to write compelling mobile applications using the current SDK, along with the flexibility to quickly adapt to future enhancements.

WHO THIS BOOK IS FOR

This book is for anyone interested in creating applications for the Android platform. It includes information that will be valuable, whether you're an experienced mobile developer or making your first foray, via Android, into writing mobile applications.

It will help if you have used smartphones (particularly phones running Android), but it's not necessary, nor is prior experience in mobile application development.

It's expected that you'll have some experience in software development and be familiar with basic object-oriented development practices. An understanding of Java syntax is a requirement, and detailed knowledge and experience is a distinct advantage, though not a strict necessity.

Chapters 1 and 2 introduce mobile development and contain instructions to get you started in Android. Beyond that, there's no requirement to read the chapters in order, although a good understanding of the core components described in Chapters 3–9 is important before you venture into the remaining chapters. Chapters 10 and 11 cover important details on how to create an application that provides a rich and consistent user experience, while Chapters 12–19 cover a variety of optional and advanced functionality and can be read in whatever order interest or need dictates.

WHAT THIS BOOK COVERS

Chapter 1 introduces Android, including what it is and how it fits into existing mobile development. What Android offers as a development platform and why it's an exciting opportunity for creating mobile phone applications are then examined in greater detail.

Chapter 2 covers some best practices for mobile development and explains how to download the Android SDK and start developing applications. It also introduces the Android Developer Tools and demonstrates how to create new applications from scratch.

Chapters 3–9 take an in-depth look at the fundamental Android application components. Starting with examining the pieces that make up an Android application and its lifecycle, you'll quickly move on to the application manifest and external resources before learning about "Activities," their lifetimes, and their lifecycles.

You'll then learn how to create basic user interfaces with layouts, Views, and Fragments, before being introduced to the Intent and Broadcast Receiver mechanisms used to perform actions and send messages between application components. Internet resources are then covered, followed by a detailed look at data storage, retrieval, and sharing. You'll start with the preference-saving mechanism and then move on to file handling, databases, and Cursors. You'll also learn how share application data using Content Providers and access data from the native Content Providers. This section finishes with an examination of how to work in the background using Services and background Threads.

Chapters 10 and 11 build on the UI lessons you learned in Chapter 4, examining how to enhance the user experience through the use of the Action Bar, Menu System, and Notifications. You'll learn how to make your applications display-agnostic (optimized for a variety of screen sizes and resolutions), how to make your applications accessible, and how to use speech recognition within your applications.

Chapters 12–18 look at more advanced topics. You'll learn how to use the compass, accelerometers, and other hardware sensors to let your application react to its environment, and then look at maps and location-based services. Next, you'll learn how your applications can interact with users directly from the home screen using dynamic Widgets, Live Wallpaper, and the Quick Search Box.

After looking at playing and recording multimedia, and using the camera, you'll be introduced to Android's communication capabilities. Bluetooth, NFC, Wi-Fi Direct, and network management (both Wi-Fi and mobile data connections) are covered, followed by the telephony APIs and the APIs used to send and receive SMS messages.

Chapter 18 discusses several advanced development topics, including security, IPC, Cloud to Device Messaging, the License Verification Library, and Strict Mode.

Finally, Chapter 19 examines the options and opportunities available for publishing, distributing, and monetizing your applications — primarily within Google Play.

HOW THIS BOOK IS STRUCTURED

This book is structured in a logical sequence to help readers of different development backgrounds learn how to write advanced Android applications. There's no requirement to read each chapter sequentially, but several of the sample projects are developed over the course of several chapters, adding new functionality and other enhancements at each stage.

Experienced mobile developers with a working Android development environment can skim the first two chapters — which are an introduction to mobile development and instructions for creating your development environment — and then dive in at Chapters 3–9. These chapters cover the fundamentals of Android development, so it's important to have a solid understanding of the concepts they describe.

With this covered, you can move on to the remaining chapters, which look at maps, location-based services, background applications, and more advanced topics, such as hardware interaction and networking.

WHAT YOU NEED TO USE THIS BOOK

To use the code samples in this book, you will need to create an Android development environment by downloading the Android SDK, developer tools, and the Java Development Kit. You may also want to download and install Eclipse and the Android Developer Tools plug-in to ease your development, but neither is a requirement.

Android development is supported in Windows, Mac OS, and Linux, with the SDK available from the Android web site.

You do not need an Android device to use this book or develop Android applications, though it can be useful — particularly when testing.

Chapter 2 outlines these requirements in more detail and describes where to download and how to install each component.

CONVENTIONS

To help you get the most from the text and keep track of what's happening, we've used a number of conventions throughout the book.

 The pencil icon indicates notes, tips, hints, tricks, and asides to the current discussion.

 Boxes with a warning icon like this one hold important, not-to-be forgotten information that is directly relevant to the surrounding text.

As for styles in the text:

➤ We show file names, URLs, and code within the text like so: `persistence.properties`.

➤ To help readability, class names in text are often represented using a regular font but capitalized like so: Content Provider.

➤ We present code in two different ways:

```
We use a monofont type with no highlighting for most code examples.
We use bold to emphasize code that is particularly important in the present context
or to show changes from a previous code snippet.
```

➤ In some code samples, you'll see lines marked as follows:

```
[ ... previous code goes here ... ]
```

or

```
[ ... implement something here ... ]
```

These represent instructions to replace the entire line (including the square brackets) with actual code, either from a previous code snippet (in the former case) or with your own implementation (in the latter).

➤ To keep the code samples reasonably concise, I have not always included every `import` statement required in the code samples. The downloadable code samples described below include all the required `import` statements. Additionally, if you are developing using Eclipse, you can use the keyboard shortcut Ctrl+Shift+O (Cmd+Shift+O) to insert the required `import` statements automatically.

SOURCE CODE

As you work through the examples in this book, you may choose either to type in all the code manually, or to use the source code files that accompany the book. All the source code used in this book is available for download at www.wrox.com. When at the site, simply locate the book's title (use the Search box or one of the title lists) and click the Download Code link on the book's detail page to obtain all the source code for the book. Code that is included on the web site is highlighted by the following icon:

Available for download on Wrox.com

Listings include the filename in the title. If it is just a code snippet, you'll find the filename in a code note such as this:

code snippet filename

> *Because many books have similar titles, you may find it easiest to search by ISBN; this book's ISBN is 978-1-118-10227-5.*

Once you download the code, just decompress it with your favorite compression tool. Alternately, you can go to the main Wrox code download page at www.wrox.com/dynamic/books/download .aspx to see the code available for this book and all other Wrox books.

ERRATA

We make every effort to ensure that there are no errors in the text or in the code. However, no one is perfect, and mistakes do occur. If you find an error in one of our books, like a spelling mistake or faulty piece of code, we would be very grateful for your feedback. By sending in errata, you may save another reader hours of frustration, and at the same time, you will be helping us provide even higher quality information.

To find the errata page for this book, go to www.wrox.com and locate the title using the Search box or one of the title lists. Then, on the book details page, click the Book Errata link. On this page, you can view all errata that has been submitted for this book and posted by Wrox editors. A complete book list, including links to each book's errata, is also available at www.wrox.com/misc-pages/ booklist.shtml.

If you don't spot "your" error on the Book Errata page, go to www.wrox.com/contact/techsupport.shtml and complete the form there to send us the error you have found. We'll check the information and, if appropriate, post a message to the book's errata page and fix the problem in subsequent editions of the book.

P2P.WROX.COM

For author and peer discussion, join the P2P forums at p2p.wrox.com. The forums are a Web-based system for you to post messages relating to Wrox books and related technologies and interact with other readers and technology users. The forums offer a subscription feature to e-mail you topics of interest of your choosing when new posts are made to the forums. Wrox authors, editors, other industry experts, and your fellow readers are present on these forums.

At http://p2p.wrox.com, you will find a number of different forums that will help you, not only as you read this book, but also as you develop your own applications. To join the forums, just follow these steps:

1. Go to p2p.wrox.com and click the Register link.

2. Read the terms of use and click Agree.

3. Complete the required information to join, as well as any optional information you wish to provide, and click Submit.

4. You will receive an e-mail with information describing how to verify your account and complete the joining process.

> *You can read messages in the forums without joining P2P, but in order to post your own messages, you must join.*

Once you join, you can post new messages and respond to messages other users post. You can read messages at any time on the Web. If you would like to have new messages from a particular forum e-mailed to you, click the Subscribe to This Forum icon by the forum name in the forum listing.

For more information about how to use the Wrox P2P, be sure to read the P2P FAQs for answers to questions about how the forum software works, as well as many common questions specific to P2P and Wrox books. To read the FAQs, click the FAQ link on any P2P page.

PROFESSIONAL

Android™ 4 Application Development

1

Hello, Android

WHAT'S IN THIS CHAPTER?

➤ A background of mobile application development

➤ What Android is (and what it isn't)

➤ An introduction to the Android SDK features

➤ Which devices Android runs on

➤ Why you should develop for mobile and Android

➤ An introduction to the Android SDK and development framework

Whether you're an experienced mobile engineer, a desktop or web developer, or a complete programming novice, Android represents an exciting new opportunity to write innovative applications for an increasingly wide range of devices.

Despite the name, Android will not help you create an unstoppable army of emotionless robot warriors on a relentless quest to cleanse the earth of the scourge of humanity. Instead, Android is an open-source software stack that includes the operating system, middleware, and key mobile applications, along with a set of API libraries for writing applications that can shape the look, feel, and function of the devices on which they run.

Small, stylish, and versatile, modern mobile devices have become powerful tools that incorporate touchscreens, cameras, media players, Global Positioning System (GPS) receivers, and Near Field Communications (NFC) hardware. As technology has evolved, mobile phones have become about much more than simply making calls. With the introduction of tablets and Google TV, Android has expanded beyond its roots as a mobile phone operating system, providing a consistent platform for application development across an increasingly wide range of hardware.

In Android, native and third-party applications are written with the same APIs and executed on the same run time. These APIs feature hardware access, video recording, location-based services, support for background services, map-based activities, relational databases, inter-application communication, Bluetooth, NFC, and 2D and 3D graphics.

This book describes how to use these APIs to create your own Android applications. In this chapter you'll learn some guidelines for mobile and embedded hardware development, as well as be introduced to some of the platform features available for Android development.

Android has powerful APIs, excellent documentation, a thriving developer community, and no development or distribution costs. As mobile devices continue to increase in popularity, and Android devices expand into exciting new form-factors, you have the opportunity to create innovative applications no matter what your development experience.

A LITTLE BACKGROUND

In the days before Twitter and Facebook, when Google was still a twinkle in its founders' eyes and dinosaurs roamed the earth, mobile phones were just that — portable phones small enough to fit inside a briefcase, featuring batteries that could last up to several hours. They did, however, offer the freedom to make calls without being physically connected to a landline.

Increasingly small, stylish, and powerful, mobile phones are now ubiquitous and indispensable. Hardware advancements have made mobiles smaller and more efficient while featuring bigger, brighter screens and including an increasing number of hardware peripherals.

After first including cameras and media players, mobiles now feature GPS receivers, accelerometers, NFC hardware, and high-definition touchscreens. These hardware innovations offer fertile ground for software development, but until relatively recently the applications available for mobile phones have lagged behind their hardware counterparts.

The Not-So-Distant Past

Historically, developers, generally coding in low-level C or C++, have needed to understand the specific hardware they were coding for, typically a single device or possibly a range of devices from a single manufacturer. As hardware technology and mobile Internet access has advanced, this closed approach has become outmoded.

Platforms such as Symbian were later created to provide developers with a wider target audience. These systems proved more successful in encouraging mobile developers to provide rich applications that better leveraged the hardware available.

Although these platforms did, and continue to, offer some access to the device hardware, they generally required developers to write complex C/C++ code and make heavy use of proprietary APIs that are notoriously difficult to work with. This difficulty is amplified for applications that must work on different hardware implementations and those that make use of a particular hardware feature, such as GPS.

In more recent years, the biggest advance in mobile phone development was the introduction of Java-hosted MIDlets. MIDlets are executed on a Java virtual machine (JVM), a process that abstracts the underlying hardware and lets developers create applications that run on the wide variety of devices that support the Java run time. Unfortunately, this convenience comes at the price of restricted access to the device hardware.

In mobile development, it was long considered normal for third-party applications to receive different hardware access and execution rights from those given to native applications written by the phone manufacturers, with MIDlets often receiving few of either.

The introduction of Java MIDlets expanded developers' audiences, but the lack of low-level hardware access and sandboxed execution meant that most mobile applications were regular desktop programs or websites designed to render on a smaller screen, and didn't take advantage of the inherent mobility of the handheld platform.

Living in the Future

Android sits alongside a new wave of modern mobile operating systems designed to support application development on increasingly powerful mobile hardware. Platforms like Microsoft's Windows Phone and the Apple iPhone also provide a richer, simplified development environment for mobile applications; however, unlike Android, they're built on proprietary operating systems. In some cases they prioritize native applications over those created by third parties, restrict communication among applications and native phone data, and restrict or control the distribution of third-party applications to their platforms.

Android offers new possibilities for mobile applications by offering an open development environment built on an open-source Linux kernel. Hardware access is available to all applications through a series of API libraries, and application interaction, while carefully controlled, is fully supported.

In Android, all applications have equal standing. Third-party and native Android applications are written with the same APIs and are executed on the same run time. Users can remove and replace any native application with a third-party developer's alternative; indeed, even the dialer and home screens can be replaced.

WHAT ANDROID ISN'T

As a disruptive addition to a mature field, it's not hard to see why there has been some confusion about what exactly Android is. Android is *not* the following:

➤ **A Java ME implementation** — Android applications are written using the Java language, but they are not run within a Java ME (Mobile Edition) VM, and Java-compiled classes and executables will not run natively in Android.

➤ **Part of the Linux Phone Standards Forum (LiPS) or the Open Mobile Alliance (OMA)** — Android runs on an open-source Linux kernel, but, while their goals are similar, Android's complete software stack approach goes further than the focus of these standards-defining organizations.

➤ **Simply an application layer (such as UIQ or S60)** — Although Android does include an application layer, "Android" also describes the entire software stack, encompassing the underlying operating system, the API libraries, and the applications themselves.

➤ **A mobile phone handset** — Android includes a reference design for mobile handset manufacturers, but there is no single "Android phone." Instead, Android has been designed to support many alternative hardware devices.

➤ **Google's answer to the iPhone** — The iPhone is a fully proprietary hardware and software platform released by a single company (Apple), whereas Android is an open-source software stack produced and supported by the Open Handset Alliance (OHA) and designed to operate on any compatible device.

ANDROID: AN OPEN PLATFORM FOR MOBILE DEVELOPMENT

Google's Andy Rubin describes Android as follows:

> *The first truly open and comprehensive platform for mobile devices. It includes an operating system, user-interface and applications — all of the software to run a mobile phone but without the proprietary obstacles that have hindered mobile innovation.*
>
> —WHERE'S MY GPHONE? *(http://googleblog.blogspot.com/2007/11/ wheres-my-gphone.html)*

More recently, Android has expanded beyond a pure mobile phone platform to provide a development platform for an increasingly wide range of hardware, including tablets and televisions.

Put simply, Android is an ecosystem made up of a combination of three components:

➤ A free, open-source operating system for embedded devices

➤ An open-source development platform for creating applications

➤ Devices, particularly mobile phones, that run the Android operating system and the applications created for it

More specifically, Android is made up of several necessary and dependent parts, including the following:

➤ A Compatibility Definition Document (CDD) and Compatibility Test Suite (CTS) that describe the capabilities required for a device to support the software stack.

➤ A Linux operating system kernel that provides a low-level interface with the hardware, memory management, and process control, all optimized for mobile and embedded devices.

➤ Open-source libraries for application development, including SQLite, WebKit, OpenGL, and a media manager.

➤ A run time used to execute and host Android applications, including the Dalvik Virtual Machine (VM) and the core libraries that provide Android-specific functionality. The run time is designed to be small and efficient for use on mobile devices.

➤ An application framework that agnostically exposes system services to the application layer, including the window manager and location manager, databases, telephony, and sensors.

➤ A user interface framework used to host and launch applications.

➤ A set of core pre-installed applications.

➤ A software development kit (SDK) used to create applications, including the related tools, plug-ins, and documentation.

What really makes Android compelling is its open philosophy, which ensures that you can fix any deficiencies in user interface or native application design by writing an extension or replacement. Android provides you, as a developer, with the opportunity to create mobile phone interfaces and applications designed to look, feel, and function exactly as you imagine them.

NATIVE ANDROID APPLICATIONS

Android devices typically come with a suite of preinstalled applications that form part of the Android Open Source Project (AOSP), including, but not necessarily limited to, the following:

➤ An e-mail client

➤ An SMS management application

➤ A full PIM (personal information management) suite, including a calendar and contacts list

➤ A WebKit-based web browser

➤ A music player and picture gallery

➤ A camera and video recording application

➤ A calculator

➤ A home screen

➤ An alarm clock

In many cases Android devices also ship with the following proprietary Google mobile applications:

➤ The Google Play Store for downloading third-party Android applications

➤ A fully featured mobile Google Maps application, including StreetView, driving directions, and turn-by-turn navigation, satellite views, and traffic conditions

➤ The Gmail email client

➤ The Google Talk instant-messaging client

➤ The YouTube video player

The data stored and used by many of these native applications — such as contact details — are also available to third-party applications. Similarly, your applications can respond to events such as incoming calls.

The exact makeup of the applications available on new Android phones is likely to vary based on the hardware manufacturer and/or the phone carrier or distributor.

The open-source nature of Android means that carriers and OEMs can customize the user interface and the applications bundled with each Android device. Several OEMs have done this, including HTC with Sense, Motorola with MotoBlur, and Samsung with TouchWiz.

It's important to note that for compatible devices, the underlying platform and SDK remain consistent across OEM and carrier variations. The look and feel of the user interface may vary, but your applications will function in the same way across all compatible Android devices.

ANDROID SDK FEATURES

The true appeal of Android as a development environment lies in its APIs.

As an application-neutral platform, Android gives you the opportunity to create applications that are as much a part of the phone as anything provided out-of-the-box. The following list highlights some of the most noteworthy Android features:

➤ GSM, EDGE, 3G, 4G, and LTE networks for telephony or data transfer, enabling you to make or receive calls or SMS messages, or to send and retrieve data across mobile networks

➤ Comprehensive APIs for location-based services such as GPS and network-based location detection

➤ Full support for applications that integrate map controls as part of their user interfaces

➤ Wi-Fi hardware access and peer-to-peer connections

➤ Full multimedia hardware control, including playback and recording with the camera and microphone

➤ Media libraries for playing and recording a variety of audio/video or still-image formats

➤ APIs for using sensor hardware, including accelerometers, compasses, and barometers

➤ Libraries for using Bluetooth and NFC hardware for peer-to-peer data transfer

➤ IPC message passing

➤ Shared data stores and APIs for contacts, social networking, calendar, and multi-media

➤ Background Services, applications, and processes

➤ Home-screen Widgets and Live Wallpaper

➤ The ability to integrate application search results into the system searches

➤ An integrated open-source HTML5 WebKit-based browser

➤ Mobile-optimized, hardware-accelerated graphics, including a path-based 2D graphics library and support for 3D graphics using OpenGL ES 2.0

➤ Localization through a dynamic resource framework

➤ An application framework that encourages the reuse of application components and the replacement of native applications

Access to Hardware, Including Camera, GPS, and Sensors

Android includes API libraries to simplify development involving the underlying device hardware. They ensure that you don't need to create specific implementations of your software for different devices, so you can create Android applications that work as expected on any device that supports the Android software stack.

The Android SDK includes APIs for location-based hardware (such as GPS), the camera, audio, network connections, Wi-Fi, Bluetooth, sensors (including accelerometers), NFC, the touchscreen, and power management. You can explore the possibilities of some of Android's hardware APIs in more detail in Chapters 12 and 15–17.

Data Transfers Using Wi-Fi, Bluetooth, and NFC

Android offers rich support for transferring data between devices, including Bluetooth, Wi-Fi Direct, and Android Beam. These technologies offer a rich variety of techniques for sharing data between paired devices, depending on the hardware available on the underlying device, allowing you to create innovative collaborative applications.

In addition, Android offers APIs to manage your network connections, Bluetooth connections, and NFC tag reading.

> *Details on using Android's communications APIs are available in Chapter 16, "Bluetooth, NFC, Networks, and Wi-Fi."*

Maps, Geocoding, and Location-Based Services

Embedded map support enables you to create a range of map-based applications that leverage the mobility of Android devices. Android lets you design user interfaces that include interactive Google Maps that you can control programmatically and annotate using Android's rich graphics library.

Android's location-based services manage technologies such as GPS and Google's network-based location technology to determine the device's current position. These services enforce an abstraction from specific location-detecting technology and let you specify minimum requirements (e.g., accuracy or cost) rather than selecting a particular technology. This also means your location-based applications will work no matter what technology the host device supports.

To combine maps with locations, Android includes an API for forward and reverse geocoding that lets you find map coordinates for an address, and the address of a map position.

> *You'll learn the details of using maps, the geocoder, and location-based services in Chapter 13, "Maps, Geocoding, and Location-Based Services."*

Background Services

Android supports applications and services designed to run in the background while your application isn't being actively used.

Modern mobiles and tablets are by nature multifunction devices; however, their screen sizes and interaction models mean that generally only one interactive application is visible at any time. Platforms that don't support background execution limit the viability of applications that don't need your constant attention.

Background services make it possible to create invisible application components that perform automatic processing without direct user action. Background execution allows your applications to become event-driven and to support regular updates, which is perfect for monitoring game scores or market prices, generating location-based alerts, or prioritizing and prescreening incoming calls and SMS messages.

Notifications are the standard means by which a mobile device traditionally alerts users to events that have happened in a background application. Using the Notification Manager, you can trigger audible alerts, cause vibration, and flash the device's LED, as well as control status bar notification icons.

> *Learn more about how to use Notifications and get the most out of background services in Chapters 9 and 10.*

SQLite Database for Data Storage and Retrieval

Rapid and efficient data storage and retrieval are essential for a device whose storage capacity is relatively limited.

Android provides a lightweight relational database for each application via SQLite. Your applications can take advantage of this managed relational database engine to store data securely and efficiently.

By default, each application database is sandboxed — its content is available only to the application that created it — but Content Providers supply a mechanism for the managed sharing of these application databases as well as providing an abstraction between your application and the underlying data source.

> *Databases and Content Providers are covered in detail in Chapter 8, "Databases and Content Providers."*

Shared Data and Inter-Application Communication

Android includes several techniques for making information from your applications available for use elsewhere, primarily: Intents and Content Providers.

Intents provide a mechanism for message-passing within and between applications. Using Intents, you can broadcast a desired action (such as dialing the phone or editing a contact) systemwide for other applications to handle. Using the same mechanism, you can register your own application to receive these messages or execute the requested actions.

You can use *Content Providers* to provide secure, managed access to your applications' private databases. The data stores for native applications, such as the contact manager, are exposed as Content Providers so you can read or modify this data from within your own applications.

> *Intents are a fundamental component of Android and are covered in depth in Chapter 5, "Intents and Broadcast Receivers."*
>
> *Chapter 8 covers content providers in detail, including the native providers, and demonstrates how to create and use providers of your own.*

Using Widgets and Live Wallpaper to Enhance the Home Screen

Widgets and Live Wallpaper let you create dynamic application components that provide a window into your applications, or offer useful and timely information, directly on the home screen.

Offering a way for users to interact with your application directly from the home screen increases user engagement by giving them instant access to interesting information without needing to open the application, as well as adding a dynamic shortcut into your application from their home screen.

> *You'll learn how to create application components for the home screen in Chapter 14, "Invading the Home Screen."*

Extensive Media Support and 2D/3D Graphics

Bigger screens and brighter, higher-resolution displays have helped make mobiles multimedia devices. To help you make the most of the hardware available, Android provides graphics libraries for 2D canvas drawing and 3D graphics with OpenGL.

Android also offers comprehensive libraries for handling still images, video, and audio files, including the MPEG4, H.264, HTTP Live Streaming, VP8, WEBP, MP3, AAC, AMR, HLS, JPG, PNG, and GIF formats.

> *2D and 3D graphics are covered in depth in Chapter 11, "Advanced User Experience," and Android media management libraries are covered in Chapter 15, "Audio, Video, and Using the Camera."*

Cloud to Device Messaging

The Android Cloud to Device Messaging (C2DM) service provides an efficient mechanism for developers to create event-driven applications based on server-side pushes.

Using C2DM you can create a lightweight, always-on connection between your mobile application and your server, allowing you to send small amounts of data directly to your device in real time.

The C2DM service is typically used to prompt applications of new data available on the server, reducing the need for polling, decreasing the battery impact of an application's updates, and improving the timeliness of those updates.

Optimized Memory and Process Management

Like Java and .NET, Android uses its own run time and VM to manage application memory. Unlike with either of these other frameworks, the Android run time also manages the process lifetimes. Android ensures application responsiveness by stopping and killing processes as necessary to free resources for higher-priority applications.

In this context, the highest priority is given to the application with which the user is interacting. Ensuring that your applications are prepared for a swift death but are still able to remain responsive, and to update or restart in the background if necessary, is an important consideration in an environment that does not allow applications to control their own lifetimes.

 You will learn more about the Android application lifecycle in Chapter 3, "Creating Applications and Activities."

INTRODUCING THE OPEN HANDSET ALLIANCE

The Open Handset Alliance (OHA) is a collection of more than 80 technology companies, including hardware manufacturers, mobile carriers, software developers, semiconductor companies, and commercialization companies. Of particular note are the prominent mobile technology companies, including Samsung, Motorola, HTC, T-Mobile, Vodafone, ARM, and Qualcomm. In their own words, the OHA represents the following:

> *A commitment to openness, a shared vision for the future, and concrete plans to make the vision a reality. To accelerate innovation in mobile and offer consumers a richer, less expensive, and better mobile experience.*
>
> —*www.openhandsetalliance.com*

The OHA hopes to deliver a better mobile software experience for consumers by providing the platform needed for innovative mobile development at a faster rate and with higher quality than existing platforms, without licensing fees for either software developers or handset manufacturers.

WHAT DOES ANDROID RUN ON?

The first Android mobile handset, the T-Mobile G1, was released in the United States in October 2008. By the beginning of 2012, more than 300 million Android-compatible devices have been sold from more than 39 manufacturers, in more than 123 countries, on 231 different carrier networks.

Rather than being a mobile OS created for a single hardware implementation, Android is designed to support a large variety of hardware platforms, from smartphones to tablets and televisions.

With no licensing fees or proprietary software, the cost to handset manufacturers for providing Android devices is comparatively low. Many people now expect that the advantages of Android as a platform for creating powerful applications will encourage device manufacturers to produce increasingly diverse and tailored hardware.

WHY DEVELOP FOR MOBILE?

In market terms, the emergence of modern mobile smartphones — multifunction devices including a phone but featuring a full-featured web browser, cameras, media players, Wi-Fi, and location-based services — has fundamentally changed the way people interact with their mobile devices and access the Internet.

Mobile-phone ownership easily surpasses computer ownership in many countries, with more than 3 billion mobile phone users worldwide. 2009 marked the year that more people accessed the Internet for the first time from a mobile phone rather than a PC. Many people believe that within the next 5 years more people will access the Internet by mobile phone rather than using personal computers.

The increasing popularity of modern smartphones, combined with the increasing availability of high-speed mobile data and Wi-Fi hotspots, has created a huge opportunity for advanced mobile applications.

The ubiquity of mobile phones, and our attachment to them, makes them a fundamentally different platform for development from PCs. With a microphone, camera, touchscreen, location detection, and environmental sensors, a phone can effectively become an extra-sensory perception device.

Smartphone applications have changed the way people use their phones. This gives you, the application developer, a unique opportunity to create dynamic, compelling new applications that become a vital part of people's lives.

WHY DEVELOP FOR ANDROID?

Android represents a clean break, a mobile framework based on the reality of modern mobile devices designed by developers, for developers.

With a simple, powerful, and open SDK, no licensing fees, excellent documentation, and a thriving developer community, Android represents an opportunity to create software that changes how and why people use their mobile phones.

The barrier to entry for new Android developers is minimal:

➤ No certification is required to become an Android developer.

➤ Google Play provides free, up-front purchase, and in-app billing options for distribution and monetization of your applications.

➤ There is no approval process for application distribution.

➤ Developers have total control over their brands.

From a commercial perspective, more than 850,000 new Android devices are activated daily, with many studies showing the largest proportion of new smartphone sales belonging to Android devices.

As of March 2012, Google Play (formerly Android Market) has expanded its support for application sales to 131 countries, supporting more than 10 billion installs at a growth rate of 1 billion downloads per month.

Factors Driving Android's Adoption

Developers have always been a critical element within the Android ecosystem, with Google and the OHA betting that the way to deliver better mobile software to consumers is to make it easier for developers to write it.

As a development platform, Android is powerful and intuitive, enabling developers who have never programmed for mobile devices to create innovative applications quickly and easily. It's easy to see how compelling Android applications have created demand for the devices necessary to run them, particularly when developers write applications for Android because they *can't* write them for other platforms.

As Android expands into more form-factors, with increasingly powerful hardware, advanced sensors, and new developer APIs, the opportunities for innovation will continue to grow.

Open access to the nuts and bolts of the underlying system is what's always driven software development and platform adoption. The Internet's inherent openness has seen it become the platform for a multibillion-dollar industry within 10 years of its inception. Before that, it was open systems such as Linux and the powerful APIs provided as part of the Windows operating system that enabled the explosion in personal computers and the movement of computer programming from the arcane to the mainstream.

This openness and power ensure that anyone with the inclination can bring a vision to life at minimal cost.

What Android Has That Other Platforms Don't Have

Many of the features listed previously, such as 3D graphics and native database support, are also available in other native mobile SDKs, as well as becoming available on mobile browsers.

The pace of innovation in mobile platforms, both Android and its competitors, makes an accurate comparison of the available features difficult. The following noncomprehensive list details some of the features available on Android that may not be available on all modern mobile development platforms:

➤ **Google Maps applications** — Google Maps for Mobile has been hugely popular, and Android offers a Google Map as an atomic, reusable control for use in your applications. The Map View lets you display, manipulate, and annotate a Google Map within your Activities to build map-based applications using the familiar Google Maps interface.

➤ **Background services and applications** — Full support for background applications and services lets you create applications based on an event-driven model, working silently while other applications are being used or while your mobile sits ignored until it rings, flashes, or vibrates to get your attention. Maybe it's a streaming music player, an application that tracks the stock market, alerting you to significant changes in your portfolio, or a service that changes your ringtone or volume depending on your current location, the time of day, and the identity of the caller. Android provides the same opportunities for all applications and developers.

➤ **Shared data and inter-process communication** — Using Intents and Content Providers, Android lets your applications exchange messages, perform processing, and share data. You can also use these mechanisms to leverage the data and functionality provided by the native Android applications. To mitigate the risks of such an open strategy, each application's process, data storage, and files are private unless explicitly shared with other applications via a full permission-based security mechanism, as detailed in Chapter 18, "Advanced Android Development."

➤ **All applications are created equal** — Android doesn't differentiate between native applications and those developed by third parties. This gives consumers unprecedented power to change the look and feel of their devices by letting them completely replace every native application with a third-party alternative that has access to the same underlying data and hardware.

➤ **Wi-Fi Direct and Android Beam** — Using these innovative new inter-device communication APIs, you can include features such as instant media sharing and streaming. Android Beam is an NFC-based API that lets you provide support for proximity-based interaction, while Wi-Fi Direct offers a wider range peer-to-peer for reliable, high-speed communication between devices.

➤ **Home-screen Widgets, Live Wallpaper, and the quick search box** — Using Widgets and Live Wallpaper, you can create windows into your application from the phone's home screen. The quick search box lets you integrate search results from your application directly into the phone's search functionality.

The Changing Mobile Development Landscape

Existing mobile development platforms have created an aura of exclusivity around mobile development. In contrast, Android allows, even encourages, radical change.

As consumer devices, Android handsets ship with a core set of the standard applications that consumers expect on a new phone, but the real power lies in users' ability to completely customize their devices' look, feel, and function — giving application developers an exciting opportunity.

All Android applications are a native part of the phone, not just software that's run in a sandbox on top of it. Rather than writing small-screen versions of software that can be run on low-power devices, you can now build mobile applications that change the way people use their phones.

The field of mobile development is currently enjoying a period of rapid innovation and incredible growth. This provides both challenges and opportunities for developers simply to keep up with the pace of change, let alone identify the opportunities these changes make possible.

Android will continue to advance and improve to compete with existing and future mobile development platforms, but as an open-source developer framework, the strength of the SDK is very much in its favor. Its free and open approach to mobile application development, with total access to the phone's resources, represents an opportunity for any mobile developer looking to seize the opportunities now available in mobile development.

INTRODUCING THE DEVELOPMENT FRAMEWORK

With the "why" covered, let's take a look at the "how."

Android applications normally are written using Java as the programming language but executed by means of a custom VM called *Dalvik*, rather than a traditional Java VM.

> *Later in this chapter you'll be introduced to the framework, starting with a technical explanation of the Android software stack, followed by a look at what's included in the SDK, an introduction to the Android libraries, and a look at the Dalvik VM.*

Each Android application runs in a separate process within its own Dalvik instance, relinquishing all responsibility for memory and process management to the Android run time, which stops and kills processes as necessary to manage resources.

Dalvik and the Android run time sit on top of a Linux kernel that handles low-level hardware interaction, including drivers and memory management, while a set of APIs provides access to all the underlying services, features, and hardware.

What Comes in the Box

The Android SDK includes everything you need to start developing, testing, and debugging Android applications:

- ➤ **The Android APIs** — The core of the SDK is the Android API libraries that provide developer access to the Android stack. These are the same libraries that Google uses to create native Android applications.

- ➤ **Development tools** — The SDK includes several development tools that let you compile and debug your applications so that you can turn Android source code into executable applications. You will learn more about the developer tools in Chapter 2, "Getting Started."

- ➤ **The Android Virtual Device Manager and emulator** — The Android emulator is a fully interactive mobile device emulator featuring several alternative skins. The emulator runs within an Android Virtual Device (AVD) that simulates a device hardware configuration. Using the emulator you can see how your applications will look and behave on a real Android device. All Android applications run within the Dalvik VM, so the software emulator is an excellent development environment — in fact, because it's hardware-neutral, it provides a better independent test environment than any single hardware implementation.

- ➤ **Full documentation** — The SDK includes extensive code-level reference information detailing exactly what's included in each package and class and how to use them. In addition to the code documentation, Android's reference documentation and developer guide explains how to get started, gives detailed explanations of the fundamentals behind Android development, highlights best practices, and provides deep-dives into framework topics.

- ➤ **Sample code** — The Android SDK includes a selection of sample applications that demonstrate some of the possibilities available with Android, as well as simple programs that highlight how to use individual API features.

> ➤ **Online support** — Android has rapidly generated a vibrant developer community. The Google Groups (`http://developer.android.com/resources/community-groups .html#ApplicationDeveloperLists`) are active forums of Android developers with regular input from the Android engineering and developer relations teams at Google. Stack Overflow (`www.stackoverflow.com/questions/tagged/android`) is also a hugely popular destination for Android questions and a great place to find answers to beginner questions.

For those of you using Eclipse, Android has released the Android Development Tools (ADT) plug-in that simplifies project creation and tightly integrates Eclipse with the Android emulator and the build and debugging tools. The features of the ADT plug-in are covered in more detail in Chapter 2.

Understanding the Android Software Stack

The Android software stack is, put simply, a Linux kernel and a collection of C/C++ libraries exposed through an application framework that provides services for, and management of, the run time and applications. The Android software stack is composed of the elements shown in Figure 1-1.

➤ **Linux kernel** — Core services (including hardware drivers, process and memory management, security, network, and power management) are handled by a Linux 2.6 kernel. The kernel also provides an abstraction layer between the hardware and the remainder of the stack.

➤ **Libraries** — Running on top of the kernel, Android includes various C/C++ core libraries such as libc and SSL, as well as the following:

> ➤ A media library for playback of audio and video media
>
> ➤ A surface manager to provide display management
>
> ➤ Graphics libraries that include SGL and OpenGL for 2D and 3D graphics
>
> ➤ SQLite for native database support
>
> ➤ SSL and WebKit for integrated web browser and Internet security

➤ **Android run time** — The run time is what makes an Android phone an Android phone rather than a mobile Linux implementation. Including the core libraries and the Dalvik VM, the Android run time is the engine that powers your applications and, along with the libraries, forms the basis for the application framework.

> ➤ **Core libraries** — Although most Android application development is written using the Java language, Dalvik is not a Java VM. The core Android libraries provide most of the functionality available in the core Java libraries, as well as the Android-specific libraries.
>
> ➤ **Dalvik VM** — Dalvik is a register-based Virtual Machine that's been optimized to ensure that a device can run multiple instances efficiently. It relies on the Linux kernel for threading and low-level memory management.

➤ **Application framework** — The application framework provides the classes used to create Android applications. It also provides a generic abstraction for hardware access and manages the user interface and application resources.

➤ **Application layer** — All applications, both native and third-party, are built on the application layer by means of the same API libraries. The application layer runs within the Android run time, using the classes and services made available from the application framework.

Application Layer

Application Framework

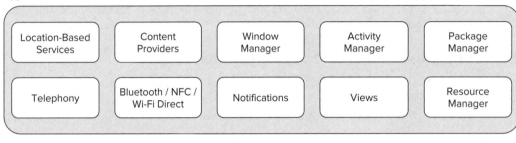

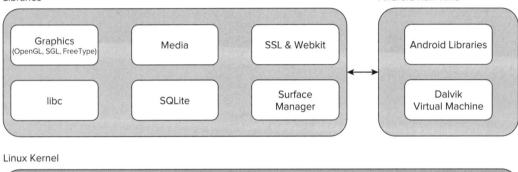

FIGURE 1-1

The Dalvik Virtual Machine

One of the key elements of Android is the Dalvik VM. Rather than using a traditional Java VM such as Java ME, Android uses its own custom VM designed to ensure that multiple instances run efficiently on a single device.

The Dalvik VM uses the device's underlying Linux kernel to handle low-level functionality, including security, threading, and process and memory management. It's also possible to write C/C++ applications that run closer to the underlying Linux OS. Although you *can* do this, in most cases there's no reason you should need to.

If the speed and efficiency of C/C++ is required for your application, Android provides a native development kit (NDK). The NDK is designed to enable you to create C++ libraries using the libc and libm libraries, along with native access to OpenGL.

>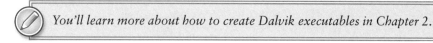
> *This book focuses exclusively on writing applications that run within Dalvik using the SDK; NDK development is not within the scope of this book. If your inclinations run toward NDK development, exploring the Linux kernel and C/C++ underbelly of Android, modifying Dalvik, or otherwise tinkering with things under the hood, check out the Android Internals Google Group at* `http://groups.google.com/group/android-internals.`

All Android hardware and system service access is managed using Dalvik as a middle tier. By using a VM to host application execution, developers have an abstraction layer that ensures they should never have to worry about a particular hardware implementation.

The Dalvik VM executes Dalvik executable files, a format optimized to ensure minimal memory footprint. You create `.dex` executables by transforming Java language compiled classes using the tools supplied within the SDK.

> *You'll learn more about how to create Dalvik executables in Chapter 2.*

Android Application Architecture

Android's architecture encourages component reuse, enabling you to publish and share Activities, Services, and data with other applications, with access managed by the security restrictions you define.

The same mechanism that enables you to produce a replacement contact manager or phone dialer can let you expose your application's components in order to let other developers build on them by creating new UI front ends or functionality extensions.

The following application services are the architectural cornerstones of all Android applications, providing the framework you'll be using for your own software:

➤ **Activity Manager and Fragment Manager** — Control the lifecycle of your Activities and Fragments, respectively, including management of the Activity stack (described in Chapters 3 and 4).

➤ **Views** — Used to construct the user interfaces for your Activities and Fragments, as described in Chapter 4.

➤ **Notification Manager** — Provides a consistent and nonintrusive mechanism for signaling your users, as described in Chapter 10.

➤ **Content Providers** — Lets your applications share data, as described in Chapter 8.

➤ **Resource Manager** — Enables non-code resources, such as strings and graphics, to be externalized, as shown in Chapter 3.

➤ **Intents** — Provides a mechanism for transferring data between applications and their components, as described in Chapter 5.

Android Libraries

Android offers a number of APIs for developing your applications. Rather than list them all here, check out the documentation at `http://developer.android.com/reference/packages.html`, which gives a complete list of packages included in the Android SDK.

Android is intended to target a wide range of mobile hardware, so be aware that the suitability and implementation of some of the advanced or optional APIs may vary depending on the host device.

2

Getting Started

WHAT'S IN THIS CHAPTER?

➤ Installing the Android SDK, creating a development environment, and debugging your projects

➤ Understanding mobile design considerations

➤ The importance of optimizing for speed and efficiency

➤ Designing for small screens and mobile data connections

➤ Using Android Virtual Devices, the Emulator, and other development tools

All you need to start writing your own Android applications is a copy of the Android SDK and the Java Development Kit (JDK). Unless you're a masochist, you'll probably want a Java integrated development environment (IDE) — Eclipse is particularly well supported — to make development a little bit less painful.

The Android SDK, the JDK, and Eclipse are each available for Windows, Mac OS, and Linux, so you can explore Android from the comfort of whatever operating system you favor. The SDK tools and Emulator work on all three OS environments, and because Android applications are run on a Dalvik virtual machine (VM), there's no advantage to developing on any particular OS.

Android code is written using Java syntax, and the core Android libraries include most of the features from the core Java APIs. Before you can run your projects, you must translate them into Dalvik bytecode. As a result, you get the familiarity of Java syntax while your applications gain the advantage of running on a VM optimized for mobile devices.

The Android SDK starter package contains the SDK platform tools, including the SDK Manager, which is necessary to download and install the rest of the SDK packages.

The Android SDK Manager is used to download Android framework SDK libraries, optional add-ons (including the Google APIs and the support library), complete documentation, and a series of excellent sample applications. It also includes the platform and development tools you will use to write and debug your applications, such as the Android Emulator to run your projects and the Dalvik Debug Monitoring Service (DDMS) to help debug them.

By the end of this chapter, you'll have downloaded the Android SDK starter package and used it to install the SDK and its add-ons, the platform tools, documentation, and sample code. You'll set up your development environment, build your first Hello World application, and run and debug it using the DDMS and the Emulator running on an Android Virtual Device (AVD).

If you've developed for mobile devices before, you already know that their small-form factor, limited battery life, and restricted processing power and memory create some unique design challenges. Even if you're new to the game, it's obvious that some of the things you can take for granted on the desktop or the Web aren't going to work on mobile or embedded devices.

The user environment brings its own challenges, in addition to those introduced by hardware limitations. Many Android devices are used on the move and are often a distraction rather than the focus of attention, so your application needs to be fast, responsive, and easy to learn. Even if your application is designed for devices more conducive to an immersive experience, such as tablets or televisions, the same design principles can be critical for delivering a high-quality user experience.

This chapter examines some of the best practices for writing Android applications that overcome the inherent hardware and environmental challenges associated with mobile development. Rather than try to tackle the whole topic, we'll focus on using the Android SDK in a way that's consistent with good design principles.

DEVELOPING FOR ANDROID

The Android SDK includes all the tools and APIs you need to write compelling and powerful mobile applications. The biggest challenge with Android, as with any new development toolkit, is learning the features and limitations of its APIs.

If you have experience in Java development, you'll find that the techniques, syntax, and grammar you've been using will translate directly into Android, although some of the specific optimization techniques may seem counterintuitive.

If you don't have experience with Java but have used other object-oriented languages (such as C#), you should find the transition straightforward. The power of Android comes from its APIs, not the language being used, so being unfamiliar with some of the Java-specific classes won't be a big disadvantage.

What You Need to Begin

Because Android applications run within the Dalvik VM, you can write them on any platform that supports the developer tools. This currently includes the following:

➤ Microsoft Windows (XP or later)

➤ Mac OS X 10.5.8 or later (Intel chips only)

➤ Linux (including GNU C Library 2.7 or later)

To get started, you'll need to download and install the following:

➤ The Android SDK starter package

➤ Java Development Kit (JDK) 5 or 6

You can download the latest JDK from Sun at `http://java.sun.com/javase/downloads/index.jsp`.

> *If you already have a JDK installed, make sure that it meets the preceding requirements, and note that the Java Runtime Environment (JRE) is not sufficient.*

In most circumstances, you'll also want to install an IDE. The following sections describe how to install the Android SDK and use Eclipse as your Android IDE.

Downloading and Installing the Android SDK

There's no cost to download or use the API, and Google doesn't require your application to pass a review to distribute your finished programs on the Google Play Store. Although the Google Play Store requires a small one-time fee to publish applications, if you chose not to distribute via the Google Play Store, you can do so at no cost.

You can download the latest version of the SDK starter package for your chosen development platform from the Android development home page at `http://developer.android.com/sdk/index.html`.

> *Unless otherwise noted, the version of the Android SDK used for writing this book was version 4.0.3 (API level 15).*
>
> *As an open-source platform, the Android SDK source is also available for you to download and compile from* `http://source.android.com`.

The starter package is a ZIP file that contains the latest version of the Android tools required to download the rest of the Android SDK packages. Install it by unzipping the SDK into a new folder. Take note of this location, as you'll need it later.

If you are developing from a Windows platform, an executable Windows installer is available (and recommended) as an alternative to the ZIP file for installing the platform tools.

Before you can begin development, you need to download at least one SDK platform release. You can do this on Windows by running the SDK Manager.exe executable, or on Mac OS or Linux by running the "android" executable in the tools subfolder of the starter package download.

The screen that appears (see Figure 2-1) shows each of the packages available for the download. This includes a node for the platform tools, each of the platform releases, and a collection of extras, such as the Android Support Package and billing/licensing packages.

You can expand each platform release node to see a list of the packages included within it, including the tools, documentation, and sample code packages.

To get started, simply check the boxes corresponding to the newest framework SDK and the latest version of the tools, compatibility/support library, documentation, and sample code.

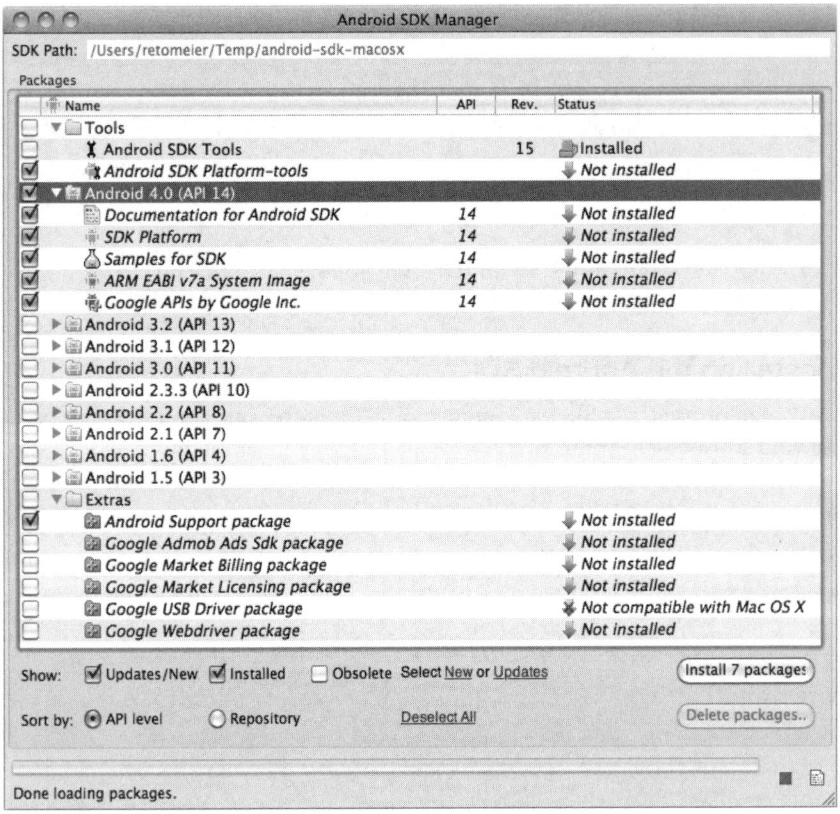

FIGURE 2-1

> *For testing the backward compatibility of your applications, it can often be useful to download the framework SDK for each version you intend to support.*

To use the Google APIs (which contain the Maps APIs), you also need to select the Google APIs by Google package from the platform releases you want to support.

When you click the Install Packages button, the packages you've chosen will be downloaded to your SDK installation folder. The result is a collection of framework API libraries, documentation, and several sample applications.

> *The examples included in the SDK are well documented and are an excellent source for full, working examples of applications written for Android. When you finish setting up your development environment, it's worth going through them.*

Downloading and Installing Updates to the SDK

As new versions of the Android framework SDK, developer tools, sample code, documentation, compatibility library, and third-party add-ons become available, you can use the Android SDK Manager to download and install those updates.

All future packages and upgrades will be placed in the same SDK location.

Developing with Eclipse

The examples and step-by-step instructions in this book are targeted at developers using Eclipse with the Android Developer Tools (ADT) plug-in. Neither is required, though; you can use any text editor or Java IDE you're comfortable with and use the developer tools in the SDK to compile, test, and debug the code snippets and sample applications.

As the recommended development platform, using Eclipse with the ADT plug-in for your Android development offers some significant advantages, primarily through the tight integration of many of the Android build and debug tools into your IDE.

Eclipse is a particularly popular open-source IDE for Java development. It's available for download for each of the development platforms supported by Android (Windows, Mac OS, and Linux) from the Eclipse foundation (www.eclipse.org/downloads).

Many variations of Eclipse are available, with Eclipse 3.5 (Galileo) or above required to use the ADT plugin. The following is the configuration for Android used in the preparation of this book:

> ➤ Eclipse 3.7 (Indigo) (Eclipse Classic download)
>> ➤ Eclipse Java Development Tools (JDT) plug-in
>> ➤ Web Standard Tools (WST)

The JDT plug-in and WST are included in most Eclipse IDE packages.

Installing Eclipse consists of uncompressing the download into a new folder, and then running the eclipse executable. When it starts for the first time, you should create a new workspace for your Android development projects.

Using the Android Developer Tools Plug-In for Eclipse

The ADT plug-in for Eclipse simplifies your Android development by integrating the developer tools, including the Emulator and .class-to-.dex converter, directly into the IDE. Although you don't have to use the ADT plug-in, it can make creating, testing, and debugging your applications faster and easier.

The ADT plug-in integrates the following into Eclipse:

➤ An Android Project Wizard, which simplifies creating new projects and includes a basic application template

➤ Forms-based manifest, layout, and resource editors to help create, edit, and validate your XML resources

➤ Automated building of Android projects, conversion to Android executables (.dex), packaging to package files (.apk), and installation of packages onto Dalvik VMs (running both within the Emulator or on physical devices)

➤ The Android Virtual Device manager, which lets you create and manage virtual devices to host Emulators that run a specific release of the Android OS and with set hardware and memory constraints

➤ The Android Emulator, including the ability to control the Emulator's appearance and network connection settings, and the ability to simulate incoming calls and SMS messages

➤ The Dalvik Debug Monitoring Service (DDMS), which includes port forwarding, stack, heap, and thread viewing, process details, and screen-capture facilities

➤ Access to the device or Emulator's filesystem, enabling you to navigate the folder tree and transfer files

➤ Runtime debugging, which enables you to set breakpoints and view call stacks

➤ All Android/Dalvik log and console outputs

Figure 2-2 shows the DDMS perspective within Eclipse with the ADT plug-in installed.

Installing the ADT Plug-In

Install the ADT plug-in by following these steps:

1. Select Help ➪ Install New Software from within Eclipse.

2. In the Available Software dialog box that appears, click the Add button.

3. In the next dialog, enter a name you will remember (e.g., **Android Developer Tools**) into the Name field, and paste the following address into the Location text entry box: https://dl-ssl.google.com/android/eclipse/.

4. Press OK and Eclipse searches for the ADT plug-in. When finished, it displays the available plug-ins, as shown in Figure 2-3. Select it by clicking the check box next to the Developer Tools root node, and then click Next.

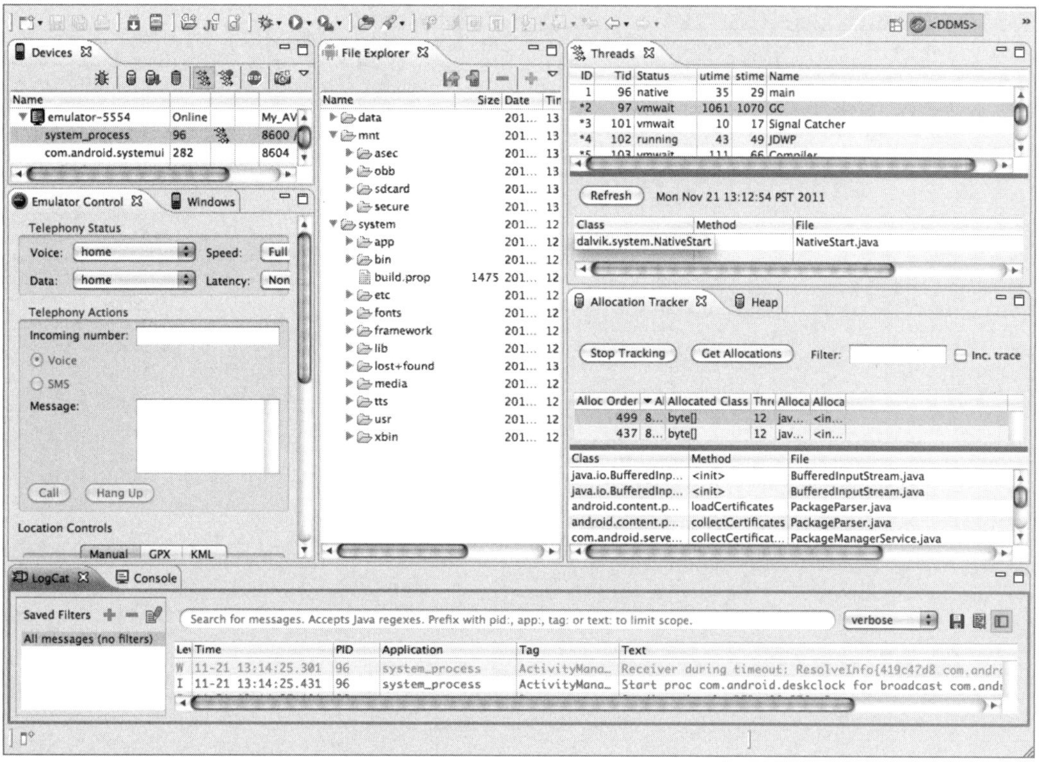

FIGURE 2-2

5. Eclipse now downloads the plug-in. When it finishes, a list of the Developer Tools displays for your review. Click Next.

6. Read and accept the terms of the license agreement, and click Next and then Finish. As the ADT plug-in is not signed, you'll be prompted before the installation continues.

7. When installation is complete, you need to restart Eclipse and update the ADT preferences. Restart and select Window ⇨ Preferences (or Eclipse ⇨ Preferences for Mac OS).

8. Select Android from the left panel.

9. Click Browse, navigate to the folder into which you installed the Android SDK, and then click Apply. The list updates to display each available SDK target, as shown in Figure 2-4. Click OK to complete the SDK installation.

> *If you move your SDK installation to a different location, you will need to update the ADT preference, as described in steps 7 to 9 above, to reflect the new path to the SDK against which the ADT should be building.*

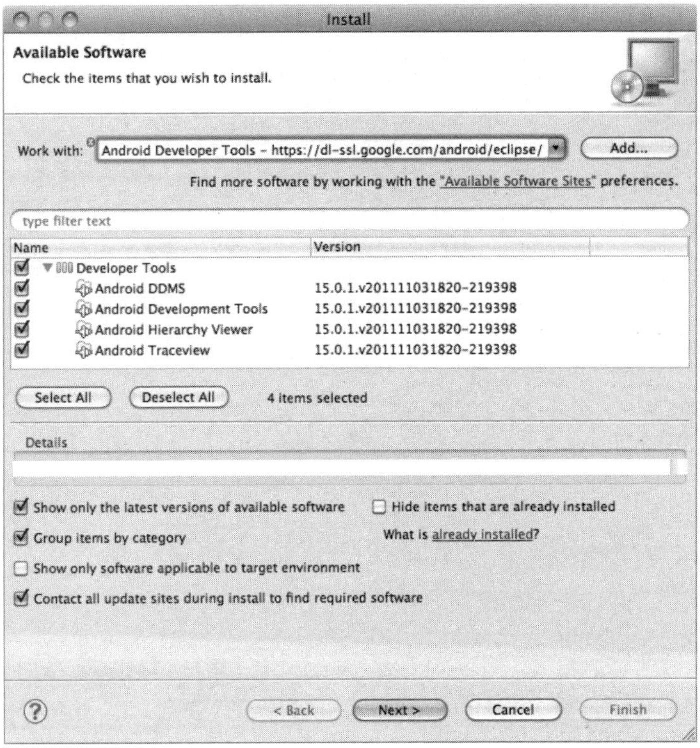

FIGURE 2-3

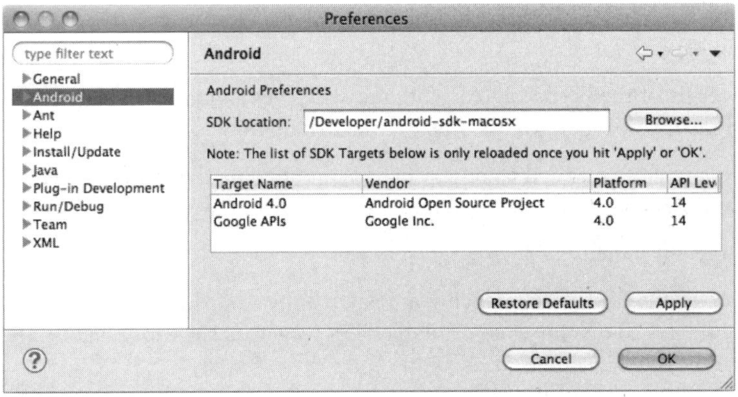

FIGURE 2-4

Updating the ADT Plug-In

In most cases, you can update your ADT plug-in simply as follows:

1. Navigate to Help ⇨ Check for Updates.

2. If there are any ADT updates available, they will be presented. Simply select them and choose Install.

> *Sometimes a plug-in upgrade may be so significant that the dynamic update mechanism can't be used. In those cases you may have to remove the previous plug-in completely before installing the newer version, as described in the previous section.*

Using the Support Package

The support library package (previously known as the compatibility library) is a set of static libraries that you can include as part of your projects to gain either convenience APIs that aren't packaged as part of the framework (such as the View Pager), or useful APIs that are not available on all platform releases (such as Fragments).

The support package enables you to use framework API features that were introduced in recent Android platform releases on any device running Android 1.6 (API level 4) and above. This helps you provide a consistent user experience and greatly simplifies your development process by reducing the burden of supporting multiple platform versions.

> *It's good practice to use the support library rather than the framework API libraries when you want to support devices running earlier platform releases and where the support library offers all the functionality you require.*
>
> *In the interest of simplicity, the examples in this book target Android API level 15 and use the framework APIs in preference to the support library, highlighting specific areas where the support library would not be a suitable alternative.*

To incorporate a support library into your project, perform the following steps:

1. Add a new `/libs` folder in the root of your project hierarchy.

2. Copy the support library JAR file from the `/extras/android/support/` folder in your Android SDK installation location.

   You'll note that the `support` folder includes multiple subfolders, each of which represents the minimum platform version supported by that library. Simply use the corresponding JAR file stored in the subfolder labeled as less than or equal to the minimum platform version you plan to support.

   For example, if you want to support all platform versions from Android 1.6 (API level 4) and above, you would copy `v4/android-support-v4.jar`.

3. After copying the file into your project's `/libs` folder, add it to your project build path by right-clicking in the Package Explorer and selecting Build Path ⇨ Add to Build Path.

> *By design, the support library classes mirror the names of their framework counterparts. Some of these classes (such as* `SimpleCursorAdapter`*) have existed since early platform releases. As a result, there's a significant risk that the code completion and automatic import-management tools in Eclipse (and other IDEs) will select the wrong library — particularly when you're building against newer versions of the SDK.*
>
> *It's good practice to set your project build target to the minimum platform version you plan to support, and to ensure the import statements are using the compatibility library for classes that also exist in the target framework.*

Creating Your First Android Application

You've downloaded the SDK, installed Eclipse, and plugged in the plug-in. You are now ready to start programming for Android. Start by creating a new Android project and setting up your Eclipse *run* and *debug* configurations, as described in the following sections.

Creating a New Android Project

To create a new Android project using the Android New Project Wizard, do the following:

1. Select File ⇨ New ⇨ Project.

2. Select the Android Project application type from the Android folder, and click Next.

3. In the wizard that appears, enter the details for your new project. On the first page (Figure 2-5), the Project Name is the name of your project file. You can also select the location your project should be saved.

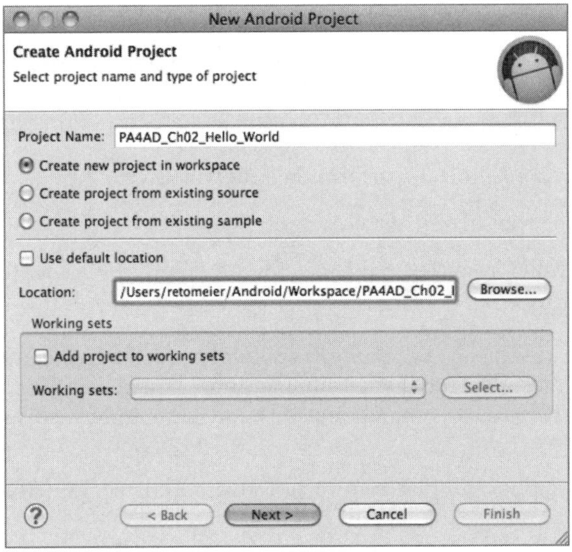

FIGURE 2-5

4. The next page (Figure 2-6) lets you select the build target for your application. The *build target* is the version of the Android framework SDK that you plan to develop with. In addition to the open sourced Android SDK libraries available as part of each platform release, Google offers a set of proprietary APIs that offer additional libraries (such as Maps). If you want to use these Google-specific APIs, you must select the Google APIs package corresponding to the platform release you want to target.

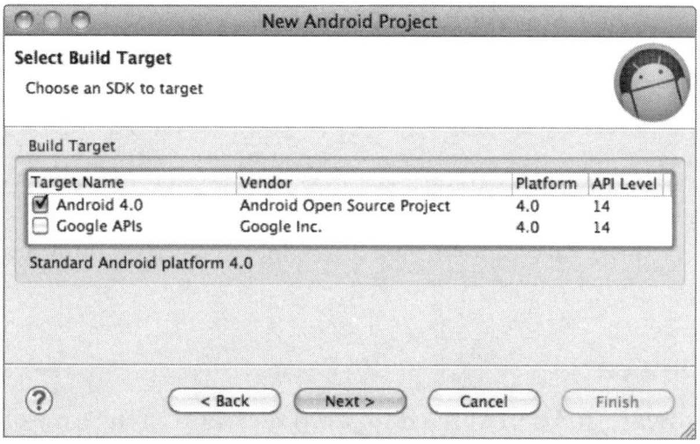

New Android Project

Select Build Target

Choose an SDK to target

Build Target

Target Name	Vendor	Platform	API Level
☑ Android 4.0	Android Open Source Project	4.0	14
☐ Google APIs	Google Inc.	4.0	14

Standard Android platform 4.0

(?)   (< Back) (Next >)   (Cancel)   (Finish)

FIGURE 2-6

Your project's build target does not need to correspond to its minimum SDK or target SDK. For new projects it's good practice to build against the newest version of the SDK to take advantage of efficiency and UI improvements in newer platform releases.

5. The final page (Figure 2-7) allows you to specify the application properties. The Application Name is the friendly name for your application; the Package Name specifies its Java package; the Create Activity option lets you specify the name of a class that will be your initial Activity; and setting the Minimum SDK lets you specify the minimum version of the SDK that your application will run on.

New Android Project

Application Info

Configure the new Android Project

Application Name: PA4AD_Ch02_Hello_World

Package Name: com.paad.helloworld

☑ Create Activity: MyActivity

Minimum SDK: 14

(?)   (< Back) (Next >)   (Cancel)   (Finish)

FIGURE 2-7

> *Selecting the minimum SDK version requires you to choose the level of backward compatibility you want to support to target a wider group of Android devices. Your application will be available from the Google Play Store on any device running the specified build or higher.*
>
> *At the time of this writing, more than 98% of Android devices were running at least Android 2.1 (API level 7). The latest Ice Cream Sandwich SDK is 4.0.3 (API level 15).*

6. When you've entered the details, click Finish.

If you selected Create Activity, the ADT plug-in will create a new project that includes a class that extends `Activity`. Rather than being completely empty, the default template implements Hello World. Before modifying the project, take this opportunity to configure launch configurations for running and debugging.

Creating an Android Virtual Device

AVDs are used to simulate the hardware and software configurations of different Android devices, allowing you test your applications on a variety of hardware platforms.

There are no prebuilt AVDs in the Android SDK, so without a physical device, you need to create at least one before you can run and debug your applications.

1. Select Window ➪ AVD Manager (or select the AVD Manager icon on the Eclipse toolbar).

2. Select the New... button.

The resulting Create new Android Virtual Device (AVD) dialog allows you to configure a name, a target build of Android, an SD card capacity, and device skin.

3. Create a new AVD called "My_AVD" that targets Android 4.0.3, includes a 16MB SD Card, and uses the Galaxy Nexus skin, as shown in Figure 2-8.

4. Click Create AVD and your new AVD will be created and ready to use.

Creating Launch Configurations

Launch configurations let you specify runtime options for running and debugging applications. Using a launch configuration you can specify the following:

➤ The Project and Activity to launch

➤ The deployment target (virtual or physical device)

➤ The Emulator's launch parameters

➤ Input/output settings (including console defaults)

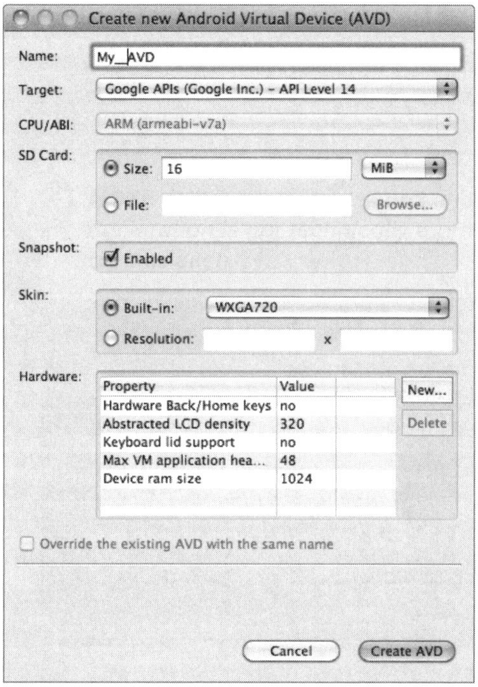

FIGURE 2-8

You can specify different launch configurations for running and debugging applications. The following steps show how to create a launch configuration for an Android application:

1. Select Run Configurations... or Debug Configurations... from the Run menu.

2. Select your application from beneath the Android Application node on the project type list, or right-click the Android Application node and select New.

3. Enter a name for the configuration. You can create multiple configurations for each project, so create a descriptive title that will help you identify this particular setup.

4. Choose your start-up options. The first (Android) tab lets you select the project to run and the Activity that you want to start when you run (or debug) the application. Figure 2-9 shows the settings for the project you created earlier.

5. Use the Target tab, as shown in Figure 2-10, to select the default virtual device to launch on, or select Manual to select a physical or virtual device each time you run the application. You can also configure the Emulator's network connection settings and optionally wipe the user data and disable the boot animation when launching a virtual device.

FIGURE 2-9

> *The Android SDK does not include a default AVD, so you need to create one before you can run or debug your applications using the Emulator. If the Virtual Device selection list in Figure 2-10 is empty, click Manager… to open the Android Virtual Device Manager and create one as described in the previous section.*
>
> *Further details on the Android Virtual Device Manager are available later in this chapter.*

6. Set any additional properties in the Common tab.

7. Click Apply, and your launch configuration will be saved.

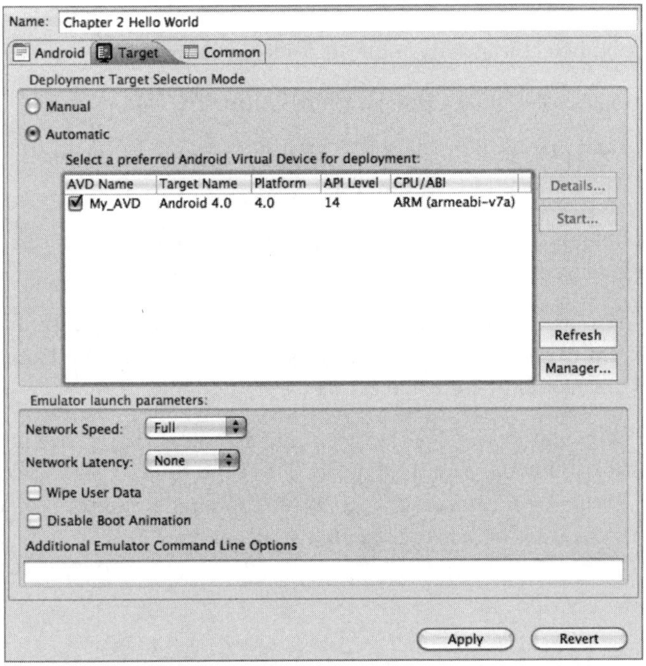

FIGURE 2-10

Running and Debugging Your Android Application

You've created your first project and created the run and debug configurations for it. Before making any changes, test your installation and configurations by running and debugging the Hello World project.

From the Run menu, select Run or Debug to launch the most recently selected configuration, or select Run Configurations... or Debug Configurations... to select a specific configuration.

If you're using the ADT plug-in, running or debugging your application does the following:

➤ Compiles the current project and converts it to an Android executable (.dex)

➤ Packages the executable and your project's resources into an Android package (.apk)

➤ Starts the virtual device (if you've targeted one and it's not already running)

➤ Installs your application onto the target device

➤ Starts your application

If you're debugging, the Eclipse debugger will then be attached, allowing you to set breakpoints and debug your code.

If everything is working correctly, you'll see a new Activity running on the device or in the Emulator, as shown in Figure 2-11.

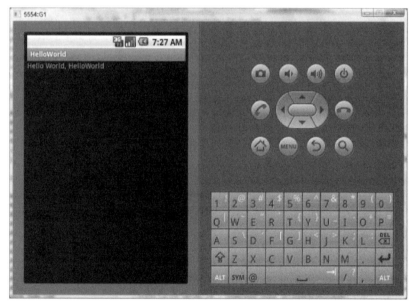

FIGURE 2-11

Understanding Hello World

Take a step back and have a good look at your first Android application.

Activity is the base class for the visual, interactive components of your application; it is roughly equivalent to a Form in traditional desktop development (and is described in detail in Chapter 3,

"Creating Applications and Activities"). Listing 2-1 shows the skeleton code for an Activity-based class; note that it extends `Activity` and overrides the `onCreate` method.

LISTING 2-1: Hello World

```
package com.paad.helloworld;

import android.app.Activity;
import android.os.Bundle;

public class MyActivity extends Activity {

  /** Called when the Activity is first created. **/
  @Override
  public void onCreate(Bundle savedInstanceState) {
    super.onCreate(savedInstanceState);

    setContentView(R.layout.main);
  }
}
```

code snippet PA4AD_Ch02_HelloWorld/src/MyActivity.java

In Android, visual components are called *Views*, which are similar to controls in traditional desktop development. The Hello World template created by the wizard overrides the `onCreate` method to call `setContentView`, which lays out the UI by inflating a layout resource, as highlighted in bold in the following snippet:

```
@Override
public void onCreate(Bundle savedInstanceState) {
  super.onCreate(savedInstanceState);
  setContentView(R.layout.main);
}
```

The resources for an Android project are stored in the `res` folder of your project hierarchy, which includes `layout`, `values`, and a series of `drawable` subfolders. The ADT plug-in interprets these resources to provide design-time access to them through the `R` variable, as described in Chapter 3.

Listing 2-2 shows the UI layout defined in the `main.xml` file created by the Android project template and stored in the project's `res/layout` folder.

LISTING 2-2: Hello World layout resource

```
<?xml version="1.0" encoding="utf-8"?>
<LinearLayout xmlns:android="http://schemas.android.com/apk/res/android"
  android:orientation="vertical"
  android:layout_width="fill_parent"
  android:layout_height="fill_parent">
  <TextView
    android:layout_width="fill_parent"
```

```
      android:layout_height="wrap_content"
      android:text="@string/hello"
  />
</LinearLayout>
```

code snippet PA4AD_Ch02_HelloWorld/res/layout/main.xml

Defining your UI in XML and inflating it is the preferred way of implementing your user interfaces (UIs), as it neatly decouples your application logic from your UI design.

To get access to your UI elements in code, you add identifier attributes to them in the XML definition. You can then use the findViewById method to return a reference to each named item. The following XML snippet shows an ID attribute added to the Text View widget in the Hello World template:

```
<TextView
  android:id="@+id/myTextView"
  android:layout_width="fill_parent"
  android:layout_height="wrap_content"
  android:text="@string/hello"
/>
```

And the following snippet shows how to get access to it in code:

```
TextView myTextView = (TextView)findViewById(R.id.myTextView);
```

Alternatively (although it's not generally considered good practice), you can create your layout directly in code, as shown in Listing 2-3.

LISTING 2-3: Creating layouts in code

```
public void onCreate(Bundle savedInstanceState) {
  super.onCreate(savedInstanceState);

  LinearLayout.LayoutParams lp;
  lp = new LinearLayout.LayoutParams(LinearLayout.LayoutParams.FILL_PARENT,
                                     LinearLayout.LayoutParams.FILL_PARENT);

  LinearLayout.LayoutParams textViewLP;
  textViewLP = new LinearLayout.LayoutParams(
    LinearLayout.LayoutParams.FILL_PARENT,
    LinearLayout.LayoutParams.WRAP_CONTENT);

  LinearLayout ll = new LinearLayout(this);
  ll.setOrientation(LinearLayout.VERTICAL);

  TextView myTextView = new TextView(this);
  myTextView.setText(getString(R.string.hello));

  ll.addView(myTextView, textViewLP);
  this.addContentView(ll, lp);
}
```

code snippet PA4AD_Ch02_Manual_Layout/src/MyActivity.java

All the properties available in code can be set with attributes in the XML layout.

More generally, keeping the visual design decoupled from the application code helps keep the code concise. With Android available on hundreds of different devices of varying screen sizes, defining your layouts as XML resources makes it easier for you to include multiple layouts optimized for different screens.

> *You'll learn how to build your user interface by creating layouts and building your own custom Views in Chapter 4, "Building User Interfaces."*

Types of Android Applications

Most of the applications you create in Android will fall into one of the following categories:

> ➤ **Foreground** — An application that's useful only when it's in the foreground and is effectively suspended when it's not visible. Games are the most common examples.

> ➤ **Background** — An application with limited interaction that, apart from when being configured, spends most of its lifetime hidden. These applications are less common, but good examples include call screening applications, SMS auto-responders, and alarm clocks.

> ➤ **Intermittent** — Most well-designed applications fall into this category. At one extreme are applications that expect limited interactivity but do most of their work in the background. A common example would be a media player. At the other extreme are applications that are typically used as foreground applications but that do important work in the background. Email and news applications are great examples.

> ➤ **Widgets and Live Wallpapers** — Some applications are represented only as a home-screen Widget or as a Live Wallpaper.

Complex applications are often difficult to pigeonhole into a single category and usually include elements of each of these types. When creating your application, you need to consider how it's likely to be used and then design it accordingly. The following sections look more closely at some of the design considerations for each application type.

Foreground Applications

When creating foreground applications, you need to consider carefully the Activity lifecycle (described in Chapter 3) so that the Activity switches seamlessly between the background and the foreground.

Applications have little control over their lifecycles, and a background application with no running Services is a prime candidate for cleanup by Android's resource management. This means that you need to save the state of the application when it leaves the foreground, and then present the same state when it returns to the front.

It's also particularly important for foreground applications to present a slick and intuitive user experience. You'll learn more about creating well-behaved and attractive foreground Activities in Chapters 3, 4, 10, and 11.

Background Applications

These applications run silently in the background with little user input. They often listen for messages or actions caused by the hardware, system, or other applications, rather than relying on user interaction.

You can create completely invisible services, but in practice it's better to provide at least a basic level of user control. At a minimum you should let users confirm that the service is running and let them configure, pause, or terminate it, as needed.

> *Services and Broadcast Receivers, the driving forces of background applications, are covered in depth in Chapter 5, "Intents and Broadcast Receivers," and Chapter 9, "Working in the Background."*

Intermittent Applications

Often you'll want to create an application that can accept user input and that also reacts to events when it's not the active foreground Activity. Chat and e-mail applications are typical examples. These applications are generally a union of visible Activities and invisible background Services and Broadcast Receivers.

Such an application needs to be aware of its state when interacting with the user. This might mean updating the Activity UI when it's visible and sending notifications to keep the user updated when it's in the background, as described in the section "Using Notifications" in Chapter 10.

You must be particularly careful to ensure that the background processes of applications of this type are well behaved and have a minimal impact on the device's battery life.

Widgets and Live Wallpapers

In some circumstances your application may consist entirely of a Widget or Live Wallpaper. By creating Widgets and Live Wallpapers, you provide interactive visual components that can add functionality to user's home screens.

Widget-only applications are commonly used to display dynamic information, such as battery levels, weather forecasts, or the date and time.

> *You'll learn how to create Widgets and Live Wallpapers in Chapter 14, "Invading the Home Screen."*

DEVELOPING FOR MOBILE AND EMBEDDED DEVICES

Android does a lot to simplify mobile- or embedded-device software development, but you need to understand the reasons behind the conventions. There are several factors to account for when writing software for mobile and embedded devices, and when developing for Android in particular.

> *In this chapter you'll learn some of the techniques and best practices for writing efficient Android code. In later examples, efficiency is sometimes compromised for clarity and brevity when new Android concepts or functionality are introduced. In the best tradition of "Do as I say, not as I do," the examples are designed to show the simplest (or easiest-to-understand) way of doing something, not necessarily the best way of doing it.*

Hardware-Imposed Design Considerations

Small and portable, mobile devices offer exciting opportunities for software development. Their limited screen size and reduced memory, storage, and processor power are far less exciting, and instead present some unique challenges.

Compared to desktop or notebook computers, mobile devices have relatively:

➤ Low processing power

➤ Limited RAM

➤ Limited permanent storage capacity

➤ Small screens with low resolution

➤ High costs associated with data transfer

➤ Intermittent connectivity, slow data transfer rates, and high latency

➤ Unreliable data connections

➤ Limited battery life

Each new generation of phones improves many of these restrictions. In particular, newer phones have dramatically improved screen resolutions and significantly cheaper data costs.

The introduction of tablet devices and Android-powered televisions has expanded the range of devices on which your application may be running and eliminating some of these restrictions. However, given the range of devices available, it's always good practice to design to accommodate the worst-case scenario to ensure your application provides a great user experience no matter what the hardware platform it's installed on.

Be Efficient

Manufacturers of embedded devices, particularly mobile devices, generally value small size and long battery life over potential improvements in processor speed. For developers, that means losing the head start traditionally afforded thanks to Moore's law (the doubling of the number of transistors placed on an integrated circuit every two years). In desktop and server hardware, this usually results directly in processor performance improvements; for mobile devices, it instead means thinner, more power-efficient mobiles, with brighter, higher resolution screens. By comparison, improvements in processor power take a back seat.

In practice, this means that you always need to optimize your code so that it runs quickly and responsively, assuming that hardware improvements over the lifetime of your software are unlikely to do you any favors.

Code efficiency is a big topic in software engineering, so I'm not going to try and cover it extensively here. Later in this chapter you'll learn some Android-specific efficiency tips, but for now note that efficiency is particularly important for resource-constrained platforms.

Expect Limited Capacity

Advances in flash memory and solid-state disks have led to a dramatic increase in mobile-device storage capacities. (MP3 collections still tend to expand to fill the available storage.) Although an 8GB flash drive or SD card is no longer uncommon in mobile devices, optical disks offer more than 32GB, and terabyte drives are now commonly available for PCs. Given that most of the available storage on a mobile device is likely to be used to store music and movies, many devices offer relatively limited storage space for your applications.

Android lets you specify that your application can be installed on the SD card as an alternative to using internal memory (described in detail in Chapter 3), but there are significant restrictions to this approach and it isn't suitable for all applications. As a result, the compiled size of your application is an important consideration, though more important is ensuring that your application is polite in its use of system resources.

You should carefully consider how you store your application data. To make life easier, you can use the Android databases and Content Providers to persist, reuse, and share large quantities of data, as described in Chapter 8, "Databases and Content Providers." For smaller data storage, such as preferences or state settings, Android provides an optimized framework, as described in Chapter 7, "Files, Saving State, and Preferences."

Of course, these mechanisms won't stop you from writing directly to the filesystem when you want or need to, but in those circumstances always consider how you're structuring these files, and ensure that yours is an efficient solution.

Part of being polite is cleaning up after yourself. Techniques such as caching, pre-fetching, and lazy loading are useful for limiting repetitive network lookups and improving application responsiveness, but don't leave files on the filesystem or records in a database when they're no longer needed.

Design for Different Screens

The small size and portability of mobiles are a challenge for creating good interfaces, particularly when users are demanding an increasingly striking and information-rich graphical user experience. Combined with the wide range of screen sizes that make up the Android device ecosystem, creating consistent, intuitive, and pleasing user interfaces can be a significant challenge.

Write your applications knowing that users will often only glance at the screen. Make your applications intuitive and easy to use by reducing the number of controls and putting the most important information front and center.

Graphical controls, such as the ones you'll create in Chapter 4, are an excellent means of displaying a lot of information in a way that's easy to understand. Rather than a screen full of text with a lot of buttons and text-entry boxes, use colors, shapes, and graphics to convey information.

You'll also need to consider how touch input is going to affect your interface design. The time of the stylus has passed; now it's all about finger input, so make sure your Views are big enough to support interaction using a finger on the screen. To support accessibility and non-touch screen devices such as Google TV, you need to ensure your application is navigable without relying purely on touch.

Android devices are now available with a variety of screen sizes, from small-screen QVGA phones to 10.1" tablets and 46" Google TVs. As display technology advances and new Android devices are released, screen sizes and resolutions will be increasingly varied. To ensure that your application looks good and behaves well on all the possible host devices, you need to design and test your application on a variety of screens, optimizing for small screens and tablets, but also ensuring that your UIs scale well on any display.

> *You'll learn some techniques for optimizing your UI for different screen sizes in Chapters 3 and 4.*

Expect Low Speeds, High Latency

The ability to incorporate some of the wealth of online information within your applications is incredibly powerful. Unfortunately, the mobile Web isn't as fast, reliable, or readily available as we would like; so, when you're developing your Internet-based applications, it's best to assume that the network connection will be slow, intermittent, and expensive.

With unlimited 4G data plans and citywide Wi-Fi, this is changing, but designing for the worst case ensures that you always deliver a high-standard user experience. This also means making sure that your applications can handle losing (or not finding) a data connection.

The Android Emulator enables you to control the speed and latency of your network connection. Figure 2-12 shows the Emulator's network connection speed and latency, simulating a distinctly suboptimal EDGE connection.

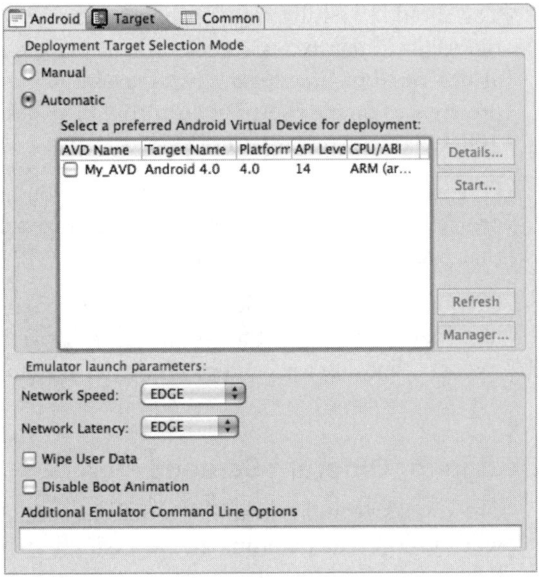

FIGURE 2-12

Experiment to ensure seamlessness and responsiveness no matter what the speed, latency, and availability of network access. Some techniques include limiting the functionality of your application, or reducing network lookups to cached bursts, when the available network connection supports only limited data transfer capabilities.

> *In Chapter 6, "Using Internet Resources," you'll learn how to use Internet resources in your applications.*
>
> *Further details, including how to detect the kind of network connections available at run time, are included in Chapter 16, "Bluetooth, NFC, Networks, and Wi-Fi."*

At What Cost?

If you're a mobile device owner, you know all too well that some of your device's functionality can literally come at a price. Services such as SMS and data transfer can incur additional fees from your service provider.

It's obvious why any costs associated with functionality in your applications should be minimized, and that users should be made aware when an action they perform might result in their being charged.

It's a good approach to assume that there's a cost associated with any action involving an interaction with the outside world. In some cases (such as with GPS and data transfer), the user can toggle Android settings to disable a potentially costly action. As a developer, it's important that you use and respect those settings within your application.

In any case, it's important to minimize interaction costs by doing the following:

➤ Transferring as little data as possible

➤ Caching data and geocoding results to eliminate redundant or repetitive lookups

➤ Stopping all data transfers and GPS updates when your Activity is not visible in the foreground (provided they're only used to update the UI)

➤ Keeping the refresh/update rates for data transfers (and location lookups) as low as practicable

➤ Scheduling big updates or transfers at off-peak times or when connected via Wi-Fi by using Alarms and Broadcast Receivers, as shown in Chapter 9

➤ Respecting the user's preferences for background data transfers

Often the best solution is to use a lower-quality option that comes at a lower cost.

When using location-based services, as described in Chapter 13, "Maps, Geocoding, and Location-Based Services," you can select a location provider based on whether there is an associated cost. Within your location-based applications, consider giving users the choice of lower cost or greater accuracy.

In some circumstances costs are either hard to define or different for different users. Charges for services vary between service providers and contract plans. Although some people will have free unlimited data transfers, others will have free SMS.

Rather than enforcing a particular technique based on which seems cheaper, consider letting your users choose. For example, when users are downloading data from the Internet, ask them if they want to use any network available or limit their transfers to times when they're connected via Wi-Fi.

Considering the User's Environment

You can't assume that your users will think of your application as the most important feature of their device.

Although Android has already expanded beyond its roots as a mobile phone platform, most Android devices are phones or tablet devices. For most people, such a device is first and foremost a phone, secondly an SMS and email communicator, thirdly a camera, and fourthly an MP3 player. The applications you write will most likely be in the fifth category of "useful stuff."

That's not a bad thing — they'll be in good company with others, including Google Maps and the web browser. That said, each user's usage model will be different; some people will never use their device to listen to music, some devices don't support telephony, and some don't include cameras — but the multitasking principle inherent in a device as ubiquitous as it is indispensable is an important consideration for usability design.

It's also important to consider when and how your users will use your applications. People use their mobiles all the time — on the train, walking down the street, or even while driving their cars. You can't make people use their phones appropriately, but you can make sure that your applications don't distract them any more than necessary.

What does this mean in terms of software design? Make sure that your application:

➤ **Is predictable and well behaved** — Start by ensuring that your Activities suspend when they're not in the foreground. Android fires event handlers when your Activity is paused or resumed, so you can pause UI updates and network lookups when your application isn't visible — there's no point updating your UI if no one can see it. If you need to continue updating or processing in the background, Android provides a Service class designed for this purpose, without the UI overheads.

➤ **Switches seamlessly from the background to the foreground** — With the multitasking nature of mobile devices, it's likely that your applications will regularly move into and out of the background. It's important that they "come to life" quickly and seamlessly. Android's nondeterministic process management means that if your application is in the background, there's every chance it will get killed to free resources. This should be invisible to the user. You can ensure seamlessness by saving the application state and queuing updates so that your users don't notice a difference between restarting and resuming your application. Switching back to it should be seamless, with users being shown the UI and application state they last saw.

➤ **Is polite** — Your application should never steal focus or interrupt a user's current Activity. Instead, use Notifications (detailed in Chapter 10) to request your user's attention when your application isn't in the foreground. There are several ways to alert users — for example, incoming calls are announced by a ringtone and/or vibration; when you have unread messages, the LED flashes; and when you have new voice mail, a small unread mail icon appears in the status bar. All these techniques and more are available to your application using the Notifications mechanism.

➤ **Presents an attractive and intuitive UI** — Your application is likely to be one of several in use at any time, so it's important that the UI you present is easy to use. Spend the time and resources necessary to produce a UI that is as attractive as it is functional, and don't force users to interpret and relearn your application every time they load it. Using it should be simple, easy, and obvious — particularly given the limited screen space and distracting user environment.

➤ **Is responsive** — Responsiveness is one of the most critical design considerations on a mobile device. You've no doubt experienced the frustration of a "frozen" piece of software; the multifunctional nature of a mobile makes this even more annoying. With the possibility of delays caused by slow and unreliable data connections, it's important that your application use worker threads and background Services to keep your Activities responsive and, more important, to stop them from preventing other applications from responding promptly.

Developing for Android

Nothing covered so far is specific to Android; the preceding design considerations are just as important in developing applications for any mobile device. In addition to these general guidelines, Android has some particular considerations.

Take a few minutes to read the design best practices included in Google's Android Dev Guide at `http://developer.android.com/guide/index.html`.

The Android design philosophy demands that applications be designed for:

➤ Performance

➤ Responsiveness

➤ Freshness

➤ Security

➤ Seamlessness

➤ Accessibility

Being Fast and Efficient

In a resource-constrained environment, being fast means being efficient. A lot of what you already know about writing efficient code will be applicable to Android, but the limitations of embedded systems and the use of the Dalvik VM mean you can't take things for granted.

The smart bet for advice is to go to the source. The Android team has published some specific guidance on writing efficient code for Android, so rather than reading a rehash of its advice, visit `http://developer.android.com/guide/practices/design/performance.html` for suggestions.

> *You may find that some of these performance suggestions contradict established design practices — for example, avoiding the use of internal setters and getters or preferring virtual classes over using interfaces. When writing software for resource-constrained systems such as embedded devices, there's often a compromise between conventional design principles and the demand for greater efficiency.*

One of the keys to writing efficient Android code is not to carry over assumptions from desktop and server environments to embedded devices.

At a time when 2 to 4GB of memory is standard for most desktop and server rigs, typical smartphones feature approximately 200MB of SDRAM. With memory such a scarce commodity, you need to take special care to use it efficiently. This means thinking about how you use the stack and heap, limiting object creation, and being aware of how variable scope affects memory use.

Being Responsive

Android takes responsiveness very seriously. Android enforces responsiveness with the Activity Manager and Window Manager. If either service detects an unresponsive application, it will display an "[Application] is not responding" dialog — previously described as a *force close* error, as shown in Figure 2-13.

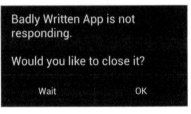

This alert is modal, steals focus, and won't go away until you press a button. It's pretty much the last thing you ever want to confront a user with.

FIGURE 2-13

Android monitors two conditions to determine responsiveness:

➤ An application must respond to any user action, such as a key press or screen touch, within five seconds.

➤ A Broadcast Receiver must return from its `onReceive` handler within 10 seconds.

The most likely culprit in cases of unresponsiveness is a lengthy task being performed on the main application thread. Network or database lookups, complex processing (such as the calculating of game moves), and file I/O should all be moved off the main thread to ensure responsiveness. There are a number of ways to ensure that these actions don't exceed the responsiveness conditions, in particular by using Services and worker threads, as shown in Chapter 9.

Android 2.3 (API level 9) introduced Strict Mode — an API that makes it easier for you to discover file I/O and network transfers being performed on the main application thread. Strict Mode is described in more detail in Chapter 18.

> *The "[Application] is not responding" dialog is a last resort of usability; the generous five-second limit is a worst-case scenario, not a target. Users will notice a regular pause of anything more than one-half second between key press and action. Happily, a side effect of the efficient code you're already writing will be more responsive applications.*

Ensuring Data Freshness

The ability to multitask is a key feature in Android. One of the most important use cases for background Services is to keep your application updated while it's not in use.

Where a responsive application reacts quickly to user interaction, a fresh application quickly displays the data users want to see and interact with. From a usability perspective, the right time to update your application is immediately before the user plans to use it. In practice, you need to weigh the update frequency against its effect on the battery and data usage.

When designing your application, it's critical that you consider how often you will update the data it uses, minimizing the time users are waiting for refreshes or updates, while limiting the effect of these background updates on the battery life.

Developing Secure Applications

Android applications have access to networks and hardware, can be distributed independently, and are built on an open-source platform featuring open communication, so it shouldn't be surprising that security is a significant consideration.

For the most part, users need to take responsibility for the applications they install and the permissions requests they accept. The Android security model sandboxes each application and restricts access to services and functionality by requiring applications to declare the permissions they require. During installation users are shown the application's required permissions before they commit to installing it.

> *You can learn more about Android's security model in Chapter 18, "Advanced Android Development,"* and at `http://developer.android.com/resources/faq/security.html`.

This doesn't get you off the hook. You not only need to make sure your application is secure for its own sake, but you also need to ensure that it doesn't "leak" permissions and hardware access to compromise the device. You can use several techniques to help maintain device security, and they'll be covered in more detail as you learn the technologies involved. In particular, you should do the following:

➤ Require permissions for any Services you publish or Intents you broadcast. Take special care when broadcasting an Intent that you aren't leaking secure information, such as location data.

➤ Take special care when accepting input to your application from external sources, such as the Internet, Bluetooth, NFC, Wi-Fi Direct, SMS messages, or instant messaging (IM). You can find out more about using Bluetooth, NFC, Wi-Fi Direct, and SMS for application messaging in Chapters 16 and 17.

➤ Be cautious when your application may expose access to lower-level hardware to third-party applications.

➤ Minimize the data your application uses and which permissions it requires.

> *For reasons of clarity and simplicity, many of the examples in this book take a relaxed approach to security. When you're creating your own applications, particularly ones you plan to distribute, this is an area that should not be overlooked.*

Ensuring a Seamless User Experience

The idea of a seamless user experience is an important, if somewhat nebulous, concept. What do we mean by *seamless*? The goal is a consistent user experience in which applications start, stop, and transition instantly and without perceptible delays or jarring transitions.

The speed and responsiveness of a mobile device shouldn't degrade the longer it's on. Android's process management helps by acting as a silent assassin, killing background applications to free resources as required. Knowing this, your applications should always present a consistent interface, regardless of whether they're being restarted or resumed.

With an Android device typically running several third-party applications written by different developers, it's particularly important that these applications interact seamlessly. Using Intents, applications can provide functionality for each other. Knowing your application may provide, or consume, third-party Activities provides additional incentive to maintain a consistent look and feel.

Use a consistent and intuitive approach to usability. You can create applications that are revolutionary and unfamiliar, but even these should integrate cleanly with the wider Android environment.

Persist data between sessions, and when the application isn't visible, suspend tasks that use processor cycles, network bandwidth, or battery life. If your application has processes that need to continue running while your Activities are out of sight, use a Service, but hide these implementation decisions from your users.

When your application is brought back to the front, or restarted, it should seamlessly return to its last visible state. As far as your users are concerned, each application should be sitting silently, ready to be used but just out of sight.

You should also follow the best-practice guidelines for using Notifications and use generic UI elements and themes to maintain consistency among applications.

There are many other techniques you can use to ensure a seamless user experience, and you'll be introduced to some of them as you discover more of the possibilities available in Android in the upcoming chapters.

Providing Accessibility

When designing and developing your applications, it's important not to assume that every user will be exactly like you. This has implications for internationalization and usability but is critical for providing accessible support for users with disabilities that require them to interact with their Android devices in different ways.

Android provides facilities to help these users navigate their devices more easily using text-to-speech, haptic feedback, and trackball or D-pad navigation.

To provide a good user experience for everyone — including people with visual, physical, or age-related disabilities that prevent them from fully using or seeing a touchscreen — you can leverage Android's accessibility layer.

> *Best practices for making your application accessible are covered in detail in Chapter 11, "Advanced User Experience."*

As a bonus, the same steps required to help make your touchscreen applications useful for users with disabilities will also make your applications easier to use on non-touch screen devices, such as GoogleTV.

ANDROID DEVELOPMENT TOOLS

The Android SDK includes several tools and utilities to help you create, test, and debug your projects. A detailed examination of each developer tool is outside the scope of this book, but it's worth briefly reviewing what's available. For additional details, check out the Android documentation at `http://developer.android.com/guide/developing/tools/index.html`.

As mentioned earlier, the ADT plug-in conveniently incorporates many of these tools into the Eclipse IDE, where you can access them from the DDMS perspective, including the following:

➤ **The Android Virtual Device and SDK Managers** — Used to create and manage AVDs and to download SDK packages, respectively. The AVD hosts an Emulator running a particular build of Android, letting you specify the supported SDK version, screen resolution, amount of SD card storage available, and available hardware capabilities (such as touchscreens and GPS).

➤ **The Android Emulator** — An implementation of the Android VM designed to run within an AVD on your development computer. Use the Emulator to test and debug your Android applications.

➤ **Dalvik Debug Monitoring Service (DDMS)** — Use the DDMS to monitor and control the Emulators on which you're debugging your applications.

➤ **Android Debug Bridge (ADB)** — A client-server application that provides a link to virtual and physical devices. It lets you copy files, install compiled application packages (`.apk`), and run shell commands.

➤ **Logcat** — A utility used to view and filter the output of the Android logging system.

➤ **Android Asset Packaging Tool (AAPT)** — Constructs the distributable Android package files (`.apk`).

The following additional tools are also available:

➤ **SQLite3** — A database tool that you can use to access the SQLite database files created and used by Android.

➤ **Traceview** and **dmtracedump** — Graphical analysis tools for viewing the trace logs from your Android application.

➤ **Hprof-conv** — A tool that converts HPROF profiling output files into a standard format to view in your preferred profiling tool.

➤ **MkSDCard** — Creates an SD card disk image that can be used by the Emulator to simulate an external storage card.

➤ **Dx** — Converts Java `.class` bytecode into Android `.dex` bytecode.

➤ **Hierarchy Viewer** — Provides both a visual representation of a layout's View hierarchy to debug and optimize your UI, and a magnified display to get your layouts pixel-perfect.

➤ **Lint** — A tool that analyzes your application and its resources to suggest improvements and optimizations.

➤ **Draw9patch:** A handy utility to simplify the creation of NinePatch graphics using a WYSIWYG editor.

➤ **Monkey** and **Monkey Runner:** Monkey runs within the VM, generating pseudo-random user and system events. Monkey Runner provides an API for writing programs to control the VM from outside your application.

➤ **ProGuard** — A tool to shrink and obfuscate your code by replacing class, variable, and method names with semantically meaningless alternatives. This is useful to make your code more difficult to reverse engineer.

Now take a look at some of the more important tools in more detail.

The Android Virtual Device Manager

The Android Virtual Device Manager is used to create and manage the virtual devices that will host instances of the Emulator.

AVDs are used to simulate the software builds and hardware configurations available on different physical devices. This lets you test your application on a variety of hardware platforms without needing to buy a variety of phones.

> The Android SDK doesn't include any prebuilt virtual devices, so you will need to create at least one device before you can run your applications within an Emulator.

Each virtual device is configured with a name, a target build of Android (based on the SDK version it supports), an SD card capacity, and screen resolution, as shown in the Create new Android Virtual Device (AVD) dialog in Figure 2-14.

You can also choose to enable snapshots to save the Emulator state when it's closed. Starting a new Emulator from a snapshot is significantly faster.

Each virtual device also supports a number of specific hardware settings and restrictions that can be added in the form of name-value pairs (NVPs) in the hardware table. Selecting one of the built-in skins will automatically configure these additional settings corresponding to the device the skin represents.

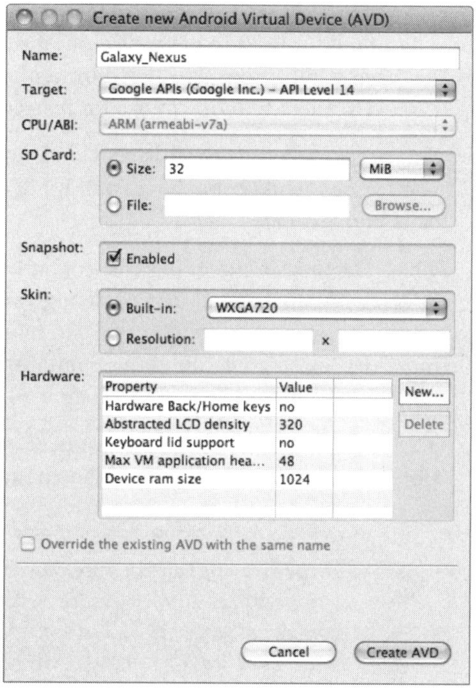

The additional settings include the following:

➤ Maximum VM heap size

➤ Screen pixel density

➤ SD card support

➤ Existence of D-pad, touchscreen, keyboard, and trackball hardware

➤ Accelerometer, GPS, and proximity sensor support

➤ Available device memory

➤ Camera hardware (and resolution)

➤ Support for audio recording

➤ Existence of hardware back and home keys

FIGURE 2-14

Different hardware settings and screen resolutions will present alternative UI skins to represent the different hardware configurations. This simulates a variety of mobile device types. Some manufacturers have made hardware presets and virtual device skins available for their devices. Some, including Samsung, are available as SDK packages.

Android SDK Manager

The Android SDK Manager can be used to see which version of the SDK you have installed and to install new SDKs when they are released.

Each platform release is displayed, along with the platform tools and a number of additional support packages. Each platform release includes the SDK platform, documentation, tools, and examples corresponding to that release.

The Android Emulator

The Emulator is available for testing and debugging your applications.

The Emulator is an implementation of the Dalvik VM, making it as valid a platform for running Android applications as any Android phone. Because it's decoupled from any particular hardware, it's an excellent baseline to use for testing your applications.

Full network connectivity is provided along with the ability to tweak the Internet connection speed and latency while debugging your applications. You can also simulate placing and receiving voice calls and SMS messages.

The ADT plug-in integrates the Emulator into Eclipse so that it's launched automatically within the selected AVD when you run or debug your projects. If you aren't using the plug-in or want to use the Emulator outside of Eclipse, you can telnet into the Emulator and control it from its console. (For more details on controlling the Emulator, check out the documentation at `http://developer .android.com/guide/developing/tools/emulator.html`.)

To execute the Emulator, you first need to create a virtual device, as described in the previous section. The Emulator will launch the virtual device and run a Dalvik instance within it.

> *At the time of this writing, the Emulator doesn't implement all the mobile hardware features supported by Android. For example, it does not implement the camera, vibration, LEDs, actual phone calls, accelerometer, USB connections, audio capture, or battery charge level.*

The Dalvik Debug Monitor Service

The Emulator enables you to see how your application will look, behave, and interact, but to actually see what's happening under the surface, you need the Dalvik Debug Monitoring Service. The DDMS is a powerful debugging tool that lets you interrogate active processes, view the stack and heap, watch and pause active threads, and explore the filesystem of any connected Android device.

The DDMS perspective in Eclipse also provides simplified access to screen captures of the Emulator and the logs generated by LogCat.

If you're using the ADT plug-in, the DDMS tool is fully integrated into Eclipse and is available from the DDMS perspective. If you aren't using the plug-in or Eclipse, you can run DDMS from the command line (it's available from the tools folder of the Android SDK), and it will automatically connect to any running device or Emulator.

The Android Debug Bridge

The *Android Debug Bridge* (ADB) is a client-service application that lets you connect with an Android device (virtual or actual). It's made up of three components:

➤   A daemon running on the device or Emulator

➤   A service that runs on your development computer

➤   Client applications (such as the DDMS) that communicate with the daemon through the service

As a communications conduit between your development hardware and the Android device/Emulator, the ADB lets you install applications, push and pull files, and run shell commands on the target device. Using the device shell, you can change logging settings and query or modify SQLite databases available on the device.

The ADT tool automates and simplifies a lot of the usual interaction with the ADB, including application installation and updating, file logging, and file transfer (through the DDMS perspective).

> *To learn more about what you can do with the ADB, check out the documentation at* `http://developer.android.com/guide/developing/tools/adb.html`.

The Hierarchy Viewer and Lint Tool

To build applications that are fast and responsive, you need to optimize your UI. The Hierarchy Viewer and Lint tools help you analyze, debug, and optimize the XML layout definitions used within your application.

The Hierarchy Viewer displays a visual representation of the structure of your UI layout. Starting at the root node, the children of each nested View (including layouts) is displayed in a hierarchy. Each View node includes its name, appearance, and identifier.

To optimize performance, the performance of the layout, measure, and draw steps of creating the UI of each View at runtime is displayed. Using these values, you can learn the actual time taken to create each View within your hierarchy, with colored "traffic light" indicators showing the relative performance for each step. You can then search within your layout for Views that appear to be taking longer to render than they should.

The Lint tool helps you to optimize your layouts by checking them for a series of common inefficiencies that can have a negative impact on your application's performance. Common issues include a surplus of nested layouts, a surplus of Views within a layout, and unnecessary parent Views.

Although a detailed investigation into optimizing and debugging your UI is beyond the scope of this book, you can find further details at `http://developer.android.com/guide/developing/debugging/debugging-ui.html`.

Monkey and Monkey Runner

Monkey and Monkey Runner can be used to test your applications stability from a UI perspective.

Monkey works from within the ADB shell, sending a stream of pseudo-random system and UI events to your application. It's particularly useful to stress test your applications to investigate edge-cases you might not have anticipated through unconventional use of the UI.

Alternatively, Monkey Runner is a Python scripting API that lets you send specific UI commands to control an Emulator or device from outside the application. It's extremely useful for performing UI, functional, and unit tests in a predictable, repeatable fashion.

3

Creating Applications and Activities

WHAT'S IN THIS CHAPTER?

➤ Introducing the Android application components and the different types of applications you can build with them

➤ Understanding the Android application lifecycle

➤ Creating your application manifest

➤ Using external resources to provide dynamic support for locations, languages, and hardware configurations

➤ Implementing and using your own Application class

➤ Creating new Activities

➤ Understanding an Activity's state transitions and lifecycle

To write high-quality applications, it's important to understand the components they consist of and how those components are bound together by the Android manifest. This chapter introduces each of the application components, with special attention paid to Activities.

Next, you'll see why and how you should use external resources and the resource hierarchy to create applications that can be customized and optimized for a variety of devices, countries, and languages.

In Chapter 2, "Getting Started," you learned that each Android application runs in a separate process, in its own instance of the Dalvik virtual machine. In this chapter, you learn more about the application lifecycle and how the Android run time can manage your application. You are also introduced to the application and Activity states, state transitions, and event handlers. The application's state determines its priority, which, in turn, affects the likelihood of its being terminated when the system requires more resources.

You should always provide the best possible experience for users, no matter which country they're in or which of the wide variety of Android device types, form factors, and screen sizes they're using. In this chapter, you learn how to use the resource framework to provide optimized resources, ensuring your applications run seamlessly on different hardware (particularly different screen resolutions and pixel densities), in different countries, and supporting multiple languages.

The `Activity` class forms the basis for all your user interface (UI) screens. You learn how to create Activities and gain an understanding of their lifecycles and how they affect the application lifetime and priority.

Finally, you are introduced to some of the `Activity` subclasses that simplify resource management for some common UI patterns, such as map- and list-based Activities.

WHAT MAKES AN ANDROID APPLICATION?

Android applications consist of loosely coupled components, bound by the application manifest that describes each component and how they interact. The manifest is also used to specify the application's metadata, its hardware and platform requirements, external libraries, and required permissions.

The following components comprise the building blocks for all your Android applications:

➤ **Activities** — Your application's presentation layer. The UI of your application is built around one or more extensions of the `Activity` class. Activities use Fragments and Views to layout and display information, and to respond to user actions. Compared to desktop development, Activities are equivalent to Forms. You'll learn more about Activities later in this chapter.

➤ **Services** — The invisible workers of your application. Service components run without a UI, updating your data sources and Activities, triggering Notifications, and broadcasting Intents. They're used to perform long running tasks, or those that require no user interaction (such as network lookups or tasks that need to continue even when your application's Activities aren't active or visible.) You'll learn more about how to create and use services in Chapter 9, "Working in the Background."

➤ **Content Providers** — Shareable persistent data storage. Content Providers manage and persist application data and typically interact with SQL databases. They're also the preferred means to share data across application boundaries. You can configure your application's Content Providers to allow access from other applications, and you can access the Content Providers exposed by others. Android devices include several native Content Providers that expose useful databases such as the media store and contacts. You'll learn how to create and use Content Providers in Chapter 8, "Databases and Content Providers."

➤ **Intents** — A powerful interapplication message-passing framework. Intents are used extensively throughout Android. You can use Intents to start and stop Activities and Services, to broadcast messages system-wide or to an explicit Activity, Service, or Broadcast Receiver, or to request an action be performed on a particular piece of data. Explicit, implicit, and broadcast Intents are explored in more detail in Chapter 5, "Intents and Broadcast Receivers."

➤ **Broadcast Receivers** — Intent listeners. Broadcast Receivers enable your application to listen for Intents that match the criteria you specify. Broadcast Receivers start your application to react to any received Intent, making them perfect for creating event-driven applications. Broadcast Receivers are covered with Intents in Chapter 5.

➤ **Widgets** — Visual application components that are typically added to the device home screen. A special variation of a Broadcast Receiver, widgets enable you to create dynamic, interactive application components for users to embed on their home screens. You'll learn how to create your own widgets in Chapter 14, "Invading the Home Screen."

➤ **Notifications** — Notifications enable you to alert users to application events without stealing focus or interrupting their current Activity. They're the preferred technique for getting a user's attention when your application is not visible or active, particularly from within a Service or Broadcast Receiver. For example, when a device receives a text message or an email, the messaging and Gmail applications use Notifications to alert you by flashing lights, playing sounds, displaying icons, and scrolling a text summary. You can trigger these notifications from your applications, as discussed in Chapter 10, "Expanding the User Experience."

By decoupling the dependencies between application components, you can share and use individual Content Providers, Services, and even Activities with other applications — both your own and those of third parties.

INTRODUCING THE APPLICATION MANIFEST FILE

Each Android project includes a manifest file, `AndroidManifest.xml`, stored in the root of its project hierarchy. The manifest defines the structure and metadata of your application, its components, and its requirements.

It includes nodes for each of the Activities, Services, Content Providers, and Broadcast Receivers that make up your application and, using Intent Filters and Permissions, determines how they interact with each other and with other applications.

The manifest can also specify application metadata (such as its icon, version number, or theme), and additional top-level nodes can specify any required permissions, unit tests, and define hardware, screen, or platform requirements (as described next).

The manifest is made up of a root `manifest` tag with a `package` attribute set to the project's package. It should also include an `xmlns:android` attribute that supplies several system attributes used within the file.

Use the `versionCode` attribute to define the current application version as an integer that increases with each version iteration, and use the `versionName` attribute to specify a public version that will be displayed to users.

You can also specify whether to allow (or prefer) for your application be installed on external storage (usually an SD card) rather than internal storage using the `installLocation` attribute. To do this specify either `preferExternal` or `auto`, where the former installs to external storage whenever possible, and the latter asks the system to decide.

> *If your application is installed on external storage, it will be immediately killed if a user mounts the USB mass storage to copy files to/from a computer, or ejects or unmounts the SD card.*

If you don't specify an install location attribute, your application will be installed in the internal storage and users won't be able to move it to external storage. The total amount of internal storage is generally limited, so it's good practice to let your application be installed on external storage whenever possible.

There are some applications for which installation to external storage is not appropriate due to the consequences of unmounting or ejecting the external storage, including:

➤ **Applications with Widgets, Live Wallpapers, and Live Folders** — Your Widgets, Live Wallpapers, and Live Folders will be removed from the home screen and may not be available until the system restarts.

➤ **Applications with ongoing Services** — Your application and its running Services will be stopped and won't be restarted automatically.

➤ **Input Method Engines** — Any IME installed on external storage will be disabled and must be reselected by the user after the external storage is once again available.

➤ **Device administrators** — Your `DeviceAdminReceiver` and any associated admin capabilities will be disabled.

A Closer Look at the Application Manifest

The following XML snippet shows a typical manifest node:

```
<manifest xmlns:android="http://schemas.android.com/apk/res/android"
          package="com.paad.myapp"
          android:versionCode="1"
          android:versionName="0.9 Beta"
          android:installLocation="preferExternal">
          [ ... manifest nodes ... ]
</manifest>
```

The `manifest` tag can include nodes that define the application components, security settings, test classes, and requirements that make up your application. The following list gives a summary of the available `manifest` sub-node tags and provides an XML snippet demonstrating how each tag is used:

➤ `uses-sdk` — This node enables you to define a minimum and maximum SDK version that must be available on a device for your application to function properly, and target SDK for which it has been designed using a combination of `minSDKVersion`, `maxSDKVersion`, and `targetSDKVersion` attributes, respectively.

The minimum SDK version specifies the lowest version of the SDK that includes the APIs you have used in your application. If you fail to specify a minimum version, it defaults to 1, and your application crashes when it attempts to access unavailable APIs.

The target SDK version attribute enables you to specify the platform against which you did your development and testing. Setting a target SDK version tells the system that there is no need to apply any forward- or backward-compatibility changes to support that particular version. To take advantage of the newest platform UI improvements, it's considered good practice to update the target SDK of your application to the latest platform release after you confirm it behaves as expected, even if you aren't making use of any new APIs.

It is usually unnecessary to specify a maximum SDK, and doing so is strongly discouraged. The maximum SDK defines an upper limit you are willing to support and your application will not be visible on the Google Play Store for devices running a higher platform release. Devices running on platforms higher than Android 2.0.1 (API level 6) will ignore any maximum SDK values at installation time.

```
<uses-sdk android:minSdkVersion="6"
          android:targetSdkVersion="15"/>
```

> *The supported SDK version is not equivalent to the platform version and cannot be derived from it. For example, Android platform release 4.0 supports the SDK version 14. To find the correct SDK version for each platform, use the table at* `http://developer.android.com/guide/appendix/api-levels.html.`

➤ `uses-configuration` — The `uses-configuration` nodes specify each combination of input mechanisms are supported by your application. You shouldn't normally need to include this node, though it can be useful for games that require particular input controls. You can specify any combination of input devices that include the following:

>   ➤ `reqFiveWayNav` — Specify `true` for this attribute if you require an input device capable of navigating up, down, left, and right and of clicking the current selection. This includes both trackballs and directional pads (D-pads).
>
>   ➤ `reqHardKeyboard` — If your application requires a hardware keyboard, specify `true`.
>
>   ➤ `reqKeyboardType` — Lets you specify the keyboard type as one of `nokeys`, `qwerty`, `twelvekey`, or `undefined`.
>
>   ➤ `reqNavigation` — Specify the attribute value as one of `nonav`, `dpad`, `trackball`, `wheel`, or `undefined` as a required navigation device.
>
>   ➤ `reqTouchScreen` — Select one of `notouch`, `stylus`, `finger`, or `undefined` to specify the required touchscreen input.

You can specify multiple supported configurations, for example, a device with a finger touchscreen, a trackball, and either a QUERTY or a twelve-key hardware keyboard, as shown here:

```
<uses-configuration android:reqTouchScreen="finger"
                    android:reqNavigation="trackball"
```

```
                      android:reqHardKeyboard="true"
                      android:reqKeyboardType="qwerty"/>
<uses-configuration android:reqTouchScreen="finger"
                      android:reqNavigation="trackball"
                      android:reqHardKeyboard="true"
                      android:reqKeyboardType="twelvekey"/>
```

> *When specifying required configurations, be aware that your application won't be installed on any device that does not have one of the combinations specified. In the preceding example, a device with a QWERTY keyboard and a D-pad (but no touchscreen or trackball) would not be supported. Ideally, you should develop your application to ensure it works with any input configuration, in which case no* uses-configuration *node is required.*

➤ uses-feature — Android is available on a wide variety of hardware platforms. Use multiple uses-feature nodes to specify which hardware features your application requires. This prevents your application from being installed on a device that does not include a required piece of hardware, such as NFC hardware, as follows:

```
<uses-feature android:name="android.hardware.nfc" />
```

You can require support for any hardware that is optional on a compatible device. Currently, optional hardware features include the following:

➤ **Audio** — For applications that requires a low-latency audio pipeline. Note that at the time of writing this book, no Android devices satisfied this requirement.

➤ **Bluetooth** — Where a Bluetooth radio is required.

➤ **Camera** — For applications that require a camera. You can also require (or set as options) autofocus, flash, or a front-facing camera.

➤ **Location** — If you require location-based services. You can also specify either network or GPS support explicitly.

➤ **Microphone** — For applications that require audio input.

➤ **NFC** — Requires NFC (near-field communications) support.

➤ **Sensors** — Enables you to specify a requirement for any of the potentially available hardware sensors.

➤ **Telephony** — Specify that either telephony in general, or a specific telephony radio (GSM or CDMA) is required.

➤ **Touchscreen** — To specify the type of touch-screen your application requires.

➤ **USB** — For applications that require either USB host or accessory mode support.

➤ **Wi-Fi** — Where Wi-Fi networking support is required.

As the variety of platforms on which Android is available increases, so too will the optional hardware. You can find a full list of uses-feature hardware at http://developer.android.com/guide/topics/manifest/uses-feature-element.html#features-reference.

To ensure compatibility, requiring some permissions implies a feature requirement. In particular, requesting permission to access Bluetooth, the camera, any of the location service permissions, audio recording, Wi-Fi, and telephony-related permissions implies the corresponding hardware features. You can override these implied requirements by adding a `required` attribute and setting it to `false` — for example, a note-taking application that supports recording an audio note:

```
<uses-feature android:name="android.hardware.microphone"
              android:required="false" />
```

The camera hardware also represents a special case. For compatibility reasons requesting permission to use the camera, or adding a uses-feature node requiring it, implies a requirement for the camera to support autofocus. You can specify it as optional as appropriate:

```
<uses-feature android:name="android.hardware.camera" />
<uses-feature android:name="android.hardware.camera.autofocus"
              android:required="false" />
<uses-feature android:name="android.hardware.camera.flash"
              android:required="false" />
```

You can also use the `uses-feature` node to specify the minimum version of OpenGL required by your application. Use the `glEsVersion` attribute, specifying the OpenGL ES version as an integer. The higher 16 bits represent the major number and the lower 16 bits represent the minor number, so version 1.1 would be represented as follows:

```
<uses-feature android:glEsVersion="0x00010001" />
```

➤ supports-screens — The first Android devices were limited to 3.2" HVGA hardware. Since then, hundreds of new Android devices have been launched including tiny 2.55" QVGA phones, 10.1" tablets, and 42" HD televisions. The supports-screen node enables you to specify the screen sizes your application has been designed and tested to. On devices with supported screens, your application is laid out normally using the scaling properties associated with the layout files you supply. On unsupported devices the system may apply a "compatibility mode," such as pixel scaling to display your application. It's best practice to create scalable layouts that adapt to all screen dimensions.

You can use two sets of attributes when describing your screen support. The first set is used primarily for devices running Android versions prior to Honeycomb MR2 (API level 13). Each attribute takes a Boolean specifying support. As of SDK 1.6 (API level 4), the default value for each attribute is `true`, so use this node to specify the screen sizes you do not support.

➤ smallScreens — Screens with a resolution smaller than traditional HVGA (typically, QVGA screens).

➤ normalScreens — Used to specify typical mobile phone screens of at least HVGA, including WVGA and WQVGA.

➤ largeScreens — Screens larger than normal. In this instance a large screen is considered to be significantly larger than a mobile phone display.

➤ xlargeScreens — Screens larger than large-typically tablet devices.

Honeycomb MR2 (API level 13) introduced additional attributes that provide a finer level of control over the size of screen your application layouts can support. It is generally good practice to use these in combination with the earlier attributes if your application is available to devices running platform releases earlier than API level 13.

➤ `requiresSmallestWidthDp` — Enables you to specify a minimum supported screen width in device independent pixels. The smallest screen width for a device is the lower dimension of its screen height and width. This attribute can potentially be used to filter applications from the Google Play Store for devices with unsupported screens, so when used it should specify the absolute minimum number of pixels required for your layouts to provide a useable user experience.

➤ `compatibleWidthLimitDp` — Specifies the upper bound beyond which your application may not scale. This can cause the system to enable a compatibility mode on devices with screen resolutions larger than you specify.

➤ `largestWidthLimitDp` — Specifies the absolute upper bound beyond which you know your application will not scale appropriately. Typically this results in the system forcing the application to run in compatibility mode (without the ability for users to disable it) on devices with screen resolutions larger than that specified.

It is generally considered a bad user experience to force your application into compatibility mode. Wherever possible, ensure that your layouts scale in a way that makes them usable on larger devices.

```
<supports-screens android:smallScreens="false"
                  android:normalScreens="true"
                  android:largeScreens="true"
                  android:xlargeScreens="true"
                  android:requiresSmallestWidthDp="480"
                  android:compatibleWidthLimitDp="600"
                  android:largestWidthLimitDp="720"/>
```

> *Where possible you should optimize your application for different screen resolutions and densities using the resources folder, as shown later in this chapter, rather than enforcing a subset of supported screens.*

➤ `supports-gl-texture` — Declares that the application is capable of providing texture assets that are compressed using a particular GL texture compression format. You must use multiple supports-gl-texture elements if your application is capable of supporting multiple texture compression formats. You can find the most up-to-date list of supported GL texture compression format values at `http://developer.android.com/guide/topics/manifest/supports-gl-texture-element.html`.

```
<supports-gl-texture android:name="GL_OES_compressed_ETC1_RGB8_texture" />
```

➤ `uses-permission` — As part of the security model, `uses-permission` tags declare the user permissions your application requires. Each permission you specify will be presented to the user before the application is installed. Permissions are required for many APIs and method calls, generally those with an associated cost or security implication (such as dialing, receiving SMS, or using the location-based services).

```
<uses-permission android:name="android.permission.ACCESS_FINE_LOCATION"/>
```

➤ `permission` — Your application components can also create permissions to restrict access to shared application components. You can use the existing platform permissions for this purpose or define your own permissions in the manifest. To do this, use the `permission` tag to create a permission definition.

Your application components can then create permissions by adding an `android:permission` attribute. Then you can include a `uses-permission` tag in your manifest to use these protected components, both in the application that includes the protected component and any other application that wants to use it.

Within the `permission` tag, you can specify the level of access the permission permits (`normal`, `dangerous`, `signature`, `signatureOrSystem`), a label, and an external resource containing the description that explains the risks of granting the specified permission. More details on creating and using your own permissions can be found in Chapter 18, "Advanced Android Development."

```
<permission android:name="com.paad.DETONATE_DEVICE"
            android:protectionLevel="dangerous"
            android:label="Self Destruct"
            android:description="@string/detonate_description">
</permission>
```

➤   `instrumentation` — Instrumentation classes provide a test framework for your application components at run time. They provide hooks to monitor your application and its interaction with the system resources. Create a new node for each of the test classes you've created for your application.

```
<instrumentation android:label="My Test"
                 android:name=".MyTestClass"
                 android:targetPackage="com.paad.apackage">
</instrumentation>
```

Note that you can use a period (.) as shorthand for prepending the manifest package to a class within your package.

➤   `application` — A manifest can contain only one application node. It uses attributes to specify the metadata for your application (including its title, icon, and theme). During development you should include a `debuggable` attribute set to `true` to enable debugging, then be sure to disable it for your release builds.

The `application` node also acts as a container for the Activity, Service, Content Provider, and Broadcast Receiver nodes that specify the application components. Later in this chapter you'll learn how to create and use your own Application class extension to manage application state. You specify the name of your custom application class using the `android:name` attribute.

```
<application android:icon="@drawable/icon"
             android:logo="@drawable/logo"
             android:theme="@android:style/Theme.Light"
             android:name=".MyApplicationClass"
             android:debuggable="true">
             [ ... application nodes ... ]
</application>
```

➤   `activity` — An `activity` tag is required for every Activity within your application. Use the `android:name` attribute to specify the `Activity` class name. You must include the main launch Activity and any other Activity that may be displayed. Trying to start an Activity that's not defined in the manifest will throw a runtime exception. Each Activity node supports `intent-filter` child tags that define the Intents that can be used to start the Activity. Later in this chapter you'll explore the Activity manifest entry in more detail.

Note, again, that a period is used as shorthand for the application's package name when specifying the Activity's class name.

```
<activity android:name=".MyActivity" android:label="@string/app_name">
  <intent-filter>
    <action android:name="android.intent.action.MAIN" />
    <category android:name=»android.intent.category.LAUNCHER» />
  </intent-filter>
</activity>
```

➤ `service` — As with the `activity` tag, add a `service` tag for each `Service` class used in your application. Service tags also support `intent-filter` child tags to allow late runtime binding.

```
<service android:name=".MyService">
</service>
```

➤ `provider` — Provider tags specify each of your application's Content Providers. Content Providers are used to manage database access and sharing.

```
<provider android:name=".MyContentProvider"
          android:authorities="com.paad.myapp.MyContentProvider"/>
```

➤ `receiver` — By adding a receiver tag, you can register a Broadcast Receiver without having to launch your application first. As you'll see in Chapter 5, Broadcast Receivers are like global event listeners that, when registered, will execute whenever a matching Intent is broadcast by the system or an application. By registering a Broadcast Receiver in the manifest you can make this process entirely autonomous. If a matching Intent is broadcast, your application will be started automatically and the registered Broadcast Receiver will be executed. Each receiver node supports `intent-filter` child tags that define the Intents that can be used to trigger the receiver:

```
<receiver android:name=".MyIntentReceiver">
  <intent-filter>
    <action android:name="com.paad.mybroadcastaction" />
  </intent-filter>
</receiver>
```

➤ `uses-library` — Used to specify a shared library that this application requires. For example, the maps APIs described in Chapter 13, "Maps, Geocoding, and Location-Based Services," are packaged as a separate library that is not automatically linked. You can specify that a particular package is required — which prevents the application from being installed on devices without the specified library — or optional, in which case your application must use reflection to check for the library before attempting to make use of it.

```
<uses-library android:name="com.google.android.maps"
              android:required="false"/>
```

> *You can find a more detailed description of the manifest and each of these nodes at* `http://developer.android.com/guide/topics/manifest/manifest-intro.html`*.*

The ADT New Project Wizard automatically creates a new manifest file when it creates a new project. You'll return to the manifest as each of the application components is introduced and explored.

USING THE MANIFEST EDITOR

The Android Development Tools (ADT) plug-in includes a Manifest Editor, so you don't have to manipulate the underlying XML directly.

To use the Manifest Editor in Eclipse, right-click the `AndroidManifest.xml` file in your project folder, and select Open With ⇨ Android Manifest Editor. This presents the Android Manifest Overview screen, as shown in Figure 3-1. This screen gives you a high-level view of your application structure, enabling you to set your application version information and root level manifest nodes, including `uses-sdk` and `uses-features`, as described previously in this chapter. It also provides shortcut links to the Application, Permissions, Instrumentation, and raw XML screens.

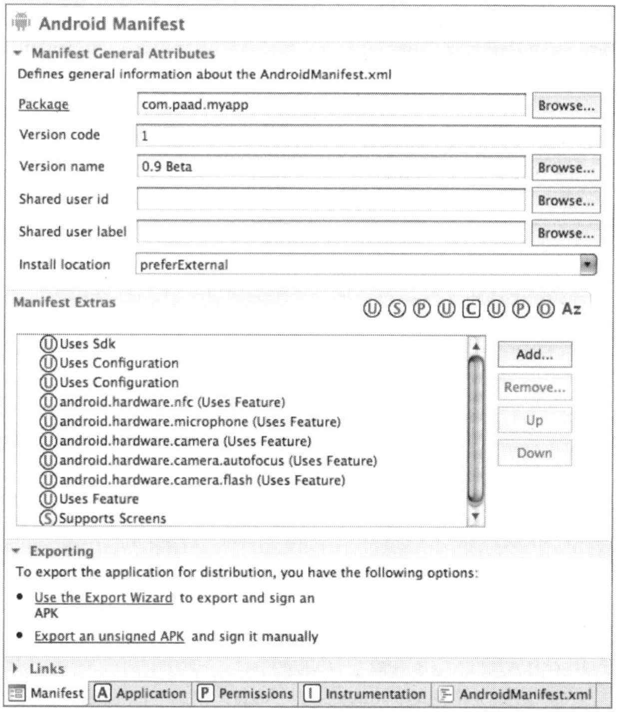

FIGURE 3-1

Each of the next three tabs contains a visual interface for managing the application, security, and instrumentation (testing) settings, while the last tab (labeled with the manifest's filename) gives access to the underlying XML.

Of particular interest is the Application tab, as shown in Figure 3-2. Use it to manage the application node and the application component hierarchy, where you specify each of your application's components.

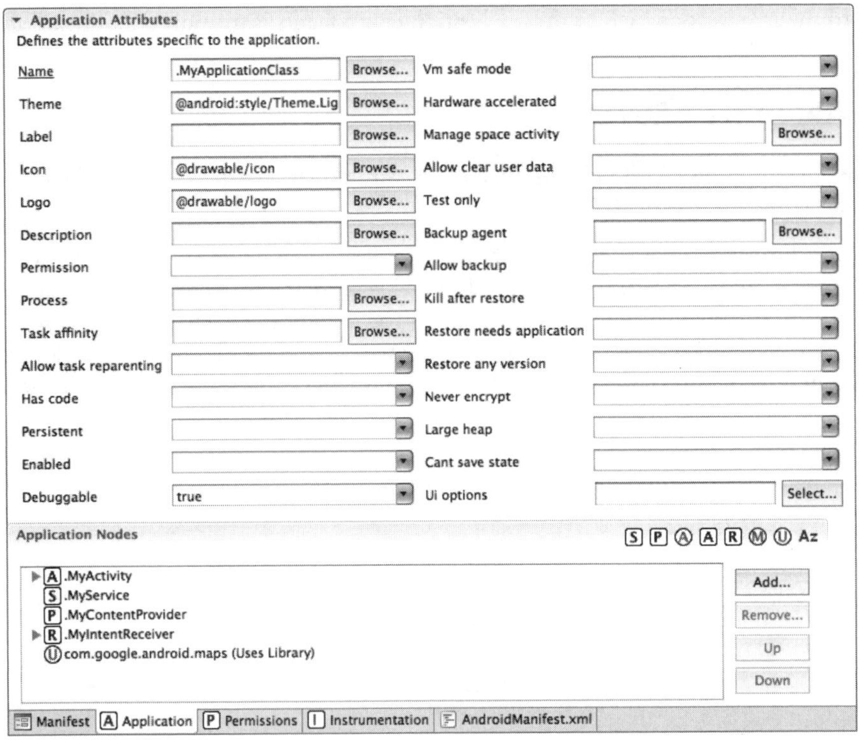

FIGURE 3-2

You can specify an application's attributes — including its icon, label, and theme — in the Application Attributes panel. The Application Nodes tree beneath it lets you manage the application components, including their attributes and any associated Intent Filters.

EXTERNALIZING RESOURCES

It's always good practice to keep non-code resources, such as images and string constants, external to your code. Android supports the externalization of resources, ranging from simple values such as strings and colors to more complex resources such as images (Drawables), animations, themes, and menus. Perhaps the most powerful externalizable resources are layouts.

By externalizing resources, you make them easier to maintain, update, and manage. This also lets you easily define alternative resource values for internationalization and to include different resources to support variations in hardware — particularly, screen size and resolution.

You'll see later in this section how Android dynamically selects resources from resource trees that contain different values for alternative hardware configurations, languages, and locations. When an application starts, Android automatically selects the correct resources without you having to write a line of code.

Among other things, this lets you change the layout based on the screen size and orientation, images based on screen density, and customize text prompts based on a user's language and country.

Creating Resources

Application resources are stored under the `res` folder in your project hierarchy. Each of the available resource types is stored in subfolders, grouped by resource type.

If you start a project using the ADT Wizard, it creates a `res` folder that contains subfolders for the `values`, `drawable-ldpi`, `drawable-mdpi`, `drawable-hdpi`, and `layout` resources that contain the default string resource definitions, application icon, and layouts respectively, as shown in Figure 3-3.

Note that three `drawable` resource folders contain three different icons: one each for low, medium, and high density displays respectively.

Each resource type is stored in a different folder: simple values, Drawables, colors, layouts, animations, styles, menus, XML files (including searchables), and raw resources. When your application is built, these resources will be compiled and compressed as efficiently as possible and included in your application package.

FIGURE 3-3

This process also generates an `R` class file that contains references to each of the resources you include in your project. This enables you to reference the resources in your code, with the advantage of design-time syntax checking.

The following sections describe many of the specific resource types available within these categories and how to create them for your applications.

In all cases, the resource filenames should contain only lowercase letters, numbers, and the period (.) and underscore (_) symbols.

Simple Values

Supported simple values include strings, colors, dimensions, styles, and string or integer arrays. All simple values are stored within XML files in the `res/values` folder.

Within each XML file, you indicate the type of value being stored using tags, as shown in the sample XML file in Listing 3-1.

LISTING 3-1: Simple values XML

```xml
<?xml version="1.0" encoding="utf-8"?>
<resources>
  <string name="app_name">To Do List</string>
  <plurals name="androidPlural">
    <item quantity="one">One android</item>
    <item quantity="other">%d androids</item>
  </plurals>
  <color name="app_background">#FF0000FF</color>
  <dimen name="default_border">5px</dimen>
  <string-array name="string_array">
    <item>Item 1</item>
    <item>Item 2</item>
    <item>Item 3</item>
  </string-array>
  <array name="integer_array">
    <item>3</item>
    <item>2</item>
    <item>1</item>
  </array>
</resources>
```

code snippet PA4AD_Ch03_Manifest_and_Resources/res/values/simple_values.xml

This example includes all the simple value types. By convention, resources are generally stored in separate files, one for each type; for example, `res/values/strings.xml` would contain only string resources.

The following sections detail the options for defining simple resources.

Strings

Externalizing your strings helps maintain consistency within your application and makes it much easier to internationalize them.

String resources are specified with the `string` tag, as shown in the following XML snippet:

```xml
<string name="stop_message">Stop.</string>
```

Android supports simple text styling, so you can use the HTML tags `<b>`, `<i>`, and `<u>` to apply bold, italics, or underlining, respectively, to parts of your text strings, as shown in the following example:

```xml
<string name="stop_message"><b>Stop.</b></string>
```

You can use resource strings as input parameters for the `String.format` method. However, `String.format` does not support the text styling previously described. To apply styling to a format string, you have to escape the HTML tags when creating your resource, as shown in the following snippet:

```xml
<string name="stop_message">&lt;b>Stop&lt;/b>. %1$s</string>
```

Within your code, use the `Html.fromHtml` method to convert this back into a styled character sequence.

```
String rString = getString(R.string.stop_message);
String fString = String.format(rString, "Collaborate and listen.");
CharSequence styledString = Html.fromHtml(fString);
```

You can also define alternative plural forms for your strings. This enables you to define different strings based on the number of items you refer to. For example, in English you would refer to "one Android" or "seven Androids."

By creating a plurals resource, you can specify an alternative string for any of zero, one, multiple, few, many, or other quantities. In English only the singular is a special case, but some languages require finer detail:

```
<plurals name="unicornCount">
  <item quantity="one">One unicorn</item>
  <item quantity="other">%d unicorns</item>
</plurals>
```

To access the correct plural in code, use the `getQuantityString` method on your application's `Resources` object, passing in the resource ID of the plural resource, and specifying the number of objects you want to describe:

```
Resources resources = getResources();
String unicornStr = resources.getQuantityString(
    R.plurals.unicornCount, unicornCount, unicornCount);
```

The object count is passed in twice — once to return the correct plural string, and again as an input parameter to complete the sentence.

Colors

Use the `color` tag to define a new color resource. Specify the color value using a # symbol followed by the (optional) alpha channel, and then the red, green, and blue values using one or two hexadecimal numbers with any of the following notations:

➤ #RGB

➤ #RRGGBB

➤ #ARGB

➤ #AARRGGBB

The following example shows how to specify a fully opaque blue and a partially transparent green:

```
<color name="opaque_blue">#00F</color>
<color name="transparent_green">#7700FF00</color>
```

Dimensions

Dimensions are most commonly referenced within style and layout resources. They're useful for creating layout constants, such as borders and font heights.

To specify a dimension resource, use the `dimen` tag, specifying the dimension value, followed by an identifier describing the scale of your dimension:

➤ px (screen pixels)

➤ in (physical inches)

➤ `pt` (physical points)

➤ `mm` (physical millimeters)

➤ `dp` (density-independent pixels)

➤ `sp` (scale-independent pixels)

Although you can use any of these measurements to define a dimension, it's best practice to use either density- or scale-independent pixels. These alternatives let you define a dimension using relative scales that account for different screen resolutions and densities to simplify scaling on different hardware.

Scale-independent pixels are particularly well suited when defining font sizes because they automatically scale if the user changes the system font size.

The following XML snippet shows how to specify dimension values for a large font size and a standard border:

```
<dimen name="standard_border">5dp</dimen>
<dimen name="large_font_size">16sp</dimen>
```

Styles and Themes

Style resources let your applications maintain a consistent look and feel by enabling you to specify the attribute values used by Views. The most common use of themes and styles is to store the colors and fonts for an application.

To create a style, use a `style` tag that includes a `name` attribute and contains one or more `item` tags. Each `item` tag should include a `name` attribute used to specify the attribute (such as font size or color) being defined. The tag itself should then contain the value, as shown in the following skeleton code.

```
<?xml version="1.0" encoding="utf-8"?>
<resources>
  <style name="base_text">
      <item name="android:textSize">14sp</item>
      <item name="android:textColor">#111</item>
  </style>
</resources>
```

Styles support inheritance using the parent attribute on the style tag, making it easy to create simple variations:

```
<?xml version="1.0" encoding="utf-8"?>
<resources>
  <style name="small_text" parent="base_text">
    <item name="android:textSize">8sp</item>
  </style>
</resources>
```

Drawables

Drawable resources include bitmaps and NinePatches (stretchable PNG images). They also include complex composite Drawables, such as `LevelListDrawables` and `StateListDrawables`, that can be defined in XML.

> *Both NinePatch Drawables and complex composite resources are covered in more detail in the next chapter.*

All Drawables are stored as individual files in the `res/drawable` folder. Note that it's good practice to store bitmap image assets in the appropriate drawable -ldpi, -mdpi, -hdpi, and -xhdpi folders, as described earlier in this chapter. The resource identifier for a Drawable resource is the lowercase file name without its extension.

> *The preferred format for a bitmap resource is PNG, although JPG and GIF files are also supported.*

Layouts

Layout resources enable you to decouple your presentation layer from your business logic by designing UI layouts in XML rather than constructing them in code.

You can use layouts to define the UI for any visual component, including Activities, Fragments, and Widgets. Once defined in XML, the layout must be "inflated" into the user interface. Within an Activity this is done using `setContentView` (usually within the `onCreate` method), whereas Fragment Views are inflated using the `inflate` method from the `Inflator` object passed in to the Fragment's `onCreateView` handler.

For more detailed information on using and creating layouts in Activities and Fragments, see Chapter 4, "Building User Interfaces."

Using layouts to construct your screens in XML is best practice in Android. The decoupling of the layout from the code enables you to create optimized layouts for different hardware configurations, such as varying screen sizes, orientation, or the presence of keyboards and touchscreens.

Each layout definition is stored in a separate file, each containing a single layout, in the `res/layout` folder. The filename then becomes the resource identifier.

A thorough explanation of layout containers and View elements is included in the next chapter, but as an example Listing 3-2 shows the layout created by the New Project Wizard. It uses a Linear Layout (described in more detail in Chapter 4) as a layout container for a Text View that displays the "Hello World" greeting.

LISTING 3-2: Hello World layout

```xml
<?xml version="1.0" encoding="utf-8"?>
<LinearLayout xmlns:android="http://schemas.android.com/apk/res/android"
    android:orientation="vertical"
    android:layout_width="fill_parent"
    android:layout_height="fill_parent">
```

continues

LISTING 3-2 *(continued)*

```
<TextView
  android:layout_width="fill_parent"
  android:layout_height="wrap_content"
  android:text="@string/hello"
/>
</LinearLayout>
```

code snippet PA4AD_Ch03_Manifest_and_Resources/res/layout/main.xml

Animations

Android supports three types of animation:

➤ **Property animations** — A tweened animation that can be used to potentially animate any property on the target object by applying incremental changes between two values. This can be used for anything from changing the color or opacity of a View to gradually fade it in or out, to changing a font size, or increasing a character's hit points.

➤ **View animations** — Tweened animations that can be applied to rotate, move, and stretch a View.

➤ **Frame animations** — Frame-by-frame "cell" animations used to display a sequence of Drawable images.

 A comprehensive overview of creating, using, and applying animations can be found in Chapter 11, "Advanced User Experience."

Defining animations as external resources enables you to reuse the same sequence in multiple places and provides you with the opportunity to present different animations based on device hardware or orientation.

Property Animations

Property animators were introduced in Android 3.0 (API level 11). It is a powerful framework that can be used to animate almost anything.

Each property animation is stored in a separate XML file in the project's `res/animator` folder. As with layouts and Drawable resources, the animation's filename is used as its resource identifier.

You can use a property animator to animate almost any property on a target object. You can define animators that are tied to a specific property, or a generic value animator that can be allocated to any property and object.

Property animators are extremely useful and are used extensively for animating Fragments in Android. You will explore them in more detail in Chapter 11.

The following simple XML snippet shows a property animator that changes the opacity of the target object by calling its `setAlpha` method incrementally between 0 and 1 over the course of a second:

```xml
<?xml version="1.0" encoding="utf-8"?>
<objectAnimator xmlns:android="http://schemas.android.com/apk/res/android"
    android:propertyName="alpha"
    android:duration="1000"
    android:valueFrom="0.0"
    android:valueTo="1.0"
/>
```

View Animations

Each view animation is stored in a separate XML file in the project's `res/anim` folder. As with layouts and Drawable resources, the animation's filename is used as its resource identifier.

An animation can be defined for changes in `alpha` (fading), `scale` (scaling), `translate` (movement), or `rotate` (rotation).

Table 3-1 shows the valid attributes, and attribute values, supported by each animation type.

TABLE 3-1: Animation type attributes

ANIMATION TYPE	ATTRIBUTES	VALID VALUES
Alpha	fromAlpha/toAlpha	Float from 0 to 1
Scale	fromXScale/toXScale	Float from 0 to 1
	fromYScale/toYScale	Float from 0 to 1
	pivotX/pivotY	String of the percentage of graphic width/height from 0% to 100%
Translate	fromX/toX	Float from 0 to 1
	fromY/toY	Float from 0 to 1
Rotate	fromDegrees/toDegrees	Float from 0 to 360
	pivotX/pivotY	String of the percentage of graphic width/height from 0% to 100%

You can create a combination of animations using the `set` tag. An animation set contains one or more animation transformations and supports various additional tags and attributes to customize when and how each animation within the set is run.

The following list shows some of the `set` tags available:

➤ `duration` — Duration of the full animation in milliseconds.

➤ `startOffset` — Millisecond delay before the animation starts.

➤ `fillBeforetrue` — Applies the animation transformation before it begins.

➤ `fillAftertrue` — Applies the animation transformation after it ends.

➤ `interpolator` — Sets how the speed of this effect varies over time. Chapter 11 explores the interpolators available. To specify one, reference the system animation resources at `android:anim/interpolatorName`.

> *If you do not use the `startOffset` tag, all the animation effects within a set will execute simultaneously.*

The following example shows an animation set that spins the target 360 degrees while it shrinks and fades out:

```xml
<?xml version="1.0" encoding="utf-8"?>
<set xmlns:android="http://schemas.android.com/apk/res/android"
     android:interpolator="@android:anim/accelerate_interpolator">
  <rotate
    android:fromDegrees="0"
    android:toDegrees="360"
    android:pivotX="50%"
    android:pivotY="50%"
    android:startOffset="500"
    android:duration="1000" />
  <scale
    android:fromXScale="1.0"
    android:toXScale="0.0"
    android:fromYScale="1.0"
    android:toYScale="0.0"
    android:pivotX="50%"
    android:pivotY="50%"
    android:startOffset="500"
    android:duration="500" />
  <alpha
    android:fromAlpha="1.0"
    android:toAlpha="0.0"
    android:startOffset="500"
    android:duration="500" />
</set>
```

Frame-by-Frame Animations

Frame-by-frame animations produce a sequence of Drawables, each of which is displayed for a specified duration.

Because frame-by-frame animations represent animated Drawables, they are stored in the `res/drawable` folder and use their filenames (without the `.xml` extension) as their resource Ids.

The following XML snippet shows a simple animation that cycles through a series of bitmap resources, displaying each one for half a second. To use this snippet, you need to create new image resources `android1` through `android3`:

```xml
<animation-list
    xmlns:android="http://schemas.android.com/apk/res/android"
    android:oneshot="false">
```

```
            <item android:drawable="@drawable/android1" android:duration="500" />
            <item android:drawable="@drawable/android2" android:duration="500" />
            <item android:drawable="@drawable/android3" android:duration="500" />
        </animation-list>
```

Note that in many cases you should include multiple resolutions of each of the drawables used within the animation list in the drawable-ldpi, -mdi, -hdpi, and -xhdpi folders, as appropriate.

To play the animation, start by assigning the resource to a host View before getting a reference to the Animation Drawable object and starting it:

```
ImageView androidIV = (ImageView)findViewById(R.id.iv_android);
androidIV.setBackgroundResource(R.drawable.android_anim);

AnimationDrawable androidAnimation =
    (AnimationDrawable) androidIV.getBackground();

androidAnimation.start();
```

Typically, this is done in two steps; assigning the resource to the background should be done within the `onCreate` handler.

Within this handler the animation is not fully attached to the window, so the animations can't be started; instead, this is usually done as a result to user action (such as a button press) or within the `onWindowFocusChanged` handler.

Menus

Create menu resources to design your menu layouts in XML, rather than constructing them in code.

You can use menu resources to define both Activity and context menus within your applications, and provide the same options you would have when constructing your menus in code. When defined in XML, a menu is inflated within your application via the `inflate` method of the `MenuInflator` Service, usually within the `onCreateOptionsMenu` method. You examine menus in more detail in Chapter 10.

Each menu definition is stored in a separate file, each containing a single menu, in the `res/menu` folder — the filename then becomes the resource identifier. Using XML to define your menus is best-practice design in Android.

A thorough explanation of menu options is included in Chapter 10, but Listing 3-3 shows a simple example.

LISTING 3-3: Simple menu layout resource

```
<?xml version="1.0" encoding="utf-8"?>
<menu xmlns:android="http://schemas.android.com/apk/res/android">
    <item android:id="@+id/menu_refresh"
          android:title="@string/refresh_mi" />
    <item android:id="@+id/menu_settings"
          android:title="@string/settings_mi" />
</menu>
```

code snippet PA4AD_Snippets_Chapter3/res/menu/menu.xml

Using Resources

In addition to the resources you supply, the Android platform includes several system resources that you can use in your applications. All resources can be used directly from your application code and can also be referenced from within other resources. For example, a dimension resource might be referenced in a layout definition.

Later in this chapter you learn how to define alternative resource values for different languages, locations, and hardware. It's important to note that when using resources, you shouldn't choose a particular specialized version. Android will automatically select the most appropriate value for a given resource identifier based on the current hardware, device, and language configurations.

Using Resources in Code

Access resources in code using the static R class. R is a generated class based on your external resources, and created when your project is compiled. The R class contains static subclasses for each of the resource types for which you've defined at least one resource. For example, the default new project includes the R.string and R.drawable subclasses.

> If you use the ADT plug-in in Eclipse, the R class will be created automatically when you make any change to an external resource file or folder. If you are not using the plug-in, use the AAPT tool to compile your project and generate the R class. R is a compiler-generated class, so don't make any manual modifications to it because they will be lost when the file is regenerated.

Each of the subclasses within R exposes its associated resources as variables, with the variable names matching the resource identifiers — for example, R.string.app_name or R.drawable.icon.

The value of these variables is an integer that represents each resource's location in the resource table, *not* an instance of the resource itself.

Where a constructor or method, such as setContentView, accepts a resource identifier, you can pass in the resource variable, as shown in the following code snippet:

```
// Inflate a layout resource.
setContentView(R.layout.main);
// Display a transient dialog box that displays the
// error message string resource.
Toast.makeText(this, R.string.app_error, Toast.LENGTH_LONG).show();
```

When you need an instance of the resource itself, you need to use helper methods to extract them from the resource table. The resource table is represented within your application as an instance of the Resources class.

These methods perform lookups on the application's current resource table, so these helper methods can't be static. Use the getResources method on your application context, as shown in the following snippet, to access your application's Resources instance:

```
Resources myResources = getResources();
```

The `Resources` class includes getters for each of the available resource types and generally works by passing in the resource ID you'd like an instance of. The following code snippet shows an example of using the helper methods to return a selection of resource values:

```
Resources myResources = getResources();

CharSequence styledText = myResources.getText(R.string.stop_message);
Drawable icon = myResources.getDrawable(R.drawable.app_icon);

int opaqueBlue = myResources.getColor(R.color.opaque_blue);

float borderWidth = myResources.getDimension(R.dimen.standard_border);

Animation tranOut;
tranOut = AnimationUtils.loadAnimation(this, R.anim.spin_shrink_fade);

ObjectAnimator animator =
  (ObjectAnimator)AnimatorInflater.loadAnimator(this,
  R.anim.my_animator);

String[] stringArray;
stringArray = myResources.getStringArray(R.array.string_array);

int[] intArray = myResources.getIntArray(R.array.integer_array);
```

Frame-by-frame animated resources are inflated into `AnimationResources`. You can return the value using `getDrawable` and casting the return value, as shown here:

```
AnimationDrawable androidAnimation;
androidAnimation =
  (AnimationDrawable)myResources.getDrawable(R.drawable.frame_by_frame);
```

Referencing Resources Within Resources

You can also use resource references as attribute values in other XML resources.

This is particularly useful for layouts and styles, letting you create specialized variations on themes and localized strings and image assets. It's also a useful way to support different images and spacing for a layout to ensure that it's optimized for different screen sizes and resolutions.

To reference one resource from another, use the @ notation, as shown in the following snippet:

```
attribute="@[packagename:]resourcetype/resourceidentifier"
```

> *Android assumes you use a resource from the same package, so you only need to fully qualify the package name if you use a resource from a different package.*

Listing 3-4 shows a layout that uses color, dimension, and string resources.

LISTING 3-4: Using resources in a layout

```xml
<?xml version="1.0" encoding="utf-8"?>
<LinearLayout
    xmlns:android="http://schemas.android.com/apk/res/android"
    android:orientation="vertical"
    android:layout_width="match_parent"
    android:layout_height="match_parent"
    android:padding="@dimen/standard_border">
    <EditText
        android:id="@+id/myEditText"
        android:layout_width="match_parent"
        android:layout_height="wrap_content"
        android:text="@string/stop_message"
        android:textColor="@color/opaque_blue"
    />
</LinearLayout>
```

code snippet PA4AD_Ch03_Manifest_and_Resources/res/layout/reslayout.xml

Using System Resources

The Android framework makes many native resources available, providing you with various strings, images, animations, styles, and layouts to use in your applications.

Accessing the system resources in code is similar to using your own resources. The difference is that you use the native Android resource classes available from `android.R`, rather than the application-specific `R` class. The following code snippet uses the `getString` method available in the application context to retrieve an error message available from the system resources:

```java
CharSequence httpError = getString(android.R.string.httpErrorBadUrl);
```

To access system resources in XML, specify `android` as the package name, as shown in this XML snippet:

```xml
<EditText
    android:id="@+id/myEditText"
    android:layout_width="match_parent"
    android:layout_height="wrap_content"
    android:text="@android:string/httpErrorBadUrl"
    android:textColor="@android:color/darker_gray"
/>
```

Referring to Styles in the Current Theme

Using themes is an excellent way to ensure consistency for your application's UI. Rather than fully define each style, Android provides a shortcut to enable you to use styles from the currently applied theme.

To do this, use `?android:` rather than `@` as a prefix to the resource you want to use. The following example shows a snippet of the preceding code but uses the current theme's text color rather than a system resource:

```xml
<EditText
    android:id="@+id/myEditText"
```

```
        android:layout_width="match_parent"
        android:layout_height="wrap_content"
        android:text="@android:string/httpErrorBadUrl"
        android:textColor="?android:textColor"
/>
```

This technique enables you to create styles that change if the current theme changes, without you modifying each individual style resource.

Creating Resources for Different Languages and Hardware

Using the directory structure described here, you can create different resource values for specific languages, locations, and hardware configurations. Android chooses from among these values dynamically at run time using its dynamic resource-selection mechanism.

You can specify alternative resource values using a parallel directory structure within the res folder. A hyphen (-) is used to separate qualifiers that specify the conditions you provide alternatives for.

The following example hierarchy shows a folder structure that features default string values, with French language and French Canadian location variations:

```
Project/
  res/
    values/
      strings.xml
    values-fr/
      strings.xml
    values-fr-rCA/
      strings.xml
```

The following list gives the qualifiers you can use to customize your resource values:

➤ **Mobile Country Code and Mobile Network Code (MCC/MNC)** — The country, and optionally the network, associated with the SIM currently used in the device. The MCC is specified by mcc followed by the three-digit country code. You can optionally add the MNC using mnc and the two- or three-digit network code (for example, mcc234-mnc20 or mcc310). You can find a list of MCC/MNC codes on Wikipedia at http://en.wikipedia.org/wiki/ MobileNetworkCode.

➤ **Language and Region** — Language specified by the lowercase two-letter ISO 639-1 language code, followed optionally by a region specified by a lowercase r followed by the uppercase two-letter ISO 3166-1-alpha-2 language code (for example, en, en-rUS, or en-rGB).

➤ **Smallest Screen Width** — The lowest of the device's screen dimensions (height and width) specified in the form sw<Dimension value>dp (for example, sw600dp, sw320dp, or sw720dp). This is generally used when providing multiple layouts, where the value specified should be the smallest screen width that your layout requires in order to render correctly. Where you supply multiple directories with different smallest screen width qualifiers, Android selects the largest value that doesn't exceed the smallest dimension available on the device.

➤ **Available Screen Width** — The minimum screen width required to use the contained resources, specified in the form w<Dimension value>dp (for example, w600dp, w320dp, or w720dp). Also used to supply multiple layouts alternatives, but unlike smallest screen width, the available screen width changes to reflect the current screen width when the device orientation changes. Android selects the largest value that doesn't exceed the currently available screen width.

➤ **Available Screen Height** — The minimum screen height required to use the contained resources, specified in the form h<Dimension value>dp (for example, h720dp, h480dp, or h1280dp). Like available screen width, the available screen height changes when the device orientation changes to reflect the current screen height. Android selects the largest value that doesn't exceed the currently available screen height.

➤ **Screen Size** — One of small (smaller than HVGA), medium (at least HVGA and typically smaller than VGA), large (VGA or larger), or xlarge (significantly larger than HVGA). Because each of these screen categories can include devices with significantly different screen sizes (particularly tablets), it's good practice to use the more specific smallest screen size, and available screen width and height whenever possible. Because they precede this screen size qualifier, where both are specified, the more specific qualifiers will be used in preference where supported.

➤ **Screen Aspect Ratio** — Specify long or notlong for resources designed specifically for wide screen. (For example, WVGA is long; QVGA is notlong.)

➤ **Screen Orientation:** One of port (portrait), land (landscape), or square (square).

➤ **Dock Mode** — One of car or desk. Introduced in API level 8.

➤ **Night Mode** — One of night (night mode) or notnight (day mode). Introduced in API level 8. Used in combination with the dock mode qualifier, this provides a simple way to change the theme and/or color scheme of an application to make it more suitable for use at night in a car dock.

➤ **Screen Pixel Density** — Pixel density in dots per inch (dpi). Best practice is to supply ldpi, mdpi, hdpi, or xhdpi to specify low (120 dpi), medium (160 dpi), high (240 dpi), or extra high (320 dpi) pixel density assets, respectively. You can specify nodpi for bitmap resources you don't want scaled to support an exact screen density. To better support applications targeting televisions running Android, you can also use the tvdpi qualifier for assets of approximately 213dpi. This is generally unnecessary for most applications, where including medium- and high-resolution assets is sufficient for a good user experience. Unlike with other resource types, Android does not require an exact match to select a resource. When selecting the appropriate folder, it chooses the nearest match to the device's pixel density and scales the resulting Drawables accordingly.

➤ **Touchscreen Type** — One of notouch, stylus, or finger, allowing you to provide layouts or dimensions optimized for the style of touchscreen input available on the host device.

➤ **Keyboard Availability** — One of keysexposed, keyshidden, or keyssoft.

➤ **Keyboard Input Type** — One of nokeys, qwerty, or 12key.

➤ **Navigation Key Availability** — One of navexposed or navhidden.

➤ **UI Navigation Type** — One of nonav, dpad, trackball, or wheel.

➤ **Platform Version** — The target API level, specified in the form v<API Level> (for example, v7). Used for resources restricted to devices running at the specified API level or higher.

You can specify multiple qualifiers for any resource type, separating each qualifier with a hyphen. Any combination is supported; however, they must be used in the order given in the preceding list, and no more than one value can be used per qualifier.

The following example shows valid and invalid directory names for alternative layout resources.

VALID

```
layout-large-land
layout-xlarge-port-keyshidden
layout-long-land-notouch-nokeys
```

INVALID

```
values-rUS-en (out of order)
values-rUS-rUK (multiple values for a single qualifier)
```

When Android retrieves a resource at run time, it finds the best match from the available alternatives. Starting with a list of all the folders in which the required value exists, it selects the one with the greatest number of matching qualifiers. If two folders are an equal match, the tiebreaker is based on the order of the matched qualifiers in the preceding list.

> If no resource matches are found on a given device, your application throws an exception when attempting to access that resource. To avoid this, you should always include default values for each resource type in a folder that includes no qualifiers.

Runtime Configuration Changes

Android handles runtime changes to the language, location, and hardware by terminating and restarting the active Activity. This forces the resource resolution for the Activity to be reevaluated and the most appropriate resource values for the new configuration to be selected.

In some special cases this default behavior may be inconvenient, particularly for applications that don't want to present a different UI based on screen orientation changes. You can customize your application's response to such changes by detecting and reacting to them yourself.

To have an Activity listen for runtime configuration changes, add an android:configChanges attribute to its manifest node, specifying the configuration changes you want to handle.

The following list describes some of the configuration changes you can specify:

➤ mcc and mnc — A SIM has been detected and the mobile country or network code (respectively) has changed.

➤ locale — The user has changed the device's language settings.

➤ `keyboardHidden` — The keyboard, d-pad, or other input mechanism has been exposed or hidden.

➤ `keyboard` — The type of keyboard has changed; for example, the phone may have a 12-key keypad that flips out to reveal a full keyboard, or an external keyboard might have been plugged in.

➤ `fontScale` — The user has changed the preferred font size.

➤ `uiMode` — The global UI mode has changed. This typically occurs if you switch between car mode, day or night mode, and so on.

➤ `orientation` — The screen has been rotated between portrait and landscape.

➤ `screenLayout` — The screen layout has changed; typically occurs if a different screen has been activated.

➤ `screenSize` — Introduced in Honeycomb MR2 (API level 12), occurs when the available screen size has changed, for example a change in orientation between landscape and portrait.

➤ `smallestScreenSize` — Introduced in Honeycomb MR2 (API level 12), occurs when the physical screen size has changed, such as when a device has been connected to an external display.

In certain circumstances multiple events will be triggered simultaneously. For example, when the user slides out a keyboard, most devices fire both the `keyboardHidden` and `orientation` events, and connecting an external display on a post-Honeycomb MR2 device is likely to trigger `orientation`, `screenLayout`, `screenSize`, and `smallestScreenSize` events.

You can select multiple events you want to handle yourself by separating the values with a pipe (|), as shown in Listing 3-5, which shows an activity node declaring that it will handle changes in screen size and orientation, and keyboard visibility.

LISTING 3-5: Activity definition for handling dynamic resource changes

```
<activity
  android:name=".MyActivity"
  android:label="@string/app_name"
  android:configChanges="screenSize|orientation|keyboardHidden">
  <intent-filter >
    <action android:name="android.intent.action.MAIN" />
    <category android:name="android.intent.category.LAUNCHER" />
  </intent-filter>
</activity>
```

code snippet PA4AD_Ch03_Config_Changes/AndroidManifest.xml

Adding an `android:configChanges` attribute suppresses the restart for the specified configuration changes, instead triggering the `onConfigurationChanged` handler in the associated Activity. Override this method to handle the configuration changes yourself, using the passed-in `Configuration` object to determine the new configuration values, as shown in Listing 3-6. Be sure to call back to the super-class and reload any resource values that the Activity uses, in case they've changed.

LISTING 3-6: Handling configuration changes in code

```
@Override
public void onConfigurationChanged(Configuration newConfig) {
    super.onConfigurationChanged(newConfig);

    // [ ... Update any UI based on resource values ... ]

    if (newConfig.orientation == Configuration.ORIENTATION_LANDSCAPE) {
      // [ ... React to different orientation ... ]
    }

    if (newConfig.keyboardHidden == Configuration.KEYBOARDHIDDEN_NO) {
      // [ ... React to changed keyboard visibility ... ]
    }
}
```

code snippet PA4AD_Ch03_Config_Changes/src/MyActivity.java

When `onConfigurationChanged` is called, the Activity's Resource variables have already been updated with the new values, so they'll be safe to use.

Any configuration change that you don't explicitly flag as being handled by your application will cause your Activity to restart, without a call to `onConfigurationChanged`.

THE ANDROID APPLICATION LIFECYCLE

Unlike many traditional application platforms, Android applications have limited control over their own lifecycles. Instead, application components must listen for changes in the application state and react accordingly, taking particular care to be prepared for untimely termination.

By default, each Android application runs in its own process, each of which is running a separate instance of Dalvik. Memory and process management is handled exclusively by the run time.

> *You can force application components within the same application to run in different processes or to have multiple applications share the same process using the* `android:process` *attribute on the affected component nodes within the manifest.*

Android aggressively manages its resources, doing whatever's necessary to ensure a smooth and stable user experience. In practice that means that processes (and their hosted applications) will be killed, in some case without warning, to free resources for higher-priority applications.

UNDERSTANDING AN APPLICATION'S PRIORITY AND ITS PROCESS' STATES

The order in which processes are killed to reclaim resources is determined by the priority of their hosted applications. An application's priority is equal to that of its highest-priority component.

If two applications have the same priority, the process that has been at that priority longest will be killed first. Process priority is also affected by interprocess dependencies; if an application has a dependency on a Service or Content Provider supplied by a second application, the secondary application has at least as high a priority as the application it supports.

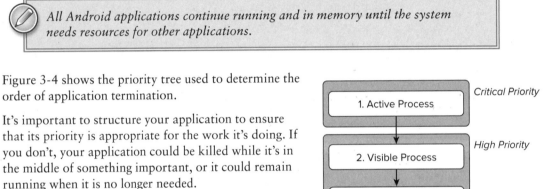

All Android applications continue running and in memory until the system needs resources for other applications.

Figure 3-4 shows the priority tree used to determine the order of application termination.

It's important to structure your application to ensure that its priority is appropriate for the work it's doing. If you don't, your application could be killed while it's in the middle of something important, or it could remain running when it is no longer needed.

The following list details each of the application states shown in Figure 3-4, explaining how the state is determined by the application components of which it comprises:

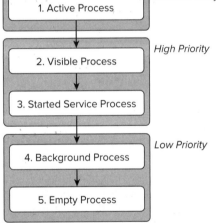

FIGURE 3-4

> **Active processes** — Active (foreground) processes have application components the user is interacting with. These are the processes Android tries to keep responsive by reclaiming resources from other applications. There are generally very few of these processes, and they will be killed only as a last resort.

Active processes include the following:

> Activities in an active state — that is, those in the foreground responding to user events. You will explore Activity states in greater detail later in this chapter.

> Broadcast Receivers executing `onReceive` event handlers as described in Chapter 5.

> Services executing `onStart`, `onCreate`, or `onDestroy` event handlers as described in Chapter 9.

> Running Services that have been flagged to run in the foreground (also described in Chapter 9.)

➤ **Visible processes** — Visible but inactive processes are those hosting "visible" Activities. As the name suggests, visible Activities are visible, but they aren't in the foreground or responding to user events. This happens when an Activity is only partially obscured (by a non-full-screen or transparent Activity). There are generally very few visible processes, and they'll be killed only under extreme circumstances to allow active processes to continue.

➤ **Started Service processes** — Processes hosting Services that have been started. Because these Services don't interact directly with the user, they receive a slightly lower priority than visible Activities or foreground Services. Applications with running Services are still considered foreground processes and won't be killed unless resources are needed for active or visible processes. When the system terminates a running Service it will attempt to restart them (unless you specify that it shouldn't) when resources become available. You'll learn more about Services in Chapter 9.

➤ **Background processes** — Processes hosting Activities that aren't visible and that don't have any running Services. There will generally be a large number of background processes that Android will kill using a last-seen-first-killed pattern in order to obtain resources for foreground processes.

➤ **Empty processes** — To improve overall system performance, Android will often retain an application in memory after it has reached the end of its lifetime. Android maintains this cache to improve the start-up time of applications when they're relaunched. These processes are routinely killed, as required.

INTRODUCING THE ANDROID APPLICATION CLASS

Your application's `Application` object remains instantiated whenever your application runs. Unlike Activities, the Application is not restarted as a result of configuration changes. Extending the `Application` class with your own implementation enables you to do three things:

➤ Respond to application level events broadcast by the Android run time such as low memory conditions.

➤ Transfer objects between application components.

➤ Manage and maintain resources used by several application components.

Of these, the latter two can be better achieved using a separate singleton class. When your `Application` implementation is registered in the manifest, it will be instantiated when your application process is created. As a result, your `Application` implementation is by nature a singleton and should be implemented as such to provide access to its methods and member variables.

Extending and Using the Application Class

Listing 3-7 shows the skeleton code for extending the `Application` class and implementing it as a singleton.

LISTING 3-7: Skeleton Application class

```java
import android.app.Application;
import android.content.res.Configuration;

public class MyApplication extends Application {

  private static MyApplication singleton;

  // Returns the application instance
  public static MyApplication getInstance() {
    return singleton;
  }

  @Override
  public final void onCreate() {
    super.onCreate();
    singleton = this;
  }
}
```

code snippet PA4AD_Ch03_Config_Changes/src/MyApplication.java

When created, you must register your new `Application` class in the manifest's `application` node using a `name` attribute, as shown in the following snippet:

```xml
<application android:icon="@drawable/icon"
             android:name=".MyApplication">
  [... Manifest nodes ...]
</application>
```

Your `Application` implementation will be instantiated when your application is started. Create new state variables and global resources for access from within the application components:

```java
MyObject value = MyApplication.getInstance().getGlobalStateValue();
MyApplication.getInstance().setGlobalStateValue(myObjectValue);
```

Although this can be an effective technique for transferring objects between your loosely coupled application components, or for maintaining application state or shared resources, it is often better to create your own static singleton class rather than extending the `Application` class specifically unless you are also handling the lifecycle events described in the following section.

Overriding the Application Lifecycle Events

The `Application` class provides event handlers for application creation and termination, low memory conditions, and configuration changes (as described in the previous section).

By overriding these methods, you can implement your own application-specific behavior for each of these circumstances:

➤   `onCreate` — Called when the application is created. Override this method to initialize your application singleton and create and initialize any application state variables or shared resources.

➤ `onLowMemory` — Provides an opportunity for well-behaved applications to free additional memory when the system is running low on resources. This will generally only be called when background processes have already been terminated and the current foreground applications are still low on memory. Override this handler to clear caches or release unnecessary resources.

➤ `onTrimMemory` — An application specific alternative to the `onLowMemory` handler introduced in Android 4.0 (API level 13). Called when the run time determines that the current application should attempt to trim its memory overhead – typically when it moves to the background. It includes a level parameter that provides the context around the request.

➤ `onConfigurationChanged` — Unlike Activities `Application` objects are not restarted due to configuration changes. If your application uses values dependent on specific configurations, override this handler to reload those values and otherwise handle configuration changes at an application level.

As shown in Listing 3-8, you must always call through to the superclass event handlers when overriding these methods.

LISTING 3-8: Overriding the Application Lifecycle Handlers

```java
public class MyApplication extends Application {

  private static MyApplication singleton;

  // Returns the application instance
  public static MyApplication getInstance() {
    return singleton;
  }

  @Override
  public final void onCreate() {
    super.onCreate();
    singleton = this;
  }

  @Override
  public final void onLowMemory() {
    super.onLowMemory();
  }

  @Override
  public final void onTrimMemory(int level) {
    super.onTrimMemory(level);
  }

  @Override
  public final void onConfigurationChanged(Configuration newConfig) {
    super.onConfigurationChanged(newConfig);
  }
}
```

code snippet PA4AD_Snippets_Chapter3/MyApplication.java

A CLOSER LOOK AT ANDROID ACTIVITIES

Each Activity represents a screen that an application can present to its users. The more complicated your application, the more screens you are likely to need.

Typically, this includes at least a primary interface screen that handles the main UI functionality of your application. This primary interface generally consists of a number of Fragments that make up your UI and is generally supported by a set of secondary Activities. To move between screens you start a new Activity (or return from one).

Most Activities are designed to occupy the entire display, but you can also create semitransparent or floating Activities.

Creating Activities

Extend `Activity` to create a new `Activity` class. Within this new class you must define the UI and implement your functionality. Listing 3-9 shows the basic skeleton code for a new `Activity`.

LISTING 3-9: Activity skeleton code

```java
package com.paad.activities;

import android.app.Activity;
import android.os.Bundle;

public class MyActivity extends Activity {

  /** Called when the activity is first created. */
  @Override
  public void onCreate(Bundle savedInstanceState) {
    super.onCreate(savedInstanceState);
  }
}
```

code snippet PA4AD_Ch03_Activities/src/MyActivity.java

The base `Activity` class presents an empty screen that encapsulates the window display handling. An empty `Activity` isn't particularly useful, so the first thing you'll want to do is create the UI with Fragments, layouts, and Views.

Views are the UI controls that display data and provide user interaction. Android provides several layout classes, called *View Groups*, which can contain multiple Views to help you layout your UIs. Fragments are used to encapsulate segments of your UI, making it simple to create dynamic interfaces that can be rearranged to optimize your layouts for different screen sizes and orientations.

> *Chapter 4 discusses Views, View Groups, layouts, and Fragments in detail, examining what's available, how to use them, and how to create your own.*

To assign a UI to an Activity, call `setContentView` from the `onCreate` method of your `Activity`.

In this first snippet, an instance of a `TextView` is used as the `Activity`'s UI:

```
@Override
public void onCreate(Bundle savedInstanceState) {
  super.onCreate(savedInstanceState);
  TextView textView = new TextView(this);
  setContentView(textView);
}
```

Usually, you'll want to use a more complex UI design. You can create a layout in code using layout View Groups, or you can use the standard Android convention of passing a resource ID for a layout defined in an external resource, as shown in the following snippet:

```
@Override
public void onCreate(Bundle savedInstanceState) {
  super.onCreate(savedInstanceState);
  setContentView(R.layout.main);
}
```

To use an `Activity` in your application, you need to register it in the manifest. Add a new `activity` tag within the `application` node of the manifest; the `activity` tag includes attributes for metadata, such as the label, icon, required permissions, and themes used by the `Activity`. An `Activity` without a corresponding `activity` tag can't be displayed — attempting to do so will result in a runtime exception.

```
<activity android:label="@string/app_name"
          android:name=".MyActivity">
</activity>
```

Within the `activity` tag you can add `intent-filter` nodes that specify the Intents that can be used to start your Activity. Each Intent Filter defines one or more actions and categories that your `Activity` supports. Intents and Intent Filters are covered in depth in Chapter 5, but it's worth noting that for an `Activity` to be available from the application launcher, it must include an Intent Filter listening for the MAIN action and the LAUNCHER category, as highlighted in Listing 3-10.

LISTING 3-10: Main Application Activity Definition

```
<activity android:label="@string/app_name"
          android:name=".MyActivity">
  <intent-filter>
    <action android:name="android.intent.action.MAIN" />
    <category android:name="android.intent.category.LAUNCHER" />
  </intent-filter>
</activity>
```

code snippet PA4AD_Ch03_Activities/AndroidManifest.xml

The Activity Lifecycle

A good understanding of the Activity lifecycle is vital to ensure that your application provides a seamless user experience and properly manages its resources.

As explained earlier, Android applications do not control their own process lifetimes; the Android run time manages the process of each application, and by extension that of each Activity within it.

Although the run time handles the termination and management of an Activity's process, the Activity's state helps determine the priority of its parent application. The application priority, in turn, influences the likelihood that the run time will terminate it and the Activities running within it.

Activity Stacks

The state of each Activity is determined by its position on the Activity stack, a last-in–first-out collection of all the currently running Activities. When a new Activity starts, it becomes active and is moved to the top of the stack. If the user navigates back using the Back button, or the foreground Activity is otherwise closed, the next Activity down on the stack moves up and becomes active. Figure 3-5 illustrates this process.

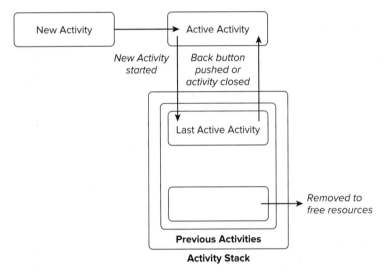

FIGURE 3-5

As described previously in this chapter, an application's priority is influenced by its highest-priority Activity. When the Android memory manager is deciding which application to terminate to free resources, it uses this Activity stack to determine the priority of applications.

Activity States

As Activities are created and destroyed, they move in and out of the stack, as shown in Figure 3-5. As they do so, they transition through four possible states:

➤ **Active** — When an Activity is at the top of the stack it is the visible, focused, foreground Activity that is receiving user input. Android will attempt to keep it alive at all costs, killing Activities further down the stack as needed, to ensure that it has the resources it needs. When another Activity becomes active, this one will be paused.

➤ **Paused** — In some cases your Activity will be visible but will not have focus; at this point it's paused. This state is reached if a transparent or non-full-screen Activity is active in front of it. When paused, an Activity is treated as if it were active; however, it doesn't receive user input events. In extreme cases Android will kill a paused Activity to recover resources for the active Activity. When an Activity becomes totally obscured, it is stopped.

➤ **Stopped** — When an Activity isn't visible, it "stops." The Activity will remain in memory, retaining all state information; however, it is now a candidate for termination when the system requires memory elsewhere. When an Activity is in a stopped state, it's important to save data and the current UI state, and to stop any non-critical operations. Once an Activity has exited or closed, it becomes inactive.

➤ **Inactive** — After an Activity has been killed, and before it's been launched, it's inactive. Inactive Activities have been removed from the Activity stack and need to be restarted before they can be displayed and used.

State transitions are nondeterministic and are handled entirely by the Android memory manager. Android will start by closing applications that contain inactive Activities, followed by those that are stopped. In extreme cases, it will remove those that are paused.

> *To ensure a seamless user experience, transitions between states should be invisible to the user. There should be no difference in an Activity moving from a paused, stopped, or inactive state back to active, so it's important to save all UI state and persist all data when an Activity is paused or stopped. Once an Activity does become active, it should restore those saved values.*
>
> *Similarly, apart from changes to the Activity's priority, transitions between the active, paused, and stopped states have little direct impact on the Activity itself. It's up to you to use these signals to pause and stop your Activities accordingly.*

Monitoring State Changes

To ensure that Activities can react to state changes, Android provides a series of event handlers that are fired when an Activity transitions through its full, visible, and active lifetimes. Figure 3-6 summarizes these lifetimes in terms of the Activity states described in the previous section.

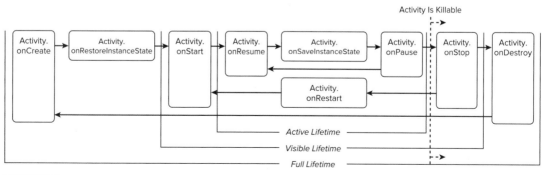

FIGURE 3-6

The skeleton code in Listing 3-11 shows the stubs for the state change method handlers available in an Activity. Comments within each stub describe the actions you should consider taking on each state change event.

LISTING 3-11: Activity state event handlers

```
package com.paad.activities;

import android.app.Activity;
import android.os.Bundle;

public class MyStateChangeActivity extends Activity {

  // Called at the start of the full lifetime.
  @Override
  public void onCreate(Bundle savedInstanceState) {
    super.onCreate(savedInstanceState);
    // Initialize Activity and inflate the UI.
  }

  // Called after onCreate has finished, use to restore UI state
  @Override
  public void onRestoreInstanceState(Bundle savedInstanceState) {
    super.onRestoreInstanceState(savedInstanceState);
    // Restore UI state from the savedInstanceState.
    // This bundle has also been passed to onCreate.
    // Will only be called if the Activity has been
    // killed by the system since it was last visible.
  }

  // Called before subsequent visible lifetimes
  // for an Activity process.
  @Override
  public void onRestart(){
    super.onRestart();
    // Load changes knowing that the Activity has already
    // been visible within this process.
  }

  // Called at the start of the visible lifetime.
  @Override
  public void onStart(){
    super.onStart();
    // Apply any required UI change now that the Activity is visible.
  }

  // Called at the start of the active lifetime.
  @Override
  public void onResume(){
    super.onResume();
    // Resume any paused UI updates, threads, or processes required
    // by the Activity but suspended when it was inactive.
```

```
    }

    // Called to save UI state changes at the
    // end of the active lifecycle.
    @Override
    public void onSaveInstanceState(Bundle savedInstanceState) {
      // Save UI state changes to the savedInstanceState.
      // This bundle will be passed to onCreate and
      // onRestoreInstanceState if the process is
      // killed and restarted by the run time.
      super.onSaveInstanceState(savedInstanceState);
    }

    // Called at the end of the active lifetime.
    @Override
    public void onPause(){
      // Suspend UI updates, threads, or CPU intensive processes
      // that don't need to be updated when the Activity isn't
      // the active foreground Activity.
      super.onPause();
    }

    // Called at the end of the visible lifetime.
    @Override
    public void onStop(){
      // Suspend remaining UI updates, threads, or processing
      // that aren't required when the Activity isn't visible.
      // Persist all edits or state changes
      // as after this call the process is likely to be killed.
      super.onStop();
    }

    // Sometimes called at the end of the full lifetime.
    @Override
    public void onDestroy(){
      // Clean up any resources including ending threads,
      // closing database connections etc.
      super.onDestroy();
    }
  }
```

code snippet PA4AD_Ch03_Activities/src/MyStateChangeActivity.java

As shown in the preceding code, you should always call back to the superclass when overriding these event handlers.

Understanding Activity Lifetimes

Within an Activity's full lifetime, between creation and destruction, it goes through one or more iterations of the active and visible lifetimes. Each transition triggers the method handlers previously described. The following sections provide a closer look at each of these lifetimes and the events that bracket them.

The Full Lifetime

The full lifetime of your Activity occurs between the first call to onCreate and the final call to onDestroy. It's not uncommon for an Activity's process to be terminated *without* the onDestroy method being called.

Use the onCreate method to initialize your Activity: inflate the user interface, get references to Fragments, allocate references to class variables, bind data to controls, and start Services and Timers. If the Activity was terminated unexpectedly by the runtime, the onCreate method is passed a Bundle object containing the state saved in the last call to onSaveInstanceState. You should use this Bundle to restore the UI to its previous state, either within the onCreate method or onRestoreInstanceState.

Override onDestroy to clean up any resources created in onCreate, and ensure that all external connections, such as network or database links, are closed.

As part of Android's guidelines for writing efficient code, it's recommended that you avoid the creation of short-term objects. The rapid creation and destruction of objects force additional garbage collection, a process that can have a direct negative impact on the user experience. If your Activity creates the same set of objects regularly, consider creating them in the onCreate method instead, as it's called only once in the Activity's lifetime.

The Visible Lifetime

An Activity's visible lifetimes are bound between calls to onStart and onStop. Between these calls your Activity will be visible to the user, although it may not have focus and may be partially obscured. Activities are likely to go through several visible lifetimes during their full lifetime because they move between the foreground and background. Although it's unusual, in extreme cases the Android run time will kill an Activity during its visible lifetime without a call to onStop.

The onStop method should be used to pause or stop animations, threads, Sensor listeners, GPS lookups, Timers, Services, or other processes that are used exclusively to update the UI. There's little value in consuming resources (such as CPU cycles or network bandwidth) to update the UI when it isn't visible. Use the onStart (or onRestart) methods to resume or restart these processes when the UI is visible again.

The onRestart method is called immediately prior to all but the first call to onStart. Use it to implement special processing that you want done only when the Activity restarts within its full lifetime.

The onStart/onStop methods are also used to register and unregister Broadcast Receivers used exclusively to update the UI.

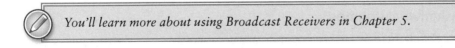

You'll learn more about using Broadcast Receivers in Chapter 5.

The Active Lifetime

The active lifetime starts with a call to onResume and ends with a corresponding call to onPause.

An active Activity is in the foreground and is receiving user input events. Your Activity is likely to go through many active lifetimes before it's destroyed, as the active lifetime will end when a new Activity is displayed, the device goes to sleep, or the Activity loses focus. Try to keep code in the onPause and onResume methods relatively fast and lightweight to ensure that your application remains responsive when moving in and out of the foreground.

Immediately before onPause, a call is made to onSaveInstanceState. This method provides an opportunity to save the Activity's UI state in a Bundle that may be passed to the onCreate and onRestoreInstanceState methods. Use onSaveInstanceState to save the UI state (such as checkbox states, user focus, and entered but uncommitted user input) to ensure that the Activity can present the same UI when it next becomes active. You can safely assume that during the active lifetime onSaveInstanceState and onPause will be called before the process is terminated.

Most Activity implementations will override at least the onSaveInstanceState method to commit unsaved changes, as it marks the point beyond which an Activity may be killed without warning. Depending on your application architecture you may also choose to suspend threads, processes, or Broadcast Receivers while your Activity is not in the foreground.

The onResume method can be lightweight. You do not need to reload the UI state here because this is handled by the onCreate and onRestoreInstanceState methods when required. Use onResume to reregister any Broadcast Receivers or other processes you may have suspended in onPause.

Android Activity Classes

The Android SDK includes a selection of Activity subclasses that wrap up the use of common UI widgets. Some of the more useful ones are listed here:

➤ MapActivity — Encapsulates the resource handling required to support a MapView widget within an Activity. Learn more about MapActivity and MapView in Chapter 13.

➤ ListActivity — Wrapper class for Activities that feature a ListView bound to a data source as the primary UI metaphor, and expose event handlers for list item selection.

➤ ExpandableListActivity — Similar to the ListActivity but supports an ExpandableListView.

4

Building User Interfaces

WHAT'S IN THIS CHAPTER?

➤ Using Views and layouts

➤ Understanding Fragments

➤ Optimizing layouts

➤ Creating resolution-independent user interfaces

➤ Extending, grouping, creating, and using Views

➤ Using Adapters to bind data to Views

To quote Stephen Fry on the role of style as part of substance in the design of digital devices:

> *As if a device can function if it has no style. As if a device can be called stylish that does not function superbly.... Yes, beauty matters. Boy, does it matter. It is not surface, it is not an extra, it is the thing itself.*
>
> —STEPHEN FRY, THE GUARDIAN (OCTOBER 27, 2007)

Although Fry was describing the style of the devices themselves, the same can be said of the applications that run on them. Bigger, brighter, and higher resolution displays with multitouch support have made applications increasingly visual. The introduction of devices optimized for a more immersive experience — including tablets and televisions — into the Android ecosystem has only served to increase the importance of an application's visual design.

In this chapter you'll discover the Android components used to create UIs. You'll learn how to use layouts, Fragments, and Views to create functional and intuitive UIs for your Activities.

The individual elements of an Android UI are arranged on screen by means of a variety of Layout Managers derived from the `ViewGroup` class. This chapter introduces several native layout classes and demonstrates how to use them, how to create your own, and how to ensure your use of layouts is as efficient as possible.

The range of screen sizes and display resolutions your application may be used on has expanded along with the range of Android devices now available to buy. Android 3.0 introduced the Fragment API to provide better support for creating dynamic layouts that can be optimized for tablets as well as a variety of different smartphone displays.

You'll learn how to use Fragments to create layouts that scale and adapt to accommodate a variety of screen sizes and resolutions, as well as the best practices for developing and testing your UIs so that they look great on all screens.

After being introduced to some of the visual controls available from the Android SDK, you'll learn how to extend and customize them. Using View Groups, you'll combine Views to create atomic, reusable UI elements made up of interacting subcontrols. You'll also create your own Views, to display data and interact with users in creative new ways.

Finally, you'll examine Adapters and learn how to use them to bind your presentation layer to the underlying data sources.

FUNDAMENTAL ANDROID UI DESIGN

User interface (UI) design, user experience (UX), human computer interaction (HCI), and usability are huge topics that can't be covered in the depth they deserve within the confines of this book. Nonetheless, the importance of creating a UI that your users will understand and enjoy using can't be overstated.

Android introduces some new terminology for familiar programming metaphors that will be explored in detail in the following sections:

➤ **Views** — Views are the base class for all visual interface elements (commonly known as *controls* or *widgets*). All UI controls, including the layout classes, are derived from `View`.

➤ **View Groups** — View Groups are extensions of the View class that can contain multiple child Views. Extend the `ViewGroup` class to create compound controls made up of interconnected child Views. The `ViewGroup` class is also extended to provide the Layout Managers that help you lay out controls within your Activities.

➤ **Fragments** — Fragments, introduced in Android 3.0 (API level 11), are used to encapsulate portions of your UI. This encapsulation makes Fragments particularly useful when optimizing your UI layouts for different screen sizes and creating reusable UI elements. Each Fragment includes its own UI layout and receives the related input events but is tightly bound to the Activity into which each must be embedded. Fragments are similar to UI View Controllers in iPhone development.

➤ **Activities** — Activities, described in detail in the previous chapter, represent the window, or screen, being displayed. Activities are the Android equivalent of Forms in traditional Windows desktop development. To display a UI, you assign a View (usually a layout or Fragment) to an Activity.

Android provides several common UI controls, widgets, and Layout Managers.

For most graphical applications, it's likely that you'll need to extend and modify these standard Views — or create composite or entirely new Views — to provide your own user experience.

ANDROID USER INTERFACE FUNDAMENTALS

All visual components in Android descend from the `View` class and are referred to generically as *Views*. You'll often see Views referred to as *controls* or *widgets* (not to be confused with home screen App Widgets described in Chapter 14, "Invading the Home Screen) — terms you're probably familiar with if you've previously done any GUI development.

The `ViewGroup` class is an extension of View designed to contain multiple Views. View Groups are used most commonly to manage the layout of child Views, but they can also be used to create atomic reusable components. View Groups that perform the former function are generally referred to as *layouts*.

In the following sections you'll learn how to put together increasingly complex UIs, before being introduced to Fragments, the Views available in the SDK, how to extend these Views, build your own compound controls, and create your own custom Views from scratch.

Assigning User Interfaces to Activities

A new Activity starts with a temptingly empty screen onto which you place your UI. To do so, call `setContentView`, passing in the View instance, or layout resource, to display. Because empty screens aren't particularly inspiring, you will almost always use `setContentView` to assign an Activity's UI when overriding its `onCreate` handler.

The `setContentView` method accepts either a layout's resource ID or a single View instance. This lets you define your UI either in code or using the preferred technique of external layout resources.

```
@Override
public void onCreate(Bundle savedInstanceState) {
  super.onCreate(savedInstanceState);

  setContentView(R.layout.main);
}
```

Using layout resources decouples your presentation layer from the application logic, providing the flexibility to change the presentation without changing code. This makes it possible to specify different layouts optimized for different hardware configurations, even changing them at run time based on hardware changes (such as screen orientation changes).

You can obtain a reference to each of the Views within a layout using the `findViewById` method:

```
TextView myTextView = (TextView)findViewById(R.id.myTextView);
```

If you prefer the more *traditional* approach, you can construct the UI in code:

```
@Override
public void onCreate(Bundle savedInstanceState) {
  super.onCreate(savedInstanceState);

  TextView myTextView = new TextView(this);
  setContentView(myTextView);

  myTextView.setText("Hello, Android");
}
```

The setContentView method accepts a single View instance; as a result, you use layouts to add multiple controls to your Activity.

If you're using Fragments to encapsulate portions of your Activity's UI, the View inflated within your Activity's onCreate handler will be a layout that describes the relative position of each of your Fragments (or their containers). The UI used for each Fragment is defined in its own layout and inflated within the Fragment itself, as described later in this chapter.

Note that once a Fragment has been inflated into an Activity, the Views it contains become part of that Activity's View hierarchy. As a result you can find any of its child Views from within the parent Activity, using findViewById as described previously.

INTRODUCING LAYOUTS

Layout Managers (or simply *layouts*) are extensions of the ViewGroup class and are used to position child Views within your UI. Layouts can be nested, letting you create arbitrarily complex UIs using a combination of layouts.

The Android SDK includes a number of layout classes. You can use these, modify them, or create your own to construct the UI for your Views, Fragments, and Activities. It's up to you to select and use the right combination of layouts to make your UI aesthetically pleasing, easy to use, and efficient to display.

The following list includes some of the most commonly used layout classes available in the Android SDK:

> ➤ FrameLayout — The simplest of the Layout Managers, the Frame Layout pins each child view within its frame. The default position is the top-left corner, though you can use the gravity attribute to alter its location. Adding multiple children stacks each new child on top of the one before, with each new View potentially obscuring the previous ones.

> ➤ LinearLayout — A Linear Layout aligns each child View in either a vertical or a horizontal line. A vertical layout has a column of Views, whereas a horizontal layout has a row of Views. The Linear Layout supports a weight attribute for each child View that can control the relative size of each child View within the available space.

> ➤ RelativeLayout — One of the most flexible of the native layouts, the Relative Layout lets you define the positions of each child View relative to the others and to the screen boundaries.

> ➤ `GridLayout` — Introduced in Android 4.0 (API level 14), the Grid Layout uses a rectangular grid of infinitely thin lines to lay out Views in a series of rows and columns. The Grid Layout is incredibly flexible and can be used to greatly simplify layouts and reduce or eliminate the complex nesting often required to construct UIs using the layouts described above. It's good practice to use the Layout Editor to construct your Grid Layouts rather than relying on tweaking the XML manually.

Each of these layouts is designed to scale to suit the host device's screen size by avoiding the use of absolute positions or predetermined pixel values. This makes them particularly useful when designing applications that work well on a diverse set of Android hardware.

The Android documentation describes the features and properties of each layout class in detail; so, rather than repeat that information here, I'll refer you to `http://developer.android.com/guide/topics/ui/layout-objects.html`.

You'll see practical example of how these layouts should be used as they're introduced in the examples throughout this book. Later in this chapter you'll also learn how to create compound controls by using and/or extending these layout classes.

Defining Layouts

The preferred way to define a layout is by using XML external resources.

Each layout XML must contain a single root element. This root node can contain as many nested layouts and Views as necessary to construct an arbitrarily complex UI.

The following snippet shows a simple layout that places a `TextView` above an `EditText` control using a vertical `LinearLayout`.

```xml
<?xml version="1.0" encoding="utf-8"?>
<LinearLayout xmlns:android="http://schemas.android.com/apk/res/android"
  android:orientation="vertical"
  android:layout_width="match_parent"
  android:layout_height="match_parent">
  <TextView
    android:layout_width="match_parent"
    android:layout_height="wrap_content"
    android:text="Enter Text Below"
  />
  <EditText
    android:layout_width="match_parent"
    android:layout_height="wrap_content"
    android:text="Text Goes Here!"
  />
</LinearLayout>
```

For each of the layout elements, the constants `wrap_content` and `match_parent` are used rather than an exact height or width in pixels. These constants, combined with layouts that scale (such as the Linear Layout, Relative Layout, and Grid Layout) offer the simplest, and most powerful, technique for ensuring your layouts are screen-size and resolution independent.

The `wrap_content` constant sets the size of a View to the minimum required to contain the contents it displays (such as the height required to display a wrapped text string). The `match_parent` constant expands the View to match the available space within the parent View, Fragment, or Activity.

Later in this chapter you'll learn how to set the minimum height and width for your own controls, as well as further best practices for resolution independence.

Implementing layouts in XML decouples the presentation layer from the View, Fragment, and Activity controller code and business logic. It also lets you create hardware configuration-specific variations that are dynamically loaded without requiring code changes.

When preferred, or required, you can implement layouts in code. When assigning Views to layouts in code, it's important to apply `LayoutParameters` using the `setLayoutParams` method, or by passing them in to the `addView` call:

```
LinearLayout ll = new LinearLayout(this);
ll.setOrientation(LinearLayout.VERTICAL);

TextView myTextView = new TextView(this);
EditText myEditText = new EditText(this);

myTextView.setText("Enter Text Below");
myEditText.setText("Text Goes Here!");

int lHeight = LinearLayout.LayoutParams.MATCH_PARENT;
int lWidth = LinearLayout.LayoutParams.WRAP_CONTENT;

ll.addView(myTextView, new LinearLayout.LayoutParams(lHeight, lWidth));
ll.addView(myEditText, new LinearLayout.LayoutParams(lHeight, lWidth));
setContentView(ll);
```

Using Layouts to Create Device Independent User Interfaces

A defining feature of the layout classes described previously, and the techniques described for using them within your apps, is their ability to scale and adapt to a wide range of screen sizes, resolutions, and orientations.

The variety of Android devices is a critical part of its success. For developers, this diversity introduces a challenge for designing UIs to ensure that they provide the best possible experience for users, regardless of which Android device they own.

Using a Linear Layout

The Linear Layout is one of the simplest layout classes. It allows you to create simple UIs (or UI elements) that align a sequence of child Views in either a vertical or a horizontal line.

The simplicity of the Linear Layout makes it easy to use but limits its flexibility. In most cases you will use Linear Layouts to construct UI elements that will be nested within other layouts, such as the Relative Layout.

Listing 4-1 shows two nested Linear Layouts — a horizontal layout of two equally sized buttons within a vertical layout that places the buttons above a List View.

LISTING 4-1: Linear Layout

```xml
<?xml version="1.0" encoding="utf-8"?>
<LinearLayout
  xmlns:android="http://schemas.android.com/apk/res/android"
  android:layout_width="match_parent"
  android:layout_height="match_parent"
  android:orientation="vertical">
  <LinearLayout
    android:layout_width="fill_parent"
    android:layout_height="wrap_content"
    android:orientation="horizontal"
    android:padding="5dp">
    <Button
      android:text="@string/cancel_button_text"
      android:layout_width="fill_parent"
      android:layout_height="wrap_content"
      android:layout_weight="1"/>
    <Button
      android:text="@string/ok_button_text"
      android:layout_width="fill_parent"
      android:layout_height="wrap_content"
      android:layout_weight="1"/>
  </LinearLayout>
  <ListView
    android:layout_width="match_parent"
    android:layout_height="match_parent"/>
</LinearLayout>
```

code snippet PA4AD_Ch4_Layouts/res/layout/linear_layout.xml

If you find yourself creating increasingly complex nesting patterns of Linear Layouts, you will likely be better served using a more flexible Layout Manager.

Using a Relative Layout

The Relative Layout provides a great deal of flexibility for your layouts, allowing you to define the position of each element within the layout in terms of its parent and the other Views.

Listing 4-2 modifies the layout described in Listing 4-1 to move the buttons below the List View.

LISTING 4-2: Relative Layout

```xml
<?xml version="1.0" encoding="utf-8"?>
<RelativeLayout
  xmlns:android="http://schemas.android.com/apk/res/android"
  android:layout_width="match_parent"
  android:layout_height="match_parent">
  <LinearLayout
    android:id="@+id/button_bar"
    android:layout_alignParentBottom="true"
```

continues

LISTING 4-2 *(continued)*

```
      android:layout_width="fill_parent"
      android:layout_height="wrap_content"
      android:orientation="horizontal"
      android:padding="5dp">
      <Button
        android:text="@string/cancel_button_text"
        android:layout_width="fill_parent"
        android:layout_height="wrap_content"
        android:layout_weight="1"/>
      <Button
        android:text="@string/ok_button_text"
        android:layout_width="fill_parent"
        android:layout_height="wrap_content"
        android:layout_weight="1"/>
    </LinearLayout>
    <ListView
      android:layout_above="@id/button_bar"
      android:layout_alignParentLeft="true"
      android:layout_width="match_parent"
      android:layout_height="match_parent">
    </ListView>
  </RelativeLayout>
```

code snippet PA4AD_Ch4_Layouts/res/layout/relative_layout.xml

Using a Grid Layout

The Grid Layout was introduced in Android 3.0 (API level 11) and provides the most flexibility of any of the Layout Managers.

The Grid Layout uses an arbitrary grid to position Views. By using row and column spanning, the Space View, and Gravity attributes, you can create complex without resorting to the often complex nesting required to construct UIs using the Relative Layout described previously.

The Grid Layout is particularly useful for constructing layouts that require alignment in two directions — for example, a form whose rows and columns must be aligned but which also includes elements that don't fit neatly into a standard grid pattern.

It's also possible to replicate all the functionality provided by the Relative Layout by using the Grid Layout and Linear Layout in combination. For performance reasons it's good practice to use the Grid Layout in preference to creating the same UI using a combination of nested layouts.

Listing 4-3 shows the same layout as described in Listing 4-2 using a Grid Layout to replace the Relative Layout.

LISTING 4-3: Grid Layout

```
<?xml version="1.0" encoding="utf-8"?>
<GridLayout
  xmlns:android="http://schemas.android.com/apk/res/android"
```

```
     android:layout_width="match_parent"
     android:layout_height="match_parent"
     android:orientation="vertical">
      <ListView
        android:background="#FF444444"
        android:layout_gravity="fill">
      </ListView>
      <LinearLayout
        android:layout_gravity="fill_horizontal"
        android:orientation="horizontal"
        android:padding="5dp">
        <Button
          android:text="Cancel"
          android:layout_width="fill_parent"
          android:layout_height="wrap_content"
          android:layout_weight="1"/>
        <Button
          android:text="OK"
          android:layout_width="fill_parent"
          android:layout_height="wrap_content"
          android:layout_weight="1"/>
      </LinearLayout>
   </GridLayout>
```

code snippet PA4AD_Ch4_Layouts/res/layout/grid_layout.xml

Note that the Grid Layout elements do not require width and height parameters to be set. Instead, each element wraps its content by default, and the `layout_gravity` attribute is used to determine in which directions each element should expand.

Optimizing Layouts

Inflating layouts is an expensive process; each additional nested layout and included View directly impacts on the performance and responsiveness of your application.

To keep your applications smooth and responsive, it's important to keep your layouts as simple as possible and to avoid inflating entirely new layouts for relatively small UI changes.

Redundant Layout Containers Are Redundant

A Linear Layout within a Frame Layout, both of which are set to MATCH_PARENT, does nothing but add extra time to inflate. Look for redundant layouts, particularly if you've been making significant changes to an existing layout or are adding child layouts to an existing layout.

Layouts can be arbitrarily nested, so it's easy to create complex, deeply nested hierarchies. Although there is no hard limit, it's good practice to restrict nesting to fewer than 10 levels.

One common example of unnecessary nesting is a Frame Layout used to create the single root node required for a layout, as shown in the following snippet:

```
<?xml version="1.0" encoding="utf-8"?>
<FrameLayout
  xmlns:android="http://schemas.android.com/apk/res/android"
  android:layout_width="match_parent"
  android:layout_height="match_parent">
```

```
  <ImageView
    android:id="@+id/myImageView"
    android:layout_width="match_parent"
    android:layout_height="match_parent"
    android:src="@drawable/myimage"
  />
  <TextView
    android:id="@+id/myTextView"
    android:layout_width="match_parent"
    android:layout_height="wrap_content"
    android:text="@string/hello"
    android:gravity="center_horizontal"
    android:layout_gravity="bottom"
  />
</FrameLayout>
```

In this example, when the Frame Layout is added to a parent, it will become redundant. A better alternative is to use the Merge tag:

```
<?xml version="1.0" encoding="utf-8"?>
<merge
  xmlns:android="http://schemas.android.com/apk/res/android">
  <ImageView
    android:id="@+id/myImageView"
    android:layout_width="match_parent"
    android:layout_height="match_parent"
    android:src="@drawable/myimage"
  />
  <TextView
    android:id="@+id/myTextView"
    android:layout_width="match_parent"
    android:layout_height="wrap_content"
    android:text="@string/hello"
    android:gravity="center_horizontal"
    android:layout_gravity="bottom"
  />
</merge>
```

When a layout containing a merge tag is added to another layout, the merge node is removed and its child Views are added directly to the new parent.

The merge tag is particularly useful in conjunction with the include tag, which is used to insert the contents of one layout into another:

```
<?xml version="1.0" encoding="utf-8"?>
<LinearLayout
  xmlns:android="http://schemas.android.com/apk/res/android"
  android:orientation="vertical"
  android:layout_width="match_parent"
  android:layout_height="match_parent">
  <include android:id="@+id/my_action_bar"
           layout="@layout/actionbar"/>
  <include android:id="@+id/my_image_text_layout"
           layout="@layout/image_text_layout"/>
</LinearLayout>
```

Combining the `merge` and `include` tags enables you to create flexible, reusable layout definitions that don't create deeply nested layout hierarchies. You'll learn more about creating and using simple and reusable layouts later in this chapter.

Avoid Using Excessive Views

Each additional View takes time and resources to inflate. To maximize the speed and responsiveness of your application, none of its layouts should include more than 80 Views. When you exceed this limit, the time taken to inflate the layout becomes significant.

To minimize the number of Views inflated within a complex layout, you can use a `ViewStub`.

A View Stub works like a lazy include — a stub that represents the specified child Views within the parent layout — but the stub is only inflated explicitly via the `inflate` method or when it's made visible.

```
// Find the stub
View stub = findViewById(R.id. download_progress_panel_stub);
// Make it visible, causing it to inflate the child layout
stub.setVisibility(View.VISIBLE);

// Find the root node of the inflated stub layout
View downloadProgressPanel = findViewById(R.id.download_progress_panel);
```

As a result, the Views contained within the child layout aren't created until they are required — minimizing the time and resource cost of inflating complex UIs.

When adding a View Stub to your layout, you can override the `id` and `layout` parameters of the root View of the layout it represents:

```
<?xml version="1.0" encoding="utf-8"?>
<FrameLayout "xmlns:android=http://schemas.android.com/apk/res/android"
  android:layout_width="match_parent"
  android:layout_height="match_parent">
  <ListView
    android:id="@+id/myListView"
    android:layout_width="match_parent"
    android:layout_height="match_parent"
  />
  <ViewStub
    android:id="@+id/download_progress_panel_stub"

    android:layout="@layout/progress_overlay_panel"
    android:inflatedId="@+id/download_progress_panel"

    android:layout_width="match_parent"
    android:layout_height="wrap_content"
    android:layout_gravity="bottom"
  />
</FrameLayout>
```

This snippet modifies the width, height, and gravity of the imported layout to suit the requirements of the parent layout. This flexibility makes it possible to create and reuse the same generic child layouts in a variety of parent layouts.

An ID has been specified for both the stub and the View Group it will become when inflated using the id and inflatedId attribute, respectively.

> *When the View Stub is inflated, it is removed from the hierarchy and replaced by the root node of the View it imported. If you need to modify the visibility of the imported Views, you must either use the reference to their root node (returned by the* inflate *call) or find the View by using* findViewById, *using the layout ID assigned to it within the corresponding View Stub node.*

Using Lint to Analyze Your Layouts

To assist you in optimizing your layout hierarchies, the Android SDK includes lint — a powerful tool that can be used to detect problems within you application, including layout performance issues.

The lint tool is available as a command-line tool or as a window within Eclipse supplied as part of the ADT plug-in, as shown in Figure 4-1.

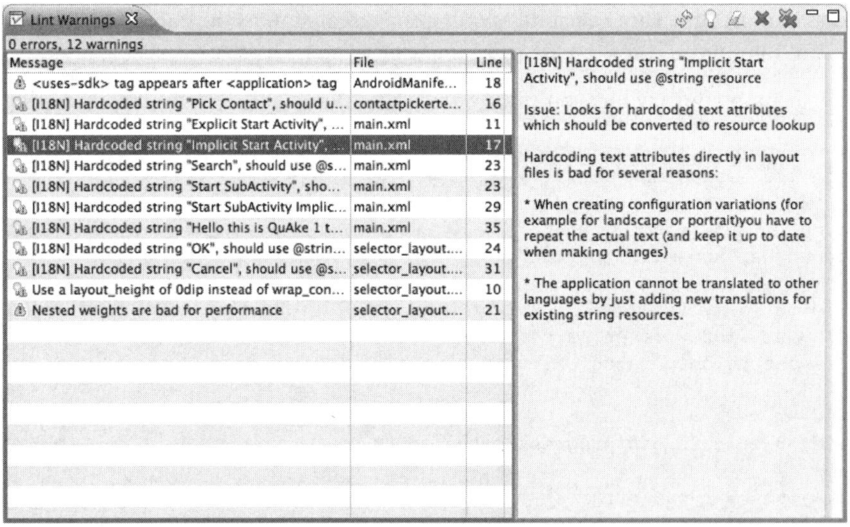

FIGURE 4-1

In addition to using Lint to detect each optimization issue described previously in this section, you can also use Lint to detect missing translations, unused resources, inconsistent array sizes, accessibility and internationalization problems, missing or duplicated image assets, usability problems, and manifest errors.

Lint is a constantly evolving tool, with new rules added regularly. A full list of the tests performed by the Lint tool can be found at http://tools.android.com/tips/lint-checks.

TO-DO LIST EXAMPLE

In this example you'll be creating a new Android application from scratch. This simple example creates a new to-do list application using native Android Views and layouts.

> Don't worry if you don't understand everything that happens in this example. Some of the features used to create this application, including ArrayAdapters, ListViews, *and* KeyListeners, *won't be introduced properly until later in this and subsequent chapters, where they'll be explained in detail. You'll also return to this example later to add new functionality as you learn more about Android.*

1. Create a new Android project. Within Eclipse, select File ➪ New ➪ Project, and then choose Android Project within the Android node (as shown in Figure 4-2) before clicking Next.

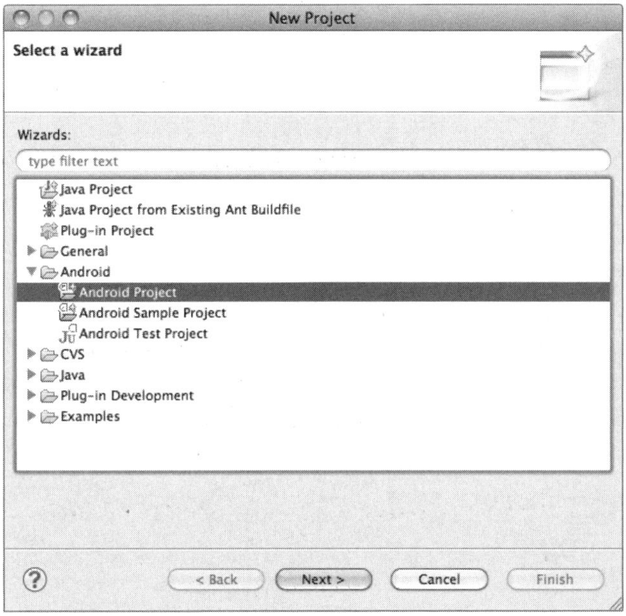

FIGURE 4-2

2. Specify the project details for your new project.

   2.1 Start by providing a project name, as shown in Figure 4-3, and then click Next.

   2.2 Select the build target. Select the newest platform release, as shown in Figure 4-4, and then click Next.

   2.3 Enter the details for your new project, as shown in Figure 4-5. The Application name is the friendly name of your application, and the Create Activity field lets you name your Activity (ToDoListActivity). When the remaining details are entered, click Finish to create your new project.

FIGURE 4-3

FIGURE 4-4

FIGURE 4-5

3. Before creating your debug and run configurations, take this opportunity to create a virtual device for testing your applications.

> **3.1** Select Window ⇨ AVD Manager. In the resulting dialog (see Figure 4-6), click the New button.

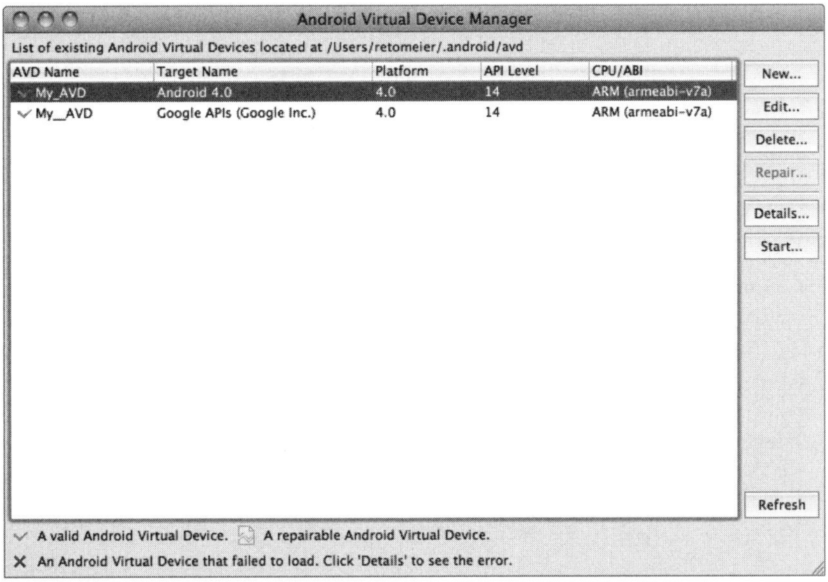

FIGURE 4-6

3.2 In the dialog displayed in Figure 4-7, enter a name for your device and choose an SDK target (use the same platform target as you selected for your project in step 2.2) and the screen resolution. Set the SD Card size to larger than 8MB, enable snapshots, and then press Create AVD.

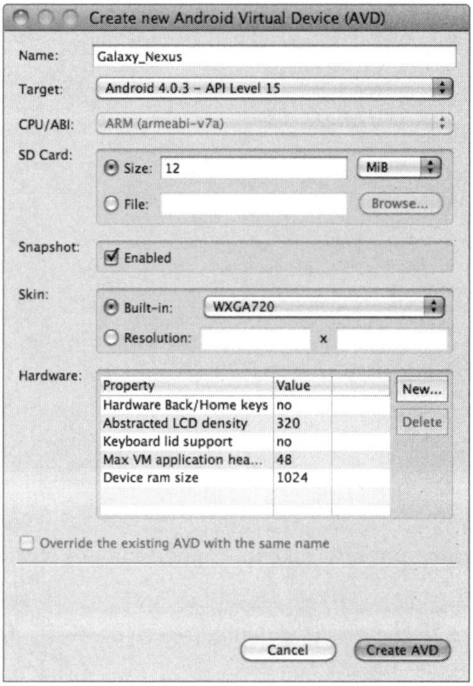

FIGURE 4-7

4. Now create your debug and run configurations. Select Run ➪ Debug Configurations and then Run ➪ Run Configurations, creating a new configuration for each specifying the `TodoList` project. If you want to debug using a virtual device, you can select the one you created in step 3 here; alternatively, if you want to debug on a device, you can select it here if it's plugged in and has debugging enabled. You can either leave the launch action as Launch Default Activity or explicitly set it to launch the new `ToDoListActivity`.

5. In this example you want to present users with a list of to-do items and a text entry box to add new ones. There's both a list and a text-entry control available from the Android libraries. (You'll learn more about the Views available in Android, and how to create new ones, later in this Chapter.)

The preferred method for laying out your UI is to create a layout resource. Open the `main.xml` layout file in the `res/layout` project folder and modify it layout to include a

ListView and an EditText within a LinearLayout. You must give both the EditText and ListView an ID so that you can get references to them both in code:

```xml
<?xml version="1.0" encoding="utf-8"?>
<LinearLayout xmlns:android="http://schemas.android.com/apk/res/android"
  android:orientation="vertical"
  android:layout_width="match_parent"
  android:layout_height="match_parent">
  <EditText
    android:id="@+id/myEditText"
    android:layout_width="match_parent"
    android:layout_height="wrap_content"
    android:hint="@string/addItemHint"
    android:contentDescription="@string/addItemContentDescription"
  />
  <ListView
    android:id="@+id/myListView"
    android:layout_width="match_parent"
    android:layout_height="wrap_content"
  />
</LinearLayout>
```

6. You'll also need to add the string resources that provide the hint text and content description included in step 5 to the strings.xml resource stored in the project's res/values folder. You can take this opportunity to remove the default "hello" string value:

```xml
<?xml version="1.0" encoding="utf-8"?>
<resources>
  <string name="app_name">ToDoList</string>
  <string name="addItemHint">New To Do Item</string>
  <string name="addItemContentDescription">New To Do Item</string>
</resources>
```

7. With your UI defined, open the ToDoListActivity Activity from your project's src folder. Start by ensuring your UI is inflated using setContentView. Then get references to the ListView and EditText using findViewById:

```java
public void onCreate(Bundle savedInstanceState) {
  super.onCreate(savedInstanceState);

  // Inflate your View
  setContentView(R.layout.main);

  // Get references to UI widgets
  ListView myListView = (ListView)findViewById(R.id.myListView);
  final EditText myEditText = (EditText)findViewById(R.id.myEditText);
}
```

> *When you add the code from step 7 into the* `ToDoListActivity`, *or when you try to compile your project, your IDE or compiler will complain that the* `ListView` *and* `EditText` *classes cannot be resolved into a type.*
>
> *You need to add import statements to your class to include the libraries that contain these Views (in this case,* `android.widget.EditText` *and* `android` `.widget.ListView`). *To ensure the code snippets and example applications listed in this book remain concise and readable, not all the necessary import statements within the code listings are included within the text (however they are all included in the downloadable source code).*
>
> *If you are using Eclipse, classes with missing import statements are highlighted with a red underline. Clicking each highlighted class will display a list of "quick fixes," which include adding the necessary import statements on your behalf.*
>
> *Eclipse also includes a handy shortcut (Ctrl+Shift+o) that will attempt to auto-matically create all the import statements required for the classes used in your code.*

8. Still within `onCreate`, define an `ArrayList` of Strings to store each to-do list item. You can bind a `ListView` to an `ArrayList` using an `ArrayAdapter`. (This process is described in more detail later in this chapter.) Create a new `ArrayAdapter` instance to bind the to-do item array to the `ListView`.

```
public void onCreate(Bundle savedInstanceState) {
  super.onCreate(savedInstanceState);

  // Inflate your View
  setContentView(R.layout.main);

  // Get references to UI widgets
  ListView myListView = (ListView)findViewById(R.id.myListView);
  final EditText myEditText = (EditText)findViewById(R.id.myEditText);

  // Create the Array List of to do items
  final ArrayList<String> todoItems = new ArrayList<String>();

  // Create the Array Adapter to bind the array to the List View
  final ArrayAdapter<String> aa;

  aa = new ArrayAdapter<String>(this,
                                android.R.layout.simple_list_item_1,
                                todoItems);

  // Bind the Array Adapter to the List View
  myListView.setAdapter(aa);
}
```

9. Let users add new to-do items. Add an `onKeyListener` to the `EditText` that listens for either a "D-pad center button" click or the Enter key being pressed. (You'll learn more about listening for key presses later in this chapter.) Either of these actions should add the contents of the `EditText` to the to-do list array created in step 8, and notify the `ArrayAdapter` of the change. Finally, clear the `EditText` to prepare for the next item.

```
public void onCreate(Bundle savedInstanceState) {
  super.onCreate(savedInstanceState);

  // Inflate your View
  setContentView(R.layout.main);

  // Get references to UI widgets
  ListView myListView = (ListView)findViewById(R.id.myListView);
  final EditText myEditText = (EditText)findViewById(R.id.myEditText);

  // Create the Array List of to do items
  final ArrayList<String> todoItems = new ArrayList<String>();

  // Create the Array Adapter to bind the array to the List View
  final ArrayAdapter<String> aa;

  aa = new ArrayAdapter<String>(this,
                                android.R.layout.simple_list_item_1,
                                todoItems);

  // Bind the Array Adapter to the List View
  myListView.setAdapter(aa);

  myEditText.setOnKeyListener(new View.OnKeyListener() {
    public boolean onKey(View v, int keyCode, KeyEvent event) {
      if (event.getAction() == KeyEvent.ACTION_DOWN)
        if ((keyCode == KeyEvent.KEYCODE_DPAD_CENTER) ||
            (keyCode == KeyEvent.KEYCODE_ENTER)) {
          todoItems.add(0, myEditText.getText().toString());
          aa.notifyDataSetChanged();
          myEditText.setText("");
          return true;
        }
      return false;
    }
  });
}
```

10. Run or debug the application and you'll see a text entry box above a list, as shown in Figure 4-8.

11. You've now finished your first Android application. Try adding breakpoints to the code to test the debugger and experiment with the DDMS perspective.

All code snippets in this example are part of the Chapter 4 To-Do List Part 1 *project, available for download at* www.wrox.com.

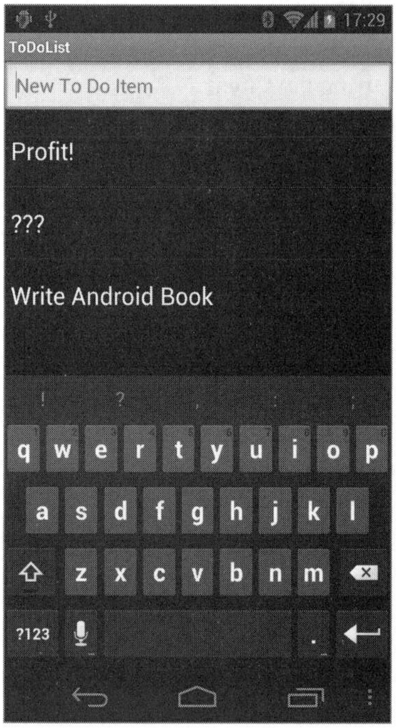

FIGURE 4-8

As it stands, this to-do list application isn't spectacularly useful. It doesn't save to-do list items between sessions; you can't edit or remove an item from the list; and typical task-list items, such as due dates and task priorities, aren't recorded or displayed. On balance, it fails most of the criteria laid out so far for a good mobile application design. You'll rectify some of these deficiencies when you return to this example.

INTRODUCING FRAGMENTS

Fragments enable you to divide your Activities into fully encapsulated reusable components, each with its own lifecycle and UI.

The primary advantage of Fragments is the ease with which you can create dynamic and flexible UI designs that can be adapted to suite a range of screen sizes — from small-screen smartphones to tablets.

Each Fragment is an independent module that is tightly bound to the Activity into which it is placed. Fragments can be reused within multiple activities, as well as laid out in a variety of combinations to suit multipane tablet UIs and added to, removed from, and exchanged within a running Activity to help build dynamic UIs.

Fragments provide a way to present a consistent UI optimized for a wide variety of Android device types, screen sizes, and device densities.

Although it is not necessary to divide your Activities (and their corresponding layouts) into Fragments, doing so will drastically improve the flexibility of your UI and make it easier for you to adapt your user experience for new device configurations.

> *Fragments were introduced to Android as part of the Android 3.0 Honeycomb (API level 11) release. They are now also available as part of the Android support library, making it possible to take advantage of Fragments on platforms from Android 1.6 (API level 4) onward.*
>
> *To use Fragments using the support library, you must make your Activity extend the* FragmentActivity *class:*
>
> ```
> public class MyActivity extends FragmentActivity
> ```
>
> *If you are using the compatibility library within a project that has a build target of API level 11 or above, it's critical that you ensure that all your Fragment-related imports and class references are using only the support library classes. The native and support library set of Fragment packages are closely related, but their classes are not interchangeable.*

Creating New Fragments

Extend the Fragment class to create a new Fragment, (optionally) defining the UI and implementing the functionality it encapsulates.

In most circumstances you'll want to assign a UI to your Fragment. It is possible to create a Fragment that *doesn't* include a UI but instead provides background behavior for an Activity. This is explored in more detail later in this chapter.

If your Fragment does require a UI, override the onCreateView handler to inflate and return the required View hierarchy, as shown in the Fragment skeleton code in Listing 4-4.

LISTING 4-4: Fragment skeleton code

```
package com.paad.fragments;

import android.app.Fragment;
import android.os.Bundle;
import android.view.LayoutInflater;
import android.view.View;
import android.view.ViewGroup;

public class MySkeletonFragment extends Fragment {
  @Override
  public View onCreateView(LayoutInflater inflater,
                           ViewGroup container,
                           Bundle savedInstanceState) {
    // Create, or inflate the Fragment's UI, and return it.
    // If this Fragment has no UI then return null.
    return inflater.inflate(R.layout.my_fragment, container, false);
  }
}
```

code snippet PA4AD_Ch04_Fragments/src/MySkeletonFragment.java

You can create a layout in code using layout View Groups; however, as with Activities, the preferred way to design Fragment UI layouts is by inflating an XML resource.

Unlike Activities, Fragments don't need to be registered in your manifest. This is because Fragments can exist only when embedded into an Activity, with their lifecycles dependent on that of the Activity to which they've been added.

The Fragment Lifecycle

The lifecycle events of a Fragment mirror those of its parent Activity; however, after the containing Activity is in its active — resumed — state adding or removing a Fragment will affect its lifecycle independently.

Fragments include a series of event handlers that mirror those in the Activity class. They are triggered as the Fragment is created, started, resumed, paused, stopped, and destroyed. Fragments also include a number of additional callbacks that signal binding and unbinding the Fragment from its parent Activity, creation (and destruction) of the Fragment's View hierarchy, and the completion of the creation of the parent Activity.

Figure 4-9 summarizes the Fragment lifecycle.

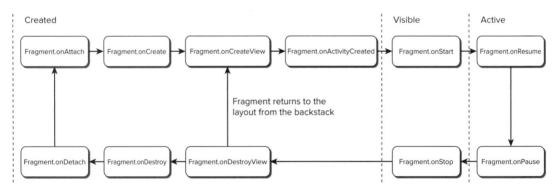

FIGURE 4-9

The skeleton code in Listing 4-5 shows the stubs for the lifecycle handlers available in a Fragment. Comments within each stub describe the actions you should consider taking on each state change event.

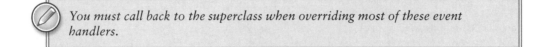

You must call back to the superclass when overriding most of these event handlers.

LISTING 4-5: Fragment lifecycle event handlers

```
package com.paad.fragments;

import android.app.Activity;
import android.app.Fragment;
import android.os.Bundle;
```

```java
import android.view.LayoutInflater;
import android.view.View;
import android.view.ViewGroup;

public class MySkeletonFragment extends Fragment {

  // Called when the Fragment is attached to its parent Activity.
  @Override
  public void onAttach(Activity activity) {
    super.onAttach(activity);
    // Get a reference to the parent Activity.
  }

  // Called to do the initial creation of the Fragment.
  @Override
  public void onCreate(Bundle savedInstanceState) {
    super.onCreate(savedInstanceState);
    // Initialize the Fragment.
  }

  // Called once the Fragment has been created in order for it to
  // create its user interface.
  @Override
  public View onCreateView(LayoutInflater inflater,
                           ViewGroup container,
                           Bundle savedInstanceState) {
    // Create, or inflate the Fragment's UI, and return it.
    // If this Fragment has no UI then return null.
    return inflater.inflate(R.layout.my_fragment, container, false);
  }



  // Called once the parent Activity and the Fragment's UI have
  // been created.
  @Override
  public void onActivityCreated(Bundle savedInstanceState) {
    super.onActivityCreated(savedInstanceState);
    // Complete the Fragment initialization - particularly anything
    // that requires the parent Activity to be initialized or the
    // Fragment's view to be fully inflated.
  }

  // Called at the start of the visible lifetime.
  @Override
  public void onStart(){
    super.onStart();
    // Apply any required UI change now that the Fragment is visible.
  }

  // Called at the start of the active lifetime.
  @Override
  public void onResume(){
    super.onResume();
    // Resume any paused UI updates, threads, or processes required
```

continues

LISTING 4-5 *(continued)*

```java
    // by the Fragment but suspended when it became inactive.
  }

  // Called at the end of the active lifetime.
  @Override
  public void onPause(){
    // Suspend UI updates, threads, or CPU intensive processes
    // that don't need to be updated when the Activity isn't
    // the active foreground activity.
    // Persist all edits or state changes
    // as after this call the process is likely to be killed.
    super.onPause();
  }

  // Called to save UI state changes at the
  // end of the active lifecycle.
  @Override
  public void onSaveInstanceState(Bundle savedInstanceState) {
    // Save UI state changes to the savedInstanceState.
    // This bundle will be passed to onCreate, onCreateView, and
    // onCreateView if the parent Activity is killed and restarted.
    super.onSaveInstanceState(savedInstanceState);
  }

  // Called at the end of the visible lifetime.
  @Override
  public void onStop(){
    // Suspend remaining UI updates, threads, or processing
    // that aren't required when the Fragment isn't visible.
    super.onStop();
  }

  // Called when the Fragment's View has been detached.
  @Override
  public void onDestroyView() {
    // Clean up resources related to the View.
    super.onDestroyView();
  }

  // Called at the end of the full lifetime.
  @Override
  public void onDestroy(){
    // Clean up any resources including ending threads,
    // closing database connections etc.
    super.onDestroy();
  }

  // Called when the Fragment has been detached from its parent Activity.
  @Override
  public void onDetach() {
    super.onDetach();
  }
}
```

code snippet PA4AD_Ch04_Fragments/src/MySkeletonFragment.java

Fragment-Specific Lifecycle Events

Most of the Fragment lifecycle events correspond to their equivalents in the Activity class, which were covered in detail in Chapter 3. Those that remain are specific to Fragments and the way in which they're inserted into their parent Activity.

Attaching and Detaching Fragments from the Parent Activity

The full lifetime of your Fragment begins when it's bound to its parent Activity and ends when it's been detached. These events are represented by the calls to onAttach and onDetach, respectively.

As with any handler called after a Fragment/Activity has become paused, it's possible that onDetach will not be called if the parent Activity's process is terminated *without* completing its full lifecycle.

The onAttach event is triggered before the Fragment's UI has been created, before the Fragment itself or its parent Activity have finished their initialization. Typically, the onAttach event is used to gain a reference to the parent Activity in preparation for further initialization tasks.

Creating and Destroying Fragments

The created lifetime of your Fragment occurs between the first call to onCreate and the final call to onDestroy. As it's not uncommon for an Activity's process to be terminated *without* the corresponding onDestroy method being called, so a Fragment can't rely on its onDestroy handler being triggered.

As with Activities, you should use the onCreate method to initialize your Fragment. It's good practice to create any class scoped objects here to ensure they're created only once in the Fragment's lifetime.

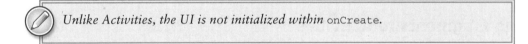

> *Unlike Activities, the UI is not initialized within* onCreate.

Creating and Destroying User Interfaces

A Fragment's UI is initialized (and destroyed) within a new set of event handlers: onCreateView and onDestroyView, respectively.

Use the onCreateView method to initialize your Fragment: Inflate the UI, get references (and bind data to) the Views it contains, and then create any required Services and Timers.

Once you have inflated your View hierarchy, it should be returned from this handler:

```
return inflater.inflate(R.layout.my_fragment, container, false);
```

If your Fragment needs to interact with the UI of its parent Activity, wait until the onActivityCreated event has been triggered. This signifies that the containing Activity has completed its initialization and its UI has been fully constructed.

Fragment States

The fate of a Fragment is inextricably bound to that of the Activity to which it belongs. As a result, Fragment state transitions are closely related to the corresponding Activity state transitions.

Like Activities, Fragments are active when they belong to an Activity that is focused and in the foreground. When an Activity is paused or stopped, the Fragments it contains are also paused and stopped, and the Fragments contained by an inactive Activity are also inactive. When an Activity is finally destroyed, each Fragment it contains is likewise destroyed.

As the Android memory manager nondeterministically closes applications to free resources, the Fragments within those Activities are also destroyed.

While Activities and their Fragments are tightly bound, one of the advantages of using Fragments to compose your Activity's UI is the flexibility to dynamically add or remove Fragments from an active Activity. As a result, each Fragment can progress through its full, visible, and active lifecycle several times within the active lifetime of its parent Activity.

Whatever the trigger for a Fragment's transition through its lifecycle, managing its state transitions is critical in ensuring a seamless user experience. There should be no difference in a Fragment moving from a paused, stopped, or inactive state back to active, so it's important to save all UI state and persist all data when a Fragment is paused or stopped. Like an Activity, when a Fragment becomes active again, it should restore that saved state.

Introducing the Fragment Manager

Each Activity includes a Fragment Manager to manage the Fragments it contains. You can access the Fragment Manager using the `getFragmentManager` method:

```
FragmentManager fragmentManager = getFragmentManager();
```

The Fragment Manager provides the methods used to access the Fragments currently added to the Activity, and to perform Fragment Transaction to add, remove, and replace Fragments.

Adding Fragments to Activities

The simplest way to add a Fragment to an Activity is by including it within the Activity's layout using the `fragment` tag, as shown in Listing 4-6.

LISTING 4-6: Adding Fragments to Activities using XML layouts

```xml
<?xml version="1.0" encoding="utf-8"?>
<LinearLayout xmlns:android="http://schemas.android.com/apk/res/android"
  android:orientation="horizontal"
  android:layout_width="match_parent"
  android:layout_height="match_parent">
  <fragment android:name="com.paad.weatherstation.MyListFragment"
    android:id="@+id/my_list_fragment"
    android:layout_width="match_parent"
    android:layout_height="match_parent"
    android:layout_weight="1"
  />
  <fragment android:name="com.paad.weatherstation.DetailsFragment"
    android:id="@+id/details_fragment"
    android:layout_width="match_parent"
```

```
      android:layout_height="match_parent"
      android:layout_weight="3"
    />
  </LinearLayout>
```

code snippet PA4AD_Ch04_Fragments/res/layout/fragment_layout.xml

Once the Fragment has been inflated, it becomes a View Group, laying out and managing its UI within the Activity.

This technique works well when you use Fragments to define a set of static layouts based on various screen sizes. If you plan to dynamically modify your layouts by adding, removing, and replacing Fragments at run time, a better approach is to create layouts that use container Views into which Fragments can be placed at runtime, based on the current application state.

Listing 4-7 shows an XML snippet that you could use to support this latter approach.

LISTING 4-7: Specifying Fragment layouts using container views

```
<?xml version="1.0" encoding="utf-8"?>
<LinearLayout xmlns:android="http://schemas.android.com/apk/res/android"
    android:orientation="horizontal"
    android:layout_width="match_parent"
    android:layout_height="match_parent">
  <FrameLayout
    android:id="@+id/ui_container"
    android:layout_width="match_parent"
    android:layout_height="match_parent"
    android:layout_weight="1"
  />
  <FrameLayout
    android:id="@+id/details_container"
    android:layout_width="match_parent"
    android:layout_height="match_parent"
    android:layout_weight="3"
  />
</LinearLayout>
```

code snippet PA4AD_Ch04_Fragments/res/layout/fragment_container_layout.xml

You then need to create and add the corresponding Fragments to their appropriate parent containers within the `onCreate` handler of your Activity using Fragment Transactions, as described in the next section.

Using Fragment Transactions

Fragment Transactions can be used to add, remove, and replace Fragments within an Activity at run time. Using Fragment Transactions, you can make your layouts dynamic — that is, they will adapt and change based on user interactions and application state.

Each Fragment Transaction can include any combination of supported actions, including adding, removing, or replacing Fragments. They also support the specification of the transition animations to display and whether to include the Transaction on the back stack.

A new Fragment Transaction is created using the `beginTransaction` method from the Activity's Fragment Manager. Modify the layout using the `add`, `remove`, and `replace` methods, as required, before setting the animations to display, and setting the appropriate back-stack behavior. When you are ready to execute the change, call `commit` to add the transaction to the UI queue.

```
FragmentTransaction fragmentTransaction = fragmentManager.beginTransaction();

// Add, remove, and/or replace Fragments.
// Specify animations.
// Add to back stack if required.

fragmentTransaction.commit();
```

Each of these transaction types and options will be explored in the following sections.

Adding, Removing, and Replacing Fragments

When adding a new UI Fragment, specify the Fragment instance to add, along with the container View into which the Fragment will be placed. Optionally, you can specify a tag that can later be used to find the Fragment by using the `findFragmentByTag` method:

```
FragmentTransaction fragmentTransaction = fragmentManager.beginTransaction();
fragmentTransaction.add(R.id.ui_container, new MyListFragment());
fragmentTransaction.commit();
```

To remove a Fragment, you first need to find a reference to it, usually using either the Fragment Manager's `findFragmentById` or `findFragmentByTag` methods. Then pass the found Fragment instance as a parameter to the `remove` method of a Fragment Transaction:

```
FragmentTransaction fragmentTransaction = fragmentManager.beginTransaction();
Fragment fragment = fragmentManager.findFragmentById(R.id.details_fragment);
fragmentTransaction.remove(fragment);
fragmentTransaction.commit();
```

You can also replace one Fragment with another. Using the `replace` method, specify the container ID containing the Fragment to be replaced, the Fragment with which to replace it, and (optionally) a tag to identify the newly inserted Fragment.

```
FragmentTransaction fragmentTransaction = fragmentManager.beginTransaction();
fragmentTransaction.replace(R.id.details_fragment,
                            new DetailFragment(selected_index));
fragmentTransaction.commit();
```

Using the Fragment Manager to Find Fragments

To find Fragments within your Activity, use the Fragment Manager's `findFragmentById` method. If you have added your Fragment to the Activity layout in XML, you can use the Fragment's resource identifier:

```
MyFragment myFragment =
    (MyFragment)fragmentManager.findFragmentById(R.id.MyFragment);
```

If you've added a Fragment using a Fragment Transaction, you should specify the resource identifier of the container View to which you added the Fragment you want to find. Alternatively, you can use the findFragmentByTag method to search for the Fragment using the tag you specified in the Fragment Transaction:

```
MyFragment myFragment =
    (MyFragment)fragmentManager.findFragmentByTag(MY_FRAGMENT_TAG);
```

Later in this chapter you'll be introduced to Fragments that don't include a UI. The find FragmentByTag method is essential for interacting with these Fragments. Because they're not part of the Activity's View hierarchy, they don't have a resource identifier or a container resource identifier to pass in to the findFragmentById method.

Populating Dynamic Activity Layouts with Fragments

If you're dynamically changing the composition and layout of your Fragments at run time, it's good practice to define only the parent containers within your XML layout and populate it exclusively using Fragment Transactions at run time to ensure consistency when configuration changes (such as screen rotations) cause the UI to be re-created.

Listing 4-8 shows the skeleton code used to populate an Activity's layout with Fragments at run time.

LISTING 4-8: Populating Fragment layouts using container views

```
public void onCreate(Bundle savedInstanceState) {
  super.onCreate(savedInstanceState);

  // Inflate the layout containing the Fragment containers
  setContentView(R.layout.fragment_container_layout);

  FragmentManager fm = getFragmentManager();

  // Check to see if the Fragment back stack has been populated
  // If not, create and populate the layout.
  DetailsFragment detailsFragment =
    (DetailsFragment)fm.findFragmentById(R.id.details_container);

  if (detailsFragment == null) {
    FragmentTransaction ft = fm.beginTransaction();
    ft.add(R.id.details_container, new DetailsFragment());
    ft.add(R.id.ui_container, new MyListFragment());
    ft.commit();
  }
}
```

code snippet PA4AD_Ch04_Fragments/src/MyFragmentActivity.java

You should first check if the UI has already been populated based on the previous state. To ensure a consistent user experience, Android persists the Fragment layout and associated back stack when an Activity is restarted due to a configuration change.

For the same reason, when creating alternative layouts for run time configuration changes, it's considered good practice to include any view containers involved in any transactions in all the layout variations. Failing to do so may result in the Fragment Manager attempting to restore Fragments to containers that don't exist in the new layout.

To remove a Fragment container in a given orientation layout, simply mark its `visibility` attribute as `gone` in your layout definition, as shown in Listing 4-9.

LISTING 4-9: Hiding Fragments in layout variations

```xml
<?xml version="1.0" encoding="utf-8"?>
<LinearLayout xmlns:android="http://schemas.android.com/apk/res/android"
    android:orientation="horizontal"
    android:layout_width="match_parent"
    android:layout_height="match_parent">
    <FrameLayout
        android:id="@+id/ui_container"
        android:layout_width="match_parent"
        android:layout_height="match_parent"
        android:layout_weight="1"
    />
    <FrameLayout
        android:id="@+id/details_container"
        android:layout_width="match_parent"
        android:layout_height="match_parent"
        android:layout_weight="3"
        android:visibility="gone"
    />
</LinearLayout>
```

code snippet PA4AD_Ch04_Fragments/res/layout-port/fragment_container_layout.xml

Fragments and the Back Stack

Chapter 3 described the concept of Activity stacks — the logical stacking of Activities that are no longer visible — which allow users to navigate back to previous screens using the back button.

Fragments enable you to create dynamic Activity layouts that can be modified to present significant changes in the UIs. In some cases these changes could be considered a new screen — in which case a user may reasonably expect the back button to return to the previous layout. This involves reversing previously executed Fragment Transactions.

Android provides a convenient technique for providing this functionality. To add the Fragment Transaction to the back stack, call `addToBackStack` on a Fragment Transaction before calling `commit`.

```
FragmentTransaction fragmentTransaction = fragmentManager.beginTransaction();

fragmentTransaction.add(R.id.ui_container, new MyListFragment());

Fragment fragment = fragmentManager.findFragmentById(R.id.details_fragment);
fragmentTransaction.remove(fragment);

String tag = null;
fragmentTransaction.addToBackStack(tag);

fragmentTransaction.commit();
```

Pressing the Back button will then reverse the previous Fragment Transaction and return the UI to the earlier layout.

When the Fragment Transaction shown above is committed, the Details Fragment is stopped and moved to the back stack, rather than simply destroyed. If the Transaction is reversed, the List Fragment is destroyed, and the Details Fragment is restarted.

Animating Fragment Transactions

To apply one of the default transition animations, use the `setTransition` method on any Fragment Transaction, passing in one of the `FragmentTransaction.TRANSIT_FRAGMENT_*` constants.

```
transaction.setTransition(FragmentTransaction.TRANSIT_FRAGMENT_OPEN);
```

You can also apply custom animations to Fragment Transactions by using the `setCustom Animations` method. This method accepts two animation XML resources: one for Fragments that are being added to the layout by this transaction, and another for Fragments being removed:

```
fragmentTransaction.setCustomAnimations(R.animator.slide_in_left,
                                        R.animator.slide_out_right);
```

This is a particularly useful way to add seamless dynamic transitions when you are replacing Fragments within your layout.

> *The Android animation libraries were significantly improved in Android 3.0 (API level 11) with the inclusion of the* `Animator` *class. As a result, the animation resource passed in to the* `setCustomAnimations` *method is different for applications built using the support library.*
>
> *Applications built for devices running on API level 11 and above should use* `Animator` *resources, whereas those using the support library to support earlier platform releases should use the older View* `Animation` *resources.*

You can find more details on creating custom Animator and Animation resources in Chapter 11, "Advanced User Experience."

Interfacing Between Fragments and Activities

Use the `getActivity` method within any Fragment to return a reference to the Activity within which it's embedded. This is particularly useful for finding the current Context, accessing other Fragments using the Fragment Manager, and finding Views within the Activity's View hierarchy.

```
TextView textView = (TextView)getActivity().findViewById(R.id.textview);
```

Although it's possible for Fragments to communicate directly using the host Activity's Fragment Manager, it's generally considered better practice to use the Activity as an intermediary. This allows the Fragments to be as independent and loosely coupled as possible, with the responsibility for deciding how an event in one Fragment should affect the overall UI falling to the host Activity.

Where your Fragment needs to share events with its host Activity (such as signaling UI selections), it's good practice to create a callback interface within the Fragment that a host Activity must implement.

Listing 4-10 shows a code snippet from within a Fragment class that defines a public event listener interface. The `onAttach` handler is overridden to obtain a reference to the host Activity, confirming that it implements the required interface.

LISTING 4-10: Defining Fragment event callback interfaces

```java
public interface OnSeasonSelectedListener {
  public void onSeasonSelected(Season season);
}

private OnSeasonSelectedListener onSeasonSelectedListener;
private Season currentSeason;

@Override
public void onAttach(Activity activity) {
  super.onAttach(activity);

  try {
    onSeasonSelectedListener = (OnSeasonSelectedListener)activity;
  } catch (ClassCastException e) {
    throw new ClassCastException(activity.toString() +
              " must implement OnSeasonSelectedListener");
  }
}

private void setSeason(Season season) {
  currentSeason = season;
  onSeasonSelectedListener.onSeasonSelected(season);
}
```

code snippet PA4AD_Ch04_Fragments/src/SeasonFragment.java

Fragments Without User Interfaces

In most circumstances, Fragments are used to encapsulate modular components of the UI; however, you can also create a Fragment without a UI to provide background behavior that persists across

Activity restarts. This is particularly well suited to background tasks that regularly touch the UI or where it's important to maintain state across Activity restarts caused by configuration changes.

You can choose to have an active Fragment retain its current instance when its parent Activity is re-created using the `setRetainInstance` method. After you call this method, the Fragment's lifecycle will change.

Rather than being destroyed and re-created with its parent Activity, the same Fragment instance is retained when the Activity restarts. It will receive the `onDetach` event when the parent Activity is destroyed, followed by the `onAttach`, `onCreateView`, and `onActivityCreated` events as the new parent Activity is instantiated.

> *Although you use this technique on Fragments with a UI, this is generally not recommended. A better alternative is to move the associated background task or required state into a new Fragment, without a UI, and have the two Fragments interact as required.*

The following snippet shows the skeleton code for a Fragment without a UI:

```java
public class NewItemFragment extends Fragment {
  @Override
  public void onAttach(Activity activity) {
    super.onAttach(activity);

    // Get a type-safe reference to the parent Activity.
  }

  @Override
  public void onCreate(Bundle savedInstanceState) {
    super.onCreate(savedInstanceState);

    // Create background worker threads and tasks.
  }

  @Override
  public void onActivityCreated(Bundle savedInstanceState) {
    super.onActivityCreated(savedInstanceState);

    // Initiate worker threads and tasks.
  }
}
```

To add this Fragment to your Activity, create a new Fragment Transaction, specifying a tag to use to identify it. Because the Fragment has no UI, it should not be associated with a container View and generally shouldn't be added to the back stack.

```java
FragmentTransaction fragmentTransaction = fragmentManager.beginTransaction();

fragmentTransaction.add(workerFragment, MY_FRAGMENT_TAG);

fragmentTransaction.commit();
```

Use the `findFragmentByTag` from the Fragment Manager to find a reference to it later.

```
MyFragment myFragment =
  (MyFragment)fragmentManager.findFragmentByTag(MY_FRAGMENT_TAG);
```

Android Fragment Classes

The Android SDK includes a number of Fragment subclasses that encapsulate some of the most common Fragment implementations. Some of the more useful ones are listed here:

➤ `DialogFragment` — A Fragment that you can use to display a floating Dialog over the parent Activity. You can customize the Dialog's UI and control its visibility directly via the Fragment API. Dialog Fragments are covered in more detail in Chapter 10, "Expanding the User Experience."

➤ `ListFragment` — A wrapper class for Fragments that feature a `ListView` bound to a data source as the primary UI metaphor. It provides methods to set the Adapter to use and exposes the event handlers for list item selection. The List Fragment is used as part of the To-Do List example in the next section.

➤ `WebViewFragment` — A wrapper class that encapsulates a WebView within a Fragment. The child WebView will be paused and resumed when the Fragment is paused and resumed.

Using Fragments for Your To-Do List

The earlier to-do list example used a Linear Layout within an Activity to define its UI.

In this example you'll break the UI into a series of Fragments that represent its component pieces — the text entry box and the list of to-do items. This will enable you to easily create optimized layouts for different screen sizes.

1. Start by creating a new layout file, `new_item_fragment.xml` in the `res/layout` folder that contains the Edit Text node from the `main.xml`.

```
<?xml version="1.0" encoding="utf-8"?>
<EditText xmlns:android="http://schemas.android.com/apk/res/android"
  android:id="@+id/myEditText"
  android:layout_width="match_parent"
  android:layout_height="wrap_content"
  android:hint="@string/addItemHint"
  android:contentDescription="@string/addItemContentDescription"
/>
```

2. You'll need to create a new Fragment for each UI component. Start by creating a `NewItemFragment` that extends `Fragment`. Override the `onCreateView` handler to inflate the layout you created in step 1.

```
package com.paad.todolist;

import android.app.Activity;
import android.app.Fragment;
import android.view.KeyEvent;
```

```
import android.os.Bundle;
import android.view.LayoutInflater;
import android.view.View;
import android.view.ViewGroup;
import android.widget.EditText;

public class NewItemFragment extends Fragment {

  @Override
  public View onCreateView(LayoutInflater inflater, ViewGroup container,
    Bundle savedInstanceState) {
    return inflater.inflate(R.layout.new_item_fragment, container, false);
  }

}
```

3. Each Fragment should encapsulate the functionality that it provides. In the case of the New Item Fragment, that's accepting new to-do items to add to your list. Start by defining an interface that the `ToDoListActivity` can implement to listen for new items being added.

```
public interface OnNewItemAddedListener {
  public void onNewItemAdded(String newItem);
}
```

4. Now create a variable to store a reference to the parent `ToDoListActivity` that will implement this interface. You can get the reference as soon as the parent Activity has been bound to the Fragment within the Fragment's `onAttach` handler.

```
private OnNewItemAddedListener onNewItemAddedListener;

@Override
public void onAttach(Activity activity) {
  super.onAttach(activity);

  try {
    onNewItemAddedListener = (OnNewItemAddedListener)activity;
  } catch (ClassCastException e) {
    throw new ClassCastException(activity.toString() +
            " must implement OnNewItemAddedListener");
  }
}
```

5. Move the `editText.onClickListener` implementation from the `ToDoListActivity` into your Fragment. When the user adds a new item, rather than adding the text directly to an array, pass it in to the parent Activity's `OnNewItemAddedListener.onNewItemAdded` implementation.

```
@Override
public View onCreateView(LayoutInflater inflater, ViewGroup container,
  Bundle savedInstanceState) {
  View view = inflater.inflate(R.layout.new_item_fragment, container, false);

  final EditText myEditText =
    (EditText)view.findViewById(R.id.myEditText);
```

```
myEditText.setOnKeyListener(new View.OnKeyListener() {
  public boolean onKey(View v, int keyCode, KeyEvent event) {
    if (event.getAction() == KeyEvent.ACTION_DOWN)
      if ((keyCode == KeyEvent.KEYCODE_DPAD_CENTER) ||
          (keyCode == KeyEvent.KEYCODE_ENTER)) {
        String newItem = myEditText.getText().toString();
        onNewItemAddedListener.onNewItemAdded(newItem);
        myEditText.setText("");
        return true;
      }
    return false;
  }
});

return view;
}
```

6. Next, create the Fragment that contains the list of to-do items. Android provides a
`ListFragment` class that you can use to easily create a simple List View based Fragment.
Create a new class that Extends `ListFragment`.

```
package com.paad.todolist;

import android.app.ListFragment;

public class ToDoListFragment extends ListFragment {
}
```

> *The List Fragment class includes a default UI consisting of a single List View,
> which is sufficient for this example. You can easily customize the default List
> Fragment UI by creating your own custom layout and inflating it within the*
> `onCreateView` *handler. Any custom layout must include a List View node with
> the ID specified as* `@android:id/list`.

7. With your Fragments completed, it's time to return to the Activity. Start by updating the
`main.xml` layout, replacing the List View and Edit Text with the ToDo List Fragment and
New Item Fragment, respectively.

```xml
<?xml version="1.0" encoding="utf-8"?>
<LinearLayout xmlns:android="http://schemas.android.com/apk/res/android"
  android:orientation="vertical"
  android:layout_width="match_parent"
  android:layout_height="match_parent">
  <fragment android:name="com.paad.todolist.NewItemFragment"
    android:id="@+id/NewItemFragment"
    android:layout_width="match_parent"
    android:layout_height="wrap_content"
  />
  <fragment android:name="com.paad.todolist.ToDoListFragment"
    android:id="@+id/TodoListFragment"
```

```
    android:layout_width="match_parent"
    android:layout_height="wrap_content"
  />
</LinearLayout>
```

8.   Return to the `ToDoListActivity`. Within the `onCreate` method, use the Fragment Manager to get a reference to the ToDo List Fragment before creating and assigning the adapter to it. Because the List View and Edit Text Views are now encapsulated within fragments, you no longer need to find references to them within your Activity. You'll need to expand the scope of the Array Adapter and Array List to class variables.

```
private ArrayAdapter<String> aa;
private ArrayList<String> todoItems;

public void onCreate(Bundle savedInstanceState) {
  super.onCreate(savedInstanceState);

  // Inflate your view
  setContentView(R.layout.main);

  // Get references to the Fragments
  FragmentManager fm = getFragmentManager();
  ToDoListFragment todoListFragment =
    (ToDoListFragment)fm.findFragmentById(R.id.TodoListFragment);

  // Create the array list of to do items
  todoItems = new ArrayList<String>();

  // Create the array adapter to bind the array to the listview
  aa = new ArrayAdapter<String>(this,
                      android.R.layout.simple_list_item_1,
                      todoItems);

  // Bind the array adapter to the listview.
  todoListFragment.setListAdapter(aa);
}
```

9.   Your List View is now connected to your Array List using an adapter, so all that's left is to add any new items created within the New Item Fragment. Start by declaring that your class will implement the `OnNewItemAddedListener` you defined within the New Item Fragment in step 3.

```
public class ToDoList extends Activity
  implements NewItemFragment.OnNewItemAddedListener {
```

10.   Finally, implement the listener by implementing an `onNewItemAdded` handler. Add the received string variable to the Array List before notifying the Array Adapter that the dataset has changed.

```
public void onNewItemAdded(String newItem) {
  todoItems.add(newItem);
  aa.notifyDataSetChanged();
}
```

> *All code snippets in this example are part of the* Chapter 4 To-Do List Part 2
> *project, available for download at* www.wrox.com.

THE ANDROID WIDGET TOOLBOX

Android supplies a toolbox of standard Views to help you create your UIs. By using these controls (and modifying or extending them, as necessary), you can simplify your development and provide consistency between applications.

The following list highlights some of the more familiar toolbox controls:

➤   TextView — A standard read-only text label that supports multiline display, string formatting, and automatic word wrapping.

➤   EditText — An editable text entry box that accepts multiline entry, word-wrapping, and hint text.

➤   Chronometer — A Text View extension that implements a simple count-up timer.

➤   ListView — A View Group that creates and manages a vertical list of Views, displaying them as rows within the list. The simplest List View displays the toString value of each object in an array, using a Text View for each item.

➤   Spinner — A composite control that displays a Text View and an associated List View that lets you select an item from a list to display in the textbox. It's made from a Text View displaying the current selection, combined with a button that displays a selection dialog when pressed.

➤   Button — A standard push button.

➤   ToggleButton — A two-state button that can be used as an alternative to a check box. It's particularly appropriate where pressing the button will initiate an action as well as changing a state (such as when turning something on or off).

➤   ImageButton — A push button for which you can specify a customized background image (Drawable).

➤   CheckBox — A two-state button represented by a checked or unchecked box.

➤   RadioButton — A two-state grouped button. A group of these presents the user with a number of possible options, of which only one can be enabled at a time.

➤   ViewFlipper — A View Group that lets you define a collection of Views as a horizontal row in which only one View is visible at a time, and in which transitions between visible views can be animated.

➤   VideoView — Handles all state management and display Surface configuration for playing videos more simply from within your Activity.

➤   QuickContactBadge — Displays a badge showing the image icon assigned to a contact you specify using a phone number, name, email address, or URI. Clicking the image will display the quick contact bar, which provides shortcuts for contacting the selected contact — including calling and sending an SMS, email, and IM.

➤ `ViewPager` — Released as part of the Compatibility Package, the View Pager implements a horizontally scrolling set of Views similar to the UI used in Google Play and Calendar. The View Pager allows users to swipe or drag left or right to switch between different Views.

This is only a selection of the widgets available. Android also supports several more advanced View implementations, including date-time pickers, auto-complete input boxes, maps, galleries, and tab sheets. For a more comprehensive list of the available widgets, head to `http://developer.android.com/guide/tutorials/views/index.html`.

CREATING NEW VIEWS

It's only a matter of time before you, as an innovative developer, encounter a situation in which none of the built-in controls meets your needs.

The ability to extend existing Views, assemble composite controls, and create unique new Views makes it possible to implement beautiful UIs optimized for your application's workflow. Android lets you subclass the existing View toolbox or implement your own View controls, giving you total freedom to tailor your UI to optimize the user experience.

> *When designing a UI, it's important to balance raw aesthetics and usability. With the power to create your own custom controls comes the temptation to rebuild all your controls from scratch. Resist that urge. The standard Views will be familiar to users from other Android applications and will update in line with new platform releases. On small screens, with users often paying limited attention, familiarity can often provide better usability than a slightly shinier control.*

The best approach to use when creating a new View depends on what you want to achieve:

➤ **Modify or extend the appearance and/or behavior of an existing View** when it supplies the basic functionality you want. By overriding the event handlers and/or `onDraw`, but still calling back to the superclass's methods, you can customize a View without having to re-implement its functionality. For example, you could customize a `TextView` to display numbers using a set number of decimal points.

➤ **Combine Views** to create atomic, reusable controls that leverage the functionality of several interconnected Views. For example, you could create a stopwatch timer by combining a `TextView` and a `Button` that resets the counter when clicked.

➤ **Create an entirely new control** when you need a completely different interface that you can't get by changing or combining existing controls.

Modifying Existing Views

The Android widget toolbox includes Views that provide many common UI requirements, but the controls are necessarily generic. By customizing these basic Views, you avoid re-implementing existing behavior while still tailoring the UI, and functionality, to your application's needs.

To create a new View based on an existing control, create a new class that extends it, as shown with the `TextView` derived class shown in Listing 4-11. In this example you extend the Text View to customize its appearance and behavior.

LISTING 4-11: Extending Text View

```java
import android.content.Context;
import android.graphics.Canvas;
import android.util.AttributeSet;
import android.view.KeyEvent;
import android.widget.TextView;

public class MyTextView extends TextView {

  public MyTextView (Context context, AttributeSet attrs, int defStyle)
  {
    super(context, attrs, defStyle);
  }

  public MyTextView (Context context) {
    super(context);
  }

  public MyTextView (Context context, AttributeSet attrs) {
    super(context, attrs);
  }
}
```

code snippet PA4AD_Ch04_Views/src/MyTextView.java

To override the appearance or behavior of your new View, override and extend the event handlers associated with the behavior you want to change.

In the following extension of the Listing 4-11 code, the `onDraw` method is overridden to modify the View's appearance, and the `onKeyDown` handler is overridden to allow custom key-press handling.

```java
public class MyTextView extends TextView {

  public MyTextView (Context context, AttributeSet ats, int defStyle) {
    super(context, ats, defStyle);
  }

  public MyTextView (Context context) {
    super(context);
  }

  public MyTextView (Context context, AttributeSet attrs) {
    super(context, attrs);
  }

  @Override
  public void onDraw(Canvas canvas) {
    [ ... Draw things on the canvas under the text ... ]
```

```
    // Render the text as usual using the TextView base class.
    super.onDraw(canvas);

    [ ... Draw things on the canvas over the text ... ]
  }

  @Override
  public boolean onKeyDown(int keyCode, KeyEvent keyEvent) {
    [ ... Perform some special processing ... ]
    [ ... based on a particular key press ... ]

    // Use the existing functionality implemented by
    // the base class to respond to a key press event.
    return super.onKeyDown(keyCode, keyEvent);
  }
}
```

The event handlers available within Views are covered in more detail later in this chapter.

Customizing Your To-Do List

The to-do list example uses `TextView` controls to represent each row in a List View. You can customize the appearance of the list by extending Text View and overriding the `onDraw` method.

In this example you'll create a new `TodoListItemView` that will make each item appear as if on a paper pad. When complete, your customized to-do list should look like Figure 4-10.

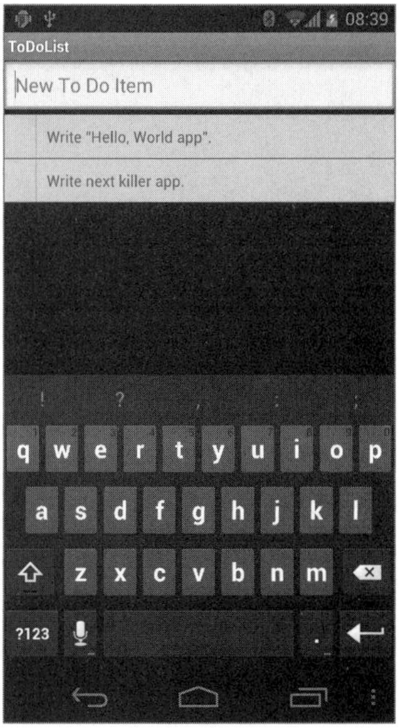

FIGURE 4-10

1. Create a new `ToDoListItemView` class that extends `TextView`. Include a stub for overriding the `onDraw` method, and implement constructors that call a new `init` method stub.

```
package com.paad.todolist;

import android.content.Context;
import android.content.res.Resources;
import android.graphics.Canvas;
import android.graphics.Paint;
import android.util.AttributeSet;
import android.widget.TextView;

public class ToDoListItemView extends TextView {

  public ToDoListItemView (Context context, AttributeSet ats, int ds) {
    super(context, ats, ds);
    init();
  }

  public ToDoListItemView (Context context) {
    super(context);
    init();
  }

  public ToDoListItemView (Context context, AttributeSet attrs) {
    super(context, attrs);
    init();
  }

  private void init() {
  }

  @Override
  public void onDraw(Canvas canvas) {
    // Use the base TextView to render the text.
    super.onDraw(canvas);
  }

}
```

2. Create a new `colors.xml` resource in the `res/values` folder. Create new color values for the paper, margin, line, and text colors.

```xml
<?xml version="1.0" encoding="utf-8"?>
<resources>
  <color name="notepad_paper">#EEF8E0A0</color>
  <color name="notepad_lines">#FF0000FF</color>
  <color name="notepad_margin">#90FF0000</color>
  <color name="notepad_text">#AA0000FF</color>
</resources>
```

3. Create a new `dimens.xml` resource file, and add a new value for the paper's margin width.

```xml
<?xml version="1.0" encoding="utf-8"?>
<resources>
  <dimen name="notepad_margin">30dp</dimen>
</resources>
```

4. With the resources defined, you're ready to customize the `ToDoListItemView` appearance. Create new private instance variables to store the `Paint` objects you'll use to draw the paper background and margin. Also create variables for the paper color and margin width values. Fill in the `init` method to get instances of the resources you created in the last two steps, and create the `Paint` objects.

```
private Paint marginPaint;
private Paint linePaint;
private int paperColor;
private float margin;

private void init() {
  // Get a reference to our resource table.
  Resources myResources = getResources();

  // Create the paint brushes we will use in the onDraw method.
  marginPaint = new Paint(Paint.ANTI_ALIAS_FLAG);
  marginPaint.setColor(myResources.getColor(R.color.notepad_margin));
  linePaint = new Paint(Paint.ANTI_ALIAS_FLAG);
  linePaint.setColor(myResources.getColor(R.color.notepad_lines));

  // Get the paper background color and the margin width.
  paperColor = myResources.getColor(R.color.notepad_paper);
  margin = myResources.getDimension(R.dimen.notepad_margin);
}
```

5. To draw the paper, override `onDraw` and draw the image using the `Paint` objects you created in step 4. After you've drawn the paper image, call the superclass's `onDraw` method and let it draw the text as usual.

```
@Override
public void onDraw(Canvas canvas) {
  // Color as paper
  canvas.drawColor(paperColor);

  // Draw ruled lines
  canvas.drawLine(0, 0, 0, getMeasuredHeight(), linePaint);
  canvas.drawLine(0, getMeasuredHeight(),
                  getMeasuredWidth(), getMeasuredHeight(),
                  linePaint);

  // Draw margin
  canvas.drawLine(margin, 0, margin, getMeasuredHeight(), marginPaint);

  // Move the text across from the margin
  canvas.save();
  canvas.translate(margin, 0);

  // Use the TextView to render the text
  super.onDraw(canvas);
  canvas.restore();
}
```

6. That completes the `ToDoListItemView` implementation. To use it in the To-Do List Activity, you need to include it in a new layout and pass that layout in to the Array Adapter constructor. Start by creating a new `todolist_item.xml` resource in the `res/layout` folder. It will specify how each of the to-do list items is displayed within the List View. For this example, your layout need only consist of the new `ToDoListItemView`, set to fill the entire available area.

```xml
<?xml version="1.0" encoding="utf-8"?>
<com.paad.todolist.ToDoListItemView
  xmlns:android="http://schemas.android.com/apk/res/android"
  android:layout_width="match_parent"
  android:layout_height="match_parent"
  android:padding="10dp"
  android:scrollbars="vertical"
  android:textColor="@color/notepad_text"
  android:fadingEdge="vertical"
/>
```

7. The final step is to change the parameters passed in to the `ArrayAdapter` in `onCreate` of the `ToDoListActivity` class. Replace the reference to the default `android.R.layout.simple_list_item_1` with a reference to the new `R.layout.todolist_item` layout created in step 6.

```java
int resID = R.layout.todolist_item;
aa = new ArrayAdapter<String>(this, resID, todoItems);
```

> *All code snippets in this example are part of the* Chapter 4 To-do List Part 3 *project, available for download at* www.wrox.com.

Creating Compound Controls

Compound controls are atomic, self-contained View Groups that contain multiple child Views laid out and connected together.

When you create a compound control, you define the layout, appearance, and interaction of the Views it contains. You create compound controls by extending a `ViewGroup` (usually a layout). To create a new compound control, choose the layout class that's most suitable for positioning the child controls and extend it:

```java
public class MyCompoundView extends LinearLayout {
  public MyCompoundView(Context context) {
    super(context);
  }

  public MyCompoundView(Context context, AttributeSet attrs) {
    super(context, attrs);
  }
}
```

As with Activities, the preferred way to design compound View UI layouts is by using an external resource.

Listing 4-12 shows the XML layout definition for a simple compound control consisting of an Edit Text for text entry, with a Clear Text button beneath it.

LISTING 4-12: A compound View layout resource

```xml
<?xml version="1.0" encoding="utf-8"?>
<LinearLayout xmlns:android="http://schemas.android.com/apk/res/android"
  android:orientation="vertical"
  android:layout_width="match_parent"
  android:layout_height="wrap_content">
  <EditText
    android:id="@+id/editText"
    android:layout_width="match_parent"
    android:layout_height="wrap_content"
  />
  <Button
    android:id="@+id/clearButton"
    android:layout_width="match_parent"
    android:layout_height="wrap_content"
    android:text="Clear"
  />
</LinearLayout>
```

code snippet PA4AD_Ch04_Views/res/layout/clearable_edit_text.xml

To use this layout in your new compound View, override its constructor to inflate the layout resource using the `inflate` method from the `LayoutInflate` system service. The `inflate` method takes the layout resource and returns the inflated View.

For circumstances such as this, in which the returned View should be the class you're creating, you can pass in the parent View and attach the result to it automatically.

Listing 4-13 demonstrates this using the `ClearableEditText` class. Within the constructor it inflates the layout resource from Listing 4-12 and then finds a reference to the Edit Text and Button Views it contains. It also makes a call to `hookupButton` that will later be used to hook up the plumbing that will implement the *clear text* functionality.

LISTING 4-13: Constructing a compound View

```java
public class ClearableEditText extends LinearLayout {

  EditText editText;
  Button clearButton;

  public ClearableEditText(Context context) {
    super(context);

    // Inflate the view from the layout resource.
    String infService = Context.LAYOUT_INFLATER_SERVICE;
    LayoutInflater li;
```

continues

LISTING 4-13 *(continued)*

```
        li = (LayoutInflater)getContext().getSystemService(infService);
        li.inflate(R.layout.clearable_edit_text, this, true);

        // Get references to the child controls.
        editText = (EditText)findViewById(R.id.editText);
        clearButton = (Button)findViewById(R.id.clearButton);

        // Hook up the functionality
        hookupButton();
    }
}
```

code snippet PA4AD_Ch04_Views/src/ClearableEditText.java

If you prefer to construct your layout in code, you can do so just as you would for an Activity:

```
public ClearableEditText(Context context) {
    super(context);

    // Set orientation of layout to vertical
    setOrientation(LinearLayout.VERTICAL);

    // Create the child controls.
    editText = new EditText(getContext());
    clearButton = new Button(getContext());
    clearButton.setText("Clear");

    // Lay them out in the compound control.
    int lHeight = LinearLayout.LayoutParams.WRAP_CONTENT;
    int lWidth = LinearLayout.LayoutParams.MATCH_PARENT;

    addView(editText, new LinearLayout.LayoutParams(lWidth, lHeight));
    addView(clearButton, new LinearLayout.LayoutParams(lWidth, lHeight));

    // Hook up the functionality
    hookupButton();
}
```

After constructing the View layout, you can hook up the event handlers for each child control to provide the functionality you need. In Listing 4-14, the `hookupButton` method is filled in to clear the Edit Text when the button is pressed.

LISTING 4-14: Implementing the Clear Text Button

```
private void hookupButton() {
    clearButton.setOnClickListener(new Button.OnClickListener() {
        public void onClick(View v) {
            editText.setText("");
```

```
        }
    });
}
```

code snippet PA4AD_Ch04_Views/src/ClearableEditText.java

Creating Simple Compound Controls Using Layouts

It's often sufficient, and more flexible, to define the layout and appearance of a set of Views without hard-wiring their interactions.

You can create a reusable layout by creating an XML resource that encapsulates the UI pattern you want to reuse. You can then import these layout patterns when creating the UI for Activities or Fragments by using the `include` tag within their layout resource definitions.

```
<include layout="@layout/clearable_edit_text"/>
```

The `include` tag also enables you to override the `id` and `layout` parameters of the root node of the included layout:

```
<include layout="@layout/clearable_edit_text"
         android:id="@+id/add_new_entry_input"
         android:layout_width="match_parent"
         android:layout_height="wrap_content"
         android:layout_gravity="top"/>
```

Creating Custom Views

Creating new Views gives you the power to fundamentally shape the way your applications look and feel. By creating your own controls, you can create UIs that are uniquely suited to your needs.

To create new controls from a blank canvas, you extend either the `View` or `SurfaceView` class. The `View` class provides a `Canvas` object with a series of draw methods and `Paint` classes. Use them to create a visual interface with bitmaps and raster graphics. You can then override user events, including screen touches or key presses to provide interactivity.

In situations in which extremely rapid repaints and 3D graphics aren't required, the `View` base class offers a powerful lightweight solution.

The `SurfaceView` class provides a `Surface` object that supports drawing from a background thread and optionally using `openGL` to implement your graphics. This is an excellent option for graphics-heavy controls that are frequently updated (such as live video) or that display complex graphical information (particularly, games and 3D visualizations).

 This section focuses on building controls based on the View class. To learn more about the `SurfaceView` *class and some of the more advanced Canvas paint features available in Android, see Chapter 10.*

Creating a New Visual Interface

The base `View` class presents a distinctly empty 100-pixel-by-100-pixel square. To change the size of the control and display a more compelling visual interface, you need to override the `onMeasure` and `onDraw` methods.

Within `onMeasure` your View will determine the height and width it will occupy given a set of boundary conditions. The `onDraw` method is where you draw onto the Canvas.

Listing 4-15 shows the skeleton code for a new `View` class, which will be examined and developed further in the following sections.

LISTING 4-15: Creating a new View

```java
public class MyView extends View {

  // Constructor required for in-code creation
  public MyView(Context context) {
    super(context);
  }

  // Constructor required for inflation from resource file
  public MyView (Context context, AttributeSet ats, int defaultStyle) {
    super(context, ats, defaultStyle );
  }

  //Constructor required for inflation from resource file
  public MyView (Context context, AttributeSet attrs) {
    super(context, attrs);
  }

  @Override
  protected void onMeasure(int wMeasureSpec, int hMeasureSpec) {
    int measuredHeight = measureHeight(hMeasureSpec);
    int measuredWidth = measureWidth(wMeasureSpec);

    // MUST make this call to setMeasuredDimension
    // or you will cause a runtime exception when
    // the control is laid out.
    setMeasuredDimension(measuredHeight, measuredWidth);
  }

  private int measureHeight(int measureSpec) {
    int specMode = MeasureSpec.getMode(measureSpec);
    int specSize = MeasureSpec.getSize(measureSpec);

    [ ... Calculate the view height ... ]

    return specSize;
  }

  private int measureWidth(int measureSpec) {
```

```
    int specMode = MeasureSpec.getMode(measureSpec);
    int specSize = MeasureSpec.getSize(measureSpec);

    [ ... Calculate the view width ... ]

    return specSize;
  }

  @Override
  protected void onDraw(Canvas canvas) {
    [ ... Draw your visual interface ... ]
  }
}
```

code snippet PA4AD_Ch04_Views/src/MyView.java

> *The* onMeasure *method calls* setMeasuredDimension. *You must always call this method within your overridden* onMeasure *method; otherwise, your control will throw an exception when the parent container attempts to lay it out.*

Drawing Your Control

The onDraw method is where the magic happens. If you're creating a new widget from scratch, it's because you want to create a completely new visual interface. The Canvas parameter in the onDraw method is the surface you'll use to bring your imagination to life.

The Android Canvas uses the *painter's algorithm*, meaning that each time you draw on to the canvas, it will cover anything previously drawn on the same area.

The drawing APIs provide a variety of tools to help draw your design on the Canvas using various Paint objects. The Canvas class includes helper methods for drawing primitive 2D objects, including circles, lines, rectangles, text, and Drawables (images). It also supports transformations that let you rotate, translate (move), and scale (resize) the Canvas while you draw on it.

When these tools are used in combination with Drawables and the Paint class (which offer a variety of customizable fills and pens), the complexity and detail that your control can render are limited only by the size of the screen and the power of the processor rendering it.

> *One of the most important techniques for writing efficient code in Android is to avoid the repetitive creation and destruction of objects. Any object created in your* onDraw *method will be created and destroyed every time the screen refreshes. Improve efficiency by making as many of these objects (particularly instances of* Paint *and* Drawable) *class-scoped and by moving their creation into the constructor.*

Listing 4-16 shows how to override the onDraw method to display a simple text string in the center of the control.

LISTING 4-16: Drawing a custom View

```
@Override
protected void onDraw(Canvas canvas) {
    // Get the size of the control based on the last call to onMeasure.
    int height = getMeasuredHeight();
    int width = getMeasuredWidth();

    // Find the center
    int px = width/2;
    int py = height/2;

    // Create the new paint brushes.
    // NOTE: For efficiency this should be done in
    // the views's constructor
    Paint mTextPaint = new Paint(Paint.ANTI_ALIAS_FLAG);
    mTextPaint.setColor(Color.WHITE);

    // Define the string.
    String displayText = "Hello World!";

    // Measure the width of the text string.
    float textWidth = mTextPaint.measureText(displayText);

    // Draw the text string in the center of the control.
    canvas.drawText(displayText, px-textWidth/2, py, mTextPaint);
}
```

code snippet PA4AD_Ch04_Views/src/MyView.java

So that we don't diverge too far from the current topic, a more detailed look at the Canvas and Paint classes, and the techniques available for drawing more complex visuals is included in Chapter 10.

> *Android does not currently support vector graphics. As a result, changes to any element of your Canvas require that the entire Canvas be repainted; modifying the color of a brush will not change your View's display until the control is invalidated and redrawn. Alternatively, you can use OpenGL to render graphics. For more details, see the discussion on* SurfaceView *in Chapter 15, "Audio, Video, and Using the Camera."*

Sizing Your Control

Unless you conveniently require a control that always occupies a space 100 pixels square, you will also need to override onMeasure.

The onMeasure method is called when the control's parent is laying out its child controls. It asks the question, "How much space will you use?" and passes in two parameters: widthMeasureSpec and heightMeasureSpec. These parameters specify the space available for the control and some metadata to describe that space.

Rather than return a result, you pass the View's height and width into the setMeasuredDimension method.

The following snippet shows how to override onMeasure. The calls to the local method stubs measureHeight and measureWidth, which are used to decode the widthHeightSpec and height MeasureSpec values and calculate the preferred height and width values, respectively.

```
@Override
protected void onMeasure(int widthMeasureSpec, int heightMeasureSpec) {

  int measuredHeight = measureHeight(heightMeasureSpec);
  int measuredWidth = measureWidth(widthMeasureSpec);

  setMeasuredDimension(measuredHeight, measuredWidth);
}

private int measureHeight(int measureSpec) {
  // Return measured widget height.
}

private int measureWidth(int measureSpec) {
  // Return measured widget width.
}
```

The boundary parameters, widthMeasureSpec and heightMeasureSpec, are passed in as integers for efficiency reasons. Before they can be used, they first need to be decoded using the static get-Mode and getSize methods from the MeasureSpec class.

```
int specMode = MeasureSpec.getMode(measureSpec);
int specSize = MeasureSpec.getSize(measureSpec);
```

Depending on the *mode* value, the *size* represents either the maximum space available for the control (in the case of AT_MOST), or the exact size that your control will occupy (for EXACTLY). In the case of UNSPECIFIED, your control does not have any reference for what the size represents.

By marking a measurement size as EXACT, the parent is insisting that the View will be placed into an area of the exact size specified. The AT_MOST mode says the parent is asking what size the View would like to occupy, given an upper boundary. In many cases the value you return will either be the same, or the size required to appropriately wrap the UI you want to display.

In either case, you should treat these limits as absolute. In some circumstances it may still be appropriate to return a measurement outside these limits, in which case you can let the parent choose how to deal with the oversized View, using techniques such as clipping and scrolling.

Listing 4-17 shows a typical implementation for handling View measurements.

LISTING 4-17: A typical View measurement implementation

```java
@Override
protected void onMeasure(int widthMeasureSpec, int heightMeasureSpec) {
  int measuredHeight = measureHeight(heightMeasureSpec);
  int measuredWidth = measureWidth(widthMeasureSpec);

  setMeasuredDimension(measuredHeight, measuredWidth);
}

private int measureHeight(int measureSpec) {
  int specMode = MeasureSpec.getMode(measureSpec);
  int specSize = MeasureSpec.getSize(measureSpec);

  // Default size if no limits are specified.
  int result = 500;

  if (specMode == MeasureSpec.AT_MOST) {
    // Calculate the ideal size of your
    // control within this maximum size.
    // If your control fills the available
    // space return the outer bound.
    result = specSize;
  } else if (specMode == MeasureSpec.EXACTLY) {
    // If your control can fit within these bounds return that value.
    result = specSize;
  }
  return result;
}

private int measureWidth(int measureSpec) {
  int specMode = MeasureSpec.getMode(measureSpec);
  int specSize = MeasureSpec.getSize(measureSpec);

  // Default size if no limits are specified.
  int result = 500;

  if (specMode == MeasureSpec.AT_MOST) {
    // Calculate the ideal size of your control
    // within this maximum size.
    // If your control fills the available space
    // return the outer bound.
    result = specSize;
  } else if (specMode == MeasureSpec.EXACTLY) {
    // If your control can fit within these bounds return that value.
    result = specSize;
  }
  return result;
}
```

code snippet PA4AD_Ch04_Views/src/MyView.java

Handling User Interaction Events

For your new View to be interactive, it will need to respond to user-initiated events such as key presses, screen touches, and button clicks. Android exposes several virtual event handlers that you can use to react to user input:

➤ onKeyDown — Called when any device key is pressed; includes the D-pad, keyboard, hang-up, call, back, and camera buttons

➤ onKeyUp — Called when a user releases a pressed key

➤ onTrackballEvent — Called when the device's trackball is moved

➤ onTouchEvent — Called when the touchscreen is pressed or released, or when it detects movement

Listing 4-18 shows a skeleton class that overrides each of the user interaction handlers in a View.

LISTING 4-18: Input event handling for Views

```
@Override
public boolean onKeyDown(int keyCode, KeyEvent keyEvent) {
  // Return true if the event was handled.
  return true;
}

@Override
public boolean onKeyUp(int keyCode, KeyEvent keyEvent) {
  // Return true if the event was handled.
  return true;
}

@Override
public boolean onTrackballEvent(MotionEvent event ) {
  // Get the type of action this event represents
  int actionPerformed = event.getAction();
  // Return true if the event was handled.
  return true;
}

@Override
public boolean onTouchEvent(MotionEvent event) {
  // Get the type of action this event represents
  int actionPerformed = event.getAction();
  // Return true if the event was handled.
  return true;
}
```

code snippet PA4AD_Ch04_Views/src/MyView.java

Further details on using each of these event handlers, including greater detail on the parameters received by each method and support for multitouch events, are available in Chapter 11.

Supporting Accessibility in Custom Views

Creating a custom View with a beautiful interface is only half the story. It's just as important to create accessible controls that can be used by users with disabilities that require them to interact with their devices in different ways.

Accessibility APIs were introduced in Android 1.6 (API level 4). They provide alternative interaction methods for users with visual, physical, or age-related disabilities that make it difficult to interact fully with a touchscreen.

The first step is to ensure that your custom View is accessible and navigable using the trackball and D-pad events, as described in the previous section. It's also important to use the content description attribute within your layout definition to describe the input widgets. (This is described in more detail in Chapter 11.)

To be accessible, custom Views must implement the `AccessibilityEventSource` interface and broadcast `AccessibilityEvents` using the `sendAccessibilityEvent` method.

The View class already implements the Accessibility Event Source interface, so you need to customize only the behavior to suit the functionality introduced by your custom View. Do this by passing the type of event that has occurred — usually one of clicks, long clicks, selection changes, focus changes, and text/content changes — to the `sendAccessibilityEvent` method. For custom Views that implement a completely new UI, this will typically include a broadcast whenever the displayed content changes, as shown in Listing 4-19.

LISTING 4-19: Broadcasting Accessibility Events

```java
public void setSeason(Season _season) {
    season = _season;
    sendAccessibilityEvent(AccessibilityEvent.TYPE_VIEW_TEXT_CHANGED);
}
```

code snippet PA4AD_Ch04_Views/src/SeasonView.java

Clicks, long-clicks, and focus and selection changes typically will be broadcast by the underlying View implementation, although you should take care to broadcast any additional events not captured by the base View class.

The broadcast Accessibility Event includes a number of properties used by the accessibility service to augment the user experience. Several of these properties, including the View's class name and event timestamp, won't need to be altered; however, by overriding the `dispatchPopulateAccessibilityEvent` handler, you can customize details such as the textual representation of the View's contents, checked state, and selection state of your View, as shown in Listing 4-20.

LISTING 4-20: Customizing Accessibility Event properties

```java
@Override
public boolean dispatchPopulateAccessibilityEvent(final
    AccessibilityEvent event) {

    super.dispatchPopulateAccessibilityEvent(event);
    if (isShown()) {
        String seasonStr = Season.valueOf(season);
        if (seasonStr.length() > AccessibilityEvent.MAX_TEXT_LENGTH)
            seasonStr = seasonStr.substring(0, AccessibilityEvent.MAX_TEXT_LENGTH-1);

        event.getText().add(seasonStr);
        return true;
    }
    else
        return false;
}
```

code snippet PA4AD_Ch04_Views/src/SeasonView.java

Creating a Compass View Example

In the following example you'll create a new Compass View by extending the `View` class. This View
will display a traditional compass rose to indicate a heading/orientation. When complete, it should
appear as in Figure 4-11.

FIGURE 4-11

A compass is an example of a UI control that requires a radically different visual display from the Text Views and Buttons available in the SDK toolbox, making it an excellent candidate for building from scratch.

> *In Chapter 11 you will learn some advanced techniques for Canvas drawing that will let you dramatically improve its appearance. Then in Chapter 12, "Hardware Sensors," you'll use this Compass View and the device's built-in accelerometer to display the user's current orientation.*

1. Create a new `Compass` project that will contain your new `CompassView`, and create a `CompassActivity` within which to display it. Within it, create a new `CompassView` class that extends `View` and add constructors that will allow the View to be instantiated, either in code or through inflation from a resource layout. Also add a new `initCompassView` method that will be used to initialize the control and call it from each constructor.

```java
package com.paad.compass;

import android.content.Context;
import android.content.res.Resources;
import android.graphics.Canvas;
import android.graphics.Paint;
import android.util.AttributeSet;
import android.view.View;
import android.view.accessibility.AccessibilityEvent;

public class CompassView extends View {
  public CompassView(Context context) {
    super(context);
    initCompassView();
  }

  public CompassView(Context context, AttributeSet attrs) {
    super(context, attrs);
    initCompassView();
  }

  public CompassView(Context context,
                     AttributeSet ats,
                     int defaultStyle) {
    super(context, ats, defaultStyle);
    initCompassView();
  }

  protected void initCompassView() {
    setFocusable(true);
  }
}
```

2. The Compass View should always be a perfect circle that takes up as much of the canvas as this restriction allows. Override the `onMeasure` method to calculate the length of the shortest side, and use `setMeasuredDimension` to set the height and width using this value.

```
@Override
protected void onMeasure(int widthMeasureSpec, int heightMeasureSpec) {
  // The compass is a circle that fills as much space as possible.
  // Set the measured dimensions by figuring out the shortest boundary,
  // height or width.
  int measuredWidth = measure(widthMeasureSpec);
  int measuredHeight = measure(heightMeasureSpec);

  int d = Math.min(measuredWidth, measuredHeight);

  setMeasuredDimension(d, d);
}

private int measure(int measureSpec) {
  int result = 0;

  // Decode the measurement specifications.
  int specMode = MeasureSpec.getMode(measureSpec);
  int specSize = MeasureSpec.getSize(measureSpec);

  if (specMode == MeasureSpec.UNSPECIFIED) {
    // Return a default size of 200 if no bounds are specified.
    result = 200;
  } else {
    // As you want to fill the available space
    // always return the full available bounds.
    result = specSize;
  }
  return result;
}
```

3.   Modify the `main.xml` layout resource and replace the `TextView` reference with your new `CompassView`:

```xml
<?xml version="1.0" encoding="utf-8"?>
<FrameLayout xmlns:android="http://schemas.android.com/apk/res/android"
  android:orientation="vertical"
  android:layout_width="match_parent"
  android:layout_height="match_parent">
  <com.paad.compass.CompassView
    android:id="@+id/compassView"
    android:layout_width="match_parent"
    android:layout_height="match_parent"
  />
</FrameLayout>
```

4.   Create two new resource files that store the colors and text strings you'll use to draw the compass.

   4.1 Create the text string resources by modifying the `res/values/strings.xml` file.

```xml
<?xml version="1.0" encoding="utf-8"?>
<resources>
  <string name="app_name">Compass</string>
  <string name="cardinal_north">N</string>
  <string name="cardinal_east">E</string>
```

```
  <string name="cardinal_south">S</string>
  <string name="cardinal_west">W</string>
</resources>
```

4.2 Create the color resource `res/values/colors.xml`.

```
<?xml version="1.0" encoding="utf-8"?>
<resources>
  <color name="background_color">#F555</color>
  <color name="marker_color">#AFFF</color>
  <color name="text_color">#AFFF</color>
</resources>
```

5. Return to the `CompassView` class. Add a new property to store the displayed bearing, and create `get` and `set` methods for it.

```
private float bearing;

public void setBearing(float _bearing) {
  bearing = _bearing;
}

public float getBearing() {
  return bearing;
}
```

6. Return to the `initCompassView` method and get references to each resource created in step 4. Store the string values as instance variables, and use the color values to create new class-scoped `Paint` objects. You'll use these objects in the next step to draw the compass face.

```
private Paint markerPaint;
private Paint textPaint;
private Paint circlePaint;
private String northString;
private String eastString;
private String southString;
private String westString;
private int textHeight;

protected void initCompassView() {
  setFocusable(true);

  Resources r = this.getResources();

  circlePaint = new Paint(Paint.ANTI_ALIAS_FLAG);
  circlePaint.setColor(r.getColor(R.color.background_color));
  circlePaint.setStrokeWidth(1);
  circlePaint.setStyle(Paint.Style.FILL_AND_STROKE);

  northString = r.getString(R.string.cardinal_north);
  eastString = r.getString(R.string.cardinal_east);
  southString = r.getString(R.string.cardinal_south);
  westString = r.getString(R.string.cardinal_west);

  textPaint = new Paint(Paint.ANTI_ALIAS_FLAG);
```

```
    textPaint.setColor(r.getColor(R.color.text_color));

    textHeight = (int)textPaint.measureText("yY");

    markerPaint = new Paint(Paint.ANTI_ALIAS_FLAG);
    markerPaint.setColor(r.getColor(R.color.marker_color));
}
```

7. The next step is to draw the compass face using the `String` and `Paint` objects you created in step 6. The following code snippet is presented with only limited commentary. You can find more detail about drawing on the Canvas and using advanced Paint effects in Chapter 11.

7.1 Start by overriding the `onDraw` method in the `CompassView` class.

```
@Override
protected void onDraw(Canvas canvas) {
```

7.2 Find the center of the control, and store the length of the smallest side as the compass's radius.

```
int mMeasuredWidth = getMeasuredWidth();
int mMeasuredHeight = getMeasuredHeight();

int px = mMeasuredWidth / 2;
int py = mMeasuredHeight / 2 ;

int radius = Math.min(px, py);
```

7.3 Draw the outer boundary, and color the background of the Compass face using the `drawCircle` method. Use the `circlePaint` object you created in step 6.

```
// Draw the background
canvas.drawCircle(px, py, radius, circlePaint);
```

7.4 This Compass displays the current heading by rotating the face so that the current direction is always at the top of the device. To achieve this, rotate the canvas in the opposite direction to the current heading.

```
// Rotate our perspective so that the 'top' is
// facing the current bearing.
canvas.save();
canvas.rotate(-bearing, px, py);
```

7.5 All that's left is to draw the markings. Rotate the canvas through a full rotation, drawing markings every 15 degrees and the abbreviated direction string every 45 degrees.

```
int textWidth = (int)textPaint.measureText("W");
int cardinalX = px-textWidth/2;
int cardinalY = py-radius+textHeight;

// Draw the marker every 15 degrees and text every 45.
for (int i = 0; i < 24; i++) {
  // Draw a marker.
  canvas.drawLine(px, py-radius, px, py-radius+10, markerPaint);

  canvas.save();
```

```
    canvas.translate(0, textHeight);

    // Draw the cardinal points
    if (i % 6 == 0) {
      String dirString = "";
      switch (i) {
        case(0)  : {
                    dirString = northString;
                    int arrowY = 2*textHeight;
                    canvas.drawLine(px, arrowY, px-5, 3*textHeight,
                                    markerPaint);
                    canvas.drawLine(px, arrowY, px+5, 3*textHeight,
                                    markerPaint);
                    break;
                   }
        case(6)  : dirString = eastString; break;
        case(12) : dirString = southString; break;
        case(18) : dirString = westString; break;
      }
      canvas.drawText(dirString, cardinalX, cardinalY, textPaint);
    }

    else if (i % 3 == 0) {
      // Draw the text every alternate 45deg
      String angle = String.valueOf(i*15);
      float angleTextWidth = textPaint.measureText(angle);

      int angleTextX = (int)(px-angleTextWidth/2);
      int angleTextY = py-radius+textHeight;
      canvas.drawText(angle, angleTextX, angleTextY, textPaint);
    }
    canvas.restore();

    canvas.rotate(15, px, py);
  }
  canvas.restore();
}
```

8. The next step is to add accessibility support. The Compass View presents a heading visually, so to make it accessible you need to broadcast an accessibility event signifying that the "text" (in this case, content) has changed when the bearing changes. Do this by modifying the `set-Bearing` method.

```
public void setBearing(float _bearing) {
  bearing = _bearing;
  sendAccessibilityEvent(AccessibilityEvent.TYPE_VIEW_TEXT_CHANGED);
}
```

9. Override the `dispatchPopulateAccessibilityEvent` to use the current heading as the content value to be used for accessibility events.

```
@Override
public boolean dispatchPopulateAccessibilityEvent(final AccessibilityEvent event) {
  super.dispatchPopulateAccessibilityEvent(event);
```

```
    if (isShown()) {
      String bearingStr = String.valueOf(bearing);
      if (bearingStr.length() > AccessibilityEvent.MAX_TEXT_LENGTH)
        bearingStr = bearingStr.substring(0, AccessibilityEvent.MAX_TEXT_LENGTH);

      event.getText().add(bearingStr);
      return true;
    }
    else
      return false;
}
```

> *All code snippets in this example are part of the* Chapter 4 Compass *project, available for download at* www.wrox.com.

Run the Activity, and you should see the `CompassView` displayed. See Chapter 12 to learn how to bind the `CompassView` to the device's compass sensor.

Using Custom Controls

Having created your own custom Views, you can use them within code and layouts as you would any other View. Note that you must specify the fully qualified class name when you create a new node in the layout definition.

```
<com.paad.compass.CompassView
  android:id="@+id/compassView"
  android:layout_width="match_parent"
  android:layout_height="match_parent"
/>
```

You can inflate the layout and get a reference to the `CompassView`, as usual, using the following code:

```
@Override
public void onCreate(Bundle savedInstanceState) {
  super.onCreate(savedInstanceState);
  setContentView(R.layout.main);
  CompassView cv = (CompassView)this.findViewById(R.id.compassView);
  cv.setBearing(45);
}
```

You can also add your new view to a layout in code:

```
@Override
public void onCreate(Bundle savedInstanceState) {
  super.onCreate(savedInstanceState);
  CompassView cv = new CompassView(this);
  setContentView(cv);
  cv.setBearing(45);
}
```

INTRODUCING ADAPTERS

Adapters are used to bind data to View Groups that extend the `AdapterView` class (such as List View or Gallery). Adapters are responsible for creating child Views that represent the underlying data within the bound parent View.

You can create your own Adapter classes and build your own `AdapterView`-derived controls.

Introducing Some Native Adapters

In most cases you won't have to create your own Adapters from scratch. Android supplies a set of Adapters that can pump data from common data sources (including arrays and Cursors) into the native controls that extend Adapter View.

Because Adapters are responsible both for supplying the data and for creating the Views that represent each item, Adapters can radically modify the appearance and functionality of the controls they're bound to.

The following list highlights two of the most useful and versatile native Adapters:

➤ `ArrayAdapter` — The Array Adapter uses generics to bind an Adapter View to an array of objects of the specified class. By default, the Array Adapter uses the `toString` value of each object in the array to create and populate Text Views. Alternative constructors enable you to use more complex layouts, or you can extend the class (as shown in the next section) to bind data to more complicated layouts.

➤ `SimpleCursorAdapter` — The Simple Cursor Adapter enables you to bind the Views within a layout to specific columns contained within a Cursor (typically returned from a Content Provider query). You specify an XML layout to inflate and populate to display each child, and then bind each column in the Cursor to a particular View within that layout. The adapter will create a new View for each Cursor entry and inflate the layout into it, populating each View within the layout using the Cursor's corresponding column value.

The following sections delve into these Adapter classes. The examples provided bind data to List Views, though the same logic will work just as well for other Adapter View classes, such as Spinners and Galleries.

Customizing the Array Adapter

By default, the Array Adapter uses the `toString` values of each item within an object array to populate a Text View within the layout you specify.

In most cases you will need to customize the Array Adapter to populate the layout used for each View to represent the underlying array data. To do so, extend `ArrayAdapter` with a type-specific variation, overriding the `getView` method to assign object properties to layout Views, as shown in Listing 4-21.

LISTING 4-21: Customizing the Array Adapter

```java
public class MyArrayAdapter extends ArrayAdapter<MyClass> {

    int resource;

    public MyArrayAdapter(Context context,
                          int _resource,
                          List<MyClass> items) {
      super(context, _resource, items);
      resource = _resource;
    }

    @Override
    public View getView(int position, View convertView, ViewGroup parent) {
      // Create and inflate the View to display
      LinearLayout newView;

      if (convertView == null) {
        // Inflate a new view if this is not an update.
        newView = new LinearLayout(getContext());
        String inflater = Context.LAYOUT_INFLATER_SERVICE;
        LayoutInflater li;
        li = (LayoutInflater)getContext().getSystemService(inflater);
        li.inflate(resource, newView, true);
      } else {
        // Otherwise we'll update the existing View
        newView = (LinearLayout)convertView;
      }

      MyClass classInstance = getItem(position);

      // TODO Retrieve values to display from the
      // classInstance variable.

      // TODO Get references to the Views to populate from the layout.
      // TODO Populate the Views with object property values.

      return newView;
    }
}
```

code snippet PA4AD_Ch04_Adapters/src/MyArrayAdapter.java

The getView method is used to construct, inflate, and populate the View that will be added to the parent Adapter View class (e.g., List View), which is being bound to the underlying array using this Adapter.

The getView method receives parameters that describe the position of the item to be displayed, the View being updated (or null), and the View Group into which this new View will be placed. A call to getItem will return the value stored at the specified index in the underlying array.

Return the newly created and populated (or updated) View instance as a result from this method.

Using Adapters to Bind Data to a View

To apply an Adapter to an `AdapterView`-derived class, call the View's `setAdapter` method, passing in an Adapter instance, as shown in Listing 4-22.

LISTING 4-22: Creating and applying an Adapter

```
ArrayList<String> myStringArray = new ArrayList<String>();

int layoutID = android.R.layout.simple_list_item_1;

ArrayAdapter<String> myAdapterInstance;
myAdapterInstance =
  new ArrayAdapter<String>(this, layoutID, myStringArray);

myListView.setAdapter(myAdapterInstance);
```

code snippet PA4AD_Ch04_Adapters/src/MyActivity.java

This snippet shows the simplest case, in which the array being bound contains Strings and each List View item is represented by a single Text View.

The following example demonstrates how to bind an array of complex objects to a List View using a custom layout.

Customizing the To-Do List Array Adapter

This example extends the To-Do List project, storing each item as a `ToDoItem` object that includes the date each item was created.

You will extend `ArrayAdapter` to bind a collection of `ToDoItem` objects to the `ListView` and customize the layout used to display each to-do item within the List View.

1. Return to the To-Do List project. Create a new `ToDoItem` class that stores the task and its creation date. Override the `toString` method to return a summary of the item data.

```
package com.paad.todolist;

import java.text.SimpleDateFormat;
import java.util.Date;

public class ToDoItem {

  String task;
  Date created;

  public String getTask() {
    return task;
  }
```

```
  public Date getCreated() {
    return created;
  }

  public ToDoItem(String _task) {
    this(_task, new Date(java.lang.System.currentTimeMillis()));
  }

  public ToDoItem(String _task, Date _created) {
    task = _task;
    created = _created;
  }

  @Override
  public String toString() {
    SimpleDateFormat sdf = new SimpleDateFormat("dd/MM/yy");
    String dateString = sdf.format(created);
    return "(" + dateString + ") " + task;
  }
}
```

2.   Open the ToDoListActivity and modify the ArrayList and ArrayAdapter variable
types to store ToDoItem objects rather than Strings. You then need to modify the onCreate
method to update the corresponding variable initialization.

```
private ArrayList<ToDoItem> todoItems;
private ArrayAdapter<ToDoItem> aa;

public void onCreate(Bundle savedInstanceState) {
  super.onCreate(savedInstanceState);

  // Inflate your view
  setContentView(R.layout.main);

  // Get references to the Fragments
  FragmentManager fm = getFragmentManager();
  ToDoListFragment todoListFragment =
    (ToDoListFragment)fm.findFragmentById(R.id.TodoListFragment);

  // Create the array list of to do items
  todoItems = new ArrayList<ToDoItem>();

  // Create the array adapter to bind the array to the listview
  int resID = R.layout.todolist_item;
  aa = new ArrayAdapter<ToDoItem>(this, resID, todoItems);

  // Bind the array adapter to the listview.
  todoListFragment.setListAdapter(aa);
}
```

3.   Update the onNewItemAdded handler to support the ToDoItem objects.

```
public void onNewItemAdded(String newItem) {
  ToDoItem newTodoItem = new ToDoItem(newItem);
```

```
    todoItems.add(0, newTodoItem);
    aa.notifyDataSetChanged();
}
```

4.   Now you can modify the `todolist_item.xml` layout to display the additional information
      stored for each to-do item. Start by modifying the custom layout you created earlier in this
      chapter to include a second `TextView`. It will be used to show the creation date of each to-do
      item.

```xml
<?xml version="1.0" encoding="utf-8"?>
<RelativeLayout xmlns:android="http://schemas.android.com/apk/res/android"
  android:layout_width="match_parent"
  android:layout_height="match_parent">
  <TextView
    android:id="@+id/rowDate"
    android:background="@color/notepad_paper"
    android:layout_width="wrap_content"
    android:layout_height="match_parent"
    android:padding="10dp"
    android:scrollbars="vertical"
    android:fadingEdge="vertical"
    android:textColor="#F000"
    android:layout_alignParentRight="true"
  />
  <com.paad.todolist.ToDoListItemView
    android:id="@+id/row"
    android:layout_width="match_parent"
    android:layout_height="match_parent"
    android:padding="10dp"
    android:scrollbars="vertical"
    android:fadingEdge="vertical"
    android:textColor="@color/notepad_text"
    android:layout_toLeftOf="@+id/rowDate"
  />
</RelativeLayout>
```

6.   To assign the ToDoItem values to each ListView Item, create a new class (`ToDoItemAdapter`)
      that extends an `ArrayAdapter` with a `ToDoItem`-specific variation. Override `getView` to
      assign the task and date properties in the `ToDoItem` object to the Views in the layout you cre-
      ated in step 4.

```java
package com.paad.todolist;

import java.text.SimpleDateFormat;
import java.util.Date;
import java.util.List;
import android.content.Context;
import android.view.LayoutInflater;
import android.view.View;
import android.view.ViewGroup;
import android.widget.ArrayAdapter;
import android.widget.LinearLayout;
import android.widget.TextView;
```

```
public class ToDoItemAdapter extends ArrayAdapter<ToDoItem> {

  int resource;

  public ToDoItemAdapter(Context context,
                         int resource,
                         List<ToDoItem> items) {
    super(context, resource, items);
    this.resource = resource;
  }

  @Override
  public View getView(int position, View convertView, ViewGroup parent) {
    LinearLayout todoView;

    ToDoItem item = getItem(position);

    String taskString = item.getTask();
    Date createdDate = item.getCreated();
    SimpleDateFormat sdf = new SimpleDateFormat("dd/MM/yy");
    String dateString = sdf.format(createdDate);

    if (convertView == null) {
      todoView = new LinearLayout(getContext());
      String inflater = Context.LAYOUT_INFLATER_SERVICE;
      LayoutInflater li;
      li = (LayoutInflater)getContext().getSystemService(inflater);
      li.inflate(resource, todoView, true);
    } else {
      todoView = (LinearLayout) convertView;
    }

    TextView dateView = (TextView)todoView.findViewById(R.id.rowDate);
    TextView taskView = (TextView)todoView.findViewById(R.id.row);

    dateView.setText(dateString);
    taskView.setText(taskString);

    return todoView;
  }
}
```

7. Return to the `ToDoListActivity` and replace the `ArrayAdapter` declaration with a `ToDoItemAdapter`:

```
private ToDoItemAdapter aa;
```

8. Within `onCreate`, replace the `ArrayAdapter<ToDoItem>` instantiation with the new `ToDoItemAdapter`:

```
aa = new ToDoItemAdapter(this, resID, todoItems);
```

If you run your Activity and add some to-do items, it should appear as shown in Figure 4-12.

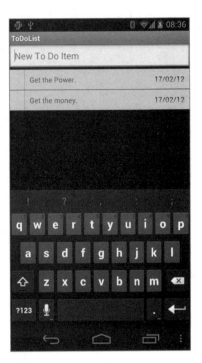

FIGURE 4-12

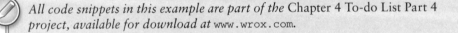

All code snippets in this example are part of the Chapter 4 To-do List Part 4 *project, available for download at* www.wrox.com.

Using the Simple Cursor Adapter

The `SimpleCursorAdapter` is used to bind a `Cursor` to an Adapter View using a layout to define the UI of each row/item. The content of each row's View is populated using the column values of the corresponding row in the underlying Cursor.

Construct a Simple Cursor Adapter by passing in the current context, a layout resource to use for each item, a Cursor that represents the data to display, and two integer arrays: one that contains the indexes of the columns from which to source the data, and a second (equally sized) array that contains resource IDs to specify which Views within the layout should be used to display the contents of the corresponding columns.

Listing 4-22 shows how to construct a Simple Cursor Adapter to display recent call information.

LISTING 4-22: Creating a Simple Cursor Adapter

```java
LoaderManager.LoaderCallbacks<Cursor> loaded =
  new LoaderManager.LoaderCallbacks<Cursor>() {

  public Loader<Cursor> onCreateLoader(int id, Bundle args) {
    CursorLoader loader = new CursorLoader(MyActivity.this,
      CallLog.CONTENT_URI, null, null, null, null);
    return loader;
  }

  public void onLoadFinished(Loader<Cursor> loader, Cursor cursor) {

    String[] fromColumns = new String[] {CallLog.Calls.CACHED_NAME,
                                         CallLog.Calls.NUMBER};

    int[] toLayoutIDs = new int[] { R.id.nameTextView, R.id.numberTextView};

    SimpleCursorAdapter myAdapter;
    myAdapter = new SimpleCursorAdapter(MyActivity.this,
                                        R.layout.mysimplecursorlayout,
                                        cursor,
                                        fromColumns,
                                        toLayoutIDs);

    myListView.setAdapter(myAdapter);
  }

  public void onLoaderReset(Loader<Cursor> loader) {}
};

getLoaderManager().initLoader(0, null, loaded);
```

code snippet PA4AD_Ch4_Adapters/src/MyActivity.java

You'll learn more about Content Providers, Cursors, and Cursor Loaders in Chapter 8, "Databases and Content Providers," where you'll also find more Simple Cursor Adapter examples.

5

Intents and Broadcast Receivers

This chapter looks at Intents — probably the most unique and important concept in Android development. You'll learn how to use Intents to broadcast data within and between applications and how to listen for them to detect changes in the system state.

You'll also learn how to define implicit and explicit Intents to start Activities or Services using late runtime binding. Using implicit Intents, you'll learn how to request that an action be performed on a piece of data, enabling Android to determine which application components can best service that request.

Broadcast Intents are used to announce events systemwide. You'll learn how to transmit these broadcasts and receive them using Broadcast Receivers.

INTRODUCING INTENTS

Intents are used as a message-passing mechanism that works both within your application and between applications. You can use Intents to do the following:

➤ Explicitly start a particular Service or Activity using its class name

➤ Start an Activity or Service to perform an action with (or on) a particular piece of data

➤ Broadcast that an event has occurred

You can use Intents to support interaction among any of the application components installed on an Android device, no matter which application they're a part of. This turns your device from a platform containing a collection of independent components into a single, interconnected system.

One of the most common uses for Intents is to start new Activities, either *explicitly* (by specifying the class to load) or *implicitly* (by requesting that an action be performed on a piece of data). In the latter case the action does not need to be performed by an Activity within the calling application.

You can also use Intents to broadcast messages across the system. Applications can register Broadcast Receivers to listen for, and react to, these Broadcast Intents. This enables you to create event-driven applications based on internal, system, or third-party application events.

Android broadcasts Intents to announce system events, such as changes in Internet connectivity or battery charge levels. The native Android applications, such as the Phone Dialer and SMS Manager, simply register components that listen for specific Broadcast Intents — such as "incoming phone call" or "SMS message received" — and react accordingly. As a result, you can replace many of the native applications by registering Broadcast Receivers that listen for the same Intents.

Using Intents, rather than explicitly loading classes, to propagate actions — even within the same application — is a fundamental Android design principle. It encourages the decoupling of components to allow the seamless replacement of application elements. It also provides the basis of a simple model for extending an application's functionality.

Using Intents to Launch Activities

The most common use of Intents is to bind your application components and communicate between them. Intents are used to start Activities, allowing you to create a workflow of different screens.

> *The instructions in this section refer to starting new Activities, but the same details also apply to Services. Details on starting (and creating) Services are available in Chapter 9, "Working in the Background."*

To create and display an Activity, call `startActivity`, passing in an `Intent`, as follows:

```
startActivity(myIntent);
```

The `startActivity` method finds and starts the single Activity that best matches your Intent.

You can construct the Intent to explicitly specify the Activity class to open, or to include an action that the target Activity must be able to perform. In the latter case, the run time will choose an Activity dynamically using a process known as *intent resolution*.

When you use `startActivity`, your application won't receive any notification when the newly launched Activity finishes. To track feedback from a sub-Activity, use `startActivityForResult`, as described later in this chapter.

Explicitly Starting New Activities

You learned in Chapter 3, "Creating Applications and Activities," that applications consist of a number of interrelated screens — Activities — that must be included in the application manifest. To transition between them, you will often need to explicitly specify which Activity to open.

To select a specific Activity class to start, create a new Intent, specifying the current Activity's Context and the class of the Activity to launch. Pass this Intent into `startActivity`, as shown in Listing 5-1.

Available for download on Wrox.com

LISTING 5-1: Explicitly starting an Activity

```java
Intent intent = new Intent(MyActivity.this, MyOtherActivity.class);
startActivity(intent);
```

code snippet PA4AD_Ch05_Intents/src/MyActivity.java

After `startActivity` is called, the new Activity (in this example, `MyOtherActivity`) will be created, started, and resumed — moving to the top of the Activity stack.

Calling `finish` on the new Activity, or pressing the hardware back button, closes it and removes it from the stack. Alternatively, you can continue to navigate to other Activities by calling `startActivity`. Note that each time you call `startActivity`, a new Activity will be added to the stack; pressing back (or calling `finish`) will remove each of these Activities, in turn.

Implicit Intents and Late Runtime Binding

An implicit Intent is a mechanism that lets anonymous application components service action requests. That means you can ask the system to start an Activity to perform an action without knowing which application, or Activity, will be started.

For example, to let users make calls from your application, you could implement a new dialer, or you could use an implicit Intent that requests the action (dialing) be performed on a phone number (represented as a URI).

```java
if (somethingWeird && itDontLookGood) {
  Intent intent =
    new Intent(Intent.ACTION_DIAL, Uri.parse("tel:555-2368"));

  startActivity(intent);
}
```

Android resolves this Intent and starts an Activity that provides the dial action on a telephone number — in this case, typically the Phone Dialer.

When constructing a new implicit Intent, you specify an action to perform and, optionally, supply the URI of the data on which to perform that action. You can send additional data to the target Activity by adding extras to the Intent.

Extras are a mechanism used to attach primitive values to an Intent. You can use the overloaded `putExtra` method on any Intent to attach a new name / value pair (NVP) that can then be retrieved using the corresponding `get[type]Extra` method in the started Activity.

The extras are stored within the Intent as a Bundle object that can be retrieved using the `getExtras` method.

When you use an implicit Intent to start an Activity, Android will — at run time — resolve it into the Activity class best suited to performing the required action on the type of data specified. This means you can create projects that use functionality from other applications without knowing exactly which application you're borrowing functionality from ahead of time.

In circumstances where multiple Activities can potentially perform a given action, the user is presented with a choice. The process of intent resolution is determined through an analysis of the registered Broadcast Receivers, which are described in detail later in this chapter.

Various native applications provide Activities capable of performing actions against specific data. Third-party applications, including your own, can be registered to support new actions or to provide an alternative provider of native actions. You'll be introduced to some of the native actions, as well as how to register your own Activities to support them, later in this chapter.

Determining If an Intent Will Resolve

Incorporating the Activities and Services of a third-party application into your own is incredibly powerful; however, there is no guarantee that any particular application will be installed on a device, or that any application capable of handling your request is available.

As a result, it's good practice to determine if your call will resolve to an Activity *before* calling `startActivity`.

You can query the Package Manager to determine which, if any, Activity will be launched to service a specific Intent by calling `resolveActivity` on your Intent object, passing in the Package Manager, as shown in Listing 5-2.

LISTING 5-2: Implicitly starting an Activity

Available for
download on
Wrox.com

```
if (somethingWeird && itDontLookGood) {
  // Create the impliciy Intent to use to start a new Activity.
  Intent intent =
    new Intent(Intent.ACTION_DIAL, Uri.parse("tel:555-2368"));

  // Check if an Activity exists to perform this action.
  PackageManager pm = getPackageManager();
```

```
ComponentName cn = intent.resolveActivity(pm);
if (cn == null) {
  // If there is no Activity available to perform the action
  // Check to see if the Google Play Store is available.
  Uri marketUri =
    Uri.parse("market://search?q=pname:com.myapp.packagename");
  Intent marketIntent = new
    Intent(Intent.ACTION_VIEW).setData(marketUri);

  // If the Google Play Store is available, use it to download an application
  // capable of performing the required action. Otherwise log an
  // error.
  if (marketIntent.resolveActivity(pm) != null)
    startActivity(marketIntent);
  else
    Log.d(TAG, "Market client not available.");
}
else
  startActivity(intent);
}
```

code snippet PA4AD_Ch05_Intents/src/MyActivity.java

If no Activity is found, you can choose to either disable the related functionality (and associated user interface controls) or direct users to the appropriate application in the Google Play Store. Note that Google Play is not available on all devices, nor the emulator, so it's good practice to check for that as well.

Returning Results from Activities

An Activity started via `startActivity` is independent of its parent and will not provide any feedback when it closes.

Where feedback is required, you can start an Activity as a sub-Activity that can pass results back to its parent. Sub-Activities are actually just Activities opened in a different way. As such, you must register them in the application manifest in the same way as any other Activity. Any manifest-registered Activity can be opened as a sub-Activity, including those provided by the system or third-party applications.

When a sub-Activity is finished, it triggers the `onActivityResult` event handler within the calling Activity. Sub-Activities are particularly useful in situations in which one Activity is providing data input for another, such as a user selecting an item from a list.

Launching Sub-Activities

The `startActivityForResult` method works much like `startActivity`, but with one important difference. In addition to passing in the explicit or implicit Intent used to determine which Activity to launch, you also pass in a *request code*. This value will later be used to uniquely identify the sub-Activity that has returned a result.

Listing 5-3 shows the skeleton code for launching a sub-Activity explicitly.

LISTING 5-3: Explicitly starting a sub-Activity for a result

```java
private static final int SHOW_SUBACTIVITY = 1;

private void startSubActivity() {
  Intent intent = new Intent(this, MyOtherActivity.class);
  startActivityForResult(intent, SHOW_SUBACTIVITY);
}
```

code snippet PA4AD_Ch05_Intents/src/MyActivity.java

Like regular Activities, you can start sub-Activities implicitly or explicitly. Listing 5-4 uses an implicit Intent to launch a new sub-Activity to pick a contact.

LISTING 5-4: Implicitly starting a sub-Activity for a result

```java
private static final int PICK_CONTACT_SUBACTIVITY = 2;

private void startSubActivityImplicitly() {
  Uri uri = Uri.parse("content://contacts/people");
  Intent intent = new Intent(Intent.ACTION_PICK, uri);
  startActivityForResult(intent, PICK_CONTACT_SUBACTIVITY);
}
```

code snippet PA4AD_Ch05_Intents/src/MyActivity.java

Returning Results

When your sub-Activity is ready to return, call `setResult` before `finish` to return a result to the calling Activity.

The `setResult` method takes two parameters: the result code and the result data itself, represented as an Intent.

The result code is the "result" of running the sub-Activity — generally, either `Activity.RESULT_OK` or `Activity.RESULT_CANCELED`. In some circumstances, where OK and cancelled don't sufficiently or accurately describe the available return results, you'll want to use your own response codes to handle application-specific choices; `setResult` supports any integer value.

The Intent returned as a result often includes a data URI that points to a piece of content (such as the selected contact, phone number, or media file) and a collection of extras used to return additional information.

Listing 5-5, taken from a sub-Activity's `onCreate` method, shows how an OK and Cancel button might return different results to the calling Activity.

LISTING 5-5: Returning a result from a sub-Activity

```java
Button okButton = (Button) findViewById(R.id.ok_button);
okButton.setOnClickListener(new View.OnClickListener() {
  public void onClick(View view) {
    long selected_horse_id = listView.getSelectedItemId();

    Uri selectedHorse = Uri.parse("content://horses/" +
                                  selected_horse_id);
    Intent result = new Intent(Intent.ACTION_PICK, selectedHorse);

    setResult(RESULT_OK, result);
    finish();
  }
});

Button cancelButton = (Button) findViewById(R.id.cancel_button);
cancelButton.setOnClickListener(new View.OnClickListener() {
  public void onClick(View view) {
    setResult(RESULT_CANCELED);
    finish();
  }
});
```

code snippet PA4AD_Ch05_Intents/src/SelectHorseActivity.java

If the Activity is closed by the user pressing the hardware back key, or `finish` is called without a prior call to `setResult`, the result code will be set to `RESULT_CANCELED` and the result Intent set to `null`.

Handling Sub-Activity Results

When a sub-Activity closes, the `onActivityResult` event handler is fired within the calling Activity. Override this method to handle the results returned by sub-Activities.

The `onActivityResult` handler receives a number of parameters:

➤ **Request code** — The request code that was used to launch the returning sub-Activity.

➤ **Result code** — The result code set by the sub-Activity to indicate its result. It can be any integer value, but typically will be either `Activity.RESULT_OK` or `Activity.RESULT_CANCELED`.

➤ **Data** — An Intent used to package returned data. Depending on the purpose of the sub-Activity, it may include a URI that represents a selected piece of content. The sub-Activity can also return information as an extra within the returned data Intent.

> If the sub-Activity closes abnormally or doesn't specify a result code before it closes, the result code is `Activity.RESULT_CANCELED`.

Listing 5-6 shows the skeleton code for implementing the `onActivityResult` event handler within an Activity.

LISTING 5-6: Implementing an On Activity Result handler

```
private static final int SELECT_HORSE = 1;
private static final int SELECT_GUN = 2;

Uri selectedHorse = null;
Uri selectedGun = null;

@Override
public void onActivityResult(int requestCode,
                             int resultCode,
                             Intent data) {

  super.onActivityResult(requestCode, resultCode, data);

  switch(requestCode) {
    case (SELECT_HORSE):
      if (resultCode == Activity.RESULT_OK)
        selectedHorse = data.getData();
      break;

    case (SELECT_GUN):
      if (resultCode == Activity.RESULT_OK)
        selectedGun = data.getData();
      break;

    default: break;
  }
}
```

code snippet PA4AD_Ch05_Intents/src/MyActivity.java

Native Android Actions

Native Android applications also use Intents to launch Activities and sub-Activities.

The following (noncomprehensive) list shows some of the native actions available as static string constants in the `Intent` class. When creating implicit Intents, you can use these actions, known as *Activity Intents*, to start Activities and sub-Activities within your own applications.

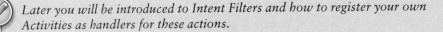

Later you will be introduced to Intent Filters and how to register your own Activities as handlers for these actions.

➤ ACTION_ALL_APPS — Opens an Activity that lists all the installed applications. Typically, this is handled by the launcher.

➤ ACTION_ANSWER — Opens an Activity that handles incoming calls. This is normally handled by the native in-call screen.

➤ ACTION_BUG_REPORT — Displays an Activity that can report a bug. This is normally handled by the native bug-reporting mechanism.

➤ ACTION_CALL — Brings up a phone dialer and immediately initiates a call using the number supplied in the Intent's data URI. This action should be used only for Activities that replace the native dialer application. In most situations it is considered better form to use ACTION_DIAL.

➤ ACTION_CALL_BUTTON — Triggered when the user presses a hardware "call button." This typically initiates the dialer Activity.

➤ ACTION_DELETE — Starts an Activity that lets you delete the data specified at the Intent's data URI.

➤ ACTION_DIAL — Brings up a dialer application with the number to dial prepopulated from the Intent's data URI. By default, this is handled by the native Android phone dialer. The dialer can normalize most number schemas — for example, tel:555-1234 and tel:(212) 555 1212 are both valid numbers.

➤ ACTION_EDIT — Requests an Activity that can edit the data at the Intent's data URI.

➤ ACTION_INSERT — Opens an Activity capable of inserting new items into the Cursor specified in the Intent's data URI. When called as a sub-Activity, it should return a URI to the newly inserted item.

➤ ACTION_PICK — Launches a sub-Activity that lets you pick an item from the Content Provider specified by the Intent's data URI. When closed, it should return a URI to the item that was picked. The Activity launched depends on the data being picked — for example, passing content://contacts/people will invoke the native contacts list.

➤ ACTION_SEARCH — Typically used to launch a specific search Activity. When it's fired without a specific Activity, the user will be prompted to select from all applications that support search. Supply the search term as a string in the Intent's extras using SearchManager.QUERY as the key.

➤ ACTION_SEARCH_LONG_PRESS — Enables you to intercept long presses on the hardware search key. This is typically handled by the system to provide a shortcut to a voice search.

➤ ACTION_SENDTO — Launches an Activity to send data to the contact specified by the Intent's data URI.

➤ ACTION_SEND — Launches an Activity that sends the data specified in the Intent. The recipient contact needs to be selected by the resolved Activity. Use setType to set the MIME type of the transmitted data. The data itself should be stored as an extra by means of the key EXTRA_TEXT or EXTRA_STREAM, depending on the type. In the case of email, the native Android applications will also accept extras via the EXTRA_EMAIL, EXTRA_CC, EXTRA_BCC, and EXTRA_SUBJECT keys. Use the ACTION_SEND action only to send data to a remote recipient (not to another application on the device).

➤ ACTION_VIEW — This is the most common generic action. View asks that the data supplied in the Intent's data URI be viewed in the most reasonable manner. Different applications will handle view requests depending on the URI schema of the data supplied. Natively http: addresses will open in the browser; tel: addresses will open the dialer to call the number; geo: addresses will be displayed in the Google Maps application; and contact content will be displayed in the Contact Manager.

➤ ACTION_WEB_SEARCH — Opens the Browser to perform a web search based on the query supplied using the SearchManager.QUERY key.

> *In addition to these Activity actions, Android includes a large number of broadcast actions to create Intents that are broadcast to announce system events. These broadcast actions are described later in this chapter.*

Introducing Linkify

Linkify is a helper class that creates hyperlinks within Text View (and Text View-derived) classes through RegEx pattern matching.

Text that matches a specified RegEx pattern will be converted into a clickable hyperlink that implicitly fires startActivity(new Intent(Intent.ACTION_VIEW, uri)), using the matched text as the target URI.

You can specify any string pattern to be treated as a clickable link; for convenience, the Linkify class provides presets for common content types.

Native Linkify Link Types

The Linkify class has presets that can detect and linkify web URLs, email addresses, and phone numbers. To apply a preset, use the static Linkify.addLinks method, passing in a View to Linkify and a bitmask of one or more of the following self-describing Linkify class constants: WEB_URLS, EMAIL_ADDRESSES, PHONE_NUMBERS, and ALL.

```
TextView textView = (TextView)findViewById(R.id.myTextView);
Linkify.addLinks(textView, Linkify.WEB_URLS|Linkify.EMAIL_ADDRESSES);
```

> *Most Android devices have at least two email applications: Gmail and Email. In situations in which multiple Activities are resolved as possible action consumers, users are asked to select their preference. In the case of the emulator, you must have the email client configured before it will respond to Linkified email addresses.*

You can also linkify Views directly within a layout using the `android:autoLink` attribute. It supports one or more of the following values: `none`, `web`, `email`, `phone`, and `all`.

```
<TextView
  android:layout_width="match_parent"
  android:layout_height="match_parent"
  android:text="@string/linkify_me"
  android:autoLink="phone|email"
/>
```

Creating Custom Link Strings

To linkify your own data, you need to define your own linkify strings. Do this by creating a new RegEx pattern that matches the text you want to display as hyperlinks.

As with the native types, you can linkify the target Text View by calling `Linkify.addLinks`; however, rather than passing in one of the preset constants, pass in your RegEx pattern. You can also pass in a prefix that will be prepended to the target URI when a link is clicked.

Listing 5-7 shows a View being linkified to support earthquake data provided by an Android Content Provider (which you will create in Chapter 8, "Databases and Content Providers"). Note that rather than include the entire schema, the specified RegEx matches any text that starts with "quake" and is followed by a number, with optional whitespace. The full schema is then prepended to the URI before the Intent is fired.

Available for download on Wrox.com

LISTING 5-7: Creating custom link strings in Linkify

```
// Define the base URI.
String baseUri = "content://com.paad.earthquake/earthquakes/";

// Contruct an Intent to test if there is an Activity capable of
// viewing the content you are Linkifying. Use the Package Manager
// to perform the test.
PackageManager pm = getPackageManager();
Intent testIntent = new Intent(Intent.ACTION_VIEW, Uri.parse(baseUri));
boolean activityExists = testIntent.resolveActivity(pm) != null;

// If there is an Activity capable of viewing the content
// Linkify the text.
if (activityExists) {
  int flags = Pattern.CASE_INSENSITIVE;
  Pattern p = Pattern.compile("\\bquake[\\s]?[0-9]+\\b", flags);
  Linkify.addLinks(myTextView, p, baseUri);
}
```

code snippet PA4AD_Ch05_Linkify/src/MyActivity.java

Note that in this example, including whitespace between "quake" and a number will return a match, but the resulting URI won't be valid. You can implement and specify one or both of a `TransformFilter` and `MatchFilter` interface to resolve this problem. These interfaces, defined in detail in the following section, offer additional control over the target URI structure and the definition of matching strings, and are used as in the following skeleton code:

```
Linkify.addLinks(myTextView, p, baseUri,
                new MyMatchFilter(), new MyTransformFilter());
```

Using the Match Filter

To add additional conditions to RegEx pattern matches, implement the `acceptMatch` method in a Match Filter. When a potential match is found, `acceptMatch` is triggered, with the match start and end index (along with the full text being searched) passed in as parameters.

Listing 5-8 shows a `MatchFilter` implementation that cancels any match immediately preceded by an exclamation mark.

LISTING 5-8: Using a Linkify Match Filter

```java
class MyMatchFilter implements MatchFilter {
    public boolean acceptMatch(CharSequence s, int start, int end) {
        return (start == 0 || s.charAt(start-1) != '!');
    }
}
```

code snippet PA4AD_Ch05_Linkify/src/MyActivity.java

Using the Transform Filter

The Transform Filter lets you modify the implicit URI generated by matching link text. Decoupling the link text from the target URI gives you more freedom in how you display data strings to your users.

To use the Transform Filter, implement the `transformUrl` method in your Transform Filter. When Linkify finds a successful match, it calls `transformUrl`, passing in the RegEx pattern used and the matched text string (before the base URI is prepended). You can modify the matched string and return it such that it can be appended to the base string as the data for a View Intent.

As shown in Listing 5-9, the `TransformFilter` implementation transforms the matched text into a lowercase URI, having also removed any whitespace characters.

LISTING 5-9: Using a Linkify Transform Filter

```java
class MyTransformFilter implements TransformFilter {
    public String transformUrl(Matcher match, String url) {
        return url.toLowerCase().replace(" ", "");
    }
}
```

code snippet PA4AD_Ch05_Linkify/src/MyActivity.java

Using Intents to Broadcast Events

So far, you've looked at using Intents to start new application components, but you can also use Intents to broadcast messages anonymously *between* components via the `sendBroadcast` method.

As a system-level message-passing mechanism, Intents are capable of sending structured messages across process boundaries. As a result, you can implement Broadcast Receivers to listen for, and respond to, these Broadcast Intents within your applications.

Broadcast Intents are used to notify applications of system or application events, extending the event-driven programming model between applications.

Broadcasting Intents helps make your application more open; by broadcasting an event using an Intent, you let yourself and third-party developers react to events without having to modify your original application. Within your applications you can listen for Broadcast Intents to to react to device state changes and third-party application events.

Android uses Broadcast Intents extensively to broadcast system events, such as changes in network connectivity, docking state, and incoming calls.

Broadcasting Events with Intents

Within your application, construct the Intent you want to broadcast and call `sendBroadcast` to send it.

Set the action, data, and category of your Intent in a way that lets Broadcast Receivers accurately determine their interest. In this scenario, the Intent *action* string is used to identify the event being broadcast, so it should be a unique string that identifies the event. By convention, action strings are constructed using the same form as Java package names:

```
public static final String NEW_LIFEFORM_DETECTED =
  "com.paad.action.NEW_LIFEFORM";
```

If you want to include data within the Intent, you can specify a URI using the Intent's `data` property. You can also include extras to add additional primitive values. Considered in terms of an event-driven paradigm, the extras equate to optional parameters passed into an event handler.

Listing 5-10 shows the basic creation of a Broadcast Intent using the action defined previously, with additional event information stored as extras.

LISTING 5-10: Broadcasting an Intent

```
Intent intent = new Intent(LifeformDetectedReceiver.NEW_LIFEFORM);
intent.putExtra(LifeformDetectedReceiver.EXTRA_LIFEFORM_NAME,
                detectedLifeform);
intent.putExtra(LifeformDetectedReceiver.EXTRA_LONGITUDE,
                currentLongitude);
intent.putExtra(LifeformDetectedReceiver.EXTRA_LATITUDE,
                currentLatitude);

sendBroadcast(intent);
```

code snippet PA4AD_Ch05_BroadcastIntents/src/MyActivity.java

Listening for Broadcasts with Broadcast Receivers

Broadcast Receivers (commonly referred to simply as Receivers) are used to listen for Broadcast Intents. For a Receiver to receive broadcasts, it must be registered, either in code or within the application manifest — the latter case is referred to as a *manifest Receiver*. In either case, use an Intent Filter to specify which Intent actions and data your Receiver is listening for.

In the case of applications that include manifest Receivers, the applications don't have to be running when the Intent is broadcast for those receivers to execute; they will be started automatically when a matching Intent is broadcast. This is excellent for resource management, as it lets you create event-driven applications that will still respond to broadcast events even after they've been closed or killed.

To create a new Broadcast Receiver, extend the `BroadcastReceiver` class and override the `onReceive` event handler:

```
import android.content.BroadcastReceiver;
import android.content.Context;
import android.content.Intent;

public class MyBroadcastReceiver extends BroadcastReceiver {
  @Override
  public void onReceive(Context context, Intent intent) {
    //TODO: React to the Intent received.
  }
}
```

The `onReceive` method will be executed on the main application thread when a Broadcast Intent is received that matches the Intent Filter used to register the Receiver. The `onReceive` handler must complete within five seconds; otherwise, the Force Close dialog will be displayed.

Typically, Broadcast Receivers will update content, launch Services, update Activity UI, or notify the user using the Notification Manager. The five-second execution limit ensures that major processing cannot, and should not, be done within the Broadcast Receiver itself.

Listing 5-11 shows how to implement a Broadcast Receiver that extracts the data and several extras from the broadcast Intent and uses them to start a new Activity. In the following sections you will learn how to register it in code or in your application manifest.

LISTING 5-11: Implementing a Broadcast Receiver

```
public class LifeformDetectedReceiver
    extends BroadcastReceiver {

  public final static String EXTRA_LIFEFORM_NAME
    = "EXTRA_LIFEFORM_NAME";
  public final static String EXTRA_LATITUDE = "EXTRA_LATITUDE";
  public final static String EXTRA_LONGITUDE = "EXTRA_LONGITUDE";

  public static final String
    ACTION_BURN = "com.paad.alien.action.BURN_IT_WITH_FIRE";
```

```
public static final String
  NEW_LIFEFORM = "com.paad.alien.action.NEW_LIFEFORM";

@Override
public void onReceive(Context context, Intent intent) {
  // Get the lifeform details from the intent.
  Uri data = intent.getData();
  String type = intent.getStringExtra(EXTRA_LIFEFORM_NAME);
  double lat = intent.getDoubleExtra(EXTRA_LATITUDE, 0);
  double lng = intent.getDoubleExtra(EXTRA_LONGITUDE, 0);
  Location loc = new Location("gps");
  loc.setLatitude(lat);
  loc.setLongitude(lng);
  if (type.equals("facehugger")) {
    Intent startIntent = new Intent(ACTION_BURN, data);
    startIntent.putExtra(EXTRA_LATITUDE, lat);
    startIntent.putExtra(EXTRA_LONGITUDE, lng);

    context.startService(startIntent);
  }
 }
}
```

code snippet PA4AD_Ch05_BroadcastIntents/src/LifeformDetectedReceiver.java

Registering Broadcast Receivers in Code

Broadcast Receivers that affect the UI of a particular Activity are typically registered in code. A Receiver registered programmatically will respond to Broadcast Intents only when the application component it is registered within is running.

This is useful when the Receiver is being used to update UI elements in an Activity. In this case, it's good practice to register the Receiver within the onResume handler and unregister it during onPause.

Listing 5-12 shows how to register and unregister a Broadcast Receiver in code using the IntentFilter class.

LISTING 5-12: Registering and unregistering a Broadcast Receiver in code

```
private IntentFilter filter =
  new IntentFilter(LifeformDetectedReceiver.NEW_LIFEFORM);

private LifeformDetectedReceiver receiver =
  new LifeformDetectedReceiver();

@Override
public void onResume() {
  super.onResume();

  // Register the broadcast receiver.
```

continues

LISTING 13-4 *(continued)*

```
    registerReceiver(receiver, filter);
}

@Override
public void onPause() {
    // Unregister the receiver
    unregisterReceiver(receiver);

    super.onPause();
}
```

code snippet PA4AD_Ch05_BroadcastIntents/src/MyActivity.java

Registering Broadcast Receivers in Your Application Manifest

To include a Broadcast Receiver in the application manifest, add a `receiver` tag within the `application` node, specifying the class name of the Broadcast Receiver to register. The receiver node needs to include an `intent-filter` tag that specifies the action string being listened for.

```
<receiver android:name=".LifeformDetectedReceiver">
  <intent-filter>
    <action android:name="com.paad.alien.action.NEW_LIFEFORM"/>
  </intent-filter>
</receiver>
```

Broadcast Receivers registered this way are always active and will receive Broadcast Intents even when the application has been killed or hasn't been started.

Broadcasting Ordered Intents

When the order in which the Broadcast Receivers receive the Intent is important — particularly where you want to allow Receivers to affect the Broadcast Intent received by future Receivers — you can use `sendOrderedBroadcast`, as follows:

```
String requiredPermission = "com.paad.MY_BROADCAST_PERMISSION";
sendOrderedBroadcast(intent, requiredPermission);
```

Using this method, your Intent will be delivered to all registered Receivers that hold the required permission (if one is specified) in the order of their specified priority. You can specify the priority of a Broadcast Receiver using the `android:priority` attribute within its Intent Filter manifest node, where higher values are considered higher priority.

```
<receiver
  android:name=".MyOrderedReceiver"
  android:permission="com.paad.MY_BROADCAST_PERMISSION">
  <intent-filter
    android:priority="100">
    <action android:name="com.paad.action.ORDERED_BROADCAST" />
  </intent-filter>
</receiver>
```

It's good practice to send ordered broadcasts, and specify Receiver priorities, only for Receivers used within your application that specifically need to impose a specific order of receipt.

One common use-case for sending ordered broadcasts is to broadcast Intents for which you want to receive result data. Using the sendOrderedBroadcast method, you can specify a Broadcast Receiver that will be placed at the end of the Receiver queue, ensuring that it will receive the Broadcast Intent after it has been handled (and modified) by the ordered set of registered Broadcast Receivers.

In this case, it's often useful to specify default values for the Intent result, data, and extras that may be modified by any of the Receivers that receive the broadcast before it is returned to the final result Receiver.

```
// Specify the default result, data, and extras.
// The may be modified by any of the Receivers who handle the broadcast
// before being received by the final Receiver.
int initialResult = Activity.RESULT_OK;
String initialData = null;
String initialExtras = null;

// A special Handler instance on which to receive the final result.
// Specify null to use the Context on which the Intent was broadcast.
Handler scheduler = null;

sendOrderedBroadcast(intent, requiredPermission, finalResultReceiver,
                  scheduler, initialResult, initialData, initialExtras);
```

Broadcasting Sticky Intents

Sticky Intents are useful variations of Broadcast Intents that persist the values associated with their last broadcast, returning them as an Intent when a new Receiver is registered to receive the broadcast.

When you call registerReceiver, specifying an Intent Filter that matches a sticky Broadcast Intent, the return value will be the last Intent broadcast, such as the battery-level changed broadcast:

```
IntentFilter battery = new IntentFilter(Intent.ACTION_BATTERY_CHANGED);
Intent currentBatteryCharge = registerReceiver(null, battery);
```

As shown in the preceding snippet, it is not necessary to specify a Receiver to obtain the current value of a sticky Intent. As a result, many of the system device state broadcasts (such as battery and docking state) use sticky Intents to improve efficiency. These are examined in more detail later in this chapter.

To broadcast your own sticky Intents, your application must have the BROADCAST_STICKY uses-permission before calling sendStickyBroadcast and passing in the relevant Intent:

```
sendStickyBroadcast(intent);
```

To remove a sticky Intent, call removeStickyBroadcast, passing in the sticky Intent to remove:

```
removeStickyBroadcast(intent);
```

Introducing the Local Broadcast Manager

The Local Broadcast Manager was introduced to the Android Support Library to simplify the process of registering for, and sending, Broadcast Intents between components within your application.

Because of the reduced broadcast scope, using the Local Broadcast Manager is more efficient than sending a global broadcast. It also ensures that the Intent you broadcast cannot be received by any components outside your application, ensuring that there is no risk of leaking private or sensitive data, such as location information.

Similarly, other applications can't transmit broadcasts to your Receivers, negating the risk of these Receivers becoming vectors for security exploits.

To use the Local Broadcast Manager, you must first include the Android Support Library in your application, as described in Chapter 2.

Use the `LocalBroadcastManager.getInstance` method to return an instance of the Local Broadcast Manager:

```
LocalBroadcastManager lbm = LocalBroadcastManager.getInstance(this);
```

To register a local broadcast Receiver, use the Local Broadcast Manager's `registerReceiver` method, much as you would register a global receiver, passing in a Broadcast Receiver and an Intent Filter:

```
lbm.registerReceiver(new BroadcastReceiver() {
  @Override
  public void onReceive(Context context, Intent intent) {
    // TODO Handle the received local broadcast
  }
}, new IntentFilter(LOCAL_ACTION));
```

Note that the Broadcast Receiver specified can also be used to handle global Intent broadcasts.

To transmit a local Broadcast Intent, use the Local Broadcast Manager's `sendBroadcast` method, passing in the Intent to broadcast:

```
lbm.sendBroadcast(new Intent(LOCAL_ACTION));
```

The Local Broadcast Manager also includes a `sendBroadcastSync` method that operates synchronously, blocking until each registered Receiver has been dispatched.

Introducing Pending Intents

The `PendingIntent` class provides a mechanism for creating Intents that can be fired on your application's behalf by another application at a later time.

A Pending Intent is commonly used to package Intents that will be fired in response to a future event, such as a Widget or Notification being clicked.

> *When used, Pending Intents execute the packaged Intent with the same permissions and identity as if you had executed them yourself, within your own application.*

The `PendingIntent` class offers static methods to construct Pending Intents used to start an Activity, to start a Service, or to broadcast an Intent:

```
int requestCode = 0;
int flags = 0;

// Start an Activity
Intent startActivityIntent = new Intent(this, MyOtherActivity.class);
PendingIntent.getActivity(this, requestCode,
                          startActivityIntent, flags);

// Start a Service
Intent startServiceIntent = new Intent(this, MyService.class);
PendingIntent.getService(this, requestCode,
                         startServiceIntent , flags);

// Broadcast an Intent
Intent broadcastIntent = new Intent(NEW_LIFEFORM_DETECTED);
PendingIntent.getBroadcast(this, requestCode,
                           broadcastIntent, flags);
```

The `PendingIntent` class includes static constants that can be used to specify flags to update or cancel any existing Pending Intent that matches your specified action, as well as to specify if this Intent is to be fired only once. The various options will be examined in more detail when Notifications and Widgets are introduced in Chapters 10 and 14, respectively.

CREATING INTENT FILTERS AND BROADCAST RECEIVERS

Having learned to use Intents to start Activities/Services and to broadcast events, it's important to understand how to create the Broadcast Receivers and Intent Filters that listen for Broadcast Intents and allow your application to respond to them.

In the case of Activities and Services, an Intent is a request for an action to be performed on a set of data, and an Intent Filter is a declaration that a particular application component is capable of performing an action on a type of data.

Intent Filters are also used to specify the actions a Broadcast Receiver is interested in receiving.

Using Intent Filters to Service Implicit Intents

If an Intent is a request for an action to be performed on a set of data, how does Android know which application (and component) to use to service that request? Using Intent Filters, application components can declare the actions and data they support.

To register an Activity or Service as a potential Intent handler, add an `intent-filter` tag to its manifest node using the following tags (and associated attributes):

➤ `action` — Uses the `android:name` attribute to specify the name of the action being serviced. Each Intent Filter must have at least one action tag. Actions should be unique strings that are self-describing. Best practice is to use a naming system based on the Java package naming conventions.

➤ `category` — Uses the `android:name` attribute to specify under which circumstances the action should be serviced. Each Intent Filter tag can include multiple category tags. You can specify your own categories or use the following standard values provided by Android:

➤ `ALTERNATIVE` — This category specifies that this action should be available as an alternative to the default action performed on an item of this data type. For example, where the default action for a contact is to view it, the alternative could be to edit it.

➤ `SELECTED_ALTERNATIVE` — Similar to the `ALTERNATIVE` category, but whereas that category will always resolve to a single action using the intent resolution described next, `SELECTED_ALTERNATIVE` is used when a list of possibilities is required. As you'll see later in this chapter, one of the uses of Intent Filters is to help populate context menus dynamically using actions.

➤ `BROWSABLE` — Specifies an action available from within the browser. When an Intent is fired from within the browser, it will always include the browsable category. If you want your application to respond to actions triggered within the browser (e.g., intercepting links to a particular website), you must include the browsable category.

➤ `DEFAULT` — Set this to make a component the default action for the data type specified in the Intent Filter. This is also necessary for Activities that are launched using an explicit Intent.

➤ `HOME` — By setting an Intent Filter category as home without specifying an action, you are presenting it as an alternative to the native home screen.

➤ `LAUNCHER` — Using this category makes an Activity appear in the application launcher.

➤ `data` — The data tag enables you to specify which data types your component can act on; you can include several data tags as appropriate. You can use any combination of the following attributes to specify the data your component supports:

➤ `android:host` — Specifies a valid hostname (e.g., `google.com`).

➤ `android:mimetype` — Specifies the type of data your component is capable of handling. For example, `<type android:value="vnd.android.cursor.dir/*"/>` would match any Android cursor.

➤ `android:path` — Specifies valid path values for the URI (e.g., `/transport/boats/`).

➤ `android:port` — Specifies valid ports for the specified host.

➤ `android:scheme` — Requires a particular scheme (e.g., `content` or `http`).

The following snippet shows an Intent Filter for an Activity that can perform the SHOW_DAMAGE action as either a primary or an alternative action based on its mime type.

```
<intent-filter>
  <action
    android:name="com.paad.earthquake.intent.action.SHOW_DAMAGE"
  />
  <category android:name="android.intent.category.DEFAULT"/>
  <category
    android:name="android.intent.category.SELECTED_ALTERNATIVE"/>
  <data android:mimeType="vnd.earthquake.cursor.item/*"/>
</intent-filter>
```

You may have noticed that clicking a link to a YouTube video or Google Maps location on an Android device prompts you to use YouTube or Google Maps, respectively, rather than the browser. This is achieved by specifying the scheme, host, and path attributes within the data tag of an Intent Filter, as shown in Listing 5-13. In this example, any link of the form that begins `http://blog.radioactiveyak.com` can be serviced by this Activity.

Available for download on Wrox.com

LISTING 5-13: Registering an Activity as an Intent Receiver for viewing content from a specific website using an Intent Filter

```
<activity android:name=".MyBlogViewerActivity">
  <intent-filter>
    <action android:name="android.intent.action.VIEW" />
    <category android:name="android.intent.category.DEFAULT" />
    <category android:name="android.intent.category.BROWSABLE" />
    <data android:scheme="http"
          android:host="blog.radioactiveyak.com"/>
  </intent-filter>
</activity>
```

code snippet PA4AD_Ch05_Intents/AndroidManifest.xml

Note that you must include the *browsable* category in order for links clicked within the browser to trigger this behavior.

How Android Resolves Intent Filters

The process of deciding which Activity to start when an implicit Intent is passed in to `start Activity` is called *intent resolution*. The aim of intent resolution is to find the best Intent Filter match possible by means of the following process:

1. Android puts together a list of all the Intent Filters available from the installed packages.

2. Intent Filters that do not match the action *or* category associated with the Intent being resolved are removed from the list.

➤ Action matches are made only if the Intent Filter includes the specified action. An Intent Filter will fail the action match check if *none* of its actions matches the one specified by the Intent.

➤ For category matching, Intent Filters must include *all* the categories defined in the resolving Intent, but can include additional categories not included in the Intent. An Intent Filter with no categories specified matches only Intents with no categories.

3. Each part of the Intent's data URI is compared to the Intent Filter's `data` tag. If the Intent Filter specifies a scheme, host/authority, path, or MIME type, these values are compared to the Intent's URI. Any mismatch will remove the Intent Filter from the list. Specifying no data values in an Intent Filter will result in a match with all Intent data values.

➤ The MIME type is the data type of the data being matched. When matching data types, you can use wildcards to match subtypes (e.g., `earthquakes/*`). If the Intent Filter specifies a data type, it must match the Intent; specifying no data types results in a match with all of them.

➤ The scheme is the "protocol" part of the URI (e.g., `http:`, `mailto:`, or `tel:`).

➤ The hostname or *data authority* is the section of the URI between the scheme and the path (e.g., `developer.android.com`). For a hostname to match, the Intent Filter's scheme must also pass.

➤ The data path is what comes after the authority (e.g., `/training`). A path can match only if the scheme and hostname parts of the data tag also match.

4. When you implicitly start an Activity, if more than one component is resolved from this process, all the matching possibilities are offered to the user. For Broadcast Receivers, each matching Receiver will receive the broadcast Intent.

Native Android application components are part of the intent-resolution process in exactly the same way as third-party applications. They do not have a higher priority and can be completely replaced with new Activities that declare Intent Filters that service the same actions.

Finding and Using Intents Received Within an Activity

When an application component is started through an implicit Intent, it needs to find the action it's to perform and the data to perform it on.

To find the Intent used to start the Activity, call `getIntent`, as shown in Listing 5-14.

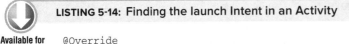

LISTING 5-14: Finding the launch Intent in an Activity

Available for
download on
Wrox.com

```
@Override
public void onCreate(Bundle savedInstanceState) {
    super.onCreate(savedInstanceState);
    setContentView(R.layout.main);

    Intent intent = getIntent();
```

```
        String action = intent.getAction();
        Uri data = intent.getData();
    }
```

code snippet PA4AD_Ch05_Intents/src/MyOtherActivity.java

Use the `getData` and `getAction` methods to find the data and action, respectively, associated with the Intent. Use the type-safe `get<type>Extra` methods to extract additional information stored in its extras Bundle.

The `getIntent` method will always return the initial Intent used to create the Activity. In some circumstances your Activity may continue to receive Intents after it has been launched. You can use widgets and Notifications to provide shortcuts to displaying data within your Activity that may still be running, though not visible.

Override the `onNewIntent` handler within your Activity to receive and handle new Intents after the Activity has been created.

```
@Override
public void onNewIntent(Intent newIntent) {
    // TODO React to the new Intent
    super.onNewIntent(newIntent);
}
```

Passing on Responsibility

To pass responsibility for action handling to the next best Activity, use `startNextMatchingActivity`.

```
Intent intent = getIntent();
if (isDuringBreak)
    startNextMatchingActivity(intent);
```

This lets you add additional conditions to your components that restrict their use beyond the ability of the Intent Filter-based intent-resolution process.

Selecting a Contact Example

In this example you'll create a new Activity that services `ACTION_PICK` for contact data. It displays each of the contacts in the contacts database and lets the user select one, before closing and returning the selected contact's URI to the calling Activity.

> *This example is somewhat contrived. Android already supplies an Intent Filter for picking a contact from a list that can be invoked by means of the* `content://contacts/people/` *URI in an implicit Intent. The purpose of this exercise is to demonstrate the form, even if this particular implementation isn't particularly useful.*

1. Create a new ContactPicker project that includes a `ContactPicker` Activity:

```
package com.paad.contactpicker;

import android.app.Activity;
import android.content.Intent;
import android.database.Cursor;
import android.net.Uri;
import android.os.Bundle;
import android.provider.ContactsContract.Contacts;
import android.view.View;
import android.widget.AdapterView;
import android.widget.ListView;
import android.widget.SimpleCursorAdapter;

public class ContactPicker extends Activity {
  @Override
  public void onCreate(Bundle savedInstanceState) {
    super.onCreate(savedInstanceState);
    setContentView(R.layout.main);
  }
}
```

2. Modify the `main.xml` layout resource to include a single `ListView` control. This control will be used to display the contacts.

```
<?xml version="1.0" encoding="utf-8"?>
<LinearLayout xmlns:android="http://schemas.android.com/apk/res/android"
  android:orientation="vertical"
  android:layout_width="match_parent"
  android:layout_height="match_parent">
  <ListView android:id="@+id/contactListView"
    android:layout_width="match_parent"
    android:layout_height="wrap_content"
  />
</LinearLayout>
```

3. Create a new `listitemlayout.xml` layout resource that includes a single `TextView` control. This control will be used to display each contact in the List View.

```
<?xml version="1.0" encoding="utf-8"?>
<LinearLayout xmlns:android="http://schemas.android.com/apk/res/android"
  android:orientation="vertical"
  android:layout_width="match_parent"
  android:layout_height="match_parent"
  >
  <TextView
    android:id="@+id/itemTextView"
    android:layout_width="match_parent"
    android:layout_height="wrap_content"
    android:padding="10dp"
    android:textSize="16dp"
    android:textColor="#FFF"
  />
</LinearLayout>
```

4. Return to the `ContactPicker` Activity. Override the `onCreate` method.

```
@Override
public void onCreate(Bundle savedInstanceState) {
  super.onCreate(savedInstanceState);
  setContentView(R.layout.main);
```

4.1 Create a new Cursor to retrieve the people stored in the contact list, and bind it to the List View using a `SimpleCursorArrayAdapter`. Note that in this example the query is executed on the main UI thread. A better approach would be to use a Cursor Loader, as shown in Chapter 8.

```
final Cursor c = getContentResolver().query(
  ContactsContract.Contacts.CONTENT_URI, null, null, null, null);

String[] from = new String[] { Contacts.DISPLAY_NAME_PRIMARY };
int[] to = new int[] { R.id.itemTextView };

SimpleCursorAdapter adapter = new SimpleCursorAdapter(this,
                                          R.layout.listitemlayout,
                                          c,
                                          from,
                                          to);
ListView lv = (ListView)findViewById(R.id.contactListView);
lv.setAdapter(adapter);
```

4.2 Add an `onItemClickListener` to the List View. Selecting a contact from the list should return a path to the item to the calling Activity.

```
lv.setOnItemClickListener(new ListView.OnItemClickListener() {
  public void onItemClick(AdapterView<?> parent, View view, int pos,
                     long id) {
    // Move the cursor to the selected item
    c.moveToPosition(pos);
    // Extract the row id.
    int rowId = c.getInt(c.getColumnIndexOrThrow("_id"));
    // Construct the result URI.
    Uri outURI =
  ContentUris.withAppendedId(ContactsContract.Contacts.CONTENT_URI, rowId);
    Intent outData = new Intent();
    outData.setData(outURI);
    setResult(Activity.RESULT_OK, outData);
    finish();
  }
});
```

c. Close off the `onCreate` method:

```
}
```

5. Modify the application manifest and replace the `intent-filter` tag of the Activity to add support for the `ACTION_PICK` action on contact data:

```
<?xml version="1.0" encoding="utf-8"?>
<manifest xmlns:android="http://schemas.android.com/apk/res/android"
    package="com.paad.contactpicker">
```

```xml
<application android:icon="@drawable/ic_launcher">
    <activity android:name=".ContactPicker" android:label="@string/app_name">
        <intent-filter>
            <action android:name="android.intent.action.PICK"></action>
            <category android:name="android.intent.category.DEFAULT"></category>
            <data android:path="contacts" android:scheme="content"></data>
        </intent-filter>
    </activity>
</application>
</manifest>
```

6. This completes the sub-Activity. To test it, create a new test harness `ContactPickerTester` Activity. Create a new layout resource — `contactpickertester.xml` — that includes a `TextView` to display the selected contact and a `Button` to start the sub-Activity:

```xml
<?xml version="1.0" encoding="utf-8"?>
<LinearLayout xmlns:android="http://schemas.android.com/apk/res/android"
  android:orientation="vertical"
  android:layout_width="match_parent"
  android:layout_height="match_parent"
  >
  <TextView
    android:id="@+id/selected_contact_textview"
    android:layout_width="match_parent"
    android:layout_height="wrap_content"
  />
  <Button
    android:id="@+id/pick_contact_button"
    android:layout_width="match_parent"
    android:layout_height="wrap_content"
    android:text="Pick Contact"
  />
</LinearLayout>
```

7. Override the `onCreate` method of the `ContactPickerTester` to add a click listener to the Button so that it implicitly starts a new sub-Activity by specifying the `ACTION_PICK` and the contact database URI (`content://contacts/`):

```java
package com.paad.contactpicker;

import android.app.Activity;
import android.content.Intent;
import android.database.Cursor;
import android.net.Uri;
import android.os.Bundle;
import android.provider.ContactsContract;
import android.view.View;
import android.view.View.OnClickListener;
import android.widget.Button;
import android.widget.TextView;

public class ContactPickerTester extends Activity {

    public static final int PICK_CONTACT = 1;
```

```
    @Override
    public void onCreate(Bundle savedInstanceState) {
      super.onCreate(savedInstanceState);
      setContentView(R.layout.contactpickertester);

      Button button = (Button)findViewById(R.id.pick_contact_button);

      button.setOnClickListener(new OnClickListener() {
        @Override
        public void onClick(View _view) {
          Intent intent = new Intent(Intent.ACTION_PICK,
            Uri.parse("content://contacts/"));
          startActivityForResult(intent, PICK_CONTACT);
        }
      });
    }
  }
```

8. When the sub-Activity returns, use the result to populate the Text View with the selected
contact's name:

```
@Override
public void onActivityResult(int reqCode, int resCode, Intent data) {
  super.onActivityResult(reqCode, resCode, data);

  switch(reqCode) {
    case (PICK_CONTACT) : {
      if (resCode == Activity.RESULT_OK) {
        Uri contactData = data.getData();
        Cursor c = getContentResolver().query(contactData, null, null, null, null);
        c.moveToFirst();
        String name = c.getString(c.getColumnIndexOrThrow(
                        ContactsContract.Contacts.DISPLAY_NAME_PRIMARY));
        c.close();
        TextView tv = (TextView)findViewById(R.id.selected_contact_textview);
        tv.setText(name);
      }
      break;
    }
    default: break;
  }
}
```

9. With your test harness complete, simply add it to your application manifest. You'll also need
to add a READ_CONTACTS permission within a uses-permission tag to allow the application
to access the contacts database.

```
<?xml version="1.0" encoding="utf-8"?>
<manifest xmlns:android="http://schemas.android.com/apk/res/android"
  package="com.paad.contactpicker">
  <uses-permission android:name="android.permission.READ_CONTACTS"/>
  <application android:icon="@drawable/ic_launcher">
    <activity android:name=".ContactPicker" android:label="@string/app_name">
      <intent-filter>
```

```
          <action android:name="android.intent.action.PICK"></action>
          <category android:name="android.intent.category.DEFAULT"></category>
          <data android:path="contacts" android:scheme="content"></data>
        </intent-filter>
      </activity>
    <activity android:name=".ContactPickerTester"
              android:label="Contact Picker Test">
      <intent-filter>
        <action android:name="android.intent.action.MAIN" />
        <category android:name="android.intent.category.LAUNCHER" />
      </intent-filter>
    </activity>
  </application>

</manifest>
```

> 🖉 *All code snippets in this example are part of the* Chapter 5 Contact Picker
> project, *available for download at* Wrox.com.

When your Activity is running, press the "pick contact" button. The contact picker Activity should
appear, as shown in Figure 5-1.

FIGURE 5-1

After you select a contact, the parent Activity should return to the foreground with the selected contact name displayed (see Figure 5-2).

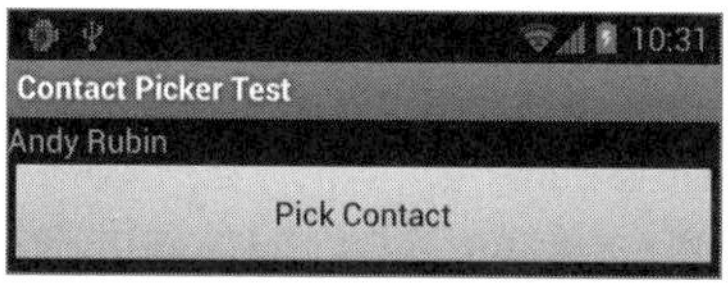

FIGURE 5-2

Using Intent Filters for Plug-Ins and Extensibility

Having used Intent Filters to declare the actions your Activities can perform on different types of data, it stands to reason that applications can also query to find which actions are available to be performed on a particular piece of data.

Android provides a plug-in model that lets your applications take advantage of functionality, provided anonymously from your own or third-party application components you haven't yet conceived of, without your having to modify or recompile your projects.

Supplying Anonymous Actions to Applications

To use this mechanism to make your Activity's actions available anonymously for existing applications, publish them using `intent-filter` tags within their manifest nodes, as described earlier.

The Intent Filter describes the `action` it performs and the `data` upon which it can be performed. The latter will be used during the intent-resolution process to determine when this action should be available. The `category` tag must be either `ALTERNATIVE` or `SELECTED_ALTERNATIVE`, or both. The `android:label` attribute should be a human-readable label that describes the action.

Listing 5-15 shows an example of an Intent Filter used to advertise an Activity's capability to nuke Moon bases from orbit.

LISTING 5-15: Advertising supported Activity actions

```
<activity android:name=".NostromoController">
  <intent-filter
    android:label="@string/Nuke_From_Orbit">
    <action android:name="com.pad.nostromo.NUKE_FROM_ORBIT"/>
    <data android:mimeType="vnd.moonbase.cursor.item/*"/>
    <category android:name="android.intent.category.ALTERNATIVE"/>
    <category
      android:name="android.intent.category.SELECTED_ALTERNATIVE"
    />
  </intent-filter>
</activity>
```

code snippet PA4AD_Ch05_Intents/AndroidManifest.xml

Discovering New Actions from Third-Party Intent Receivers

Using the Package Manager, you can create an Intent that specifies a type of data and a category of action, and have the system return a list of Activities capable of performing an action on that data.

The elegance of this concept is best explained by an example. If the data your Activity displays is a list of places, you might include functionality to View them on a map or "Show directions to" each. Jump a few years ahead and you've created an application that interfaces with your car, allowing your phone to handle driving. Thanks to the runtime menu generation, when a new Intent Filter — with a DRIVE_CAR action — is included within the new Activity's node, Android will resolve this new action and make it available to your earlier application.

This provides you with the ability to retrofit functionality to your application when you create new components capable of performing actions on a given type of data. Many of Android's native applications use this functionality, enabling you to provide additional actions to native Activities.

The Intent you create will be used to resolve components with Intent Filters that supply actions for the data you specify. The Intent is being used to find actions, so don't assign it one; it should specify only the data to perform actions on. You should also specify the category of the action, either CATEGORY_ALTERNATIVE or CATEGORY_SELECTED_ALTERNATIVE.

The skeleton code for creating an Intent for menu-action resolution is shown here:

```
Intent intent = new Intent();
intent.setData(MyProvider.CONTENT_URI);
intent.addCategory(Intent.CATEGORY_ALTERNATIVE);
```

Pass this Intent into the Package Manager method queryIntentActivityOptions, specifying any options flags.

Listing 5-16 shows how to generate a list of actions to make available within your application.

LISTING 5-16: Generating a list of possible actions to be performed on specific data

```
PackageManager packageManager = getPackageManager();

// Create the intent used to resolve which actions
// should appear in the menu.
Intent intent = new Intent();
intent.setData(MoonBaseProvider.CONTENT_URI);
intent.addCategory(Intent.CATEGORY_SELECTED_ALTERNATIVE);

// Specify flags. In this case, to return only filters
// with the default category.
int flags = PackageManager.MATCH_DEFAULT_ONLY;

// Generate the list
List<ResolveInfo> actions;
actions = packageManager.queryIntentActivities(intent, flags);

// Extract the list of action names
ArrayList<String> labels = new ArrayList<String>();
```

```
Resources r = getResources();
for (ResolveInfo action : actions )
  labels.add(r.getString(action.labelRes));
```

code snippet PA4AD_Ch05_Intents/src/MyActivity.java

Incorporating Anonymous Actions as Menu Items

The most common way to incorporate actions from third-party applications is to include them within your Menu Items or Action Bar Actions.

The addIntentOptions method, available from the Menu class, lets you specify an Intent that describes the data acted upon within your Activity, as described previously; however, rather than simply returning a list of possible Receivers, a new Menu Item will be created for each, with the text populated from the matching Intent Filters' labels.

To add Menu Items to your Menus dynamically at run time, use the addIntentOptions method on the Menu object in question: Pass in an Intent that specifies the data for which you want to provide actions. Generally, this will be handled within your Activities' onCreateOptionsMenu or onCreate-ContextMenu handlers.

As in the previous section, the Intent you create will be used to resolve components with Intent Filters that supply actions for the data you specify. The Intent is being used to find actions, so don't assign it one; it should specify only the data to perform actions on. You should also specify the category of the action, either CATEGORY_ALTERNATIVE or CATEGORY_SELECTED_ALTERNATIVE.

The skeleton code for creating an Intent for menu-action resolution is shown here:

```
Intent intent = new Intent();
intent.setData(MyProvider.CONTENT_URI);
intent.addCategory(Intent.CATEGORY_ALTERNATIVE);
```

Pass this Intent in to addIntentOptions on the Menu you want to populate, as well as any options flags, the name of the calling class, the Menu group to use, and the Menu ID values. You can also specify an array of Intents you'd like to use to create additional Menu Items.

Listing 5-17 gives an idea of how to dynamically populate an Activity Menu.

LISTING 5-17: Dynamic Menu population from advertised actions

```
@Override
public boolean onCreateOptionsMenu(Menu menu) {
  super.onCreateOptionsMenu(menu);

  // Create the intent used to resolve which actions
  // should appear in the menu.
  Intent intent = new Intent();
  intent.setData(MoonBaseProvider.CONTENT_URI);
  intent.addCategory(Intent.CATEGORY_SELECTED_ALTERNATIVE);

  // Normal menu options to let you set a group and ID
```

continues

LISTING 5-17 *(continued)*

```
    // values for the menu items you're adding.
    int menuGroup = 0;
    int menuItemId = 0;
    int menuItemOrder = Menu.NONE;

    // Provide the name of the component that's calling
    // the action -- generally the current Activity.
    ComponentName caller = getComponentName();

    // Define intents that should be added first.
    Intent[] specificIntents = null;
    // The menu items created from the previous Intents
    // will populate this array.
    MenuItem[] outSpecificItems = null;

    // Set any optional flags.
    int flags = Menu.FLAG_APPEND_TO_GROUP;

    // Populate the menu
    menu.addIntentOptions(menuGroup,
                          menuItemId,
                          menuItemOrder,
                          caller,
                          specificIntents,
                          intent,
                          flags,
                          outSpecificItems);

    return true;
}
```

code snippet PA4AD_Ch05_Intents/src/MyActivity.java

Listening for Native Broadcast Intents

Many of the system Services broadcast Intents to signal changes. You can use these messages to add functionality to your own projects based on system events, such as time-zone changes, data-connection status, incoming SMS messages, or phone calls.

The following list introduces some of the native actions exposed as constants in the Intent class; these actions are used primarily to track device status changes:

➤ ACTION_BOOT_COMPLETED — Fired once when the device has completed its startup sequence. An application requires the RECEIVE_BOOT_COMPLETED permission to receive this broadcast.

➤ ACTION_CAMERA_BUTTON — Fired when the camera button is clicked.

➤ ACTION_DATE_CHANGED and ACTION_TIME_CHANGED — These actions are broadcast if the date or time on the device is manually changed (as opposed to changing through the inexorable progression of time).

➤ `ACTION_MEDIA_EJECT` — If the user chooses to eject the external storage media, this event is fired first. If your application is reading or writing to the external media storage, you should listen for this event to save and close any open file handles.

➤ `ACTION_MEDIA_MOUNTED` and `ACTION_MEDIA_UNMOUNTED` — These two events are broadcast whenever new external storage media are successfully added to or removed from the device, respectively.

➤ `ACTION_NEW_OUTGOING_CALL` — Broadcast when a new outgoing call is about to be placed. Listen for this broadcast to intercept outgoing calls. The number being dialed is stored in the `EXTRA_PHONE_NUMBER` extra, whereas the `resultData` in the returned Intent will be the number actually dialed. To register a Broadcast Receiver for this action, your application must declare the `PROCESS_OUTGOING_CALLS` uses-permission.

➤ `ACTION_SCREEN_OFF` and `ACTION_SCREEN_ON` — Broadcast when the screen turns off or on, respectively.

➤ `ACTION_TIMEZONE_CHANGED` — This action is broadcast whenever the phone's current time zone changes. The Intent includes a `time-zone` extra that returns the ID of the new `java.util.TimeZone`.

> A comprehensive list of the broadcast actions used and transmitted natively by Android to notify applications of system state changes is available at http://developer.android.com/reference/android/content/Intent.html.

Android also uses Broadcast Intents to announce application-specific events, such as incoming SMS messages, changes in dock state, and battery level. The actions and Intents associated with these events will be discussed in more detail in later chapters when you learn more about the associated Services.

Monitoring Device State Changes Using Broadcast Intents

Monitoring the device state is an important part of creating efficient and dynamic applications whose behavior can change based on connectivity, battery charge state, and docking status.

Android broadcasts Intents for changes in each of these device states. The following sections examine how to create Intent Filters to register Broadcast Receivers that can react to such changes, and how to extract the device state information accordingly.

Listening for Battery Changes

To monitor changes in the battery level or charging status within an Activity, you can register a Receiver using an Intent Filter that listens for the `Intent.ACTION_BATTERY_CHANGED` broadcast by the Battery Manager.

The Broadcast Intent containing the current battery charge and charging status is a sticky Intent, so you can retrieve the current battery status at any time without needing to implement a Broadcast Receiver, as shown in Listing 5-18.

LISTING 5-18: Determining battery and charge state information

```
IntentFilter batIntentFilter = new IntentFilter(Intent.ACTION_BATTERY_CHANGED);
Intent battery = context.registerReceiver(null, batIntentFilter);
int status = battery.getIntExtra(BatteryManager.EXTRA_STATUS, -1);
boolean isCharging =
  status == BatteryManager.BATTERY_STATUS_CHARGING ||
  status == BatteryManager.BATTERY_STATUS_FULL;
```

code snippet PA4AD_Ch05_Intents/src/DeviceStateActivity.java

Note that you can't register the battery changed action within a manifest Receiver; however, you can monitor connection and disconnection from a power source and a low battery level using the following action strings, each prefixed with `android.intent.action`:

➤ `ACTION_BATTERY_LOW`

➤ `ACTION_BATTERY_OKAY`

➤ `ACTION_POWER_CONNECTED`

➤ `ACTION_POWER_DISCONNECTED`

Listening for Connectivity Changes

Changes in connectivity, including the bandwidth, latency, and availability of an Internet connection, can be significant signals for your application. In particular, you might choose to suspend recurring updates when you lose connectivity or to delay downloads of significant size until you have a Wi-Fi connection.

To monitor changes in connectivity, register a Broadcast Receiver (either within your application or within the manifest) to listen for the `android.net.conn.CONNECTIVITY_CHANGE` (`ConnectivityManager.CONNECTIVITY_ACTION`) action.

The connectivity change broadcast isn't sticky and doesn't contain any additional information regarding the change. To extract details on the current connectivity status, you need to use the Connectivity Manager, as shown in Listing 5-19.

LISTING 5-19: Determining connectivity state information

```
String svcName = Context.CONNECTIVITY_SERVICE;
ConnectivityManager cm = (ConnectivityManager)context.getSystemService(svcName);

NetworkInfo activeNetwork = cm.getActiveNetworkInfo();
boolean isConnected = activeNetwork.isConnectedOrConnecting();
boolean isMobile = activeNetwork.getType() ==
                  ConnectivityManager.TYPE_MOBILE;
```

code snippet PA4AD_Ch05_Intents/src/DeviceStateActivity.java

> *The Connectivity Manager is examined in more detail in Chapter 16,*
> *"Bluetooth, NFC, Networks, and Wi-Fi."*

Listening for Docking Changes

Android devices can be docked in either a car dock or desk dock. These, in term, can be either analog or digital docks. By registering a Receiver to listen for the `Intent.ACTION_DOCK_EVENT` (`android.intent.action.ACTION_DOCK_EVENT`), you can determine the docking status and type of dock.

Like the battery status, the dock event Broadcast Intent is sticky. Listing 5-20 shows how to extract the current docking status from the Intent returned when registering a Receiver for docking events.

LISTING 5-20: Determining docking state information

Available for
download on
Wrox.com

```java
IntentFilter dockIntentFilter =
  new IntentFilter(Intent.ACTION_DOCK_EVENT);
Intent dock = registerReceiver(null, dockIntentFilter);

int dockState = dock.getIntExtra(Intent.EXTRA_DOCK_STATE,
                 Intent.EXTRA_DOCK_STATE_UNDOCKED);
boolean isDocked = dockState != Intent.EXTRA_DOCK_STATE_UNDOCKED;
```

code snippet PA4AD_Ch05_Intents/src/DeviceStateActivity.java

Managing Manifest Receivers at Run Time

Using the Package Manager, you can enable and disable any of your application's manifest Receivers at run time using the `setComponentEnabledSetting` method. You can use this technique to enable or disable any application component (including Activities and Services), but it is particularly useful for manifest Receivers.

To minimize the footprint of your application, it's good practice to disable manifest Receivers that listen for common system events (such as connectivity changes) when your application doesn't need to respond to those events. This technique also enables you to schedule an action based on a system event — such as downloading a large file when the device is connected to Wi-Fi — without gaining the overhead of having the application launch every time a connectivity change is broadcast.

Listing 5-21 shows how to enable and disable a manifest Receiver at run time.

LISTING 5-21: Dynamically toggling manifest Receivers

```java
ComponentName myReceiverName = new ComponentName(this, MyReceiver.class);
PackageManager pm = getPackageManager();

// Enable a manifest receiver
```

continues

LISTING 5-21 *(continued)*

```java
pm.setComponentEnabledSetting(myReceiverName,
  PackageManager.COMPONENT_ENABLED_STATE_ENABLED,
  PackageManager.DONT_KILL_APP);

// Disable a manifest receiver
pm.setComponentEnabledSetting(myReceiverName,
  PackageManager.COMPONENT_ENABLED_STATE_DISABLED,
  PackageManager.DONT_KILL_APP);
```

code snippet PA4AD_Ch05_Intents/src/DeviceStateActivity.java

6

Using Internet Resources

WHAT'S IN THIS CHAPTER?

➤ Connecting to Internet resources

➤ Parsing XML resources

➤ Using the Download Manager to download files

➤ Querying the Download Manager

➤ Using the Account Manager to authenticate with Google App Engine

This chapter introduces Android's Internet connectivity model and some of the Java techniques for parsing Internet data feeds. You'll learn how to connect to an Internet resource and how to use the SAX Parser and the XML Pull Parser to parse XML resources.

An earthquake-monitoring example will demonstrate how to tie together all these features, and forms the basis of an ongoing example that you'll improve and extend in later chapters.

This chapter introduces the Download Manager, and you learn how to use it to schedule and manage long-running downloads. You'll also learn how to customize its notifications and query the Downloads Content Provider to determine the status of your downloads.

Finally, this chapter introduces how to use the Account Manager to make authenticated requests from Google App Engine backends.

DOWNLOADING AND PARSING INTERNET RESOURCES

Android offers several ways to leverage Internet resources. At one extreme you can use a WebView to include a WebKit-based browser within an Activity. At the other extreme you can use client-side APIs, such as the Google APIs, to interact directly with server processes.

Somewhere in between, you can process remote XML feeds to extract and process data using a Java-based XML parser, such as SAX or the XML Pull Parser.

With Internet connectivity and a WebKit browser, you might ask if there's any reason to create native Internet-based applications when you could make a web-based version instead.

There are a number of benefits to creating thick- and thin-client native applications rather than relying on entirely web-based solutions:

➤ **Bandwidth** — Static resources such as images, layouts, and sounds can be expensive on devices with bandwidth restraints. By creating a native application, you can limit the bandwidth requirements to changed data only.

➤ **Caching** — With a browser-based solution, a patchy Internet connection can result in intermittent application availability. A native application can cache data and user actions to provide as much functionality as possible without a live connection and synchronize with the cloud when a connection is reestablished.

➤ **Reducing battery drain** — Each time your application opens a connection to a server, the wireless radio will be turned on (or kept on). A native application can bundle its connections, minimizing the number of connections initiated. The longer the period between network requests, the longer the wireless radio can be left off.

➤ **Native features** — Android devices are more than simple platforms for running a browser. They include location-based services, Notifications, widgets, camera hardware, background Services, and hardware sensors. By creating a native application, you can combine the data available online with the hardware features available on the device to provide a richer user experience.

Modern mobile devices offer a number of alternatives for accessing the Internet. Broadly speaking, Android provides two connection techniques for Internet connectivity. Each is offered transparently to the application layer.

➤ **Mobile Internet** — GPRS, EDGE, 3G, 4G, and LTE Internet access is available through carriers that offer mobile data.

➤ **Wi-Fi** — Wi-Fi receivers and mobile hotspots are becoming increasingly common.

If you use Internet resources in your application, remember that your users' data connections are dependent on the communications technology available to them. EDGE and GSM connections are notoriously low-bandwidth, whereas a Wi-Fi connection may be unreliable in a mobile setting.

Optimize the user experience by limiting the quantity of data transmitted and ensure that your application is robust enough to handle network outages and bandwidth limitations.

Connecting to an Internet Resource

Before you can access Internet resources, you need to add an INTERNET uses-permission node to your application manifest, as shown in the following XML snippet:

```
<uses-permission android:name="android.permission.INTERNET"/>
```

Listing 6-1 shows the basic pattern for opening an Internet data stream.

LISTING 6-1: Opening an Internet data stream

```
String myFeed = getString(R.string.my_feed);
try {
  URL url = new URL(myFeed);

  // Create a new HTTP URL connection
  URLConnection connection = url.openConnection();
  HttpURLConnection httpConnection = (HttpURLConnection)connection;

  int responseCode = httpConnection.getResponseCode();
  if (responseCode == HttpURLConnection.HTTP_OK) {
    InputStream in = httpConnection.getInputStream();
    processStream(in);
  }
}
catch (MalformedURLException e) {
  Log.d(TAG, "Malformed URL Exception.");
}
catch (IOException e) {
  Log.d(TAG, "IO Exception.");
}
```

code snippet PA4AD_Ch06_Internet/src/MyActivity.java

> *Attempting to perform network operations on the main UI thread will cause a* `NetworkOnMainThreadException` *on the latest Android platform releases. Be sure to execute code, such as that shown in Listing 6-1, in a background thread, as described in Chapter 9, "Working in the Background."*

Android includes several classes to help you handle network communications. They are available in the `java.net.*` and `android.net.*` packages.

> *Later in this chapter is a working example that shows how to obtain and process an Internet feed to get a list of earthquakes felt in the last 24 hours. Chapter 16, "Bluetooth, NFC, Networks, and Wi-Fi," features more information on managing specific Internet connections, including monitoring connection status and configuring Wi-Fi access point connections.*

Parsing XML Using the XML Pull Parser

Although detailed instructions for parsing XML and interacting with specific web services are outside the scope of this book, it's important to understand the available technologies.

This section provides a brief overview of the XML Pull Parser, whereas the next section demonstrates the use of the DOM parser to retrieve earthquake details from the United States Geological Survey (USGS).

The XML Pull Parser API is available from the following libraries:

```
import org.xmlpull.v1.XmlPullParser;
import org.xmlpull.v1.XmlPullParserException;
import org.xmlpull.v1.XmlPullParserFactory;
```

It enables you to parse an XML document in a single pass. Unlike the DOM parser, the Pull Parser presents the elements of your document in a sequential series of events and tags.

Your location within the document is represented by the current event. You can determine the current event by calling getEventType. Each document begins at the START_DOCUMENT event and ends at END_DOCUMENT.

To proceed through the tags, simply call next, which causes you to progress through a series of matched (and often nested) START_TAG and END_TAG events. You can extract the name of each tag by calling getName and extract the text between each set of tags using getNextText.

Listing 6-2 demonstrates how to use the XML Pull Parser to extract details from the points of interest list returned by the Google Places API.

LISTING 6-2: Parsing XML using the XML Pull Parser

```java
private void processStream(InputStream inputStream) {
    // Create a new XML Pull Parser.
    XmlPullParserFactory factory;
    try {
        factory = XmlPullParserFactory.newInstance();
        factory.setNamespaceAware(true);
        XmlPullParser xpp = factory.newPullParser();

        // Assign a new input stream.
        xpp.setInput(inputStream, null);
        int eventType = xpp.getEventType();

        // Continue until the end of the document is reached.
        while (eventType != XmlPullParser.END_DOCUMENT) {
            // Check for a start tag of the results tag.
            if (eventType == XmlPullParser.START_TAG &&
                xpp.getName().equals("result")) {
                eventType = xpp.next();
                String name = "";
                // Process each result within the result tag.
                while (!(eventType == XmlPullParser.END_TAG &&
                        xpp.getName().equals("result"))) {
                    // Check for the name tag within the results tag.
                    if (eventType == XmlPullParser.START_TAG &&
                        xpp.getName().equals("name"))
                        // Extract the POI name.
                        name = xpp.nextText();
```

```
      // Move on to the next tag.
      eventType = xpp.next();
    }
    // Do something with each POI name.
  }
  // Move on to the next result tag.
  eventType = xpp.next();
  }
} catch (XmlPullParserException e) {
  Log.d("PULLPARSER", "XML Pull Parser Exception", e);
} catch (IOException e) {
  Log.d("PULLPARSER", "IO Exception", e);
}
}
```

code snippet PA4AD_ Ch6_Internet/src/MyActivity.java

Creating an Earthquake Viewer

In the following example you'll create a tool that uses a USGS earthquake feed to display a list of recent earthquakes. You will return to this earthquake application several times in the following chapters, gradually adding more features and functionality.

The earthquake feed XML is parsed here by the DOM parser. Several alternatives exist, including the XML Pull Parser described in the previous section. As noted, a detailed analysis of the alternative XML parsing techniques is beyond the scope of this book.

In this example you'll create a list-based Activity that connects to an earthquake feed and displays the location, magnitude, and time of the earthquakes it contains.

> *To simplify readability, each of these examples excludes the import statements. If you are using Eclipse, you can press Ctrl+Shift+o (or Cmd+Shift+o on Mac) to automatically populate the import statements required to support the classes used in your code.*

1. Start by creating an Earthquake project featuring an Earthquake Activity.

2. Create a new EarthquakeListFragment that extends ListFragment. This Fragment displays your list of earthquakes.

```
public class EarthquakeListFragment extends ListFragment {
}
```

3. Modify the main.xml layout resource to include the Fragment you created in Step 2. Be sure to name it so that you can reference it from the Activity code.

```
<?xml version="1.0" encoding="utf-8"?>
<LinearLayout xmlns:android="http://schemas.android.com/apk/res/android"
```

```
      android:orientation="vertical"
      android:layout_width="match_parent"
      android:layout_height="match_parent">
      <fragment android:name="com.paad.earthquake.EarthquakeListFragment"
        android:id="@+id/EarthquakeListFragment"
        android:layout_width="match_parent"
        android:layout_height="match_parent"
      />
  </LinearLayout>
```

4.   Create a new public Quake class. This class will be used to store the details (date, details, location, magnitude, and link) of each earthquake. Override the toString method to provide the string that will be used to represent each quake in the List View.

```java
package com.paad.earthquake;

import java.util.Date;
import java.text.SimpleDateFormat;
import android.location.Location;

public class Quake {
  private Date date;
  private String details;
  private Location location;
  private double magnitude;
  private String link;

  public Date getDate() { return date; }
  public String getDetails() { return details; }
  public Location getLocation() { return location; }
  public double getMagnitude() { return magnitude; }
  public String getLink() { return link; }

  public Quake(Date _d, String _det, Location _loc, double _mag, String _link) {
    date = _d;
    details = _det;
    location = _loc;
    magnitude = _mag;
    link = _link;
  }

  @Override
  public String toString() {
    SimpleDateFormat sdf = new SimpleDateFormat("HH.mm");
    String dateString = sdf.format(date);
    return dateString + ": " + magnitude + " " + details;
  }

}
```

5.   In the EarthquakeListFragment, override the onActivityCreated method to store an ArrayList of Quake objects, and bind that to the underlying ListView using an ArrayAdapter:

```java
public class EarthquakeListFragment extends ListFragment {
```

```
ArrayAdapter<Quake> aa;
ArrayList<Quake> earthquakes = new ArrayList<Quake>();

@Override
public void onActivityCreated(Bundle savedInstanceState) {
  super.onActivityCreated(savedInstanceState);

  int layoutID = android.R.layout.simple_list_item_1;
  aa = new ArrayAdapter<Quake>(getActivity(), layoutID , earthquakes);
  setListAdapter(aa);
  }
}
```

6. Start processing the earthquake feed. For this example, the feed used is the one-day USGS feed for earthquakes with a magnitude greater than 2.5. Add the location of your feed as an external string resource. This lets you potentially specify a different feed based on a user's location.

```
<?xml version="1.0" encoding="utf-8"?>
<resources>
  <string name="app_name">Earthquake</string>
  <string name="quake_feed">
    http://earthquake.usgs.gov/eqcenter/catalogs/1day-M2.5.xml
  </string>
</resources>
```

7. Before your application can access the Internet, it needs to be granted permission for Internet access. Add the Internet uses-permission to the manifest:

```
<uses-permission android:name="android.permission.INTERNET"/>
```

8. Returning to the Earthquake List Fragment, create a new refreshEarthquakes method that connects to and parses the earthquake feed. Extract each earthquake and parse the details to obtain the date, magnitude, link, and location. As you finish parsing each earthquake, pass it in to a new addNewQuake method. Note that the addNewQuake method is executed within a Runnable posted from a Handler object. This allows you to execute the refreshEarthquakes method on a background thread before updating the UI within addNewQuake. This will be explored in more detail in Chapter 9.

```
private static final String TAG = "EARTHQUAKE";
private Handler handler = new Handler();

public void refreshEarthquakes() {
  // Get the XML
  URL url;
  try {
    String quakeFeed = getString(R.string.quake_feed);
    url = new URL(quakeFeed);

    URLConnection connection;
    connection = url.openConnection();

    HttpURLConnection httpConnection = (HttpURLConnection)connection;
    int responseCode = httpConnection.getResponseCode();
```

```java
if (responseCode == HttpURLConnection.HTTP_OK) {
  InputStream in = httpConnection.getInputStream();

  DocumentBuilderFactory dbf = DocumentBuilderFactory.newInstance();
  DocumentBuilder db = dbf.newDocumentBuilder();

  // Parse the earthquake feed.
  Document dom = db.parse(in);
  Element docEle = dom.getDocumentElement();

  // Clear the old earthquakes
  earthquakes.clear();

  // Get a list of each earthquake entry.
  NodeList nl = docEle.getElementsByTagName("entry");
  if (nl != null && nl.getLength() > 0) {
    for (int i = 0 ; i < nl.getLength(); i++) {
      Element entry = (Element)nl.item(i);
      Element title = (Element)entry.getElementsByTagName("title").item(0);
      Element g = (Element)entry.getElementsByTagName("georss:point").item(0);
      Element when = (Element)entry.getElementsByTagName("updated").item(0);
      Element link = (Element)entry.getElementsByTagName("link").item(0);

      String details = title.getFirstChild().getNodeValue();
      String hostname = "http://earthquake.usgs.gov";
      String linkString = hostname + link.getAttribute("href");

      String point = g.getFirstChild().getNodeValue();
      String dt = when.getFirstChild().getNodeValue();
      SimpleDateFormat sdf = new SimpleDateFormat("yyyy-MM-dd'T'hh:mm:ss'Z'");
      Date qdate = new GregorianCalendar(0,0,0).getTime();
      try {
        qdate = sdf.parse(dt);
      } catch (ParseException e) {
        Log.d(TAG, "Date parsing exception.", e);
      }

      String[] location = point.split(" ");
      Location l = new Location("dummyGPS");
      l.setLatitude(Double.parseDouble(location[0]));
      l.setLongitude(Double.parseDouble(location[1]));

      String magnitudeString = details.split(" ")[1];
      int end =  magnitudeString.length()-1;
      double magnitude = Double.parseDouble(magnitudeString.substring(0, end));

      details = details.split(",")[1].trim();

      final Quake quake = new Quake(qdate, details, l, magnitude, linkString);

      // Process a newly found earthquake
      handler.post(new Runnable() {
        public void run() {
```

```
          addNewQuake(quake);
        }
      });
    }
  }
}
} catch (MalformedURLException e) {
  Log.d(TAG, "MalformedURLException");
} catch (IOException e) {
  Log.d(TAG, "IOException");
} catch (ParserConfigurationException e) {
  Log.d(TAG, "Parser Configuration Exception");
} catch (SAXException e) {
  Log.d(TAG, "SAX Exception");
}
finally {
}
}

private void addNewQuake(Quake _quake) {
  // TODO Add the earthquakes to the array list.
}
```

9. Update the `addNewQuake` method so that it takes each newly processed quake and adds it to the earthquake Array List. It should also notify the Array Adapter that the underlying data has changed.

```
private void addNewQuake(Quake _quake) {
  // Add the new quake to our list of earthquakes.
  earthquakes.add(_quake);

  // Notify the array adapter of a change.
  aa.notifyDataSetChanged();
}
```

10. Modify your `onActivityCreated` method to call `refreshEarthquakes` on startup. Network operations should always be performed in a background thread — a requirement that is enforced in API level 11 onwards.

```
@Override
public void onActivityCreated(Bundle savedInstanceState) {
  super.onActivityCreated(savedInstanceState);

  int layoutID = android.R.layout.simple_list_item_1;
  aa = new ArrayAdapter<Quake>(getActivity(), layoutID , earthquakes);
  setListAdapter(aa);

  Thread t = new Thread(new Runnable() {
    public void run() {
      refreshEarthquakes();
    }
  });
  t.start();
}
```

> *If your application is targeting API level 11 or above, attempting to perform network operations on the main UI thread will cause a* `NetworkOnMainThreadException`. *In this example a simple Thread is used to post the* `refreshEarthquakes` *method on a background thread.*
>
> *This will be explored in more detail in Chapter 9, where you will learn more technique for moving expensive or time-consuming operations like this into a Service and onto background threads.*

11.　When you run your project, you should see a List View that features the earthquakes from the last 24 hours with a magnitude greater than 2.5 (Figure 6-1).

FIGURE 6-1

> *All code snippets in this example are part of the* Chapter 6 Earthquake *project, available for download at* www.wrox.com.

USING THE DOWNLOAD MANAGER

The Download Manager was introduced in Android 2.3 (API level 9) as a Service to optimize the handling of long-running downloads. The Download Manager handles the HTTP connection and monitors connectivity changes and system reboots to ensure each download completes successfully.

It's good practice to use the Download Manager in most situations, particularly where a download is likely to continue in the background between user sessions, or when successful completion is important.

To access the Download Manager, request the DOWNLOAD_SERVICE using the getSystemService method, as follows:

```
String serviceString = Context.DOWNLOAD_SERVICE;
DownloadManager downloadManager;
downloadManager = (DownloadManager)getSystemService(serviceString);
```

Downloading Files

To request a download, create a new DownloadManager.Request, specifying the URI of the file to download and passing it in to the Download Manager's enqueue method, as shown in Listing 6-3.

LISTING 6-3: Downloading files using the Download Manager

```
String serviceString = Context.DOWNLOAD_SERVICE;
DownloadManager downloadManager;
downloadManager = (DownloadManager)getSystemService(serviceString);

Uri uri = Uri.parse("http://developer.android.com/shareables/icon_templates-v4.0.zip");
DownloadManager.Request request = new Request(uri);
long reference = downloadManager.enqueue(request);
```

code snippet PA4AD_ Ch6_DownloadManager/src/MyActivity.java

You can use the returned reference value to perform future actions or queries on the download, including checking its status or canceling it.

You can add an HTTP header to your request, or override the mime type returned by the server, by calling addRequestHeader and setMimeType, respectively, on your Request object.

You can also specify the connectivity conditions under which to execute the download. The setAllowedNetworkTypes method enables you to restrict downloads to either Wi-Fi or mobile networks, whereas the setAllowedOverRoaming method predictably enables you to prevent downloads while the phone is roaming.

The following snippet shows how to ensure a large file is downloaded only when connected to Wi-Fi:

```
request.setAllowedNetworkTypes(Request.NETWORK_WIFI);
```

Android API level 11 introduced the getRecommendedMaxBytesOverMobile convenience method, which is useful to determine if you should restrict a download to Wi-Fi by returning a recommended maximum number of bytes to transfer over a mobile data connection.

After calling enqueue, the download begins as soon as connectivity is available and the Download Manager is free.

To receive a notification when the download is completed, register a Receiver to receive an ACTION_ DOWNLOAD_COMPLETE broadcast. It will include an EXTRA_DOWNLOAD_ID extra that contains the reference ID of the download that has completed, as shown in Listing 6-4.

LISTING 6-4: Monitoring downloads for completion

```java
IntentFilter filter = new IntentFilter(DownloadManager.ACTION_DOWNLOAD_COMPLETE);

BroadcastReceiver receiver = new BroadcastReceiver() {
  @Override
  public void onReceive(Context context, Intent intent) {
    long reference = intent.getLongExtra(DownloadManager.EXTRA_DOWNLOAD_ID, -1);
    if (myDownloadReference == reference) {
      // Do something with downloaded file.
    }
  }
};

registerReceiver(receiver, filter);
```

code snippet PA4AD_ Ch6_DownloadManager/src/MyActivity.java

You can use Download Manager's openDownloadedFile method to receive a Parcel File Descriptor to your file, to query the Download Manager to obtain its location, or to manipulate it directly if you've specified a filename and location yourself.

It's also good practice to register a Receiver for the ACTION_NOTIFICATION_CLICKED action, as shown in Listing 6-5. This Intent will be broadcast whenever a user selects a download from the Notification tray or the Downloads app.

LISTING 6-5: Responding to download notification clicks

```java
IntentFilter filter = new IntentFilter(DownloadManager.ACTION_NOTIFICATION_CLICKED);

BroadcastReceiver receiver = new BroadcastReceiver() {
  @Override
  public void onReceive(Context context, Intent intent) {
    String extraID = DownloadManager.EXTRA_NOTIFICATION_CLICK_DOWNLOAD_IDS;
    long[] references = intent.getLongArrayExtra(extraID);
    for (long reference : references)
      if (reference == myDownloadReference) {
        // Do something with downloading file.
      }
  }
};

registerReceiver(receiver, filter);
```

code snippet PA4AD_ Ch6_DownloadManager/src/MyActivity.java

Customizing Download Manager Notifications

By default, ongoing Notifications will be displayed for each download managed by the Download Manager. Each Notification will show the current download progress and the filename (Figure 6-2).

FIGURE 6-2

The Download Manager enables you to customize the Notification displayed for each download request, including hiding it completely. The following snippet shows how to use the `setTitle` and `setDescription` methods to customize the text displayed in the file download Notification. Figure 6-3 shows the result.

```
request.setTitle("Earthquakes");
request.setDescription("Earthquake XML");
```

FIGURE 6-3

The `setNotificationVisibility` method lets you control when, and if, a Notification should be displayed for your request using one of the following flags:

➤ `Request.VISIBILITY_VISIBLE` — An ongoing Notification will be visible for the duration that the download is in progress. It will be removed when the download is complete. This is the default option.

➤ `Request.VISIBILITY_VISIBLE_NOTIFY_COMPLETED` — An ongoing Notification will be displayed during the download and will continue to be displayed (until selected or dismissed) once the download has completed.

➤ `Request.VISIBILITY_VISIBLE_NOTIFY_ONLY_COMPLETION` — The notification will be displayed only after the download is complete.

➤ `Request.VISIBILITY_HIDDEN` — No Notification will be displayed for this download. In order to set this flag, your application must have the `DOWNLOAD_WITHOUT_NOTIFICATION` uses-permission specified in its manifest.

> *You will learn more about creating your own custom Notifications in Chapter 9.*

Specifying a Download Location

By default, all Download Manager downloads are saved to the shared download cache using system-generated filenames. Each Request object can specify a download location, though all downloads

must be stored somewhere on external storage and the calling application must have the WRITE_
EXTERNAL_STORAGE uses-permission in its manifest:

```
<uses-permission android:name="android.permission.WRITE_EXTERNAL_STORAGE"/>
```

The following code snippet shows how to specify an arbitrary path on external storage:

```
request.setDestinationUri(Uri.fromFile(f));
```

If the downloaded file is to your application, you may want to place it in your application's external
storage folder. Note that access control is not applied to this folder, and other applications will be
able to access it. If your application is uninstalled, files stored in these folders will also be removed.

The following snippet specifies storing a file in your application's external downloads folder:

```
request.setDestinationInExternalFilesDir(this,
    Environment.DIRECTORY_DOWNLOADS, "Bugdroid.png");
```

For files that can or should be shared with other applications — particularly those you want to scan
with the Media Scanner — you can specify a folder within the public folder on the external storage.
The following snippet requests a file be stored in the public music folder:

```
request.setDestinationInExternalPublicDir(Environment.DIRECTORY_MUSIC,
    "Android_Rock.mp3");
```

> *See Chapter 7, "Files, Saving State, and Preferences," for more details about
> external storage and the Environment static variables you can use to specify
> folders within it.*

It's important to note that by default files downloaded by the Download Manager are not scanned
by Media Scanner, so they might not appear in apps such as Gallery and Music Player.

To make downloaded files scannable, call allowScaningByMediaScanner on the Request object.

If you want your files to be visible and manageable by the system's Downloads app, you need to call
setVisibleInDownloadsUi, passing in true.

Cancelling and Removing Downloads

The Download Manager's remove method lets you cancel a pending download, abort a download in
progress, or delete a completed download.

As shown in the following code snippet, the remove method accepts download IDs as optional arguments, enabling you to specify one or many downloads to cancel:

```
downloadManager.remove(REFERENCE_1, REFERENCE_2, REFERENCE_3);
```

It returns the number of downloads successfully canceled. If a download is canceled, all associated
files — both partial and complete — are removed.

Querying the Download Manager

You can query the Download Manager to find the status, progress, and details of your download requests by using the query method that returns a Cursor of downloads.

> *Cursors are a data construct used by Android to return data stored in a Content Provider or SQLite database. You will learn more about Content Providers, Cursors, and how to find data stored in them in Chapter 8, "Databases and Content Providers."*

The query method takes a DownloadManager.Query object as a parameter. Use the setFilterById method on a Query object to specify a sequence of download reference IDs, or use the setFilterByStatus method to filter on a download status using one of the DownloadManager .STATUS_* constants to specify running, paused, failed, or successful downloads.

The Download Manager includes a number of COLUMN_* static String constants that you can use to query the result Cursor. You can find details for each download, including the status, files size, bytes downloaded so far, title, description, URI, local filename and URI, media type, and Media Provider download URI.

Listing 6-6 expands on Listing 6-4 to demonstrate how to find the local filename and URI of a completed downloads from within a Broadcast Receiver registered to listen for download completions.

LISTING 6-6: Finding details of completed downloads

```java
@Override
public void onReceive(Context context, Intent intent) {
    long reference = intent.getLongExtra(DownloadManager.EXTRA_DOWNLOAD_ID, -1);

    if (reference == myDownloadReference) {
        Query myDownloadQuery = new Query();
        myDownloadQuery.setFilterById(reference);

        Cursor myDownload = downloadManager.query(myDownloadQuery);
        if (myDownload.moveToFirst()) {
            int fileNameIdx =
                myDownload.getColumnIndex(DownloadManager.COLUMN_LOCAL_FILENAME);
            int fileUriIdx =
                myDownload.getColumnIndex(DownloadManager.COLUMN_LOCAL_URI);

            String fileName = myDownload.getString(fileNameIdx);
            String fileUri = myDownload.getString(fileUriIdx);

            // TODO Do something with the file.
        }
        myDownload.close();
    }
}
```

code snippet PA4AD_ Ch6_DownloadManager/src/MyActivity.java

For downloads that are either paused or have failed, you can query the COLUMN_REASON column to find the cause represented as an integer.

In the case of STATUS_PAUSED downloads, you can interpret the reason code by using one of the DownloadManager.PAUSED_* static constants to determine if the download has been paused while waiting for network connectivity, a Wi-Fi connection, or pending a retry.

For STATUS_FAILED downloads, you can determine the cause of failure using the DownloadManager.ERROR_* codes. Possible error codes include lack of a storage device, insufficient free space, duplicate filenames, or HTTP errors.

Listing 6-7 shows how to find a list of the currently paused downloads, extracting the reason the download was paused, the filename, its title, and the current progress.

LISTING 6-7: Finding details of paused downloads

```java
// Obtain the Download Manager Service.
String serviceString = Context.DOWNLOAD_SERVICE;
DownloadManager downloadManager;
downloadManager = (DownloadManager)getSystemService(serviceString);

// Create a query for paused downloads.
Query pausedDownloadQuery = new Query();
pausedDownloadQuery.setFilterByStatus(DownloadManager.STATUS_PAUSED);

// Query the Download Manager for paused downloads.
Cursor pausedDownloads = downloadManager.query(pausedDownloadQuery);

// Find the column indexes for the data we require.
int reasonIdx = pausedDownloads.getColumnIndex(DownloadManager.COLUMN_REASON);
int titleIdx = pausedDownloads.getColumnIndex(DownloadManager.COLUMN_TITLE);
int fileSizeIdx =
  pausedDownloads.getColumnIndex(DownloadManager.COLUMN_TOTAL_SIZE_BYTES);
int bytesDLIdx =
  pausedDownloads.getColumnIndex(DownloadManager.COLUMN_BYTES_DOWNLOADED_SO_FAR);

// Iterate over the result Cursor.
while (pausedDownloads.moveToNext()) {
  // Extract the data we require from the Cursor.
  String title = pausedDownloads.getString(titleIdx);
  int fileSize = pausedDownloads.getInt(fileSizeIdx);
  int bytesDL = pausedDownloads.getInt(bytesDLIdx);

  // Translate the pause reason to friendly text.
  int reason = pausedDownloads.getInt(reasonIdx);
  String reasonString = "Unknown";
  switch (reason) {
    case DownloadManager.PAUSED_QUEUED_FOR_WIFI :
      reasonString = "Waiting for WiFi"; break;
    case DownloadManager.PAUSED_WAITING_FOR_NETWORK :
      reasonString = "Waiting for connectivity"; break;
    case DownloadManager.PAUSED_WAITING_TO_RETRY :
```

```
        reasonString = "Waiting to retry"; break;
      default : break;
  }

  // Construct a status summary
  StringBuilder sb = new StringBuilder();
  sb.append(title).append("\n");
  sb.append(reasonString).append("\n");
  sb.append("Downloaded ").append(bytesDL).append(" / " ).append(fileSize);

  // Display the status
  Log.d("DOWNLOAD", sb.toString());
}

// Close the result Cursor.
pausedDownloads.close();
```

code snippet PA4AD_ Ch6_DownloadManager/src/MyActivity.java

USING INTERNET SERVICES

Software as a service (SaaS) and *cloud computing* are becoming increasingly popular as companies try to reduce the cost overheads associated with installing, upgrading, and maintaining deployed software. The result is a range of rich Internet services with which you can build thin mobile applications that enrich online services with the personalization available from your smartphone or tablet.

The idea of using a middle tier to reduce client-side load is not a novel one, and happily there are many Internet-based options to supply your applications with the level of service you need.

The sheer volume of Internet services available makes it impossible to list them all here (let alone look at them in any detail), but the following list shows some of the more mature and interesting Internet services currently available.

➤ **Google Services APIs** — In addition to the native Google applications, Google offers web APIs for access to their Calendar, Docs, Blogger, and Picasa Web Albums platforms. These APIs collectively make use of a form of XML for data communication.

➤ **Yahoo! Pipes** — Yahoo! Pipes offers a graphical web-based approach to XML feed manipulation. Using pipes, you can filter, aggregate, analyze, and otherwise manipulate XML feeds and output them in a variety of formats to be consumed by your applications.

➤ **Google App Engine** — Using the Google App Engine, you can create cloud-hosted web services that shift complex processing away from your mobile client. Doing so reduces the load on your system resources but comes at the price of Internet-connection dependency. Google also offers Cloud Storage and Prediction API services.

➤ **Amazon Web Services** — Amazon offers a range of cloud-based services, including a rich API for accessing its media database of books, CDs, and DVDs. Amazon also offers a distributed storage solution (S3) and Elastic Compute Cloud (EC2).

CONNECTING TO GOOGLE APP ENGINE

To use the Google Play Store, users must be signed in to a Google account on their phones; therefore, if your application connects to a Google App Engine backend to store and retrieve data related to a particular user, you can use the Account Manager to handle the authentication.

The Account Manager enables you to ask users for permission to retrieve an authentication token, which, in turn, can be used to obtain a cookie from your server that can then be used to make future authenticated requests.

To retrieve accounts and authentication tokens from the Account Manager, your application requires the GET_ACCOUNTS uses-permission:

```
<uses-permission android:name="android.permission.GET_ACCOUNTS"/>
```

Making authenticated Google App Engine requests is a three-part process:

1. Request an auth token.

2. Use the auth token to request an auth cookie.

3. Use the auth cookie to make authenticated requests.

Listing 6-8 demonstrates how to request an auth token for Google accounts using the Account Manager.

LISTING 6-8: Requesting an auth token

```java
String acctSvc = Context.ACCOUNT_SERVICE;
AccountManager accountManager = (AccountManager)getSystemService(acctSvc);

Account[] accounts = accountManager.getAccountsByType("com.google");

if (accounts.length > 0)
  accountManager.getAuthToken(accounts[0], "ah", false,
                              myAccountManagerCallback, null);
```

code snippet PA4AD_Ch6_AppEngine/src/MyActivity.java

The Account Manager then checks to see if the user has approved your request for an auth token. The result is returned to your application via the Account Manager Callback you specified when making the request.

In the following extension to Listing 6-8, the returned bundle is inspected for an Intent stored against the AccountManager.KEY_INTENT key. If this key's value is null, the user has approved your application's request, and you can retrieve the auth token from the bundle.

```java
private static int ASK_PERMISSION = 1;

private class GetAuthTokenCB implements AccountManagerCallback<Bundle> {
  public void run(AccountManagerFuture<Bundle> result) {
    try {
      Bundle bundle = result.getResult();
      Intent launch = (Intent)bundle.get(AccountManager.KEY_INTENT);
      if (launch != null)
```

```
            startActivityForResult(launch, ASK_PERMISSION);
        else {
          // Extract the auth token and request an auth cookie.
        }
      }
    catch (Exception ex) {}
  }
};
```

If the key's value is not null, you must start a new Activity using the bundled Intent to request the user's permission. The user will be prompted to approve or deny your request. After control has been passed back to your application, you should request the auth token again.

The auth token is stored within the Bundle parameter against the `AccountManager.KEY_AUTHTOKEN`, as follows:

```
String auth_token = bundle.getString(AccountManager.KEY_AUTHTOKEN);
```

You can use this token to request an auth cookie from Google App Engine by configuring an `httpClient` and using it to transmit an `HttpGet` request, as follows:

```
DefaultHttpClient http_client = new DefaultHttpClient();
http_client.getParams().setBooleanParameter(ClientPNames.HANDLE_REDIRECTS, false);

String getString = "https://[yourappsubdomain].appspot.com/_ah/login?" +
                   "continue=http://localhost/&auth=" +
                   auth_token;
HttpGet get = new HttpGet(getString);

HttpResponse response = http_client.execute(get);
```

If the request was successful, simply iterate over the Cookies stored in the HTTP Client's Cookie Store to confirm the auth cookie has been set. The HTTP Client used to make the request has the authenticated cookie, and all future requests to Google App Engine using it will be properly authenticated.

```
if (response.getStatusLine().getStatusCode() != 302)
  return false;
else {
  for (Cookie cookie : http_client.getCookieStore().getCookies())
    if (cookie.getName().equals("ACSID")) {
      // Make authenticated requests to your Google App Engine server.
    }
}
```

BEST PRACTICES FOR DOWNLOADING DATA WITHOUT DRAINING THE BATTERY

The timing and techniques you use to download data can have a significant effect on battery life. The wireless radio on mobile devices draws significant power when active, so it's important to consider how your application's connectivity model may impact the operation of the underlying radio hardware.

Every time you create a new connection to download additional data, you risk waking the wireless radio from standby mode to active mode. In general, it's good practice to bundle your connections and associated downloads to perform them concurrently and infrequently.

To use a converse example, creating frequent, short-lived connections that download small amounts of data can have the most dramatic impact on the battery.

You can use the following techniques to minimize your application's battery cost.

➤ **Aggressively prefetch** — The more data you download in a single connection, the less frequently the radio will need to be powered up to download more data. This will need to be balanced with downloading too much data that won't be used.

➤ **Bundle your connections and downloads** — Rather than sending time-insensitive data such as analytics as they're received, bundle them together and schedule them to transmit concurrently with other connections, such as when refreshing content or prefetching data. Remember, each new connection has the potential of powering up the radio.

➤ **Reuse existing connections rather than creating new ones** — Using existing connections rather than initiating new ones for each transfer can dramatically improve network performance, reduce latency, and allow the network to intelligently react to congestion and related issues

➤ **Schedule repeated downloads as infrequently as possible** — It's good practice to set the default refresh frequency to as low as usability will allow, rather than as fast as possible. For users who require their updates to be more frequent, provide preferences that allow them to sacrifice battery life in exchange for freshness.

7

Files, Saving State, and Preferences

WHAT'S IN THIS CHAPTER?

➤ Persisting simple application data using Shared Preferences

➤ Saving Activity instance data between sessions

➤ Managing application preferences and building Preference Screens

➤ Saving and loading files and managing the local filesystem

➤ Including static files as external resources

This chapter introduces some of the simplest and most versatile data-persistence techniques in Android: Shared Preferences, instance-state Bundles, and local files.

Saving and loading data is essential for most applications. At a minimum, an Activity should save its user interface (UI) state before it becomes inactive to ensure the same UI is presented when it restarts. It's also likely that you'll need to save user preferences and UI selections.

Android's nondeterministic Activity and application lifetimes make persisting UI state and application data between sessions particularly important, as your application process may have been killed and restarted before it returns to the foreground. Android offers several alternatives for saving application data, each optimized to fulfill a particular need.

Shared Preferences are a simple, lightweight name/value pair (NVP) mechanism for saving primitive application data, most commonly a user's application preferences. Android also offers a mechanism for recording application state within the Activity lifecycle handlers, as well as for providing access to the local filesystem, through both specialized methods and the `java.io` classes.

Android also offers a rich framework for user preferences, allowing you to create settings screens consistent with the system settings.

SAVING SIMPLE APPLICATION DATA

The data-persistence techniques in Android provide options for balancing speed, efficiency, and robustness.

➤ **Shared Preferences** — When storing UI state, user preferences, or application settings, you want a lightweight mechanism to store a known set of values. Shared Preferences let you save groups of name/value pairs of primitive data as named preferences.

➤ **Saved application UI state** — Activities and Fragments include specialized event handlers to record the current UI state when your application is moved to the background.

➤ **Files** — It's not pretty, but sometimes writing to and reading from files is the only way to go. Android lets you create and load files on the device's internal or external media, providing support for temporary caches and storing files in publicly accessible folders.

There are two lightweight techniques for saving simple application data for Android applications: Shared Preferences and a set of event handlers used for saving Activity instance state. Both mechanisms use an NVP mechanism to store simple primitive values. Both techniques support primitive types Boolean, string, float, long, and integer, making them ideal means of quickly storing default values, class instance variables, the current UI state, and user preferences.

CREATING AND SAVING SHARED PREFERENCES

Using the `SharedPreferences` class, you can create named maps of name/value pairs that can be persisted across sessions and shared among application components running within the same application sandbox.

To create or modify a Shared Preference, call `getSharedPreferences` on the current Context, passing in the name of the Shared Preference to change.

```
SharedPreferences mySharedPreferences = getSharedPreferences(MY_PREFS,
                                  Activity.MODE_PRIVATE);
```

Shared Preferences are stored within the application's sandbox, so they can be shared between an application's components but aren't available to other applications.

To modify a Shared Preference, use the `SharedPreferences.Editor` class. Get the Editor object by calling `edit` on the Shared Preferences object you want to change.

```
SharedPreferences.Editor editor = mySharedPreferences.edit();
```

Use the `put<type>` methods to insert or update the values associated with the specified name:

```
// Store new primitive types in the shared preferences object.
editor.putBoolean("isTrue", true);
editor.putFloat("lastFloat", 1f);
editor.putInt("wholeNumber", 2);
editor.putLong("aNumber", 31);
editor.putString("textEntryValue", "Not Empty");
```

To save edits, call `apply` or `commit` on the Editor object to save the changes asynchronously or synchronously, respectively.

```
// Commit the changes.
editor.apply();
```

> *The `apply` method was introduced in Android API level 9 (Android 2.3). Calling it causes a safe asynchronous write of the Shared Preference Editor object to be performed. Because it is asynchronous, it is the preferred technique for saving Shared Preferences.*
>
> *If you require confirmation of success or want to support earlier Android releases, you can call the `commit` method, which blocks the calling thread and returns `true` once a successful write has completed, or `false` otherwise.*

RETRIEVING SHARED PREFERENCES

Accessing Shared Preferences, like editing and saving them, is done using the `getSharedPreferences` method.

Use the type-safe `get<type>` methods to extract saved values. Each getter takes a key and a default value (used when no value has yet been saved for that key.)

```
// Retrieve the saved values.
boolean isTrue = mySharedPreferences.getBoolean("isTrue", false);
float lastFloat = mySharedPreferences.getFloat("lastFloat", 0f);
int wholeNumber = mySharedPreferences.getInt("wholeNumber", 1);
long aNumber = mySharedPreferences.getLong("aNumber", 0);
String stringPreference =
  mySharedPreferences.getString("textEntryValue", "");
```

You can return a map of all the available Shared Preferences keys values by calling `getAll`, and check for the existence of a particular key by calling the `contains` method.

```
Map<String, ?> allPreferences = mySharedPreferences.getAll();
boolean containsLastFloat = mySharedPreferences.contains("lastFloat");
```

CREATING A SETTINGS ACTIVITY FOR THE EARTHQUAKE VIEWER

In the following example you build an Activity to set application preferences for the earthquake viewer last seen in the previous chapter. The Activity lets users configure settings for a more personalized experience. You'll provide the option to toggle automatic updates, control the frequency of updates, and filter the minimum earthquake magnitude displayed.

> *Creating your own Activity to control user preferences is considered bad prac-
> tice. Later in this chapter you'll replace this Activity with a standard settings
> screen using the Preferences Screen classes.*

1. Open the Earthquake project you created in Chapter 6, "Using Internet Resources." Add
    new string resources to the `res/values/strings.xml` file for the labels to be displayed in
    the Preference Screen. Also, add a string for the new Menu Item that will let users open the
    Preference Screen:

```xml
<?xml version="1.0" encoding="utf-8"?>
<resources>
  <string name="app_name">Earthquake</string>
  <string name="quake_feed">
    http://earthquake.usgs.gov/eqcenter/catalogs/1day-M2.5.xml
  </string>
  <string name="menu_update">Refresh Earthquakes</string>
  <string name="auto_update_prompt">Auto Update?</string>
  <string name="update_freq_prompt">Update Frequency</string>
  <string name="min_quake_mag_prompt">Minimum Quake Magnitude</string>
  <string name="menu_preferences">Preferences</string>
</resources>
```

2. Create a new `preferences.xml` layout resource in the `res/layout` folder for the
    `Preferences` Activity. Include a check box for indicating the "automatic update" toggle,
    and spinners to select the update rate and magnitude filter:

```xml
<?xml version="1.0" encoding="utf-8"?>
<LinearLayout xmlns:android="http://schemas.android.com/apk/res/android"
    android:orientation="vertical"
    android:layout_width="fill_parent"
    android:layout_height="fill_parent">
  <TextView
    android:layout_width="fill_parent"
    android:layout_height="wrap_content"
    android:text="@string/auto_update_prompt"
  />
  <CheckBox android:id="@+id/checkbox_auto_update"
    android:layout_width="fill_parent"
    android:layout_height="wrap_content"
  />
  <TextView
    android:layout_width="fill_parent"
    android:layout_height="wrap_content"
    android:text="@string/update_freq_prompt"
  />
  <Spinner android:id="@+id/spinner_update_freq"
    android:layout_width="fill_parent"
    android:layout_height="wrap_content"
    android:drawSelectorOnTop="true"
  />
```

```xml
<TextView
  android:layout_width="fill_parent"
  android:layout_height="wrap_content"
  android:text="@string/min_quake_mag_prompt"
/>
<Spinner android:id="@+id/spinner_quake_mag"
  android:layout_width="fill_parent"
  android:layout_height="wrap_content"
  android:drawSelectorOnTop="true"
/>
<LinearLayout
  android:orientation="horizontal"
  android:layout_width="fill_parent"
  android:layout_height="wrap_content">
  <Button android:id="@+id/okButton"
    android:layout_width="wrap_content"
    android:layout_height="wrap_content"
    android:text="@android:string/ok"
  />
  <Button android:id="@+id/cancelButton"
    android:layout_width="wrap_content"
    android:layout_height="wrap_content"
    android:text="@android:string/cancel"
  />
</LinearLayout>
</LinearLayout>
```

3. Create four array resources in a new `res/values/arrays.xml` file. They will provide the values to use for the update frequency and minimum magnitude spinners:

```xml
<?xml version="1.0" encoding="utf-8"?>
<resources>
  <string-array name="update_freq_options">
    <item>Every Minute</item>
    <item>5 minutes</item>
    <item>10 minutes</item>
    <item>15 minutes</item>
    <item>Every Hour</item>
  </string-array>

  <string-array name="magnitude">
    <item>3</item>
    <item>5</item>
    <item>6</item>
    <item>7</item>
    <item>8</item>
  </string-array>

  <string-array name="magnitude_options">
    <item>3</item>
    <item>5</item>
    <item>6</item>
    <item>7</item>
    <item>8</item>
  </string-array>
```

```
     <string-array name="update_freq_values">
       <item>1</item>
       <item>5</item>
       <item>10</item>
       <item>15</item>
       <item>60</item>
     </string-array>
   </resources>
```

4. Create a `PreferencesActivity` Activity. Override `onCreate` to inflate the layout you created in step 2, and get references to the check box and both the spinner controls. Then make a call to the `populateSpinners` stub:

```java
package com.paad.earthquake;

import android.app.Activity;
import android.content.Context;
import android.content.SharedPreferences;
import android.content.SharedPreferences.Editor;
import android.os.Bundle;
import android.preference.PreferenceManager;
import android.view.View;
import android.widget.ArrayAdapter;
import android.widget.Button;
import android.widget.CheckBox;
import android.widget.Spinner;

public class PreferencesActivity extends Activity {

  CheckBox autoUpdate;
  Spinner updateFreqSpinner;
  Spinner magnitudeSpinner;

  @Override
  public void onCreate(Bundle savedInstanceState) {
    super.onCreate(savedInstanceState);
    setContentView(R.layout.preferences);

    updateFreqSpinner = (Spinner)findViewById(R.id.spinner_update_freq);
    magnitudeSpinner = (Spinner)findViewById(R.id.spinner_quake_mag);
    autoUpdate = (CheckBox)findViewById(R.id.checkbox_auto_update);

    populateSpinners();
  }

  private void populateSpinners() {
  }
}
```

5. Fill in the `populateSpinners` method, using Array Adapters to bind each spinner to its corresponding array:

```java
private void populateSpinners() {
  // Populate the update frequency spinner
```

```
  ArrayAdapter<CharSequence> fAdapter;
  fAdapter = ArrayAdapter.createFromResource(this, R.array.update_freq_options,
    android.R.layout.simple_spinner_item);
  int spinner_dd_item = android.R.layout.simple_spinner_dropdown_item;
  fAdapter.setDropDownViewResource(spinner_dd_item);
  updateFreqSpinner.setAdapter(fAdapter);
  // Populate the minimum magnitude spinner
  ArrayAdapter<CharSequence> mAdapter;
  mAdapter = ArrayAdapter.createFromResource(this,
    R.array.magnitude_options,
    android.R.layout.simple_spinner_item);
  mAdapter.setDropDownViewResource(spinner_dd_item);
  magnitudeSpinner.setAdapter(mAdapter);
}
```

6.   Add public static string values that you'll use to identify the Shared Preference keys you'll use to store each preference value. Update the onCreate method to retrieve the named preference and call updateUIFromPreferences. The updateUIFromPreferences method uses the get<type> methods on the Shared Preference object to retrieve each preference value and apply it to the current UI.

Use the default application Shared Preference object to save your settings values:

```
public static final String USER_PREFERENCE = "USER_PREFERENCE";
public static final String PREF_AUTO_UPDATE = "PREF_AUTO_UPDATE";
public static final String PREF_MIN_MAG_INDEX = "PREF_MIN_MAG_INDEX";
public static final String PREF_UPDATE_FREQ_INDEX = "PREF_UPDATE_FREQ_INDEX";

SharedPreferences prefs;

@Override
public void onCreate(Bundle savedInstanceState) {
  super.onCreate(savedInstanceState);
  setContentView(R.layout.preferences);

  updateFreqSpinner = (Spinner)findViewById(R.id.spinner_update_freq);
  magnitudeSpinner = (Spinner)findViewById(R.id.spinner_quake_mag);
  autoUpdate = (CheckBox)findViewById(R.id.checkbox_auto_update);

  populateSpinners();

  Context context = getApplicationContext();
  prefs = PreferenceManager.getDefaultSharedPreferences(context);
  updateUIFromPreferences();
}

private void updateUIFromPreferences() {
  boolean autoUpChecked = prefs.getBoolean(PREF_AUTO_UPDATE, false);
  int updateFreqIndex = prefs.getInt(PREF_UPDATE_FREQ_INDEX, 2);
  int minMagIndex = prefs.getInt(PREF_MIN_MAG_INDEX, 0);

  updateFreqSpinner.setSelection(updateFreqIndex);
  magnitudeSpinner.setSelection(minMagIndex);
  autoUpdate.setChecked(autoUpChecked);
}
```

7. Still in the `onCreate` method, add event handlers for the OK and Cancel buttons. The Cancel button should close the Activity, whereas the OK button should call `savePreferences` first:

```
@Override
public void onCreate(Bundle savedInstanceState) {
  super.onCreate(savedInstanceState);
  setContentView(R.layout.preferences);
  updateFreqSpinner = (Spinner)findViewById(R.id.spinner_update_freq);
  magnitudeSpinner = (Spinner)findViewById(R.id.spinner_quake_mag);
  autoUpdate = (CheckBox)findViewById(R.id.checkbox_auto_update);

  populateSpinners();

  Context context = getApplicationContext();
  prefs = PreferenceManager.getDefaultSharedPreferences(context);
  updateUIFromPreferences();

  Button okButton = (Button) findViewById(R.id.okButton);
  okButton.setOnClickListener(new View.OnClickListener() {

    public void onClick(View view) {
      savePreferences();
      PreferencesActivity.this.setResult(RESULT_OK);
      finish();
    }
  });

  Button cancelButton = (Button) findViewById(R.id.cancelButton);
  cancelButton.setOnClickListener(new View.OnClickListener() {

    public void onClick(View view) {
      PreferencesActivity.this.setResult(RESULT_CANCELED);
      finish();
    }
  });
}

private void savePreferences() {
}
```

8. Fill in the `savePreferences` method to record the current preferences, based on the UI selections, to the Shared Preference object:

```
private void savePreferences() {
  int updateIndex = updateFreqSpinner.getSelectedItemPosition();
  int minMagIndex = magnitudeSpinner.getSelectedItemPosition();
  boolean autoUpdateChecked = autoUpdate.isChecked();

  Editor editor = prefs.edit();
  editor.putBoolean(PREF_AUTO_UPDATE, autoUpdateChecked);
  editor.putInt(PREF_UPDATE_FREQ_INDEX, updateIndex);
  editor.putInt(PREF_MIN_MAG_INDEX, minMagIndex);
  editor.commit();
}
```

9. That completes the `Preferences` Activity. Make it accessible in the application by adding it to the manifest:

```
<activity android:name=".PreferencesActivity"
        android:label="Earthquake Preferences">
</activity>
```

10. Return to the `Earthquake` Activity, and add support for the new Shared Preferences file and a Menu Item to display the Preferences Activity. Start by adding the new Menu Item. Override the `onCreateOptionsMenu` method to include a new item that opens the Preferences Activity and another to refresh the earthquake list:

```
static final private int MENU_PREFERENCES = Menu.FIRST+1;
static final private int MENU_UPDATE = Menu.FIRST+2;

@Override
public boolean onCreateOptionsMenu(Menu menu) {
  super.onCreateOptionsMenu(menu);

  menu.add(0, MENU_PREFERENCES, Menu.NONE, R.string.menu_preferences);

  return true;
}
```

11. Override the `onOptionsItemSelected` method to display the `PreferencesActivity` Activity when the new Menu Item is selected. To launch the Preferences Activity, create an explicit Intent, and pass it in to the `startActivityForResult` method. This will launch the Activity and alert the Earthquake class when the preferences are saved through the `onActivityResult` handler:

```
private static final int SHOW_PREFERENCES = 1;

public boolean onOptionsItemSelected(MenuItem item){
  super.onOptionsItemSelected(item);
  switch (item.getItemId()) {
    case (MENU_PREFERENCES): {
      Intent i = new Intent(this,
  PreferencesActivity.class);
      startActivityForResult(i, SHOW_PREFERENCES);
      return true;
    }
  }
  return false;
}
```

12. Launch your application and select Preferences from the Activity menu. The Preferences Activity should be displayed, as shown in Figure 7-1.

FIGURE 7-1

13. All that's left is to apply the preferences to the earthquake functionality. Implementing the automatic updates will be left until Chapter 9, "Working in the Background," where you'll learn to use Services and background threads. For now you can put the framework in place and apply the magnitude filter. Start by creating a new `updateFromPreferences` method in the Earthquake Activity that reads the Shared Preference values and creates instance variables for each of them:

```java
public int minimumMagnitude = 0;
public boolean autoUpdateChecked = false;
public int updateFreq = 0;

private void updateFromPreferences() {
  Context context = getApplicationContext();
  SharedPreferences prefs =
    PreferenceManager.getDefaultSharedPreferences(context);

  int minMagIndex = prefs.getInt(PreferencesActivity.PREF_MIN_MAG_INDEX, 0);
  if (minMagIndex < 0)
    minMagIndex = 0;

  int freqIndex = prefs.getInt(PreferencesActivity.PREF_UPDATE_FREQ_INDEX, 0);
  if (freqIndex < 0)
    freqIndex = 0;

  autoUpdateChecked = prefs.getBoolean(PreferencesActivity.PREF_AUTO_UPDATE, false);

  Resources r = getResources();
  // Get the option values from the arrays.
  String[] minMagValues = r.getStringArray(R.array.magnitude);
  String[] freqValues = r.getStringArray(R.array.update_freq_values);

  // Convert the values to ints.
  minimumMagnitude = Integer.valueOf(minMagValues[minMagIndex]);
  updateFreq = Integer.valueOf(freqValues[freqIndex]);
}
```

14. Apply the magnitude filter by updating the `addNewQuake` method from the `EarthquakeListFragment` to check a new earthquake's magnitude before adding it to the list:

```java
private void addNewQuake(Quake _quake) {
  Earthquake earthquakeActivity = (Earthquake)getActivity();
  if (_quake.getMagnitude() > earthquakeActivity.minimumMagnitude) {
    // Add the new quake to our list of earthquakes.
    earthquakes.add(_quake);

  }

  // Notify the array adapter of a change.
  aa.notifyDataSetChanged();
}
```

15. Return to the Earthquake Activity and override the `onActivityResult` handler to call `updateFromPreferences` and refresh the earthquakes whenever the `Preferences` Activity saves changes. Note that once again you are creating a new Thread on which to execute the earthquake refresh code.

```
@Override
public void onActivityResult(int requestCode, int resultCode, Intent data) {
  super.onActivityResult(requestCode, resultCode, data);

  if (requestCode == SHOW_PREFERENCES)
    if (resultCode == Activity.RESULT_OK) {
      updateFromPreferences();
      FragmentManager fm = getFragmentManager();
      final EarthquakeListFragment earthquakeList =

(EarthquakeListFragment)fm.findFragmentById(R.id.EarthquakeListFragment);

      Thread t = new Thread(new Runnable() {
        public void run() {
          earthquakeList.refreshEarthquakes();
        }
      });
      t.start();
    }
}
```

16. Finally, call `updateFromPreferences` in `onCreate` of the Earthquake Activity to ensure the preferences are applied when the Activity starts:

```
@Override
public void onCreate(Bundle savedInstanceState) {
  super.onCreate(savedInstanceState);
  setContentView(R.layout.main);

  updateFromPreferences();
}
```

> *All code snippets in this example are part of the* Chapter 7 Earthquake Part 1 *project, available for download at* www.wrox.com.

INTRODUCING THE PREFERENCE FRAMEWORK AND THE PREFERENCE ACTIVITY

Android offers an XML-driven framework to create system-style Preference Screens for your applications. By using this framework you can create Preference Activities that are consistent with those used in both native and other third-party applications.

This has two distinct advantages:

➤ Users will be familiar with the layout and use of your settings screens.

➤ You can integrate settings screens from other applications (including system settings such as location settings) into your application's preferences.

The preference framework consists of four parts:

➤ **Preference Screen layout** — An XML file that defines the hierarchy of items displayed in your Preference screens. It specifies the text and associated controls to display, the allowed values, and the Shared Preference keys to use for each control.

➤ **Preference Activity** and **Preference Fragment** — Extensions of `PreferenceActivity` and `PreferenceFragment` respectively, that are used to host the Preference Screens. Prior to Android 3.0, Preference Activities hosted the Preference Screen directly; since then, Preference Screens are hosted by Preference Fragments, which, in turn, are hosted by Preference Activities.

➤ **Preference Header definition** — An XML file that defines the Preference Fragments for your application and the hierarchy that should be used to display them.

➤ **Shared Preference Change Listener** — An implementation of the `OnSharedPreferenceChangeListener` class used to listen for changes to Shared Preferences.

> *Android API level 11 (Android 3.0) introduced significant changes to the preference framework by introducing the concept of Preference Fragments and Preference Headers. This is now the preferred technique for creating Activity Preference screens.*
>
> *As of the time of writing, Preference Fragments are not included in the support library, restricting their use to devices Android 3.0 and above.*
>
> *The following sections describe the best practice techniques for creating Activity screens for Android 3.0+ devices, making note of how to achieve similar functionality for older devices.*

Defining a Preference Screen Layout in XML

Unlike in the standard UI layout, preference definitions are stored in the `res/xml` resources folder.

Although conceptually they are similar to the UI layout resources described in Chapter 4, "Building User Interfaces," Preference Screen layouts use a specialized set of controls designed specifically for preferences. These native preference controls are described in the next section.

Each preference layout is defined as a hierarchy, beginning with a single `PreferenceScreen` element:

```
<?xml version="1.0" encoding="utf-8"?>
<PreferenceScreen
  xmlns:android="http://schemas.android.com/apk/res/android">
</PreferenceScreen>
```

You can include additional Preference Screen elements, each of which will be represented as a selectable element that will display a new screen when clicked.

Within each Preference Screen you can include any combination of `PreferenceCategory` and `Preference<control>` elements. Preference Category elements, as shown in the following snippet, are used to break each Preference Screen into subcategories using a title bar separator:

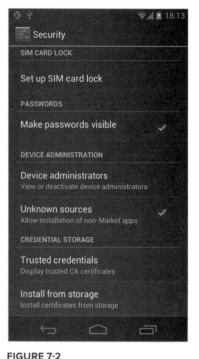

```
<PreferenceCategory
    android:title="My Preference Category"/>
```

Figure 7-2 shows the SIM card lock, device administration, and credential storage Preference Categories used on the Security Preference Screen.

All that remains is to add the preference controls that will be used to set the preferences. Although the specific attributes available for each preference control vary, each of them includes at least the following four:

> `android:key` — The Shared Preference key against which the selected value will be recorded.

> `android:title` — The text displayed to represent the preference.

> `android:summary` — The longer text description displayed in a smaller font below the title text.

FIGURE 7-2

> `android:defaultValue` — The default value that will be displayed (and selected) if no preference value has been assigned to the associated preference key.

Listing 7-1 shows a sample Preference Screen that includes a Preference Category and CheckBox Preference.

LISTING 7-1: A simple Shared Preferences screen

```xml
<?xml version="1.0" encoding="utf-8"?>
<PreferenceScreen
  xmlns:android="http://schemas.android.com/apk/res/android">
  <PreferenceCategory
    android:title="My Preference Category">
    <CheckBoxPreference
      android:key="PREF_CHECK_BOX"
      android:title="Check Box Preference"
      android:summary="Check Box Preference Description"
      android:defaultValue="true"
    />
  </PreferenceCategory>
</PreferenceScreen>
```

code snippet PA4AD_Ch07_Preferences/res/xml/userpreferences.xml

When displayed, this Preference Screen will appear as shown in Figure 7-3. You'll learn how to display a Preference Screen later in this chapter.

MY PREFERENCE CATEGORY

Check Box Preference ✓
Check Box Preference Description

FIGURE 7-3

Native Preference Controls

Android includes several preference controls to build your Preference Screens:

➤ `CheckBoxPreference` — A standard preference check box control used to set preferences to true or false.

➤ `EditTextPreference` — Allows users to enter a string value as a preference. Selecting the preference text at run time will display a text-entry dialog.

➤ `ListPreference` — The preference equivalent of a spinner. Selecting this preference will display a dialog box containing a list of values from which to select. You can specify different arrays to contain the display text and selection values.

➤ `MultiSelectListPreference` — Introduced in Android 3.0 (API level 11), this is the preference equivalent of a check box list.

➤ `RingtonePreference` — A specialized List Preference that presents the list of available ringtones for user selection. This is particularly useful when you're constructing a screen to configure notification settings.

You can use each preference control to construct your Preference Screen hierarchy. Alternatively, you can create your own specialized preference controls by extending the `Preference` class (or any of the subclasses listed above).

> *You can find further details about preference controls at* `http://developer` `.android.com/reference/android/preference/Preference.html`.

Using Intents to Import System Preferences into Preference Screens

In addition to including your own Preference Screens, preference hierarchies can include Preference Screens from other applications — including system preferences.

You can invoke any Activity within your Preference Screen using an Intent. If you add an Intent node within a Preference Screen element, the system will interpret this as a request to call `start Activity` using the specified action. The following XML snippet adds a link to the system display settings:

```
<?xml version="1.0" encoding="utf-8"?>
<PreferenceScreen xmlns:android="http://schemas.android.com/apk/res/android"
  android:title="Intent preference"
  android:summary="System preference imported using an intent">
```

```
    <intent android:action="android.settings.DISPLAY_SETTINGS "/>
  </PreferenceScreen>
```

The `android.provider.Settings` class includes a number of `android.settings.*` constants that can be used to invoke the system settings screens. To make your own Preference Screens available for invocation using this technique, simply add an Intent Filter to the manifest entry for the host Preference Activity (described in detail in the following section):

```
<activity android:name=".UserPreferences" android:label="My User Preferences">
  <intent-filter>
    <action android:name="com.paad.myapp.ACTION_USER_PREFERENCE" />
  </intent-filter>
</activity>
```

Introducing the Preference Fragment

Since Android 3.0, the `PreferenceFragment` class has been used to host the preference screens defined by Preferences Screen resources. To create a new Preference Fragment, extend the `PreferenceFragment` class, as follows:

```
public class MyPreferenceFragment extends PreferenceFragment
```

To inflate the preferences, override the `onCreate` handler and call `addPreferencesFromResource`, as shown here:

```
@Override
public void onCreate(Bundle savedInstanceState) {
  super.onCreate(savedInstanceState);
  addPreferencesFromResource(R.xml.userpreferences);
}
```

Your application can include several different Preference Fragments, which will be grouped according to the Preference Header hierarchy and displayed within a Preference Activity, as described in the following sections.

Defining the Preference Fragment Hierarchy Using Preference Headers

Preference headers are XML resources that describe how your Preference Fragments should be grouped and displayed within a Preference Activity. Each header identifies and allows you to select a particular Preference Fragment.

The layout used to display the headers and their associated Fragments can vary depending on the screen size and OS version. Figure 7-4 shows examples of how the same Preference Header definition is displayed on a phone and tablet.

Preference Headers are XML resources stored in the `res/xml` folder of your project hierarchy. The resource ID for each header is the filename (without extension).

FIGURE 7-4

Each header must be associated with a particular Preference Fragment that will be displayed when its header is selected. You must also specify a title and, optionally, a summary and icon resource to represent each Fragment and the Preference Screen it contains, as shown in Listing 7-2.

LISTING 7-2: Defining a Preference Headers resource

```xml
<preference-headers xmlns:android="http://schemas.android.com/apk/res/android">
  <header android:fragment="com.paad.preferences.MyPreferenceFragment"
          android:icon="@drawable/preference_icon"
          android:title="My Preferences"
          android:summary="Description of these preferences" />
</preference-headers>
```

code snippet PA4AD_Ch07_Preferences/res/xml/preferenceheaders.xml

Like Preference Screens, you can invoke any Activity within your Preference Headers using an Intent. If you add an Intent node within a header element, as shown in the following snippet, the system will interpret this as a request to call `startActivity` using the specified action:

```xml
<header android:icon="@drawable/ic_settings_display"
        android:title="Intent"
        android:summary="Launches an Intent.">
        <intent android:action="android.settings.DISPLAY_SETTINGS " />
</header>
```

Introducing the Preference Activity

The `PreferenceActivity` class is used to host the Preference Fragment hierarchy defined by a preference headers resource. Prior to Android 3.0, the Preference Activity was used to host Preference Screens directly. For applications that target devices prior to Android 3.0, you may still need to use the Preference Activity in this way.

To create a new Preference Activity, extend the `PreferenceActivity` class as follows:

```
public class MyFragmentPreferenceActivity extends PreferenceActivity
```

When using Preference Fragments and headers, override the `onBuildHeaders` handler, calling `load-HeadersFromResource` and specifying your preference headers resource file:

```
public void onBuildHeaders(List<Header> target) {
  loadHeadersFromResource(R.xml.userpreferenceheaders, target);
}
```

For legacy applications, you can inflate the Preference Screen directly in the same way as you would from a Preference Fragment — by overriding the `onCreate` handler and calling `add PreferencesFromResource`, specifying the Preference Screen layout XML resource to display within that Activity:

```
@Override
public void onCreate(Bundle savedInstanceState) {
  super.onCreate(savedInstanceState);
  addPreferencesFromResource(R.xml.userpreferences);
}
```

Like all Activities, the Preference Activity must be included in the application manifest:

```
<activity android:name=".MyPreferenceActivity"
          android:label="My Preferences">
</activity>
```

To display the application settings hosted in this Activity, open it by calling `startActivity` or `startActivityForResult`:

```
Intent i = new Intent(this, MyPreferenceActivity.class);
startActivityForResult(i, SHOW_PREFERENCES);
```

Backward Compatibility and Preference Screens

As noted earlier, the Preference Fragment and associated Preference Headers are not supported on Android platforms prior to Android 3.0 (API level 11). As a result, if you want to create applications that support devices running on both pre- and post-Honeycomb devices, you need to implement separate Preference Activities to support both, and launch the appropriate Activity at run time, as shown in Listing 7-3.

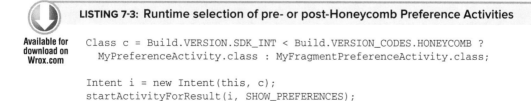

LISTING 7-3: Runtime selection of pre- or post-Honeycomb Preference Activities

```
Class c = Build.VERSION.SDK_INT < Build.VERSION_CODES.HONEYCOMB ?
  MyPreferenceActivity.class : MyFragmentPreferenceActivity.class;

Intent i = new Intent(this, c);
startActivityForResult(i, SHOW_PREFERENCES);
```

code snippet PA4AD Ch07_Preferences/src/MyActivity.java

Finding and Using the Shared Preferences Set by Preference Screens

The Shared Preference values recorded for the options presented in a Preference Activity are stored within the application's sandbox. This lets any application component, including Activities, Services, and Broadcast Receivers, access the values, as shown in the following snippet:

```
Context context = getApplicationContext();
SharedPreferences prefs = PreferenceManager.getDefaultSharedPreferences(context);
// TODO Retrieve values using get<type> methods.
```

Introducing On Shared Preference Change Listeners

The onSharedPreferenceChangeListener can be implemented to invoke a callback whenever a particular Shared Preference value is added, removed, or modified.

This is particularly useful for Activities and Services that use the Shared Preference framework to set application preferences. Using this handler, your application components can listen for changes to user preferences and update their UIs or behavior, as required.

Register your On Shared Preference Change Listeners using the Shared Preference you want to monitor:

```
public class MyActivity extends Activity implements
  OnSharedPreferenceChangeListener {

  @Override
  public void onCreate(Bundle savedInstanceState) {
    super.onCreate(savedInstanceState);

    // Register this OnSharedPreferenceChangeListener
    SharedPreferences prefs =
      PreferenceManager.getDefaultSharedPreferences(this);
    prefs.registerOnSharedPreferenceChangeListener(this);
  }

  public void onSharedPreferenceChanged(SharedPreferences prefs,
                                        String key) {
    // TODO Check the shared preference and key parameters
    // and change UI or behavior as appropriate.
  }
}
```

CREATING A STANDARD PREFERENCE ACTIVITY FOR THE EARTHQUAKE VIEWER

Previously in this chapter you created a custom Activity to let users modify the application settings for the earthquake viewer. In this example you replace this custom Activity with the standard application settings framework described in the previous section.

This example describes two ways of creating a Preference Activity — first, using the legacy PreferencesActivity, and then a backward-compatible alternative using the newer PreferenceFragment techniques.

1. Start by creating a new XML resource folder at res/xml. Within it create a new userpreferences.xml file. This file will define the settings UI for your earthquake application settings. Use the same controls and data sources as in the previous Activity, but this time create them using the standard application settings framework. Note that in this example difference key names are selected. This is because where you were previously recording integers, you're now recording strings. To avoid type mismatches when the application attempts to read the saved preferences, use a different key name.

```xml
<?xml version="1.0" encoding="utf-8"?>
<PreferenceScreen
  xmlns:android="http://schemas.android.com/apk/res/android">
  <CheckBoxPreference
    android:key="PREF_AUTO_UPDATE"
    android:title="Auto refresh"
    android:summary="Select to turn on automatic updating"
    android:defaultValue="true"
  />
  <ListPreference
   android:key="PREF_UPDATE_FREQ"
   android:title="Refresh frequency"
   android:summary="Frequency at which to refresh earthquake list"
   android:entries="@array/update_freq_options"
   android:entryValues="@array/update_freq_values"
   android:dialogTitle="Refresh frequency"
   android:defaultValue="60"
  />
  <ListPreference
    android:key="PREF_MIN_MAG"
    android:title="Minimum magnitude"
    android:summary="Select the minimum magnitude earthquake to report"
    android:entries="@array/magnitude_options"
    android:entryValues="@array/magnitude"
    android:dialogTitle="Magnitude"
    android:defaultValue="3"
  />
</PreferenceScreen>
```

2. Open the PreferencesActivity Activity and modify its inheritance to extend PreferenceActivity:

```
public class PreferencesActivity extends PreferenceActivity {
```

3. The Preference Activity will handle the controls used in the UI, so you can remove the variables used to store the check box and spinner objects. You can also remove the populateSpinners, updateUIFromPreferences, and savePreferences methods. Update the preference name strings to match those used in the user preferences definition in step 1.

```
public static final String PREF_MIN_MAG = "PREF_MIN_MAG";
public static final String PREF_UPDATE_FREQ = "PREF_UPDATE_FREQ";
```

4. Update `onCreate` by removing all the references to the UI controls and the OK and Cancel buttons. Instead of using these, inflate the `userpreferences.xml` file you created in step 1:

```
@Override
public void onCreate(Bundle savedInstanceState) {
  super.onCreate(savedInstanceState);
  addPreferencesFromResource(R.xml.userpreferences);
}
```

5. Open the Earthquake Activity and update the `updateFromPreferencesMethod`. Using this technique, the selected value itself is stored in the preferences, so there's no need to perform the array lookup steps.

```
private void updateFromPreferences() {
  Context context = getApplicationContext();
  SharedPreferences prefs =
    PreferenceManager.getDefaultSharedPreferences(context);

  minimumMagnitude =
    Integer.parseInt(prefs.getString(PreferencesActivity.PREF_MIN_MAG, "3"));
  updateFreq =
    Integer.parseInt(prefs.getString(PreferencesActivity.PREF_UPDATE_FREQ, "60"));

  autoUpdateChecked = prefs.getBoolean(PreferencesActivity.PREF_AUTO_UPDATE, false);
}
```

6. Update the `onActivityResult` handler to remove the check for the return value. Using this mechanism, all changes to user preferences are applied as soon as they are made.

```
public void onActivityResult(int requestCode, int
resultCode, Intent data) {
  super.onActivityResult(requestCode, resultCode,
  data);

  if (requestCode == SHOW_PREFERENCES)
    updateFromPreferences();

    FragmentManager fm = getFragmentManager();
    EarthquakeListFragment earthquakeList =
  (EarthquakeListFragment)
  fm.findFragmentById(R.id.EarthquakeListFragment);

    Thread t = new Thread(new Runnable() {
      public void run() {
        earthquakeList.refreshEarthquakes();
      }
    });
    t.start();
}
```

FIGURE 7-5

7. If you run your application and select the Preferences Menu Item, your new "native" settings screen should be visible, as shown in Figure 7-5.

Now create an backward-compatible alternative implementation using the newer Preference Fragments and Preference Headers.

1. Start by creating a new `UserPreferenceFragment` class that extends the Preference Fragment:

```
public class UserPreferenceFragment extends PreferenceFragment
```

2. Override its `onCreate` handler to populate the Fragment with the Preference screen, as you did in step 4 above to populate the legacy Preference Activity:

```
@Override
public void onCreate(Bundle savedInstanceState) {
  super.onCreate(savedInstanceState);
  addPreferencesFromResource(R.xml.userpreferences);
}
```

3. Add your Preference Fragment to a new `preference_headers.xml` file in the `res/xml` folder.

```
<preference-headers xmlns:android="http://schemas.android.com/apk/res/android">
  <header android:fragment="com.paad.earthquake.UserPreferenceFragment"
          android:title="Settings"
          android:summary="Earthquake Refresh Settings" />
</preference-headers>
```

4. Make a copy of the `PreferencesActivity` class, naming the copy `FragmentPreferences`:

```
public class FragmentPreferences extends PreferenceActivity
```

5. Add the new User Fragment Preferences Activity to the application manifest.

```
<activity android:name=".FragmentPreferences"/>
```

6. Open the User Fragment Preferences Activity and remove the `onCreate` handler completely. Instead, override the `onBuildHeaders` method, inflating the headers you defined in step 3:

```
@Override
public void onBuildHeaders(List<Header> target) {
  loadHeadersFromResource(R.xml.preference_headers, target);
}
```

7. Finally, open the Earthquake Activity and modify the `onOptionsItemSelected` method to select the appropriate Preference Activity. Create an explicit Intent based on the host platform version and pass it in to the `startActivityForResult` method:

```
private static final int SHOW_PREFERENCES = 1;
public boolean onOptionsItemSelected(MenuItem item){
  super.onOptionsItemSelected(item);
  switch (item.getItemId()) {

    case (MENU_PREFERENCES): {
      Class c = Build.VERSION.SDK_INT < Build.VERSION_CODES.HONEYCOMB ?
        PreferencesActivity.class : FragmentPreferences.class;
      Intent i = new Intent(this, c);
```

```
        startActivityForResult(i, SHOW_PREFERENCES);
        return true;
      }
    }
    return false;
}
```

All the code snippets in this example are part of the Chapter 7 Earthquake Part 2 project, available for download at www.wrox.com.

PERSISTING THE APPLICATION INSTANCE STATE

To save Activity instance variables, Android offers two specialized variations of Shared Preferences. The first uses a Shared Preference named specifically for your Activity, whereas the other relies on a series of lifecycle event handlers.

Saving Activity State Using Shared Preferences

If you want to save Activity information that doesn't need to be shared with other components (e.g., class instance variables), you can call `Activity.getPreferences()` without specifying a Shared Preferences name. This returns a Shared Preference using the calling Activity's class name as the Shared Preference name.

```
// Create or retrieve the activity preference object.
SharedPreferences activityPreferences =
  getPreferences(Activity.MODE_PRIVATE);

// Retrieve an editor to modify the shared preferences.
SharedPreferences.Editor editor = activityPreferences.edit();

// Retrieve the View
TextView myTextView = (TextView)findViewById(R.id.myTextView);

// Store new primitive types in the shared preferences object.
editor.putString("currentTextValue",
                 myTextView.getText().toString());

// Commit changes.
editor.apply();
```

Saving and Restoring Activity Instance State Using the Lifecycle Handlers

Activities offer the `onSaveInstanceState` handler to persist data associated with UI state across sessions. It's designed specifically to persist UI state should an Activity be terminated by the run time, either in an effort to free resources for foreground applications or to accommodate restarts caused by hardware configuration changes.

If an Activity is closed by the user (by pressing the Back button), or programmatically with a call to finish, the instance state bundle will not be passed in to onCreate or onRestoreInstanceState when the Activity is next created. Data that should be persisted across user sessions should be stored using Shared Preferences, as described in the previous sections.

By overriding an Activity's onSaveInstanceState event handler, you can use its Bundle parameter to save UI instance values. Store values using the same put methods as shown for Shared Preferences, before passing the modified Bundle into the superclass's handler:

```java
private static final String TEXTVIEW_STATE_KEY = "TEXTVIEW_STATE_KEY";

@Override
public void onSaveInstanceState(Bundle saveInstanceState) {
  // Retrieve the View
  TextView myTextView = (TextView)findViewById(R.id.myTextView);

  // Save its state
  saveInstanceState.putString(TEXTVIEW_STATE_KEY,
    myTextView.getText().toString());

  super.onSaveInstanceState(saveInstanceState);
}
```

This handler will be triggered whenever an Activity completes its active lifecycle, but only when it's not being explicitly finished (with a call to finish). As a result, it's used to ensure a consistent Activity state between active lifecycles of a single user session.

The saved Bundle is passed in to the onRestoreInstanceState and onCreate methods if the application is forced to restart during a session.

```java
@Override
public void onCreate(Bundle savedInstanceState) {
  super.onCreate(savedInstanceState);
  setContentView(R.layout.main);

  TextView myTextView = (TextView)findViewById(R.id.myTextView);

  String text = "";
  if (savedInstanceState != null &&
      savedInstanceState.containsKey(TEXTVIEW_STATE_KEY))
    text = savedInstanceState.getString(TEXTVIEW_STATE_KEY);

  myTextView.setText(text);
}
```

Saving and Restoring Fragment Instance State Using the Lifecycle Handlers

The UI for most applications will be encapsulated within Fragments. Accordingly, Fragments also include an onSaveInstanceState handler that works in much the same way as its Activity counterpart.

The instance state persisted in the bundle is passed as a parameter to the Fragment's onCreate, onCreateView, and onActivityCreated handlers.

If an Activity is destroyed and restarted to handle a hardware configuration change, such as the screen orientation changing, you can request that your Fragment instance be retained. By calling setRetainInstance within a Fragment's onCreate handler, you specify that Fragment's instance should not be killed and restarted when its associated Activity is re-created.

As a result, the onDestroy and onCreate handlers for a retained Fragment will not be called when the device configuration changes and the attached Activity is destroyed and re-created. This can provide a significant efficiency improvement if you move the majority of your object creation into onCreate, while using onCreateView to update the UI with the values stored within those persisted instance values.

Note that the rest of the Fragment's lifecycle handlers, including onAttach, onCreateView, onActivityCreated, onStart, onResume, and their corresponding tear-down handlers, will still be called.

Listing 7-4 shows how to use the lifecycle handlers to record the current UI state while taking advantage of the efficiency gains associated with retaining the Fragment instance.

LISTING 7-4: Persisting UI state by using lifecycle handlers and retaining Fragment instances

```
public class MyFragment extends Fragment {

    private static String USER_SELECTION = "USER_SELECTION";
    private int userSelection = 0;
    private TextView tv;

    @Override
    public void onCreate(Bundle savedInstanceState) {
      super.onCreate(savedInstanceState);
      setRetainInstance(true);
      if (savedInstanceState != null)
        userSelection = savedInstanceState.getInt(USER_SELECTION);
    }

    @Override
    public View onCreateView(LayoutInflater inflater,
                             ViewGroup container,
                             Bundle savedInstanceState) {
      View v = inflater.inflate(R.layout.mainfragment, container, false);

      tv = (TextView)v.findViewById(R.id.text);
      setSelection(userSelection);

      Button b1 = (Button)v.findViewById(R.id.button1);
      Button b2 = (Button)v.findViewById(R.id.button2);
      Button b3 = (Button)v.findViewById(R.id.button3);

      b1.setOnClickListener(new OnClickListener() {
        public void onClick(View arg0) {
          setSelection(1);
        }
```

```
    });

    b2.setOnClickListener(new OnClickListener() {
      public void onClick(View arg0) {
        setSelection(2);
      }
    });

    b3.setOnClickListener(new OnClickListener() {
      public void onClick(View arg0) {
        setSelection(3);
      }
    });

    return v;
  }

  private void setSelection(int selection) {
    userSelection = selection;
    tv.setText("Selected: " + selection);
  }

  @Override
  public void onSaveInstanceState(Bundle outState) {
    outState.putInt(USER_SELECTION, userSelection);
    super.onSaveInstanceState(outState);
  }
}
```

code snippet PA4AD_Ch07_Preferences/src/MyFragment.java

INCLUDING STATIC FILES AS RESOURCES

If your application requires external file resources, you can include them in your distribution package by placing them in the res/raw folder of your project hierarchy.

To access these read-only file resources, call the openRawResource method from your application's Resource object to receive an InputStream based on the specified file. Pass in the filename (without the extension) as the variable name from the R.raw class, as shown in the following skeleton code:

```
Resources myResources = getResources();
InputStream myFile = myResources.openRawResource(R.raw.myfilename);
```

Adding raw files to your resources hierarchy is an excellent alternative for large, preexisting data sources (such as dictionaries) for which it's not desirable (or even possible) to convert them into Android databases.

Android's resource mechanism lets you specify alternative resource files for different languages, locations, and hardware configurations. For example, you could create an application that loads a different dictionary resource based on the user's language settings.

WORKING WITH THE FILE SYSTEM

It's good practice to use Shared Preferences or a database to store your application data, but there may still be times when you'll want to use files directly rather than rely on Android's managed mechanisms — particularly when working with multimedia files.

File-Management Tools

Android supplies some basic file-management tools to help you deal with the file system. Many of these utilities are located within the `java.io.File` package.

Complete coverage of Java file-management utilities is beyond the scope of this book, but Android does supply some specialized utilities for file management that are available from the application Context.

➤ `deleteFile` — Enables you to remove files created by the current application

➤ `fileList` — Returns a string array that includes all the files created by the current application

These methods are particularly useful for cleaning up temporary files left behind if your application crashes or is killed unexpectedly.

Using Application-Specific Folders to Store Files

Many applications will create or download files that are specific to the application. There are two options for storing these application-specific files: internally or externally.

When referring to the external storage, we refer to the shared/media storage that is accessible by all applications and can typically be mounted to a computer file system when the device is connected via USB. Although it is typically located on the SD Card, some devices implement this as a separate partition on the internal storage.

The most important thing to remember when storing files on external storage is that no security is enforced on files stored here. Any application can access, over-write, or delete files stored on the external storage.

It's also important to remember that files stored on external storage may not always be available. If the SD Card is ejected, or the device is mounted for access via a computer, your application will be unable to read (or create) files on the external storage.

Android offers two corresponding methods via the application Context, `getDir` and `getExternalFilesDir`, both of which return a File object that contains the path to the internal and external application file storage directory, respectively.

All files stored in these directories or the subfolders will be erased when your application is uninstalled.

> The `getExternalFilesDir` *method was introduced in Android API level 8 (Android 2.2). To support earlier platform releases, you can call* `Environment` `.getExternalStorageDirectory` *to return a path to the root of the external storage.*
>
> *It's good practice to store your application-specific data in its own subdirectory using the same style as* `getExternalFilesDir` *— that is,* `/Android/data/[Your Package Name]/files`*.*
>
> *Note that this work-around will not automatically delete your application files when it is uninstalled.*

Both of these methods accept a string parameter that can be used to specify the subdirectory into which you want to place your files. In Android 2.2 (API level 8) the `Environment` class introduced a number of `DIRECTORY_[Category]` string constants that represent standard directory names, including downloads, images, movies, music, and camera files.

Files stored in the application folders should be specific to the parent application and are typically not detected by the media-scanner, and therefore won't be added to the Media Library automatically. If your application downloads or creates files that should be added to the Media Library or otherwise made available to other applications, consider putting them in the public external storage directory, as described later in this chapter.

Creating Private Application Files

Android offers the `openFileInput` and `openFileOutput` methods to simplify reading and writing streams from and to files stored in the application's sandbox.

```
String FILE_NAME = "tempfile.tmp";

// Create a new output file stream that's private to this application.
FileOutputStream fos = openFileOutput(FILE_NAME, Context.MODE_PRIVATE);
// Create a new file input stream.
FileInputStream fis = openFileInput(FILE_NAME);
```

These methods support only those files in the current application folder; specifying path separators will cause an exception to be thrown.

If the filename you specify when creating a `FileOutputStream` does not exist, Android will create it for you. The default behavior for existing files is to overwrite them; to append an existing file, specify the mode as `Context.MODE_APPEND`.

By default, files created using the `openFileOutput` method are private to the calling application — a different application will be denied access. The standard way to share a file between applications is to use a Content Provider. Alternatively, you can specify either `Context.MODE_WORLD_READABLE` or

`Context.MODE_WORLD_WRITEABLE` when creating the output file, to make it available in other applications, as shown in the following snippet:

```
String OUTPUT_FILE = "publicCopy.txt";
FileOutputStream fos = openFileOutput(OUTPUT_FILE, Context.MODE_WORLD_WRITEABLE);
```

You can find the location of files stored in your sandbox by calling `getFilesDir`. This method will return the absolute path to the files created using `openFileOutput`:

```
File file = getFilesDir();
Log.d("OUTPUT_PATH_", file.getAbsolutePath());
```

Using the Application File Cache

Should your application need to cache temporary files, Android offers both a managed internal cache, and (since Android API level 8) an unmanaged external cache. You can access them by calling the `getCacheDir` and `getExternalCacheDir` methods, respectively, from the current Context.

Files stored in either cache location will be erased when the application is uninstalled. Files stored in the internal cache will potentially be erased by the system when it is running low on available storage; files stored on the external cache will not be erased, as the system does not track available storage on external media.

In either case it's good form to monitor and manage the size and age of your cache, deleting files when a reasonable maximum cache size is exceeded.

Storing Publicly Readable Files

Android 2.2 (API level 8) also includes a convenience method, `Environment.getExternal StoragePublicDirectory`, that can be used to find a path in which to store your application files. The returned location is where users will typically place and manage their own files of each type.

This is particularly useful for applications that provide functionality that replaces or augments system applications, such as the camera, that store files in standard locations.

The `getExternalStoragePublicDirectory` method accepts a String parameter that determines which subdirectory you want to access using a series of Environment static constants:

➤ `DIRECTORY_ALARMS` — Audio files that should be available as user-selectable alarm sounds

➤ `DIRECTORY_DCIM` — Pictures and videos taken by the device

➤ `DIRECTORY_DOWNLOADS` — Files downloaded by the user

➤ `DIRECTORY_MOVIES` — Movies

➤ `DIRECTORY_MUSIC` — Audio files that represent music

➤ `DIRECTORY_NOTIFICATIONS` — Audio files that should be available as user-selectable notification sounds

➤ `DIRECTORY_PICTURES` — Pictures

➤ `DIRECTORY_PODCASTS` — Audio files that represent podcasts

➤ `DIRECTORY_RINGTONES` — Audio files that should be available as user-selectable ringtones

Note that if the returned directory doesn't exit, you must create it before writing files to the directory, as shown in the following snippet:

```
String FILE_NAME = "MyMusic.mp3";

File path = Environment.getExternalStoragePublicDirectory(
          Environment.DIRECTORY_MUSIC);

File file = new File(path, FILE_NAME);

try {
  path.mkdirs();
  [... Write Files ...]
} catch (IOException e) {
  Log.d(TAG, "Error writing " + FILE_NAME, e);
}
```

8

Databases and Content Providers

WHAT'S IN THIS CHAPTER?

➤ Creating databases and using SQLite

➤ Using Content Providers, Cursors, and Content Values to store, share, and consume application data

➤ Asynchronously querying Content Providers using Cursor Loaders

➤ Adding search capabilities to your applications

➤ Using the native Media Store, Contacts, and Calendar Content Providers

This chapter introduces persistent data storage in Android, starting with the SQLite database library. SQLite offers a powerful SQL database library that provides a robust persistence layer over which you have total control.

You'll also learn how to build and use Content Providers to store, share, and consume structured data within and between applications. Content Providers offer a generic interface to any data source by decoupling the data storage layer from the application layer. You'll see how to query Content Providers asynchronously to ensure your application remains responsive.

Although access to a database is restricted to the application that created it, Content Providers offer a standard interface your applications can use to share data with and consume data from other applications — including many of the native data stores.

Having created an application with data to store, you'll learn how to add search functionality to your application and how to build Content Providers that can provide real-time search suggestions.

Because Content Providers can be used across application boundaries, you have the opportunity to integrate your own application with several native Content Providers, including contacts, calendar, and the Media Store. You'll learn how to store and retrieve data from these core Android applications to provide your users with a richer, more consistent, and fully integrated user experience.

INTRODUCING ANDROID DATABASES

Android provides structured data persistence through a combination of SQLite databases and Content Providers.

SQLite databases can be used to store application data using a managed, structured approach. Android offers a full SQLite relational database library. Every application can create its own databases over which it has complete control.

Having created your underlying data store, Content Providers offer a generic, well-defined interface for using and sharing data that provides a consistent abstraction from the underlying data source.

SQLite Databases

Using SQLite you can create fully encapsulated relational databases for your applications. Use them to store and manage complex, structured application data.

Android databases are stored in the `/data/data/<package_name>/databases` folder on your device (or emulator). All databases are private, accessible only by the application that created them.

Database design is a big topic that deserves more thorough coverage than is possible within this book. It is worth highlighting that standard database best practices still apply in Android. In particular, when you're creating databases for resource-constrained devices (such as mobile phones), it's important to normalize your data to minimize redundancy.

Content Providers

Content Providers provide an interface for publishing and consuming data, based around a simple URI addressing model using the `content://` schema. They enable you to decouple your application layers from the underlying data layers, making your applications data-source agnostic by abstracting the underlying data source.

Content Providers can be shared between applications, queried for results, have their existing records updated or deleted, and have new records added. Any application — with the appropriate permissions — can add, remove, or update data from any other application, including the native Android Content Providers.

Several native Content Providers have been made accessible for access by third-party applications, including the contact manager, media store, and calendar, as described later in this chapter.

By publishing your own Content Providers, you make it possible for you (and other developers) to incorporate and extend your data in new applications.

INTRODUCING SQLITE

SQLite is a well-regarded relational database management system (RDBMS). It is:

➤ Open-source

➤ Standards-compliant

➤ Lightweight

➤ Single-tier

It has been implemented as a compact C library that's included as part of the Android software stack.

By being implemented as a library, rather than running as a separate ongoing process, each SQLite database is an integrated part of the application that created it. This reduces external dependencies, minimizes latency, and simplifies transaction locking and synchronization.

SQLite has a reputation for being extremely reliable and is the database system of choice for many consumer electronic devices, including many MP3 players and smartphones.

Lightweight and powerful, SQLite differs from many conventional database engines by loosely typing each column, meaning that column values are not required to conform to a single type; instead, each value is typed individually in each row. As a result, type checking isn't necessary when assigning or extracting values from each column within a row.

> *For more comprehensive coverage of SQLite, including its particular strengths and limitations, check out the official site, at* www.sqlite.org.

CONTENT VALUES AND CURSORS

Content Values are used to insert new rows into tables. Each `ContentValues` object represents a single table row as a map of column names to values.

Database queries are returned as `Cursor` objects. Rather than extracting and returning a copy of the result values, Cursors are pointers to the result set within the underlying data. Cursors provide a managed way of controlling your position (row) in the result set of a database query.

The `Cursor` class includes a number of navigation functions, including, but not limited to, the following:

➤ `moveToFirst` — Moves the cursor to the first row in the query result

➤ `moveToNext` — Moves the cursor to the next row

➤ `moveToPrevious` — Moves the cursor to the previous row

➤ `getCount` — Returns the number of rows in the result set

➤ `getColumnIndexOrThrow` — Returns the zero-based index for the column with the specified name (throwing an exception if no column exists with that name)

➤ `getColumnName` — Returns the name of the specified column index

➤ `getColumnNames` — Returns a string array of all the column names in the current Cursor

➤ `moveToPosition` — Moves the cursor to the specified row

➤ `getPosition` — Returns the current cursor position

Android provides a convenient mechanism to ensure queries are performed asynchronously. The `CursorLoader` class and associated Loader Manager (described later in this chapter) were introduced in Android 3.0 (API level 11) and are now also available as part of the support library, allowing you to leverage them while still supporting earlier Android releases.

Later in this chapter you'll learn how to query a database and how to extract specific row/column values from the resulting Cursors.

WORKING WITH SQLITE DATABASES

This section shows you how to create and interact with SQLite databases within your applications.

When working with databases, it's good form to encapsulate the underlying database and expose only the public methods and constants required to interact with that database, generally using what's often referred to as a contract or helper class. This class should expose database constants, particularly column names, which will be required for populating and querying the database. Later in this chapter you'll be introduced to Content Providers, which can also be used to expose these interaction constants.

Listing 8-1 shows a sample of the type of database constants that should be made public within a helper class.

LISTING 8-1: Skeleton code for contract class constants

```
// The index (key) column name for use in where clauses.
public static final String KEY_ID = "_id";

// The name and column index of each column in your database.
// These should be descriptive.
public static final String KEY_GOLD_HOARD_NAME_COLUMN =
  "GOLD_HOARD_NAME_COLUMN";
public static final String KEY_GOLD_HOARD_ACCESSIBLE_COLUMN =
  "OLD_HOARD_ACCESSIBLE_COLUMN";
public static final String KEY_GOLD_HOARDED_COLUMN =
  "GOLD_HOARDED_COLUMN";
// TODO: Create public field for each column in your table.
```

---

code snippet PA4AD_ Ch08_DatabaseSkeleton/src/MyHoardDatabase.java

Introducing the SQLiteOpenHelper

`SQLiteOpenHelper` is an abstract class used to implement the best practice pattern for creating, opening, and upgrading databases.

By implementing an SQLite Open Helper, you hide the logic used to decide if a database needs to be created or upgraded before it's opened, as well as ensure that each operation is completed efficiently.

It's good practice to defer creating and opening databases until they're needed. The SQLite Open Helper caches database instances after they've been successfully opened, so you can make requests to open the database immediately prior to performing a query or transaction. For the same reason, there is no need to close the database manually unless you no longer need to use it again.

> *Database operations, especially opening or creating databases, can be time-consuming. To ensure this doesn't impact the user experience, make all database transactions asynchronous.*

Listing 8-2 shows how to extend the `SQLiteOpenHelper` class by overriding the constructor, `onCreate`, and `onUpgrade` methods to handle the creation of a new database and upgrading to a new version, respectively.

LISTING 8-2: Implementing an SQLite Open Helper

```java
private static class HoardDBOpenHelper extends SQLiteOpenHelper {

  private static final String DATABASE_NAME = "myDatabase.db";
  private static final String DATABASE_TABLE = "GoldHoards";
  private static final int DATABASE_VERSION = 1;

  // SQL Statement to create a new database.
  private static final String DATABASE_CREATE = "create table " +
    DATABASE_TABLE + " (" + KEY_ID +
    " integer primary key autoincrement, " +
    KEY_GOLD_HOARD_NAME_COLUMN + " text not null, " +
    KEY_GOLD_HOARDED_COLUMN + " float, " +
    KEY_GOLD_HOARD_ACCESSIBLE_COLUMN + " integer);";

  public HoardDBOpenHelper(Context context, String name,
                   CursorFactory factory, int version) {
    super(context, name, factory, version);
  }

  // Called when no database exists in disk and the helper class needs
  // to create a new one.
  @Override
  public void onCreate(SQLiteDatabase db) {
    db.execSQL(DATABASE_CREATE);
  }
```

continues

LISTING 8-2 *(continued)*

```
// Called when there is a database version mismatch meaning that
// the version of the database on disk needs to be upgraded to
// the current version.
@Override
public void onUpgrade(SQLiteDatabase db, int oldVersion,
                      int newVersion) {
  // Log the version upgrade.
  Log.w("TaskDBAdapter", "Upgrading from version " +
    oldVersion + " to " +
    newVersion + ", which will destroy all old data");

  // Upgrade the existing database to conform to the new
  // version. Multiple previous versions can be handled by
  // comparing oldVersion and newVersion values.

  // The simplest case is to drop the old table and create a new one.
  db.execSQL("DROP TABLE IF EXISTS " + DATABASE_TABLE);
  // Create a new one.
  onCreate(db);
  }
}
```

code snippet PA4AD_ Ch08_DatabaseSkeleton/src/MyHoardDatabase.java

> In this example onUpgrade *simply drops the existing table and replaces it with the new definition. This is often the simplest and most practical solution; however, for important data that is not synchronized with an online service or is hard to recapture, a better approach may be to migrate existing data into the new table.*

To access a database using the SQLite Open Helper, call getWritableDatabase or getReadableDatabase to open and obtain a writable or read-only instance of the underlying database, respectively.

Behind the scenes, if the database doesn't exist, the helper executes its onCreate handler. If the database version has changed, the onUpgrade handler will fire. In either case, the get<read/writ>ableDatabase call will return the cached, newly opened, newly created, or upgraded database, as appropriate.

When a database has been successfully opened, the SQLite Open Helper will cache it, so you can (and should) use these methods each time you query or perform a transaction on the database, rather than caching the open database within your application.

A call to getWritableDatabase can fail due to disk space or permission issues, so it's good practice to fall back to the getReadableDatabase method for database queries if necessary. In most cases this method will provide the same, cached writeable database instance as getWritableDatabase unless it does not yet exist or the same permission or disk space issues occur, in which case a read-only copy will be returned.

> *To create or upgrade the database, it must be opened in a writeable form; therefore, it's generally good practice to attempt to open a writeable database first, falling back to a read-only alternative if it fails.*

Opening and Creating Databases Without the SQLite Open Helper

If you would prefer to manage the creation, opening, and version control of your databases directly, rather than using the SQLite Open Helper, you can use the application Context's `openOrCreateDatabase` method to create the database itself:

```
SQLiteDatabase db = context.openOrCreateDatabase(DATABASE_NAME,
                                                 Context.MODE_PRIVATE,
                                                 null);
```

After you have created the database, you must handle the creation and upgrade logic handled within the `onCreate` and `onUpgrade` handlers of the SQLite Open Helper — typically using the database's `execSQL` method to create and drop tables, as required.

It's good practice to defer creating and opening databases until they're needed, and to cache database instances after they're successfully opened to limit the associated efficiency costs.

At a minimum, any such operations must be handled asynchronously to avoid impacting the main application thread.

Android Database Design Considerations

You should keep the following Android-specific considerations in mind when designing your database.

➤   Files (such as bitmaps or audio files) are not usually stored within database tables. Use a string to store a path to the file, preferably a fully qualified URI.

➤   Although not strictly a requirement, it's strongly recommended that all tables include an auto-increment key field as a unique index field for each row. If you plan to share your table using a Content Provider, a unique ID field is required.

Querying a Database

Each database query is returned as a `Cursor`. This lets Android manage resources more efficiently by retrieving and releasing row and column values on demand.

To execute a query on a Database object, use the `query` method, passing in the following:

➤   An optional Boolean that specifies if the result set should contain only unique values.

➤   The name of the table to query.

➤ A projection, as an array of strings, that lists the columns to include in the result set.

➤ A where clause that defines the rows to be returned. You can include ? wildcards that will be replaced by the values passed in through the selection argument parameter.

➤ An array of selection argument strings that will replace the ? wildcards in the where clause.

➤ A group by clause that defines how the resulting rows will be grouped.

➤ A having clause that defines which row groups to include if you specified a group by clause.

➤ A string that describes the order of the returned rows.

➤ A string that defines the maximum number of rows in the result set.

Listing 8-3 shows how to return a selection of rows from within an SQLite database table.

LISTING 8-3: Querying a database

```
// Specify the result column projection. Return the minimum set
// of columns required to satisfy your requirements.
String[] result_columns = new String[] {
  KEY_ID, KEY_GOLD_HOARD_ACCESSIBLE_COLUMN, KEY_GOLD_HOARDED_COLUMN };

// Specify the where clause that will limit our results.
String where = KEY_GOLD_HOARD_ACCESSIBLE_COLUMN + "=" + 1;

// Replace these with valid SQL statements as necessary.
String whereArgs[] = null;
String groupBy = null;
String having = null;
String order = null;

SQLiteDatabase db = hoardDBOpenHelper.getWritableDatabase();
Cursor cursor = db.query(HoardDBOpenHelper.DATABASE_TABLE,
                         result_columns, where,
                         whereArgs, groupBy, having, order);
```

code snippet PA4AD_ Ch08_GoldHoarder/src/MyHoardDatabase.java

---

In this Listing 8-3, a database instance is opened using an SQLite Open Helper implementation. The SQLite Open Helper defers the creation and opening of database instances until they are first required and caches them after they are successfully opened.

As a result, it's good practice to request a database instance each time you perform a query or transaction on the database. For efficiency reasons, you should close your database instance only when you believe you will no longer require it — typically, when the Activity or Service using it is stopped.

Extracting Values from a Cursor

To extract values from a Cursor, first use the `moveTo<location>` methods described earlier to position the cursor at the correct row of the result Cursor, and then use the type-safe `get<type>` methods (passing in a column index) to return the value stored at the current row for the specified column. To find the column index of a particular column within a result Cursor, use its `getColumnIndexOrThrow` and `getColumnIndex` methods.

It's good practice to use `getColumnIndexOrThrow` when you expect the column to exist in all cases. Using `getColumnIndex` and checking for a –1 result, as shown in the following snippet, is a more efficient technique than catching exceptions when the column might not exist in every case.

```
int columnIndex = cursor.getColumnIndex(KEY_COLUMN_1_NAME);
if (columnIndex > -1) {
  String columnValue = cursor.getString(columnIndex);
  // Do something with the column value.
}
else {
  // Do something else if the column doesn't exist.
}
```

> *Database implementations should publish static constants that provide the column names. These static constants are typically exposed from within the database contract class or the Content Provider.*

Listing 8-4 shows how to iterate over a result Cursor, extracting and averaging a column of float values.

LISTING 8-4: Extracting values from a Cursor

```
float totalHoard = 0f;
float averageHoard = 0f;

// Find the index to the column(s) being used.
int GOLD_HOARDED_COLUMN_INDEX =
  cursor.getColumnIndexOrThrow(KEY_GOLD_HOARDED_COLUMN);

// Iterate over the cursors rows.
// The Cursor is initialized at before first, so we can
// check only if there is a "next" row available. If the
// result Cursor is empty this will return false.
while (cursor.moveToNext()) {
  float hoard = cursor.getFloat(GOLD_HOARDED_COLUMN_INDEX);
  totalHoard += hoard;
}

// Calculate an average -- checking for divide by zero errors.
float cursorCount = cursor.getCount();
```

continues

LISTING 8-4 *(continued)*

```
averageHoard = cursorCount > 0 ?
                   (totalHoard / cursorCount) : Float.NaN;

// Close the Cursor when you've finished with it.
cursor.close();
```

code snippet PA4AD_ Ch08_GoldHoarder/src/MyHoardDatabase.java

Because SQLite database columns are loosely typed, you can cast individual values into valid types, as required. For example, values stored as floats can be read back as strings.

When you have finished using your result Cursor, it's important to close it to avoid memory leaks and reduce your application's resource load:

```
cursor.close();
```

Adding, Updating, and Removing Rows

The SQLiteDatabase class exposes insert, delete, and update methods that encapsulate the SQL statements required to perform these actions. Additionally, the execSQL method lets you execute any valid SQL statement on your database tables, should you want to execute these (or any other) operations manually.

Any time you modify the underlying database values, you should update your Cursors by running a new query.

Inserting Rows

To create a new row, construct a ContentValues object and use its put methods to add name/value pairs representing each column name and its associated value.

Insert the new row by passing the Content Values into the insert method called on the target database — along with the table name — as shown in Listing 8-5.

LISTING 8-5: Inserting new rows into a database

```
// Create a new row of values to insert.
ContentValues newValues = new ContentValues();

// Assign values for each row.
newValues.put(KEY_GOLD_HOARD_NAME_COLUMN, hoardName);
newValues.put(KEY_GOLD_HOARDED_COLUMN, hoardValue);
newValues.put(KEY_GOLD_HOARD_ACCESSIBLE_COLUMN, hoardAccessible);
// [ ... Repeat for each column / value pair ... ]

// Insert the row into your table
SQLiteDatabase db = hoardDBOpenHelper.getWritableDatabase();
db.insert(HoardDBOpenHelper.DATABASE_TABLE, null, newValues);
```

code snippet PA4AD_ Ch08_GoldHoarder/src/MyHoardDatabase.java

The second parameter used in the insert method shown in Listing 8-5 is known as the null column hack.

If you want to add an empty row to an SQLite database, by passing in an empty Content Values object, you must also pass in the name of a column whose value can be explicitly set to null.

When inserting a new row into an SQLite database, you must always explicitly specify at least one column and a corresponding value, the latter of which can be null. If you set the null column hack parameter to null, as shown in Listing 8-5, when inserting an empty Content Values object SQLite will throw an exception.

It's generally good practice to ensure that your code doesn't attempt to insert empty Content Values into an SQLite database.

Updating Rows

Updating rows is also done with Content Values. Create a new `ContentValues` object, using the `put` methods to assign new values to each column you want to update. Call the `update` method on the database, passing in the table name, the updated Content Values object, and a `where` clause that specifies the row(s) to update, as shown in Listing 8-6.

LISTING 8-6: Updating a database row

```
// Create the updated row Content Values.
ContentValues updatedValues = new ContentValues();

// Assign values for each row.
updatedValues.put(KEY_GOLD_HOARDED_COLUMN, newHoardValue);
// [ ... Repeat for each column to update ... ]

// Specify a where clause the defines which rows should be
// updated. Specify where arguments as necessary.
String where = KEY_ID + "=" + hoardId;
String whereArgs[] = null;

// Update the row with the specified index with the new values.
SQLiteDatabase db = hoardDBOpenHelper.getWritableDatabase();
db.update(HoardDBOpenHelper.DATABASE_TABLE, updatedValues,
          where, whereArgs);
```

code snippet PA4AD_ Ch08_GoldHoarder/src/MyHoardDatabase.java

Deleting Rows

To delete a row, simply call the `delete` method on a database, specifying the table name and a `where` clause that returns the rows you want to delete, as shown in Listing 8-7.

LISTING 8-7: Deleting a database row

```
// Specify a where clause that determines which row(s) to delete.
// Specify where arguments as necessary.
String where = KEY_GOLD_HOARDED_COLUMN + "=" + 0;
String whereArgs[] = null;

// Delete the rows that match the where clause.
SQLiteDatabase db = hoardDBOpenHelper.getWritableDatabase();
db.delete(HoardDBOpenHelper.DATABASE_TABLE, where, whereArgs);
```

code snippet PA4AD_ Ch08_GoldHoarder/src/MyHoardDatabase.java

CREATING CONTENT PROVIDERS

Content Providers provide an interface for publishing data that will be consumed using a Content Resolver. They allow you to decouple the application components that consume data from their underlying data sources, providing a generic mechanism through which applications can share their data or consume data provided by others.

To create a new Content Provider, extend the abstract `ContentProvider` class:

```
public class MyContentProvider extends ContentProvider
```

Like the database contract class described in the previous section, it's good practice to include static database constants — particularly column names and the Content Provider authority — that will be required for transacting with, and querying, the database.

You will also need to override the `onCreate` handler to initialize the underlying data source, as well as the `query`, `update`, `delete`, `insert`, and `getType` methods to implement the interface used by the Content Resolver to interact with the data, as described in the following sections.

Registering Content Providers

Like Activities and Services, Content Providers must be registered in your application manifest before the Content Resolver can discover them. This is done using a `provider` tag that includes a `name` attribute describing the Provider's class name and an `authorities` tag.

Use the `authorities` tag to define the base URI of the Provider's authority. A Content Provider's authority is used by the Content Resolver as an address and used to find the database you want to interact with.

Each Content Provider authority must be unique, so it's good practice to base the URI path on your package name. The general form for defining a Content Provider's authority is as follows:

```
com.<CompanyName>.provider.<ApplicationName>
```

The completed `provider` tag should follow the format show in the following XML snippet:

```
<provider android:name=".MyContentProvider"
          android:authorities="com.paad.skeletondatabaseprovider"/>
```

Publishing Your Content Provider's URI Address

Each Content Provider should expose its authority using a public static CONTENT_URI property to make it more easily discoverable. This should include a data path to the primary content — for example:

```
public static final Uri CONTENT_URI =
  Uri.parse("content://com.paad.skeletondatabaseprovider/elements");
```

These content URIs will be used when accessing your Content Provider using a Content Resolver. A query made using this form represents a request for all rows, whereas an appended trailing /<rownumber>, as shown in the following snippet, represents a request for a single record:

```
content://com.paad.skeletondatabaseprovider/elements/5
```

It's good practice to support access to your provider for both of these forms. The simplest way to do this is to use a UriMatcher, a useful class that parses URIs and determines their forms.

Listing 8-8 shows the implementation pattern for defining a URI Matcher that analyzes the form of a URI — specifically determining if a URI is a request for all data or for a single row.

LISTING 8-8: Defining a UriMatcher to determine if a request is for all elements or a single row

```
// Create the constants used to differentiate between the different URI
// requests.
private static final int ALLROWS = 1;
private static final int SINGLE_ROW = 2;

private static final UriMatcher uriMatcher;

// Populate the UriMatcher object, where a URI ending in
// 'elements' will correspond to a request for all items,
// and 'elements/[rowID]' represents a single row.
static {
  uriMatcher = new UriMatcher(UriMatcher.NO_MATCH);
  uriMatcher.addURI("com.paad.skeletondatabaseprovider",
                    "elements", ALLROWS);
  uriMatcher.addURI("com.paad.skeletondatabaseprovider",
                    "elements/#", SINGLE_ROW);
}
```

code snippet PA4AD_ Ch08_DatabaseSkeleton/src/MyContentProvider.java

You can use the same technique to expose alternative URIs within the same Content Provider that represent different subsets of data, or different tables within your database.

Having distinguished between full table and single row queries, you can use the SQLiteQueryBuilder class to easily apply the additional selection condition to a query, as shown in the following snippet:

```
SQLiteQueryBuilder queryBuilder = new SQLiteQueryBuilder();

// If this is a row query, limit the result set to the passed in row.
```

```
switch (uriMatcher.match(uri)) {
  case SINGLE_ROW :
    String rowID = uri.getPathSegments().get(1);
    queryBuilder.appendWhere(KEY_ID + "=" + rowID);
  default: break;
}
```

You'll learn how to perform a query using the SQLite Query Builder later in the "Implementing Content Provider Queries" section.

Creating the Content Provider's Database

To initialize the data source you plan to access through the Content Provider, override the `onCreate` method, as shown in Listing 8-9. This is typically handled using an SQLite Open Helper implementation, of the type described in the previous section, allowing you to effectively defer creating and opening the database until it's required.

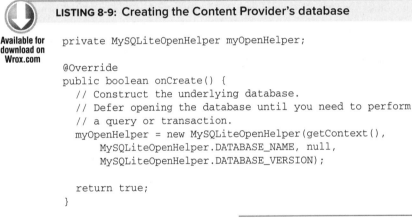

LISTING 8-9: Creating the Content Provider's database

```
private MySQLiteOpenHelper myOpenHelper;

@Override
public boolean onCreate() {
    // Construct the underlying database.
    // Defer opening the database until you need to perform
    // a query or transaction.
    myOpenHelper = new MySQLiteOpenHelper(getContext(),
        MySQLiteOpenHelper.DATABASE_NAME, null,
        MySQLiteOpenHelper.DATABASE_VERSION);

    return true;
}
```

code snippet PA4AD_ Ch08_DatabaseSkeleton/src/MyContentProvider.java

> When your application is launched, the `onCreate` handler of each of its Content Providers is called on the main application thread.
>
> Like the database examples in the previous section, it's best practice to use an SQLite Open Helper to defer opening (and where necessary, creating) the underlying database until it is required within the query or transaction methods of your Content Provider.
>
> For efficiency reasons, it's preferable to leave your Content Provider open while your application is running; it's not necessary to manually close the database at any stage. If the system requires additional resources, your application will be killed and the associated databases closed.

Implementing Content Provider Queries

To support queries with your Content Provider, you must implement the `query` and `getType` methods. Content Resolvers use these methods to access the underlying data, without knowing its structure or implementation. These methods enable applications to share data across application boundaries without having to publish a specific interface for each data source.

The most common scenario is to use a Content Provider to provide access to an SQLite database, but within these methods you can access any source of data (including files or application instance variables).

Notice that the `UriMatcher` object is used to refine the transaction and query requests, and the SQLite Query Builder is used as a convenient helper for performing row-based queries.

Listing 8-10 shows the skeleton code for implementing queries within a Content Provider using an underlying SQLite database.

LISTING 8-10: Implementing queries and transactions within a Content Provider

```
@Override
public Cursor query(Uri uri, String[] projection, String selection,
    String[] selectionArgs, String sortOrder) {

  // Open the database.
  SQLiteDatabase db;
  try {
    db = myOpenHelper.getWritableDatabase();
  } catch (SQLiteException ex) {
    db = myOpenHelper.getReadableDatabase();
  }

  // Replace these with valid SQL statements if necessary.
  String groupBy = null;
  String having = null;

  // Use an SQLite Query Builder to simplify constructing the
  // database query.
  SQLiteQueryBuilder queryBuilder = new SQLiteQueryBuilder();

  // If this is a row query, limit the result set to the passed in row.
  switch (uriMatcher.match(uri)) {
    case SINGLE_ROW :
      String rowID = uri.getPathSegments().get(1);
      queryBuilder.appendWhere(KEY_ID + "=" + rowID);
    default: break;
  }

  // Specify the table on which to perform the query. This can
  // be a specific table or a join as required.
  queryBuilder.setTables(MySQLiteOpenHelper.DATABASE_TABLE);

  // Execute the query.
  Cursor cursor = queryBuilder.query(db, projection, selection,
      selectionArgs, groupBy, having, sortOrder);

  // Return the result Cursor.
  return cursor;
}
```

code snippet PA4AD_ Ch08_DatabaseSkeleton/src/MyContentProvider.java

Having implemented queries, you must also specify a MIME type to identify the data returned. Override the `getType` method to return a string that uniquely describes your data type.

The type returned should include two forms, one for a single entry and another for all the entries, following these forms:

➤ Single item:

```
vnd.android.cursor.item/vnd.<companyname>.<contenttype>
```

➤ All items:

```
vnd.android.cursor.dir/vnd.<companyname>.<contenttype>
```

Listing 8-11 shows how to override the `getType` method to return the correct MIME type based on the URI passed in.

LISTING 8-11: Returning a Content Provider MIME type

Available for download on Wrox.com

```java
@Override
public String getType(Uri uri) {
  // Return a string that identifies the MIME type
  // for a Content Provider URI
  switch (uriMatcher.match(uri)) {
    case ALLROWS:
      return "vnd.android.cursor.dir/vnd.paad.elemental";
    case SINGLE_ROW:
      return "vnd.android.cursor.item/vnd.paad.elemental";
    default:
      throw new IllegalArgumentException("Unsupported URI: " +
                                         uri);

  }
}
```

code snippet PA4AD_ Ch08_DatabaseSkeleton/src/MyContentProvider.java

Content Provider Transactions

To expose delete, insert, and update transactions on your Content Provider, implement the corresponding `delete`, `insert`, and `update` methods.

Like the `query` method, these methods are used by Content Resolvers to perform transactions on the underlying data without knowing its implementation — allowing applications to update data across application boundaries.

When performing transactions that modify the dataset, it's good practice to call the Content Resolver's `notifyChange` method. This will notify any Content Observers, registered for a given Cursor using the `Cursor.registerContentObserver` method, that the underlying table (or a particular row) has been removed, added, or updated.

As with Content Provider queries, the most common use case is performing transactions on an SQLite database, though this is not a requirement. Listing 8-12 shows the skeleton code for implementing transactions within a Content Provider on an underlying SQLite database.

LISTING 8-12: Typical Content Provider transaction implementations

```java
@Override
public int delete(Uri uri, String selection, String[] selectionArgs) {
  // Open a read / write database to support the transaction.
  SQLiteDatabase db = myOpenHelper.getWritableDatabase();

  // If this is a row URI, limit the deletion to the specified row.
  switch (uriMatcher.match(uri)) {
    case SINGLE_ROW :
      String rowID = uri.getPathSegments().get(1);
      selection = KEY_ID + "=" + rowID
          + (!TextUtils.isEmpty(selection) ?
            " AND (" + selection + ')' : "");
    default: break;
  }

  // To return the number of deleted items you must specify a where
  // clause. To delete all rows and return a value pass in "1".
  if (selection == null)
    selection = "1";

  // Perform the deletion.
  int deleteCount = db.delete(MySQLiteOpenHelper.DATABASE_TABLE,
    selection, selectionArgs);

  // Notify any observers of the change in the data set.
  getContext().getContentResolver().notifyChange(uri, null);

  // Return the number of deleted items.
  return deleteCount;
}


@Override
public Uri insert(Uri uri, ContentValues values) {
  // Open a read / write database to support the transaction.
  SQLiteDatabase db = myOpenHelper.getWritableDatabase();

  // To add empty rows to your database by passing in an empty
  // Content Values object you must use the null column hack
  // parameter to specify the name of the column that can be
  // set to null.
  String nullColumnHack = null;

  // Insert the values into the table
  long id = db.insert(MySQLiteOpenHelper.DATABASE_TABLE,
      nullColumnHack, values);

  // Construct and return the URI of the newly inserted row.
  if (id > -1) {
    // Construct and return the URI of the newly inserted row.
    Uri insertedId = ContentUris.withAppendedId(CONTENT_URI, id);
```

continues

LISTING 8-12 *(continued)*

```java
      // Notify any observers of the change in the data set.
      getContext().getContentResolver().notifyChange(insertedId, null);

      return insertedId;
    }
    else
      return null;
}

@Override
public int update(Uri uri, ContentValues values, String selection,
  String[] selectionArgs) {

  // Open a read / write database to support the transaction.
  SQLiteDatabase db = myOpenHelper.getWritableDatabase();

  // If this is a row URI, limit the deletion to the specified row.
  switch (uriMatcher.match(uri)) {
    case SINGLE_ROW :
      String rowID = uri.getPathSegments().get(1);
      selection = KEY_ID + "=" + rowID
          + (!TextUtils.isEmpty(selection) ?
            " AND (" + selection + ')' : "");
    default: break;
  }

  // Perform the update.
  int updateCount = db.update(MySQLiteOpenHelper.DATABASE_TABLE,
    values, selection, selectionArgs);

  // Notify any observers of the change in the data set.
  getContext().getContentResolver().notifyChange(uri, null);

  return updateCount;
}
```

code snippet PA4AD_ Ch08_DatabaseSkeleton/src/MyContentProvider.java

> When working with content URIs, the ContentUris *class includes the* with-AppendedId *convenience method to easily append a specific row ID to the* CONTENT_URI *of a Content Provider. This is used in Listing 8-12 to construct the URI of newly insert rows and will be used in the following sections to address a particular row when making database queries and transactions.*

Storing Files in a Content Provider

Rather than store large files within your Content Provider, you should represent them within a table as fully qualified URIs to a file stored somewhere else on the filesystem.

To support files within your table, you must include a column labeled _data that will contain the path to the file represented by that record. This column should not be used by client applications. Override the openFile handler to provide a ParcelFileDescriptor when the Content Resolver requests the file associated with that record.

It's typical for a Content Provider to include two tables, one that is used only to store the external files, and another that includes a user-facing column containing a URI reference to the rows in the file table.

Listing 8-13 shows the skeleton code for overriding the openFile handler within a Content Provider. In this instance, the name of the file will be represented by the ID of the row to which it belongs.

LISTING 8-13: Storing files within your Content Provider

```java
@Override
public ParcelFileDescriptor openFile(Uri uri, String mode)
    throws FileNotFoundException {

  // Find the row ID and use it as a filename.
  String rowID = uri.getPathSegments().get(1);

  // Create a file object in the application's external
  // files directory.
  String picsDir = Environment.DIRECTORY_PICTURES;
  File file =
    new File(getContext().getExternalFilesDir(picsDir), rowID);

  // If the file doesn't exist, create it now.
  if (!file.exists()) {
    try {
      file.createNewFile();
    } catch (IOException e) {
      Log.d(TAG, "File creation failed: " + e.getMessage());
    }
  }

  // Translate the mode parameter to the corresponding Parcel File
  // Descriptor open mode.
  int fileMode = 0;
  if (mode.contains("w"))
    fileMode |= ParcelFileDescriptor.MODE_WRITE_ONLY;
  if (mode.contains("r"))
    fileMode |= ParcelFileDescriptor.MODE_READ_ONLY;
  if (mode.contains("+"))
    fileMode |= ParcelFileDescriptor.MODE_APPEND;

  // Return a Parcel File Descriptor that represents the file.
  return ParcelFileDescriptor.open(file, fileMode);
}
```

code snippet PA4AD_ Ch08_DatabaseSkeleton/src/MyHoardContentProvider.java

> *Because the files associated with rows in the database are stored externally, it's important to consider what the effect of deleting a row should have on the underlying file.*

A Skeleton Content Provider Implementation

Listing 8-14 shows a skeleton implementation of a Content Provider. It uses an SQLite Open Helper to manage the database, and simply passes each query or transaction directly to the underlying SQLite database.

LISTING 8-14: A skeleton Content Provider implementation

```java
import android.content.ContentProvider;
import android.content.ContentUris;
import android.content.ContentValues;
import android.content.Context;
import android.content.UriMatcher;
import android.database.Cursor;
import android.database.sqlite.SQLiteDatabase;
import android.database.sqlite.SQLiteDatabase.CursorFactory;
import android.database.sqlite.SQLiteOpenHelper;
import android.database.sqlite.SQLiteQueryBuilder;
import android.net.Uri;
import android.text.TextUtils;
import android.util.Log;

public class MyContentProvider extends ContentProvider {

  public static final Uri CONTENT_URI =
    Uri.parse("content://com.paad.skeletondatabaseprovider/elements");

  // Create the constants used to differentiate between
  // the different URI requests.
  private static final int ALLROWS = 1;
  private static final int SINGLE_ROW = 2;

  private static final UriMatcher uriMatcher;

  // Populate the UriMatcher object, where a URI ending
  // in 'elements' will correspond to a request for all
  // items, and 'elements/[rowID]' represents a single row.
  static {
   uriMatcher = new UriMatcher(UriMatcher.NO_MATCH);
   uriMatcher.addURI("com.paad.skeletondatabaseprovider",
     "elements", ALLROWS);
   uriMatcher.addURI("com.paad.skeletondatabaseprovider",
     "elements/#", SINGLE_ROW);
  }
```

```
// The index (key) column name for use in where clauses.
public static final String KEY_ID = "_id";

// The name and column index of each column in your database.
// These should be descriptive.
public static final String KEY_COLUMN_1_NAME = "KEY_COLUMN_1_NAME";
// TODO: Create public field for each column in your table.

// SQLite Open Helper variable
private MySQLiteOpenHelper myOpenHelper;

@Override
public boolean onCreate() {
  // Construct the underlying database.
  // Defer opening the database until you need to perform
  // a query or transaction.
  myOpenHelper = new MySQLiteOpenHelper(getContext(),
      MySQLiteOpenHelper.DATABASE_NAME, null,
      MySQLiteOpenHelper.DATABASE_VERSION);

  return true;
}

@Override
public Cursor query(Uri uri, String[] projection, String selection,
    String[] selectionArgs, String sortOrder) {
  // Open the database.
  SQLiteDatabase db = myOpenHelper.getWritableDatabase();

  // Replace these with valid SQL statements if necessary.
  String groupBy = null;
  String having = null;

  SQLiteQueryBuilder queryBuilder = new SQLiteQueryBuilder();
  queryBuilder.setTables(MySQLiteOpenHelper.DATABASE_TABLE);

  // If this is a row query, limit the result set to the
  // passed in row.
  switch (uriMatcher.match(uri)) {
    case SINGLE_ROW :
      String rowID = uri.getPathSegments().get(1);
      queryBuilder.appendWhere(KEY_ID + "=" + rowID);
    default: break;
  }

  Cursor cursor = queryBuilder.query(db, projection, selection,
      selectionArgs, groupBy, having, sortOrder);

  return cursor;
}

@Override
public int delete(Uri uri, String selection, String[] selectionArgs)
```

continues

LISTING 8-14 *(continued)*

```
{
  // Open a read / write database to support the transaction.
  SQLiteDatabase db = myOpenHelper.getWritableDatabase();

  // If this is a row URI, limit the deletion to the specified row.
  switch (uriMatcher.match(uri)) {
    case SINGLE_ROW :
      String rowID = uri.getPathSegments().get(1);
      selection = KEY_ID + "=" + rowID
          + (!TextUtils.isEmpty(selection) ?
            " AND (" + selection + ')' : "");
    default: break;
  }

  // To return the number of deleted items, you must specify a where
  // clause. To delete all rows and return a value, pass in "1".
  if (selection == null)
    selection = "1";

  // Execute the deletion.
  int deleteCount = db.delete(MySQLiteOpenHelper.DATABASE_TABLE,
    selection, selectionArgs);

  // Notify any observers of the change in the data set.
  getContext().getContentResolver().notifyChange(uri, null);

  return deleteCount;
}


@Override
public Uri insert(Uri uri, ContentValues values) {
  // Open a read / write database to support the transaction.
  SQLiteDatabase db = myOpenHelper.getWritableDatabase();

  // To add empty rows to your database by passing in an empty
  // Content Values object, you must use the null column hack
  // parameter to specify the name of the column that can be
  // set to null.
  String nullColumnHack = null;

  // Insert the values into the table
  long id = db.insert(MySQLiteOpenHelper.DATABASE_TABLE,
      nullColumnHack, values);

  if (id > -1) {
    // Construct and return the URI of the newly inserted row.
    Uri insertedId = ContentUris.withAppendedId(CONTENT_URI, id);

    // Notify any observers of the change in the data set.
    getContext().getContentResolver().notifyChange(insertedId, null);
```

```
        return insertedId;
    }
    else
      return null;
  }

  @Override
  public int update(Uri uri, ContentValues values, String selection,
    String[] selectionArgs) {

    // Open a read / write database to support the transaction.
    SQLiteDatabase db = myOpenHelper.getWritableDatabase();

    // If this is a row URI, limit the deletion to the specified row.
    switch (uriMatcher.match(uri)) {
      case SINGLE_ROW :
        String rowID = uri.getPathSegments().get(1);
        selection = KEY_ID + "=" + rowID
            + (!TextUtils.isEmpty(selection) ?
              " AND (" + selection + ')' : "");
      default: break;
    }

    // Perform the update.
    int updateCount = db.update(MySQLiteOpenHelper.DATABASE_TABLE,
      values, selection, selectionArgs);

    // Notify any observers of the change in the data set.
    getContext().getContentResolver().notifyChange(uri, null);

    return updateCount;
  }

  @Override
  public String getType(Uri uri) {
    // Return a string that identifies the MIME type
    // for a Content Provider URI
    switch (uriMatcher.match(uri)) {
      case ALLROWS:
        return "vnd.android.cursor.dir/vnd.paad.elemental";
      case SINGLE_ROW:
        return "vnd.android.cursor.item/vnd.paad.elemental";
      default:
        throw new IllegalArgumentException("Unsupported URI: " + uri);
    }
  }

  private static class MySQLiteOpenHelper extends SQLiteOpenHelper {
    // [ ... SQLite Open Helper Implementation ... ]
  }
}
```

code snippet PA4AD_ Ch08_DatabaseSkeleton/src/MyContentProvider.java

USING CONTENT PROVIDERS

The following sections introduce the `ContentResolver` class and how to use it to query and transact with a Content Provider.

Introducing the Content Resolver

Each application includes a `ContentResolver` instance, accessible using the `getContentResolver` method, as follows:

```
ContentResolver cr = getContentResolver();
```

When Content Providers are used to expose data, Content Resolvers are the corresponding class used to query and perform transactions on those Content Providers. Whereas Content Providers provide an abstraction from the underlying data, Content Resolvers provide an abstraction from the Content Provider being queried or transacted.

The Content Resolver includes query and transaction methods corresponding to those defined within your Content Providers. The Content Resolver does not need to know the implementation of the Content Providers it is interacting with — each query and transaction method simply accepts a URI that specifies the Content Provider to interact with.

A Content Provider's URI is its *authority* as defined by its manifest node and typically published as a static constant on the Content Provider implementation.

Content Providers usually accept two forms of URI, one for requests against all data and another that specifies only a single row. The form for the latter appends the row identifier (in the form `/<rowID>`) to the base URI.

Querying Content Providers

Content Provider queries take a form very similar to that of database queries. Query results are returned as Cursors over a result set in the same way as described previously in this chapter for databases.

You can extract values from the result Cursor using the same techniques described in the section "Extracting Results from a Cursor."

Using the `query` method on the `ContentResolver` object, pass in the following:

➤ A URI to the Content Provider you want to query.

➤ A projection that lists the columns you want to include in the result set.

➤ A `where` clause that defines the rows to be returned. You can include `?` wildcards that will be replaced by the values passed into the selection argument parameter.

➤ An array of selection argument strings that will replace the `?` wildcards in the `where` clause.

➤ A string that describes the order of the returned rows.

Listing 8-15 shows how to use a Content Resolver to apply a query to a Content Provider.

LISTING 8-15: Querying a Content Provider with a Content Resolver

```
// Get the Content Resolver.
ContentResolver cr = getContentResolver();

// Specify the result column projection. Return the minimum set
// of columns required to satisfy your requirements.
String[] result_columns = new String[] {
    MyHoardContentProvider.KEY_ID,
    MyHoardContentProvider.KEY_GOLD_HOARD_ACCESSIBLE_COLUMN,
    MyHoardContentProvider.KEY_GOLD_HOARDED_COLUMN };

// Specify the where clause that will limit your results.
String where = MyHoardContentProvider.KEY_GOLD_HOARD_ACCESSIBLE_COLUMN
               + "=" + 1;

// Replace these with valid SQL statements as necessary.
String whereArgs[] = null;
String order = null;

// Return the specified rows.
Cursor resultCursor = cr.query(MyHoardContentProvider.CONTENT_URI,
  result_columns, where, whereArgs, order);
```

code snippet PA4AD_ Ch08_DatabaseSkeleton/src/DatabaseSkeletonActivity.java

In this example the query is made using static constants provided by the `MyHoardContentProvider` class; however, it's worth noting that a third-party application can perform the same query, provided it knows the content URI and column names, and has the appropriate permissions.

Most Content Providers also include a shortcut URI pattern that allows you to address a particular row by appending a row ID to the content URI. You can use the static `withAppendedId` method from the `ContentUris` class to simplify this, as shown in Listing 8-16.

LISTING 8-16: Querying a Content Provider for a particular row

```
// Get the Content Resolver.
ContentResolver cr = getContentResolver();

// Specify the result column projection. Return the minimum set
// of columns required to satisfy your requirements.
String[] result_columns = new String[] {
    MyHoardContentProvider.KEY_ID,
    MyHoardContentProvider.KEY_GOLD_HOARD_NAME_COLUMN,
    MyHoardContentProvider.KEY_GOLD_HOARDED_COLUMN };

// Append a row ID to the URI to address a specific row.
```

continues

LISTING 8-16 *(continued)*

```
Uri rowAddress =
  ContentUris.withAppendedId(MyHoardContentProvider.CONTENT_URI,
  rowId);

// These are null as we are requesting a single row.
String where = null;
String whereArgs[] = null;
String order = null;

// Return the specified rows.
Cursor resultCursor = cr.query(rowAddress,
  result_columns, where, whereArgs, order);
```

code snippet PA4AD_ Ch08_DatabaseSkeleton/src/DatabaseSkeletonActivity.java

To extract values from a result Cursor, use the same techniques described earlier in this chapter, using the moveTo<location> methods in combination with the get<type> methods to extract values from the specified row and column.

Listing 8-17 extends the code from Listing 8-15, by iterating over a result Cursor and displaying the name of the largest hoard.

LISTING 8-17: Extracting values from a Content Provider result Cursor

```
float largestHoard = 0f;
String hoardName = "No Hoards";

// Find the index to the column(s) being used.
int GOLD_HOARDED_COLUMN_INDEX = resultCursor.getColumnIndexOrThrow(
  MyHoardContentProvider.KEY_GOLD_HOARDED_COLUMN);
int HOARD_NAME_COLUMN_INDEX = resultCursor.getColumnIndexOrThrow(
  MyHoardContentProvider.KEY_GOLD_HOARD_NAME_COLUMN);


// Iterate over the cursors rows.
// The Cursor is initialized at before first, so we can
// check only if there is a "next" row available. If the
// result Cursor is empty, this will return false.
while (resultCursor.moveToNext()) {
  float hoard = resultCursor.getFloat(GOLD_HOARDED_COLUMN_INDEX);
  if (hoard > largestHoard) {
    largestHoard = hoard;
    hoardName = resultCursor.getString(HOARD_NAME_COLUMN_INDEX);
  }
}

// Close the Cursor when you've finished with it.
resultCursor.close();
```

code snippet PA4AD_ Ch08_DatabaseSkeleton/src/DatabaseSkeletonActivity.java

When you have finished using your result Cursor it's important to close it to avoid memory leaks and reduce your application's resource load.

```
resultCursor.close();
```

You'll see more examples of querying for content later in this chapter when the native Android Content Providers are introduced.

> *Database queries can take significant time to execute. By default, the Content Resolver will execute queries — as well as other transactions — on the main application thread.*
>
> *To ensure your application remains smooth and responsive, you must execute all queries asynchronously, as described in the following section.*

Querying for Content Asynchronously Using the Cursor Loader

Database operations can be time-consuming, so it's particularly important that any database and Content Provider queries are not performed on the main application thread.

It can be difficult to manage Cursors, synchronize correctly with the UI thread, and ensure all queries occur on a background. To help simplify the process, Android 3.0 (API level 11) introduced the `Loader` class. Loaders are now also available within the Android Support Library, making them available for use with every Android platform back to Android 1.6.

Introducing Loaders

Loaders are available within every Activity and Fragment via the `LoaderManager`. They are designed to asynchronously load data and monitor the underlying data source for changes.

While loaders can be implemented to load any kind of data from any data source, of particular interest is the `CursorLoader` class. The Cursor Loader allows you to perform asynchronous queries against Content Providers, returning a result Cursor and notifications of any updates to the underlying provider.

> *To maintain concise and encapsulated code, not all the examples in this chapter utilize a Cursor Loader when making a Content Provider query. For your own applications it's best practice to always use a Cursor Loader to manage Cursors within your Activities and Fragments.*

Using the Cursor Loader

The Cursor Loader handles all the management tasks required to use a Cursor within an Activity or Fragment, effectively deprecating the `managedQuery` and `startManagingCursor` Activity methods.

This includes managing the Cursor lifecycle to ensure Cursors are closed when the Activity is terminated.

Cursor Loaders also observe changes in the underlying query, so you no longer need to implement your own Content Observers.

Implementing Cursor Loader Callbacks

To use a Cursor Loader, create a new `LoaderManager.LoaderCallbacks` implementation. Loader Callbacks are implemented using generics, so you should specify the explicit type being loaded, in this case Cursors, when implementing your own.

```
LoaderManager.LoaderCallbacks<Cursor> loaderCallback
  = new LoaderManager.LoaderCallbacks<Cursor>() {
```

If you require only a single Loader implementation within your Fragment or Activity, this is typically done by having that component implement the interface.

The Loader Callbacks consist of three handlers:

➤ `onCreateLoader` — Called when the loader is initialized, this handler should create and return new Cursor Loader object. The Cursor Loader constructor arguments mirror those required for executing a query using the Content Resolver. Accordingly, when this handler is executed, the query parameters you specify will be used to perform a query using the Content Resolver.

➤ `onLoadFinished` — When the Loader Manager has completed the asynchronous query, the `onLoadFinished` handler is called, with the result Cursor passed in as a parameter. Use this Cursor to update adapters and other UI elements.

➤ `onLoaderReset` — When the Loader Manager resets your Cursor Loader, `onLoaderReset` is called. Within this handler you should release any references to data returned by the query and reset the UI accordingly. The Cursor will be closed by the Loader Manager, so you shouldn't attempt to close it.

> The `onLoadFinished` and `onLoaderReset` are not synchronized to the UI thread. If you want to modify UI elements directly, you will first need to synchronize with the UI thread using a Handler or similar mechanism. Synchronizing with the UI thread is covered in more details in Chapter 9, "Working in the Background."

Listing 8-18 show a skeleton implementation of the Cursor Loader Callbacks.

Available for download on Wrox.com

LISTING 8-18: Implementing Loader Callbacks

```
public Loader<Cursor> onCreateLoader(int id, Bundle args) {
    // Construct the new query in the form of a Cursor Loader. Use the id
    // parameter to construct and return different loaders.
    String[] projection = null;
```

```
         String where = null;
         String[] whereArgs = null;
         String sortOrder = null;

         // Query URI
         Uri queryUri = MyContentProvider.CONTENT_URI;

         // Create the new Cursor loader.
         return new CursorLoader(DatabaseSkeletonActivity.this, queryUri,
           projection, where, whereArgs, sortOrder);
       }

       public void onLoadFinished(Loader<Cursor> loader, Cursor cursor) {
         // Replace the result Cursor displayed by the Cursor Adapter with
         // the new result set.
         adapter.swapCursor(cursor);

         // This handler is not synchronized with the UI thread, so you
         // will need to synchronize it before modifying any UI elements
         // directly.
       }

       public void onLoaderReset(Loader<Cursor> loader) {
         // Remove the existing result Cursor from the List Adapter.
         adapter.swapCursor(null);

         // This handler is not synchronized with the UI thread, so you
         // will need to synchronize it before modifying any UI elements
         // directly.
       }
```

code snippet PA4AD_ Ch08_DatabaseSkeleton/src/DatabaseSkeletonActivity.java

Initializing and Restarting the Cursor Loader

Each Activity and Fragment provides access to its Loader Manager through a call to
getLoaderManager.

```
       LoaderManager loaderManager = getLoaderManager();
```

To initialize a new Loader, call the Loader Manager's initLoader method, passing in a reference to
your Loader Callback implementation, an optional arguments Bundle, and a loader identifier.

```
       Bundle args = null;
       loaderManager.initLoader(LOADER_ID, args, myLoaderCallbacks);
```

This is generally done within the onCreate method of the host Activity (or the onActivityCreated
handler in the case of Fragments).

If a loader corresponding to the identifier used doesn't already exist, it is created within the associated Loader Callback's onCreateLoader handler as described in the previous section.

In most circumstances this is all that is required. The Loader Manager will handle the lifecycle of
any Loaders you initialize and the underlying queries and cursors. Similarly, it will manage changes
to the query results.

After a Loader has been created, repeated calls to `initLoader` will simply return the existing Loader. Should you want to discard the previous Loader and re-create it, use the `restartLoader` method.

```
loaderManager.restartLoader(LOADER_ID, args, myLoaderCallbacks);
```

This is typically necessary where your query parameters change, such as search queries or changes in sort order.

Adding, Deleting, and Updating Content

To perform transactions on Content Providers, use the `insert`, `delete`, and `update` methods on the Content Resolver. Like queries, unless moved to a worker thread, Content Provider transactions will execute on the main application thread.

> *Database operations can be time-consuming, so it's important to execute each transaction asynchronously.*

Inserting Content

The Content Resolver offers two methods for inserting new records into a Content Provider: `insert` and `bulkInsert`. Both methods accept the URI of the Content Provider into which you're inserting; the `insert` method takes a single new `ContentValues` object, and the `bulkInsert` method takes an array.

The `insert` method returns a URI to the newly added record, whereas the `bulkInsert` method returns the number of successfully added rows.

Listing 8-19 shows how to use the `insert` method to add new rows to a Content Provider.

LISTING 8-19: Inserting new rows into a Content Provider

```java
// Create a new row of values to insert.
ContentValues newValues = new ContentValues();

// Assign values for each row.
newValues.put(MyHoardContentProvider.KEY_GOLD_HOARD_NAME_COLUMN,
              hoardName);
newValues.put(MyHoardContentProvider.KEY_GOLD_HOARDED_COLUMN,
              hoardValue);
newValues.put(MyHoardContentProvider.KEY_GOLD_HOARD_ACCESSIBLE_COLUMN,
              hoardAccessible);
// [ ... Repeat for each column / value pair ... ]

// Get the Content Resolver
ContentResolver cr = getContentResolver();

// Insert the row into your table
Uri myRowUri = cr.insert(MyHoardContentProvider.CONTENT_URI,
                         newValues);
```

code snippet PA4AD_ Ch08_DatabaseSkeleton/src/DatabaseSkeletonActivity.java

Deleting Content

To delete a single record, call `delete` on the Content Resolver, passing in the URI of the row you want to remove. Alternatively, you can specify a `where` clause to remove multiple rows. Listing 8-20 demonstrates how to delete a number of rows matching a given condition.

LISTING 8-20: Deleting rows from a Content Provider

```
// Specify a where clause that determines which row(s) to delete.
// Specify where arguments as necessary.
String where = MyHoardContentProvider.KEY_GOLD_HOARDED_COLUMN +
                "=" + 0;
String whereArgs[] = null;

// Get the Content Resolver.
ContentResolver cr = getContentResolver();

// Delete the matching rows
int deletedRowCount =
  cr.delete(MyHoardContentProvider.CONTENT_URI, where, whereArgs);
```

code snippet PA4AD_ Ch08_DatabaseSkeleton/src/DatabaseSkeletonActivity.java

Updating Content

You can update rows by using the Content Resolver's `update` method. The `update` method takes the URI of the target Content Provider, a `ContentValues` object that maps column names to updated values, and a `where` clause that indicates which rows to update.

When the update is executed, every row matched by the `where` clause is updated using the specified Content Values, and the number of successful updates is returned.

Alternatively, you can choose to update a specific row by specifying its unique URI, as shown in Listing 8-21.

LISTING 8-21: Updating a record in a Content Provider

```
// Create the updated row content, assigning values for each row.
ContentValues updatedValues = new ContentValues();
updatedValues.put(MyHoardContentProvider.KEY_GOLD_HOARDED_COLUMN,
                  newHoardValue);
// [ ... Repeat for each column to update ... ]

// Create a URI addressing a specific row.
Uri rowURI =
  ContentUris.withAppendedId(MyHoardContentProvider.CONTENT_URI,
  hoardId);

// Specify a specific row so no selection clause is required.
String where = null;
String whereArgs[] = null;
```

continues

LISTING 8-21 *(continued)*

```
// Get the Content Resolver.
ContentResolver cr = getContentResolver();

// Update the specified row.
int updatedRowCount =
  cr.update(rowURI, updatedValues, where, whereArgs);
```

code snippet PA4AD_ Ch08_DatabaseSkeleton/src/DatabaseSkeletonActivity.java

Accessing Files Stored in Content Providers

Content Providers represent large files as fully qualified URIs rather than raw file blobs; however, this is abstracted away when using the Content Resolver.

To access a file stored in, or to insert a new file into, a Content Provider, simply use the Content Resolver's openOutputStream or openInputStream methods, respectively, passing in the URI to the Content Provider row containing the file you require. The Content Provider will interpret your request and return an input or output stream to the requested file, as shown in Listing 8-22.

LISTING 8-22: Reading and writing files from and to a Content Provider

```
public void addNewHoardWithImage(String hoardName, float hoardValue,
    boolean hoardAccessible, Bitmap bitmap) {

  // Create a new row of values to insert.
  ContentValues newValues = new ContentValues();

  // Assign values for each row.
  newValues.put(MyHoardContentProvider.KEY_GOLD_HOARD_NAME_COLUMN,
            hoardName);
  newValues.put(MyHoardContentProvider.KEY_GOLD_HOARDED_COLUMN,
            hoardValue);
  newValues.put(
    MyHoardContentProvider.KEY_GOLD_HOARD_ACCESSIBLE_COLUMN,
    hoardAccessible);

  // Get the Content Resolver
  ContentResolver cr = getContentResolver();

  // Insert the row into your table
  Uri myRowUri =
    cr.insert(MyHoardContentProvider.CONTENT_URI, newValues);

  try {
    // Open an output stream using the new row's URI.
    OutputStream outStream = cr.openOutputStream(myRowUri);
    // Compress your bitmap and save it into your provider.
```

```
      bitmap.compress(Bitmap.CompressFormat.JPEG, 80, outStream);
    }
    catch (FileNotFoundException e) {
      Log.d(TAG, "No file found for this record.");
    }
  }

  public Bitmap getHoardImage(long rowId) {
    Uri myRowUri =
      ContentUris.withAppendedId(MyHoardContentProvider.CONTENT_URI,
                                 rowId);

    try {
      // Open an input stream using the new row's URI.
      InputStream inStream =
        getContentResolver().openInputStream(myRowUri);

      // Make a copy of the Bitmap.
      Bitmap bitmap = BitmapFactory.decodeStream(inStream);
      return bitmap;
    }
    catch (FileNotFoundException e) {
      Log.d(TAG, "No file found for this record.");
    }

    return null;
  }
```

code snippet PA4AD_ Ch08_DatabaseSkeleton/src/DatabaseSkeletonActivity.java

Creating a To-Do List Database and Content Provider

In Chapter 4, "Building User Interfaces," you created a To-Do List application. In the following example, you'll create a database and Content Provider to save each of the to-do items added to the list.

1. Start by creating a new `ToDoContentProvider` class. It will be used to host the database using an `SQLiteOpenHelper` and manage your database interactions by extending the `ContentProvider` class. Include stub methods for the `onCreate`, `query`, `update`, `insert`, `delete`, and `getType` methods, and a private skeleton implementation of an `SQLiteOpenHelper`.

```
package com.paad.todolist;

import android.content.ContentProvider;
import android.content.ContentUris;
import android.content.ContentValues;
import android.content.Context;
import android.content.UriMatcher;
import android.database.Cursor;
import android.database.sqlite.SQLiteDatabase;
import android.database.sqlite.SQLiteQueryBuilder;
import android.database.sqlite.SQLiteDatabase.CursorFactory;
import android.database.sqlite.SQLiteOpenHelper;
```

```java
import android.net.Uri;
import android.text.TextUtils;
import android.util.Log;

public class ToDoContentProvider extends ContentProvider {

  @Override
  public boolean onCreate() {
    return false;
  }

  @Override
  public String getType(Uri url) {
    return null;
  }

  @Override
  public Cursor query(Uri url, String[] projection, String selection,
                      String[] selectionArgs, String sort) {
    return null;
  }

  @Override
  public Uri insert(Uri url, ContentValues initialValues) {
    return null;
  }

  @Override
  public int delete(Uri url, String where, String[] whereArgs) {
    return 0;
  }

  @Override
  public int update(Uri url, ContentValues values,
                    String where, String[]wArgs) {
    return 0;
  }

  private static class MySQLiteOpenHelper extends SQLiteOpenHelper {

    public MySQLiteOpenHelper(Context context, String name,
                      CursorFactory factory, int version) {
      super(context, name, factory, version);
    }

    // Called when no database exists in disk and the helper class needs
    // to create a new one.
    @Override
    public void onCreate(SQLiteDatabase db) {
      // TODO Create database tables.
    }

    // Called when there is a database version mismatch meaning that the version
    // of the database on disk needs to be upgraded to the current version.
    @Override
```

```
      public void onUpgrade(SQLiteDatabase db, int oldVersion, int newVersion) {
        // TODO Upgrade database.
      }
    }
  }
```

2. Publish the URI for this provider. This URI will be used to access this Content Provider from within other application components via the ContentResolver.

```
public static final Uri CONTENT_URI =
  Uri.parse("content://com.paad.todoprovider/todoitems");
```

3. Create public static variables that define the column names. They will be used within the SQLite Open Helper to create the database, and from other application components to extract values from your queries.

```
public static final String KEY_ID = "_id";
public static final String KEY_TASK = "task";
public static final String KEY_CREATION_DATE = "creation_date";
```

4. Within the `MySQLiteOpenHelper`, create variables to store the database name and version, along with the table name of the to-do list item table.

```
private static final String DATABASE_NAME = "todoDatabase.db";
private static final int DATABASE_VERSION = 1;
private static final String DATABASE_TABLE = "todoItemTable";
```

5. Still in the `MySQLiteOpenHelper`, overwrite the `onCreate` and `onUpgrade` methods to handle the database creation using the columns from step 3 and standard upgrade logic.

```
// SQL statement to create a new database.
private static final String DATABASE_CREATE = "create table " +
  DATABASE_TABLE + " (" + KEY_ID +
  " integer primary key autoincrement, " +
  KEY_TASK + " text not null, " +
  KEY_CREATION_DATE + "long);";

// Called when no database exists in disk and the helper class needs
// to create a new one.
@Override
public void onCreate(SQLiteDatabase db) {
  db.execSQL(DATABASE_CREATE);
}

// Called when there is a database version mismatch, meaning that the version
// of the database on disk needs to be upgraded to the current version.
@Override
public void onUpgrade(SQLiteDatabase db, int oldVersion, int newVersion) {
  // Log the version upgrade.
  Log.w("TaskDBAdapter", "Upgrading from version " +
                         oldVersion + " to " +
                         newVersion + ", which will destroy all old data");

  // Upgrade the existing database to conform to the new version. Multiple
  // previous versions can be handled by comparing oldVersion and newVersion
```

```
        // values.

        // The simplest case is to drop the old table and create a new one.
        db.execSQL("DROP TABLE IF IT EXISTS " + DATABASE_TABLE);
        // Create a new one.
        onCreate(db);
    }
```

6. Returning to the `ToDoContentProvider`, add a private variable to store an instance of the `MySQLiteOpenHelper` class, and create it within the `onCreate` handler.

```
private MySQLiteOpenHelper myOpenHelper;

@Override
public boolean onCreate() {
    // Construct the underlying database.
    // Defer opening the database until you need to perform
    // a query or transaction.
    myOpenHelper = new MySQLiteOpenHelper(getContext(),
        MySQLiteOpenHelper.DATABASE_NAME, null,
        MySQLiteOpenHelper.DATABASE_VERSION);

    return true;
}
```

7. Still in the Content Provider, create a new `UriMatcher` to allow your Content Provider to differentiate between a query against the entire table and one that addresses a particular row. Use it within the `getType` handler to return the correct MIME type, depending on the query type.

```
private static final int ALLROWS = 1;
private static final int SINGLE_ROW = 2;

private static final UriMatcher uriMatcher;

//Populate the UriMatcher object, where a URI ending in 'todoitems' will
//correspond to a request for all items, and 'todoitems/[rowID]'
//represents a single row.
static {
 uriMatcher = new UriMatcher(UriMatcher.NO_MATCH);
 uriMatcher.addURI("com.paad.todoprovider", "todoitems", ALLROWS);
 uriMatcher.addURI("com.paad.todoprovider", "todoitems/#", SINGLE_ROW);
}

@Override
public String getType(Uri uri) {
    // Return a string that identifies the MIME type
    // for a Content Provider URI
    switch (uriMatcher.match(uri)) {
      case ALLROWS: return "vnd.android.cursor.dir/vnd.paad.todos";
      case SINGLE_ROW: return "vnd.android.cursor.item/vnd.paad.todos";
      default: throw new IllegalArgumentException("Unsupported URI: " + uri);
    }
}
```

8. Implement the `query` method stub. Start by requesting an instance of the database, before constructing a query based on the parameters passed in. In this simple instance, you need to apply the same query parameters only to the underlying database — modifying the query only to account for the possibility of a URI that addresses a single row.

```
@Override
public Cursor query(Uri uri, String[] projection, String selection,
    String[] selectionArgs, String sortOrder) {
  // Open a read-only database.
  SQLiteDatabase db = myOpenHelper.getWritableDatabase();

  // Replace these with valid SQL statements if necessary.
  String groupBy = null;
  String having = null;

  SQLiteQueryBuilder queryBuilder = new SQLiteQueryBuilder();
  queryBuilder.setTables(MySQLiteOpenHelper.DATABASE_TABLE);

  // If this is a row query, limit the result set to the passed in row.
  switch (uriMatcher.match(uri)) {
    case SINGLE_ROW :
      String rowID = uri.getPathSegments().get(1);
      queryBuilder.appendWhere(KEY_ID + "=" + rowID);
    default: break;
  }

  Cursor cursor = queryBuilder.query(db, projection, selection,
      selectionArgs, groupBy, having, sortOrder);

  return cursor;
}
```

9. Implement the `delete`, `insert`, and `update` methods using the same approach — pass through the received parameters while handling the special case of single-row URIs.

```
@Override
public int delete(Uri uri, String selection, String[] selectionArgs) {
  // Open a read / write database to support the transaction.
  SQLiteDatabase db = myOpenHelper.getWritableDatabase();

  // If this is a row URI, limit the deletion to the specified row.
  switch (uriMatcher.match(uri)) {
    case SINGLE_ROW :
      String rowID = uri.getPathSegments().get(1);
      selection = KEY_ID + "=" + rowID
          + (!TextUtils.isEmpty(selection) ?
            " AND (" + selection + ')' : "");
    default: break;
  }

  // To return the number of deleted items, you must specify a where
  // clause. To delete all rows and return a value, pass in "1".
  if (selection == null)
    selection = "1";
```

```
  // Execute the deletion.
  int deleteCount = db.delete(MySQLiteOpenHelper.DATABASE_TABLE, selection,
                              selectionArgs);

  // Notify any observers of the change in the data set.
  getContext().getContentResolver().notifyChange(uri, null);

  return deleteCount;
}

@Override
public Uri insert(Uri uri, ContentValues values) {
  // Open a read / write database to support the transaction.
  SQLiteDatabase db = myOpenHelper.getWritableDatabase();

  // To add empty rows to your database by passing in an empty Content Values
  // object, you must use the null column hack parameter to specify the name of
  // the column that can be set to null.
  String nullColumnHack = null;

  // Insert the values into the table
  long id = db.insert(MySQLiteOpenHelper.DATABASE_TABLE,
      nullColumnHack, values);

  if (id > -1) {
    // Construct and return the URI of the newly inserted row.
    Uri insertedId = ContentUris.withAppendedId(CONTENT_URI, id);

    // Notify any observers of the change in the data set.
    getContext().getContentResolver().notifyChange(insertedId, null);

    return insertedId;
  }
  else
    return null;
}

@Override
public int update(Uri uri, ContentValues values, String selection,
  String[] selectionArgs) {

  // Open a read / write database to support the transaction.
  SQLiteDatabase db = myOpenHelper.getWritableDatabase();

  // If this is a row URI, limit the deletion to the specified row.
  switch (uriMatcher.match(uri)) {
    case SINGLE_ROW :
      String rowID = uri.getPathSegments().get(1);
      selection = KEY_ID + "=" + rowID
          + (!TextUtils.isEmpty(selection) ?
            " AND (" + selection + ')' : "");
    default: break;
  }

  // Perform the update.
```

```
      int updateCount = db.update(MySQLiteOpenHelper.DATABASE_TABLE,
        values, selection, selectionArgs);

      // Notify any observers of the change in the data set.
      getContext().getContentResolver().notifyChange(uri, null);

      return updateCount;
    }
```

10. That completes the Content Provider class. Add it to your application Manifest, specifying the base URI to use as its authority.

```
<provider android:name=".ToDoContentProvider"
          android:authorities="com.paad.todoprovider"/>
```

11. Return to the `ToDoList` Activity and update it to persist the to-do list array. Start by modifying the Activity to implement `LoaderManager.LoaderCallbacks<Cursor>`, and then add the associated stub methods.

```
public class ToDoList extends Activity implements
    NewItemFragment.OnNewItemAddedListener, LoaderManager.LoaderCallbacks<Cursor> {

    // [... Existing ToDoList Activity code ...]

    public Loader<Cursor> onCreateLoader(int id, Bundle args) {
      return null;
    }

    public void onLoadFinished(Loader<Cursor> loader, Cursor cursor) {
    }

    public void onLoaderReset(Loader<Cursor> loader) {
    }
}
```

12. Complete the `onCreateLoader` handler by building and returning a Loader that queries the `ToDoListContentProvider` for all of its elements.

```
public Loader<Cursor> onCreateLoader(int id, Bundle args) {
  CursorLoader loader = new CursorLoader(this,
    ToDoContentProvider.CONTENT_URI, null, null, null, null);

  return loader;
}
```

13. When the Loader's query completes, the result Cursor will be returned to the `onLoadFinished` handler. Update it to iterate over the result Cursor and repopulate the to-do list Array Adapter accordingly.

```
public void onLoadFinished(Loader<Cursor> loader, Cursor cursor) {
  int keyTaskIndex = cursor.getColumnIndexOrThrow(ToDoContentProvider.KEY_TASK);

  todoItems.clear();
  while (cursor.moveToNext()) {
    ToDoItem newItem = new ToDoItem(cursor.getString(keyTaskIndex));
    todoItems.add(newItem);
  }
```

```
        aa.notifyDataSetChanged();
    }
```

14. Update the `onCreate` handler to initiate the Loader when the Activity is created, and the `onResume` handler to restart the Loader when the Activity is restarted.

```
public void onCreate(Bundle savedInstanceState) {

    // [... Existing onCreate code …]

    getLoaderManager().initLoader(0, null, this);
}

@Override
protected void onResume() {
    super.onResume();
    getLoaderManager().restartLoader(0, null, this);
}
```

15. The final step is to modify the behavior of the `onNewItemAdded` handler. Rather than adding the item to the to-do Array List directly, use the `ContentResolver` to add it to the Content Provider.

```
public void onNewItemAdded(String newItem) {
    ContentResolver cr = getContentResolver();

    ContentValues values = new ContentValues();
    values.put(ToDoContentProvider.KEY_TASK, newItem);

    cr.insert(ToDoContentProvider.CONTENT_URI, values);
    getLoaderManager().restartLoader(0, null, this);
}
```

> *All code snippets in this example are part of the* Chapter 8 Todo List *project,
> available for download at* www.wrox.com.

You have now created a database into which to save your to-do items. A better approach than copying Cursor rows to an Array List is to use a Simple Cursor Adapter. You'll do this later in the chapter, in the section "Creating a Searchable Earthquake Provider."

To make this To-Do List application more useful, consider adding functionality to delete and update list items, change the sort order, and store additional information.

ADDING SEARCH TO YOUR APPLICATION

Surfacing your application's content through search is a simple and powerful way to make your content more discoverable, increase user engagement, and improve the visibility of your application. On mobile devices speed is everything, and search provides a mechanism for users to quickly find the content they need.

Android includes a framework that simplifies the process of making your Content Providers searchable, adding search functionality to your Activities, and surfacing application search results on the home screen.

Until Android 3.0 (API level 11) most Android devices featured a hardware *search* key. In more recent releases this has been replaced with on-screen widgets, typically placed on your application's Action Bar.

By implementing search within your application, you can expose your application-specific search functionality whenever a user presses the search button or uses the search widget.

You can provide search capabilities for your application in three ways:

➤ **Search bar** — When activated, the search bar (often referred to as the *search dialog*) is displayed over the title bar of your Activity, as shown in Figure 8-1. The search bar is activated when the user presses the hardware search button, or it can be initiated programmatically with a call to your Activity's `onSearchRequested` method.

FIGURE 8-1

Not all Android devices include a hardware search key, particularly newer devices and tablets, so it's good practice to also include a software trigger to initiate search.

FIGURE 8-2

➤ **Search View** — Introduced in Android 3.0 (API level 11), the Search View is a search widget that can be placed anywhere within your Activity.

FIGURE 8-3

Typically represented as an icon in the Action Bar, it is shown expanded in Figure 8-2.

➤ **Quick Search Box** — The Quick Search Box, as shown in Figure 8-3, is a home screen search Widget that performs searches across all supported applications. You can configure your application's search results to be surfaced for searches initiated through the Quick Search Box.

The search bar, Search View, and Quick Search Box support the display of search suggestions, providing a powerful mechanism for improving the responsiveness of your application.

Making Your Content Provider Searchable

Before you can enable the search dialog or use a Search View widget within your application, you need to define what is searchable.

To do this, the first step is to create a new searchable metadata XML resource in your project's `res/xml` folder. As shown in Listing 8-23, you must specify the `android:label` attribute (typically your application name), and best practice suggests you also include an `android:hint` attribute to help users understand what they can search for. The hint is typically in the form of "Search for [content type or product name]."

LISTING 8-23: Defining application search metadata

```xml
<?xml version="1.0" encoding="utf-8"?>
<searchable xmlns:android="http://schemas.android.com/apk/res/android"
  android:label="@string/app_name"
  android:hint="@string/search_hint">
</searchable>
```

code snippet PA4AD_ Ch08_DatabaseSkeleton/res/xml/searchable.xml

Creating a Search Activity for Your Application

Having defined the Content Provider to search, you must now create an Activity that will be used to display search results. This will most commonly be a simple List View-based Activity, but you can use any user interface, provided that it has a mechanism for displaying search results.

Users will not generally expect multiple searches to be added to the back stack, so it's good practice to set a search Activity as "single top," ensuring that the same instance will be used repeatedly rather than creating a new instance for each search.

To indicate that an Activity can be used to provide search results, include an Intent Filter registered for the android.intent.action.SEARCH action and the DEFAULT category.

You must also include a meta-data tag that includes a name attribute that specifies android.app .searchable, and a resource attribute that specifies a searchable XML resource, as shown in Listing 8-24.

LISTING 8-24: Registering a search results Activity

```xml
<activity android:name=".DatabaseSkeletonSearchActivity"
          android:label="Element Search"
          android:launchMode="singleTop">
  <intent-filter>
    <action android:name="android.intent.action.SEARCH" />
    <category android:name="android.intent.category.DEFAULT" />
  </intent-filter>
  <meta-data
    android:name="android.app.searchable"
    android:resource="@xml/searchable"
  />
</activity>
```

code snippet PA4AD_ Ch08_DatabaseSkeleton/AndroidManifest.xml

To enable the search dialog for a given Activity, you need to specify which search results Activity should be used to handle search requests. You can do this by adding a meta-data tag to its activity node in the manifest. Set the name attribute to android.app.

`default_searchable` and specify your search Activity using the `value` attribute, as shown in the following snippet:

```
<meta-data
  android:name="android.app.default_searchable"
  android:value=".DatabaseSkeletonSearchResultsActivity"
/>
```

Searches initiated from within the search results Activity are automatically handled by it, so there's no need to annotate it specifically.

After users have initiated a search, your Activity will be started and their search queries will be available from within the Intent that started it, accessible through the `SearchManager.QUERY` extra. Searches initiated from within the search results Activity will result in new Intents being received — you can capture those Intents and extract the new queries from the `onNewIntent` handler, as shown in Listing 8-25.

LISTING 8-25: Extracting the search query

```java
@Override
public void onCreate(Bundle savedInstanceState) {
  super.onCreate(savedInstanceState);

  // Get the launch Intent
  parseIntent(getIntent());
}

@Override
protected void onNewIntent(Intent intent) {
  super.onNewIntent(intent);
  parseIntent(getIntent());
}

private void parseIntent(Intent intent) {
  // If the Activity was started to service a Search request,
  // extract the search query.
  if (Intent.ACTION_SEARCH.equals(intent.getAction())) {
    String searchQuery = intent.getStringExtra(SearchManager.QUERY);
    // Perform the search
    performSearch(searchQuery);
  }
}
```

code snippet PA4AD_ Ch08_DatabaseSkeleton/src/DatabaseSkeletonSearchActivity.java

Making Your Search Activity the Default Search Provider for Your Application

It's generally good practice to use the same search results form for your entire application. To set a search Activity as the default search result provider for all Activities within your application, add a `meta-data` tag within the `application` manifest node. Set the `name` attribute to `android.app.default_searchable` and specify your search Activity using the `value` attribute, as shown in Listing 8-26.

LISTING 8-26: Setting a default search result Activity for an application

```
<meta-data
  android:name="android.app.default_searchable"
  android:value=".DatabaseSkeletonSearchActivity"
/>
```

code snippet PA4AD_ Ch08_DatabaseSkeleton/AndroidManifest.xml

Performing a Search and Displaying the Results

When your search Activity receives a new search query, you must execute the search and display the results within the Activity. How you choose to implement your search query and display its results depends on your application, what you're searching, and where the searchable content is stored.

If you are searching a Content Provider, it's good practice to use a Cursor Loader to execute a query whose result Cursor is bound to a List View, as shown in Listing 8-27.

LISTING 8-27: Performing a search and displaying the results

```java
import android.app.ListActivity;
import android.app.LoaderManager;
import android.app.SearchManager;
import android.content.ContentUris;
import android.content.CursorLoader;
import android.content.Intent;
import android.content.Loader;
import android.database.Cursor;
import android.net.Uri;
import android.os.Bundle;
import android.view.View;
import android.widget.ListView;
import android.widget.SimpleCursorAdapter;

public class DatabaseSkeletonSearchActivity extends ListActivity
  implements LoaderManager.LoaderCallbacks<Cursor> {

  private static String QUERY_EXTRA_KEY = "QUERY_EXTRA_KEY";

  private SimpleCursorAdapter adapter;

  @Override
  public void onCreate(Bundle savedInstanceState) {
    super.onCreate(savedInstanceState);

    // Create a new adapter and bind it to the List View
    adapter = new SimpleCursorAdapter(this,
            android.R.layout.simple_list_item_1, null,
```

```
              new String[] { MyContentProvider.KEY_COLUMN_1_NAME },
              new int[] { android.R.id.text1 }, 0);
  setListAdapter(adapter);

  // Initiate the Cursor Loader
  getLoaderManager().initLoader(0, null, this);

  // Get the launch Intent
  parseIntent(getIntent());
}

@Override
protected void onNewIntent(Intent intent) {
  super.onNewIntent(intent);
  parseIntent(getIntent());
}

private void parseIntent(Intent intent) {
  // If the Activity was started to service a Search request,
  // extract the search query.
  if (Intent.ACTION_SEARCH.equals(intent.getAction())) {
    String searchQuery = intent.getStringExtra(SearchManager.QUERY);
    // Perform the search
    performSearch(searchQuery);
  }
}

// Execute the search.
private void performSearch(String query) {
  // Pass the search query as an argument to the Cursor Loader
  Bundle args = new Bundle();
  args.putString(QUERY_EXTRA_KEY, query);

  // Restart the Cursor Loader to execute the new query.
  getLoaderManager().restartLoader(0, args, this);
}

public Loader<Cursor> onCreateLoader(int id, Bundle args) {
  String query = "0";

  // Extract the search query from the arguments.
  if (args != null)
    query = args.getString(QUERY_EXTRA_KEY);

  // Construct the new query in the form of a Cursor Loader.
  String[] projection = {
      MyContentProvider.KEY_ID,
      MyContentProvider.KEY_COLUMN_1_NAME
  };
  String where = MyContentProvider.KEY_COLUMN_1_NAME
                 + " LIKE \"%" + query + "%\"";
  String[] whereArgs = null;
  String sortOrder = MyContentProvider.KEY_COLUMN_1_NAME +
                     " COLLATE LOCALIZED ASC";

  // Create the new Cursor loader.
```

continues

LISTING 8-27 *(continued)*

```
    return new CursorLoader(this, MyContentProvider.CONTENT_URI,
      projection, where, whereArgs, sortOrder);
  }

  public void onLoadFinished(Loader<Cursor> loader, Cursor cursor) {
    // Replace the result Cursor displayed by the Cursor Adapter with
    // the new result set.
    adapter.swapCursor(cursor);
  }

  public void onLoaderReset(Loader<Cursor> loader) {
    // Remove the existing result Cursor from the List Adapter.
    adapter.swapCursor(null);
  }
}
```

code snippet PA4AD_ Ch08_DatabaseSkeleton/DatabaseSkeletonSearchActivity.java

---

This example uses a simple like-based search against a single column in a local Content Provider. Although outside the scope of this book, it's often more effective to perform full text searches on local databases, and to incorporate search results from cloud-based data sources.

In most circumstances you'll need to provide some functionality beyond simply displaying the search results. If you are using a List Activity or List Fragment, you can override the onListItemClick handler to react to user's selecting a search result, such as displaying the result details, as shown in Listing 8-28.

LISTING 8-28: Providing actions for search result selection

```
@Override
protected void onListItemClick(ListView listView, View view, int position, long id) {
  super.onListItemClick(listView, view, position, id);

  // Create a URI to the selected item.
  Uri selectedUri =
    ContentUris.withAppendedId(MyContentProvider.CONTENT_URI, id);

  // Create an Intent to view the selected item.
  Intent intent = new Intent(Intent.ACTION_VIEW);
  intent.setData(selectedUri);

  // Start an Activity to view the selected item.
  startActivity(intent);
}
```

code snippet PA4AD_ Ch08_DatabaseSkeleton/DatabaseSkeletonSearchActivity.java

Using the Search View Widget

Android 3.0 (API level 11) introduced the `SearchView` widget as an alternative to the Activity search bar. The Search View appears and behaves as an Edit Text View, but it can be configured to offer search suggestions and to initiate search queries within your application in the same way as the search bar in earlier versions of Android.

> *You can add the Search View anywhere in your View hierarchy and config-ure it in the same way; however, it's best practice to add it as an action View within your Activity's Action Bar, as described in more detail in Chapter 10, "Expanding the User Experience."*

To connect your Search View to your search Activity, you must first extract a reference to its `SearchableInfo` using the Search Manager's `getSearchableInfo` method. Use the Search View's `setSearchableInfo` method to bind this object to your Search View, as shown in Listing 8-29.

LISTING 8-29: Binding a Search View to your searchable Activity

```java
// Use the Search Manager to find the SearchableInfo related
// to this Activity.
SearchManager searchManager =
  (SearchManager)getSystemService(Context.SEARCH_SERVICE);
SearchableInfo searchableInfo =
  searchManager.getSearchableInfo(getComponentName());

// Bind the Activity's SearchableInfo to the Search View
SearchView searchView = (SearchView)findViewById(R.id.searchView);
searchView.setSearchableInfo(searchableInfo);
```

code snippet PA4AD_ Ch08_DatabaseSkeleton/DatabaseSkeletonSearchActivity.java

When connected, your Search View will work like the search bar, providing search suggestions (where possible) and displaying the Search Activity after a query has been entered.

By default, the Search View will be displayed as an icon that, when clicked, expands to the search edit box. You can use its `setIconifiedByDefault` method to disable this and have it always display as an edit box.

```java
searchView.setIconifiedByDefault(false);
```

By default a Search View query is initiated when the user presses Enter. You can choose to also dis-play a button to submit a search using the `setSubmitButtonEnabled` method.

```java
searchView.setSubmitButtonEnabled(true);
```

Supporting Search Suggestions from a Content Provider

Beyond the simple case of submitting a search and listing the results in your Activities, one of the most engaging innovations in search is the provision of real-time search suggestions as users type their queries.

Search suggestions display a simple list of possible search results beneath the search bar/Search View widget as users enter their queries, allowing them to bypass the search result Activity and jump directly to the search result.

Although your search Activity can structure its query and display the results Cursor data in any way, if you want to provide search suggestions, you need to create (or modify) a Content Provider to receive search queries and return suggestions using the expected projection.

To support search suggestions, you need to configure your Content Provider to recognize specific URI paths as search queries. Listing 8-30 shows a URI Matcher that compares a requested URI to the known search-query path values.

LISTING 8-30: Detecting search suggestion requests in Content Providers

```java
private static final int ALLROWS = 1;
private static final int SINGLE_ROW = 2;
private static final int SEARCH = 3;

private static final UriMatcher uriMatcher;

static {
  uriMatcher = new UriMatcher(UriMatcher.NO_MATCH);
  uriMatcher.addURI("com.paad.skeletondatabaseprovider",
                    "elements", ALLROWS);
  uriMatcher.addURI("com.paad.skeletondatabaseprovider",
                    "elements/#", SINGLE_ROW);

  uriMatcher.addURI("com.paad.skeletondatabaseprovider",
    SearchManager.SUGGEST_URI_PATH_QUERY, SEARCH);
  uriMatcher.addURI("com.paad.skeletondatabaseprovider",
    SearchManager.SUGGEST_URI_PATH_QUERY + "/*", SEARCH);
  uriMatcher.addURI("com.paad.skeletondatabaseprovider",
    SearchManager.SUGGEST_URI_PATH_SHORTCUT, SEARCH);
  uriMatcher.addURI("com.paad.skeletondatabaseprovider",
    SearchManager.SUGGEST_URI_PATH_SHORTCUT + "/*", SEARCH);
}
```

---

code snippet PA4AD_ Ch08_DatabaseSkeleton/src/MySearchSuggestionsContentProvider.java

Within your Content Provider use the Uri Matcher to return the search suggestion MIME type for search queries, as shown in Listing 8-31.

LISTING 8-31: Returning the correct MIME type for search results

```java
@Override
public String getType(Uri uri) {
  // Return a string that identifies the MIME type
  // for a Content Provider URI
  switch (uriMatcher.match(uri)) {
    case ALLROWS:
      return "vnd.android.cursor.dir/vnd.paad.elemental";
    case SINGLE_ROW:
      return "vnd.android.cursor.item/vnd.paad.elemental";
    case SEARCH :
      return SearchManager.SUGGEST_MIME_TYPE;
    default:
      throw new IllegalArgumentException("Unsupported URI: " + uri);
  }
}
```

code snippet PA4AD_ Ch08_DatabaseSkeleton/src/MySearchSuggestionsContentProvider.java

The Search Manager requests your search suggestions by initiating a query on your Content Provider, passing in the query value as the last element in the URI path. To provide suggestions, you must return a Cursor using a set of predefined columns.

There are two required columns, SUGGEST_COLUMN_TEXT_1, which displays the search result text, and _id, which indicates the unique row ID. You can supply up to two columns containing text, and an icon to be displayed on either the left or right of the text results.

It's also useful to include a SUGGEST_COLUMN_INTENT_DATA_ID column. The value returned in this column can be appended to a specified URI path and used to populate an Intent that will be fired if the suggestion is selected.

As speed is critical for real-time search results, in many cases it's good practice to create a separate table specifically to store and provide them. Listing 8-32 shows the skeleton code for creating a projection that returns a Cursor suitable for search results.

LISTING 8-32: Creating a projection for returning search suggestions

```java
public static final String KEY_SEARCH_COLUMN = KEY_COLUMN_1_NAME;

private static final HashMap<String, String> SEARCH_SUGGEST_PROJECTION_MAP;
static {
  SEARCH_SUGGEST_PROJECTION_MAP = new HashMap<String, String>();
  SEARCH_SUGGEST_PROJECTION_MAP.put(
    "_id", KEY_ID + " AS " + "_id");
  SEARCH_SUGGEST_PROJECTION_MAP.put(
    SearchManager.SUGGEST_COLUMN_TEXT_1,
```

continues

LISTING 8-32 *(continued)*

```
        KEY_SEARCH_COLUMN + " AS " + SearchManager.SUGGEST_COLUMN_TEXT_1);
    SEARCH_SUGGEST_PROJECTION_MAP.put(
        SearchManager.SUGGEST_COLUMN_INTENT_DATA_ID, KEY_ID +
        " AS " + "_id");
    }
```

code snippet PA4AD_ Ch08_DatabaseSkeleton/src/MySearchSuggestionsContentProvider.java

To perform the query that will supply the search suggestions, use the Uri Matcher within your query implementation, applying the projection map of the form defined in the previous listing, as shown in Listing 8-33.

LISTING 8-33: Returning search suggestions for a query

```
@Override
public Cursor query(Uri uri, String[] projection, String selection,
        String[] selectionArgs, String sortOrder) {
    // Open a read-only database.
    SQLiteDatabase db = myOpenHelper.getWritableDatabase();

    // Replace these with valid SQL statements if necessary.
    String groupBy = null;
    String having = null;

    SQLiteQueryBuilder queryBuilder = new SQLiteQueryBuilder();
    queryBuilder.setTables(MySQLiteOpenHelper.DATABASE_TABLE);

    // If this is a row query, limit the result set to the passed in row.
    switch (uriMatcher.match(uri)) {
      case SINGLE_ROW :
        String rowID = uri.getPathSegments().get(1);
        queryBuilder.appendWhere(KEY_ID + "=" + rowID);
        break;
      case SEARCH :
        String query = uri.getPathSegments().get(1);
        queryBuilder.appendWhere(KEY_SEARCH_COLUMN +
          " LIKE \"%" + query + "%\"");
        queryBuilder.setProjectionMap(SEARCH_SUGGEST_PROJECTION_MAP);
        break;
      default: break;
    }

    Cursor cursor = queryBuilder.query(db, projection, selection,
        selectionArgs, groupBy, having, sortOrder);

    return cursor;
}
```

code snippet PA4AD_ Ch08_DatabaseSkeleton/src/MySearchSuggestionsContentProvider.java

The final step is to update your searchable resource to specify the authority of the Content Provider that should be used to supply search suggestions for your search bar and/or Search View. This can be the same Content Provider used to execute regular queries (if you've mapped the columns as required), or an entirely different Provider.

Listing 8-34 shows how to specify the authority, as well as to define the `searchSuggestIntentAction` to determine which action to perform if a suggestion is clicked, and the `searchSuggestIntentData` attribute to specify the base URI that will be used in the action Intent's data value.

If you have included an Intent data ID column in your search suggestion result Cursor, it will be appended to this base URI.

LISTING 8-34: Configuring a searchable resource for search suggestions

```xml
<?xml version="1.0" encoding="utf-8"?>
<searchable xmlns:android="http://schemas.android.com/apk/res/android"
    android:label="@string/app_name"
    android:searchSuggestAuthority=
      "com.paad.skeletonsearchabledatabaseprovider"
    android:searchSuggestIntentAction="android.intent.action.VIEW"
    android:searchSuggestIntentData=
      "content://com.paad.skeletonsearchabledatabaseprovider/elements">
</searchable>
```

code snippet PA4AD_ Ch08_DatabaseSkeleton/res/xml/searchablewithsuggestions.xml

Surfacing Search Results in the Quick Search Box

The Quick Search Box (QSB) is a home screen Widget designed to provide universal search across every application installed on the host device, as well as to initiate web searches. Inclusion in QSB results is opt in — that is, developers can choose to supply search results, and users can select which supported application's results they want to see.

> *To supply results to the QSB, your application must be able to provide search suggestions, as described in the previous section, "Supporting Search Suggestions from a Content Provider." Chapter 14, "Invading the Home Screen," provides more details on how to surface your search results to the QSB.*

CREATING A SEARCHABLE EARTHQUAKE CONTENT PROVIDER

In this example you will modify the earthquake application you created in Chapter 6, "Using Internet Resources," by storing the earthquake data in a Content Provider. In this three-part example, you will start by moving the data to a Content Provider, and then update the application to use that Provider, and, finally, add support for search.

Creating the Content Provider

Start by creating a new Content Provider that will be used to store each earthquake once it has been parsed out of the Internet feed.

1. Open the Earthquake project and create a new `EarthquakeProvider` class that extends `ContentProvider`. Include stubs to override the `onCreate`, `getType`, `query`, `insert`, `delete`, and `update` methods.

```java
package com.paad.earthquake;

import android.content.ContentProvider;
import android.content.ContentUris;
import android.content.ContentValues;
import android.content.Context;
import android.content.UriMatcher;
import android.database.Cursor;
import android.database.SQLException;
import android.database.sqlite.SQLiteDatabase;
import android.database.sqlite.SQLiteDatabase.CursorFactory;
import android.database.sqlite.SQLiteOpenHelper;
import android.database.sqlite.SQLiteQueryBuilder;
import android.net.Uri;
import android.text.TextUtils;
import android.util.Log;

public class EarthquakeProvider extends ContentProvider {

  @Override
  public boolean onCreate() {
    return false;
  }

  @Override
  public String getType(Uri url) {
    return null;
  }

  @Override
  public Cursor query(Uri url, String[] projection, String selection,
                      String[] selectionArgs, String sort) {
    return null;
  }

  @Override
  public Uri insert(Uri _url, ContentValues _initialValues) {
    return null;
  }

  @Override
  public int delete(Uri url, String where, String[] whereArgs) {
    return 0;
  }
```

```
  @Override
  public int update(Uri url, ContentValues values,
                    String where, String[]wArgs) {
    return 0;
  }
}
```

2. Publish the URI for this provider. This URI will be used to access this Content Provider from within other application components via the `ContentResolver`.

```
public static final Uri CONTENT_URI =
  Uri.parse("content://com.paad.earthquakeprovider/earthquakes");
```

3. Create a set of public variables that describe the column names to be used within your database table.

```
// Column Names
public static final String KEY_ID = "_id";
public static final String KEY_DATE = "date";
public static final String KEY_DETAILS = "details";
public static final String KEY_SUMMARY = "summary";
public static final String KEY_LOCATION_LAT = "latitude";
public static final String KEY_LOCATION_LNG = "longitude";
public static final String KEY_MAGNITUDE = "magnitude";
public static final String KEY_LINK = "link";
```

4. Create the database that will be used to store the earthquakes. Within the `EarthquakeProvider` create a new `SQLiteOpenHelper` implementation that creates and updates the database.

```
// Helper class for opening, creating, and managing database version control
private static class EarthquakeDatabaseHelper extends SQLiteOpenHelper {

  private static final String TAG = "EarthquakeProvider";

  private static final String DATABASE_NAME = "earthquakes.db";
  private static final int DATABASE_VERSION = 1;
  private static final String EARTHQUAKE_TABLE = "earthquakes";

  private static final String DATABASE_CREATE =
    "create table " + EARTHQUAKE_TABLE + " ("
    + KEY_ID + " integer primary key autoincrement, "
    + KEY_DATE + " INTEGER, "
    + KEY_DETAILS + " TEXT, "
    + KEY_SUMMARY + " TEXT, "
    + KEY_LOCATION_LAT + " FLOAT, "
    + KEY_LOCATION_LNG + " FLOAT, "
    + KEY_MAGNITUDE + " FLOAT, "
    + KEY_LINK + " TEXT);";

  // The underlying database
  private SQLiteDatabase earthquakeDB;

  public EarthquakeDatabaseHelper(Context context, String name,
```

```
                                     CursorFactory factory, int version) {
      super(context, name, factory, version);
    }

    @Override
    public void onCreate(SQLiteDatabase db) {
      db.execSQL(DATABASE_CREATE);
    }

    @Override
    public void onUpgrade(SQLiteDatabase db, int oldVersion, int newVersion) {
      Log.w(TAG, "Upgrading database from version " + oldVersion + " to "
                 + newVersion + ", which will destroy all old data");

      db.execSQL("DROP TABLE IF EXISTS " + EARTHQUAKE_TABLE);
      onCreate(db);
    }
}
```

5. Override the Provider's onCreate handler to create a new instance of the database helper you created in step 4.

```
EarthquakeDatabaseHelper dbHelper;

@Override
public boolean onCreate() {
  Context context = getContext();

  dbHelper = new EarthquakeDatabaseHelper(context,
    EarthquakeDatabaseHelper.DATABASE_NAME, null,
    EarthquakeDatabaseHelper.DATABASE_VERSION);

  return true;
}
```

6. Create a UriMatcher to handle requests using different URIs. Include support for queries and transactions over the entire dataset (QUAKES) and a single record matching a quake index value (QUAKE_ID). Also override the getType method to return a MIME type for each of the URI structures supported.

```
// Create the constants used to differentiate between the different URI
// requests.
private static final int QUAKES = 1;
private static final int QUAKE_ID = 2;

private static final UriMatcher uriMatcher;

// Allocate the UriMatcher object, where a URI ending in 'earthquakes' will
// correspond to a request for all earthquakes, and 'earthquakes' with a
// trailing '/[rowID]' will represent a single earthquake row.
static {
  uriMatcher = new UriMatcher(UriMatcher.NO_MATCH);
  uriMatcher.addURI("com.paad.earthquakeprovider", "earthquakes", QUAKES);
  uriMatcher.addURI("com.paad.earthquakeprovider", "earthquakes/#", QUAKE_ID);
}
```

```java
@Override
public String getType(Uri uri) {
  switch (uriMatcher.match(uri)) {
    case QUAKES: return "vnd.android.cursor.dir/vnd.paad.earthquake";
    case QUAKE_ID: return "vnd.android.cursor.item/vnd.paad.earthquake";
    default: throw new IllegalArgumentException("Unsupported URI: " + uri);
  }
}
```

7. Implement the query and transaction stubs. Start by requesting a read / write version of the database using the SQLite Open Helper. Then implement the `query` method, which should decode the request being made based on the URI (either all content or a single row), and apply the selection, projection, and sort-order parameters to the database before returning a result Cursor.

```java
@Override
public Cursor query(Uri uri,
                    String[] projection,
                    String selection,
                    String[] selectionArgs,
                    String sort) {

  SQLiteDatabase database = dbHelper.getWritableDatabase();

  SQLiteQueryBuilder qb = new SQLiteQueryBuilder();

  qb.setTables(EarthquakeDatabaseHelper.EARTHQUAKE_TABLE);

  // If this is a row query, limit the result set to the passed in row.
  switch (uriMatcher.match(uri)) {
    case QUAKE_ID: qb.appendWhere(KEY_ID + "=" + uri.getPathSegments().get(1));
                   break;
    default      : break;
  }

  // If no sort order is specified, sort by date / time
  String orderBy;
  if (TextUtils.isEmpty(sort)) {
    orderBy = KEY_DATE;
  } else {
    orderBy = sort;
  }

  // Apply the query to the underlying database.
  Cursor c = qb.query(database,
                      projection,
                      selection, selectionArgs,
                      null, null,
                      orderBy);

  // Register the contexts ContentResolver to be notified if
  // the cursor result set changes.
  c.setNotificationUri(getContext().getContentResolver(), uri);
```

```
    // Return a cursor to the query result.
    return c;
}
```

8. Now implement methods for inserting, deleting, and updating content. In this case the
    process is an exercise in mapping Content Provider transaction requests to their database
    equivalents.

```java
@Override
public Uri insert(Uri _uri, ContentValues _initialValues) {
  SQLiteDatabase database = dbHelper.getWritableDatabase();

  // Insert the new row. The call to database.insert will return the row number
  // if it is successful.
  long rowID = database.insert(
    EarthquakeDatabaseHelper.EARTHQUAKE_TABLE, "quake", _initialValues);

  // Return a URI to the newly inserted row on success.
  if (rowID > 0) {
    Uri uri = ContentUris.withAppendedId(CONTENT_URI, rowID);
    getContext().getContentResolver().notifyChange(uri, null);
    return uri;
  }

  throw new SQLException("Failed to insert row into " + _uri);
}

@Override
public int delete(Uri uri, String where, String[] whereArgs) {
  SQLiteDatabase database = dbHelper.getWritableDatabase();

  int count;
  switch (uriMatcher.match(uri)) {
    case QUAKES:
      count = database.delete(
        EarthquakeDatabaseHelper.EARTHQUAKE_TABLE, where, whereArgs);
      break;
    case QUAKE_ID:
      String segment = uri.getPathSegments().get(1);
      count = database.delete(EarthquakeDatabaseHelper.EARTHQUAKE_TABLE,
              KEY_ID + "="
              + segment
              + (!TextUtils.isEmpty(where) ? " AND ("
              + where + ')' : ""), whereArgs);
      break;

    default: throw new IllegalArgumentException("Unsupported URI: " + uri);
  }

  getContext().getContentResolver().notifyChange(uri, null);
  return count;
}
```

```
@Override
public int update(Uri uri, ContentValues values,
            String where, String[] whereArgs) {
  SQLiteDatabase database = dbHelper.getWritableDatabase();

  int count;
  switch (uriMatcher.match(uri)) {
    case QUAKES:
      count = database.update(EarthquakeDatabaseHelper.EARTHQUAKE_TABLE,
                              values, where, whereArgs);
      break;
    case QUAKE_ID:
      String segment = uri.getPathSegments().get(1);
      count = database.update(EarthquakeDatabaseHelper.EARTHQUAKE_TABLE,
                              values, KEY_ID
                                + "=" + segment
                                + (!TextUtils.isEmpty(where) ? " AND ("
                                + where + ')' : ""), whereArgs);
      break;
    default: throw new IllegalArgumentException("Unknown URI " + uri);
  }

  getContext().getContentResolver().notifyChange(uri, null);
  return count;
}
```

9. With the Content Provider complete, register it in the manifest by creating a new `provider` node within the application tag.

```
<provider android:name=".EarthquakeProvider"
          android:authorities="com.paad.earthquakeprovider" />
```

> *All code snippets in this example are part of the* Chapter 8 Earthquake Part 1 *project, available for download at* www.wrox.com.

Using the Earthquake Provider

You can now update the Earthquake List Fragment to store each earthquake using the Earthquake Provider, and use that Content Provider to populate the associated List View.

1. Within the `EarthquakeListFragment`, update the `addNewQuake` method. It should use the application's Content Resolver to insert each new Earthquake into the provider.

```
private void addNewQuake(Quake _quake) {
  ContentResolver cr = getActivity().getContentResolver();
  // Construct a where clause to make sure we don't already have this
  // earthquake in the provider.
  String w = EarthquakeProvider.KEY_DATE + " = " + _quake.getDate().getTime();

  // If the earthquake is new, insert it into the provider.
```

```
Cursor query = cr.query(EarthquakeProvider.CONTENT_URI, null, w, null, null);
if (query.getCount()==0) {
  ContentValues values = new ContentValues();

  values.put(EarthquakeProvider.KEY_DATE, _quake.getDate().getTime());
  values.put(EarthquakeProvider.KEY_DETAILS, _quake.getDetails());
  values.put(EarthquakeProvider.KEY_SUMMARY, _quake.toString());

  double lat = _quake.getLocation().getLatitude();
  double lng = _quake.getLocation().getLongitude();
  values.put(EarthquakeProvider.KEY_LOCATION_LAT, lat);
  values.put(EarthquakeProvider.KEY_LOCATION_LNG, lng);
  values.put(EarthquakeProvider.KEY_LINK, _quake.getLink());
  values.put(EarthquakeProvider.KEY_MAGNITUDE, _quake.getMagnitude());

  cr.insert(EarthquakeProvider.CONTENT_URI, values);
}
query.close();
}
```

2. Now that you're storing each earthquake in a Content Provider, you should replace your Array Adapter with a Simple Cursor Adapter. This adapter will manage applying changes to the underlying table directly to your List View. Take the opportunity to remove the Array Adapter and array as well. (You'll need to remove the reference to the earthquake array from the refreshEarthquakes method.)

```
SimpleCursorAdapter adapter;

@Override
public void onActivityCreated(Bundle savedInstanceState) {
  super.onActivityCreated(savedInstanceState);

  // Create a new Adapter and bind it to the List View
  adapter = new SimpleCursorAdapter(getActivity(),
    android.R.layout.simple_list_item_1, null,
    new String[] { EarthquakeProvider.KEY_SUMMARY },
    new int[] { android.R.id.text1 }, 0);
  setListAdapter(adapter);

  Thread t = new Thread(new Runnable() {
    public void run() {
      refreshEarthquakes();
    }
  });
  t.start();
}
```

3. Use a Cursor Loader to query the database and supply a Cursor to the Cursor Adapter you created in step 2. Start by modifying the Fragment inheritance to implement LoaderManager.LoaderCallbacks<Cursor> and add the associated method stubs.

```
public class EarthquakeListFragment extends ListFragment implements
  LoaderManager.LoaderCallbacks<Cursor> {
```

```
// [... Existing EarthquakeListFragment code ...]

public Loader<Cursor> onCreateLoader(int id, Bundle args) {
  return null;
}

public void onLoadFinished(Loader<Cursor> loader, Cursor cursor) {
}

public void onLoaderReset(Loader<Cursor> loader) {
}
}
```

4. Complete the `onCreateLoader` handler by building and returning a Loader that queries the `EarthquakeProvider` for all its elements. Be sure to add a `where` clause that restricts the result Cursor to only earthquakes of the minimum magnitude specified by the user preferences.

```
public Loader<Cursor> onCreateLoader(int id, Bundle args) {
  String[] projection = new String[] {
    EarthquakeProvider.KEY_ID,
    EarthquakeProvider.KEY_SUMMARY
  };

  Earthquake earthquakeActivity = (Earthquake)getActivity();
  String where = EarthquakeProvider.KEY_MAGNITUDE + " > " +
                 earthquakeActivity.minimumMagnitude;

  CursorLoader loader = new CursorLoader(getActivity(),
    EarthquakeProvider.CONTENT_URI, projection, where, null, null);

  return loader;
}
```

5. When the Loader's query completes, the result Cursor will be returned to the `onLoad Finished` handler, so you need to swap out the previous Cursor with the new result. Similarly, remove the reference to the Cursor when the Loader resets.

```
public void onLoadFinished(Loader<Cursor> loader, Cursor cursor) {
  adapter.swapCursor(cursor);
}

public void onLoaderReset(Loader<Cursor> loader) {
  adapter.swapCursor(null);
}
```

6. Update the `onActivityCreated` handler to initiate the Loader when the Activity is created, and the `refreshEarthquakes` method to restart it. Note that you must initialize and restart the loader from the main UI thread, so use a Handler to post the restart from within the `refreshEarthquakes` thread.

```
Handler handler = new Handler();
@Override
public void onActivityCreated(Bundle savedInstanceState) {
```

```
      super.onActivityCreated(savedInstanceState);

      // Create a new Adapter and bind it to the List View
      adapter = new SimpleCursorAdapter(getActivity(),
        android.R.layout.simple_list_item_1, null,
        new String[] { EarthquakeProvider.KEY_SUMMARY },
        new int[] { android.R.id.text1 }, 0);
      setListAdapter(adapter);

      getLoaderManager().initLoader(0, null, this);

      Thread t = new Thread(new Runnable() {
        public void run() {
          refreshEarthquakes();
        }
      });
      t.start();
  }

  public void refreshEarthquakes() {
    handler.post(new Runnable() {
      public void run() {
        getLoaderManager().restartLoader(0, null, EarthquakeListFragment.this);
      }
    });

    // [... Existing refreshEarthquakes code ...]
  }
```

> *All code snippets in this example are part of the* Chapter 8 Earthquake Part 2
> *project, available for download at* www.wrox.com.

Searching the Earthquake Provider

In the following example you'll add search functionality to the Earthquake project and make sure results are available from the home screen Quick Search Box.

1. Start by adding a new string resource to the `strings.xml` file (in the `res/values` folder) that describes the earthquake search description.

```
<string name="search_description">Search earthquake locations</string>
```

2. Create a new `searchable.xml` file in the `res/xml` folder that defines the metadata for your Earthquake search results provider. Specify the string from step 1 as the description. Specify the Earthquake Content Provider's authority and set the `searchSuggestIntentAction` and `searchSuggestIntentData` attributes.

```
<searchable xmlns:android="http://schemas.android.com/apk/res/android"
  android:label="@string/app_name"
  android:searchSettingsDescription="@string/search_description"
```

```
    android:searchSuggestAuthority="com.paad.earthquakeprovider"
    android:searchSuggestIntentAction="android.intent.action.VIEW"
    android:searchSuggestIntentData=
      "content://com.paad.earthquakeprovider/earthquakes">
</searchable>
```

3. Open the Earthquake Content Provider and create a new Hash Map that will be used to supply a projection to support search suggestions.

```
private static final HashMap<String, String> SEARCH_PROJECTION_MAP;
static {
  SEARCH_PROJECTION_MAP = new HashMap<String, String>();
  SEARCH_PROJECTION_MAP.put(SearchManager.SUGGEST_COLUMN_TEXT_1, KEY_SUMMARY +
    " AS " + SearchManager.SUGGEST_COLUMN_TEXT_1);
  SEARCH_PROJECTION_MAP.put("_id", KEY_ID +
    " AS " + "_id");
}
```

4. Modify the `UriMatcher` to include search queries.

```
private static final int QUAKES = 1;
private static final int QUAKE_ID = 2;
private static final int SEARCH = 3;

private static final UriMatcher uriMatcher;

//Allocate the UriMatcher object, where a URI ending in 'earthquakes' will
//correspond to a request for all earthquakes, and 'earthquakes' with a
//trailing '/[rowID]' will represent a single earthquake row.
static {
 uriMatcher = new UriMatcher(UriMatcher.NO_MATCH);
 uriMatcher.addURI("com.paad.earthquakeprovider", "earthquakes", QUAKES);
 uriMatcher.addURI("com.paad.earthquakeprovider", "earthquakes/#", QUAKE_ID);
 uriMatcher.addURI("com.paad.earthquakeprovider",
   SearchManager.SUGGEST_URI_PATH_QUERY, SEARCH);
 uriMatcher.addURI("com.paad.earthquakeprovider",
   SearchManager.SUGGEST_URI_PATH_QUERY + "/*", SEARCH);
 uriMatcher.addURI("com.paad.earthquakeprovider",
   SearchManager.SUGGEST_URI_PATH_SHORTCUT, SEARCH);
 uriMatcher.addURI("com.paad.earthquakeprovider",
   SearchManager.SUGGEST_URI_PATH_SHORTCUT + "/*", SEARCH);
}
```

5. Also modify the `getType` method to return the appropriate MIME type for the search results.

```
@Override
public String getType(Uri uri) {
  switch (uriMatcher.match(uri)) {
    case QUAKES  : return "vnd.android.cursor.dir/vnd.paad.earthquake";
    case QUAKE_ID: return "vnd.android.cursor.item/vnd.paad.earthquake";
    case SEARCH  : return SearchManager.SUGGEST_MIME_TYPE;
    default: throw new IllegalArgumentException("Unsupported URI: " + uri);
  }
}
```

6. The final change to the Content Provider is to modify the `query` method to apply the search term and return the result Cursor using the projection you created in step 3.

```
@Override
public Cursor query(Uri uri,
                    String[] projection,
                    String selection,
                    String[] selectionArgs,
                    String sort) {

  SQLiteDatabase database = dbHelper.getWritableDatabase();

  SQLiteQueryBuilder qb = new SQLiteQueryBuilder();

  qb.setTables(EarthquakeDatabaseHelper.EARTHQUAKE_TABLE);

  // If this is a row query, limit the result set to the passed in row.
  switch (uriMatcher.match(uri)) {
    case QUAKE_ID: qb.appendWhere(KEY_ID + "=" + uri.getPathSegments().get(1));
                   break;
    case SEARCH  : qb.appendWhere(KEY_SUMMARY + " LIKE \"%" +
                      uri.getPathSegments().get(1) + "%\"");
                   qb.setProjectionMap(SEARCH_PROJECTION_MAP);
                   break;
    default      : break;
  }

  [ ... existing query method ... ]
}
```

7. Now create a Search Results Activity. Create a simple `EarthquakeSearchResults` Activity that extends `ListActivity` and is populated using a Simple Cursor Adapter. The Activity will use a Cursor Loader to perform the search query, so it must also implement the Loader Manager Loader Callbacks.

```
import android.app.ListActivity;
import android.app.LoaderManager;
import android.app.SearchManager;
import android.content.CursorLoader;
import android.content.Intent;
import android.content.Loader;
import android.database.Cursor;
import android.os.Bundle;
import android.widget.SimpleCursorAdapter;

public class EarthquakeSearchResults extends ListActivity implements
  LoaderManager.LoaderCallbacks<Cursor> {

  private SimpleCursorAdapter adapter;

  @Override
  public void onCreate(Bundle savedInstanceState) {
    super.onCreate(savedInstanceState);
```

```
      // Create a new adapter and bind it to the List View
      adapter = new SimpleCursorAdapter(this,
              android.R.layout.simple_list_item_1, null,
              new String[] { EarthquakeProvider.KEY_SUMMARY },
              new int[] { android.R.id.text1 }, 0);
      setListAdapter(adapter);
    }

    public Loader<Cursor> onCreateLoader(int id, Bundle args) {
      return null;
    }

    public void onLoadFinished(Loader<Cursor> loader, Cursor cursor) {
    }

    public void onLoaderReset(Loader<Cursor> loader) {
    }
  }
```

8. Update the `onCreate` method to initialize the Cursor Loader. Create a new `parseIntent`
stub method that will be used to parse the Intents containing the search query and pass in the
launch Intents from within `onCreate` and `onNewIntent`.

```
@Override
public void onCreate(Bundle savedInstanceState) {
  super.onCreate(savedInstanceState);

  // Create a new adapter and bind it to the List View
  adapter = new SimpleCursorAdapter(this,
    android.R.layout.simple_list_item_1, null,
    new String[] { EarthquakeProvider.KEY_SUMMARY },
    new int[] { android.R.id.text1 }, 0);
  setListAdapter(adapter);

  // Initiate the Cursor Loader
  getLoaderManager().initLoader(0, null, this);

  // Get the launch Intent
  parseIntent(getIntent());
}

@Override
protected void onNewIntent(Intent intent) {
  super.onNewIntent(intent);
  parseIntent(getIntent());
}

private void parseIntent(Intent intent) {
}
```

9. Update the `parseIntent` method to extract the search query from within the Intent and
restart the Cursor Loader to apply the new query, passing in the query value using a Bundle.

```
private static String QUERY_EXTRA_KEY = "QUERY_EXTRA_KEY";
```

```
private void parseIntent(Intent intent) {
  // If the Activity was started to service a Search request,
  // extract the search query.
  if (Intent.ACTION_SEARCH.equals(intent.getAction())) {
    String searchQuery = intent.getStringExtra(SearchManager.QUERY);

    // Perform the search, passing in the search query as an argument
    // to the Cursor Loader
    Bundle args = new Bundle();
    args.putString(QUERY_EXTRA_KEY, searchQuery);

    // Restart the Cursor Loader to execute the new query.
    getLoaderManager().restartLoader(0, args, this);
  }
}
```

10. Implement the Loader Manager Loader Callback handlers to execute the search query, and assign the results to the Simple Cursor Adapter.

```
public Loader<Cursor> onCreateLoader(int id, Bundle args) {
  String query = "0";

  if (args != null) {
    // Extract the search query from the arguments.
    query = args.getString(QUERY_EXTRA_KEY);
  }

  // Construct the new query in the form of a Cursor Loader.
  String[] projection = { EarthquakeProvider.KEY_ID,
      EarthquakeProvider.KEY_SUMMARY };
  String where = EarthquakeProvider.KEY_SUMMARY
                  + " LIKE \"%" + query + "%\"";
  String[] whereArgs = null;
  String sortOrder = EarthquakeProvider.KEY_SUMMARY + " COLLATE LOCALIZED ASC";

  // Create the new Cursor loader.
  return new CursorLoader(this, EarthquakeProvider.CONTENT_URI,
        projection, where, whereArgs,
        sortOrder);
}

public void onLoadFinished(Loader<Cursor> loader, Cursor cursor) {
  // Replace the result Cursor displayed by the Cursor Adapter with
  // the new result set.
  adapter.swapCursor(cursor);
}

public void onLoaderReset(Loader<Cursor> loader) {
  // Remove the existing result Cursor from the List Adapter.
  adapter.swapCursor(null);
}
```

11. Open the application Manifest, and add the new EarthquakeSearchResults Activity. Make sure you add an Intent Filter for the SEARCH action in the DEFAULT category. You will also need to add a meta-data tag that specifies the searchable XML resource you created in step 2.

```
<activity android:name=".EarthquakeSearchResults"
  android:label="Earthquake Search"
  android:launchMode="singleTop">
  <intent-filter>
    <action android:name="android.intent.action.SEARCH" />
    <category android:name="android.intent.category.DEFAULT" />
  </intent-filter>
  <meta-data
    android:name="android.app.searchable"
    android:resource="@xml/searchable"
  />
</activity>
```

12. Still in the manifest, add a new `meta-data` tag to the `application` node that describes the Earthquake Search Results Activity as the default search provider for the application.

```
<application android:icon="@drawable/icon"
             android:label="@string/app_name">
  <meta-data
    android:name="android.app.default_searchable"
    android:value=".EarthquakeSearchResults"
  />
  [ ... existing application node ... ]
</application>
```

13. For Android devices that feature a hardware search key, you're finished. To add support for devices without hardware search keys, you can add a Search View to the `main.xml` layout definition for the Earthquake Activity.

```
<?xml version="1.0" encoding="utf-8"?>
<LinearLayout xmlns:android="http://schemas.android.com/apk/res/android"
  android:orientation="vertical"
  android:layout_width="match_parent"
  android:layout_height="match_parent">
  <SearchView
    android:id="@+id/searchView"
    android:iconifiedByDefault="false"
    android:background="#FFF"
    android:layout_width="wrap_content"
    android:layout_height="wrap_content">
  </SearchView>
  <fragment android:name="com.paad.earthquake.EarthquakeListFragment"
    android:id="@+id/EarthquakeListFragment"
    android:layout_width="match_parent"
    android:layout_height="match_parent"
  />
</LinearLayout>
```

14. Return to the Earthquake Activity and connect the Search View to the searchable definition within the `onCreate` handler of the Earthquake Activity.

```
@Override
public void onCreate(Bundle savedInstanceState) {
  super.onCreate(savedInstanceState);
```

```
    setContentView(R.layout.main);

    updateFromPreferences();

    // Use the Search Manager to find the SearchableInfo related to this
    // Activity.
    SearchManager searchManager =
      (SearchManager)getSystemService(Context.SEARCH_SERVICE);
    SearchableInfo searchableInfo =
      searchManager.getSearchableInfo(getComponentName());

    // Bind the Activity's SearchableInfo to the Search View
    SearchView searchView = (SearchView)findViewById(R.id.searchView);
    searchView.setSearchableInfo(searchableInfo);
}
```

> *All code snippets in this example are part of the* Chapter 8 Earthquake Part 3 *project, available for download at* www.wrox.com.

NATIVE ANDROID CONTENT PROVIDERS

Android exposes several native Content Providers, which you can access directly using the techniques described earlier in this chapter. Alternatively, the android.provider package includes APIs that can simplify access to many of the most useful Content Providers, including the following:

➤ **Media Store** — Provides centralized, managed access to the multimedia on your device, including audio, video, and images. You can store your own multimedia within the Media Store and make it globally available, as shown in Chapter 15, "Audio, Video, and Using the Camera."

➤ **Browser** — Reads or modifies browser and browser search history.

➤ **Contacts Contract** — Retrieves, modifies, or stores contact details and associated social stream updates.

➤ **Calendar** — Creates new events, and deletes or updates existing calendar entries. That includes modifying the attendee lists and setting reminders.

➤ **Call Log** — Views or updates the call history, including incoming and outgoing calls, missed calls, and call details, including caller IDs and call durations.

These Content Providers, with the exception of the Browser and Call Log, are covered in more detail in the following sections.

You should use these native Content Providers wherever possible to ensure your application integrates seamlessly with other native and third-party applications.

Using the Media Store Content Provider

The Android Media Store is a managed repository of audio, video, and image files.

Whenever you add a new multimedia file to the filesystem, it should also be added to the Media Store using the Content Scanner, as described in Chapter 15; this will expose it to other applications, including media players. In most circumstances it's not necessary (or recommended) to modify the contents of the Media Store Content Provider directly.

To access the media available within the Media Store, the MediaStore class includes Audio, Video, and Images subclasses, which in turn contain subclasses that are used to provide the column names and content URIs for the corresponding media providers.

The Media Store segregates media kept on the internal and external volumes of the host device. Each Media Store subclass provides a URI for either the internally or externally stored media using the forms:

➤ `MediaStore.<mediatype>.Media.EXTERNAL_CONTENT_URI`

➤ `MediaStore.<mediatype>.Media.INTERNAL_CONTENT_URI`

Listing 8-35 shows a simple code snippet used to find the song title and album name for each piece of audio stored on the external volume.

LISTING 8-35: Accessing the Media Store Content Provider

```
// Get a Cursor over every piece of audio on the external volume,
// extracting the song title and album name.
String[] projection = new String[] {
  MediaStore.Audio.AudioColumns.ALBUM,
  MediaStore.Audio.AudioColumns.TITLE
};

Uri contentUri = MediaStore.Audio.Media.EXTERNAL_CONTENT_URI;

Cursor cursor =
  getContentResolver().query(contentUri, projection,
                             null, null, null);

// Get the index of the columns we need.
int albumIdx =
  cursor.getColumnIndexOrThrow(MediaStore.Audio.AudioColumns.ALBUM);
int titleIdx =
  cursor.getColumnIndexOrThrow(MediaStore.Audio.AudioColumns.TITLE);

// Create an array to store the result set.
String[] result = new String[cursor.getCount()];

// Iterate over the Cursor, extracting each album name and song title.
while (cursor.moveToNext()) {
```

continues

LISTING 8-35 *(continued)*

```
    // Extract the song title.
    String title = cursor.getString(titleIdx);
    // Extract the album name.
    String album = cursor.getString(albumIdx);

    result[cursor.getPosition()] = title + " (" + album + ")";
}

// Close the Cursor.
cursor.close();
```

code snippet PA4AD_ Ch08_ContentProviders/src/Ch08_ContentProvidersActivity.java

 In Chapter 15 you'll learn how to play audio and video resources stored in the Media Store by specifying the URI of a particular multimedia item.

Using the Contacts Contract Content Provider

Android makes the full database of contact information available to any application that has been granted the READ_CONTACTS permission.

The Contacts Contract Provider provides an extensible database of contact-related information. This allows users to specify multiple sources for their contact information. More importantly, it allows developers to arbitrarily extend the data stored against each contact, or even become an alternative provider for contacts and contact details.

 Android 2.0 (API level 5) introduced the ContactsContract *class, which super-seded the deprecated* Contacts *class that had previously been used to store and manage the contacts stored on the device.*

Introducing the Contacts Contract Content Provider

Rather than providing a single, fully defined table of contact detail columns, the Contacts Contract provider uses a three-tier data model to store data, associate it with a contact, and aggregate it to a single person using the following ContactsContract subclasses:

➤ Data — Each row in the underlying table defines a set of personal data (phone numbers, email addresses, and so on), separated by MIME type. Although there is a predefined set of common column names for each personal data-type available (along with the appropriate MIME types from subclasses within ContactsContract.CommonDataKinds), this table can be used to store *any* value.

The kind of data stored in a particular row is determined by the MIME type specified for that row. A series of generic columns is then used to store up to 15 different pieces of data varying by MIME type.

When adding new data to the Data table, you specify a Raw Contact to which a set of data will be associated.

➤   `RawContacts` — From Android 2.0 (API level 5) forward, users can add multiple contact account providers to their device. Each row in the Raw Contacts table defines an account to which a set of `Data` values is associated.

➤   `Contacts` — The Contacts table aggregates rows from Raw Contacts that all describe the same person.

The contents of each of these tables are aggregated as shown in Figure 8-4.

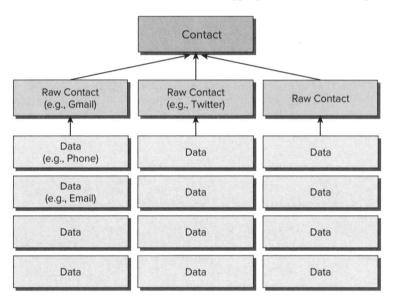

FIGURE 8-4

Typically, you will use the Data table to add, delete, or modify data stored against an existing contact account, the Raw Contacts table to create and manage accounts, and both the Contact and Data tables to query the database to extract contact details.

Reading Contact Details

To access any contact details, you need to include the READ_CONTACTS uses-permission in your application manifest:

```
<uses-permission android:name="android.permission.READ_CONTACTS"/>
```

Use the Content Resolver to query any of the three Contact Contracts Providers previously described using their respective CONTENT_URI static constants. Each class includes their column names as static properties.

Listing 8-36 queries the Contacts table for a Cursor to every person in the address book, creating an array of strings that holds each contact's name and unique ID.

LISTING 8-36: Accessing the Contacts Contract Contact Content Provider

```java
// Create a projection that limits the result Cursor
// to the required columns.
String[] projection = {
    ContactsContract.Contacts._ID,
    ContactsContract.Contacts.DISPLAY_NAME
};

// Get a Cursor over the Contacts Provider.
Cursor cursor =
  getContentResolver().query(ContactsContract.Contacts.CONTENT_URI,
                             projection, null, null, null);

// Get the index of the columns.
int nameIdx =
  cursor.getColumnIndexOrThrow(ContactsContract.Contacts.DISPLAY_NAME);
int idIdx =
  cursor.getColumnIndexOrThrow(ContactsContract.Contacts._ID);

// Initialize the result set.
String[] result = new String[cursor.getCount()];

// Iterate over the result Cursor.
while(cursor.moveToNext()) {
  // Extract the name.
  String name = cursor.getString(nameIdx);
  // Extract the unique ID.
  String id = cursor.getString(idIdx);

  result[cursor.getPosition()] = name + " (" + id + ")";
}

// Close the Cursor.
cursor.close();
```

code snippet PA4AD_ Ch08_ContentProviders/src/Ch08_ContentProvidersActivity.java

The `ContactsContract.Data` Content Provider is used to store all the contact details, such as addresses, phone numbers, and email addresses. In most cases, you will likely be querying for contact details based on a full or partial contact name.

To simplify this lookup, Android provides the `ContactsContract.Contacts.CONTENT_FILTER_URI` query URI. Append the full or partial name to this lookup as an additional path segment to the URI. To extract the associated contact details, find the `_ID` value from the returned Cursor, and use it to create a query on the Data table.

The content of each column with a row in the Data table depends on the MIME type specified for that row. As a result, any query on the Data table must filter the rows by MIME type to meaningfully extract data.

Listing 8-37 shows how to use the contact-detail column names available in the `CommonDataKinds` subclasses to extract the display name and mobile phone number from the Data table for a particular contact.

LISTING 8-37: Finding contact details for a contact name

```
ContentResolver cr = getContentResolver();
String[] result = null;

// Find a contact using a partial name match
String searchName = "andy";
Uri lookupUri =
  Uri.withAppendedPath(ContactsContract.Contacts.CONTENT_FILTER_URI,
                       searchName);

// Create a projection of the required column names.
String[] projection = new String[] {
  ContactsContract.Contacts._ID
};

// Get a Cursor that will return the ID(s) of the matched name.
Cursor idCursor = cr.query(lookupUri,
  projection, null, null, null);

// Extract the first matching ID if it exists.
String id = null;
if (idCursor.moveToFirst()) {
  int idIdx =
    idCursor.getColumnIndexOrThrow(ContactsContract.Contacts._ID);
  id = idCursor.getString(idIdx);
}

// Close that Cursor.
idCursor.close();

// Create a new Cursor searching for the data associated with the returned Contact ID.
if (id != null) {
  // Return all the PHONE data for the contact.
  String where = ContactsContract.Data.CONTACT_ID +
    " = " + id + " AND " +
    ContactsContract.Data.MIMETYPE + " = '" +
    ContactsContract.CommonDataKinds.Phone.CONTENT_ITEM_TYPE +
    "'";

  projection = new String[] {
    ContactsContract.Data.DISPLAY_NAME,
    ContactsContract.CommonDataKinds.Phone.NUMBER
  };

  Cursor dataCursor =
    getContentResolver().query(ContactsContract.Data.CONTENT_URI,
      projection, where, null, null);

  // Get the indexes of the required columns.
```

continues

LISTING 8-37 *(continued)*

```
    int nameIdx =
      dataCursor.getColumnIndexOrThrow(ContactsContract.Data.DISPLAY_NAME);
    int phoneIdx =
      dataCursor.getColumnIndexOrThrow(
        ContactsContract.CommonDataKinds.Phone.NUMBER);

    result = new String[dataCursor.getCount()];

    while(dataCursor.moveToNext()) {
      // Extract the name.
      String name = dataCursor.getString(nameIdx);
      // Extract the phone number.
      String number = dataCursor.getString(phoneIdx);

      result[dataCursor.getPosition()] = name + " (" + number + ")";
    }

    dataCursor.close();
}
```

code snippet PA4AD_ Ch08_ContentProviders/src/Ch08_ContentProvidersActivity.java

The Contacts subclass also offers a phone number lookup URI to help find a contact associated with a particular phone number. This query is highly optimized to return fast results for caller-ID notification.

Use `ContactsContract.PhoneLookup.CONTENT_FILTER_URI`, appending the number to look up as an additional path segment, as shown in Listing 8-38.

LISTING 8-38: Performing a caller-ID lookup

```
String incomingNumber = "(650)253-0000";
String result = "Not Found";

Uri lookupUri =
  Uri.withAppendedPath(ContactsContract.PhoneLookup.CONTENT_FILTER_URI,
                       incomingNumber);

String[] projection = new String[] {
  ContactsContract.Contacts.DISPLAY_NAME
};

Cursor cursor = getContentResolver().query(lookupUri,
  projection, null, null, null);

if (cursor.moveToFirst()) {
  int nameIdx =
    cursor.getColumnIndexOrThrow(ContactsContract.Contacts.DISPLAY_NAME);
```

```
      result = cursor.getString(nameIdx);
   }

   cursor.close();
```

code snippet PA4AD_ Ch08_ContentProviders/src/Ch08_ContentProvidersActivity.java

Creating and Picking Contacts Using Intents

The Contacts Contract Content Provider includes an Intent-based mechanism that can be used to view, insert, or select a contact using an existing contact application (typically, the native application).

This is the best practice approach and has the advantage of presenting the user with a consistent interface for performing the same task, avoiding ambiguity and improving the overall user experience.

To display a list of contacts for your users to select from, you can use the `Intent.ACTION_PICK` action along with the `ContactsContract.Contacts.CONTENT_URI`, as shown in Listing 8-39.

LISTING 8-39: Picking a contact

```
private static int PICK_CONTACT = 0;

private void pickContact() {
   Intent intent = new Intent(Intent.ACTION_PICK,
                              ContactsContract.Contacts.CONTENT_URI);
   startActivityForResult(intent, PICK_CONTACT);
}
```

code snippet PA4AD_ Ch08_ContentProviders/src/Ch08_ContentProvidersActivity.java

This will display a List View of the contacts available (as shown in Figure 8-5).

When the user selects a contact, it will be returned as a URI within the data property of the returned Intent, as shown in this extension to Listing 8-39.

```
@Override
protected void onActivityResult(int requestCode, int resultCode, Intent data) {
   super.onActivityResult(requestCode, resultCode, data);
   if ((requestCode == PICK_CONTACT) && (resultCode == RESULT_OK)) {
      resultTextView.setText(data.getData().toString());
   }
}
```

There are two alternatives to insert a new contact, both of which will prepopulate the new contact form using the values you specify as extras in your Intent.

The `ContactsContract.Intents.SHOW_OR_CREATE_CONTACT` action will search the contacts Provider for a particular email address or telephone number URI, offering to insert a new entry only if a contact with the specified contact address doesn't exist.

FIGURE 8-5

Use the constants in the `ContactsContract.Intents.Insert` class to include Intent extras that can be used to prepopulate contact details, including the name, company, email, phone number, notes, and postal address of the new contact, as shown in Listing 8-40.

LISTING 8-40: Inserting a new contact using an Intent

Available for download on Wrox.com

```
Intent intent =
  new Intent(ContactsContract.Intents.SHOW_OR_CREATE_CONTACT,
             ContactsContract.Contacts.CONTENT_URI);
intent.setData(Uri.parse("tel:(650)253-0000"));

intent.putExtra(ContactsContract.Intents.Insert.COMPANY, "Google");
intent.putExtra(ContactsContract.Intents.Insert.POSTAL,
  "1600 Amphitheatre Parkway, Mountain View, California");

startActivity(intent);
```

code snippet PA4AD_ Ch08_ContentProviders/src/Ch08_ContentProvidersActivity.java

Modifying and Augmenting Contact Details Directly

If you want to build your own Sync Adapter to insert server-synchronized contacts into the contacts Provider, you can modify the contact tables directly.

You can use the contact Content Providers to modify, delete, or insert contact records after adding the WRITE_CONTACTS uses-permission to your application manifest.

```
<uses-permission android:name="android.permission.WRITE_CONTACTS"/>
```

The extensible nature of the Contacts Contract provider allows you to add arbitrary Data table rows to any account stored as a Raw Contact.

In practice it's inadvisable to extend a Contacts Contract provider belonging to a third-party account with custom data. Such extensions won't be synchronized with the data owner's online server. It's better practice to create your own synchronized contact adapter that will be aggregated with the other accounts within the Contacts Content Provider.

The process for creating your own syncing contact account adapter is beyond the scope of this book. However, in general terms, by creating a record in the Raw Contacts Provider, it's possible for you to create a contacts account type for your own custom data.

You can add new records into the Contacts Contract Content Provider that are associated with your custom contact account. When added, your custom contact data will be aggregated with the details provided by native and other third-party contact information adapters and made available when developers query the Contacts Content Provider, as described in the previous section.

Using the Calendar Content Provider

Android 4.0 (API level 14) introduced a supported API for accessing the Calendar Content Provider. The Calendar API allows you to insert, view, and edit the complete Calendar database, providing access to calendars, events, attendees, and event reminders using either Intents or through direct manipulation of the Calendar Content Providers.

Like the Contacts Contract Content Provider, the Calendar Content Provider is designed to support multiple synchronized accounts. As a result, you can choose to read from, and contribute to, existing calendar applications and accounts; develop an alternative Calendar Provider by creating a calendar Sync Adapter; or create an alternative calendar application.

Querying the Calendar

To access the Calendar Content Provider, you must include the READ_CALENDAR uses-permission in your application manifest:

```
<uses-permission android:name="android.permission.READ_CALENDAR"/>
```

Use the Content Resolver to query any of the Calendar Provider tables using their CONTENT_URI static constant. Each table is exposed from within the CalendarContract class, including:

➤ Calendars — The Calendar application can display multiple calendars associated with multiple accounts. This table holds each calendar that can be displayed, as well as details such as the calendar's display name, time zone, and color.

➤ Events — The Events table includes an entry for each scheduled calendar event, including the name, description, location, and start/end times.

➤ `Instances` — Each event has one or (in the case of recurring events) multiple instances. The Instances table is populated with entries generated by the contents of the Events table and includes a reference to the event that generated it.

➤ `Attendees` — Each entry in the Attendees table represents a single attendee of a given event. Each attendee can include a name, email address, and attendance status, and if they are optional or required guests.

➤ `Reminders` — Event reminders are represented within the Reminders table, with each row representing one reminder for a particular event.

Each class includes its column names as static properties.

Listing 8-41 queries the Events table for every event, creating an array of strings that holds each event's name and unique ID.

LISTING 8-41: Querying the Events table

```java
// Create a projection that limits the result Cursor
// to the required columns.
String[] projection = {
    CalendarContract.Events._ID,
    CalendarContract.Events.TITLE
};

// Get a Cursor over the Events Provider.
Cursor cursor =
  getContentResolver().query(CalendarContract.Events.CONTENT_URI,
                             projection, null, null, null);

// Get the index of the columns.
int nameIdx =
 cursor.getColumnIndexOrThrow(CalendarContract.Events.TITLE);
int idIdx = cursor. getColumnIndexOrThrow(CalendarContract.Events._ID);

// Initialize the result set.
String[] result = new String[cursor.getCount()];

// Iterate over the result Cursor.
while(cursor.moveToNext()) {
   // Extract the name.
   String name = cursor.getString(nameIdx);
   // Extract the unique ID.
   String id = cursor.getString(idIdx);

   result[cursor.getPosition()] = name + " (" + id + ")";
 }

// Close the Cursor.
cursor.close();
```

code snippet PA4AD_ Ch08_ContentProviders/src/Ch08_ContentProvidersActivity.java

Creating and Editing Calendar Entries Using Intents

The Calendar Content Provider includes an Intent-based mechanism that allows you to perform common actions without the need for special permissions using the Calendar application. Using Intents, you can open the Calendar application to a specific time, view event details, insert a new event, or edit an existing event.

Like the Contacts API, using Intents is the best practice approach for manipulating calendar entries and should be used in preference to direct manipulation of the underlying tables whenever possible.

Creating New Calendar Events

Using the `Intent.ACTION_INSERT` action, specifying the `CalendarContract.Events.CONTENT_URI`, you can add new events to an existing calendar without requiring any special permissions.

Your Intent can include extras that define each of the event attributes, including the title, start and end time, location, and description, as shown in Listing 8-42. When triggered, the Intent will be received by the Calendar application, which will create a new entry prepopulated with the data provided.

LISTING 8-42: Inserting a new calendar event using an Intent

```
// Create a new insertion Intent.
Intent intent = new Intent(Intent.ACTION_INSERT, CalendarContract.Events.CONTENT_URI);

// Add the calendar event details
intent.putExtra(CalendarContract.Events.TITLE, "Launch!");
intent.putExtra(CalendarContract.Events.DESCRIPTION,
                "Professional Android 4 " +
                "Application Development release!");
intent.putExtra(CalendarContract.Events.EVENT_LOCATION, "Wrox.com");

Calendar startTime = Calendar.getInstance();
startTime.set(2012, 2, 13, 0, 30);
intent.putExtra(CalendarContract.EXTRA_EVENT_BEGIN_TIME, startTime.getTimeInMillis());

intent.putExtra(CalendarContract.EXTRA_EVENT_ALL_DAY, true);

// Use the Calendar app to add the new event.
startActivity(intent);
```

code snippet PA4AD_ Ch08_ContentProviders/src/Ch08_ContentProvidersActivity.java

Editing Calendar Events

To edit a calendar event, you must first know its row ID. To find this, you need to query the Events Content Provider, as described earlier in this section.

When you have the ID of the event you want to edit, create a new Intent using the `Intent.ACTION_EDIT` action and a URI that appends the event's row ID to the end of the Events table's `CONTENT_URI`, as shown in Listing 8-43.

Note that the Intent mechanism provides support only for editing the start and end times of an event.

LISTING 8-43: Editing a calendar event using an Intent

```
// Create a URI addressing a specific event by its row ID.
// Use it to  create a new edit Intent.
long rowID = 760;
Uri uri = ContentUris.withAppendedId(
  CalendarContract.Events.CONTENT_URI, rowID);

Intent intent = new Intent(Intent.ACTION_EDIT, uri);

// Modify the calendar event details
Calendar startTime = Calendar.getInstance();
startTime.set(2012, 2, 13, 0, 30);
intent.putExtra(CalendarContract.EXTRA_EVENT_BEGIN_TIME, startTime.getTimeInMillis());

intent.putExtra(CalendarContract.EXTRA_EVENT_ALL_DAY, true);

// Use the Calendar app to edit the event.
startActivity(intent);
```

code snippet PA4AD_ Ch08_ContentProviders/src/Ch08_ContentProvidersActivity.java

Displaying the Calendar and Calendar Events

You can also use Intents to display a particular event or to open the Calendar application to display a specific date and time using the `Intent.ACTION_VIEW` action.

To view an existing event, specify the Intent's URI using a row ID, as you would when editing an event, as shown in Listing 8-43. To view a specific date and time, the URI should be of the form `content://com.android.calendar/time/[milliseconds since epoch]`, as shown in Listing 8-44.

LISTING 8-44: Displaying a calendar event using an Intent

```
// Create a URI that specifies a particular time to view.
Calendar startTime = Calendar.getInstance();
startTime.set(2012, 2, 13, 0, 30);

Uri uri = Uri.parse("content://com.android.calendar/time/" +
  String.valueOf(startTime.getTimeInMillis()));
Intent intent = new Intent(Intent.ACTION_VIEW, uri);

// Use the Calendar app to view the time.
startActivity(intent);
```

code snippet PA4AD_ Ch08_ContentProviders/src/Ch08_ContentProvidersActivity.java

Modifying Calendar Entries Directly

If you are building your own contacts application, or want to build a Sync Adapter to integrate events from your own cloud-based calendar service, you can use the Calendar Content Providers to modify, delete, or insert contact records after adding the WRITE_CONTACTS uses-permission to your application manifest.

```
<uses-permission android:name="android.permission.WRITE_CALENDAR"/>
```

The process for creating your own syncing calendar account adapter is beyond the scope of this book; however, the process for adding, modifying, and deleting rows from the associated Calendar Content Providers is the same as that described for your own Content Providers earlier in this chapter.

> *You can find further details on performing transactions on the Calendar Content Providers and building Sync Adapters in the Android Dev Guide* (http://developer.android.com/guide/topics/providers/calendar-provider.html).

9

Working in the Background

WHAT'S IN THIS CHAPTER?

➤ Creating, starting, and stopping Services

➤ Binding Services to Activities

➤ Creating ongoing foreground Services

➤ Extending the Intent Service

➤ Using AsyncTasks to manage background processing

➤ Creating background Threads and using Handlers to synchronize with the GUI Thread

➤ Using Alarms to schedule application events

Android offers the `Service` class to create application components that handle long-lived operations and include functionality that doesn't require a user interface.

Android accords Services a higher priority than inactive Activities, so they're less likely to be killed when the system requires resources. In fact, should the run time prematurely terminate a Service that's been started, it can be configured to restart as soon as sufficient resources become available. When necessary a Service's priority can be raised to the equivalent of a foreground Activity. This is reserved for extreme cases, where the termination of a Service will noticeably affect the user experience — such as an interruption in music playback.

By using Services, you can ensure that your applications can continue to run even when their UI isn't visible.

Although Services run without a dedicated GUI, they still execute in the main Thread of the application's process — just like Activities and Broadcast Receivers. To keep your applications responsive, you'll learn to move time-consuming processes onto background Threads using the `Thread` and `AsyncTask` classes.

This chapter also introduces Alarms, a mechanism for firing Intents at set intervals or set times, outside the scope of your application's lifecycle. You'll learn to use Alarms to start Services, open Activities, or broadcast Intents based on either the clock time or the time elapsed since device boot. An Alarm will fire even after its owner application has been closed and can (if required) wake a device from sleep.

INTRODUCING SERVICES

Unlike Activities, which display graphical interfaces, Services run invisibly — doing Internet look-ups, processing data, updating your Content Providers, firing Intents, and triggering Notifications. While Activities are started, stopped, and re-created regularly as part of their lifecycle, Services are designed to be longer-lived — specifically, to perform ongoing and potentially time-consuming operations.

Services are started, stopped, and controlled from other application components, including Activities, Broadcast Receivers, and other Services. If your application provides functionality that doesn't depend directly on user input, or includes time-consuming operations, Services may be the answer.

Running Services have a higher priority than inactive or invisible (stopped) Activities, making them less likely to be terminated by the run time's resource management. The only reason Android will stop a Service prematurely is to provide additional resources for a foreground component (usually an Activity). When that happens, your Service can be configured to restart automatically when resources become available.

If your Service is interacting directly with the user (for example, by playing music), it may be necessary to increase its priority by labeling it as a foreground component. This will ensure that your Service isn't terminated except in extreme circumstances, but it reduces the run time's ability to manage its resources, potentially degrading the overall user experience.

Creating and Controlling Services

The following sections describe how to create a new Service, and how to start and stop it using Intents with the `startService` and `stopService` methods, respectively. Later you'll learn how to bind a Service to an Activity to provide a richer interface.

Creating Services

To define a Service, create a new class that extends `Service`. You'll need to override the `onCreate` and `onBind` methods, as shown in Listing 9-1.

LISTING 9-1: A skeleton Service class

```
import android.app.Service;
import android.content.Intent;
import android.os.IBinder;

public class MyService extends Service {
  @Override
```

```
public void onCreate() {
  super.onCreate();
  // TODO: Actions to perform when service is created.
}

@Override
public IBinder onBind(Intent intent) {
  // TODO: Replace with service binding implementation.
  return null;
}
}
```

code snippet PA4AD_Ch09_MyService/src/MyService.java

After you've constructed a new Service, you must register it in the application manifest. Do this by including a `service` tag within the `application` node, as shown in Listing 9-2.

LISTING 9-2: Adding a Service node to the application manifest

```
<service android:enabled="true" android:name=".MyService"/>
```

code snippet PA4AD_Ch09_MyService/AndroidManifest.xml

To ensure your Service can be started and stopped only by your own application, add a `permission` attribute to its Service node.

```
<service android:enabled="true"
         android:name=".MyService"
         android:permission="com.paad.MY_SERVICE_PERMISSION"/>
```

This will require any third-party applications to include a uses-permission in their manifests in order to access this Service. You'll learn more about creating and using permissions in Chapter 18, "Advanced Android Development."

Executing a Service and Controlling Its Restart Behavior

Override the `onStartCommand` event handler to execute the task (or begin the ongoing operation) encapsulated by your Service. You can also specify your Service's restart behavior within this handler.

The `onStartCommand` method is called whenever the Service is started using `startService`, so it may be executed several times within a Service's lifetime. You should ensure that your Service accounts for this.

The `onStartCommand` handler was introduced in Android 2.0 (API level 5) and replaces the deprecated `onStart` event. It provides the same functionality as the deprecated method, but in addition it enables you specify how to handle restarts if the Service is killed by the system prior to an explicit call to `stopService` or `stopSelf`.

Services are launched on the main Application Thread, meaning that any processing done in the `onStartCommand` handler will happen on the main GUI Thread. The standard pattern for implementing a Service is to create and run a new Thread from `onStartCommand` to perform the processing in the background, and then stop the Service when it's been completed. (You will be shown how to create and manage background Threads later in this chapter.)

Listing 9-3 extends the skeleton code shown in Listing 9-1 by overriding the `onStartCommand` handler. Note that it returns a value that controls how the system will respond if the Service is restarted after being killed by the run time.

LISTING 9-3: Overriding Service restart behavior

```
@Override
public int onStartCommand(Intent intent, int flags, int startId) {
    startBackgroundTask(intent, startId);
    return Service.START_STICKY;
}
```

code snippet PA4AD_Ch09_MyService/src/MyService.java

This pattern lets `onStartCommand` complete quickly, and it enables you to control the restart behavior by returning one of the following `Service` constants:

➤ `START_STICKY` — Describes the standard behavior, which is similar to the way in which `onStart` was implemented prior to Android 2.0. If you return this value, `onStartCommand` will be called any time your Service restarts after being terminated by the run time. Note that on a restart the Intent parameter passed in to `onStartCommand` will be `null`.

This mode typically is used for Services that handle their own states and that are explicitly started and stopped as required (via `startService` and `stopService`). This includes Services that play music or handle other ongoing background tasks.

➤ `START_NOT_STICKY` — This mode is used for Services that are started to process specific actions or commands. Typically, they will use `stopSelf` to terminate once that command has been completed.

Following termination by the run time, Services set to this mode restart only if there are pending start calls. If no `startService` calls have been made since the Service was terminated, the Service will be stopped without a call being made to `onStartCommand`.

This mode is ideal for Services that handle specific requests, particularly regular processing such as updates or network polling. Rather than restarting the Service during a period of resource contention, it's often more prudent to let the Service stop and retry at the next scheduled interval.

➤ `START_REDELIVER_INTENT` — In some circumstances you will want to ensure that the commands you have requested from your Service are completed — for example when timeliness is important.

This mode is a combination of the first two; if the Service is terminated by the run time, it will restart only if there are pending start calls *or* the process was killed prior to its calling `stopSelf`. In the latter case, a call to `onStartCommand` will be made, passing in the initial Intent whose processing did not properly complete.

Note that each mode requires you to explicitly stop your Service, through a call to `stopService` or `stopSelf`, when your processing has completed. Both methods are discussed in more detail later in this chapter.

> *Prior to Android SDK 2.0 (API level 5), the Service class triggered the* `onStart` *event handler to let you perform actions when the Service started. Implementing the* `onStart` *handler is now the equivalent of overriding* `onStartCommand` *and returning* `START_STICKY`.

The restart mode you specify in your `onStartCommand` return value will affect the parameter values passed in to it on subsequent calls. Initially, the Intent will be the parameter you passed in to `startService` to start your Service. After system-based restarts it will be either null, in the case of `START_STICKY` mode, or the original Intent if the mode is set to `START_REDELIVER_INTENT`.

The `flag` parameter can be used to discover how the Service was started. In particular, you determine if either of the following cases is true:

➤ `START_FLAG_REDELIVERY` — Indicates that the Intent parameter is a redelivery caused by the system run time's having terminated the Service before it was explicitly stopped by a call to `stopSelf`.

➤ `START_FLAG_RETRY` — Indicates that the Service has been restarted after an abnormal termination. It is passed in when the Service was previously set to `START_STICKY`.

Starting and Stopping Services

To start a Service, call `startService`. Much like Activities, you can either use an action to implicitly start a Service with the appropriate Intent Receiver registered, or you can explicitly specify the Service using its class. If the Service requires permissions that your application does not have, the call to `startService` will throw a `SecurityException`.

In both cases you can pass values in to the Service's `onStart` handler by adding extras to the Intent, as shown in Listing 9-4, which demonstrates both techniques available for starting a Service.

LISTING 9-4: Starting a Service

```
private void explicitStart() {
    // Explicitly start My Service
    Intent intent = new Intent(this, MyService.class);
    // TODO Add extras if required.
    startService(intent);
}

private void implicitStart() {
    // Implicitly start a music Service
    Intent intent = new Intent(MyMusicService.PLAY_ALBUM);
    intent.putExtra(MyMusicService.ALBUM_NAME_EXTRA, "United");
```

continues

LISTING 9-4 *(continued)*

```
    intent.putExtra(MyMusicService.ARTIST_NAME_EXTRA, "Pheonix");
    startService(intent);
}
```

code snippet PA4AD_Ch9_MyService/src/MyActivity.java

To stop a Service, use `stopService`, specifying an Intent that defines the Service to stop (in the same way you specified which Service to start), as shown in Listing 9-5.

LISTING 9-5: Stopping a Service

Available for
download on
Wrox.com

```
// Stop a service explicitly.
stopService(new Intent(this, MyService.class));

// Stop a service implicitly.
Intent intent = new Intent(MyMusicService.PLAY_ALBUM);
stopService(intent);
```

code snippet PA4AD_Ch09_MyService/src/MyActivity.java

Calls to `startService` do not nest, so a single call to `stopService` will terminate the running Service it matches, no matter how many times `startService` has been called.

Self-Terminating Services

Due to the high priority of Services, they are not commonly killed by the run time, so self-termination can significantly improve the resource footprint of your application.

By explicitly stopping the Service when your processing is complete, you allow the system to recover the resources otherwise required to keep it running.

When your Service has completed the actions or processing for which it was started, you should terminate it by making a call to `stopSelf`. You can call `stopSelf` either without a parameter to force an immediate stop, or by passing in a `startId` value to ensure processing has been completed for each instance of `startService` called so far.

Binding Services to Activities

Services can be bound to Activities, with the latter maintaining a reference to an instance of the former, enabling you to make method calls on the running Service as you would on any other instantiated class.

Binding is useful for Activities that would benefit from a more detailed interface with a Service. To support binding for a Service, implement the `onBind` method, returning the current instance of the Service being bound, as shown in Listing 9-6.

LISTING 9-6: Implementing binding on a Service

```java
@Override
public IBinder onBind(Intent intent) {
  return binder;
}

public class MyBinder extends Binder {
  MyMusicService getService() {
    return MyMusicService.this;
  }
}
private final IBinder binder = new MyBinder();
```

code snippet PA4AD_Ch09_MyService/src/MyMusicService.java

The connection between the Service and another component is represented as a
`ServiceConnection`.

To bind a Service to another application component, you need to implement a new
`ServiceConnection`, overriding the `onServiceConnected` and `onServiceDisconnected` methods
to get a reference to the Service instance after a connection has been established, as shown in
Listing 9-7.

LISTING 9-7: Creating a Service Connection for Service binding

```java
// Reference to the service
private MyMusicService serviceRef;

// Handles the connection between the service and activity
private ServiceConnection mConnection = new ServiceConnection() {
  public void onServiceConnected(ComponentName className,
                                 IBinder service) {
    // Called when the connection is made.
    serviceRef = ((MyMusicService.MyBinder)service).getService();
  }

  public void onServiceDisconnected(ComponentName className) {
    // Received when the service unexpectedly disconnects.
    serviceRef = null;
  }
};
```

code snippet PA4AD_Ch09_MyService/src/MyActivity.java

To perform the binding, call `bindService` within your Activity, passing in an Intent (either explicit
or implicit) that selects the Service to bind to, and an instance of a `ServiceConnection` implementation. You can also specify a number of binding flags, as shown in Listing 9-8. In this example you
specify that the target Service should be created when the binding is initiated.

LISTING 9-8: Binding to a Service

```
// Bind to the service
Intent bindIntent = new Intent(MyActivity.this, MyMusicService.class);
bindService(bindIntent, mConnection, Context.BIND_AUTO_CREATE);
```

code snippet PA4AD_Ch09_MyService/src/MyActivity.java

Android 4.0 (API level 14) introduced a number of new flags that can be used and combined when binding a Service to an application:

➤ BIND_ADJUST_WITH_ACTIVITY — Causes the Service's priority to be adjusted based on the relative importance of the Activity to which it is bound. As a result, the run time will increase the priority of the Service when the Activity is in the foreground.

➤ BIND_ABOVE_CLIENT and BIND_IMPORTANT — Specify that the bound Service is so important to the binding client that it should be become a foreground process when the client is in the foreground — in the case of BIND_ABOVE_CLIENT, you are specifying that the run time should terminate the Activity before the bound Service in cases of low memory.

➤ BIND_NOT_FOREGROUND — Ensures the bound Service is never brought to foreground priority. By default, the act of binding a Service increases its relative priority.

➤ BIND_WAIVE_PRIORITY — Indicates that binding the specified Service shouldn't alter its priority.

When the Service has been bound, all its public methods and properties are available through the serviceBinder object obtained from the onServiceConnected handler.

Android applications do not (normally) share memory, but in some cases your application may want to interact with (and bind to) Services running in different application processes.

You can communicate with a Service running in a different process by using broadcast Intents or through the extras Bundle in the Intent used to start the Service. If you need a more tightly coupled connection, you can make a Service available for binding across application boundaries by using Android Interface Definition Language (AIDL). AIDL defines the Service's interface in terms of OS-level primitives, allowing Android to transmit objects across process boundaries. AIDL definitions are covered in Chapter 18.

An Earthquake-Monitoring Service Example

In this chapter you'll modify the Earthquake example you started in Chapter 6 (and continued to enhance in Chapters 7 and 8). In this example you'll move the earthquake updating and processing functionality into its own Service component.

> *In the sections "Using Repeating Alarms to Schedule Network Refreshes"
> and "Using the Intent Service to Simplify the Earthquake Update Service,"
> you'll extend this Service by improving its efficiency and simplifying the
> implementation.*

1. Start by creating a new `EarthquakeUpdateService` that extends `Service`:

```
package com.paad.earthquake;

import android.app.Service;
import android.content.Intent;
import android.os.IBinder;

public class EarthquakeUpdateService extends Service {

  public static String TAG = "EARTHQUAKE_UPDATE_SERVICE";

  @Override
  public IBinder onBind(Intent intent) {
    return null;
  }
}
```

2. Add this new Service to the manifest by adding a new `service` tag within the `application` node:

```
<service android:enabled="true" android:name=".EarthquakeUpdateService"/>
```

3. Move the `addNewQuake` method out of the `EarthquakeListFragment` and into the `EarthquakeUpdateService`. Modify the first line in the method to obtain the Content Resolver from the Service rather than a parent Activity:

```
private void addNewQuake(Quake quake) {
  ContentResolver cr = getContentResolver();

  // Construct a where clause to make sure we don't already have this
  // earthquake in the provider.
  String w = EarthquakeProvider.KEY_DATE + " = " + quake.getDate().getTime();

  // If the earthquake is new, insert it into the provider.
  Cursor query = cr.query(EarthquakeProvider.CONTENT_URI, null, w, null, null);

  if (query.getCount()==0) {
    ContentValues values = new ContentValues();

    values.put(EarthquakeProvider.KEY_DATE, quake.getDate().getTime());
    values.put(EarthquakeProvider.KEY_DETAILS, quake.getDetails());
    values.put(EarthquakeProvider.KEY_SUMMARY, quake.toString());

    double lat = quake.getLocation().getLatitude();
    double lng = quake.getLocation().getLongitude();
    values.put(EarthquakeProvider.KEY_LOCATION_LAT, lat);
    values.put(EarthquakeProvider.KEY_LOCATION_LNG, lng);
    values.put(EarthquakeProvider.KEY_LINK, quake.getLink());
    values.put(EarthquakeProvider.KEY_MAGNITUDE, quake.getMagnitude());

    cr.insert(EarthquakeProvider.CONTENT_URI, values);
  }
  query.close();
}
```

4. Create a new `refreshEarthquakes` method in the `EarthquakeUpdateService`. You will move most of the functionality from the method of the same name in the Earthquake List Fragment into this new method:

```
public void refreshEarthquakes() {
}
```

4.1 Start by moving all the XML processing code into the Service's `refreshEarthquakes` method:

```
public void refreshEarthquakes() {
  // Get the XML
  URL url;
  try {
    String quakeFeed = getString(R.string.quake_feed);
    url = new URL(quakeFeed);

    URLConnection connection;
    connection = url.openConnection();

    HttpURLConnection httpConnection = (HttpURLConnection)connection;
    int responseCode = httpConnection.getResponseCode();

    if (responseCode == HttpURLConnection.HTTP_OK) {
      InputStream in = httpConnection.getInputStream();

      DocumentBuilderFactory dbf = DocumentBuilderFactory.newInstance();
      DocumentBuilder db = dbf.newDocumentBuilder();

      // Parse the earthquake feed.
      Document dom = db.parse(in);
      Element docEle = dom.getDocumentElement();

      // Get a list of each earthquake entry.
      NodeList nl = docEle.getElementsByTagName("entry");
      if (nl != null && nl.getLength() > 0) {
        for (int i = 0 ; i < nl.getLength(); i++) {
          Element entry = (Element)nl.item(i);
          Element title = (Element)entry.getElementsByTagName("title").item(0);
          Element g = (Element)entry.getElementsByTagName("georss:point").item(0);
          Element when = (Element)entry.getElementsByTagName("updated").item(0);
          Element link = (Element)entry.getElementsByTagName("link").item(0);

          String details = title.getFirstChild().getNodeValue();
          String hostname = "http://earthquake.usgs.gov";
          String linkString = hostname + link.getAttribute("href");

          String point = g.getFirstChild().getNodeValue();
          String dt = when.getFirstChild().getNodeValue();
          SimpleDateFormat sdf = new SimpleDateFormat("yyyy-MM-dd'T'hh:mm:ss'Z'");
          Date qdate = new GregorianCalendar(0,0,0).getTime();
          try {
            qdate = sdf.parse(dt);
          } catch (ParseException e) {
```

```
            Log.e(TAG, "Date parsing exception.", e);
          }

          String[] location = point.split(" ");
          Location l = new Location("dummyGPS");
          l.setLatitude(Double.parseDouble(location[0]));
          l.setLongitude(Double.parseDouble(location[1]));

          String magnitudeString = details.split(" ")[1];
          int end =  magnitudeString.length()-1;
          double magnitude = Double.parseDouble(magnitudeString.substring(0, end));

          details = details.split(",")[1].trim();

          Quake quake = new Quake(qdate, details, l, magnitude, linkString);

          // Process a newly found earthquake
          addNewQuake(quake);
        }
      }
    }
  } catch (MalformedURLException e) {
    Log.e(TAG, "Malformed URL Exception", e);
  } catch (IOException e) {
    Log.e(TAG, "IO Exception", e);
  } catch (ParserConfigurationException e) {
    Log.e(TAG, "Parser Configuration Exception", e);
  } catch (SAXException e) {
    Log.e(TAG, "SAX Exception", e);
  }
  finally {
  }
}
```

4.2 With the XML processing moved out of the refreshEarthquakes method in the Earthquake List Fragment, there's no longer a need to execute it on a background thread. Update the onActivityCreated handler to remove the Thread creation code:

```
@Override
public void onActivityCreated(Bundle savedInstanceState) {
  super.onActivityCreated(savedInstanceState);

  // Create a new Adapter and bind it to the List View
  adapter = new SimpleCursorAdapter(getActivity(),
    android.R.layout.simple_list_item_1, null,
    new String[] { EarthquakeProvider.KEY_SUMMARY },
    new int[] { android.R.id.text1 }, 0);
  setListAdapter(adapter);

  getLoaderManager().initLoader(0, null, this);

  refreshEarthquakes();
}
```

4.3 The Earthquake List Fragment's `refreshEarthquake` method should still contain the code used to restart the Cursor Loader, but it no longer needs to synchronize it to the UI thread. Remove that code and add a new call to `startService` that will explicitly start the `EarthquakeUpdateService`:

```
public void refreshEarthquakes() {
  getLoaderManager().restartLoader(0, null, EarthquakeListFragment.this);

  getActivity().startService(new Intent(getActivity(),
                                   EarthquakeUpdateService.class));
}
```

5. Return to the `EarthquakeService`. Override the `onStartCommand` and `onCreate` methods to refresh the earthquake from the server, and to create a new Timer that will be used to regularly update the earthquake list.

The `onStartCommand` handler should return `START_STICKY` because you are using a timer to trigger multiple refreshes. This is generally poor form — the Timer behavior should be triggered by Alarms and/or an Intent Service. You'll learn how to do both of these things later in this chapter. Use the `SharedPreference` object created in Chapter 7 to determine if the earthquakes should be updated regularly.

```
private Timer updateTimer;

@Override
public int onStartCommand(Intent intent, int flags, int startId) {
  // Retrieve the shared preferences
  Context context = getApplicationContext();
  SharedPreferences prefs =
    PreferenceManager.getDefaultSharedPreferences(context);

  int updateFreq =
    Integer.parseInt(prefs.getString(PreferencesActivity.PREF_UPDATE_FREQ, "60"));
  boolean autoUpdateChecked =
    prefs.getBoolean(PreferencesActivity.PREF_AUTO_UPDATE, false);

  updateTimer.cancel();
  if (autoUpdateChecked) {
    updateTimer = new Timer("earthquakeUpdates");
    updateTimer.scheduleAtFixedRate(doRefresh, 0,
      updateFreq*60*1000);
  }
  else {
    Thread t = new Thread(new Runnable() {
      public void run() {
        refreshEarthquakes();
      }
    });
    t.start();
  }

  return Service.START_STICKY;
};
```

```
private TimerTask doRefresh = new TimerTask() {
  public void run() {
    refreshEarthquakes();
  }
};

@Override
public void onCreate() {
  super.onCreate();
  updateTimer = new Timer("earthquakeUpdates");
}
```

> *All code snippets in this example are part of the* Chapter 9 Earthquake Part 1
> *project, available for download at* www.wrox.com.

Now when the Earthquake Activity is launched, it will start the Earthquake Service. This Service
will then continue to run, updating the Content Provider in the background, even after the Activity
is suspended or closed. Because the Earthquake List Fragment is using a Cursor Loader, each new
Earthquake will automatically be added to the List View.

> *At this stage the earthquake Service is constantly running, taking up valuable
> resources. Later sections will explain how to replace the Timer with Alarms and
> the Intent Service.*

Creating Foreground Services

As you learned in Chapter 3, "Creating Applications and Activities," Android uses a dynamic
approach to managing resources that can result in your application's components being terminated
with little or no warning.

When calculating which applications and application components should be killed, Android assigns
running Services the second-highest priority. Only active, foreground Activities are considered a
higher priority.

In cases where your Service is interacting directly with the user, it may be appropriate to lift its priority to the equivalent of a foreground Activity's. You can do this by setting your Service to run in
the foreground by calling its `startForeground` method.

Because foreground Services are expected to be interacting directly with the user (for example, by
playing music), calls to `startForeground` must specify an ongoing Notification (described in more
detail in Chapter 10, "Expanding the User Experience"), as shown in Listing 9-9. This notification
will be displayed for as long as your Service is running in the foreground.

LISTING 9-9: Moving a Service to the foreground

```java
private void startPlayback(String album, String artist) {
  int NOTIFICATION_ID = 1;

  // Create an Intent that will open the main Activity
  // if the notification is clicked.
  Intent intent = new Intent(this, MyActivity.class);
  PendingIntent pi = PendingIntent.getActivity(this, 1, intent, 0);

  // Set the Notification UI parameters
  Notification notification = new Notification(R.drawable.icon,
    "Starting Playback", System.currentTimeMillis());
  notification.setLatestEventInfo(this, album, artist, pi);

  // Set the Notification as ongoing
  notification.flags = notification.flags |
                   Notification.FLAG_ONGOING_EVENT;

  // Move the Service to the Foreground
  startForeground(NOTIFICATION_ID, notification);
}
```

code snippet PA4AD_Ch09_MyService/src/MyMusicService.java

> *Moving a Service to the foreground effectively makes it impossible for the run time to kill it in order to free resources. Having multiple unkillable Services running simultaneously can make it extremely difficult for the system to recover from resource-starved situations.*
>
> *Use this technique only if it is necessary in order for your Service to function properly, and even then keep the Service in the foreground only as long as absolutely necessary.*

It's good practice to provide a simple way for users to disable a foreground Service — typically from whichever Activity is opened by clicking the ongoing Notification (or from the Notification itself).

When your Service no longer requires foreground priority, you can move it back to the background, and optionally remove the ongoing notification using the `stopForeground` method, as shown in Listing 9-10. The Notification will be canceled automatically if your Service stops or is terminated.

LISTING 9-10: Moving a Service back to the background

```java
public void pausePlayback() {
  // Move to the background and remove the Notification
  stopForeground(true);
}
```

code snippet PA4AD_Ch09_MyService/src/MyMusicService.java

> Prior to Android 2.0 it was possible to set a Service to the foreground using the `setForeground` method. This method has now been deprecated and will result in a NOP (no operation performed), effectively doing nothing.

USING BACKGROUND THREADS

Responsiveness is one of the most critical attributes of a good Android application. To ensure that your application responds quickly to any user interaction or system event, it's vital that you move all processing and I/O operations off the main application Thread and into a child Thread.

> All Android application components — including Activities, Services, and Broadcast Receivers — start on the main application Thread. As a result, time-consuming processing in any component will block all other components, including Services and the visible Activity.

In Android, Activities that don't respond to an input event (such as a key press) within 5 seconds, and Broadcast Receivers that don't complete their `onReceive` handlers within 10 seconds, are considered unresponsive.

Not only do you want to avoid this scenario, but you don't even want to come close. In practice, users will notice input delays and UI pauses of more than a couple of hundred milliseconds.

It's important to use background Threads for any nontrivial processing that doesn't directly interact with the user interface. It's particularly important to schedule file operations, network lookups, database transactions, and complex calculations on a background Thread.

Android offers a number of alternatives for moving your processing to the background. You can implement your own Threads and use the Handler class to synchronize with the GUI Thread before updating the UI. Alternatively, the `AsyncTask` class lets you define an operation to be performed in the background and provides event handlers that enable you to monitor progress and post the results on the GUI Thread.

Using AsyncTask to Run Asynchronous Tasks

The `AsyncTask` class implements a best practice pattern for moving your time-consuming operations onto a background Thread and synchronizing with the UI Thread for updates and when the processing is complete. It offers the convenience of event handlers synchronized with the GUI Thread to let you update Views and other UI elements to report progress or publish results when your task is complete.

AsyncTask handles all the Thread creation, management, and synchronization, enabling you to create an asynchronous task consisting of processing to be done in the background and UI updates to be performed both during the processing, and once it's complete.

AsyncTasks are a good solution for short-lived background processing whose progress and results need to be reflected on the UI. However, they aren't persisted across Activity restarts — meaning that your AsyncTask will be cancelled if the orientation of the device changes, causing the Activity to be destroyed and recreated. For longer running background processes, such as downloading data from the Internet, a Service component is a better approach.

Similarly, Cursor Loaders are better optimized for the use-case of Content Provider or database results.

Creating New Asynchronous Tasks

Each AsyncTask implementation can specify parameter types that will be used for input parameters, the progress-reporting values, and result values. If you don't need or want to take input parameters, update progress, or report a final result, simply specify Void for any or all the types required.

To create a new asynchronous task, extend the AsyncTask class, specifying the parameter types to use, as shown in the skeleton code of Listing 9-11.

LISTING 9-11: AsyncTask implementation using a string parameter and result, with an integer progress value

```java
private class MyAsyncTask extends AsyncTask<String, Integer, String> {
  @Override
  protected String doInBackground(String... parameter) {
    // Moved to a background thread.
    String result = "";
    int myProgress = 0;

    int inputLength = parameter[0].length();

    // Perform background processing task, update myProgress]
    for (int i = 1; i <= inputLength; i++) {
      myProgress = i;
      result = result + parameter[0].charAt(inputLength-i);
      try {
        Thread.sleep(100);
      } catch (InterruptedException e) { }
      publishProgress(myProgress);
    }

    // Return the value to be passed to onPostExecute
    return result;
  }

  @Override
  protected void onProgressUpdate(Integer... progress) {
    // Synchronized to UI thread.
    // Update progress bar, Notification, or other UI elements
    asyncProgress.setProgress(progress[0]);
  }
```

```
  @Override
  protected void onPostExecute(String result) {
    // Synchronized to UI thread.
    // Report results via UI update, Dialog, or notifications
    asyncTextView.setText(result);
  }
}
```

code snippet PA4AD_Ch09_MyService/src/MyActivity.java

Your subclass should also override the following event handlers:

➤ `doInBackground` — This method will be executed on the background Thread, so place your long-running code here, and don't attempt to interact with UI objects from within this handler. It takes a set of parameters of the type defined in your class implementation.

You can use the `publishProgress` method from within this handler to pass parameter values to the `onProgressUpdate` handler, and when your background task is complete, you can return the final result as a parameter to the `onPostExecute` handler, which can update the UI accordingly.

➤ `onProgressUpdate` — Override this handler to update the UI with interim progress updates. This handler receives the set of parameters passed in to `publishProgress` (typically from within the `doInBackground` handler).

This handler is synchronized with the GUI Thread when executed, so you can safely modify UI elements.

➤ `onPostExecute` — When `doInBackground` has completed, the return value from that method is passed in to this event handler.

Use this handler to update the UI when your asynchronous task has completed. This handler is synchronized with the GUI Thread when executed, so you can safely modify UI elements.

Running Asynchronous Tasks

After you've implemented an asynchronous task, execute it by creating a new instance and calling `execute`, as shown in Listing 9-12. You can pass in a number of parameters, each of the type specified in your implementation.

LISTING 9-12: Executing an asynchronous task

```
String input = "redrum ... redrum";
new MyAsyncTask().execute(input);
```

code snippet PA4AD_Ch09_MyService/src/MyActivity.java

> Each `AsyncTask` *instance can be executed only once. If you attempt to call* `execute` *a second time, an exception will be thrown.*

Introducing the Intent Service

The Intent Service is a convenient wrapper class that implements the best practice pattern for background Services that perform set tasks on demand, such as recurring Internet updates or data processing.

Other application components request an Intent Service complete a task by starting the Service and passing in an Intent containing the parameters necessary to complete the task.

The Intent Service queues request Intents as they are received and processes them consecutively on an asynchronous background Thread. After every received Intent has been processed, the Intent Service will terminate itself.

The Intent Service handles all the complexities around queuing multiple requests, background Thread creation, and UI Thread synchronization.

To implement a Service as an Intent Service, extend `IntentService` and override the `onHandleIntent` handler, as shown in Listing 9-13.

LISTING 9-13: Implementing an Intent Service

```
import android.app.IntentService;
import android.content.Intent;

public class MyIntentService extends IntentService {

  public MyIntentService(String name) {
    super(name);
    // TODO Complete any required constructor tasks.
  }

  @Override
  public void onCreate() {
    super.onCreate();
    // TODO: Actions to perform when service is created.
  }

  @Override
  protected void onHandleIntent(Intent intent) {
    // This handler occurs on a background thread.
    // TODO The time consuming task should be implemented here.
    // Each Intent supplied to this IntentService will be
    // processed consecutively here. When all incoming Intents
    // have been processed the Service will terminate itself.
  }
}
```

code snippet PA4AD_Ch09_MyService/src/MyIntentService.java

The `onHandleIntent` handler will be executed on a worker Thread, once for each Intent received. The Intent Service is the best-practice approach to creating Services that perform set tasks either on-demand or at regular intervals.

The "Using the Intent Service to Simplify the Earthquake Update Service" section demonstrates a practical example of how to use the Intent Service for recurring tasks.

Introducing Loaders

The abstract `Loader` class was introduced in Android 3.0 (API level 11) to encapsulate the best practice technique for asynchronous data loading within UI elements, such as Activities and Fragments. Loaders are also available within the Android Support Library.

The `CursorLoader` class, discussed in more detail in Chapter 8, is a concrete implementation used to asynchronously query the Content Resolver and return a Cursor.

When creating your own Loader implementation, it is typically best practice to extend the `AsyncTaskLoader` class rather than the Loader class directly. Although a Loader implementation is outside the scope of this book, in general your custom Loaders should:

➤   Asynchronously load data

➤   Monitor the source of the loaded data and automatically provide updated results

Manual Thread Creation and GUI Thread Synchronization

Although using Intent Services and creating `AsyncTasks` are useful shortcuts, there are times when you will want to create and manage your own Threads to perform background processing. This is often the case when you have long-running or inter-related Threads that require more subtle or complex management than is provided by the two techniques described so far.

In this section you learn how to create and start new Thread objects, and how to synchronize with the GUI Thread before updating the UI.

You can create and manage child Threads using Android's `Handler` class and the Threading classes available within `java.lang.Thread`. Listing 9-14 shows the simple skeleton code for moving processing onto a child Thread.

LISTING 9-14: Moving processing to a background Thread

```
// This method is called on the main GUI thread.
private void backgroundExecution() {
  // This moves the time consuming operation to a child thread.
  Thread thread = new Thread(null, doBackgroundThreadProcessing,
                             "Background");
  thread.start();
}

// Runnable that executes the background processing method.
private Runnable doBackgroundThreadProcessing = new Runnable() {
  public void run() {
    backgroundThreadProcessing();
  }
};
```

continues

LISTING 9-14 *(continued)*

```
// Method which does some processing in the background.
private void backgroundThreadProcessing() {
  // [ ... Time consuming operations ... ]
}
```

code snippet PA4AD_Ch09_MyService/src/MyService.java

Whenever you're using background Threads in a GUI environment, it's important to synchronize child Threads with the main application (GUI) Thread before attempting to create or modify UI elements.

Within your application components, Notifications and Intents are always received and handled on the GUI Thread. In all other cases, operations that explicitly interact with objects created on the GUI Thread (such as Views) or that display messages (such as Toasts) must be invoked on the main Thread.

If you are running within an Activity, you can also use the runOnUiThread method, which lets you force a method to execute on the same Thread as the Activity UI, as shown in the following code snippet:

```
runOnUiThread(new Runnable() {
  public void run() {
    // Update a View or other Activity UI element.
  }
});
```

You can also use the Handler class to post methods onto the Thread in which the Handler was created.

Using the Handler class, you can post updates to the user interface from a background Thread using the Post method. Listing 9-15 updates Listing 9-14 to demonstrate the outline for using the Handler to update the GUI Thread.

LISTING 9-15: Using a Handler to synchronize with the GUI Thread

```
//This method is called on the main GUI thread.
private void backgroundExecution() {
  // This moves the time consuming operation to a child thread.
  Thread thread = new Thread(null, doBackgroundThreadProcessing,
                             "Background");
  thread.start();
}

// Runnable that executes the background processing method.
private Runnable doBackgroundThreadProcessing = new Runnable() {
  public void run() {
    backgroundThreadProcessing();
  }
};
```

```
// Method which does some processing in the background.
private void backgroundThreadProcessing() {
  // [ ... Time consuming operations ... ]

  // Use the Handler to post the doUpdateGUI
  // runnable on the main UI thread.
  handler.post(doUpdateGUI);
}

//Initialize a handler on the main thread.
private Handler handler = new Handler();

// Runnable that executes the updateGUI method.
private Runnable doUpdateGUI = new Runnable() {
  public void run() {
    updateGUI();
  }
};

// This method must be called on the UI thread.
private void updateGUI() {
  // [ ... Open a dialog or modify a GUI element ... ]
}
```

code snippet PA4AD_Ch09_MyService/src/MyActivity.java

The Handler class also enables you to delay posts or execute them at a specific time, using the postDelayed and postAtTime methods, respectively:

```
// Post a method on the UI thread after 1sec.
handler.postDelayed(doUpdateGUI, 1000);

// Post a method on the UI thread after the device has been in
// use for 5mins.
int upTime = 1000*60*5;
handler.postAtTime(doUpdateGUI, SystemClock.uptimeMillis()+upTime);
```

USING ALARMS

Alarms are a means of firing Intents at predetermined times or intervals. Unlike Timers, Alarms operate outside the scope of your application, so you can use them to trigger application events or actions even after your application has been closed. Alarms are particularly powerful when used in combination with Broadcast Receivers, enabling you to set Alarms that fire broadcast Intents, start Services, or even open Activities, without your application needing to be open or running.

Alarms are an effective means to reducing your application's resource requirements, by enabling you to stop Services and eliminate timers while maintaining the ability to perform scheduled actions. You can use Alarms to schedule regular updates based on network lookups, to schedule time-consuming or cost-bound operations at "off-peak" times, or to schedule retries for failed operations.

> *For timing operations that occur only during the lifetime of your applications, using the* Handler *class in combination with Timers and Threads is a better approach than using Alarms, as this allows Android better control over system resources. Alarms provide a mechanism to reduce the lifetime of your applications by moving scheduled events out of their control.*

Alarms in Android remain active while the device is in sleep mode and can optionally be set to wake the device; however, all Alarms are canceled whenever the device is rebooted.

Alarm operations are handled through the AlarmManager, a system Service accessed via getSystemService, as follows:

```
AlarmManager alarmManager =
  (AlarmManager)getSystemService(Context.ALARM_SERVICE);
```

Creating, Setting, and Canceling Alarms

To create a new one-shot Alarm, use the set method and specify an alarm type, a trigger time, and a Pending Intent to fire when the Alarm triggers. If the trigger time you specify for the Alarm occurs in the past, the Alarm will be triggered immediately.

The following four alarm types are available:

➤ RTC_WAKEUP — Wakes the device from sleep to fire the Pending Intent at the clock time specified.

➤ RTC — Fires the Pending Intent at the time specified but does not wake the device.

➤ ELAPSED_REALTIME — Fires the Pending Intent based on the amount of time elapsed since the device was booted but does not wake the device. The elapsed time includes any period of time the device was asleep.

➤ ELAPSED_REALTIME_WAKEUP — Wakes the device from sleep and fires the Pending Intent after a specified length of time has passed since device boot.

Your selection will determine if the time value passed in the set method represents a specific time or an elapsed wait.

Listing 9-16 shows the Alarm-creation process.

LISTING 9-16: Creating a waking Alarm that triggers in 10 seconds

```
// Get a reference to the Alarm Manager
AlarmManager alarmManager =
  (AlarmManager)getSystemService(Context.ALARM_SERVICE);

// Set the alarm to wake the device if sleeping.
int alarmType = AlarmManager.ELAPSED_REALTIME_WAKEUP;

// Trigger the device in 10 seconds.
```

```
long timeOrLengthofWait = 10000;

// Create a Pending Intent that will broadcast and action
String ALARM_ACTION = "ALARM_ACTION";
Intent intentToFire = new Intent(ALARM_ACTION);
PendingIntent alarmIntent = PendingIntent.getBroadcast(this, 0,
  intentToFire, 0);

// Set the alarm
alarmManager.set(alarmType, timeOrLengthofWait, alarmIntent);
```

code snippet PA4AD_Ch09_MyService/src/MyActivity.java

When the Alarm goes off, the Pending Intent you specified will be broadcast. Setting a second Alarm using the same Pending Intent replaces the preexisting Alarm.

To cancel an Alarm, call `cancel` on the Alarm Manager, passing in the Pending Intent you no longer want to trigger, as shown in the Listing 9-17.

LISTING 9-17: Canceling an Alarm

```
alarmManager.cancel(alarmIntent);
```

code snippet PA4AD_Ch09_MyService/src/MyActivity.java

Setting Repeating Alarms

Repeating alarms work in the same way as the one-shot alarms but will trigger repeatedly at the specified interval.

Because alarms are set outside your Application lifecycle, they are perfect for scheduling regular updates or data lookups so that they don't require a Service to be constantly running in the background.

To set a repeating alarm, use the `setRepeating` or `setInexactRepeating` method on the Alarm Manager. Both methods support an alarm type, an initial trigger time, and a Pending Intent to fire when the alarm triggers (as described in the previous section).

Use `setRepeating` when you need fine-grained control over the exact interval of your repeating alarm. The interval value passed in to this method lets you specify an exact interval for your alarm, down to the millisecond.

The `setInexactRepeating` method helps to reduce the battery drain associated with waking the device on a regular schedule to perform updates. At run time Android will synchronize multiple inexact repeating alarms and trigger them simultaneously.

Rather than specifying an exact interval, the `setInexactRepeating` method accepts one of the following Alarm Manager constants:

- ➤ `INTERVAL_FIFTEEN_MINUTES`
- ➤ `INTERVAL_HALF_HOUR`

➤ INTERVAL_HOUR

➤ INTERVAL_HALF_DAY

➤ INTERVAL_DAY

Using an inexact repeating alarm, as shown in Listing 9-18, prevents each application from separately waking the device in a similar but nonoverlapping period. By synchronizing these alarms, the system is able to limit the impact of regularly repeating events on battery resources.

LISTING 9-18: Setting an inexact repeating alarm

```
// Get a reference to the Alarm Manager
AlarmManager alarmManager =
  (AlarmManager)getSystemService(Context.ALARM_SERVICE);

// Set the alarm to wake the device if sleeping.
int alarmType = AlarmManager.ELAPSED_REALTIME_WAKEUP;

// Schedule the alarm to repeat every half hour.
long timeOrLengthofWait = AlarmManager.INTERVAL_HALF_HOUR;

// Create a Pending Intent that will broadcast and action
String ALARM_ACTION = "ALARM_ACTION";
Intent intentToFire = new Intent(ALARM_ACTION);
PendingIntent alarmIntent = PendingIntent.getBroadcast(this, 0,
  intentToFire, 0);

// Wake up the device to fire an alarm in half an hour, and every
// half-hour after that.
alarmManager.setInexactRepeating(alarmType,
                    timeOrLengthofWait,
                    timeOrLengthofWait,
                    alarmIntent);
```

code snippet PA4AD_Ch09_MyService/src/MyActivity.java

> *The battery impact of setting regularly repeating alarms can be significant. It is good practice to limit your alarm frequency to the slowest acceptable rate, wake the device only if necessary, and use an inexact repeating alarm whenever possible.*

Repeating Alarms are canceled in the same way as one-shot Alarms, by calling `cancel` on the Alarm Manager and passing in the Pending Intent you no longer want to trigger.

Using Repeating Alarms to Schedule Network Refreshes

In this modification to the Earthquake example, you use Alarms to replace the Timer currently used to schedule Earthquake network refreshes.

One of the most significant advantages of this approach is that it allows the Service to stop itself when it has completed a refresh, freeing significant system resources.

1. Start by creating a new `EarthquakeAlarmReceiver` class that extends `BroadcastReceiver`:

```
package com.paad.earthquake;

import android.content.BroadcastReceiver;
import android.content.Context;
import android.content.Intent;

public class EarthquakeAlarmReceiver extends BroadcastReceiver {

  @Override
  public void onReceive(Context context, Intent intent) {
  }

}
```

2. Override the `onReceive` method to explicitly start the `EarthquakeUpdateService`:

```
@Override
public void onReceive(Context context, Intent intent) {
  Intent startIntent = new Intent(context, EarthquakeUpdateService.class);
  context.startService(startIntent);
}
```

3. Create a new public static String to define the action that will be used to trigger this Broadcast Receiver:

```
public static final String ACTION_REFRESH_EARTHQUAKE_ALARM =
  "com.paad.earthquake.ACTION_REFRESH_EARTHQUAKE_ALARM";
```

4. Add the new `EarthquakeAlarmReceiver` to the manifest, including an `intent-filter` tag that listens for the action defined in step 3:

```
<receiver android:name=".EarthquakeAlarmReceiver">
  <intent-filter>
    <action
      android:name="com.paad.earthquake.ACTION_REFRESH_EARTHQUAKE_ALARM"
    />
  </intent-filter>
</receiver>
```

5. Within the Earthquake Update Service, override the `onCreate` method to get a reference to the `AlarmManager`, and create a new `PendingIntent` that will be fired when the Alarm is triggered. You can also remove the `timerTask` initialization.

```
private AlarmManager alarmManager;
private PendingIntent alarmIntent;

@Override
public void onCreate() {
  super.onCreate();
  alarmManager = (AlarmManager)getSystemService(Context.ALARM_SERVICE);

  String ALARM_ACTION =
    EarthquakeAlarmReceiver.ACTION_REFRESH_EARTHQUAKE_ALARM;
```

```
    Intent intentToFire = new Intent(ALARM_ACTION);
    alarmIntent =
      PendingIntent.getBroadcast(this, 0, intentToFire, 0);
}
```

6. Modify the `onStartCommand` handler to set an inexact repeating Alarm rather than use a Timer to schedule the refreshes (if automated updates are enabled). Setting a new Intent with the same action automatically cancels any previous Alarms. Take this opportunity to modify the return result. Rather than setting the Service to sticky, return `Service.START_NOT_STICKY`. In step 7 you will stop the Service when the background refresh is complete; the use of alarms guarantees that another refresh will occur at the specified update frequency, so there's no need for the system to restart the Service if it is killed mid-refresh.

```
@Override
public int onStartCommand(Intent intent, int flags, int startId) {
  // Retrieve the shared preferences
  Context context = getApplicationContext();
  SharedPreferences prefs =
    PreferenceManager.getDefaultSharedPreferences(context);

  int updateFreq =
    Integer.parseInt(prefs.getString(PreferencesActivity.PREF_UPDATE_FREQ, "60"));
  boolean autoUpdateChecked =
    prefs.getBoolean(PreferencesActivity.PREF_AUTO_UPDATE, false);

  if (autoUpdateChecked) {
    int alarmType = AlarmManager.ELAPSED_REALTIME_WAKEUP;
    long timeToRefresh = SystemClock.elapsedRealtime() +
                         updateFreq*60*1000;
    alarmManager.setInexactRepeating(alarmType, timeToRefresh,
                                     updateFreq*60*1000, alarmIntent);
  }
  else
    alarmManager.cancel(alarmIntent);

  Thread t = new Thread(new Runnable() {
    public void run() {
      refreshEarthquakes();
    }
  });
  t.start();

  return Service.START_NOT_STICKY;
};
```

7. Within the `refreshEarthquakes` method, update the last try-finally case to call `stopSelf` when the background refresh has completed:

```
private void refreshEarthquakes() {
  [... existing refreshEarthquakes method ...]
  finally {
    stopSelf();
```

```
    }
  }
```

8. Remove the `updateTimer` instance variable and the Timer Task instance `doRefresh`.

When you run the updated application, the behavior should appear identical to the previous iteration of the application. Behind the scenes, however, the Service is being terminated when each update is complete, reducing the application's memory footprint and improving overall performance.

In the next section you'll use the Intent Service to further simplify and optimize this Service component.

 All code snippets in this example are part of the Chapter 9 Earthquake Part 2 *project, available for download at* www.wrox.com.

USING THE INTENT SERVICE TO SIMPLIFY THE EARTHQUAKE UPDATE SERVICE

The following example shows how to further simplify the `EarthquakeUpdateService` using an Intent Service.

1. Modify the inheritance of the Earthquake Update Service so that it extends `IntentService`:

```
public class EarthquakeUpdateService extends IntentService {
```

2. Create a new constructor that passes the name parameter to the super class:

```
public EarthquakeUpdateService() {
  super("EarthquakeUpdateService");
}

public EarthquakeUpdateService(String name) {
  super(name);
}
```

3. Override the `onHandleIntent` handler, moving all the code currently within `onStartCommand` into this handler. Note that you don't have to explicitly create a background Thread to execute the refresh; the Intent Service base class will do this for you.

```
@Override
protected void onHandleIntent(Intent intent) {
  // Retrieve the shared preferences
  Context context = getApplicationContext();
  SharedPreferences prefs =
    PreferenceManager.getDefaultSharedPreferences(context);

  int updateFreq =
```

```
      Integer.parseInt(prefs.getString(PreferencesActivity.PREF_UPDATE_FREQ, "60"));
    boolean autoUpdateChecked =
      prefs.getBoolean(PreferencesActivity.PREF_AUTO_UPDATE, false);

    if (autoUpdateChecked) {
      int alarmType = AlarmManager.ELAPSED_REALTIME_WAKEUP;
      long timeToRefresh = SystemClock.elapsedRealtime() +
                           updateFreq*60*1000;
      alarmManager.setInexactRepeating(alarmType, timeToRefresh,
                                       updateFreq*60*1000, alarmIntent);
    }
    else
      alarmManager.cancel(alarmIntent);

    refreshEarthquakes();
  }
```

The Intent Service implementation will queue Intents as they are received and process them consecutively, so there's no need to check for stacking refresh requests. After every received Intent has been processed, the Intent Service will terminate itself.

4. Remove the now empty `onStartCommand` handler, and remove the call to `stopSelf` you added to the `finally` clause of the `refreshEarthquakes` method step 7 of the previous example.

```
private void refreshEarthquakes() {
  [... existing refreshEarthquakes method ...]
  finally {
  }
}
```

 All code snippets in this example are part of the Chapter 9 Earthquake 3 *project, available for download at* www.wrox.com.

10

Expanding the User Experience

WHAT'S IN THIS CHAPTER?

➤ Customizing the Action Bar

➤ Using the Action Bar for application navigation

➤ Using the Android menu system

➤ Choosing Action Bar actions

➤ Creating immersive applications

➤ Creating and displaying Dialogs

➤ Displaying Toasts

➤ Using the Notification Manager to notify users of application events

➤ Creating insistent and ongoing Notifications

In Chapter 4, "Building User Interfaces," you learned how to use Activities, Fragments, layouts, and Views to construct a user interface (UI). To ensure that your UI is stylish, easy to use, and provides a user experience consistent with the underlying platform and other applications running in it, this chapter looks at ways to expand the user experience beyond the UI elements you design.

You'll start with the Action Bar, introduced in Android 3.0, a system UI component used to provide a consistent pattern for branding, navigation, and displaying common actions within your Activities. You'll learn how to customize the look of the Action Bar, as well as how to use it to provide navigation with tabs and drop-down lists.

Action Bar actions, application Menus, and Popup Menus use a new approach to menus, optimized for modern touch screen devices. As part of an examination of the Android UI model, this chapter looks at how to create and use them within your applications. In particular, you'll learn how to identify which Menu Items should be displayed as actions on your Action Bar.

Android offers several techniques for applications to communicate with users without an Activity. You'll learn how to use Notifications and Toasts to alert and update users without interrupting the active application.

A *Toast* is a transient, nonmodal dialog-box mechanism used to display information to users without stealing focus from the active application. You'll learn to display Toasts from any application component to send unobtrusive on-screen messages to your users.

Whereas a Toast is silent and transient, a *Notification* represents a more robust mechanism for alerting users. In many cases, when the user isn't actively using the mobile phone, it sits silent and unwatched in a pocket or on a desk until it rings, vibrates, or flashes. If a user misses these alerts, status bar icons are used to indicate that an event has occurred. All these attention-grabbing antics are available to your Android application through Notifications.

You'll also learn how to customize the appearance and functionality of your Notification when it appears in the notification tray — providing a mechanism for users to interact with your application without needing to open it first.

INTRODUCING THE ACTION BAR

The Action Bar component, shown in Figure 10-1, was introduced in Android 3.0 (API level 11). It's a navigation panel that replaces the title bar at the top of every Activity and that formalizes a common Android design pattern.

FIGURE 10-1

It's possible to hide the Action Bar, but best practice is to keep it and customize it to suit the style and navigation requirements of your application.

The Action Bar can be added to each Activity within your application and is designed to provide a consistent UI between applications and within a particular application's Activities.

The Action Bar provides a consistent framework for providing branding, navigation, and surfacing the key actions to be performed within an Activity. Although the Action Bar provides a framework for presenting this functionality consistently across applications, the following sections describe how you can select which options are suitable for your application — and how they can be implemented.

The Action Bar is enabled by default in any Activity that uses the (default) `Theme.Holo` theme and whose application has a target (or minimum) SDK version of 11 or higher.

Listing 10-1 shows how to enable the Action Bar by setting the target SDK to Android 4.0.3 (API level 15) and not modifying the default theme.

LISTING 10-1: Enabling the Action Bar

```
<uses-sdk android:targetSdkVersion="15" />
```

code snippet PA4AD_Ch10_ActionBar/AndroidManifest.java

To toggle the visibility of the Action Bar at run time, you can use its `show` and `hide` methods:

```
ActionBar actionBar = getActionBar();

// Hide the Action Bar
actionBar.hide();

// Show the Action Bar
actionBar.show();
```

Alternatively, you can apply a theme that doesn't include the Action Bar, such as the `Theme.Holo`
`.NoActionBar` theme, as shown in Listing 10-2.

LISTING 10-2: Disabling the Action Bar

```
<activity
  android:name=".MyNonActionBarActivity"
  android:theme="@android:style/Theme.Holo.NoActionBar">
```

code snippet PA4AD_Ch10_ActionBar/AndroidManifest.java

You can create or customize your own theme that removes the Action Bar by setting the
`android:windowActionBar` style property to `false`:

```
<?xml version="1.0" encoding="utf-8"?>
<resources>
  <style name="NoActionBar" parent="@style/ActivityTheme">
    <item name="android:windowActionBar">false</item>
  </style>
</resources>
```

When you apply a theme that excludes the Action Bar from an Activity, you can't programmatically
display it at run time. A call to `getActionBar` will return null.

> *The Action Bar was introduced in Android 3.0 (API level 11) and is not cur-*
> *rently included in the support library. As a result, you can only use the Action*
> *Bar when running on a host platform with at least Android 3.0. One alternative*
> *is to create a different layout for platforms running pre-Android 3.0. The alter-*
> *native layout would need to implement its own custom Action Bar — typically*
> *in the form of a Fragment — to offer similar functionality.*

Customizing the Action Bar

In addition to controlling the implementation of this standard functionality, each application can modify the appearance of the Action Bar while maintaining the same consistent behavior and general layout.

One of the primary purposes of the Action Bar is to provide a consistent UI between applications. As such, the customization options are purposefully limited, though you can customize the Action Bar to provide your own application branding and identity.

You can control your branding by specifying the image to appear (if any) at the far left, the application title to display, and the background Drawable to use. Figure 10-2 shows a customized Action Bar that uses a logo bitmap to identify the application and a Gradient Drawable as a background image.

FIGURE 10-2

Modifying the Icon and Title Text

By default, the Action Bar displays the Drawable you specify using your application or Activity's `android:icon` attribute, alongside the corresponding `android:label` attribute on a black background.

You can specify an alternative graphic using the `android:logo` attribute. Unlike the square icon, there is no limit to the width of the logo graphic — though it's good practice to limit it to approximately double the width of the icon image.

The logo image typically is used to provide the top-level branding for your application, so it's good practice to hide the title label when using a logo image. You can do this at run time by setting the Action Bar's `setDisplayShowTitleEnabled` method to `false`:

```
ActionBar actionBar = getActionBar();
actionBar.setDisplayShowTitleEnabled(false);
```

Where both an icon and logo image are supplied, you can switch between them at run time by using the `setDisplayUseLogoEnabled` method:

```
actionBar.setDisplayUseLogoEnabled(displayLogo);
```

If you choose to hide the icon and logo, you can do so by setting the `setDisplayShowHomeEnabled` method to `false`:

```
actionBar.setDisplayShowHomeEnabled(false);
```

> *The application icon/logo is typically used as a navigation shortcut to the application's main Activity, so it's good practice to always have it visible.*

You also can use the icon and title text to provide navigation and context cues. Use the `setTitle` and `setSubTitle` methods at run time to modify the text displayed alongside the icon, as demonstrated in Listing 10-3 and shown in Figure 10-3.

LISTING 10-3: Customizing the Action Bar titles

```
actionBar.setSubtitle("Inbox");
actionBar.setTitle("Label:important");
```

code snippet PA4AD_Ch10_ActionBar/src/ActionBarActivity.java

Label:important
Inbox

FIGURE 10-3

These text strings can be used to describe the users' location within the application and the context within which they're working. This is particularly useful when using Fragments to change context rather than the traditional Activity stack. The followings sections provide more details regarding navigation options.

Customizing the Background

The default background color of the Action Bar depends on the underlying theme. The native Android Action Bar background is transparent, with the Holo theme background set to black.

You can specify any Drawable as the background image for your Action Bar by using the `setBackgroundDrawable` method, as shown in Listing 10-4.

LISTING 10-4: Customizing the Action Bar background

```
ActionBar actionBar = getActionBar();
Resources r = getResources();

Drawable myDrawable = r.getDrawable(R.drawable.gradient_header);

actionBar.setBackgroundDrawable(myDrawable);
```

code snippet PA4AD_Ch10_ActionBar/src/ActionBarActivity.java

The Action Bar will scale your image, so it's best practice to create a scalable Drawable, typically using either a 9-patch or XML defined Drawable. Both alternatives are explored in more detail in Chapter 11, "Advanced User Experience."

Under normal circumstances the Action Bar will reserve space at the top of your Activity, with your layout being inflated into the remaining space. Alternatively, you can choose to overlay the Action Bar above your Activity layout by requesting the FEATURE_ACTION_BAR_OVERLAY window feature.

```
@Override
public void onCreate(Bundle savedInstanceState) {
  super.onCreate(savedInstanceState);

  getWindow().requestFeature(Window.FEATURE_ACTION_BAR_OVERLAY);

  setContentView(R.layout.main);
}
```

When the overlay mode is enabled, the Action Bar will float above your Activity, potentially obscuring content at the top of your layout.

Enabling the Split Action Bar Mode

The Action Bar was initially introduced in Android 3.0 — a platform release that was focused on providing the best user experience possible for tablet devices. Android 4.0 (API level 14) sought to optimize many of the features initially designed for tablets for use on smaller, smartphone devices.

For the Action Bar, this meant the introduction of the split Action Bar. You can enable the split Action Bar by setting the `android:uiOptions` attribute within your application or Activity manifest nodes to `splitActionBarWhenNarrow`, as shown in Listing 10-5.

LISTING 10-5: Enabling the split Action Bar

```
<activity
    android:label="My Activity"
    android:name=".ActionBarActivity"
    android:logo="@drawable/ic_launcher"
    android:uiOptions="splitActionBarWhenNarrow">
```

code snippet PA4AD_Ch10_ActionBar/AndroidManifest.xml

On supported devices with narrow screens (such as a smartphone in portrait mode), enabling the split Action Bar mode will allow the system to split the Action Bar into separate sections. Figure 10-4 shows an example of an Action Bar that has been laid out with the branding and navigation sections layered at the top of the screen, with the action sections aligned to the bottom of the screen.

The layout is calculated and performed by the run time and may change depending on the orientation of the host device and any Action Bar configuration changes you make at run time.

FIGURE 10-4

Customizing the Action Bar to Control Application Navigation Behavior

The Action Bar introduces a several options for providing consistent and predictable navigation within your application. Broadly speaking, those options can be divided into two categories:

➤ **Application icons** — The application icon or logo is used to provide a consistent navigation path, typically by resetting the application to its home Activity. You can also configure the icon to represent moving "up" one level of context.

➤   **Tabs and drop-downs** — The Action Bar supports built-in tabs or drop-down lists that can be used to replace the visible Fragments within an Activity.

Icon navigation can be considered a way to navigate the Activity stack, whereas tabs and drop-downs are used for Fragment transitions within an Activity. In practice, the actions you perform when the application icon is clicked or a tab is changed will depend on the way you've implemented your UI.

Selecting the application icon should change the overall context of your UI in the same way that an Activity switch might do, whereas changing a tab or selecting a drop-down should change the data being displayed.

Configuring Action Bar Icon Navigation Behavior

In most cases, the application icon should act as a shortcut to return to the "home" Activity, typically the root of your Activity stack. To make the application icon clickable, you must call the Action Bar's `setHomeButtonEnabled` method:

```
actionBar.setHomeButtonEnabled(true);
```

Clicking the application icon/logo is broadcast by the system as a special Menu Item click. Menu Item selections are handled within the `onOptionsItemSelected` handler of your Activity, with the ID of the Menu Item parameter set to `android.R.id.home`, as shown in Listing 10-6.

The process of creating and handling Menu Item selections is described in more detail later in this chapter.

LISTING 10-6: Handling application icon clicks

Available for
download on
Wrox.com

```java
@Override
public boolean onOptionsItemSelected(MenuItem item) {
    switch (item.getItemId()) {
      case (android.R.id.home) :
        Intent intent = new Intent(this, ActionBarActivity.class);
        intent.addFlags(Intent.FLAG_ACTIVITY_CLEAR_TOP);
        startActivity(intent);
        return true;
      default:
        return super.onOptionsItemSelected(item);
    }
}
```

code snippet PA4AD_Ch10_ActionBar/src/ActionBarActivity.java

Traditionally, Android applications have started a new Activity to transition between different contexts. In turn, pressing the back button closes the active Activity and returns to the previous one.

To supplement this behavior, you can configure the application icon to offer "up" navigation.

The back button should always move the user back through contexts (typically in the form of Activities) that they have already seen, effectively reversing the navigation path they followed to arrive at the current Activity or screen. This might result in navigation between "siblings" in your application structure.

In contrast, "up" navigation should always move users to the parent of the current Activity. As a result, it can move users to a screen they have not previously visited. This is particularly useful for applications with multiple entry points, allowing users to navigate within an application without having to return to the application that spawned it.

To enable up navigation for your application icon, call the Action Bar's `setDisplayHomeAsUp-Enabled` method:

```
actionBar.setDisplayUseLogoEnabled(false);
actionBar.setDisplayHomeAsUpEnabled(true);
```

This has the effect of overlaying an "up" graphic over your application icon, as shown in Figure 10-5. Note that it's good practice to use the icon rather than the logo when enabling up navigation.

FIGURE 10-5

Handling the navigation is left to you to implement. The Action Bar will still trigger the `onOptions-ItemSelected` handler with a Menu Item that uses `android.R.id.home` as its identifier, as shown in Listing 10-6.

Such behavior introduces certain risks, particularly if there are multiple ways a user may have navigated to a particular Activity. If in doubt, the up behavior should mirror the back button. In all cases, the navigation behavior should be predictable.

Using Navigation Tabs

In addition to the application icon navigation, the Action Bar also offers navigation tabs and drop-down lists. Note that only one of these forms of navigation can be enabled at once. These navigation options are designed to work closely with Fragments, providing a mechanism for altering the context of the current Activity by replacing the visible Fragments.

Navigation tabs (shown in Figure 10-6) can be considered a replacement for the `TabWidget` control.

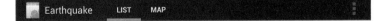

FIGURE 10-6

To configure your Action Bar to display tabs, call its `setNavigationMode` method, specifying `ActionBar.NAVIGATION_MODE_TABS`. The tabs should provide the application context, so it's good practice to disable the title text as well, as shown in Listing 10-7.

LISTING 10-7: Enabling Action Bar navigation tabs

```
actionBar.setNavigationMode(ActionBar.NAVIGATION_MODE_TABS);
actionBar.setDisplayShowTitleEnabled(false);
```

code snippet PA4AD_Ch10_ActionBar/src/ActionBarTabActivity.java

Tabs are added to the Action Bar using its `addTab` method, as shown in Listing 10-8. Start by creating a new Tab and using its `setText` and `setIcon` methods to determine the title and image to be displayed, respectively. Alternatively, you can use the `setCustomView` method to replace the standard text and image layout with your own custom View.

LISTING 10-8: Adding Action Bar navigation tabs

```
Tab tabOne = actionBar.newTab();

tabOne.setText("First Tab")
      .setIcon(R.drawable.ic_launcher)
      .setContentDescription("Tab the First")
      .setTabListener(
          new TabListener<MyFragment>
              (this, R.id.fragmentContainer, MyFragment.class));

actionBar.addTab(tabOne);
```

code snippet PA4AD_Ch10_ActionBar/src/ActionBarTabActivity.java

> *Android 4.0 (API level 14) introduced the* `setContentDescription` *method, which allows you include a more detailed content description to better support accessibility.*

The tab switching is handled using a `TabListener`, allowing you to create Fragment Transactions in response to tabs being selected, unselected, and reselected, as shown in Listing 10-9. Note that you are not required to execute the Fragment Transaction created in each handler — the Action Bar will execute it for you when necessary.

LISTING 10-9: Handling Action Bar tab switching

```
public static class TabListener<T extends Fragment>
  implements ActionBar.TabListener {

  private MyFragment fragment;
  private Activity activity;
  private Class<T> fragmentClass;
```

continues

LISTING 10-9 *(continued)*

```java
    private int fragmentContainer;

    public TabListener(Activity activity, int fragmentContainer,
                       Class<T> fragmentClass) {

      this.activity = activity;
      this.fragmentContainer = fragmentContainer;
      this.fragmentClass = fragmentClass;
    }

    // Called when a new tab has been selected
    public void onTabSelected(Tab tab, FragmentTransaction ft) {
      if (fragment == null) {
        String fragmentName = fragmentClass.getName();
        fragment =
          (MyFragment)Fragment.instantiate(activity, fragmentName);
        ft.add(fragmentContainer, fragment, null);
        fragment.setFragmentText(tab.getText());
      } else {
        ft.attach(fragment);
      }
    }

    // Called on the currently selected tab when a different tag is
    // selected.
    public void onTabUnselected(Tab tab, FragmentTransaction ft) {
      if (fragment != null) {
        ft.detach(fragment);
      }
    }

    // Called when the selected tab is selected.
    public void onTabReselected(Tab tab, FragmentTransaction ft) {
      // TODO React to a selected tab being selected again.
    }
  }
```

code snippet PA4AD_Ch10_ActionBar/src/ActionBarTabActivity.java

The basic workflow used within this Tab Listener is to instantiate, configure, and then add a new Fragment to your layout within the `onTab-Selected` handler. The Fragment associated with the unselected tab should be detached from your layout and recycled if its tab is reselected.

Using Drop-Down Lists for Navigation

You can use an Action Bar drop-down list, as shown in Figure 10-7, as an alternative to the navigation tabs or as ideal solutions for applying in-place filters to content being displayed within your Activity.

FIGURE 10-7

To configure your Action Bar to display a drop-down list, call its `setNavigationMode` method, specifying `ActionBar.NAVIGATION_MODE_LIST`:

```
actionBar.setNavigationMode(ActionBar.NAVIGATION_MODE_LIST);
```

The drop-down list is implemented much like a Spinner — a view that displays one child at a time and lets the user pick from among them. Populate the drop-down list by creating a new Adapter that implements the `SpinnerAdapter` interface, such as an Array Adapter or Simple Cursor Adapter:

```
ArrayList<CharSequence> al = new ArrayList<CharSequence>();
al.add("Item 1");
al.add("Item 2");

ArrayAdapter<CharSequence> dropDownAdapter =
  new ArrayAdapter<CharSequence>(this,
    android.R.layout.simple_list_item_1,
    al);
```

To assign the Adapter to your Action Bar, and handle selections, call the Action Bar's `setList-NavigationCallbacks`, passing in your adapter and an `OnNavigationListener`, as shown in Listing 10-10.

LISTING 10-10: Creating an Action Bar drop-down list

```
// Select the drop-down navigation mode.
actionBar.setNavigationMode(ActionBar.NAVIGATION_MODE_LIST);

// Create a new Spinner Adapter that contains the values to
// be displayed in the drop down.
ArrayAdapter dropDownAdapter =
  ArrayAdapter.createFromResource(this,
                        R.array.my_dropdown_values,
                        android.R.layout.simple_list_item_1);

// Assign the callbacks to handle drop-down selections.
actionBar.setListNavigationCallbacks(dropDownAdapter,
  new OnNavigationListener() {
    public boolean onNavigationItemSelected(int itemPosition,
                                      long itemId) {
    // TODO Modify your UI based on the position
    // of the drop down item selected.
    return true;
  }
});
```

code snippet PA4AD_Ch10_ActionBar/src/ActionBarDropDownActivity.java

---

When a user selects an item from the drop-down list, the `onNavigationItemSelected` handler will be triggered. Use the `itemPosition` and `itemId` parameters to determine how your UI should be adapted based on the new selection.

Drop-down list selections typically are used to refine existing content, such as to select a particular account or label within an email client.

Using Custom Navigation Views

For situations where neither tabs nor drop-down lists are appropriate, the Action Bar allows you to add your own custom View (including layouts) using the `setCustomView` method:

```
actionBar.setDisplayShowCustomEnabled(true);
actionBar.setCustomView(R.layout.my_custom_navigation);
```

Custom Views will appear in the same place as the tabs or drop-down lists — to the right of the application icon but to the left of any actions. To ensure consistency between applications, it's generally good form to use the standard navigation modes.

Introducing Action Bar Actions

The right side of the Action Bar is used to display "actions" and the associated overflow menu, as shown in Figure 10-8.

FIGURE 10-8

Action Bar actions and the overflow menu were introduced, along with the Action Bar itself, in Android 3.0 (API level 11) as an alternative to the hardware menu button and its associated options menu. As such, they are populated using the same APIs that were previously used to create and manage the options menu. This process is described in detail later in this chapter.

Actions, then, are Menu Items that are important enough to make them visible and easily available to users at all times. Action items should be menu options that are either most frequently used, most important for users to discover, or most expected based on the actions available in similar applications. Generic and seldom used options, such as settings, help, or "about this app" options, should never be presented as action items.

Generally speaking, action items should be global actions that don't depend on the current context. Navigating within an Activity — for example, changing tabs or selecting an item from a navigation drop-down — should not alter the available action items.

ADDING AN ACTION BAR TO THE EARTHQUAKE MONITOR

In the following example, the earthquake-monitoring application, whose processing you moved to the background in Chapter 9, "Working in the Background," will be enhanced to include an Action Bar.

In Chapter 13, "Maps, Geocoding, and Location-Based Services," you will add a map to the earthquake monitor, so take this opportunity to add some navigation elements to the application to support a map.

1. Start by modifying the manifest. Add a `uses-sdk` node that specifies the target SDK as API level 15 and the minimum SDK level as 11 — the first platform release to support the Action Bar:

```xml
<?xml version="1.0" encoding="utf-8"?>
<manifest xmlns:android="http://schemas.android.com/apk/res/android"
    package="com.paad.earthquake"
    android:versionCode="1"
    android:versionName="1.0">

    <uses-sdk android:targetSdkVersion="15"
            android:minSdkVersion="11" />


    [... Existing Manifest nodes ...]

</manifest>
```

2. You can take this opportunity to create custom branding by adding a logo and Action Bar background. Creating the artwork is left as an exercise for you. Enable the split Action Bar for handset screens by updating the Earthquake Activity node in the manifest:

```xml
<activity
  android:name=".Earthquake"
  android:label="@string/app_name"
  android:uiOptions="splitActionBarWhenNarrow">
  <intent-filter>
    <action android:name="android.intent.action.MAIN" />
    <category android:name="android.intent.category.LAUNCHER" />
  </intent-filter>
</activity>
```

3. The map will be displayed within its own Fragment. Start by creating a new `map_fragment` `.xml` layout in the `res/layout` folder. You will update this in Chapter 13 with a Map View, but for now use a Text View as a placeholder.

```xml
<?xml version="1.0" encoding="utf-8"?>
<FrameLayout xmlns:android="http://schemas.android.com/apk/res/android"
  android:layout_width="match_parent"
  android:layout_height="match_parent">
  <TextView
    android:id="@+id/textView1"
    android:layout_width="match_parent"
    android:layout_height="match_parent"
    android:text="Map Goes Here!"
  />
</FrameLayout>
```

4. Create the Map Fragment. Create a new `EarthquakeMapFragment` class that extends Fragment and then override the `onCreateView` handler to inflate the `map_fragment` layout.

```java
import android.app.Fragment;
import android.os.Bundle;
import android.view.LayoutInflater;
import android.view.View;
import android.view.ViewGroup;

public class EarthquakeMapFragment extends Fragment  {

  @Override
  public View onCreateView(LayoutInflater inflater, ViewGroup container,
      Bundle savedInstanceState) {

    View view = inflater.inflate(R.layout.map_fragment, container, false);
    return view;
  }
}
```

5. Now consider the layouts to use. On handset devices it makes sense to display only the list or the map at any given time. On tablet devices a multipanel approach that displays both side by side would create a more engaging UI. Create a variation of the `main.xml` layout in the `res/layout-sw720dp` folder. This folder decoration requires a display to have at least 720 device independent pixels (dp) of screen width available in order to be displayed. The new layout should display the Earthquake List Fragment and Earthquake Map Fragment side by side. Limit the width of the list Fragment to half the minimum width for this layout (360dp).

```xml
<?xml version="1.0" encoding="utf-8"?>
<LinearLayout xmlns:android="http://schemas.android.com/apk/res/android"
  android:orientation="horizontal"
  android:layout_width="match_parent"
  android:layout_height="match_parent">
  <SearchView
    android:id="@+id/searchView"
    android:iconifiedByDefault="false"
    android:background="#FFF"
    android:layout_width="wrap_content"
    android:layout_height="wrap_content">
  </SearchView>
  <fragment
    android:name="com.paad.earthquake.EarthquakeListFragment"
    android:id="@+id/EarthquakeListFragment"
    android:layout_width="360dp"
    android:layout_height="match_parent"
  />
  <fragment android:name="com.paad.earthquake.EarthquakeMapFragment"
    android:id="@+id/EarthquakeMapFragment"
    android:layout_width="fill_parent"
    android:layout_height="match_parent"
  />
</LinearLayout>
```

6. To support earlier platform releases, copy the new tablet layout into the `res/layout-xlarge` folder.

7. For smaller screens, you'll be switching between the list and map fragments based on Action Bar tabs. Start by modifying the `main.xml` layout in the `res/layout` folder. Replace the `fragment` node that contains the Earthquake List Fragment, replacing it with a Frame Layout that will act as a container for either the list or map Fragments:

```
<?xml version="1.0" encoding="utf-8"?>
<LinearLayout xmlns:android="http://schemas.android.com/apk/res/android"
  android:orientation="vertical"
  android:layout_width="match_parent"
  android:layout_height="match_parent">
  <SearchView
    android:id="@+id/searchView"
    android:iconifiedByDefault="false"
    android:background="#FFF"
    android:layout_width="wrap_content"
    android:layout_height="wrap_content">
  </SearchView>
  <FrameLayout
    android:id="@+id/EarthquakeFragmentContainer"
    android:layout_width="match_parent"
    android:layout_height="match_parent">
  </FrameLayout>
</LinearLayout>
```

8. Your new layout means that the Earthquake List Fragment won't always be available, so return to the Earthquake Activity and update the `onActivityResult` handler to update the earthquakes by using the Service directly:

```
@Override
public void onActivityResult(int requestCode, int resultCode, Intent data) {
  super.onActivityResult(requestCode, resultCode, data);

  if (requestCode == SHOW_PREFERENCES) {
    updateFromPreferences();
    startService(new Intent(this, EarthquakeUpdateService.class));
  }
}
```

9. Now add navigation support for switching between the list and map when only one is visible at a time. Start by creating a new `TabListener` that extends the `ActionBar.TabListener`. It should take a container and a Fragment class, expanding the latter into the former when the tab is selected and detaching it from the UI when the tab is unselected.

```
public static class TabListener<T extends Fragment>
  implements ActionBar.TabListener {

  private Fragment fragment;
  private Activity activity;
  private Class<T> fragmentClass;
```

```
    private int fragmentContainer;

    public TabListener(Activity activity, int fragmentContainer,
                       Class<T> fragmentClass) {

      this.activity = activity;
      this.fragmentContainer = fragmentContainer;
      this.fragmentClass = fragmentClass;
    }

    // Called when a new tab has been selected
    public void onTabSelected(Tab tab, FragmentTransaction ft) {
      if (fragment == null) {
        String fragmentName = fragmentClass.getName();
        fragment = Fragment.instantiate(activity, fragmentName);
        ft.add(fragmentContainer, fragment, fragmentName);
      } else
        ft.attach(fragment);
    }

    // Called on the currently selected tab when a different tag is
    // selected.
    public void onTabUnselected(Tab tab, FragmentTransaction ft) {
      if (fragment != null)
        ft.detach(fragment);
    }

    // Called when the selected tab is selected.
    public void onTabReselected(Tab tab, FragmentTransaction ft) {
      if (fragment != null)
        ft.attach(fragment);
    }
  }
```

10. Still within the Earthquake Activity, modify the `onCreate` handler to detect if tab navigation is required; if so, enable tab mode and create new tabs for the list and map Fragments, using the `TabListener` created in step 8 to handle the navigation:

```
TabListener<EarthquakeListFragment> listTabListener;
TabListener<EarthquakeMapFragment> mapTabListener;

@Override
public void onCreate(Bundle savedInstanceState) {
  [... Existing onCreate ...]

  ActionBar actionBar = getActionBar();

  View fragmentContainer = findViewById(R.id.EarthquakeFragmentContainer);

  // Use tablet navigation if the list and map fragments are both available.
  boolean tabletLayout = fragmentContainer == null;

  // If it's not a tablet, use the tab Action Bar navigation.
  if (!tabletLayout) {
    actionBar.setNavigationMode(ActionBar.NAVIGATION_MODE_TABS);
```

```
      actionBar.setDisplayShowTitleEnabled(false);

      // Create and add the list tab.
      Tab listTab = actionBar.newTab();

      listTabListener = new TabListener<EarthquakeListFragment>
        (this, R.id.EarthquakeFragmentContainer, EarthquakeListFragment.class);

      listTab.setText("List")
             .setContentDescription("List of earthquakes")
             .setTabListener(listTabListener);

      actionBar.addTab(listTab);

      // Create and add the map tab.
      Tab mapTab = actionBar.newTab();

      mapTabListener = new TabListener<EarthquakeMapFragment>
        (this, R.id.EarthquakeFragmentContainer, EarthquakeMapFragment.class);

      mapTab.setText("Map")
            .setContentDescription("Map of earthquakes")
            .setTabListener(mapTabListener);

      actionBar.addTab(mapTab);
    }
  }
```

11. The Fragment Manager will attempt to restore the Fragments displayed within an Activity when the Activity is restarted due to a configuration change. Ensure that the Action Bar tabs and related tab listeners are synchronized with the visible tabs by overriding the onSaveInstanceState, onRestoreInstanceState, and onResume handlers.

11.1 Start by overriding the onSaveInstanceState handler to save the current Action Bar tab selection and detach each of the Fragments from the current view:

```
private static String ACTION_BAR_INDEX = "ACTION_BAR_INDEX";

@Override
public void onSaveInstanceState(Bundle outState) {
  View fragmentContainer = findViewById(R.id.EarthquakeFragmentContainer);
  boolean tabletLayout = fragmentContainer == null;

  if (!tabletLayout) {
    // Save the current Action Bar tab selection
    int actionBarIndex = getActionBar().getSelectedTab().getPosition();
    SharedPreferences.Editor editor = getPreferences(Activity.MODE_PRIVATE).edit();
    editor.putInt(ACTION_BAR_INDEX, actionBarIndex);
    editor.apply();

    // Detach each of the Fragments
    FragmentTransaction ft = getFragmentManager().beginTransaction();
    if (mapTabListener.fragment != null)
      ft.detach(mapTabListener.fragment);
    if (listTabListener.fragment != null)
```

```
    ft.detach(listTabListener.fragment);
  ft.commit();
}

super.onSaveInstanceState(outState);
}
```

11.2 Override the `onRestoreInstanceState` handler to find any Fragments that have been created and assign them to their associated Tab Listeners:

```
@Override
public void onRestoreInstanceState(Bundle savedInstanceState) {
  super.onRestoreInstanceState(savedInstanceState);

  View fragmentContainer = findViewById(R.id.EarthquakeFragmentContainer);
  boolean tabletLayout = fragmentContainer == null;

  if (!tabletLayout) {
    // Find the recreated Fragments and assign them to their associated Tab Listeners.
    listTabListener.fragment =
      getFragmentManager().findFragmentByTag(EarthquakeListFragment.class.getName());
    mapTabListener.fragment =
      getFragmentManager().findFragmentByTag(EarthquakeMapFragment.class.getName());

    // Restore the previous Action Bar tab selection.
    SharedPreferences sp = getPreferences(Activity.MODE_PRIVATE);
    int actionBarIndex = sp.getInt(ACTION_BAR_INDEX, 0);
    getActionBar().setSelectedNavigationItem(actionBarIndex);
  }
}
```

11.3 Finally, override the `onResume` handler to restore the previous Action Bar tab selection:

```
@Override
public void onResume() {
  super.onResume();
  View fragmentContainer = findViewById(R.id.EarthquakeFragmentContainer);
  boolean tabletLayout = fragmentContainer == null;

  if (!tabletLayout) {
    SharedPreferences sp = getPreferences(Activity.MODE_PRIVATE);
    int actionBarIndex = sp.getInt(ACTION_BAR_INDEX, 0);
    getActionBar().setSelectedNavigationItem(actionBarIndex);
  }
}
```

> *All code snippets in this example are part of the* Chapter 10 Earthquake Part 1 *project, available for download at* www.wrox.com.

Running the application on a phone should display the Action Bar with two tabs — one to display the list of earthquakes, the other a map. On a tablet device it should display two fragments side-by-side. We'll return to this example in Chapter 13 to add the Map View itself.

CREATING AND USING MENUS AND ACTION BAR ACTION ITEMS

Menus offer a way to expose application functions without sacrificing valuable screen space. Each Activity can specify its own menu that's displayed when the device's hardware menu button is pressed.

In Android 3.0 (API level 11) the hardware menu button was made optional, and the Activity menu was deprecated. To replace them, Action Bar actions and the overflow menu were introduced.

Android also supports Context Menus and Popup Menus that can be assigned to any View. Context Menus are normally triggered when a user holds the middle D-pad button, depresses the trackball, or long-presses the touch screen for approximately 3 seconds when the View has focus.

Actions, Activity Menus, and Context Menus each support a number of different options, including a subset of submenus, check boxes, radio buttons, shortcut keys, and icons.

Introducing the Android Menu System

If you've ever tried to navigate a mobile phone menu system using a stylus or trackball, you know that traditional menu systems are awkward to use on mobile devices. To improve the usability of application menus, Android uses a three-stage menu system optimized for small screens. Android 3.0 (API level 11) further refined this concept.

➤ **The icon menu and Action Bar actions** — The icon menu is a compact display (shown in Figure 10-9) that appears along the bottom of the screen when the menu button is pressed on Android devices earlier than Android 3.0. It displays the icons and text for a limited number of Menu Items (typically six), selected based on the order in which they were added to the menu.

The icon menu has been deprecated in Android 3.0, effectively replaced with Action Bar actions (refer to Figure 10-8). Rather than displaying a subset of all the Menu Items based on order, you explicitly select which Menu Items should be displayed as Action Bar actions.

FIGURE 10-9

This icon menu and Action Bar actions display icons and, optionally, their associated text (using the condensed text if it has been specified). By convention, menu icons are flat, pictured face on, and are generally grayscale — they should not look three-dimensional.

Menu Items in the icon menu and Action Bar do *not* display check boxes, radio buttons, or shortcut keys, so it's generally good practice not to depend on check boxes or radio buttons in icon Menu Items or actions because they will not be visible.

If the Activity menu contains more than the maximum number of visible Menu Items, a *More* Menu Item is displayed. When selected, it displays the expanded menu. Pressing the back button closes the icon menu.

In Android 3.0 and above, any actions that could not fit into the Action Bar — along with any Menu Items not flagged as actions — will be displayed in the overflow menu.

➤ **The expanded menu and overflow menu** — Prior to Android 3.0, the expanded menu was triggered when a user selected the *More* Menu Item from the icon menu. The expanded menu (shown in Figure 10-10) displays a scrollable list of only the Menu Items that *weren't* visible in the icon menu.

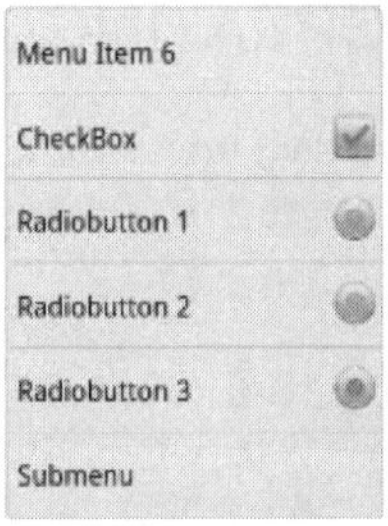

In Android 3.0 the expanded menu is represented by the overflow menu (see Figure 10-11). The overflow menu contains any Menu Item not flagged as an action and any action that was moved to the overflow menu due to a lack of room on the Action Bar.

FIGURE 10-10

The extended and overflow menus display the full Menu Item text, along with any associated check boxes and radio buttons. They do not, however, display icons. Pressing back from the expanded menu returns you to the icon menu. Pressing back when the overflow menu is displayed closes it.

FIGURE 10-11

> *You cannot force the expanded menu to be displayed instead of the icon menu. Special care must be taken with Menu Items that feature check boxes or radio buttons to ensure they aren't displayed within the icon menu. The maximum number of icon Menu Items can vary by device, so it's good practice to ensure that their state information is also indicated by an icon or a change in text.*

➤ **Submenus** — A traditional expanding hierarchical tree can be awkward to navigate using a mouse, so it's no surprise that this metaphor is particularly ill-suited for use on mobile devices. The Android alternative is to display each submenu in a floating window. For example, when a user selects a submenu, its items are displayed in a floating menu dialog box, as shown in Figure 10-12.

Note that the name of the submenu is shown in the header bar and that each Menu Item is displayed with its full text, checkbox (if any) and shortcut key. As with the extended menu, icons

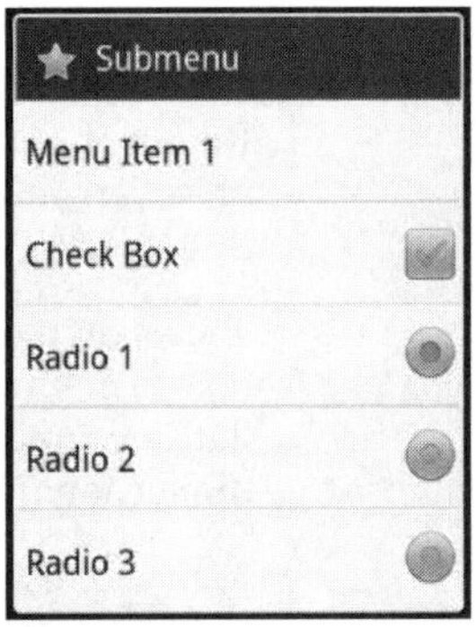

FIGURE 10-12

are not displayed in the submenu, so it's good practice to avoid assigning icons to submenu items.

Because Android does not support nested submenus, you can't add a submenu to a submenu (trying to do so will result in an exception), nor can you specify a submenu to be an action. Pressing the back button closes the floating window/menu.

Creating a Menu

To add a menu to an Activity, override its onCreateOptionsMenu handler. Prior to Android 3.0 this handler is triggered the first time an Activity's menu is displayed; in Android 3.0 and above it's triggered as part of creating the Action Bar each time the Activity is laid out.

The onCreateOptionsMenu receives a Menu object as a parameter. You can store a reference to, and continue to use, the Menu reference elsewhere in your code until the next time onCreateOptions-Menu is called.

You should always call through to the superclass implementation because it can add additional system menu options where appropriate.

Use the add method on the Menu object to populate your menu. For each new Menu Item, you must specify the following:

➤ A group value to separate Menu Items for batch processing and ordering.

➤ A unique identifier for each Menu Item. For efficiency reasons, Menu Item selections normally are handled using the onOptionsItemSelected event handler, so this unique identifier makes it possible for you to determine which Menu Item was selected. It is conventional to declare each menu ID as a private static variable within the Activity class. You can use the Menu.FIRST static constant and simply increment that value for each subsequent item.

➤ An order value that defines the order in which the Menu Items are displayed.

➤ The Menu Item display text, either as a character string or as a string resource.

When you have finished populating the Menu, return true to indicate that you have handled the Menu creation.

Listing 10-11 shows how to add a single Menu Item to an Activity Menu.

LISTING 10-11: Adding a Menu Item

```java
static final private int MENU_ITEM = Menu.FIRST;

@Override
public boolean onCreateOptionsMenu(Menu menu) {
  super.onCreateOptionsMenu(menu);

  // Group ID
  int groupId = 0;
  // Unique Menu Item identifier. Used for event handling
  int menuItemId = MENU_ITEM;
  // The order position of the item
  int menuItemOrder = Menu.NONE;
  // Text to be displayed for this Menu Item
  int menuItemText = R.string.menu_item;

  // Create the Menu Item and keep a reference to it
  MenuItem menuItem = menu.add(groupId, menuItemId,
                                menuItemOrder, menuItemText);

  return true;
}
```

code snippet PA4AD_Ch10_ActionBar/src/ActionBarActivity.java

Like the `Menu` object, each `MenuItem` returned by an `add` call is valid until the next call to `onCreateOptionsMenu`. Rather than maintaining a reference to each item, you can find a particular Menu Item by passing its ID into the Menu's `findItem` method:

```java
MenuItem menuItem = menu.findItem(MENU_ITEM);
```

Specifying Action Bar Actions

To specify a Menu Item as an Action Bar action, use its `setShowAsActionFlags` method, passing in one of the following options:

➤ `SHOW_AS_ACTION` — Forces the Menu Item to always be displayed as an action.

➤ `SHOW_AS_IF_SPACE` — Specifies that the Menu Item should be available as an action provided there is enough space in the Action Bar to display it. It is good practice to always use this option to provide the system with maximum flexibility on how to layout the available actions.

By default, actions display only their associated icon. You can optionally OR either of the preceding flags with `SHOW_AS_ACTION_WITH_TEXT` to make the Menu Item's text visible as well, as shown in Listing 10-12.

LISTING 10-12: Making a Menu Item an action

```
menuItem.setShowAsAction(MenuItem.SHOW_AS_ACTION_IF_ROOM |
                         MenuItem.SHOW_AS_ACTION_WITH_TEXT);
```

code snippet PA4AD_Ch10_ActionBar/src/ActionBarActivity.java

Menu Item Options

Android supports most of the traditional Menu Item options you're probably familiar with, including icons, shortcuts, check boxes, and radio buttons, as listed here:

➤ **Check boxes** — Check boxes on Menu Items are visible in the overflow and expanded menus, as well as within submenus. To set a Menu Item as a check box, use the `setCheckable` method. The state of that check box is controlled via `setChecked`.

```
// Create a new check box item.
menu.add(0, CHECKBOX_ITEM, Menu.NONE, "CheckBox").setCheckable(true);
```

➤ **Radio buttons** — A *radio button group* is a group of items displaying circular buttons, in which only one item can be selected at any given time. Checking one of these items will automatically uncheck any checked item in the same group.

To create a radio button group, assign the same group identifier to each item and then call `Menu.setGroupCheckable`, passing in that group identifier and setting the exclusive parameter to `true`:

```
// Create a radio button group.
menu.add(RB_GROUP, RADIOBUTTON_1, Menu.NONE, "Radiobutton 1");
menu.add(RB_GROUP, RADIOBUTTON_2, Menu.NONE, "Radiobutton 2");
menu.add(RB_GROUP, RADIOBUTTON_3, Menu.NONE,
        "Radiobutton 3").setChecked(true);

menu.setGroupCheckable(RB_GROUP, true, true);
```

➤ **Shortcut keys** — You can specify a keyboard shortcut for a Menu Item by using the `setShortcut` method. Each call to `setShortcut` requires two shortcut keys — one for use with the numeric keypad and another to support a full keyboard. Neither key is case-sensitive.

```
// Add a shortcut to this Menu Item, '0' if using the numeric keypad
// or 'b' if using the full keyboard.
menuItem.setShortcut('0', 'b');
```

➤ **Condensed titles** — The `setTitleCondensed` method lets you specify text to be displayed only in the icon menu or as Action Bar actions. The normal title will only be used when the Menu Item is displayed in the overflow or extended menu.

```
menuItem.setTitleCondensed("Short Title");
```

➤ **Icons** — Icons are displayed only in the icon menu or as an action; they are not visible in the extended menu or submenus. You can specify any Drawable resource as a menu icon.

```
menuItem.setIcon(R.drawable.menu_item_icon);
```

➤ **Menu item click listener** — An event handler that will execute when the Menu Item is selected. For efficiency, the use of such an event handler is discouraged; instead, Menu Item selections should be handled by the onOptionsItemSelected handler, as shown in the "Handling Menu Selections" section later in this chapter.

```
menuItem.setOnMenuItemClickListener(new OnMenuItemClickListener() {
  public boolean onMenuItemClick(MenuItem _menuItem) {
    [ ... execute click handling, return true if handled ... ]
    return true;
  }
});
```

➤ **Intents** — An Intent assigned to a Menu Item is triggered when a Menu Item click isn't handled by a MenuItemClickListener or the Activity's onOptionsItemSelected handler. When the Intent is triggered, Android will execute startActivity, passing in the specified Intent.

```
menuItem.setIntent(new Intent(this, MyOtherActivity.class));
```

Adding Action Views and Action Providers

The introduction of actions and the Action Bar in Android 3.0 (API level 11) made it possible to add richer interaction modes to the menu system. In particular, it's now possible to add interactive Views to your Action Bar actions in the form of action Views and Action Providers.

You can replace the icon/text used to represent an action with any View or layout using the Menu Item's setActionView method, passing in either a View instance or a layout resource, as shown in Listing 10-13.

LISTING 10-13: Adding an action View

```
menuItem.setActionView(R.layout.my_action_view)
  .setShowAsActionFlags(MenuItem.SHOW_AS_ACTION_IF_ROOM|
    MenuItem.SHOW_AS_ACTION_COLLAPSE_ACTION_VIEW);
```

code snippet PA4AD_Ch10_ActionBar/src/ActionBarActivity.java

Once added, the action View will be displayed whenever the associated Menu Item is displayed as an action in the Action Bar, but will never be displayed if the Menu Item is relegated to the overflow menu.

A better alternative, introduced in Android 4.0 (API level 14), is to add the MenuItem.SHOW_AS_ACTION_COLLAPSE_ACTION_VIEW flag. When this flag is set, the Menu Item will be represented using its standard icon and/or text properties until it's pressed. At that point, it will be expanded to fill the Action Bar, as shown in Figure 10-13.

FIGURE 10-13

In either case, it's up to you to wire the View's interaction handlers. Typically, this is done within the `onCreateMenuOptions` handler:

```
View myView = menuItem.getActionView();
Button button = (Button)myView.findViewById(R.id.goButton);

button.setOnClickListener(new OnClickListener() {
  public void onClick(View v) {
    // TODO React to the button press.
  }
});
```

Android 4.0 (API level 14) introduced a new alternative to manually creating and configuring action Views within each Activity. Instead, you can create Action Providers by extending the `ActionProvider` class. Action Providers are similar to action Views but encapsulate both the appearance and interaction models associated with the View. For example, Android 4.0 includes the `ShareActionProvider` to encapsulate the "share" action.

To assign an Action Provider to a Menu Item, use the `setActionProvider` method, assigning it an Intent to use to perform the sharing action, as shown in Listing 10-14.

LISTING 10-14: Adding a Share Action Provider to a menu

```
// Create the sharing Intent
Intent shareIntent = new Intent(Intent.ACTION_SEND);
shareIntent.setType("image/*");
Uri uri = Uri.fromFile(new File(getFilesDir(), "test_1.jpg"));
shareIntent.putExtra(Intent.EXTRA_STREAM, uri.toString());

ShareActionProvider shareProvider = new ShareActionProvider(this);
shareProvider.setShareIntent(shareIntent);

menuItem.setActionProvider(shareProvider)
        .setShowAsActionFlags(MenuItem.SHOW_AS_ACTION_ALWAYS);
```

code snippet PA4AD_Ch10_ActionBar/src/ActionBarActivity.java

Adding Menu Items from Fragments

With most of your UI encapsulated within Fragments, it makes sense to encapsulate any related Activity Menu Items and Action Bar actions within those Fragments.

To register your Fragment as a contributor to the options Menu, call `setHasOptionsMenu` within its `onCreate` hander:

```
@Override
public void onCreate(Bundle savedInstanceState) {
  super.onCreate(savedInstanceState);
  setHasOptionsMenu(true);
}
```

You can then override the `onCreateOptionsMenu` handler, as described in the previous section, to populate the menu and Action Bar. At run time, the system will aggregate the Menu Items supplied by the Activity and each of its component Fragments.

Defining Menu Hierarchies in XML

Rather than constructing your Menus in code, it's best practice to define your Menu hierarchies as XML resources. As with layouts and other resources, this gives you the ability to create different Menus for alternative hardware configurations, languages, or locations.

Menu resources are stored as XML files in the `res/menu` folder of your project. Each menu hierarchy must be created as a separate file, for which the lowercase filename becomes the resource identifier.

Create your Menu hierarchy using the `menu` tag as the root node and a series of `item` tags to specify each Menu Item. Each `item` node supports attributes to specify each of the available Menu Item options. This includes the text, icon, shortcut, and check box options, as well as collapsible action Views and Action Providers.

To create a submenu, place a new `menu` tag as a subnode within an `item`. Listing 10-15 shows how to create a simple Menu hierarchy as an XML resource.

LISTING 10-15: Defining a Menu Hierarchy in XML

```xml
<menu xmlns:android="http://schemas.android.com/apk/res/android">
    <item
        android:id="@+id/action_item"
        android:icon="@drawable/action_item_icon"
        android:title="@string/action_item_title"
        android:showAsAction="ifRoom">
    </item>
    <item
        android:id="@+id/action_view_item"
        android:icon="@drawable/action_view_icon"
        android:title="@string/action_view_title"
        android:showAsAction="ifRoom|collapseActionView"
        android:actionLayout="@layout/my_action_view">
    </item>
    <item
        android:id="@+id/action_provider_item"
        android:title="Share"
        android:showAsAction="always"
```

```
          android:actionProviderClass="android.widget.ShareActionProvider">
        </item>
        <item
          android:id="@+id/item02"
          android:checkable="true"
          android:title="@string/menu_item_two">
        </item>
        <item
          android:id="@+id/item03"
          android:numericShortcut="3"
          android:alphabeticShortcut="3"
          android:title="@string/menu_item_three">
        </item>
        <item
          android:id="@+id/item04"
          android:title="@string/submenu_title">
          <menu>
            <item
              android:id="@+id/item05"
              android:title="@string/submenu_item">
            </item>
          </menu>
        </item>
      </menu>
```

code snippet PA4AD_Ch10_ActionBar/res/menu/my_menu.xml

To use your Menu resource, use the MenuInflater class within your onCreateOptionsMenu or onCreateContextMenu event handlers, as shown in Listing 10-16.

LISTING 10-16: Inflating an XML menu resource

```
public boolean onCreateOptionsMenu(Menu menu) {
    super.onCreateOptionsMenu(menu);

    MenuInflater inflater = getMenuInflater();
    inflater.inflate(R.menu.my_menu, menu);

    return true;
}
```

code snippet PA4AD_Ch10_ActionBar/src/ActionBarActivity.java

Updating Menu Items Dynamically

By overriding your Activity's onPrepareOptionsMenu method, you can modify a Menu based on an application's current state immediately before the Menu is displayed. This lets you dynamically disable/enable Menu Items, set visibility, and modify text.

Note that the onPrepareOptionsMenu method is triggered whenever the menu button is clicked, the overflow menu displayed, or the Action Bar is created.

To modify Menu Items dynamically, you can either record a reference to them from within the onCreateOptionsMenu method when they're created, or you can use the findItem method on the Menu object, as shown in Listing 10-17, where onPrepareOptionsMenu is overridden.

Available for
download on
Wrox.com

LISTING 10-17: Modifying Menu Items dynamically

```
@Override
public boolean onPrepareOptionsMenu(Menu menu) {
  super.onPrepareOptionsMenu(menu);

  MenuItem menuItem = menu.findItem(MENU_ITEM);

  [ ... modify Menu Items ... ]

  return true;
}
```

code snippet PA4AD_Ch10_ActionBar/src/ActionBarActivity.java

Handling Menu Selections

Android handles the Action Bar actions, overflow menu, and Activity menu selections using a single event handler, onOptionsItemSelected. The Menu Item selected is passed in to this method as the MenuItem parameter.

To react to the menu selection, compare the item.getItemId value to the Menu Item identifiers you used when populating the Menu (or their resource identifiers if defining your Menu in XML), as shown in Listing 10-18, and perform the corresponding action.

LISTING 10-18: Handling Menu Item selections

```
public boolean onOptionsItemSelected(MenuItem item) {
  super.onOptionsItemSelected(item);

  // Find which Menu Item has been selected
  switch (item.getItemId()) {

    // Check for each known Menu Item
    case (MENU_ITEM):
      [ ... Perform menu handler actions ... ]
      return true;

    // Return false if you have not handled the Menu Item
    default: return false;
  }
}
```

code snippet PA4AD_Ch10_ActionBar/src/ActionBarActivity.java

If you have supplied Menu Items from within a Fragment, you can choose to handle them within the `onOptionsItemSelected` handler of either the Activity or the Fragment. Note that the Activity will receive the selected Menu Item first, and that the Fragment will not receive it if the Activity handles it and returns `true`.

Introducing Submenus and Context Menus

Context Menus use the same floating window as the submenus shown in Figure 10-12. Although their appearance is the same, the two menu types are populated differently.

> *Although Context Menus are still supported in Android 4.0, their use has become limited, with long-press functionality now used more commonly to support operations like drag and drop.*
>
> *Users are unlikely to find options supplied by the Context Menu, so they should be used sparingly.*

Creating Submenus

Submenus are displayed as regular Menu Items that, when selected, reveal more items. Traditionally, submenus are displayed in a hierarchical tree layout. Android uses a different approach to simplify menu navigation for touch-screen devices. Rather than a tree structure, selecting a submenu presents either a single floating window (in the case of the legacy Menu system) or replaces the overflow menu (in the case of Android 3.0 and above), both of which display all its Menu Items.

You can add submenus by using the `addSubMenu` method. It supports the same parameters as the `add` method used to add normal Menu Items, enabling you to specify a group, unique identifier, and text string for each submenu. You can also use the `setHeaderIcon` and `setIcon` methods to specify an icon to display in the submenu's header bar or icon menu, respectively.

The Menu Items within a submenu support the same options as those assigned to the icon or extended menus, with the exception of the Action Bar action-related properties.

> *Submenus can't be used as actions, nor does Android support nested submenus.*

The following code snippet shows an extract from an implementation of the `onCreateMenuOptions` code that adds a submenu to the main menu, sets the header icon, and then adds a submenu Menu Item:

```
SubMenu sub = menu.addSubMenu(0, 0, Menu.NONE, "Submenu");
sub.setHeaderIcon(R.drawable.icon);
sub.setIcon(R.drawable.icon);

MenuItem submenuItem = sub.add(0, 0, Menu.NONE, "Submenu Item");
```

Using Context Menus and Popup Menus

Context Menus are contextualized by the currently focused View and are triggered when a user long-presses the trackball, middle D-pad button, or a View (typically for approximately 3 seconds). A Context Menu is displayed as a floating window above your Activity.

Android 3.0 (API level 11) introduced the `PopupMenu` class, a lighter-weight alternative to the `ContextMenu` that anchors itself to a specific View.

You define and populate Context Menus and Popup Menus as you define and populate Activity Menus. There are two options available for creating Context Menus for a particular View.

Creating Context Menus

One option is to create a generic `ContextMenu` object for a `View` class by overriding a View's `onCreateContextMenu` handler, as shown here:

```
@Override
public void onCreateContextMenu(ContextMenu menu) {
  super.onCreateContextMenu(menu);
  menu.add("ContextMenuItem1");
}
```

The Context Menu created here will be available within any Activity that includes this `View` class.

The more common alternative is to create Activity-specific Context Menus by overriding the Activity's `onCreateContextMenu` method, and registering the Views that should use it using the `registerForContextMenu` method, as shown in Listing 10-19.

LISTING 10-19: Assigning a Context Menu to a View

```
@Override
public void onCreate(Bundle savedInstanceState) {
  super.onCreate(savedInstanceState);

  EditText view = new EditText(this);
  setContentView(view);

  registerForContextMenu(view);
}
```

code snippet PA4AD_Ch10_ActionBar/src/ActionBarActivity.java

Once a View has been registered, the `onCreateContextMenu` handler will be triggered the first time a Context Menu is displayed for that View.

To populate the Context Menu parameter with the appropriate Menu Items, override `onCreateContextMenu` and check which View has triggered the menu creation.

```
@Override
public void onCreateContextMenu(ContextMenu menu, View v,
                                ContextMenu.ContextMenuInfo menuInfo) {
  super.onCreateContextMenu(menu, v, menuInfo);
```

```
    menu.setHeaderTitle("Context Menu");
    menu.add(0, Menu.FIRST, Menu.NONE,
            "Item 1").setIcon(R.drawable.menu_item);
    menu.add(0, Menu.FIRST+1, Menu.NONE, "Item 2").setCheckable(true);
    menu.add(0, Menu.FIRST+2, Menu.NONE, "Item 3").setShortcut('3', '3');
    SubMenu sub = menu.addSubMenu("Submenu");
    sub.add("Submenu Item");
}
```

As shown in the preceding code, the `ContextMenu` class supports the same `add` method as the `Menu` class, so you can populate a Context Menu in the same way that you populate Activity menus — using the `add` method. This includes using the `add` method to add submenus to your Context Menus. Note that icons will never be displayed; however, you can specify the title and icon to display in the Context Menu's header bar.

Android also supports late runtime population of Context Menus via Intent Filters. This mechanism lets you populate a Context Menu by specifying the kind of data presented by the current View and asking other Android applications if they support any actions for it. The most common examples of this mechanism are the cut/copy/paste Menu Items available on Edit Text controls.

Handling Context Menu Selections

Context Menu Item selections are handled much the same as Activity Menu selections. You can attach an Intent or Menu Item Click Listener directly to each Menu Item or use the preferred technique of overriding the `onContextItemSelected` method on the Activity, as follows:

```
@Override
public boolean onContextItemSelected(MenuItem item) {
  super.onContextItemSelected(item);

  // TODO [ ... Handle Menu Item selection ... ]

  return false;
}
```

The `onContextItemSelected` event handler is triggered whenever a Context Menu Item is selected.

Using Popup Menus

An alternative to Context Menus, Popup Menus are displayed alongside a particular View instance, rather than above the entire Activity (see Figure 10-14). When targeting devices running Android 3.0 or above, it's best practice to use Popup Menus rather than Context Menus.

To assign a Popup Menu to a View, you must create a new Popup Menu, specifying the Activity Context and the View to which it should be anchored:

```
final PopupMenu popupMenu = new PopupMenu(this,
myView);
```

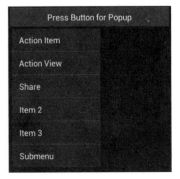

FIGURE 10-14

Assign or inflate a Menu resource as you would for an Activity or Context Menu, and add a new `OnMenuItemClickListener` to handle Menu Item selections, as shown in Listing 10-20.

LISTING 10-20: Assigning a Popup Menu to a View

```java
final PopupMenu popupMenu = new PopupMenu(this, button);

popupMenu.inflate(R.menu.my_popup_menu);
popupMenu.setOnMenuItemClickListener(new OnMenuItemClickListener() {
  public boolean onMenuItemClick(MenuItem item) {
    switch (item.getItemId()) {
      case (POPUP_ITEM_1) :
        // TODO Handle popup menu clicks.
        return true;
      default: return false;
    }
  }
});
```

code snippet PA4AD_Ch10_ActionBar/src/ActionBarActivity.java

To display the Popup Menu, call its `show` method:

```java
popupMenu.show();
```

REFRESHING THE EARTHQUAKE MONITOR

In the following example you'll add a Menu Item to refresh the Earthquake monitor.

1. Create a new string resource that defines the menu text in the `res/values/strings.xml` file:

```xml
<string name="menu_refresh">Refresh</string>
```

2. Create a new `main_menu.xml` resource in the `res/menu` folder that contains the "refresh" and "preferences" Menu Items. The former should be specified as an action to be displayed on the Action Bar:

```xml
<menu xmlns:android="http://schemas.android.com/apk/res/android">
  <item
    android:id="@+id/menu_refresh"
    android:title="@string/menu_refresh"
    android:showAsAction="ifRoom|withText">
  </item>
  <item
    android:id="@+id/menu_preferences"
    android:title="@string/menu_preferences"
    android:showAsAction="never">
  </item>
</menu>
```

3. Modify the `onCreateOptionsMenu` method in the Earthquake Activity to inflate the menu resource from step 2:

```
@Override
public boolean onCreateOptionsMenu(Menu menu) {
  super.onCreateOptionsMenu(menu);

  MenuInflater inflater = getMenuInflater();
  inflater.inflate(R.menu.main_menu, menu);

  return true;
}
```

4. Having populated the Activity Menu and Action Bar actions, the next step is to handle the selection of these items. Modify the `onOptionsItemSelected` handler. Update the "preferences" selection to refer to its resource ID. When the "refresh" item is selected, start the update Service.

```
@Override
public boolean onOptionsItemSelected(MenuItem item) {
  super.onOptionsItemSelected(item);

  switch (item.getItemId()) {
    case (R.id.menu_refresh): {
      startService(new Intent(this, EarthquakeUpdateService.class));
      return true;
    }
    case (R.id.menu_preferences): {
      Class c = Build.VERSION.SDK_INT < Build.VERSION_CODES.HONEYCOMB ?
        PreferencesActivity.class : FragmentPreferences.class;
      Intent i = new Intent(this, c);

      startActivityForResult(i, SHOW_PREFERENCES);
      return true;
    }
    default: return false;
  }
}
```

5. Take this opportunity to move the Search View to the Action Bar. Start by updating the menu definition to include a Search View:

```
<menu xmlns:android="http://schemas.android.com/apk/res/android">
  <item
    android:id="@+id/menu_search"
    android:icon="@android:drawable/ic_menu_search"
    android:actionViewClass="android.widget.SearchView"
    android:showAsAction="ifRoom|collapseActionView">
  </item>
  <item
    android:id="@+id/menu_refresh"
    android:title="@string/menu_refresh"
    android:showAsAction="ifRoom|withText">
  </item>
```

```
<item
  android:id="@+id/menu_preferences"
  android:title="@string/menu_preferences"
  android:showAsAction="never">
</item>
</menu>
```

6. Modify each of the `main.xml` layouts, removing the reference to the Search View.

7. Update the `onCreateOptionsMenu` handler to configure the Search View, and remove the corresponding code from the `onCreate` handler:

```
@Override
public boolean onCreateOptionsMenu(Menu menu) {
  super.onCreateOptionsMenu(menu);

  MenuInflater inflater = getMenuInflater();
  inflater.inflate(R.menu.main_menu, menu);

  // Moved from onCreate -- Retreive the Search View and configure/enable it.
  SearchManager searchManager =
    (SearchManager) getSystemService(Context.SEARCH_SERVICE);
  SearchView searchView = (SearchView) menu.findItem(R.id.menu_search).getActionView();
  searchView.setSearchableInfo(searchManager.getSearchableInfo(getComponentName()));

  return true;
}
```

> *All code snippets in this example are part of the* Chapter 10 Earthquake Part 2 *project, available for download at* www.wrox.com.

GOING FULL SCREEN

For specific situations, it makes sense for your application to occupy the entire screen, hiding or obscuring navigation controls and status information such as the time and Notifications. This is the case if, and only if, you are building an application that is designed to be fully immersive. Valid examples of immersive applications include immersive games such as first-person racers or shooters, eLearning applications, and video.

> *Hiding status information and navigation cues is a disruptive action likely to frustrate many users. If you choose to make your application "full screen," you should make it easy for users to disable such behavior.*

The UI of every Android device includes space managed by the system, dedicated to displaying status information such as the time, connectivity, and Notifications (new and ongoing). The system-controlled UI elements of Android have changed as the platform has evolved.

Prior to the introduction of tablets, this space was known as the "status bar," and resided at the top of the screen for each handset, as shown in Figure 10-15.

FIGURE 10-15

The extra screen real-estate available for tablets, combined with a lack of hardware navigation keys, led to the introduction of a "system bar" in Android 3.0 — a UI section at the bottom of the screen that contains both the contents normally displayed in the status bar, as well as software implementations of the *back* and *home* keys, as shown in Figure 10-16.

FIGURE 10-16

Android 4.0 saw the introduction of phone hardware that, like tablets, uses onscreen software buttons for navigation rather than hardware keys. As a result, a new "navigation bar" was introduced to house the *back* and *home* buttons, as shown in Figure 10-17. Unlike tablets, Android smartphones continue to use the status bar to display status information, just as they did in previous versions.

FIGURE 10-17

The result is that for tablets a single piece of screen is dedicated to displaying status information and navigation buttons, whereas on handsets status is displayed separately from the navigation.

To control the visibility of the navigation bar on handsets, or the appearance of the system bar in tablets, you can use the `setSystemUiVisibility` method on any View visible within your Activity hierarchy. Note that any user interaction with the Activity will revert these changes.

In Android 3.0 (API level 11) you can obscure, but not remove, the navigation bar on handsets and the system bar on tablets using the `STATUS_BAR_HIDDEN` flag.

```
myView.setSystemUiVisibility(View.STATUS_BAR_HIDDEN);
```

Android 4.0 (API level 14) deprecated this flag, replacing it with the following flags to better support handsets that use a separate navigation and status bar:

➤ `SYSTEM_UI_FLAG_LOW_PROFILE` — Obscures the navigation buttons in the same way as `STATUS_BAR_HIDDEN`

➤ `SYSTEM_UI_FLAG_HIDE_NAVIGATION` — Removes the navigation bar on handset devices, and obscures the navigation buttons used in the system bar on tablets

```
myView.setSystemUiVisibility(View.SYSTEM_UI_FLAG_LOW_PROFILE);
```

It's generally good practice to synchronize other changes within your UI with changes in navigation visibility. For example, you may choose to hide and display the Action Bar and other navigational controls based on entering and exiting "full screen mode."

You can do this by registering an `OnSystemUiVisibilityChangeListener` to your View — generally, the View you are using to control the navigation visibility, as shown in Listing 10-21.

LISTING 10-21: Reacting to changes in system UI visibility

```
myView.setOnSystemUiVisibilityChangeListener(
  new OnSystemUiVisibilityChangeListener() {

  public void onSystemUiVisibilityChange(int visibility) {
    if (visibility == View.SYSTEM_UI_FLAG_VISIBLE) {
      // TODO Display Action Bar and Status Bar
    }
    else {
      // TODO Hide Action Bar and Status Bar
    }
  }
});
```

code snippet PA4AD_Ch10_ActionBar/src/ActionBarActivity.java

You also can hide the status bar along the top of all handset devices. This should be done cautiously because it can disrupt how people use their phones. In many cases — particularly for watching video — it's best practice to enable and disable the status bar from within an On System UI Visibility Change Listener.

To hide the status bar, add the `LayoutParams.FLAG_FULLSCREEN` flag to the Window:

```
myView.setSystemUiVisibility(View.SYSTEM_UI_FLAG_HIDE_NAVIGATION);
getWindow().addFlags(WindowManager.LayoutParams.FLAG_FULLSCREEN);
```

Note that this will not affect tablet devices, which use a system bar rather than a separate navigation and status bars.

INTRODUCING DIALOGS

Dialog boxes are a common UI metaphor in desktop, web, and mobile applications. They're used to help users answer questions, make selections, and confirm actions, and to display warning or error messages. Dialog boxes in Android are partially transparent, floating Activities or Fragments that partially obscure the UI that launched them.

In terms of Android UX design, Dialogs should be used to represent system-level events, such as displaying errors or supporting account selection. It is good practice to limit the use of Dialogs within your applications, and when using them to limit the degree of customization.

Depending on the platform and hardware configuration, dialogs may obscure the Activities behind them using a blur or dim filter, as shown in Figure 10-18.

There are three ways to implement a dialog in Android:

➤ **Using the Dialog class (or its extensions)** — In addition to the general-purpose `AlertDialog` class, Android includes a number of classes that extend `Dialog`. Each is designed to provide specific dialog-box functionality. A Dialog class-based screen is constructed and controlled entirely within its calling Activity, so it doesn't need to be registered in the manifest.

➤ **Dialog-themed Activities** — You can apply the dialog theme to a regular Activity to give it the appearance of a standard dialog box.

➤ **Toasts** — Toasts are special nonmodal transient message boxes, often used by Broadcast Receivers and Services to notify users of events occurring in the background. You learn more about Toasts in the section "Let's Make a Toast."

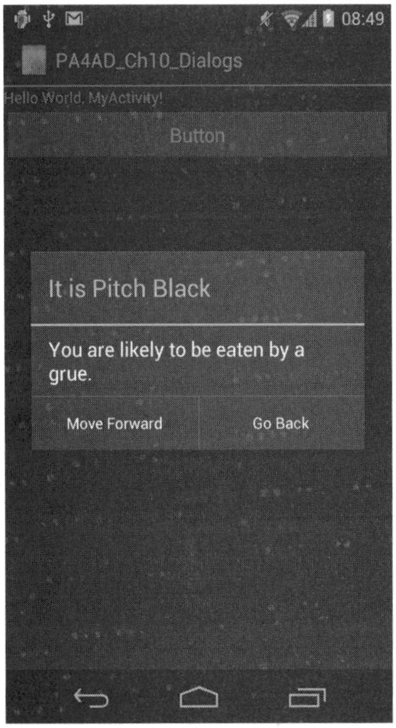

FIGURE 10-18

Creating a Dialog

To create a new Dialog, instantiate a new `Dialog` instance and set the title and layout, using the `setTitle` and `setContentView` methods, respectively, as shown in Listing 10-22. The `setContentView` method accepts a resource identifier for a layout that will be inflated to display the Dialog's UI.

Once the Dialog is configured to your liking, use the `show` method to display it.

LISTING 10-22: Creating a new Dialog using the Dialog class

```
// Create the new Dialog.
Dialog dialog = new Dialog(MyActivity.this);

// Set the title.
dialog.setTitle("Dialog Title");

// Inflate the layout.
dialog.setContentView(R.layout.dialog_view);

// Update the Dialog's contents.
TextView text = (TextView)dialog.findViewById(R.id.dialog_text_view);
text.setText("This is the text in my dialog");
```

continues

LISTING 10-22 *(continued)*

```
// Display the Dialog.
dialog.show();
```

code snippet PA4AD_Ch10_Dialogs/src/MyActivity.java

Using the Alert Dialog Class

The `AlertDialog` class is one of the most versatile Dialog-class implementations. It offers a number of options that let you construct dialogs for some of the most common use cases, including the following:

➤ Presenting a message to users offering them one to three options in the form of buttons. This functionality is probably familiar to you if you've done any desktop programming for which the buttons presented are usually a combination of OK, Cancel, Yes, and No.

➤ Offering a list of options in the form of check boxes or radio buttons.

➤ Providing a text entry box for user input.

To construct the Alert Dialog UI, create a new `AlertDialog.Builder` object:

```
AlertDialog.Builder ad = new AlertDialog.Builder(context);
```

You can then assign values for the title and message to display, and optionally assign values to be used for any buttons, selection items, and text input boxes you want to display. That includes setting event listeners to handle user interaction.

Listing 10-23 gives an example of an Alert Dialog used to display a message with two buttons. Clicking either button will close the Dialog after executing the attached On Click Listeners.

LISTING 10-23: Configuring an Alert Dialog

```
Context context = MyActivity.this;
String title = "It is Pitch Black";
String message = "You are likely to be eaten by a Grue.";
String button1String = "Go Back";
String button2String = "Move Forward";

AlertDialog.Builder ad = new AlertDialog.Builder(context);
ad.setTitle(title);
ad.setMessage(message);

ad.setPositiveButton(
  button1String,
  new DialogInterface.OnClickListener() {
    public void onClick(DialogInterface dialog, int arg1) {
      eatenByGrue();
    }
  }
);
```

```
ad.setNegativeButton(
  button2String,
  new DialogInterface.OnClickListener(){
    public void onClick(DialogInterface dialog, int arg1) {
      // do nothing
    }
  }
);
```

code snippet PA4AD_Ch10_Dialogs/src/MyActivity.java

Use the `setCancelable` method to determine if the user should be able to close the dialog by pressing the back button without making a selection. If you choose to make the Dialog cancelable, you can use the `setOnCancelListener` method to attach an On Cancel Listener to react to this event:

```
ad.setCancelable(true);

ad.setOnCancelListener(
  new DialogInterface.OnCancelListener() {
    public void onCancel(DialogInterface dialog) {
      eatenByGrue();
    }
  }
);
```

Using Specialized Input Dialogs

Android includes several specialized dialog boxes that encapsulate controls designed to facilitate common user-input requests. In order to maintain consistency, they should be used in preference to customized Dialogs wherever possible. They include the following:

➤ `CharacterPickerDialog` — Lets users select an accented character based on a regular character source.

➤ `DatePickerDialog` — Lets users select a date from a `DatePicker` View. The constructor includes a callback listener to alert your calling Activity when the date has been set.

➤ `TimePickerDialog` — Similar to the Date Picker Dialog, this dialog lets users select a time from a `TimePicker` View.

➤ `ProgressDialog` — Displays a progress bar beneath a message text box. This can be used to keep users informed of the ongoing progress of a time-consuming operation, though best practice is to allow users to interact with the application when such long-running processes are underway.

In each case, to use the specialist Dialog, construct a new instance of it, setting its properties and event handlers, before displaying the Dialog:

```
DatePickerDialog datePickerDialog =
  new DatePickerDialog(
    MyActivity.this,
```

```
        new OnDateSetListener() {
          public void onDateSet(DatePicker view, int year,
                                int monthOfYear, int dayOfMonth) {
            // TODO Use the selected date.
          }
        },
        1978, 6, 19);

    datePickerDialog.show();
```

Managing and Displaying Dialogs Using Dialog Fragments

You can use the `show` method of each Dialog instance to display it, but a better alternative is to use Dialog Fragments. A Dialog Fragment is a Fragment that contains a Dialog.

Dialog Fragments were introduced in Android 3.0 (API level 11) and replace the deprecated `Activity.onCreateDialog` and `Activity.onPrepareDialog` handlers (described in more detail in the next section). Dialog Fragments are included as part of the Android Support Package, making it possible to use them for projects targeting all Android platforms down to Android 1.6 (API level 4).

A Dialog Fragment efficiently encapsulates and manages the Dialog's lifecycle and ensures that the Fragment and the containing Dialog states remain consistent.

To use a Dialog Fragment, extend the `DialogFragment` class, as shown in Listing 10-24. Override the `onCreateDialog` handler to return a Dialog constructed as described in the previous sections.

LISTING 10-24: Using the On Create Dialog event handler

```
public class MyDialogFragment extends DialogFragment {

  private static String CURRENT_TIME = "CURRENT_TIME";

  public static MyDialogFragment newInstance(String currentTime) {
    // Create a new Fragment instance with the specified
    // parameters.
    MyDialogFragment fragment = new MyDialogFragment();
    Bundle args = new Bundle();
    args.putString(CURRENT_TIME, currentTime);
    fragment.setArguments(args);

    return fragment;
  }

  @Override
  public Dialog onCreateDialog(Bundle savedInstanceState) {
    // Create the new Dialog using the AlertBuilder.
    AlertDialog.Builder timeDialog =
      new AlertDialog.Builder(getActivity());

    // Configure the Dialog UI.
    timeDialog.setTitle("The Current Time Is...");
    timeDialog.setMessage(getArguments().getString(CURRENT_TIME));
```

```
        // Return the configured Dialog.
        return timeDialog.create();
    }
}
```

You can display the Dialog Fragment using the Fragment Manager and Fragment Transactions the same way as you would any other Fragment, as described in Chapter 4 and shown in Listing 10-25. The Fragment's application appearance will depend on the Dialog it contains.

LISTING 10-25: Displaying a Dialog Fragment

```
String tag = "my_dialog";
DialogFragment myFragment =
    MyDialogFragment.newInstance(dateString);

myFragment.show(getFragmentManager(), tag);
```

Any listeners you attach to the dialog must be handled within the containing Fragment — typically by calling a method in the parent Activity.

Alternatively, you can override the `onCreateView` handler to inflate a custom Dialog layout within your Dialog Fragment, just as you would your custom Dialog class, as shown in Listing 10-26.

LISTING 10-26: Using the On Create View handler

```
@Override
public View onCreateView(LayoutInflater inflater, ViewGroup container,
    Bundle savedInstanceState) {

    // Inflate the Dialog's UI.
    View view = inflater.inflate(R.layout.dialog_view, container, false);

    // Update the Dialog's contents.
    TextView text = (TextView)view.findViewById(R.id.dialog_text_view);
    text.setText("This is the text in my dialog");

    return view;
}
```

Note that you must choose to override only one of `onCreateView` or `onCreateDialog`. Overriding both will result in an exception being thrown.

In addition to providing improved resource use, this technique lets your Activity handle the persistence of state information within Dialogs. Any selection or data input (such as item selection and text entry) will be persisted if the Fragment is re-created due to a configuration change, such as screen rotation.

Managing and Displaying Dialogs Using Activity Event Handlers

Prior to the introduction of Fragments, the best practice way to display Dialogs was by overriding your Activity's onCreateDialog and onPrepareDialog handlers to prepare each Dialog, and showDialog to display them on demand.

By overriding the onCreateDialog handler, you can specify Dialogs that will be created on demand when showDialog is used to display a specific Dialog. As shown in Listing 10-27, the overridden method includes a switch statement that lets you determine which dialog is required.

LISTING 10-27: Using the On Create Dialog event handler

```
static final private int TIME_DIALOG = 1;

@Override
public Dialog onCreateDialog(int id) {
  switch(id) {
    case (TIME_DIALOG) :
      AlertDialog.Builder timeDialog = new AlertDialog.Builder(this);
      timeDialog.setTitle("The Current Time Is...");
      timeDialog.setMessage("Now");
      return timeDialog.create();
  }
  return null;
}
```

code snippet PA4AD_Ch10_Dialogs/src/MyActivity.java

After the initial creation, each time showDialog is called, it will trigger the onPrepareDialog handler. By overriding this method you can modify a dialog each time it is displayed. This lets you contextualize any of the display values, as shown in Listing 10-28, which assigns the current time to the dialog created in Listing 10-27.

LISTING 10-28: Using the On Prepare Dialog event handler

```
@Override
public void onPrepareDialog(int id, Dialog dialog) {
  switch(id) {
    case (TIME_DIALOG) :
      SimpleDateFormat sdf = new SimpleDateFormat("HH:mm:ss");
      Date currentTime =
        new Date(java.lang.System.currentTimeMillis());
      String dateString = sdf.format(currentTime);
```

```
        AlertDialog timeDialog = (AlertDialog)dialog;
        timeDialog.setMessage(dateString);

        break;
    }
}
```

code snippet PA4AD_Ch10_Dialogs/src/MyActivity.java

After overriding these methods, you can display the Dialogs by calling `showDialog`:

```
showDialog(TIME_DIALOG);
```

Pass in the identifier for the Dialog you want to display, and Android will create (if necessary) and prepare the Dialog before displaying it.

Although you can use the `onCreateDialog` and `onPrepareDialog` handlers, they have been deprecated in favor of Dialog Fragments, as described in the previous section.

Using Activities as Dialogs

Dialogs and Dialog Fragments offer a simple and lightweight technique for displaying screens, but you can also style an Activity so that it appears as a Dialog.

Note that in must circumstances you can gain the same level of control over the appearance and life-cycle of your Dialog by using a Dialog Fragment.

The easiest way to make an Activity look like a Dialog is to apply the `android:style/Theme.Dialog` theme when you add the Activity to your manifest, as shown in the following XML snippet:

```
<activity android:name="MyDialogActivity"
          android:theme="@android:style/Theme.Dialog">
</activity>
```

This will cause your Activity to behave as a Dialog, floating on top of, and partially obscuring, the Activity beneath it.

LET'S MAKE A TOAST

Toasts are transient notifications that remain visible for only a few seconds before fading out. Toasts don't steal focus and are nonmodal, so they don't interrupt the active application.

Toasts are perfect for informing your users of events without forcing them to open an Activity or read a Notification. They provide an ideal mechanism for alerting users to events occurring in background Services without interrupting foreground applications.

Generally, your application should display Toasts only when one of its Activities is active.

The `Toast` class includes a static `makeText` method that creates a standard Toast display window. To construct a new Toast, pass the current Context, the text message to display, and the length of time to display it (LENGTH_SHORT or LENGTH_LONG) into the makeText method. After creating a Toast, you can display it by calling show, as shown in Listing 10-29.

LISTING 10-29: Displaying a Toast

```
Context context = this;
String msg = "To health and happiness!";
int duration = Toast.LENGTH_SHORT;

Toast toast = Toast.makeText(context, msg, duration);
toast.show();
```

code snippet PA4AD_Ch10_Dialogs/src/MyActivity.java

Figure 10-19 shows a Toast. It will remain on-screen for approximately 2 seconds before fading out. The application behind it remains fully responsive and interactive while the Toast is visible.

FIGURE 10-19

Customizing Toasts

The standard Toast message window is often sufficient, but in many situations you'll want to customize its appearance and screen position. You can modify a Toast by setting its display position and assigning it alternative Views or layouts.

Listing 10-30 shows how to align a Toast to the bottom of the screen using the `setGravity` method.

LISTING 10-30: Aligning Toast text

```
Context context = this;
String msg = "To the bride and groom!";
int duration = Toast.LENGTH_SHORT;
Toast toast = Toast.makeText(context, msg, duration);
int offsetX = 0;
int offsetY = 0;

toast.setGravity(Gravity.BOTTOM, offsetX, offsetY);
toast.show();
```

code snippet PA4AD_Ch10_Dialogs/src/MyActivity.java

When a text message just isn't going to get the job done, you can specify a custom View or layout to use a more complex, or more visual, display. Using `setView` on a Toast object, you can specify any View (including a layout) to display using the Toast mechanism. For example, Listing 10-31 assigns a layout, containing the `CompassView` Widget from Chapter 4 along with a `TextView`, to be displayed as a Toast.

LISTING 10-31: Using Views to customize a Toast

```
Context context = getApplicationContext();
String msg = "Cheers!";
int duration = Toast.LENGTH_LONG;
Toast toast = Toast.makeText(context, msg, duration);
toast.setGravity(Gravity.TOP, 0, 0);

LinearLayout ll = new LinearLayout(context);
ll.setOrientation(LinearLayout.VERTICAL);

TextView myTextView = new TextView(context);
CompassView cv = new CompassView(context);

myTextView.setText(msg);

int lHeight = LinearLayout.LayoutParams.FILL_PARENT;
int lWidth = LinearLayout.LayoutParams.WRAP_CONTENT;

ll.addView(cv, new LinearLayout.LayoutParams(lHeight, lWidth));
ll.addView(myTextView, new LinearLayout.LayoutParams(lHeight, lWidth));

ll.setPadding(40, 50, 0, 50);

toast.setView(ll);
toast.show();
```

code snippet PA4AD_Ch10_Dialogs/src/MyActivity.java

The resulting Toast will appear, as shown in Figure 10-20.

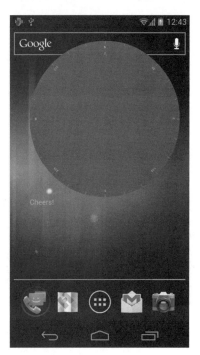

FIGURE 10-20

Using Toasts in Worker Threads

As GUI components, Toasts must be created and shown on the GUI thread; otherwise, you risk throwing a cross-thread exception. In Listing 10-32 a Handler is used to ensure that the Toast is opened on the GUI thread.

LISTING 10-32: Opening a Toast on the GUI thread

```
Handler handler = new Handler();

private void mainProcessing() {
  Thread thread = new Thread(null, doBackgroundThreadProcessing,
                             "Background");
  thread.start();
}

private Runnable doBackgroundThreadProcessing = new Runnable() {
  public void run() {
    backgroundThreadProcessing();
  }
};
```

```
private void backgroundThreadProcessing() {
  handler.post(doUpdateGUI);
}

// Runnable that executes the update GUI method.
private Runnable doUpdateGUI = new Runnable() {
  public void run() {
    Context context = getApplicationContext();
    String msg = "To open mobile development!";
    int duration = Toast.LENGTH_SHORT;
    Toast.makeText(context, msg, duration).show();
  }
};
```

code snippet PA4AD_Ch10_Dialogs/src/MyActivity.java

INTRODUCING NOTIFICATIONS

Your application can use Notifications to alert users of events that may require their attention without one of its Activity's being visible.

Notifications are handled by the Notification Manager and currently have the ability to

➤ Display a status bar icon

➤ Flash the lights/LEDs

➤ Vibrate the phone

➤ Sound audible alerts (ringtones, Media Store audio)

➤ Display additional information within the notification tray

➤ Broadcast Intents using interactive controls from within the notification tray

Notifications are the preferred mechanism for invisible application components (Broadcast Receivers, Services, and inactive Activities) to alert users that events have occurred that may require attention. They are also used to indicate ongoing background Services — and are required to indicate a Service that has foreground priority.

Notifications are particularly well suited to mobile devices. It's likely that your users will have their phones with them at all times but quite unlikely that they will be paying attention to them, or your application, at any given time. Generally, users will have several applications open in the background, and they won't be paying attention to any of them.

In this environment it's important that your applications be able to alert users when specific events occur that require their attention.

Notifications can be persisted through insistent repetition, being marked ongoing, or simply by displaying an icon on the status bar. Status bar icons can be updated regularly or expanded to show additional information using the expanded notification tray, as shown in Figure 10-21.

FIGURE 10-21

> To display the expanded notification tray on smartphones, press anywhere on the status bar and drag it toward the bottom of the screen. On tablet devices, click the time on the lower-right corner of the system bar.

Introducing the Notification Manager

The NotificationManager is a system Service used to manage Notifications. Get a reference to it using the getSystemService method, as shown in Listing 10-33.

LISTING 10-33: Using the Notification Manager

```
String svcName = Context.NOTIFICATION_SERVICE;

NotificationManager notificationManager;
notificationManager = (NotificationManager)getSystemService(svcName);
```

code snippet PA4AD_Ch10_Notifications/src/MyActivity.java

Using the Notification Manager, you can trigger new Notifications, modify existing ones, or cancel those that are no longer required.

Creating Notifications

Android offers a number of ways to convey information to users using Notifications:

➤ Status bar icon

➤ Sounds, lights, and vibrations

➤ Details displayed within the extended notification tray

This section examines the first two options. In the section "Setting and Customizing the Notification Tray UI," you'll learn how to configure the UI displayed for your Notifications within the notification tray.

Creating a Notification and Configuring the Status Bar Display

Start by creating a new Notification object, passing in an icon to display on the status bar along with the ticker text to display on the status bar when the Notification is triggered, as shown in Listing 10-34.

Available for download on Wrox.com

LISTING 10-34: Creating a Notification

```
// Choose a drawable to display as the status bar icon
int icon = R.drawable.icon;
// Text to display in the status bar when the notification is launched
String tickerText = "Notification";
// The extended status bar orders notification in time order
long when = System.currentTimeMillis();

Notification notification = new Notification(icon, tickerText, when);
```

code snippet PA4AD_Ch10_Notifications/src/MyActivity.java

The ticker text should be a short summary that describes what you are notifying the user of (for example, an SMS message or email subject line).

You also need to specify the timestamp of the Notification; the Notification Manager will sort Notifications in this order.

You can also set the Notification object's `number` property to display the number of events a status bar icon represents. Setting this value to a number greater than 1, as shown in the following line of code, overlays the values as a small number over the status bar icon:

```
notification.number++;
```

Before you can trigger the Notification, you must update its contextual information, as described in the section, "Setting and Customizing the Notification Tray UI." Once that's done you can trigger the Notification as described in the section, "Triggering, Updating, and Canceling Notifications." This process will be explored in more detail later in this chapter.

In the following sections you'll learn to enhance Notifications to provide additional alerts through hardware, particularly by making the device ring, flash, and vibrate. Android 3.0 (API level 11) introduced the `Notification.Builder` class to simplify the process of adding these additional features and will be covered in detail within the "Using the Notification Builder" section.

> To use the Notification techniques described in the following sections without also displaying the status bar icon, simply cancel the Notification directly after triggering it. This stops the icon from displaying but doesn't interrupt the other effects.

Using the Default Notification Sounds, Lights, and Vibrations

The simplest and most consistent way to add sounds, lights, and vibrations to your Notifications is to use the default settings. Using the `defaults` property, you can combine the following constants:

➤ `Notification.DEFAULT_LIGHTS`

➤ `Notification.DEFAULT_SOUND`

➤ `Notification.DEFAULT_VIBRATE`

For example, the following code snippet assigns the default sound and vibration settings to a Notification:

```
notification.defaults = Notification.DEFAULT_SOUND |
                        Notification.DEFAULT_VIBRATE;
```

If you want to use all the default values, you can use the `Notification.DEFAULT_ALL` constant.

Making Sounds

Most native phone events, from incoming calls to new messages and low battery, are announced by audible ringtones.

Android lets you assign any available audio file to signal a Notification. Assign a new sound to a Notification using its `sound` property, specifying a URI to the audio file, as shown in the following snippet:

```
Uri ringURI =
    RingtoneManager.getDefaultUri(RingtoneManager.TYPE_NOTIFICATION);

notification.sound = ringURI;
```

To use your own custom audio, push the file onto your device or include it as a raw resource, as described in Chapter 15, "Audio, Video, and Using the Camera."

Vibrating the Device

You can use the device's vibrator to execute a vibration pattern specific to your Notification. Android lets you control the pattern of a vibration; you can use vibration to alert the user to new information being available, or use a specific pattern to convey the information directly.

Before you can use vibration in your application, you need to request the VIBRATE uses-permission in your manifest:

```
<uses-permission android:name="android.permission.VIBRATE"/>
```

To set a vibration pattern, assign a long[] to the Notification's vibrate property. Construct the array so that values representing the length of time (in milliseconds) to vibrate alternate with values representing the length of time to pause.

The following example shows how to modify a Notification to vibrate in a repeating pattern of 1 second on and 1 second off, for 5 seconds total:

```
long[] vibrate = new long[] { 1000, 1000, 1000, 1000, 1000 };
notification.vibrate = vibrate;
```

You can take advantage of this fine-grained control to pass contextual information to your users.

Flashing the Lights

Notifications also include properties to configure the color and flash frequency of the device's LED.

> *Each device may have different limitations with regard to control over the LED. If the color you specify is not available, as close an approximation as possible will be used. When using LEDs to convey information to the user, keep this limitation in mind and avoid making it the only way such information is made available.*

The ledARGB property can be used to set the LED's color, whereas the ledOffMS and ledOnMS properties let you set the frequency and pattern of the flashing LED. You can turn on the LED by setting the ledOnMS property to 1 and the ledOffMS property to 0, or turn it off by setting both properties to 0.

After configuring the LED settings, you must also add the FLAG_SHOW_LIGHTS flag to the Notification's flags property. The following code snippet shows how to turn on the red device LED:

```
notification.ledARGB = Color.RED;
notification.ledOffMS = 0;
notification.ledOnMS = 1;
notification.flags = notification.flags | Notification.FLAG_SHOW_LIGHTS;
```

Controlling the color and flash frequency gives you another opportunity to pass additional information to users.

Using the Notification Builder

The Notification Builder, introduced in Android 3.0 (API level 11) to simplify the process of config-uring the flags, options, content, and layout of Notifications, is the preferred alternative when con-structing Notifications for newer Android platforms.

Listing 10-35 shows how to use the Notification Builder to construct a Notification using each of the options selected in the preceding sections.

LISTING 10-35: Setting Notification options using the Notification Builder

Available for
download on
Wrox.com

```java
Notification.Builder builder =
  new Notification.Builder(MyActivity.this);

builder.setSmallIcon(R.drawable.ic_launcher)
       .setTicker("Notification")
       .setWhen(System.currentTimeMillis())
       .setDefaults(Notification.DEFAULT_SOUND |
                    Notification.DEFAULT_VIBRATE)
       .setSound(
          RingtoneManager.getDefaultUri(
            RingtoneManager.TYPE_NOTIFICATION))
       .setVibrate(new long[] { 1000, 1000, 1000, 1000, 1000 })
       .setLights(Color.RED, 0, 1);

Notification notification = builder.getNotification();
```

code snippet PA4AD_Ch10_Notifications/src/MyActivity.java

Setting and Customizing the Notification Tray UI

You can configure the appearance of the Notification within the extended notification tray in a number of ways:

➤ Use the `setLatestEventInfo` method to update the details displayed in the standard notifi-cation tray display.

➤ Use the Notification Builder to create and control one of several alternative notification tray UIs.

➤ Set the `contentView` and `contentIntent` properties to assign a custom UI for the extended status display using a Remote Views object.

➤ From Android 3.0 (API level 11) onward, you can assign Broadcast Intents to each View within the Remote Views object that describes your custom UI to make them fully interactive.

It's good form to use one Notification icon to represent multiple instances of the same event (e.g., receiving multiple SMS messages). To do this, create a new Notification that will update the values displayed in the notification tray UI to reflect the most recent message (or a summary of multiple messages) and retrigger the Notification to update the displayed values.

Using the Standard Notification UI

The simplest approach is to use the `setLatestE-`
`ventInfo` method to specify the title and text
fields used to populate the default notification tray
layout (see Figure 10-22).

FIGURE 10-22

```
notification.setLatestEventInfo(context,
                                expandedTitle,
                                expandedText,
                                launchIntent);
```

The `PendingIntent` you specify will be fired if a user clicks the Notification item. In most cases that
Intent should open your application and navigate to the Activity that provides context for the notification (e.g., showing an unread SMS or email message).

Android 3.0 (API level 11) expanded the size used for each Notification, introducing support for a
larger icon to be displayed within the notification tray. You can assign the large icon by assigning it
to the `largeIcon` property of your Notification.

Alternatively, you can use the Notification Builder
to populate these details, as shown in Listing
10-36. Note that using the Builder provides the
ability to set the info text that will be displayed
at the lower right of the Notification, as shown in
Figure 10-23.

FIGURE 10-23

LISTING 10-36: Applying a custom layout to the Notification status window

```
builder.setSmallIcon(R.drawable.ic_launcher)
       .setTicker("Notification")
       .setWhen(System.currentTimeMillis())
       .setContentTitle("Title")
       .setContentText("Subtitle")
       .setContentInfo("Info")
       .setLargeIcon(myIconBitmap)
       .setContentIntent(pendingIntent);
```

code snippet PA4AD_Ch10_Notifications/src/MyActivity.java

The Notification Builder also provides support for displaying a progress bar within your
Notification. Using the `setProgress` method,
you can specify the current progress in relation to a maximum value, as shown in Figure
10-24, or indicate that the progress should be
indeterminate:

FIGURE 10-24

```
builder.setSmallIcon(R.drawable.ic_launcher)
       .setTicker("Notification")
```

```
.setWhen(System.currentTimeMillis())
.setContentTitle("Progress")
.setProgress(100, 50, false)
.setContentIntent(pendingIntent);
```

Creating a Custom Notification UI

If the details available in the standard Notification display are insufficient (or unsuitable) for your needs, you can create your own layout and assign it to your Notification using a Remote Views object, as shown in Figure 10-25.

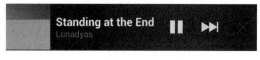

FIGURE 10-25

Listing 10-37 defines a custom layout that includes an icon, Text View, and progress bar.

LISTING 10-37: Creating a custom layout for the Notification status window

```xml
<?xml version="1.0" encoding="utf-8"?>
<RelativeLayout
    xmlns:android="http://schemas.android.com/apk/res/android"
    android:padding="5dp"
    android:layout_width="fill_parent"
    android:layout_height="fill_parent">
    <ImageView
        android:id="@+id/status_icon"
        android:layout_width="wrap_content"
        android:layout_height="fill_parent"
        android:layout_alignParentLeft="true"
    />
    <RelativeLayout
        android:layout_width="fill_parent"
        android:layout_height="fill_parent"
        android:paddingLeft="10dp"
        android:layout_toRightOf="@id/status_icon">
        <TextView
            android:id="@+id/status_text"
            android:layout_width="fill_parent"
            android:layout_height="wrap_content"
            android:layout_alignParentTop="true"
            android:textColor="#000"
            android:textSize="14sp"
            android:textStyle="bold"
        />
        <ProgressBar
            android:id="@+id/status_progress"
            android:layout_width="fill_parent"
            android:layout_height="wrap_content"
            android:layout_below="@id/status_text"
            android:progressDrawable="@android:drawable/progress_horizontal"
            android:indeterminate="false"
            android:indeterminateOnly="false"
        />
```

```
      </RelativeLayout>
    </RelativeLayout>
```

code snippet PA4AD_Ch10_Notifications/res/layout/my_status_window.xml

To use this layout within a Notification, you must package it within a Remote Views object:

```
RemoteViews myView =
  new RemoteViews(this.getPackageName(),
                 R.layout.my_status_window_layout);
```

Remote Views are a mechanism that enables you to embed and control a layout embedded within a separate application, most commonly when creating home screen Widgets. There are strict limits on the Views you can use when creating a layout to be used for Remote Views. These are covered in some detail in Chapter 14.

If you are using the Notification Builder, you can assign your custom View using the setContent method, as shown in Listing 10-38.

LISTING 10-38: Applying a custom layout to the Notification status window

```
RemoteViews myRemoteView =
  new RemoteViews(this.getPackageName(),
                 R.layout.my_notification_layout);

builder.setSmallIcon(R.drawable.notification_icon)
       .setTicker("Notification")
       .setWhen(System.currentTimeMillis())
       .setContentTitle("Progress")
       .setProgress(100, 50, false)
       .setContent(myRemoteView);
```

code snippet PA4AD_Ch10_Notifications/src/MyActivity.java

When targeting platform releases earlier than Android 3.0 (API level 11), you can assign your custom View to the Notification's contentView property. You will also need to assign a Pending Intent to the contentIntent property:

```
Intent intent = new Intent(this, MyActivity.class);
PendingIntent pendingIntent
  = PendingIntent.getActivity(this, 0, intent, 0);

notification.contentView = new RemoteViews(this.getPackageName(),
  R.layout.my_status_window_layout);

notification.contentIntent = pendingIntent;
```

> *When you manually set the* contentView *property, you must also set the* contentIntent *property; otherwise, an exception will be thrown when the notification is triggered.*

You can modify the properties and appearance of the Views used in your Notification layout using the set* methods on the Remote Views object, as shown in Listing 10-39, which modifies each View used in the layout defined in Listing 10-38.

LISTING 10-39: Customizing your extended Notification window layout

Available for
download on
Wrox.com

```
notification.contentView.setImageViewResource(R.id.status_icon,
                                      R.drawable.icon);
notification.contentView.setTextViewText(R.id.status_text,
                                 "Current Progress:");
notification.contentView.setProgressBar(R.id.status_progress,
                               100, 50, false);
```

code snippet PA4AD_Ch10_Notifications/src/MyActivity.java

Note that to modify these views, you will need to broadcast a new Notification with the updated Remote Views object.

Android 4.0 (API level 14) introduced the ability to attach click listeners to the Views contained within your custom Notification layout. To assign a click listener to a View within your Remote Views layout, use the setOnClickPendingIntent method, passing in the resource id of the View to bind to, and a Pending Intent to broadcast when the View is clicked, as shown in Listing 10-40.

LISTING 10-40: Adding click handlers to your customized extended Notification window layout

```
Intent newIntent = new Intent(BUTTON_CLICK);
PendingIntent newPendingIntent =
  PendingIntent.getBroadcast(MyActivity.this, 2, newIntent, 0);

notification.contentView.setOnClickPendingIntent(
  R.id.status_progress, newPendingIntent);
```

code snippet PA4AD_Ch10_Notifications/src/MyActivity.java

Clicking anywhere on the Notification layout that isn't bound in this way will trigger the Notification's content Intent.

Using this mechanism, you can make your notifications fully interactive — effectively allowing you to embed a home screen Widget within the Notification tray.

This technique is particularly useful when used with ongoing events such as notifications associated with media players, allowing users to control the playback with the pause and skip buttons.

Customizing the Ticker View

On some devices, particularly tablet devices, you can specify a Remote Views object that will be displayed within the system bar instead of the Notification ticker text.

Use the `setTicker` method on the Notification Builder to specify a Remote Views object to display, as shown in Listing 10-41. Note that you must still specify the ticker text to display on devices that don't support the custom ticker view.

LISTING 10-41: Applying a custom layout to the Notification ticker

```
RemoteViews myTickerView =
  new RemoteViews(this.getPackageName(),
                    R.layout.my_ticker_layout);

builder.setSmallIcon(R.drawable.notification_icon)
       .setTicker("Notification", myTickerView)
       .setWhen(System.currentTimeMillis())
       .setContent(myRemoteView);
```

code snippet PA4AD_Ch10_Notifications/src/MyActivity.java

Configuring Ongoing and Insistent Notifications

You can configure Notifications as insistent and/or ongoing by setting the `FLAG_INSISTENT` and `FLAG_ONGOING_EVENT` flags, respectively.

Notifications flagged as ongoing are used to represent events that are currently in progress (such as a download in progress or music playing in the background).

Using the Notification Builder, you can mark a Notification as ongoing using the `setOngoing` method, as shown in Listing 10-42.

LISTING 10-42: Setting an ongoing Notification

```
builder.setSmallIcon(R.drawable.notification_icon)
       .setTicker("Notification")
       .setWhen(System.currentTimeMillis())
       .setContentTitle("Progress")
       .setProgress(100, 50, false)
       .setContent(myRemoteView)
       .setOngoing(true);
```

code snippet PA4AD_Ch10_Notifications/src/MyActivity.java

If you aren't using the Notification Builder, you can apply the `Notification.FLAG_ONGOING_EVENT` flag directly to the Notification's `flags` property:

```
notification.flags = notification.flags |
                     Notification.FLAG_ONGOING_EVENT;
```

An ongoing Notification is a requirement for a foreground Service, as described in Chapter 9.

Insistent Notifications repeat their audio, vibration, and light settings continuously until canceled. These Notifications should be used only for events that require immediate and timely attention — such as an incoming call or the ringing of a user-set alarm clock.

To make a Notification insistent, apply the `Notification.FLAG_INSISTENT` flag directly to the Notification's `flags` property:

```
notification.flags = notification.flags |
                     Notification.FLAG_INSISTENT;
```

Note that insistent Notifications are particularly intrusive and should seldom be used within third-party applications. This is reflected in the lack of a corresponding Notification Builder method for setting this flag.

Triggering, Updating, and Canceling Notifications

To fire a Notification, pass it in to the `notify` method of the `NotificationManager` along with an integer reference ID, as shown in Listing 10-43. If you've used a Notification Builder to construct the Notification, use its `getNotification` method to obtain the Notification to broadcast.

LISTING 10-43: Triggering a Notification

```
String svc = Context.NOTIFICATION_SERVICE;

NotificationManager notificationManager
  = (NotificationManager)getSystemService(svc);

int NOTIFICATION_REF = 1;
Notification notification = builder.getNotification();

notificationManager.notify(NOTIFICATION_REF, notification);
```

code snippet PA4AD_Ch10_Notifications/src/MyActivity.java

To update a Notification that's already been fired, including updating the UI of any attached content View, retrigger it using the Notification Manager, passing the `notify` method the same reference ID.

You can pass in either the same Notification object or an entirely new one. As long as the ID values are the same, the new Notification will be used to replace the status icon and extended status window details.

To update a Notification without triggering any of the associated lights, audio, or vibration settings, use the Notification Builder's `setOnlyAlertOnce` method, as shown in Listing 10-44.

LISTING 10-44: Updating a Notification without replaying the alerts

```
builder.setSmallIcon(R.drawable.notification_icon)
       .setTicker("Updated Notification")
       .setWhen(System.currentTimeMillis())
       .setContentTitle("More Progress")
       .setProgress(100, 75, false)
```

```
        .setContent(myRemoteView)
        .setOngoing(true)
        .setOnlyAlertOnce(true);

Notification notification = builder.getNotification();

notificationManager.notify(NOTIFICATION_REF, notification);
```

code snippet PA4AD_Ch10_Notifications/src/MyActivity.java

Alternatively, you can apply the FLAG_ONLY_ALERT_ONCE flag directly to the Notification:

```
notification.flags = notification.flags |
                Notification.FLAG_ONLY_ALERT_ONCE;
```

Canceling a Notification removes its icon from the status bar and its extended details from the Notification tray. It's good practice to cancel a Notification after the user has acted upon it — typically either by clicking it or by manually navigating to the application that launched it.

You can configure a Notification to automatically cancel itself when it's clicked by using the Notification Builder's setAutoCancel flag, as shown in Listing 10-45.

LISTING 10-45: Setting an auto-cancel Notification

```
builder.setSmallIcon(R.drawable.ic_launcher)
        .setTicker("Notification")
        .setWhen(System.currentTimeMillis())
        .setContentTitle("Title")
        .setContentText("Subtitle")
        .setContentInfo("Info")
        .setLargeIcon(myIconBitmap)
        .setContentIntent(pendingIntent)
        .setAutoCancel(true);
```

code snippet PA4AD_Ch10_Notifications/src/MyActivity.java

Alternatively, apply the FLAG_AUTO_CANCEL flag when not using the Notification Builder:

```
notification.flags = notification.flags |
                Notification.FLAG_AUTO_CANCEL;
```

To cancel the Notification, use the Notification Manager's cancel method, passing in the reference id of the Notification you want to cancel, as shown in Listing 10-46.

LISTING 10-46: Canceling a Notification

```
notificationManager.cancel(NOTIFICATION_REF);
```

code snippet PA4AD_Ch10_Notifications/src/MyActivity.java

Canceling a Notification removes its status bar icon and clears it from the extended status window.

ADDING NOTIFICATIONS AND DIALOGS TO THE EARTHQUAKE MONITOR

The following example enhances the `EarthquakeUpdateService` to trigger a Notification for each new earthquake. In addition to displaying a status bar icon, the Notification tray view will display the magnitude and location of the latest quake, and selecting the notification will open the Earthquake Activity.

You'll also update the `EarthquakeListFragment` to display a summary dialog when an Earthquake is selected.

1. Start within the `EarthquakeUpdateService`. Create a new Notification Builder variable to help construct the Notifications that will be used to create each Notification:

```
private Notification.Builder earthquakeNotificationBuilder;
public static final int NOTIFICATION_ID = 1;
```

2. Extend the `onCreate` method to create the Notification Builder object with the standard Notification items to be used. Note that you will need to create a Notification icon and store it in your `res/drawable` folder.

```
@Override
public void onCreate() {
  super.onCreate();

  alarmManager = (AlarmManager)getSystemService(Context.ALARM_SERVICE);

  String ALARM_ACTION;
  ALARM_ACTION =
    EarthquakeAlarmReceiver.ACTION_REFRESH_EARTHQUAKE_ALARM;
  Intent intentToFire = new Intent(ALARM_ACTION);
  alarmIntent =
    PendingIntent.getBroadcast(this, 0, intentToFire, 0);

  earthquakeNotificationBuilder = new Notification.Builder(this);
  earthquakeNotificationBuilder
    .setAutoCancel(true)
    .setTicker("Earthquake detected")
    .setSmallIcon(R.drawable.notification_icon);
}
```

3. Create a new `broadcastNotification` method that will update the Notification Builder instance using a Quake object. Use it to create and broadcast a Notification.

```
private void broadcastNotification(Quake quake) {
  Intent startActivityIntent = new Intent(this, Earthquake.class);
  PendingIntent launchIntent =
    PendingIntent.getActivity(this, 0, startActivityIntent, 0);

  earthquakeNotificationBuilder
    .setContentIntent(launchIntent)
    .setWhen(quake.getDate().getTime())
    .setContentTitle("M:" + quake.getMagnitude())
```

```
      .setContentText(quake.getDetails());

    NotificationManager notificationManager
      = (NotificationManager)getSystemService(Context.NOTIFICATION_SERVICE);

    notificationManager.notify(NOTIFICATION_ID,
      earthquakeNotificationBuilder.getNotification());
  }
```

4. Update the `addNewQuake` method to broadcast the Notification. Insert a call the `broadcast-Notification` method immediately before the call to insert the new quake into the Content Provider:

```
private void addNewQuake(Quake quake) {
  ContentResolver cr = getContentResolver();

  // Construct a where clause to make sure we don't already have this
  // earthquake in the provider.
  String w = EarthquakeProvider.KEY_DATE + " = " + quake.getDate().getTime();

  // If the earthquake is new, insert it into the provider.
  Cursor query = cr.query(EarthquakeProvider.CONTENT_URI, null, w, null, null);

  if (query.getCount()==0) {
    ContentValues values = new ContentValues();

    values.put(EarthquakeProvider.KEY_DATE, quake.getDate().getTime());
    values.put(EarthquakeProvider.KEY_DETAILS, quake.getDetails());
    values.put(EarthquakeProvider.KEY_SUMMARY, quake.toString());

    double lat = quake.getLocation().getLatitude();
    double lng = quake.getLocation().getLongitude();
    values.put(EarthquakeProvider.KEY_LOCATION_LAT, lat);
    values.put(EarthquakeProvider.KEY_LOCATION_LNG, lng);
    values.put(EarthquakeProvider.KEY_LINK, quake.getLink());
    values.put(EarthquakeProvider.KEY_MAGNITUDE, quake.getMagnitude());

    // Trigger a notification.
    broadcastNotification(quake);

    // Add the new quake to the Earthquake provider.
    cr.insert(EarthquakeProvider.CONTENT_URI, values);
  }
  query.close();
}
```

5. To make the Notification more interesting, modify the `broadcastNotification` method to customize the extended Notification settings such as lights and vibration based on the size of the earthquake.

> **5.1** Add an audio component to the Notification, ringing the default notification ringtone if a significant earthquake (one with a magnitude greater than 6) occurs:

```
if (quake.getMagnitude() > 6) {
```

```
Uri ringURI =
  RingtoneManager.getDefaultUri(RingtoneManager.TYPE_NOTIFICATION);

earthquakeNotificationBuilder.setSound(ringURI);
}
```

5.2 Set the device to vibrate in a pattern based on the power of the quake. Earthquakes are measured on an exponential scale, so you'll use the same scale when creating the vibration pattern.

For a barely perceptible magnitude 1 quake, the phone will vibrate for a fraction of a second; for one of magnitude 10, an earthquake that would split the earth in two, your users will have a head start on the Apocalypse when their devices vibrate for a full 20 seconds.

Most significant quakes fall between 3 and 7 on the Richter scale, or a more reasonable 200-millisecond-to-4-second range of vibration duration.

```
double vibrateLength = 100*Math.exp(0.53*quake.getMagnitude());
long[] vibrate = new long[] {100, 100, (long)vibrateLength };
earthquakeNotificationBuilder.setVibrate(vibrate);
```

5.3 Help your users perceive the nuances of an exponential scale by also using the device's LED to help convey the magnitude. Here you color the LED based on the size of the quake, and the frequency of the flashing is inversely related to the power of the quake:

```
int color;
if (quake.getMagnitude() < 5.4)
  color = Color.GREEN;
else if (quake.getMagnitude() < 6)
  color = Color.YELLOW;
else
  color = Color.RED;

earthquakeNotificationBuilder.setLights(
  color,
  (int)vibrateLength,
  (int)vibrateLength);
```

6. Add the vibrate uses-permission to your manifest:

```
<uses-permission android:name="android.permission.VIBRATE"/>
```

7. Let users find more details by opening a Dialog when they select an earthquake from the list. Create a new `quake_details.xml` layout resource for the Dialog you'll display when an item is clicked:

```
<?xml version="1.0" encoding="utf-8"?>
<LinearLayout xmlns:android="http://schemas.android.com/apk/res/android"
  android:orientation="vertical"
  android:layout_width="match_parent"
  android:layout_height="match_parent"
  android:padding="10dp">
```

```
    <TextView
      android:id="@+id/quakeDetailsTextView"
      android:layout_width="match_parent"
      android:layout_height="match_parent"
      android:textSize="14sp"
    />
</LinearLayout>
```

8. Create a new `EarthquakeDialog` class that extends `DialogFragment`. It should accept a Quake object and use that to populate the dialog.

```java
package com.paad.earthquake;

import java.text.SimpleDateFormat;
import android.app.Dialog;
import android.app.DialogFragment;
import android.content.Context;
import android.os.Bundle;
import android.view.LayoutInflater;
import android.view.View;
import android.view.ViewGroup;
import android.widget.TextView;

public class EarthquakeDialog extends DialogFragment {

  private static String DIALOG_STRING = "DIALOG_STRING";

  public static EarthquakeDialog newInstance(Context context, Quake quake) {
    // Create a new Fragment instance with the specified
    // parameters.
    EarthquakeDialog fragment = new EarthquakeDialog();
    Bundle args = new Bundle();

    SimpleDateFormat sdf = new SimpleDateFormat("dd/MM/yyyy HH:mm:ss");
    String dateString = sdf.format(quake.getDate());
    String quakeText = dateString + "\n" + "Magnitude " + quake.getMagnitude() +
                       "\n" + quake.getDetails() + "\n" +
                       quake.getLink();


    args.putString(DIALOG_STRING, quakeText);
    fragment.setArguments(args);

    return fragment;
  }

  @Override
  public View onCreateView(LayoutInflater inflater, ViewGroup container,
      Bundle savedInstanceState) {

    View view = inflater.inflate(R.layout.quake_details, container, false);

    String title = getArguments().getString(DIALOG_STRING);
    TextView tv = (TextView)view.findViewById(R.id.quakeDetailsTextView);
```

```
    tv.setText(title);

    return view;
  }

  @Override
  public Dialog onCreateDialog(Bundle savedInstanceState) {
    Dialog dialog = super.onCreateDialog(savedInstanceState);
    dialog.setTitle("Earthquake Details");
    return dialog;
  }
}
```

9. Finally, open the `EarthquakeListFragment` and override the `onListItemClick` handler to create a new Quake object, and use it to create and show the Earthquake Dialog.

```
@Override
public void onListItemClick(ListView l, View v, int position, long id) {
  super.onListItemClick(l, v, position, id);

  ContentResolver cr = getActivity().getContentResolver();

  Cursor result =
    cr.query(ContentUris.withAppendedId(EarthquakeProvider.CONTENT_URI, id),
             null, null, null, null);

  if (result.moveToFirst()) {
    Date date =
      new Date(result.getLong(
        result.getColumnIndex(EarthquakeProvider.KEY_DATE)));

    String details =
      result.getString(
        result.getColumnIndex(EarthquakeProvider.KEY_DETAILS));

    double magnitude =
      result.getDouble(
        result.getColumnIndex(EarthquakeProvider.KEY_MAGNITUDE));

    String linkString =
      result.getString(
        result.getColumnIndex(EarthquakeProvider.KEY_LINK));

    double lat =
      result.getDouble(
        result.getColumnIndex(EarthquakeProvider.KEY_LOCATION_LAT));

    double lng =
      result.getDouble(
        result.getColumnIndex(EarthquakeProvider.KEY_LOCATION_LNG));

    Location location = new Location("db");
    location.setLatitude(lat);
    location.setLongitude(lng);
```

```
Quake quake = new Quake(date, details, location, magnitude, linkString);

DialogFragment newFragment = EarthquakeDialog.newInstance(getActivity(), quake);
newFragment.show(getFragmentManager(), "dialog");
    }
}
```

All code snippets in this example are part of the Chapter 10 Earthquake 3 *project, available for download at* www.wrox.com.

With these changes complete, any new earthquake will trigger a Notification, accompanied by flashing lights, vibration, and a ringtone. Selecting any of the earthquakes from the list will display their details in a Dialog.

11

Advanced User Experience

WHAT'S IN THIS CHAPTER?

➤ Resolution independence and designing for every screen

➤ Creating image assets in XML

➤ Making applications accessible

➤ Using the Text-to-Speech and speech recognition libraries

➤ Using animations

➤ Controlling hardware acceleration

➤ Using Surface Views

➤ Copy, paste, and the clipboard

In Chapter 4, "Building User Interfaces," you learned the basics of creating user interfaces (UIs) in Android with an introduction to Activities, Fragments, layouts, and Views. In Chapter 10, "Expanding the User Experience," you expanded the user experience through using the Action Bar, menu system, Dialogs, and Notifications.

It's important to think beyond the bounds of necessity and create applications that combine purpose with beauty and simplicity, even when they provide complex functionality.

> *As you design apps to work with Android, consider these goals: Enchant me. Simplify my life. Make me amazing.*
>
> — ANDROID DESIGN CREATIVE VISION, HTTP://DEVELOPER.ANDROID.COM/DESIGN/
> GET-STARTED/CREATIVE-VISION.HTML

This chapter introduces you to some best practices and techniques to create user experiences that are compelling and aesthetically pleasing on a diverse range of devices and for an equally diverse range of users.

You start with an introduction to the best practices for creating resolution- and density-independent UIs, and how to use Drawables to create scalable image assets, before learning how to ensure your applications are accessible and use the text-to-speech and speech recognition APIS.

You also discover how to use animations to make your UIs more dynamic, and how to enhance the custom Views you created in Chapter 4 using advanced canvas-drawing techniques.

When designing and implementing your application's UX design, be sure to refer to the guidelines on the Android Design site at `http://developer.android.com/design`.

DESIGNING FOR EVERY SCREEN SIZE AND DENSITY

The first four Android handsets all featured 3.2" HVGA screens. By the start of 2010, the number of devices running Android exploded, with the increased diversity of handsets heralding variations in screen sizes and pixel densities. In 2011, tablets and Google TV introduced further variation with significantly larger screens and even greater variation in resolution and pixel density.

To provide a great user experience on all Android devices, it's important to create your UIs knowing that your applications can run on a broad variety of screen resolutions and physical screen sizes. In practice, this means that just as with websites and desktop applications, you must design and build your applications with the expectation that they can run an infinitely varied set of devices. That means supplying scalable image assets for a variety of pixel densities, creating layouts that scale to fit the available display, and designing layouts optimized for different device categories based on the screen size and interaction model.

The following sections begin by describing the range of screens you need to consider, and how to support them, before summarizing some of the best practices to ensure your applications are resolution- and density-independent, and optimized for different screen sizes and layouts.

> *The Android Developer site includes some excellent tips for supporting multiple screen types. You can find this documentation at* `http://developer.android` `.com/guide/practices/screens_support.html`.

Resolution Independence

A display's pixel density is calculated as a function of the physical screen size and resolution, referring to the number of physical pixels on a display relative to the physical size of that display. It's typically measured in dots per inch (dpi).

Using Density-Independent Pixels

As a result of the variations in screen size and resolution for Android devices, the same number of pixels can correspond to different physical sizes on different devices based on the screen's DPI. This makes it impossible to create consistent layouts by specifying pixels. Instead, Android uses density-independent pixels (dp) to specify screen dimensions that scale to appear the same on screens of the same size but which use different pixel densities.

In practical terms, one density-independent pixel (dp) is equivalent to one pixel on a 160dpi screen. For example, a line specified as 2dp wide appears as 3 pixels on a display with 240dpi.

Within your application you should always use density-independent pixels, avoiding specifying any layout dimensions, View sizes, or Drawable dimensions using pixel values.

In addition to dp units, Android also uses a scale-independent pixel (sp) for the special case of font sizes. Scale-independent pixels use the same base unit as density-independent pixels but are additionally scaled according to the user's preferred text size.

Resource Qualifiers for Pixel Density

Scaling bitmap images can result in either lost detail (when scaling downward) or pixilation (when scaling upward). To ensure that your UI is crisp, clear, and devoid of artifacts, it's good practice to include multiple image assets for different pixel densities.

Chapter 3, "Creating Applications and Activities," introduced you to the Android resource framework, which enables you to create a parallel directory structure to store external resources for different host hardware configurations.

When using Drawable resources that cannot be dynamically scaled well, you should create and include image assets optimized for each pixel density category.

➤ `res/drawable-ldpi` — Low-density resources for screens approximately 120dpi

➤ `res/drawable-mdpi` — Medium-density resources for screens approximately 160pi

➤ `res/drawable-tvdpi` — Medium- to high-density resources for screens approximately 213dpi; introduced in API level 13 as a specific optimization for applications targeting televisions

➤ `res/drawable-hdpi` — High-density resources for screens approximately 240dpi

➤ `res/drawable-xhdpi` — Extra-high density resources for screens approximately 320dpi

➤ `res/drawable-nodpi` — Used for resources that must not be scaled regardless of the host screen's density

Supporting and Optimizing for Different Screen Sizes

Android devices can come in all shapes and sizes, so when designing your UI it's important to ensure that your layouts not only support different screen sizes, orientations, and aspect ratios, but also that they are optimized for each.

It's neither possible nor desirable to create a different absolute layout for each specific screen configuration; instead, it's best practice to take a two-phased approach:

➤ Ensure that all your layouts are capable of scaling within a reasonable set of bounds.

➤ Create a set of alternative layouts whose bounds overlap such that all possible screen configurations are considered.

In practice this approach is similar to that taken by most websites and desktop applications. After a fling with fixed-width pages in the '90s, websites now scale to fit the available space on desktop browsers and offer an alternative CSS definition to provide an optimized layout on tablets or mobile devices.

Using the same approach, you can create optimized layouts for certain categories of screen configurations, which are capable of scaling to account for variation within that category.

Creating Scalable Layouts

The layout managers provided by the framework are designed to support the implementation of UIs that scale to fit the available space. In all cases, you should avoid defining the location of your layout elements in absolute terms.

Using the Linear Layout you can create layouts represented by simple columns or rows that fill the available width or height of the screen, respectively.

The Relative Layout is a flexible alternative that enables you to define the position of each UI element relative to the parent Activity and the other elements used within the layout.

When defining the height or width of your scalable UI elements (such as Buttons and Text Views) it's good practice to avoid providing specific dimensions. Instead, you can define the height and width of Views using `wrap_content` or `match_parent` attributes, as appropriate.

```
<Button
  android:id="@+id/button"
  android:layout_width="match_parent"
  android:layout_height="wrap_content"
  android:text="@string/buttonText"
/>
```

The `wrap_content` flag enables the View to define its size based on the amount of space potentially available to it, whereas the `match_parent` flag (formally `fill_parent`) enables the element to expand as necessary to fill the available space.

Deciding which screen element should expand (or contract) when the screen size changes is one of the most important factors in optimizing your layouts for variable screen dimensions.

Android 4.0 (API level 14) introduced the Grid Layout, a highly flexible layout designed to reduce nesting and simplify the creation of adaptive and dynamic layouts.

Optimizing Layouts for Different Screen Types

In addition to providing layouts that scale, you should consider creating alternative layout definitions optimized for different screen sizes.

There is a significant difference in screen available on a 3" QVGA smartphone display compared to a high-resolution 10.1" tablet. Similarly, and particularly for devices with significant aspect ratios, a layout that works well viewed in landscape mode might be unsuitable when the device is rotated into portrait.

Creating a layout that scales to accommodate the space available is a good first step; it's good practice to consider ways that you can take advantage of the extra space (or consider the effect of reduced space) to create a better user experience.

This is a similar approach to websites that provide a specialized layout for users on smartphones, tablets, or desktop browsers. For Android users, the lines between each device category are blurred, so it's best practice to optimize your layouts based on the available space rather than the type of device.

The Android resource framework provides several options to supply different layouts based on the screen size and properties.

Use the `long` and `notlong` decorators to supply layouts optimized for normal versus widescreen displays, and use the `port` and `land` decorators to indicate layouts to be used when the screen is viewed in portrait or landscape modes, respectively.

```
res/layout-long-land/      // Layouts for long screens in landscape mode.
res/layout-notlong-port/   // Layouts for not-long screens in portrait mode.
```

In terms of screen size, two options are available. Android 3.2 (API level 13) introduced the capability to provide layouts based on the current screen width/height, or the smallest available screen width:

```
res/layout-w600dp
res/layout-h720dp
res/layout-sw320dp
```

These decorators enable you to determine the lowest number of device-independent pixels your layout requires in terms of height and width, and supply an alternative layout for devices that fall outside those bounds.

If you plan to make your application available to earlier versions of Android, it's good practice to use these modifiers in conjunction with the `small`, `medium`, `large`, and `xlarge` decorators.

```
res/layout-small
res/layout-normal
res/layout-large
res/layout-xlarge
```

These buckets, although less specific, enable you to supply a different layout based on the size of the host device relative to a "normal" HVGA smartphone display.

Typically, you can use these various decorators together to create layouts optimized for various sizes and orientations. This can lead to situations in which two or more screen configurations should use the same layout. To avoid duplication, you can define aliases.

An alias enables you to create an empty layout definition that can be configured to return a specific resource when another one is requested. For example, within your resources hierarchy, you could include a `res/layout/main_multipanel.xml` layout that contains a multipanel layout and a `res/layout/main_singlepanel.xml` resource that contains a single-panel layout.

Create a `res/values/layout.xml` file that uses an alias to select the single panel layout:

```
<?xml version="1.0" encoding="utf-8"?>
<resources>
  <item name="main" type="layout">@layout/main_singlepanel</item>
</resources>
```

For each specific configuration that should use the multi-panel resource, create a corresponding values folder:

```
res/values-large-land
res/values-xlarge
```

And create and add a new `layout.xml` resource to them:

```
<?xml version="1.0" encoding="utf-8"?>
<resources>
  <item name="main" type="layout">@layout/main_multipanel</item>
</resources>
```

Within your code, simply refer to the `R.layout.main` resource to let the system decide which underlying layout resource to use. Note that you cannot use the alias name you specify as resource identifier for any layouts stored within the `res/layout` folder; if you do, there will be a naming collision.

Specifying Supported Screen Sizes

For some applications it may not be possible to optimize your UI to support all possible screen sizes. You can use the `supports-screens` manifest element to specify on which screens your application can be run:

```
<supports-screens android:smallScreens="false"
                   android:normalScreens="true"
                   android:largeScreens="true"
                   android:xlargeScreens="true"/>
```

In this context a small screen is any display with a resolution smaller than HVGA; a large screen is larger than a smartphone; an extra large screen is significantly larger (such as a tablet); and normal screens encompass the majority of smartphone handsets.

A `false` value forces Android to use compatibility scaling to attempt to scale your application UI correctly. This generally results in a UI with degraded image assets that show scaling artifacts.

Mirroring the new resource decorators described in the previous section, Android 3.2 (API level 13) introduced the `requiresSmallestWidthDp`, `compatibleWidthLimitDp`, and `largestWidth LimitDp` attributes to the `supports-screen` node:

```
<supports-screens android:requiresSmallestWidthDp="480"
                  android:compatibleWidthLimitDp="600"
                  android:largestWidthLimitDp="720"/>
```

Although neither the Android run time nor the Google Play Store currently use these parameters to enforce compatibility, they will eventually be used on the Google Play Store in preference to the small, normal, large, and extra large parameters on supported devices.

Creating Scalable Graphics Assets

Android includes a number of simple Drawable resource types that can be defined entirely in XML. These include the `ColorDrawable`, `ShapeDrawable`, and `GradientDrawable` classes. These resources are stored in the `res/drawable` folder and can be identified in code by their lowercase XML filenames.

When these Drawables are defined in XML, and you specify their attributes using density-independent pixels, the run time smoothly scales them. Like vector graphics, these Drawables can be scaled dynamically to display correctly and without scaling artifacts regardless of screen size, resolution, or pixel density. The notable exceptions to this rule are Gradient Drawables, which require a gradient radius defined in pixels.

As you see later in this chapter, you can use these Drawables in combination with transformative Drawables and composite Drawables. Together, they can result in dynamic, scalable UI elements that require fewer resources and appear crisp on any screen. They are ideal to use as backgrounds for Views, layouts, Activities, and the Action Bar.

Android also supports NinePatch PNG images that enable you to mark the parts of an image that can be stretched.

Color Drawables

A `ColorDrawable`, the simplest of the XML-defined Drawables, enables you to specify an image asset based on a single solid color. Color Drawables, such as this solid red Drawable, are defined as XML files using the `color` tag in the `res/drawable` folder:

```
<color xmlns:android="http://schemas.android.com/apk/res/android"
    android:color="#FF0000"
/>
```

Shape Drawables

Shape Drawable resources let you define simple primitive shapes by defining their dimensions, background, and stroke/outline using the `shape` tag.

Each shape consists of a type (specified via the `shape` attribute), attributes that define the dimensions of that shape, and subnodes to specify padding, stroke (outline), and background color values.

Android currently supports the following shape types as values for the `shape` attribute:

➤ `line` — A horizontal line spanning the width of the parent View. The line's width and style are described by the shape's stroke.

➤ `oval` — A simple oval shape.

➤ `rectangle` — A simple rectangle shape. Also supports a `corners` subnode that uses a `radius` attribute to create a rounded rectangle.

➤ `ring` — Supports the `innerRadius` and `thickness` attributes to let you specify the inner radius of the ring shape and its thickness, respectively. Alternatively, you can use `innerRadiusRatio` and `thicknessRatio` to define the ring's inner radius and thickness, respectively, as a proportion of its width (where an inner radius of a quarter of the width would use the value 4).

Use the `stroke` subnode to specify an outline for your shapes using `width` and `color` attributes.

You can also include a `padding` node to offset the positioning of your shape on the canvas.

More usefully, you can include a subnode to specify the background color. The simplest case involves using the `solid` node, including the `color` attribute, to define a solid background color.

The following snippet shows a rectangular Shape Drawable with a solid fill, rounded edges, 10dp outline, and 10dp of padding around each edge. Figure 11-1 shows the result.

```xml
<?xml version="1.0" encoding="utf-8"?>
<shape xmlns:android="http://schemas.android.com/apk/res/android"
  android:shape="rectangle">
    <solid
      android:color="#f0600000"/>
    <stroke
      android:width="10dp"
      android:color="#00FF00"/>
    <corners
      android:radius="15dp" />
    <padding
      android:left="10dp"
      android:top="10dp"
      android:right="10dp"
      android:bottom="10dp"
    />
</shape>
```

The following section describes the `GradientDrawable` class and how to specify a gradient fill for your Shape Drawables.

Gradient Drawables

FIGURE 11-1

A `GradientDrawable` lets you design complex gradient fills. Each gradient defines a smooth transition between two or three colors in a linear, radial, or sweep pattern.

Gradient Drawables are defined using the `gradient` tag as a subnode within a Shape Drawable definition (such as those defined in the preceding section).

Each Gradient Drawable requires at least a `startColor` and `endColor` attribute and supports an optional `middleColor`. Using the `type` attribute you can define your gradient as one of the following:

➤ `linear` — The default gradient type, it draws a straight color transition from `startColor` to `endColor` at an angle defined by the `angle` attribute.

➤ `radial` — Draws a circular gradient from `startColor` to `endColor` from the outer edge of the shape to the center. It requires a `gradientRadius` attribute that specifies the radius of the gradient transition in pixels. It also optionally supports `centerX` and `centerY` attributes to offset the location of the center of the gradient.

Because the gradient radius is defined in pixels, it does not dynamically scale for different pixel densities. To minimize banding, you may need to specify different gradient radius values for different screen resolutions and pixel densities.

➤ sweep – Draws a sweep gradient that transitions from startColor to endColor along the outer edge of the parent shape (typically a ring).

The following snippets show the XML for a linear gradient within a rectangle, a radial gradient within an oval, and a sweep gradient within a ring, as shown in Figure 11-2. Note that each would need to be created in a separate file within the res/drawable folder.

```
<!-- Rectangle with linear gradient -->
<?xml version="1.0" encoding="utf-8"?>
<shape xmlns:android="http://schemas.android.com/apk/res/android"
  android:shape="rectangle"
  android:useLevel="false">
  <gradient
    android:startColor="#ffffff"
    android:endColor="#ffffff"
    android:centerColor="#000000"
    android:useLevel="false"
    android:type="linear"
    android:angle="45"
  />
</shape>

<!-- Oval with radial gradient -->
<?xml version="1.0" encoding="utf-8"?>
<shape xmlns:android="http://schemas.android.com/apk/res/android"
  android:shape="oval"
  android:useLevel="false">
  <gradient
    android:type="radial"
    android:startColor="#ffffff"
    android:endColor="#ffffff"
    android:centerColor="#000000"
    android:useLevel="false"
    android:gradientRadius="300"
  />
</shape>

<!-- Ring with sweep gradient -->
<?xml version="1.0" encoding="utf-8"?>
<shape xmlns:android="http://schemas.android.com/apk/res/android"
  android:shape="ring"
  android:useLevel="false"
  android:innerRadiusRatio="3"
  android:thicknessRatio="8">
  <gradient
    android:startColor="#ffffff"
    android:endColor="#ffffff"
    android:centerColor="#000000"
    android:useLevel="false"
    android:type="sweep"
  />
</shape>
```

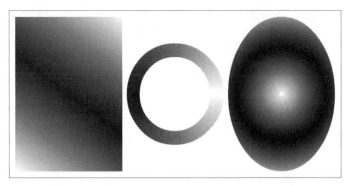

FIGURE 11-2

NinePatch Drawables

NinePatch (or stretchable) images are PNG files that mark the parts of an image that can be stretched. They're stored in your `res/drawable` folders with names ending in `.9.png` extensions.

```
res/drawable/stretchable_background.9.png
```

NinePatches use a one-pixel border to define the area of the image that can be stretched if the image is enlarged. This makes them particularly useful for creating backgrounds for Views or Activities that may have a variable size.

To create a NinePatch, draw single-pixel black lines that represent stretchable areas along the left and top borders of your image, as shown in Figure 11-3.

FIGURE 11-3

The unmarked sections won't be resized, and the relative size of each of the marked sections remains the same as the image size changes, as shown in Figure 11-4.

To simplify the process to create NinePatch images for your application, the Android SDK includes a WYSIWIG `draw9patch` tool in the `/tools` folder.

NinePatch Sample

FIGURE 11-4

Creating Optimized, Adaptive, and Dynamic Designs

When designing your UI, it's important to ensure that not only are your assets and layouts scalable, but also that they are optimized for a variety of different device types and screen sizes. A layout that looks great on a smartphone may suffer from excessive whitespace or line lengths on a tablet. Conversely, a layout optimized for a tablet device may appear cramped on a smartphone.

It's good practice to build optimized layouts for several different screen sizes that take advantage of their relative size and aspect ratio. The specific techniques used to design such UIs are beyond the scope of this book, but they are covered in detail at the Android Training site: `http://developer.android.com/training/design-navigation/index.html`.

Testing, Testing, Testing

With hundreds of Android devices of varying screen sizes and pixel densities now available, it's impractical (and in some cases impossible) to physically test your application on every device.

Android Virtual Devices (AVDs) are ideal platforms for testing your application with a number of different screen configurations. AVDs also have the advantage to let you configure alternative platform releases and hardware configurations.

You learned how to create and use AVDs in Chapter 2, "Getting Started," so this section focuses on how to create AVDs representative of different screens.

Using Emulator Skins

The simplest way to test your application's UI is to use the built-in skins. Each skin emulates a known device configuration with a resolution, pixel density, and physical screen size.

As of Android 4.0.3, the following built-in skins are available for testing:

- ➤ **QVGA** — 320 × 240, 120dpi, 3.3"
- ➤ **WQVGA43** — 432 × 240, 120dpi, 3.9"
- ➤ **WQVGA400** — 240 × 400, 120dpi, 3.9"
- ➤ **WSVGA** — 1024 × 600, 160dpi, 7"
- ➤ **WXGA720** — 720 ×1280, 320dpi, 4.8" (Galaxy Nexus)
- ➤ **WXGA800** — 1280 × 800, 160dpi, 10.1" (Motorola Xoom)
- ➤ **HVGA** — 480 × 320, 160dpi, 3.6"
- ➤ **WVGA800** — 800 × 480, 240dpi, 3.9" (Nexus One)
- ➤ **WVGA854** — 854 × 480, 240dpi, 4.1"

Testing for Custom Resolutions and Screen Sizes

One of the advantages of using an AVD to evaluate devices is the ability to define arbitrary screen resolutions and pixel densities.

When you start a new AVD, you see the Launch Options dialog, as shown in Figure 11-5. If you check the Scale Display to Real Size check box and specify a screen size for your virtual device, as well as the dpi of your development monitor, the emulator scales to approximately the physical size you specified.

This enables you to evaluate your UI against a variety of screen sizes and pixel densities as well as resolutions and skins — an ideal way to see how your application appears on a small, high-resolution phone or a large, low-resolution tablet.

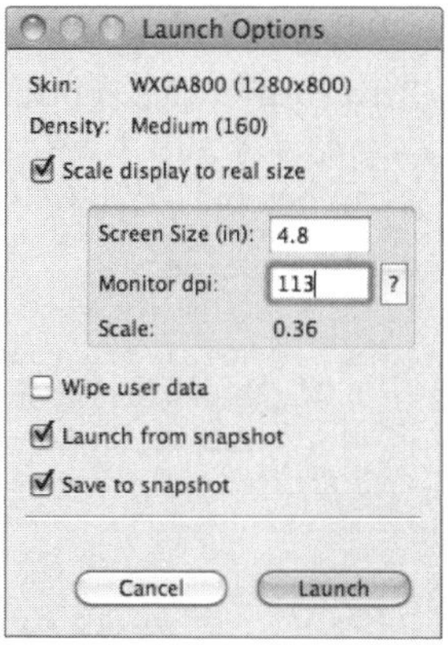

FIGURE 11-5

ENSURING ACCESSIBILITY

An important part of creating an inclusive and compelling UI is to ensure that it can be used by people with disabilities that require them to interact with their devices in different ways.

Accessibility APIs were introduced in Android 1.6 (API level 4) to provide alternative interaction methods for users with visual, physical, or age-related disabilities that make it difficult to interact fully with a touch screen.

In Chapter 4 you learned how to make your custom Views accessible and navigable. This section summarizes some of the best practices to ensure your entire user experience is accessible.

Supporting Navigation Without a Touch Screen

Directional controllers, such as trackballs, D-pads, and arrow keys, are the primary means of navigation for many users. To ensure that your UI is navigable without requiring a touch screen, it's important that your application supports each of these input mechanisms.

The first step is to ensure that each input View is focusable and clickable. Pressing the center or OK button should then affect the focused control in the same way as touching it using the touch screen.

It's good practice to visually indicate when a control has the input focus, allowing users to know which control they are interacting with. All the Views included in the Android SDK are focusable.

The Android run time determines the focus order for each control in your layout based on an algorithm that finds the nearest neighbor in a given direction. You can manually override that order using the `android:nextFocusDown`, `android:nextFocusLeft`, `android:nextFocusRight`, and `android:nextFocusUp` attributes for any View within your layout definition. It's good practice to ensure that consecutive navigation movements in the opposite direction should return you to your original location.

Providing a Textual Description of Each View

Context is of critical importance when designing your UI. Button images, text labels, or even the relative location of each control can be used to indicate the purpose of each input View.

To ensure your application is accessible, consider how a user without visual context can navigate and use your UI. To assist, each View can include an `android:contentDescription` attribute that can be read aloud to users who have enabled the accessibility speech tools:

```
<Button
  android:id="@+id/pick_contact_button"
  android:layout_width="match_parent"
  android:layout_height="wrap_content"
  android:text="@string/pick_contact_button"
  android:contentDescription="@string/pick_contact_button_description"
/>
```

Every View within your layout that can hold focus should have a content description that provides the entire context necessary for a user to act on it.

INTRODUCING ANDROID TEXT-TO-SPEECH

The text-to-speech (TTS) libraries, also known as *speech synthesis*, enable you to output synthesized speech from within your applications, allowing them to "talk" to your users.

> *Android 4.0 (API level 14) introduced the ability for application developers to implement their own text-to-speech engines and make them available to other applications. Creating a speech synthesis engine is beyond the scope of this book and won't be covered here. You can find further resources on the Android Developer site, at* `http://developer.android.com/resources/articles/tts.html`.

Due to storage space constraints on some Android devices, the language packs are not always preinstalled on each device. Before using the TTS engine, it's good practice to confirm the language packs are installed.

To check for the TTS libraries, start a new Activity for a result using the `ACTION_CHECK_TTS_DATA` action from the `TextToSpeech.Engine` class:

```
Intent intent = new Intent(TextToSpeech.Engine.ACTION_CHECK_TTS_DATA);
startActivityForResult(intent, TTS_DATA_CHECK);
```

The `onActivityResult` handler receives `CHECK_VOICE_DATA_PASS` if the voice data has been installed successfully. If the voice data is not currently available, start a new Activity using the `ACTION_INSTALL_TTS_DATA` action from the TTS Engine class to initiate its installation.

```
Intent installVoice = new Intent(Engine.ACTION_INSTALL_TTS_DATA);
startActivity(installVoice);
```

After confirming the voice data is available, you need to create and initialize a new `TextToSpeech` instance. Note that you cannot use the new Text To Speech object until initialization is complete. Pass an `OnInitListener` into the constructor that will be fired when the TTS engine has been initialized.

```
boolean ttsIsInit = false;
TextToSpeech tts = null;

protected void onActivityResult(int requestCode,
                                int resultCode, Intent data) {
  if (requestCode == TTS_DATA_CHECK) {
    if (resultCode == Engine.CHECK_VOICE_DATA_PASS) {
      tts = new TextToSpeech(this, new OnInitListener() {
        public void onInit(int status) {
          if (status == TextToSpeech.SUCCESS) {
            ttsIsInit = true;
            // TODO Speak!
          }
        }
```

```
      });
    }
  }
}
```

After initializing Text To Speech, you can use the `speak` method to synthesize voice data using the default device audio output:

```
HashMap parameters = null;
tts.speak("Hello, Android", TextToSpeech.QUEUE_ADD, parameters);
```

The `speak` method enables you to specify a parameter either to add the new voice output to the existing queue or to flush the queue and start speaking immediately.

You can affect the way the voice output sounds using the `setPitch` and `setSpeechRate` methods. Each method accepts a float parameter that modifies the pitch and speed, respectively, of the voice output.

You can also change the pronunciation of your voice output using the `setLanguage` method. This method takes a `Locale` parameter to specify the country and language of the text to speak. This affects the way the text is spoken to ensure the correct language and pronunciation models are used.

When you have finished speaking, use `stop` to halt voice output and `shutdown` to free the TTS resources:

```
tts.stop();
tts.shutdown();
```

Listing 11-1 determines whether the TTS voice library is installed, initializes a new TTS engine, and uses it to speak in UK English.

LISTING 11-1: Using Text-to-Speech

```
private static int TTS_DATA_CHECK = 1;

private TextToSpeech tts = null;
private boolean ttsIsInit = false;

private void initTextToSpeech() {
  Intent intent = new Intent(Engine.ACTION_CHECK_TTS_DATA);
  startActivityForResult(intent, TTS_DATA_CHECK);
}

protected void onActivityResult(int requestCode,
                                int resultCode, Intent data) {
  if (requestCode == TTS_DATA_CHECK) {
    if (resultCode == Engine.CHECK_VOICE_DATA_PASS) {
      tts = new TextToSpeech(this, new OnInitListener() {
        public void onInit(int status) {
          if (status == TextToSpeech.SUCCESS) {
            ttsIsInit = true;
            if (tts.isLanguageAvailable(Locale.UK) >= 0)
```

```
                  tts.setLanguage(Locale.UK);
              tts.setPitch(0.8f);
              tts.setSpeechRate(1.1f);
              speak();
          }
        }
      });
    } else {
      Intent installVoice = new Intent(Engine.ACTION_INSTALL_TTS_DATA);
      startActivity(installVoice);
    }
  }
}

private void speak() {
  if (tts != null && ttsIsInit) {
    tts.speak("Hello, Android", TextToSpeech.QUEUE_ADD, null);
  }
}

@Override
public void onDestroy() {
  if (tts != null) {
    tts.stop();
    tts.shutdown();
  }
  super.onDestroy();
}
```

code snippet PA4AD_Ch11_TextToSpeach/src/MyActivity.java

USING SPEECH RECOGNITION

Android supports voice input and speech recognition using the
RecognizerIntent class. This API enables you to accept voice
input into your application using the standard voice input dialog, as
shown in Figure 11-6.

To initialize voice recognition, call startNewActivityFor
Result, passing in an Intent that specifies the RecognizerIntent
.ACTION_RECOGNIZE_SPEECH or RecognizerIntent.ACTION_WEB_
SEARCH actions. The former action enables you to receive the input
speech within your application, whereas the latter action enables
you to trigger a web search or voice action using the native
providers.

The launch Intent must include the RecognizerIntent.EXTRA_
LANGUAGE_MODEL extra to specify the language model used to parse
the input audio. This can be either LANGUAGE_MODEL_FREE_FORM
or LANGUAGE_MODEL_WEB_SEARCH; both are available as static constants from the RecognizerIntent class.

FIGURE 11-6

You can also specify a number of optional extras to control the language, potential result count, and display prompt using the following Recognizer Intent constants:

➤ EXTRA_LANGUAGE — Specifies a language constant from the `Locale` class to use an input language other than the device default. You can find the current default by calling the static `getDefault` method on the `Locale` class.

➤ EXTRA_MAXRESULTS — Uses an integer value to limit the number of potential recognition results returned.

➤ EXTRA_PROMPT — Specifies a string that displays in the voice input dialog (shown in Figure 11-6) to prompt the user to speak.

> *The engine that handles the speech recognition may not be capable of under-standing spoken input from all the languages available from the* `Locale` *class.*
>
> *Not all devices include support for speech recognition. In such cases it is generally possible to download the voice recognition library from the Google Play Store.*

Using Speech Recognition for Voice Input

When using voice recognition to receive the spoken words, call `startNewActivityForResult` using the `RecognizerIntent.ACTION_RECOGNIZE_SPEECH` action, as shown in Listing 11-2.

LISTING 11-2: Initiating a speech recognition request

```
Intent intent = new Intent(RecognizerIntent.ACTION_RECOGNIZE_SPEECH);
// Specify free form input
intent.putExtra(RecognizerIntent.EXTRA_LANGUAGE_MODEL,
                RecognizerIntent.LANGUAGE_MODEL_FREE_FORM);
intent.putExtra(RecognizerIntent.EXTRA_PROMPT,
                "or forever hold your peace");
intent.putExtra(RecognizerIntent.EXTRA_MAX_RESULTS, 1);
intent.putExtra(RecognizerIntent.EXTRA_LANGUAGE, Locale.ENGLISH);
startActivityForResult(intent, VOICE_RECOGNITION);
```

code snippet PA4AD_Ch11_Speech/src/MyActivity.java

When the user finishes speaking, the speech recognition engine analyzes and processes the result-ing audio and then returns the results through the `onActivityResult` handler as an Array List of strings in the `EXTRA_RESULTS` extra, as shown in Listing 11-3.

LISTING 11-3: Finding the results of a speech recognition request

```
@Override
protected void onActivityResult(int requestCode,
                                int resultCode,
                                Intent data) {
```

```
    if (requestCode == VOICE_RECOGNITION && resultCode == RESULT_OK) {
      ArrayList<String> results;

      results =
        data.getStringArrayListExtra(RecognizerIntent.EXTRA_RESULTS);

      float[] confidence;

      String confidenceExtra = RecognizerIntent.EXTRA_CONFIDENCE_SCORES;
      confidence =
        data.getFloatArrayExtra(confidenceExtra);

      // TODO Do something with the recognized voice strings
    }
    super.onActivityResult(requestCode, resultCode, data);
  }
```

code snippet PA4AD_Ch11_Speech/src/MyActivity.java

Each string returned in the Array List represents a potential match for the spoken input. You can find the recognition engine's confidence in each result using the float array returned in the EXTRA_ CONFIDENCE_SCORES extra. Each value in the array is the confidence score between 0 (no confidence) and 1 (high confidence) that the speech has been correctly recognized.

Using Speech Recognition for Search

Rather than handling the received speech yourself, you can use the RecognizerIntent.ACTION_ WEB_SEARCH action to display a web search result or to trigger another type of voice action based on the user's speech, as shown in Listing 11-4.

LISTING 11-4: Finding the results of a speech recognition request

```
Intent intent = new Intent(RecognizerIntent.ACTION_WEB_SEARCH);
intent.putExtra(RecognizerIntent.EXTRA_LANGUAGE_MODEL,
                RecognizerIntent.LANGUAGE_MODEL_WEB_SEARCH);
startActivityForResult(intent, 0);
```

code snippet PA4AD_Ch11_Speech/src/MyActivity.java

CONTROLLING DEVICE VIBRATION

In Chapter 10 you learned how to create Notifications that can use vibration to enrich event feedback. In some circumstances, you may want to vibrate the device independently of Notifications. For example, vibrating the device is an excellent way to provide haptic user feedback and is particularly popular as a feedback mechanism for games.

To control device vibration, your applications needs the VIBRATE permission:

```
<uses-permission android:name="android.permission.VIBRATE"/>
```

Device vibration is controlled through the `Vibrator` Service, accessible via the `getSystemService` method:

```
String vibratorService = Context.VIBRATOR_SERVICE;
Vibrator vibrator = (Vibrator)getSystemService(vibratorService);
```

Call `vibrate` to start device vibration; you can pass in either a vibration duration or a pattern of alternating vibration/pause sequences along with an optional index parameter that repeats the pattern starting at the index specified:

```
long[] pattern = {1000, 2000, 4000, 8000, 16000 };
vibrator.vibrate(pattern, 0); // Execute vibration pattern.
vibrator.vibrate(1000);        // Vibrate for 1 second.
```

To cancel vibration, call `cancel`; exiting your application automatically cancels any vibration it has initiated.

```
vibrator.cancel();
```

WORKING WITH ANIMATIONS

In Chapter 3, you learned how to define animations as external resources. Now, you get the opportunity to put them to use.

Android offers three kinds of animation:

➤ **Tweened View Animations** — Tweened animations are applied to Views, letting you define a series of changes in position, size, rotation, and opacity that animate the View contents.

➤ **Frame Animations** — Traditional cell-based animations in which a different Drawable is displayed in each frame. Frame-by-frame animations are displayed within a View, using its Canvas as a projection screen.

➤ **Interpolated Property Animations** — The property animation system enables you to animate almost anything within your application. It's a framework designed to affect any object property over a period of time using the specified interpolation technique.

Tweened View Animations

Tweened animations offer a simple way to provide depth, movement, or feedback to your users at a minimal resource cost.

Using animations to apply a set of orientation, scale, position, and opacity changes is much less resource-intensive than manually redrawing the Canvas to achieve similar effects, not to mention far simpler to implement.

Tweened animations are commonly used to:

➤ Transition between Activities

➤ Transition between layouts within an Activity

➤ Transition between different content displayed within the same View

➤ Provide user feedback, such as indicating progress or "shaking" an input box to indicate an incorrect or invalid data entry

Creating Tweened View Animations

Tweened animations are created using the `Animation` class. The following list explains the animation types available:

➤ `AlphaAnimation` — Lets you animate a change in the View's transparency (opacity or alpha blending)

➤ `RotateAnimation` — Lets you spin the selected View canvas in the XY plane

➤ `ScaleAnimation` — Lets you to zoom in to or out from the selected View

➤ `TranslateAnimation` — Lets you move the selected View around the screen (although it will only be drawn within its original bounds)

Android offers the `AnimationSet` class, shown in Listing 11-5, to group and configure animations to be run as a set. You can define the start time and duration of each animation used within a set to control the timing and order of the animation sequence.

LISTING 11-5: Defining an interpolated View animation

```
<set xmlns:android="http://schemas.android.com/apk/res/android"
     android:interpolator="@android:anim/accelerate_interpolator">
  <scale
    android:fromXScale="0.0" android:toXScale="1.0"
    android:fromYScale="0.0" android:toYScale="1.0"
    android:pivotX="50%"
    android:pivotY="50%"
    android:duration="1000"
  />
</set>
```

code snippet PA4AD_Ch11_Animation/res/anim/popin.xml

> *It's important to set the start offset and duration for each child animation; otherwise, they will all start and complete at the same time.*

Applying Tweened Animations

You can apply animations to any View by calling its `startAnimation` method and passing in the Animation or Animation Set to apply.

Animation sequences run once and then stop, unless you modify this behavior using the
`setRepeatMode` and `setRepeatCount` methods on the Animation or Animation Set. You can
force an animation to loop or repeat in reverse by setting the repeat mode of `RESTART` or
`REVERSE`, respectively. Setting the repeat count controls the number of times the animation
repeats.

```
myAnimation.setRepeatMode(Animation.RESTART);
myAnimation.setRepeatCount(Animation.INFINITE);
myView.startAnimation(myAnimation);
```

Using Animation Listeners

The `AnimationListener` lets you create an event handler that's fired when an animation begins or
ends. This lets you perform actions before or after an animation has completed, such as changing
the View contents or chaining multiple animations.

Call `setAnimationListener` on an Animation object, and pass in a new implementation of
`AnimationListener`, overriding `onAnimationEnd`, `onAnimationStart`, and `onAnimationRepeat`,
as required:

```
myAnimation.setAnimationListener(new AnimationListener() {
  public void onAnimationEnd(Animation animation) {
    // TODO Do something after animation is complete.
  }

  public void onAnimationStart(Animation animation) {
    // TODO Do something when the animation starts.
  }

  public void onAnimationRepeat(Animation animation) {
    // TODO Do something when the animation repeats.
  }
});
```

Animating Layouts and View Groups

A `LayoutAnimation` is used to animate View Groups, applying a single Animation (or Animation
Set) to each child View in a predetermined sequence.

Use a `LayoutAnimationController` to specify an Animation (or Animation Set) that's applied
to each child View in a View Group. Each View it contains will have the same animation
applied, but you can use the Layout Animation Controller to specify the order and start time for
each View.

Android includes two `LayoutAnimationController` classes:

➤ `LayoutAnimationController` — Lets you select the start offset of each View (in milliseconds) and the order (`forward`, `reverse`, and `random`) to apply the animation to each child
View.

➤ `GridLayoutAnimationController` — A derived class that lets you assign the animation
sequence of the child Views using grid row and column references.

Creating Layout Animations

To create a new Layout Animation, start by defining the Animation to apply to each child View. Then create a new `LayoutAnimation`, either in code or as an external animation resource, that references the animation to apply and defines the order and timing in which to apply it.

Listing 11-6 shows a Layout Animation definition stored as `popinlayout.xml`. The Layout Animation applies a simple "pop-in" animation randomly to each child View of any View Group it's assigned to.

LISTING 11-6: Defining a layout animation

```xml
<layoutAnimation
  xmlns:android="http://schemas.android.com/apk/res/android"
  android:delay="0.5"
  android:animationOrder="random"
  android:animation="@anim/popin"
/>
```

code snippet PA4AD_Ch11_Animation/res/anim/popinlayout.xml

Using Layout Animations

After defining a Layout Animation, you can apply it to a View Group either in code or in the layout XML resource. In XML this is done using the `android:layoutAnimation` tag in the layout definition:

```
android:layoutAnimation="@anim/popinlayout"
```

To set a Layout Animation in code, call `setLayoutAnimation` on the View Group, passing in a reference to the `LayoutAnimation` object you want to apply. In each case, the Layout Animation will execute once, when the View Group is first laid out. You can force it to execute again by calling `scheduleLayoutAnimation` on the `ViewGroup` object. The animation will then be executed the next time the View Group is laid out. Layout Animations also support Animation Listeners.

```java
aViewGroup.setLayoutAnimationListener(new AnimationListener() {
  public void onAnimationEnd(Animation _animation) {
    // TODO: Actions on animation complete.
  }
  public void onAnimationRepeat(Animation _animation) {}
  public void onAnimationStart(Animation _animation) {}
});

aViewGroup.scheduleLayoutAnimation();
```

Creating and Using Frame-by-Frame Animations

Frame-by-frame animations are akin to traditional cel-based cartoons in which an image is chosen for each frame. Whereas tweened animations use the target View to supply the content of the animation, frame-by-frame animations enable you to specify a series of `Drawable` objects that are used as the background to a View.

The `AnimationDrawable` class is used to create a new frame-by-frame animation presented as a `Drawable` resource. You can define your Animation Drawable resource as an external resource in your project's `res/drawable` folder using XML.

Use the `animation-list` tag to group a collection of `item` nodes, each of which uses a `drawable` attribute to define an image to display and a `duration` attribute to specify the time (in milliseconds) to display it.

Listing 11-7 shows how to create a simple animation that displays a rocket taking off. (Rocket images are not included.)

LISTING 11-7: Defining a frame-by-frame animation

```
<animation-list
  xmlns:android="http://schemas.android.com/apk/res/android"
  android:oneshot="false">
  <item android:drawable="@drawable/rocket1" android:duration="500" />
  <item android:drawable="@drawable/rocket2" android:duration="500" />
  <item android:drawable="@drawable/rocket3" android:duration="500" />
</animation-list>
```

code snippet PA4AD_Ch11_Animation/res/drawable/animated_rocket.xml

To display your animation, set it as the background to a View using the `setBackgroundResource` method:

```
ImageView image = (ImageView)findViewById(R.id.my_animation_frame);
image.setBackgroundResource(R.drawable.animated_rocket);
```

Alternatively, use the `setBackgroundDrawable` to use a Drawable instance instead of a resource reference. Run the animation calling its `start` method.

```
AnimationDrawable animation = (AnimationDrawable)image.getBackground();
animation.start();
```

Interpolated Property Animations

Android 3.0 (API level 11) introduced a new animation technique that animates object properties. Although the tweened View animations described in the earlier section modified the appearance of the affected view, without modifying the object itself, property animations modify the properties of the underlying object directly.

As a result, you can modify any property of any object — visual or otherwise — using a property animator to transition it from one value to another, over a given period of time, using the interpolation algorithm of your choice, and setting the repeat behavior as required. The *value* can be any object, from a regular integer to a complex Class instance.

As a result, you can use property animators to create a smooth transition for anything within your code; the target property doesn't even need to represent something visual. Property animations are effectively iterators implemented using a background timer to increment or decrement a value according to a given interpolation path over a given period of time.

This is an incredibly powerful tool that can be used for anything from a simple View effect, such as moving, scaling, or fading a View, to complex animations, including runtime layout changes and curved transitions.

Creating Property Animations

The simplest technique for creating property animations is using an `ObjectAnimator`. The Object Animator class includes the `ofFloat`, `ofInt`, and `ofObject` static methods to easily create an animation that transitions the specified property of the target object between the values provided:

```
String propertyName = "alpha";
float from = 1f;
float to = 0f;
ObjectAnimator anim = ObjectAnimator.ofFloat(targetObject, propertyName, from, to);
```

Alternatively, you can provide a single value to animate the property from its current value to its final value:

```
ObjectAnimator anim = ObjectAnimator.ofFloat(targetObject, propertyName, to);
```

> To animate a given property, there must be associated getter/setter functions on the underlying object. In the preceding example, the `targetObject` *must include* `getAlpha` *and* `setAlpha` *methods that return and accept a float value, respectively.*

To target a property of a type other than integer or float, use the `ofObject` method. This method requires that you supply an implementation of the `TypeEvaluator` class. Implement the `evaluate` method to return an object that should be returned when the animation is a given fraction of the way through animating between the start and end objects:

```
TypeEvaluator<MyClass> evaluator = new TypeEvaluator<MyClass>() {
  public MyClass evaluate(float fraction,
                          MyClass startValue,
                          MyClass endValue) {
    MyClass result = new MyClass();
    // TODO Modify the new object to represent itself the given
    // fraction between the start and end values.
    return result;
  }
};

// Animate between two instances
ValueAnimator  oa
  = ObjectAnimator.ofObject(evaluator, myClassFromInstance, myClassToInstance);

oa.setTarget(myClassInstance);
oa.start();
```

By default, each animation will run once with a 300ms duration. Use the `setDuration` method to alter the amount of time the interpolator should use to complete the transition:

```
anim.setDuration(500);
```

You can use the `setRepeatMode` and `setRepeatCount` methods to cause the animation to be applied either a set number of times or infinitely:

```
anim.setRepeatCount(ValueAnimator.INFINITE);
```

You can set the repeat mode either to restart from the beginning or to apply the animation in reverse:

```
anim.setRepeatMode(ValueAnimator.REVERSE);
```

To create the same Object Animator as an XML resource, create a new XML file in the `res/animator` folder:

```
<objectAnimator xmlns:android="http://schemas.android.com/apk/res/android"
    android:valueTo="0"
    android:propertyName="alpha"
    android:duration="500"
    android:valueType="floatType"
    android:repeatCount="-1"
    android:repeatMode="reverse"
/>
```

The filename can then be used as the resource identifier. To affect a particular object with an XML animator resource, use the `AnimatorInflator.loadAnimator` method, passing in the current context and the resource ID of the animation to apply to obtain a copy of the Object Animator, and then use the `setTarget` method to apply it to an object:

```
Animator anim = AnimatorInflater.loadAnimator(context, resID);
anim.setTarget(targetObject);
```

By default, the interpolator used to transition between the start and end values of each animation uses a nonlinear `AccelerateDecelerateInterpolator`, which provides the effect of accelerating at the beginning of the transition and decelerating when approaching the end.

You can use the `setInterpolator` method to apply one of the following SDK interpolators:

➤ `AccelerateDecelerateInterpolator` — The rate of change starts and ends slowly but accelerates through the middle.

➤ `AccelerateInterpolator` — The rate of change starts slowly but accelerates through the middle.

➤ `AnticipateInterpolator` — The change starts backward and then flings forward.

➤ `AnticipateOvershootInterpolator` — The change starts backward, flings forward, overshoots the target value, and finally goes back to the final value.

➤ `BounceInterpolator` — The change bounces at the end.

➤ `DecelerateInterpolator` — The rate of change starts out quickly and then decelerates.

➤ `LinearInterpolator` — The rate of change is constant.

➤ `OvershootInterpolator` — The change flings forward, overshoots the last value, and then comes back.

```
anim.setInterpolator(new AnticipateOvershootInterpolator());
```

You can also extend your own `TimeInterpolator` class to specify a custom interpolation algorithm.

To execute an animation, call its `start` method:

```
anim.start();
```

Creating Property Animation Sets

Android includes the `AnimatorSet` class to make it easier to create complex, interrelated animations.

```
AnimatorSet bouncer = new AnimatorSet();
```

To add a new animation to an Animator Set, use the `play` method. This returns an `AnimatorSet`
`.Builder` object that lets you specify when to play the specified animation in relation to another:

```
AnimatorSet mySet = new AnimatorSet();
mySet.play(firstAnimation).before(concurrentAnim1);
mySet.play(concurrentAnim1).with(concurrentAnim2);
mySet.play(lastAnim).after(concurrentAnim2);
```

Use the `start` method to execute the sequence of animations.

```
mySet.start();
```

Using Animation Listeners

The `Animator.AnimationListener` class lets you create event handlers that are fired when an animation begins, ends, repeats, or is canceled:

```
Animator.AnimatorListener l = new AnimatorListener() {

  public void onAnimationStart(Animator animation) {
    // TODO Auto-generated method stub
  }

  public void onAnimationRepeat(Animator animation) {
    // TODO Auto-generated method stub
  }

  public void onAnimationEnd(Animator animation) {
    // TODO Auto-generated method stub
  }

  public void onAnimationCancel(Animator animation) {
    // TODO Auto-generated method stub
  }
};
```

To apply an Animation Listener to your property animation, use the `addListener` method:

```
anim.addListener(l);
```

ENHANCING YOUR VIEWS

The explosive growth in the smartphone and tablet market has led to equally dramatic changes and improvements to mobile UIs.

This section describes how to use more advanced UI visual effects such as Shaders, translucency, touch screens with multiple touch, OpenGL, and hardware acceleration to improve the performance and aesthetics of your Activities and Views.

Advanced Canvas Drawing

You were introduced to the Canvas class in Chapter 4, where you learned how to create your own Views. The Canvas is also used in Chapter 13, "Maps, Geocoding, and Location-Based Services," to annotate Overlays for MapViews.

The concept of the canvas is a common metaphor used in graphics programming and generally consists of three basic drawing components:

➤ Canvas — Supplies the draw methods that paint drawing primitives onto the underlying bitmap.

➤ Paint — Also referred to as a "brush," Paint lets you specify how a primitive is drawn on the bitmap.

➤ Bitmap — The surface being drawn on.

Most of the advanced techniques described in this chapter involve variations and modifications to the Paint object that enable you to add depth and texture to otherwise flat raster drawings.

The Android drawing API supports translucency, gradient fills, rounded rectangles, and anti-aliasing.

Owing to resource limitations, Android does not support vector graphics; instead, it uses traditional raster-style repaints. The result of this raster approach is improved efficiency, but changing a Paint object does not affect primitives that have already been drawn; it affects only new elements.

> *For those of you with a Windows development background, the two-dimensional (2D) drawing capabilities of Android are roughly equivalent to those available in GDI+.*

What Can You Draw?

The Canvas class encapsulates the bitmap used as a surface for your artistic endeavors; it also exposes the draw* methods used to implement your designs.

Without going into detail about each draw method, the following list provides a taste of the primitives available:

➤ drawARGB/drawRGB/drawColor — Fills the canvas with a single color.

➤ drawArc — Draws an arc between two angles within an area bounded by a rectangle.

➤ drawBitmap — Draws a bitmap on the Canvas. You can alter the appearance of the target bitmap by specifying a target size or using a matrix to transform it.

➤ drawBitmapMesh — Draws a bitmap using a mesh that lets you manipulate the appearance of the target by moving points within it.

➤ drawCircle — Draws a circle of a specified radius centered on a given point.

➤ drawLine(s) — Draws a line (or series of lines) between two points.

➤ drawOval — Draws an oval bounded by the rectangle specified.

➤ drawPaint — Fills the entire Canvas with the specified Paint.

➤ drawPath — Draws the specified Path. A Path object is often used to hold a collection of drawing primitives within a single object.

➤ drawPicture — Draws a Picture object within the specified rectangle (not supported when using hardware acceleration.)

➤ drawPosText — Draws a text string specifying the offset of each character (not supported when using hardware acceleration).

➤ drawRect — Draws a rectangle.

➤ drawRoundRect — Draws a rectangle with rounded edges.

➤ drawText — Draws a text string on the Canvas. The text font, size, color, and rendering properties are set in the Paint object used to render the text.

➤ drawTextOnPath — Draws text that follows along a specified path (not supported when using hardware acceleration).

➤ drawVertices — Draws a series of tri-patches specified as a series of vertex points (not supported when using hardware acceleration).

Each drawing method lets you specify a Paint object to render it. In the following sections, you learn how to create and modify Paint objects to get the most out of your drawings.

Getting the Most from Your Paint

The Paint class represents a paintbrush and palette. It lets you choose how to render the primitives you draw onto the Canvas using the draw methods described in the previous section. By modifying the Paint object, you can control the color, style, font, and special effects used when drawing.

> *Not all the Paint options described here are available if you're using hardware acceleration to improve 2D drawing performance. As a result, it's important to check how hardware acceleration affects your 2D drawing.*

Most simply, `setColor` enables you to select the color of a Paint, whereas the style of a `Paint` object (controlled using `setStyle`) enables you to decide if you want to draw only the outline of a drawing object (`STROKE`), just the filled portion (`FILL`), or both (`STROKE_AND_FILL`).

Beyond these simple controls, the `Paint` class also supports transparency and can be modified with a variety of Shaders, filters, and effects to provide a rich palette of complex paints and brushes.

The Android SDK includes several excellent projects that demonstrate most of the features available in the `Paint` class. They are available in the graphics subfolder of the API demos at:

```
[sdk root folder]\samples\android-15\ApiDemos\src\com\example\android\apis\graphics
```

In the following sections, you learn what some of these features are and how to use them. These sections outline what can be achieved (such as gradients and edge embossing) without exhaustively listing all possible alternatives.

Using Translucency

All colors in Android include an opacity component (alpha channel). You define an alpha value for a color when you create it using the `argb` or `parseColor` methods:

```
// Make color red and 50% transparent
int opacity = 127;
int intColor = Color.argb(opacity, 255, 0, 0);
int parsedColor = Color.parseColor("#7FFF0000");
```

Alternatively, you can set the opacity of an existing `Paint` object using the `setAlpha` method:

```
// Make color 50% transparent
int opacity = 127;
myPaint.setAlpha(opacity);
```

Creating a paint color that's not 100 percent opaque means that any primitive drawn with it will be partially transparent — making whatever is drawn beneath it partially visible.

You can use transparency effects in any class or method that uses colors including Paint colors, Shaders, and Mask Filters.

Introducing Shaders

Extensions of the `Shader` class let you create Paints that fill drawn objects with more than a single solid color.

The most common use of Shaders is to define gradient fills; gradients are an excellent way to add depth and texture to 2D drawings. Android includes three gradient Shaders as well as a Bitmap Shader and a Compose Shader.

Trying to describe painting techniques seems inherently futile, so Figure 11-7 shows how each Shader works. Represented from left to right are `LinearGradient`, `RadialGradient`, and `SweepGradient`.

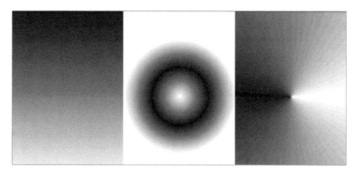

FIGURE 11-7

 Not included in the image in Figure 11-7 is the ComposeShader, *which lets you create a composite of multiple Shaders, nor the* BitmapShader, *which lets you create a brush based on a bitmap image.*

Creating Gradient Shaders

Gradient Shaders let you fill drawings with an interpolated color range. You can define the gradient in two ways. The first is a simple transition between two colors:

```
int colorFrom = Color.BLACK;
int colorTo = Color.WHITE;

LinearGradient myLinearGradient =
  new LinearGradient(x1, y1, x2, y2,
                     colorFrom, colorTo, TileMode.CLAMP);
```

The second alternative is to specify a more complex series of colors distributed at set proportions:

```
int[] gradientColors = new int[3];
gradientColors[0] = Color.GREEN;
gradientColors[1] = Color.YELLOW;
gradientColors[2] = Color.RED;

float[] gradientPositions = new float[3];
gradientPositions[0] = 0.0f;
gradientPositions[1] = 0.5f;
gradientPositions[2] = 1.0f;

RadialGradient radialGradientShader
  = new RadialGradient(centerX, centerY,
                       radius,
                       gradientColors,
                       gradientPositions,
                       TileMode.CLAMP);
```

Each gradient Shader (linear, radial, and sweep) lets you define the gradient fill using either of these techniques.

Applying Shaders to Paint

To use a Shader when drawing, apply it to a Paint using the `setShader` method:

```
shaderPaint.setShader(myLinearGradient);
```

Anything you draw with this Paint will be filled with the Shader you specified rather than the paint color.

Using Shader Tile Modes

The brush sizes of the gradient Shaders are defined using explicit bounding rectangles or center points and radius lengths; the Bitmap Shader implies a brush size through its bitmap size.

If the area defined by your Shader brush is smaller than the area being filled, the `TileMode` determines how the remaining area will be covered. You can define which tile mode to use with the following static constants:

➤ `CLAMP` — Uses the edge colors of the Shader to fill the extra space

➤ `MIRROR` — Flips the Shader image horizontally and vertically so that each image seams with the last

➤ `REPEAT` — Repeats the Shader image horizontally and vertically, but doesn't flip it

Using Mask Filters

The `MaskFilter` classes let you assign edge effects to your Paint. Mask Filters are not supported when the Canvas is hardware-accelerated.

Extensions to `MaskFilter` apply transformations to the alpha-channel of a Paint along its outer edge. Android includes the following Mask Filters:

➤ `BlurMaskFilter` — Specifies a blur style and radius to feather the edges of your Paint

➤ `EmbossMaskFilter` — Specifies the direction of the light source and ambient light level to add an embossing effect

To apply a Mask Filter, use the `setMaskFilter` method, passing in a `MaskFilter` object:

```
// Set the direction of the light source
float[] direction = new float[]{ 1, 1, 1 };
// Set the ambient light level
float light = 0.4f;
// Choose a level of specularity to apply
float specular = 6;
// Apply a level of blur to apply to the mask
float blur = 3.5f;
EmbossMaskFilter emboss = new EmbossMaskFilter(direction, light,
                                               specular, blur);
```

```
  // Apply the mask
  if (canvas.isHardwareAccelerated())
    myPaint.setMaskFilter(emboss);
```

The `FingerPaint` API demo included in the SDK is an excellent example of how to use `MaskFilters`. It demonstrates the effect of both the emboss and blur filters.

Using Color Filters

Whereas Mask Filters are transformations of a Paint's alpha-channel, a `ColorFilter` applies a transformation to each of the RGB channels. All `ColorFilter`-derived classes ignore the alpha-channel when performing their transformations.

Android includes three Color Filters:

➤ `ColorMatrixColorFilter` — Lets you specify a 4 x 5 `ColorMatrix` to apply to a Paint. Color Matrixes are commonly used to perform image processing programmatically and are useful because they support chaining transformations using matrix multiplication.

➤ `LightingColorFilter` — Multiplies the RGB channels by the first color before adding the second. The result of each transformation will be clamped between 0 and 255.

➤ `PorterDuffColorFilter` — Lets you use any one of the 16 Porter-Duff rules for digital image compositing to apply a specified color to the Paint. The Porter-Duff rules are defined here at `http://developer.android.com/reference/android/graphics/PorterDuff .Mode.html`.

Apply `ColorFilters` using the `setColorFilter` method:

```
  myPaint.setColorFilter(new LightingColorFilter(Color.BLUE, Color.RED));
```

An excellent example of using a Color Filter and Color Matrixes is in the `ColorMatrixSample` API example:

```
  samples\android-15\ApiDemos\src\com\example\android\apis\graphics\ColorMatrixSample.java
```

Using Path Effects

The effects described so far affect the way the Paint *fills* a drawing; Path Effects are used to control how its outline (or stroke) is drawn.

Path Effects are particularly useful for drawing Path primitives, but they can be applied to any Paint to affect the way the stroke is drawn.

Using Path Effects, you can change the appearance of a shape's corners and control the appearance of the outline. Android includes several Path Effects, including the following:

➤ `CornerPathEffect` — Lets you smooth sharp corners in the shape of a primitive by replacing them with rounded corners.

➤ `DashPathEffect` — Rather than drawing a solid outline, you can use the `DashPathEffect` to create an outline of broken lines (dashes/dots). You can specify any repeating pattern of solid/empty line segments.

➤ `DiscretePathEffect` — Similar to the `DashPathEffect`, but with added randomness. Specifies the length of each segment and a degree of deviation from the original path to use when drawing it.

➤ `PathDashPathEffect` — Enables you to define a new shape (path) to use as a stamp to outline the original path.

The following effects let you combine multiple Path Effects to a single Paint:

➤ `SumPathEffect` — Adds two effects to a path in sequence, such that each effect is applied to the original path and the two results are combined.

➤ `ComposePathEffect` — Applies first one effect and then applies the second effect to the result of the first.

Path Effects that modify the shape of the object being drawn change the area of the affected shape. This ensures that any fill effects applied to the same shape are drawn within the new bounds.

Path Effects are applied to `Paint` objects using the `setPathEffect` method:

```
borderPaint.setPathEffect(new CornerPathEffect(5));
```

The Path Effects API sample gives an excellent guide to how to apply each of these effects:

```
samples\android-15\ApiDemos\src\com\example\android\apis\graphics\PathEffects.java
```

Changing the Transfer Mode

Change a Paint's `Xfermode` to affect the way it paints new colors on top of what's already on the Canvas. Under normal circumstances, painting on top of an existing drawing layers the new shape on top. If the new Paint is fully opaque, it totally obscures the paint underneath; if it's partially transparent, it tints the colors underneath.

The following `Xfermode` subclasses let you change this behavior:

➤ `AvoidXfermode` — Specifies a color and tolerance to force your Paint to avoid drawing over (or only draw over) it.

➤ `PixelXorXfermode` — Applies a simple pixel XOR operation when covering existing colors.

➤ `PorterDuffXfermode` — This is a very powerful transfer mode with which you can use any of the 16 Porter-Duff rules for image composition to control how the paint interacts with the existing canvas image.

To apply transfer modes, use the `setXferMode` method:

```
AvoidXfermode avoid = new AvoidXfermode(Color.BLUE, 10,
                                        AvoidXfermode.Mode.AVOID);
borderPen.setXfermode(avoid);
```

Improving Paint Quality with Anti-Aliasing

When you create a new `Paint` object, you can pass in several flags that affect the way the Paint will be rendered. One of the most interesting is the `ANTI_ALIAS_FLAG`, which ensures that diagonal lines drawn with this paint are anti-aliased to give a smooth appearance (at the cost of performance).

Anti-aliasing is particularly important when drawing text, as anti-aliased text can be significantly easier to read. To create even smoother text effects, you can apply the SUBPIXEL_TEXT_FLAG, which applies subpixel anti-aliasing.

```
Paint paint = new Paint(Paint.ANTI_ALIAS_FLAG|Paint.SUBPIXEL_TEXT_FLAG);
```

You can also set both of these flags manually using the setSubpixelText and setAntiAlias methods:

```
myPaint.setSubpixelText(true);
myPaint.setAntiAlias(true);
```

Canvas Drawing Best Practice

2D owner-draw operations tend to be expensive in terms of processor use; inefficient drawing routines can block the GUI thread and have a detrimental effect on application responsiveness. This is particularly true for resource-constrained mobile devices.

In Chapter 4 you learned how to create your own Views by overriding the onDraw method of new View-derived classes. You need to be aware of the resource drain and CPU-cycle cost of your onDraw method to ensure you don't end up with an attractive application that's unresponsive, laggy, or "janky."

A lot of techniques exist to help minimize the resource drain associated with owner-drawn controls. Rather than focus on general principles, I'll describe some Android-specific considerations for ensuring that you can create activities that look good and remain interactive. (Note that list is not exhaustive.)

➤ **Consider size and orientation** — When you design your Views and Overlays, be sure to consider (and test!) how they look at different resolutions, pixel densities, and sizes.

➤ **Create static objects once** — Object creation and garbage collection are particularly expensive operations. Where possible, create drawing objects such as Paint objects, Paths, and Shaders once, rather than re-creating them each time the View is invalidated.

➤ **Remember that onDraw is expensive** — Performing the onDraw method is an expensive process that forces Android to perform several image composition and bitmap construction operations. Many of the following points suggest ways to modify the appearance of your Canvas without having to redraw it:

   ➤ **Use Canvas transforms** — Use Canvas transforms, such as rotate and translate, to simplify complex relational positioning of elements on your canvas. For example, rather than positioning and rotating each text element around a clock face, simply rotate the canvas 22.5 degrees, and draw the text in the same place.

   ➤ **Use Animations** — Consider using Animations to perform preset transformations of your View rather than manually redrawing it. Scale, rotation, and translation Animations can be performed on any View within an Activity and provide a resource-efficient way to provide zoom, rotate, or shake effects.

   ➤ **Consider using bitmaps, NinePatches, and Drawable resources** — If your Views feature static backgrounds, you should consider using a Drawable such as a bitmap, scalable NinePatch, or static XML Drawable rather than dynamically creating it.

➤ **Avoid overdrawing** — A combination of raster painting and layered Views can result in many layers being drawn on top of each other. Before drawing a layer or object, check to confirm if it will be completely obscured by a layer above it. It's good practice to avoid drawing more than 2.5 times the number of pixels on screen per frame. Transparent pixels still count — and are more expensive to draw than opaque colors.

Advanced Compass Face Example

In Chapter 4, you created a simple compass UI. In the following example, you make some significant changes to the Compass View's `onDraw` method to change it from a simple, flat compass to a dynamic artificial horizon, as shown in Figure 11-8. Because the image in Figure 11-8 is limited to black and white, you need to create the control to see the full effect.

1. Start by adding properties to store the pitch and roll values:

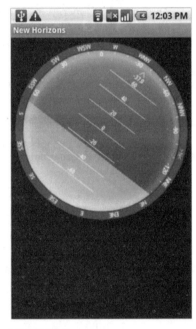

```
private float pitch;

public void setPitch(float _pitch) {
  pitch = _pitch;
  sendAccessibilityEvent(AccessibilityEvent.TYPE_
VIEW_TEXT_CHANGED);
}

public float getPitch() {
  return pitch;
}

private float roll;

public void setRoll(float _roll) {
  roll = _roll;
  sendAccessibilityEvent(AccessibilityEvent.TYPE_
VIEW_TEXT_CHANGED);
}

public float getRoll() {
  return roll;
}
```

FIGURE 11-8

2. Modify the `colors.xml` resource file to include color values for the border gradient, the glass compass shading, the sky, and the ground. Also update the colors used for the border and the face markings:

```
<?xml version="1.0" encoding="utf-8"?>
<resources>
  <color name="background_color">#F000</color>
  <color name="marker_color">#FFFF</color>
  <color name="text_color">#FFFF</color>


  <color name="shadow_color">#7AAA</color>
  <color name="outer_border">#FF444444</color>
```

```
    <color name="inner_border_one">#FF323232</color>
    <color name="inner_border_two">#FF414141</color>
    <color name="inner_border">#FFFFFFFF</color>
    <color name="horizon_sky_from">#FFA52A2A</color>
    <color name="horizon_sky_to">#FFFC125</color>
    <color name="horizon_ground_from">#FF5F9EA0</color>
    <color name="horizon_ground_to">#FF00008B</color>
</resources>
```

3.   The `Paint` and `Shader` objects used for the sky and ground in the artificial horizon are created based on the size of the current View, so they can't be static like the Paint objects you created in Chapter 4. Instead of creating `Paint` objects, update the `initCompassView` method in the `CompassView` class to construct the gradient arrays and colors they use. The existing method code can be left largely intact, with some changes to the `textPaint`, `circlePaint`, and `markerPaint` variables, as highlighted in the following code:

```
int[] borderGradientColors;
float[] borderGradientPositions;

int[] glassGradientColors;
float[] glassGradientPositions;

int skyHorizonColorFrom;
int skyHorizonColorTo;
int groundHorizonColorFrom;
int groundHorizonColorTo;

protected void initCompassView() {
  setFocusable(true);

  // Get external resources
  Resources r = this.getResources();

  circlePaint = new Paint(Paint.ANTI_ALIAS_FLAG);
  circlePaint.setColor(R.color.background_color);
  circlePaint.setStrokeWidth(1);
  circlePaint.setStyle(Paint.Style.STROKE);

  northString = r.getString(R.string.cardinal_north);
  eastString = r.getString(R.string.cardinal_east);
  southString = r.getString(R.string.cardinal_south);
  westString = r.getString(R.string.cardinal_west);

  textPaint = new Paint(Paint.ANTI_ALIAS_FLAG);
  textPaint.setColor(r.getColor(R.color.text_color));
  textPaint.setFakeBoldText(true);
  textPaint.setSubpixelText(true);
  textPaint.setTextAlign(Align.LEFT);

  textHeight = (int)textPaint.measureText("yY");

  markerPaint = new Paint(Paint.ANTI_ALIAS_FLAG);
  markerPaint.setColor(r.getColor(R.color.marker_color));
  markerPaint.setAlpha(200);
```

```
    markerPaint.setStrokeWidth(1);
    markerPaint.setStyle(Paint.Style.STROKE);
    markerPaint.setShadowLayer(2, 1, 1, r.getColor(R.color.shadow_color));
}
```

3.1 Still within the `initCompassView` method, create the color and position arrays that will be used by a radial Shader to paint the outer border:

```
protected void initCompassView() {
  [ ... Existing code ... ]

  borderGradientColors = new int[4];
  borderGradientPositions = new float[4];

  borderGradientColors[3] = r.getColor(R.color.outer_border);
  borderGradientColors[2] = r.getColor(R.color.inner_border_one);
  borderGradientColors[1] = r.getColor(R.color.inner_border_two);
  borderGradientColors[0] = r.getColor(R.color.inner_border);
  borderGradientPositions[3] = 0.0f;
  borderGradientPositions[2] = 1-0.03f;
  borderGradientPositions[1] = 1-0.06f;
  borderGradientPositions[0] = 1.0f;
}
```

3.2 Then create the radial gradient color and position arrays that will be used to create the semitransparent "glass dome" that sits on top of the View to give it the illusion of depth:

```
protected void initCompassView() {
  [ ... Existing code ... ]

  glassGradientColors = new int[5];
  glassGradientPositions = new float[5];

  int glassColor = 245;
  glassGradientColors[4] = Color.argb(65, glassColor,
                                      glassColor, glassColor);
  glassGradientColors[3] = Color.argb(100, glassColor,
                                      glassColor, glassColor);
  glassGradientColors[2] = Color.argb(50, glassColor,
                                      glassColor, glassColor);
  glassGradientColors[1] = Color.argb(0, glassColor,
                                      glassColor, glassColor);
  glassGradientColors[0] = Color.argb(0, glassColor,
                                      glassColor, glassColor);
  glassGradientPositions[4] = 1-0.0f;
  glassGradientPositions[3] = 1-0.06f;
  glassGradientPositions[2] = 1-0.10f;
  glassGradientPositions[1] = 1-0.20f;
  glassGradientPositions[0] = 1-1.0f;
}
```

3.3 Finally, get the colors you'll use to create the linear gradients that will represent the sky and the ground in the artificial horizon:

```
protected void initCompassView() {
  [ ... Existing code ... ]
```

```
skyHorizonColorFrom = r.getColor(R.color.horizon_sky_from);
skyHorizonColorTo = r.getColor(R.color.horizon_sky_to);

groundHorizonColorFrom = r.getColor(R.color.horizon_ground_from);
groundHorizonColorTo = r.getColor(R.color.horizon_ground_to);
}
```

4. Before you start drawing the face, create a new `enum` that stores each of the cardinal directions:

```
private enum CompassDirection { N, NNE, NE, ENE,
                                E, ESE, SE, SSE,
                                S, SSW, SW, WSW,
                                W, WNW, NW, NNW }
```

5. Now you need to completely replace the existing `onDraw` method. You start by figuring out some size-based values, including the center of the View, the radius of the circular control, and the rectangles that will enclose the outer (heading) and inner (tilt and roll) face elements. To start, replace the existing `onDraw` method:

```
@Override
protected void onDraw(Canvas canvas) {
```

6. Calculate the width of the outer (heading) ring based on the size of the font used to draw the heading values:

```
float ringWidth = textHeight + 4;
```

7. Calculate the height and width of the View, and use those values to establish the radius of the inner and outer face dials, as well as to create the bounding boxes for each face:

```
int height = getMeasuredHeight();
int width =getMeasuredWidth();

int px = width/2;
int py = height/2;
Point center = new Point(px, py);

int radius = Math.min(px, py)-2;

RectF boundingBox = new RectF(center.x - radius,
                              center.y - radius,
                              center.x + radius,
                              center.y + radius);

RectF innerBoundingBox = new RectF(center.x - radius + ringWidth,
                                   center.y - radius + ringWidth,
                                   center.x + radius - ringWidth,
                                   center.y + radius - ringWidth);

float innerRadius = innerBoundingBox.height()/2;
```

8. With the dimensions of the View established, it's time to start drawing the faces.

Start from the bottom layer at the outside, and work your way in and up, starting with the outer face (heading). Create a new `RadialGradient` Shader using the colors and positions you defined in step 3.2, and assign that Shader to a new Paint before using it to draw a circle:

```
RadialGradient borderGradient = new RadialGradient(px, py, radius,
borderGradientColors, borderGradientPositions, TileMode.CLAMP);

Paint pgb = new Paint();
pgb.setShader(borderGradient);

Path outerRingPath = new Path();
outerRingPath.addOval(boundingBox, Direction.CW);

canvas.drawPath(outerRingPath, pgb);
```

9. Now you need to draw the artificial horizon. You do this by dividing the circular face into two sections, one representing the sky and the other the ground. The proportion of each section depends on the current pitch.

Start by creating the `Shader` and `Paint` objects that will be used to draw the sky and earth:

```
LinearGradient skyShader = new LinearGradient(center.x,
    innerBoundingBox.top, center.x, innerBoundingBox.bottom,
    skyHorizonColorFrom, skyHorizonColorTo, TileMode.CLAMP);

Paint skyPaint = new Paint();
skyPaint.setShader(skyShader);

LinearGradient groundShader = new LinearGradient(center.x,
    innerBoundingBox.top, center.x, innerBoundingBox.bottom,
    groundHorizonColorFrom, groundHorizonColorTo, TileMode.CLAMP);

Paint groundPaint = new Paint();
groundPaint.setShader(groundShader);
```

10. Normalize the pitch and roll values to clamp them within ±90 degrees and ±180 degrees, respectively:

```
float tiltDegree = pitch;
while (tiltDegree > 90 || tiltDegree < -90)
{
  if (tiltDegree > 90) tiltDegree = -90 + (tiltDegree - 90);
    if (tiltDegree < -90) tiltDegree = 90 - (tiltDegree + 90);
}

float rollDegree = roll;
while (rollDegree > 180 || rollDegree < -180)
{
  if (rollDegree > 180) rollDegree = -180 + (rollDegree - 180);
   if (rollDegree < -180) rollDegree = 180 - (rollDegree + 180);
}
```

11. Create paths that will fill each segment of the circle (ground and sky). The proportion of each segment should be related to the clamped pitch:

```
Path skyPath = new Path();
skyPath.addArc(innerBoundingBox,
```

```
                                -tiltDegree,
                                (180 + (2 * tiltDegree))));
```

12. Spin the canvas around the center in the opposite direction to the current roll, and draw the sky and ground paths using the Paints you created in step 4:

```
canvas.save();
canvas.rotate(-rollDegree, px, py);
canvas.drawOval(innerBoundingBox, groundPaint);
canvas.drawPath(skyPath, skyPaint);
canvas.drawPath(skyPath, markerPaint);
```

13. Next is the face marking. Start by calculating the start and endpoints for the horizontal horizon markings:

```
int markWidth = radius / 3;
int startX = center.x - markWidth;
int endX = center.x + markWidth;
```

14. To make the horizon values easier to read, you should ensure that the pitch scale always starts at the current value. The following code calculates the position of the UI between the ground and sky on the horizon face:

```
double h = innerRadius*Math.cos(Math.toRadians(90-tiltDegree));
double justTiltY = center.y - h;
```

15. Find the number of pixels representing each degree of tilt:

```
float pxPerDegree = (innerBoundingBox.height()/2)/45f;
```

16. Iterate over 180 degrees, centered on the current tilt value, to give a sliding scale of possible pitch:

```
for (int i = 90; i >= -90; i -= 10) {
  double ypos = justTiltY + i*pxPerDegree;

  // Only display the scale within the inner face.
  if ((ypos < (innerBoundingBox.top + textHeight)) ||
      (ypos > innerBoundingBox.bottom - textHeight))
    continue;

  // Draw a line and the tilt angle for each scale increment.
  canvas.drawLine(startX, (float)ypos,
                  endX, (float)ypos,
                  markerPaint);
  int displayPos = (int)(tiltDegree - i);
  String displayString = String.valueOf(displayPos);
  float stringSizeWidth = textPaint.measureText(displayString);
  canvas.drawText(displayString,
                  (int)(center.x-stringSizeWidth/2),
                  (int)(ypos)+1,
                  textPaint);
}
```

17. Draw a thicker line at the earth/sky interface. Change the stroke thickness of the `marker-Paint` object before drawing the line (and then set it back to the previous value):

```
markerPaint.setStrokeWidth(2);
canvas.drawLine(center.x - radius / 2,
                (float)justTiltY,
                center.x + radius / 2,
                (float)justTiltY,
                markerPaint);
markerPaint.setStrokeWidth(1);
```

18. To make it easier to read the exact roll, you should draw an arrow and display a text string that shows the value.

Create a new `Path`, and use the `moveTo/lineTo` methods to construct an open arrow that points straight up. Draw the path and a text string that shows the current roll:

```
// Draw the arrow
Path rollArrow = new Path();
rollArrow.moveTo(center.x - 3, (int)innerBoundingBox.top + 14);
rollArrow.lineTo(center.x, (int)innerBoundingBox.top + 10);
rollArrow.moveTo(center.x + 3, innerBoundingBox.top + 14);
rollArrow.lineTo(center.x, innerBoundingBox.top + 10);
canvas.drawPath(rollArrow, markerPaint);
// Draw the string
String rollText = String.valueOf(rollDegree);
double rollTextWidth = textPaint.measureText(rollText);
canvas.drawText(rollText,
                (float)(center.x - rollTextWidth / 2),
                innerBoundingBox.top + textHeight + 2,
                textPaint);
```

19. Spin the canvas back to upright so that you can draw the rest of the face markings:

```
canvas.restore();
```

20. Draw the roll dial markings by rotating the canvas 10 degrees at a time, drawing a value every 30 degrees and otherwise draw a mark. When you've completed the face, restore the canvas to its upright position:

```
canvas.save();
canvas.rotate(180, center.x, center.y);
for (int i = -180; i < 180; i += 10)
{
  // Show a numeric value every 30 degrees
  if (i % 30 == 0) {
    String rollString = String.valueOf(i*-1);
    float rollStringWidth = textPaint.measureText(rollString);
    PointF rollStringCenter =
      new PointF(center.x-rollStringWidth/2,
                 innerBoundingBox.top+1+textHeight);
    canvas.drawText(rollString,
                    rollStringCenter.x, rollStringCenter.y,
                    textPaint);
  }
```

```
  // Otherwise draw a marker line
  else {
    canvas.drawLine(center.x, (int)innerBoundingBox.top,
                    center.x, (int)innerBoundingBox.top + 5,
                    markerPaint);
  }

  canvas.rotate(10, center.x, center.y);
}
canvas.restore();
```

21. The final step in creating the face is drawing the heading markers around the outside edge:

```
canvas.save();
canvas.rotate(-1*(bearing), px, py);

// Should this be a double?
double increment = 22.5;

for (double i = 0; i < 360; i += increment) {
  CompassDirection cd = CompassDirection.values()
                        [(int)(i / 22.5)];
  String headString = cd.toString();

  float headStringWidth = textPaint.measureText(headString);
  PointF headStringCenter =
    new PointF(center.x - headStringWidth / 2,
               boundingBox.top + 1 + textHeight);

  if (i % increment == 0)
    canvas.drawText(headString,
                    headStringCenter.x, headStringCenter.y,
                    textPaint);
  else
    canvas.drawLine(center.x, (int)boundingBox.top,
                    center.x, (int)boundingBox.top + 3,
                    markerPaint);

  canvas.rotate((int)increment, center.x, center.y);
}
canvas.restore();
```

22. With the face complete, you can add some finishing touches.

Start by adding a "glass dome" over the top to give the illusion of a watch face. Using the radial gradient array you constructed earlier, create a new `Shader` and `Paint` object. Use them to draw a circle over the inner face that makes it look like it's covered in glass:

```
RadialGradient glassShader =
  new RadialGradient(px, py, (int)innerRadius,
                     glassGradientColors,
                     glassGradientPositions,
                     TileMode.CLAMP);
Paint glassPaint = new Paint();
```

```
glassPaint.setShader(glassShader);

canvas.drawOval(innerBoundingBox, glassPaint);
```

23. All that's left is to draw two more circles as clean borders for the inner and outer face boundaries. Then restore the canvas to upright, and finish the onDraw method:

```
// Draw the outer ring
canvas.drawOval(boundingBox, circlePaint);

// Draw the inner ring
circlePaint.setStrokeWidth(2);
canvas.drawOval(innerBoundingBox, circlePaint);
}
```

If you run the parent activity, you will see an artificial horizon, as shown at the beginning of this
example in Figure 11-9.

> *All code snippets in this example are part of the* Chapter 11 Compass *project,*
> *available for download at* www.wrox.com.

Hardware Acceleration

Android 3.0 (API level 11) introduced a new rendering pipeline to allow applications to benefit from
hardware-accelerated 2D graphics.

The hardware-accelerated rendering pipeline supports most of the existing Canvas and Paint drawing options, with several exceptions, as described in the preceding sections. All the SDK Views, layouts, and effects support hardware acceleration, so in most cases it is safe to enable for your entire
application — the primary exception being Views that you create yourself.

> *For a complete list of the unsupported drawing operations see the Android*
> *Developer Guide:* http://developer.android.com/guide/topics/graphics/
> hardware-accel.html#unsupported.

Managing Hardware Acceleration Use in Your Applications

You can explicitly enable or disable hardware acceleration for your application by adding an
android:hardwareAccelerated attribute to the application node in your manifest:

```
<application android:hardwareAccelerated="true">
```

To enable or disable hardware acceleration for a specific Activity, use the same attribute on that
Activity's manifest node:

```
<activity android:name=".MyActivity"
          android:hardwareAccelerated="false" />
```

It's also possible to disable hardware acceleration for a particular View within an Activity. To do so, set the layer type of the view to render using software using the `setLayerType` method:

```
view.setLayerType(View.LAYER_TYPE_SOFTWARE, null);
```

Checking If Hardware Acceleration Is Enabled

Not all devices support hardware acceleration, and not all 2D graphics features are supported on a hardware-accelerated Canvas. As a result, you might choose to alter the UI presented by a View based on whether hardware acceleration is currently enabled.

You can confirm hardware acceleration is active by using the `isHardwareAccelerated` method on either a View object or its underlying Canvas. If you are checking for hardware acceleration within your `onDraw` code, it's best practice to use the `Canvas.isHardwareAccelerated` method:

```
@Override
public void onDraw(Canvas canvas) {
  if (canvas.isHardwareAccelerated()) {
    // TODO Hardware accelerated drawing routine.
  }
  else {
    // TODO Unaccelerated drawing routine.
  }
}
```

Introducing the Surface View

Under normal circumstances, all your application's Views are drawn on the same GUI thread. This main application thread is also used for all user interaction (such as button clicks or text entry).

In Chapter 9, "Working in the Background," you learned how to move blocking processes onto background threads. Unfortunately, you can't do this with the `onDraw` method of a View; modifying a GUI element from a background thread is explicitly disallowed.

When you need to update the View's UI rapidly, or the rendering code blocks the GUI thread for too long, the `SurfaceView` class is the answer. A Surface View wraps a `Surface` object rather than a `Canvas` object. This is important because Surfaces can be drawn on from background threads. This is particularly useful for resource-intensive operations, or where rapid updates or high frame rates are required, such as when using 3D graphics, creating games, or previewing the camera in real time.

The ability to draw independently of the GUI thread comes at the price of additional memory consumption, so although it's a useful — sometimes necessary — way to create custom Views, you should use Surface Views with caution.

When to Use a Surface View

You can use a Surface View in exactly the same way you use any `View`-derived class. You can apply animations and place them in layouts as you would any other View.

The `Surface` encapsulated by the Surface View supports drawing, using most of the standard Canvas methods described previously in this chapter, and also supports the full OpenGL ES library.

Surface Views are particularly useful for displaying dynamic 3D images, such as those featured in interactive games that provide immersive experiences. They're also the best choice for displaying real-time camera previews.

Creating Surface Views

To create a new Surface View, create a new class that extends `SurfaceView` and implements `SurfaceHolder.Callback`. The `SurfaceHolder` callback notifies the View when the underlying Surface is created, destroyed, or modified. It passes a reference to the `SurfaceHolder` object that contains a valid Surface. A typical Surface View design pattern includes a `Thread`-derived class that accepts a reference to the current `SurfaceHolder` and independently updates it.

Listing 11-8 shows a Surface View implementation for drawing using a Canvas. A new Thread-derived class is created within the Surface View control, and all UI updates are handled within this new class.

LISTING 11-8: Surface View skeleton implementation

```java
import android.content.Context;
import android.graphics.Canvas;
import android.view.SurfaceHolder;
import android.view.SurfaceView;

public class MySurfaceView extends SurfaceView implements
  SurfaceHolder.Callback {

  private SurfaceHolder holder;
  private MySurfaceViewThread mySurfaceViewThread;
  private boolean hasSurface;

  MySurfaceView(Context context) {
    super(context);
    init();
  }

  private void init() {
    // Create a new SurfaceHolder and assign this
    // class as its callback.
    holder = getHolder();
    holder.addCallback(this);
    hasSurface = false;
  }

  public void resume() {
    // Create and start the graphics update thread.
    if (mySurfaceViewThread == null) {
      mySurfaceViewThread = new MySurfaceViewThread();

      if (hasSurface == true)
        mySurfaceViewThread.start();
    }
  }
```

```java
public void pause() {
  // Kill the graphics update thread
  if (mySurfaceViewThread != null) {
    mySurfaceViewThread.requestExitAndWait();
    mySurfaceViewThread = null;
  }
}

public void surfaceCreated(SurfaceHolder holder) {
  hasSurface = true;
  if (mySurfaceViewThread != null)
    mySurfaceViewThread.start();
}

public void surfaceDestroyed(SurfaceHolder holder) {
  hasSurface = false;
  pause();
}


public void surfaceChanged(SurfaceHolder holder, int format,
                           int w, int h) {
  if (mySurfaceViewThread != null)
    mySurfaceViewThread.onWindowResize(w, h);
}

class MySurfaceViewThread extends Thread {
  private boolean done;

  MySurfaceViewThread() {
    super();
    done = false;
  }

  @Override
  public void run() {
    SurfaceHolder surfaceHolder = holder;

    // Repeat the drawing loop until the thread is stopped.
    while (!done) {
      // Lock the surface and return the canvas to draw onto.
      Canvas canvas = surfaceHolder.lockCanvas();
      // TODO: Draw on the canvas!
      // Unlock the canvas and render the current image.
      surfaceHolder.unlockCanvasAndPost(canvas);
    }
  }

  public void requestExitAndWait() {
    // Mark this thread as complete and combine into
    // the main application thread.
    done = true;
    try {
      join();
    } catch (InterruptedException ex) { }
```

```
      }

      public void onWindowResize(int w, int h) {
        // Deal with a change in the available surface size.
      }
    }
  }
```

---

code snippet PA4AD_Ch11_SurfaceView/src/MySurfaceView.java

Creating 3D Views with a Surface View

Android includes full support for the OpenGL ES 3D rendering framework, including support for hardware acceleration on devices that offer it. The `SurfaceView` provides a Surface onto which you can render your OpenGL scenes.

OpenGL is commonly used in desktop applications to provide dynamic 3D UIs and animations. Resource-constrained devices don't have the capacity for polygon handling that's available on desktop PCs and gaming devices that feature dedicated 3D graphics processors. Within your applications, consider the load your 3D Surface View will be placing on your processor, and attempt to keep the total number of polygons being displayed, and the rate at which they're updated, as low as possible.

> *Creating a Doom clone for Android is well out of the scope of this book, so I'll leave it to you to test the limits of what's possible in a mobile 3D UI. Check out the `GLSurfaceView` API demo example included in the SDK distribution to see an example of the OpenGL ES framework in action.*

Creating Interactive Controls

Anyone who has used a mobile phone is painfully aware of the challenges associated with designing intuitive UIs for mobile devices. Touch screens have been available on mobiles for many years, but it's only recently that touch-enabled UIs have been designed to be used by fingers rather than styluses. Full physical keyboards have also become common, with the compact size of the slide-out or flip-out keyboard introducing its own challenges.

As an open framework, Android is available on a wide variety of devices featuring many different permutations of input technologies, including touch screens, D-pads, trackballs, and keyboards.

The challenge for you as a developer is to create intuitive UIs that make the most of whatever input hardware is available, while introducing as few hardware dependencies as possible.

The techniques described in this section show how to listen for (and react to) user input from touch-screen taps, key presses, and trackball events using the following event handlers in Views and Activities:

➤ `onTouchEvent` — The touch-screen event handler, triggered when the touch screen is touched, released, or dragged

➤ `onKeyDown` — Called when any hardware key is pressed

➤ onKeyUp — Called when any hardware key is released

➤ onTrackballEvent — Triggered by movement on the trackball

Using the Touch Screen

Mobile touch screens have existed since the days of the Apple Newton and the Palm Pilot, although their usability has had mixed reviews. Modern mobile devices are now all about finger input — a design principle that assumes users will use their fingers rather than a specialized stylus to touch the screen and navigate your UI.

Finger-based touch makes interaction less precise and is often based more on movement than simple contact. Android's native applications make extensive use of finger-based, touch-screen UIs, including the use of dragging motions to scroll through lists, swipe between screens, or perform actions.

To create a View or Activity that uses touch-screen interaction, override the onTouchEvent handler:

```
@Override
public boolean onTouchEvent(MotionEvent event) {
  return super.onTouchEvent(event);
}
```

Return true if you have handled the screen press; otherwise, return false to pass events down through the View stack until the touch has been successfully handled.

Processing Single and Multiple Touch Events

For each gesture, the onTouchEvent handler is fired several times. Starting when the user touches the screen, multiple times while the system tracks the current finger position, and, finally, once more when the contact ends.

Android 2.0 (API level 5) introduced platform support for processing an arbitrary number of simultaneous touch events. Each touch event is allocated a separate pointer identifier that is referenced in the Motion Event parameter of the onTouchEvent handler.

> *Not all touch-screen hardware reports multiple simultaneous screen presses. In cases in which the hardware does not support multiple touches, the platform returns a single touch event.*

Call getAction on the MotionEvent parameter to find the event type that triggered the handler. For either a single touch device, or the first touch event on a multitouch device, you can use the ACTION_UP/DOWN/MOVE/CANCEL/OUTSIDE constants to find the event type:

```
@Override
public boolean onTouchEvent(MotionEvent event) {
  int action = event.getAction();
  switch (action) {
    case (MotionEvent.ACTION_DOWN):
      // Touch screen pressed
      return true;
```

```
      case (MotionEvent.ACTION_MOVE):
        // Contact has moved across screen
        return true;
      case (MotionEvent.ACTION_UP):
        // Touch screen touch ended
        return true;
      case (MotionEvent.ACTION_CANCEL):
        // Touch event cancelled
        return true;
      case (MotionEvent.ACTION_OUTSIDE):
        // Movement has occurred outside the
        // bounds of the current screen element
        return true;
      default: return super.onTouchEvent(event);
    }
  }
```

To track touch events from multiple pointers, you need to apply the `MotionEvent.ACTION_MASK` and `MotionEvent.ACTION_POINTER_ID_MASK` constants to find the touch event (either `ACTION_POINTER_DOWN` or `ACTION_POINTER_UP`) and the pointer ID that triggered it, respectively. Call `getPointerCount` to find if this is a multiple-touch event.

```
@Override
public boolean onTouchEvent(MotionEvent event) {
  int action = event.getAction();

  if (event.getPointerCount() > 1) {
    int actionPointerId = action & MotionEvent.ACTION_POINTER_ID_MASK;
    int actionEvent = action & MotionEvent.ACTION_MASK;
    // Do something with the pointer ID and event.
  }
  return super.onTouchEvent(event);
}
```

The Motion Event also includes the coordinates of the current screen contact. You can access these coordinates using the `getX` and `getY` methods. These methods return the coordinate relative to the responding View or Activity.

In the case of multiple-touch events, each Motion Event includes the current position of each pointer. To find the position of a given pointer, pass its index into the `getX` or `getY` methods. Note that its index is *not* equivalent to the pointer ID. To find the index for a given pointer, use the `findPointerIndex` method, passing in the pointer ID whose index you need:

```
int xPos = -1;
int yPos = -1;

if (event.getPointerCount() > 1) {
  int actionPointerId = action & MotionEvent.ACTION_POINTER_ID_MASK;
  int actionEvent = action & MotionEvent.ACTION_MASK;

  int pointerIndex = event.findPointerIndex(actionPointerId);
  xPos = (int)event.getX(pointerIndex);
  yPos = (int)event.getY(pointerIndex);
}
```

```
else {
  // Single touch event.
  xPos = (int)event.getX();
  yPos = (int)event.getY();
}
```

The Motion Event parameter also includes the pressure being applied to the screen using get Pressure, a method that returns a value usually between 0 (no pressure) and 1 (normal pressure).

> *Depending on the calibration of the hardware, it may be possible to return values greater than 1.*

Finally, you can also determine the normalized size of the current contact area by using the getSize method. This method returns a value between 0 and 1, where 0 suggests a precise measurement and 1 indicates a possible "fat touch" event in which the user may not have intended to press anything.

Tracking Movement

Whenever the current touch contact position, pressure, or size changes, a new onTouchEvent is triggered with an ACTION_MOVE action.

The Motion Event parameter can include historical values, in addition to the fields described previously. This history represents all the movement events that have occurred between the previously handled onTouchEvent and this one, allowing Android to buffer rapid movement changes to provide fine-grained capture of movement data.

You can find the size of the history by calling getHistorySize, which returns the number of movement positions available for the current event. You can then obtain the times, pressures, sizes, and positions of each of the historical events by using a series of getHistorical* methods and passing in the position index. Note that as with the getX and getY methods described earlier, you can pass in a pointer index value to track historical touch events for multiple cursors.

```
int historySize = event.getHistorySize();
long time = event.getHistoricalEventTime(i);

if (event.getPointerCount() > 1) {
  int actionPointerId = action & MotionEvent.ACTION_POINTER_ID_MASK;
  int pointerIndex = event.findPointerIndex(actionPointerId);
  for (int i = 0; i < historySize; i++) {
    float pressure = event.getHistoricalPressure(pointerIndex, i);
    float x = event.getHistoricalX(pointerIndex, i);
    float y = event.getHistoricalY(pointerIndex, i);
    float size = event.getHistoricalSize(pointerIndex, i);
    // TODO: Do something with each point
  }
}
else {
  for (int i = 0; i < historySize; i++) {
    float pressure = event.getHistoricalPressure(i);
```

```
      float x = event.getHistoricalX(i);
      float y = event.getHistoricalY(i);
      float size = event.getHistoricalSize(i);
      // TODO: Do something with each point
    }
  }
```

The normal pattern for handling movement events is to process each of the historical events first, followed by the current Motion Event values, as shown in Listing 11-9.

LISTING 11-9: Handling touch screen movement events

```
@Override
public boolean onTouchEvent(MotionEvent event) {

  int action = event.getAction();

  switch (action) {
    case (MotionEvent.ACTION_MOVE):
    {
      int historySize = event.getHistorySize();
      for (int i = 0; i < historySize; i++) {
        float x = event.getHistoricalX(i);
        float y = event.getHistoricalY(i);
        processMovement(x, y);
      }

      float x = event.getX();
      float y = event.getY();
      processMovement(x, y);

      return true;
    }
  }

  return super.onTouchEvent(event);
}

private void processMovement(float _x, float _y) {
  // Todo: Do something on movement.
}
```

code snippet PA4AD_Ch11_Touch/src/MyView.java

Using an On Touch Listener

You can listen for touch events without subclassing an existing View by attaching an OnTouchListener to any View object, using the setOnTouchListener method:

```
myView.setOnTouchListener(new OnTouchListener() {
  public boolean onTouch(View _view, MotionEvent _event) {
```

```
      // TODO Respond to motion events
      return false;
    }
  });
```

Using the Device Keys, Buttons, and D-Pad

Button and key-press events for all hardware keys are handled by the `onKeyDown` and `onKeyUp` handlers of the active Activity or the focused View. This includes keyboard keys, the D-pad, and the volume, back, dial, and hang-up buttons. The only exception is the *home* key, which is reserved to ensure that users can never get locked within an application.

To have your View or Activity react to button presses, override the `onKeyUp` and `onKeyDown` event handlers:

```
@Override
public boolean onKeyDown(int _keyCode, KeyEvent _event) {
  // Perform on key pressed handling, return true if handled
  return false;
}

@Override
public boolean onKeyUp(int _keyCode, KeyEvent _event) {
  // Perform on key released handling, return true if handled
  return false;
}
```

The `keyCode` parameter contains the value of the key being pressed; compare it to the static key code values available from the `KeyEvent` class to perform key-specific processing.

The `KeyEvent` parameter also includes the `isAltPressed`, `isShiftPressed`, and `isSymPressed` methods to determine if the alt, shift, or symbols keys are also being held. Android 3.0 (API level 11) introduced the `isCtrlPressed` and `isFunctionPressed` methods to determine if the control or function keys are pressed. The static `isModifierKey` method accepts the `keyCode` and determines whether this key event was triggered by the user pressing one of these modifier keys.

Using the On Key Listener

To respond to key presses within existing Views in your Activities, implement an `OnKeyListener`, and assign it to a View using the `setOnKeyListener` method. Rather than implementing a separate method for key-press and key-release events, the `OnKeyListener` uses a single `onKey` event.

```
myView.setOnKeyListener(new OnKeyListener() {
  public boolean onKey(View v, int keyCode, KeyEvent event) {
    // TODO Process key press event, return true if handled
    return false;
  }
});
```

Use the `keyCode` parameter to find the key pressed. The `KeyEvent` parameter is used to determine if the key has been pressed or released, where `ACTION_DOWN` represents a key press and `ACTION_UP` signals its release.

Using the Trackball

Many mobile devices offer a trackball as a useful alternative (or addition) to the touch screen and D-pad. Trackball events are handled by overriding the `onTrackballEvent` method in your View or Activity.

Like touch events, trackball movement is included in a `MotionEvent` parameter. In this case, the `MotionEvent` contains the relative movement of the trackball since the last trackball event, normalized so that 1 represents the equivalent movement caused by the user pressing the D-pad key.

You can find the vertical change by using the `getY` method, and find the horizontal scrolling through the `getX` method:

```
@Override
public boolean onTrackballEvent(MotionEvent _event) {
  float vertical = _event.getY();
  float horizontal = _event.getX();
  // TODO Process trackball movement.
  return false;
}
```

ADVANCED DRAWABLE RESOURCES

Earlier in this chapter you examined a number of scalable Drawable resources, including shapes, gradients, and colors. This section introduces a number of additional XML-defined Drawables.

Composite Drawables

Use composite Drawables to combine and manipulate other Drawable resources. You can use any Drawable resource within the following composite resource definitions, including bitmaps, shapes, and colors. Similarly, you can use these new Drawables within each other and assign them to Views in the same way as all other Drawable assets.

Transformative Drawables

You can scale and rotate existing Drawable resources using the aptly named `ScaleDrawable` and `RotateDrawable` classes. These transformative Drawables are particularly useful for creating progress bars or animating Views.

➤ **ScaleDrawable** — Within the `scale` tag, use the `scaleHeight` and `scaleWidth` attributes to define the target height and width relative to the bounding box of the original Drawable, respectively. Use the `scaleGravity` attribute to control the anchor point for the scaled image.

```
<?xml version="1.0" encoding="utf-8"?>
<scale xmlns:android="http://schemas.android.com/apk/res/android"
  android:drawable="@drawable/icon"
```

```
    android:scaleHeight="100%"
    android:scaleWidth="100%"
    android:scaleGravity="center_vertical|center_horizontal"
/>
```

➤ **RotateDrawable** — Within the `rotate` tag, use `fromDegrees` and `toDegrees` to define the start and end rotation angle around a pivot point, respectively. Define the pivot using the `pivotX` and `pivotY` attributes, specifying a percentage of the Drawable's width and height, respectively, using nn% notation.

```
<?xml version="1.0" encoding="utf-8"?>
<rotate xmlns:android="http://schemas.android.com/apk/res/android"
    android:drawable="@drawable/icon"
    android:fromDegrees="0"
    android:toDegrees="90"
    android:pivotX="50%"
    android:pivotY="50%"
/>
```

To apply the scaling and rotation at run time, use the `setImageLevel` method on the View object hosting the Drawable to move between the start and finish values on a scale of 0 to 10,000. This allows you to define a single Drawable that can be modified to suit particular circumstances — such as an arrow that can point in multiple directions.

When moving through levels, level 0 represents the start angle (or smallest scale result). Level 10,000 represents the end of the transformation (the finish angle or highest scale). If you do not specify the image level, it will default to 0.

```
ImageView rotatingImage
    = (ImageView)findViewById(R.id.RotatingImageView);
ImageView scalingImage
    = (ImageView)findViewById(R.id.ScalingImageView);

// Rotate the image 50% of the way to its final orientation.
rotatingImage.setImageLevel(5000);

// Scale the image to 50% of its final size.
scalingImage.setImageLevel(5000);
```

Layer Drawables

A `LayerDrawable` lets you composite several Drawable resources on top of one another. If you define an array of partially transparent Drawables, you can stack them on top of one another to create complex combinations of dynamic shapes and transformations.

Similarly, you can use Layer Drawables as the source for the transformative Drawable resources described in the preceding section, or the State List and Level List Drawables that follow.

Layer Drawables are defined via the `layer-list` node tag. Within that tag, create a new `item` sub-node using the `drawable` attribute to specify each Drawables to add. Each Drawable will be stacked in index order, with the first item in the array at the bottom of the stack.

```xml
<?xml version="1.0" encoding="utf-8"?>
<layer-list xmlns:android="http://schemas.android.com/apk/res/android">
  <item android:drawable="@drawable/bottomimage"/>
  <item android:drawable="@drawable/image2"/>
  <item android:drawable="@drawable/image3"/>
  <item android:drawable="@drawable/topimage"/>
</layer-list>
```

State List Drawables

A State List Drawable is a composite resource that enables you to specify a different Drawable to display based on the state of the View to which it has been assigned.

Most native Android Views use State List Drawables, including the image used on Buttons and the background used for standard List View items.

To define a State List Drawable, create an XML file containing a root `selector` tag. Add a series of item subnodes, each of which uses an `android:state_*` attribute and `android:drawable` attribute to assign a specific Drawable to a particular state:

```xml
<selector xmlns:android="http://schemas.android.com/apk/res/android">
<item android:state_pressed="true"
      android:drawable="@drawable/widget_bg_pressed"/>
  <item android:state_focused="true"
      android:drawable="@drawable/widget_bg_selected"/>
  <item android:state_window_focused="false"
      android:drawable="@drawable/widget_bg_normal"/>
  <item android:drawable="@drawable/widget_bg_normal"/>
</selector>
```

Each state attribute can be set to `true` or `false`, allowing you to specify a different Drawable for each combination of the following list View states:

- `android:state_pressed` — Pressed or not pressed.

- `android:state_focused` — Has focus or does not have focus.

- `android:state_hovered` — Introduced in API level 11, the cursor is hovering over the view or is not hovering.

- `android:state_selected` — Selected or not selected.

- `android:state_checkable` — Can or can't be checked.

- `android:state_checked` — Is or isn't checked.

- `android:state_enabled` — Enabled or disabled.

- `android:state_activated` — Activated or not activated.

- `android:state_window_focused` — The parent window has focus or does not have focus.

When deciding which Drawable to display for a given View, Android will apply the first item in the state list that matches the current state of the object. As a result, your default value should be the last in the list.

Level List Drawables

Using a Level List Drawable you can create an array of Drawable resources, assigning an integer index value for each layer. Use the `level-list` node to create a new Level List Drawable, using `item` subnodes to define each layer, with `android:drawable` / `android:maxLevel` attributes defining the Drawable for each layer and its corresponding index.

```
<level-list xmlns:android="http://schemas.android.com/apk/res/android">
  <item android:maxLevel="0"  android:drawable="@drawable/earthquake_0"/>
  <item android:maxLevel="1"  android:drawable="@drawable/earthquake_1"/>
  <item android:maxLevel="2"  android:drawable="@drawable/earthquake_2"/>
  <item android:maxLevel="4"  android:drawable="@drawable/earthquake_4"/>
  <item android:maxLevel="6"  android:drawable="@drawable/earthquake_6"/>
  <item android:maxLevel="8"  android:drawable="@drawable/earthquake_8"/>
  <item android:maxLevel="10" android:drawable="@drawable/earthquake_10"/>
</level-list>
```

To select which image to display in code, call `setImageLevel` on the View displaying the Level List Drawable resource, passing in the index of the Drawable you want to display:

```
imageView.setImageLevel(5);
```

The View will display the image corresponding to the index with an equal or greater value to the one specified.

COPY, PASTE, AND THE CLIPBOARD

Android 3.0 (API level 11) introduced support for full copy and paste operations within (and between) Android applications using the Clipboard Manager:

```
ClipboardManager clipboard = (ClipboardManager)getSystemService(CLIPBOARD_SERVICE);
```

The clipboard supports text strings, URIs (typically directed at a Content Provider item), and Intents (for copying application shortcuts). To copy an object to the clipboard, create a new `ClipData` object that contains a `ClipDescription` that describes the meta data related to the copied object, and any number of `ClipData.Item` objects, as described in the following section. Add it to the clipboard using the `setPrimaryClip` method:

```
clipboard.setPrimaryClip(newClip);
```

The clipboard can contain only one Clip Data object at any time. Copying a new object replaces the previously held clipboard item. As a result, you can assume neither that your application will be the last to have copied something to the clipboard nor that it will be the only application that pastes it.

Copying Data to the Clipboard

The `ClipData` class includes a number of static convenience methods to simplify the creation of typical Clip Data object. Use the `newPlainText` method to create a new Clip Data that includes the specified string, sets the description to the label provided, and sets the MIME type to `MIMETYPE_TEXT_PLAIN`:

```
ClipData newClip = ClipData.newPlainText("copied text","Hello, Android!");
```

For Content Provider-based items, use the `newUri` method, specifying a Content Resolver, label, and URI from which the data is to be pasted:

```
ClipData newClip = ClipData.newUri(getContentResolver(),"URI", myUri);
```

Pasting Clipboard Data

To provide a good user experience, you should enable and disable the paste option from your UI based on whether there is data copied to the clipboard. You can do this by querying the clipboard service using the `hasPrimaryClip` method:

```
if (!(clipboard.hasPrimaryClip())) {
  // TODO Disable paste UI option.
```

It's also possible to query the data type of the Clip Data object currently in the clipboard. Use the `getPrimaryClipDescription` method to extract the metadata for the clipboard data, using its `hasMimeType` method to specify the MIME type you support pasting into your application:

```
if (!(clipboard.getPrimaryClipDescription().hasMimeType(MIMETYPE_TEXT_PLAIN)))
{
  // TODO Disable the paste UI option if the content in
  // the clipboard is not of a supported type.
}
else {
  // TODO Enable the paste UI option if the clipboard contains data
  // of a supported type.
}
```

To access the data itself, use the `getItemAt` method, passing in the index of the item you want to retrieve:

```
ClipData.Item item = clipboard.getPrimaryClip().getItemAt(0);
```

You can extract the text, URI, or Intent using the `getText`, `getUri`, and `getIntent` methods, respectively:

```
CharSequence pasteData = item.getText();
Intent pastIntent = item.getIntent();
Uri pasteUri = item.getUri();
```

It's also possible to paste the content of any clipboard item, even if your application supports only text. Using the `coerceToText` method you can transform the contents of a `ClipData.Item` object into a string.

```
CharSequence pasteText = item.coerceToText(this);
```

Hardware Sensors

Modern Android devices are much more than simple communications or web browsing platforms. They are now extra-sensory devices that use hardware sensors, including accelerometers, gyroscopes, and barometers, to provide a platform to extend your perceptions.

Sensors that detect physical and environmental properties offer an exciting avenue for innovations that enhance the user experience of mobile applications. The incorporation of an increasingly rich array of sensor hardware in modern devices provides new possibilities for user interaction and application development, including augmented reality, movement-based input, and environmental customizations.

In this chapter you'll be introduced to the sensors currently available in Android and how to use the Sensor Manager to monitor them.

You'll take a closer look at the accelerometer, orientation, and gyroscopic sensors, and use them to determine changes in the device orientation and acceleration, regardless of the natural orientation of the host device. This is particularly useful for creating motion-based user interfaces (UIs).

You'll also explore the environmental sensors, including how to use the barometer to detect the current altitude, the light Sensor to determine the level of cloud cover, and the temperature Sensor to measure the ambient temperature.

Finally, you'll learn about the virtual and composite Sensors, which amalgamate the output of several hardware sensors to provide smoother and more accurate results.

USING SENSORS AND THE SENSOR MANAGER

The Sensor Manager is used to manage the sensor hardware available on Android devices. Use `getSystemService` to return a reference to the Sensor Manager Service, as shown in the following snippet:

```
String service_name = Context.SENSOR_SERVICE;
SensorManager sensorManager = (SensorManager)getSystemService(service_name);
```

Rather than interacting with the sensor hardware directly, they are represented by `Sensor` objects that describe the properties of the hardware sensor they represent, including its type, name, manufacturer, and details on its accuracy and range.

The Sensor class includes a set of constants that describe which type of hardware sensor is being represented by a particular Sensor object. These constants take the form of `Sensor.TYPE_<TYPE>`. The following section describes each supported sensor type, after which you'll learn how to find and use these sensors.

Supported Android Sensors

The following sections describe each sensor type currently available. Note that the hardware available on the host device determines which of these sensors will be available to your application.

➤ `Sensor.TYPE_AMBIENT_TEMPERATURE` — Introduced in Android 4.0 (API level 14) to replace the ambiguous — and deprecated — `Sensor.TYPE_TEMPERATURE`. This is a thermometer that returns the temperature in degrees Celsius; the temperature returned will be the ambient room temperature.

➤ `Sensor.TYPE_ACCELEROMETER` — A three-axis accelerometer that returns the current acceleration along three axes in m/s^2 (meters per second, per second.) The accelerometer is explored in greater detail later in this chapter.

➤ `Sensor.TYPE_GRAVITY` — A three-axis gravity sensor that returns the current direction and magnitude of gravity along three axes in m/s^2. The gravity sensor typically is implemented as a virtual sensor by applying a low-pass filter to the accelerometer sensor results.

➤ `Sensor.TYPE_LINEAR_ACCELERATION` — A three-axis linear acceleration Sensor that returns the acceleration, not including gravity, along three axes in m/s^2. Like the gravity sensor, the linear acceleration typically is implemented as a virtual sensor using the accelerometer output. In this case, to obtain the linear acceleration, a high-pass filter is applied to the accelerometer output.

➤ `Sensor.TYPE_GYROSCOPE` — A three-axis gyroscope that returns the rate of device rotation along three axes in radians/second. You can integrate the rate of rotation over time to determine the current orientation of the device; however, it generally is better practice to use this in combination with other sensors (typically the accelerometers) to provide asmoothed and corrected orientation. You'll learn more about the gyroscope Sensor later in this chapter.

➤ `Sensor.TYPE_ROTATION_VECTOR` — Returns the orientation of the device as a combination of an angle around an axis. It typically is used as an input to the `getRotationMatrixFromVector` method from the Sensor Manager to convert the returned rotation vector into a rotation matrix. The rotation vector Sensor typically is implemented as a virtual sensor that can combine and correct the results obtained from multiple sensors, such as the accelerometers and gyroscopes, to provide a smoother rotation matrix.

➤ `Sensor.TYPE_MAGNETIC_FIELD` — A magnetometer that finds the current magnetic field in microteslas (µT) along three axes.

➤ `Sensor.TYPE_PRESSURE` — An atmospheric pressure sensor, or barometer, that returns the current atmospheric pressure in millibars (mbars) as a single value. The pressure Sensor can be used to determine altitude using the `getAltitude` method on the Sensor Manager to compare the atmospheric pressure in two locations. Barometers can also be used in weather forecasting by measuring changes in atmospheric pressure in the same location.

➤ `Sensor.TYPE_RELATIVE_HUMIDITY` — A relative humidity sensor that returns the current relative humidity as a percentage. This Sensor was introduced in Android 4.0 (API level 14).

➤ `Sensor.TYPE_PROXIMITY` — A proximity sensor that indicates the distance between the device and the target object in centimeters. How a target object is selected, and the distances supported, will depend on the hardware implementation of the proximity detector. Some proximity sensors can return only "near" or "far" results, in which case the latter will be represented as the Sensor's maximum range, and the former using any lower value. Typical uses for the proximity sensor are to detect when the device is being held up against the user's ear, to automatically adjust screen brightness, or to initiate a voice command.

➤ `Sensor.TYPE_LIGHT` — An ambient light sensor that returns a single value describing the ambient illumination in lux. A light sensor commonly is used to control the screen brightness dynamically.

Introducing Virtual Sensors

Android Sensors typically work independently of each other, each reporting the results obtained from a particular piece of hardware without applying any filtering or smoothing. In some cases it can be helpful to use virtual Sensors that present simplified, corrected, or composite sensor data in a way that makes them easier to use within some applications.

The gravity, linear-acceleration, and rotation-vector Sensors described previously are examples of virtual Sensors provided by the framework. They may use a combination of accelerometers, magnetic-field sensors, and gyroscopes, rather than the output of a specific piece of hardware.

In some cases the underlying hardware will also provide virtual sensors. In such cases both the framework and hardware virtual Sensors are offered, with the default sensor being the best available.

Corrected gyroscope and orientation Sensors are also available as virtual sensors that attempt to improve the quality and performance of their respective hardware sensors. This involves using filters and the output of multiple Sensors to smooth, correct, or filter the raw output.

To ensure predictability and consistency across platforms and devices, the Sensor Manager always offers you the hardware Sensors by default. It's good practice to experiment with all the available Sensors of a given type to determine the best alternative for your particular application.

Finding Sensors

In addition to including virtual sensors, any Android device potentially could include several hardware implementations of a particular sensor type.

To find every Sensor available on the host platform, use `getSensorList` on the Sensor Manager, passing in `Sensor.TYPE_ALL`:

```
List<Sensor> allSensors = sensorManager.getSensorList(Sensor.TYPE_ALL);
```

To find a list of all the available Sensors of a particular type, use `getSensorList`, specifying the type of Sensor you require, as shown in the following code that returns all the available gyroscopes:

```
List<Sensor> gyroscopes = sensorManager.getSensorList(Sensor.TYPE_GYROSCOPE);
```

If there are multiple Sensor implementations for a given sensor type, you can decide which of the returned Sensors to use by querying each returned Sensor object. Each Sensor reports its name, power use, minimum delay latency, maximum range, resolution, and vendor type. By convention, any hardware Sensor implementations are returned at the top of the list, with virtual corrected implementations last.

You can find the default Sensor implementation for a given type by using the Sensor Manager's `getDefaultSensor` method. If no default Sensor exists for the specified type, the method returns null.

The following snippet returns the default pressure sensor:

```
Sensor defaultBarometer = sensorManager.getDefaultSensor(Sensor.TYPE_PRESSURE);
```

The following code snippet shows how to select a light sensor with the highest maximum range and lowest power requirement, and the corrected gyroscope, if it's available:

```
List<Sensor> lightSensors
  = sensorManager.getSensorList(Sensor.TYPE_LIGHT);
List<Sensor> gyroscopes
  = sensorManager.getSensorList(Sensor.TYPE_GYROSCOPE);

Sensor bestLightSensor
  = sensorManager.getDefaultSensor(Sensor.TYPE_LIGHT);
Sensor correctedGyro
  = sensorManager.getDefaultSensor(Sensor.TYPE_GYROSCOPE);

if (bestLightSensor != null)
  for (Sensor lightSensor : lightSensors) {
```

```
        float range = lightSensor.getMaximumRange();
        float power = lightSensor.getPower();

        if (range >= bestLightSensor.getMaximumRange())
          if (power < bestLightSensor.getPower() ||
             range > bestLightSensor.getMaximumRange())
            bestLightSensor = lightSensor;
  }

if (gyroscopes != null && gyroscopes.size() > 1)
  correctedGyro = gyroscopes.get(gyroscopes.size()-1);
```

Where the sensor type describes a physical hardware sensor, such as a gyroscope, the unfiltered hardware Sensor will be returned as the default in preference to any virtual implementations. In many cases the smoothing, filtering, and corrections applied to the virtual Sensor will provide better results for your applications.

It's also worth noting that some Android devices may also have multiple independent hardware sensors.

The default Sensor will always provide a Sensor implementation consistent with the typical use-case and, in most cases, will be the best alternative for your application. However, it can be useful to experiment with the available Sensors or to provide users with the ability to select which sensor to use in order to utilize the most appropriate implementation for their needs.

Monitoring Sensors

To monitor a Sensor, implement a SensorEventListener, using the onSensorChanged method to monitor Sensor values, and onAccuracyChanged to react to changes in a Sensor's accuracy.

Listing 12-1 shows the skeleton code for implementing a Sensor Event Listener.

LISTING 12-1: Sensor Event Listener skeleton code

```
final SensorEventListener mySensorEventListener = new SensorEventListener() {
  public void onSensorChanged(SensorEvent sensorEvent) {
    // TODO Monitor Sensor changes.
  }

  public void onAccuracyChanged(Sensor sensor, int accuracy) {
    // TODO React to a change in Sensor accuracy.
  }
};
```

code snippet PA4AD_Ch12_Sensors/src/MyActivity.java

The `SensorEvent` parameter in the `onSensorChanged` method includes the following four properties to describe each Sensor Event:

➤   `sensor` — The Sensor object that triggered the event.

➤   `accuracy` — The accuracy of the Sensor when the event occurred (low, medium, high, or unreliable, as described in the next list).

➤   `values` — A float array that contains the new value(s) observed. The next section explains the values returned for each sensor type.

➤   `timestamp` — The time (in nanoseconds) at which the Sensor Event occurred.

You can monitor changes in the accuracy of a Sensor separately, using the `onAccuracyChanged` method.

In both handlers the `accuracy` value represents the Sensor's accuracy, using one of the following constants:

➤   `SensorManager.SENSOR_STATUS_ACCURACY_LOW` — Indicates that the Sensor is reporting with low accuracy and needs to be calibrated

➤   `SensorManager.SENSOR_STATUS_ACCURACY_MEDIUM` — Indicates that the Sensor data is of average accuracy and that calibration might improve the accuracy of the reported results

➤   `SensorManager.SENSOR_STATUS_ACCURACY_HIGH` — Indicates that the Sensor is reporting with the highest possible accuracy

➤   `SensorManager.SENSOR_STATUS_UNRELIABLE` — Indicates that the Sensor data is unreliable, meaning that either calibration is required or readings are not currently possible

To listen for Sensor Events, register your Sensor Event Listener with the Sensor Manager. Specify the Sensor to observe, and the rate at which you want to receive updates.

> *Remember that not all Sensors will be available on every device, so be sure to check for the availability of any Sensors you use, and make sure your applications fail gracefully if they are missing. Where a Sensor is required for your application to function, you can specify it as a required feature in the application's manifest, as described in Chapter 3, "Creating Applications and Activities."*

Listing 12-2 registers a Sensor Event Listener for the default proximity Sensor at the default update rate.

LISTING 12-2: Registering a Sensor Event Listener

```
Sensor sensor = sensorManager.getDefaultSensor(Sensor.TYPE_PROXIMITY);
sensorManager.registerListener(mySensorEventListener,
                        sensor,
                        SensorManager.SENSOR_DELAY_NORMAL);
```

code snippet PA4AD_Ch12_Sensors/src/MyActivity.java

The Sensor Manager includes the following static constants (shown in descending order of responsiveness) to let you specify a suitable update rate:

➤ `SENSOR_DELAY_FASTEST` — Specifies the fastest possible update rate

➤ `SENSOR_DELAY_GAME` — Specifies an update rate suitable for use in controlling games

➤ `SENSOR_DELAY_NORMAL` — Specifies the default update rate

➤ `SENSOR_DELAY_UI` — Specifies a rate suitable for updating UI features

The rate you select is not binding; the Sensor Manager may return results faster or slower than you specify, though it will tend to be faster. To minimize the associated resource cost of using the Sensor in your application, it is best practice to select the slowest acceptable rate.

It's also important to unregister your Sensor Event Listeners when your application no longer needs to receive updates:

```
sensorManager.unregisterListener(mySensorEventListener);
```

It's good practice to register and unregister your Sensor Event Listener in the `onResume` and `onPause` methods of your Activities to ensure they're being used only when the Activity is active.

Interpreting Sensor Values

The length and composition of the values returned in the `onSensorChanged` handler vary, depending on the Sensor being monitored. The details are summarized in Table 12-1. Further details on the use of the accelerometer, orientation, magnetic field, gyroscopic, and environmental Sensors can be found in the following sections.

> The Android documentation describes the values returned by each sensor type with some additional commentary at `http://developer.android.com/reference/android/hardware/SensorEvent.html`.

TABLE 12-1: Sensor Return Values

SENSOR TYPE	VALUE COUNT	VALUE COMPOSITION	COMMENTARY
TYPE_ ACCELEROMETER	3	value[0] : X-axis (Lateral) value[1] : Y-axis (Longitudinal) value[2] : Z-axis (Vertical)	Acceleration along three axes in m/s^2. The Sensor Manager includes a set of gravity constants of the form `SensorManager.GRAVITY_*`.

continues

TABLE 12-1 *(continued)*

SENSOR TYPE	VALUE COUNT	VALUE COMPOSITION	COMMENTARY
TYPE_GRAVITY	3	value[0] : X-axis (Lateral) value[1] : Y-axis (Longitudinal) value[2] : Z-axis (Vertical)	Force of gravity along three axes in m/s². The Sensor Manager includes a set of gravity constants of the form `SensorManager.GRAVITY_*`.
TYPE_HUMIDITY	1	value[0]: Relative humidity	Relative humidity as a percentage (%).
TYPE_LINEAR_ ACCELERATION	3	value[0] : X-axis (Lateral) value[1] : Y-axis (Longitudinal) value[2] : Z-axis (Vertical)	Linear acceleration along three axes in m/s² without the force of gravity.
TYPE_GYROSCOPE	3	value[0] : X-axis value[1] : Y-axis value[2] : Z-axis	Rate of rotation around three axes in radians/second (r/s).
TYPE_ROTATION_ VECTOR	3 (+1 optional)	values[0]: $x*\sin(\theta/2)$ values[1]: $y*\sin(\theta/2)$ values[2]: $z*\sin(\theta/2)$ values[3]: $\cos(\theta/2)$ (optional)	Device orientation described as an angle of rotation around an axis (°).
TYPE_MAGNETIC_ FIELD	3	value[0] : X-axis (Lateral) value[1] : Y-axis (Longitudinal) value[2] : Z-axis (Vertical)	Ambient magnetic field measured in microteslas (µT).
TYPE_LIGHT	1	value[0] : Illumination	Ambient light measured in lux (lx). The Sensor Manager includes a set of constants representing different standard illuminations of the form `SensorManager.LIGHT_*`.

SENSOR TYPE	VALUE COUNT	VALUE COMPOSITION	COMMENTARY
TYPE_PRESSURE	1	value[0] : Atmospheric Pressure	Atmospheric pressure measured in millibars (mbars).
TYPE_PROXIMITY	1	value[0] : Distance	Distance from target measured in centimeters (cm).
TYPE_AMBIENT_ TEMPERATURE	1	value[0] : Temperature	Ambient temperature measured in degrees Celsius (°C).

MONITORING A DEVICE'S MOVEMENT AND ORIENTATION

Accelerometers, compasses, and (more recently) gyroscopes offer the ability to provide functionality based on device direction, orientation, and movement. You can use these Sensors to offer new and innovative input mechanisms, in addition to (or as an alternative to) traditional touch screen, trackball, and keyboard input.

The availability of specific Sensors depends on the hardware platform on which your application runs. A 70" flat screen weighs more than 150 pounds, making it difficult to lift and awkward to maneuver. As a result Android-powered TVs are unlikely to include orientation or movement sensors — so it's good practice to offer users alternatives in case their devices don't support such Sensors.

Where they are available, movement and orientation sensors can be used by your application to:

➤ Determine the device orientation

➤ React to changes in orientation

➤ React to movement or acceleration

➤ Understand which direction the user is facing

➤ Monitor gestures based on movement, rotation, or acceleration

This opens some intriguing possibilities for your applications. By monitoring orientation, direction, and movement, you can:

➤ Use the compass and accelerometers to determine your heading and orientation. Use these with a map, camera, and location-based service to create augmented-reality UIs that overlay location-based data over a real-time camera feed.

➤ Create UIs that adjust dynamically as the orientation of the device changes. In the most simple case, Android alters the screen orientation when the device is rotated from portrait to landscape or vice versa, but applications such as the native Gallery use orientation changes to provide a 3D effect on stacks of photos.

➤ Monitor for rapid acceleration to detect if a device has been dropped or thrown.

➤ Measure movement or vibration. For example, you could create an application that lets a user lock his or her device; if any movement is detected while it's locked, it could send an alert SMS that includes the current location.

➤ Create UI controls that use physical gestures and movement as input.

Determining the Natural Orientation of a Device

Before calculating the device's orientation, you must first understand its "at rest" (natural) orientation. The natural orientation of a device is the orientation in which the orientation is 0 on all three axes. The natural orientation can be either portrait or landscape, but it typically is identifiable by the placement of branding and hardware buttons.

For a typical smartphone, the natural orientation is with the device lying on its back on a desk, with the top of the device pointing due north.

More creatively, you can imagine yourself perched on top of a jet fuselage during level flight. An Android device has been strapped to the fuselage in front of you. In its natural orientation the screen is pointing up into space, the top of the device pointing towards the nose of the plane, and the plane is heading due north, as shown in Figure 12-1.

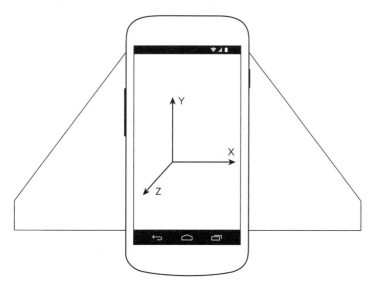

FIGURE 12-1

> *Before you head out to an airfield, note that this example is contrived to provide a useful metaphor for understanding the standard reference frame. The electronic compass and accelerometers included in most Android devices make them unsuitable for determining the heading, pitch, and roll of an aircraft in flight.*

Android can reorient the display for use in any orientation; however, the Sensor axes described in Table 12-1 do not change as the device rotates. As a result, the display orientation and device orientation can be different.

Sensor values are always returned relative to the natural orientation of the device, whereas your application is likely to want the current orientation relative to the display orientation. As a result, if your application uses device orientation or linear acceleration as an input, it may be necessary to adjust your Sensor inputs based on the display orientation relative to the natural orientation. This is particularly important because the natural orientation of most early Android phones was portrait; however, with the range of Android devices having expanded to also include tablets and televisions, many Android devices (including smartphones) are naturally oriented when the display is in landscape.

To ensure that you are interpreting the orientation correctly, you need to determine the current display orientation relative to the natural orientation, rather than relying on the current display mode being either portrait or landscape.

You can find the current screen rotation using the `getRotation` method on the default Display object, as shown in Listing 12-3.

LISTING 12-3: Finding the screen orientation relative to the natural orientation

```java
String windowSrvc = Context.WINDOW_SERVICE;
WindowManager wm = ((WindowManager) getSystemService(windowSrvc));
Display display = wm.getDefaultDisplay();
int rotation = display.getRotation();
switch (rotation) {
  case (Surface.ROTATION_0) : break; // Natural
  case (Surface.ROTATION_90) : break; // On its left side
  case (Surface.ROTATION_180) : break; // Upside down
  case (Surface.ROTATION_270) : break; // On its right side
  default: break;
}
```

code snippet PA4AD_Ch12_Sensors/src/MyActivity.java

Introducing Accelerometers

Acceleration is defined as the rate of change of velocity; that means accelerometers measure how quickly the speed of the device is changing in a given direction. Using an accelerometer you can detect movement and, more usefully, the rate of change of the speed of that movement (also known as *linear acceleration*).

> *Accelerometers are also known as gravity sensors because they measure acceleration caused both by movement and by gravity. As a result, an accelerometer detecting acceleration on an axis perpendicular to the earth's surface will read $-9.8m/s^2$ when it's at rest. (This value is available as the* `SensorManager.STANDARD_GRAVITY` *constant.)*

Generally, you'll be interested in acceleration changes relative to a rest state, or rapid movement (signified by rapid changes in acceleration), such as gestures used for user input. In the former case you'll often need to calibrate the device to calculate the initial acceleration to take those effects into account for future results.

> *It's important to note that accelerometers do not measure velocity, so you can't measure speed directly based on a single accelerometer reading. Instead, you need to integrate the acceleration over time to find the velocity. You can then integrate the velocity over time to determine the distance traveled.*

Because accelerometers can also measure gravity, you can use them in combination with the magnetic field sensors to calculate the device orientation. You will learn more about how to find the orientation of the device later in this section.

Detecting Acceleration Changes

Acceleration can be measured along three directional axes:

➤ Left-right (lateral)

➤ Forward-backward (longitudinal)

➤ Up-down (vertical)

The Sensor Manager reports accelerometer sensor changes along all three axes.

The sensor values passed in via the `values` property of the Sensor Event Listener's Sensor Event parameter represent lateral, longitudinal, and vertical acceleration, in that order.

Figure 12-2 illustrates the mapping of the three directional acceleration axes in relation to the device at rest in its natural orientation. Note that for the remainder of this section, I will refer to the movement of the device in relation to its natural orientation, which may be either landscape or portrait.

➤ **x-axis (lateral)** — Sideways (left or right) acceleration, for which positive values represent movement toward the right, and negative values indicate movement to the left.

➤ **y-axis (longitudinal)** — Forward or backward acceleration, for which forward acceleration, such as the device being pushed in the direction of the top of the device, is represented by a positive value and acceleration backwards represented by negative values.

➤ **z-axis (vertical)** — Upward or downward acceleration, for which positive represents upward movement, such as the device being lifted. While at rest at the device's natural orientation, the vertical accelerometer will register $-9.8m/s2$ as a result of gravity.

As described earlier, you can monitor changes in acceleration using a Sensor Event Listener. Register an implementation of `SensorEventListener` with the Sensor Manager, using a Sensor object of type `Sensor.TYPE_ACCELEROMETER` to request accelerometer updates. Listing 12-4 registers the default accelerometer using the default update rate.

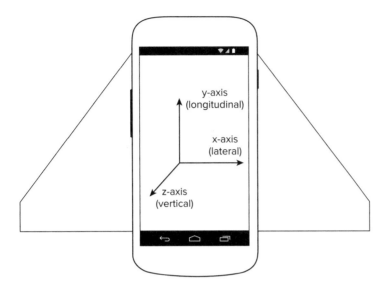

FIGURE 12-2

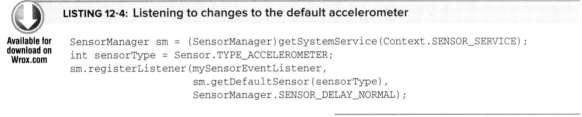

LISTING 12-4: Listening to changes to the default accelerometer

```
SensorManager sm = (SensorManager)getSystemService(Context.SENSOR_SERVICE);
int sensorType = Sensor.TYPE_ACCELEROMETER;
sm.registerListener(mySensorEventListener,
                    sm.getDefaultSensor(sensorType),
                    SensorManager.SENSOR_DELAY_NORMAL);
```

code snippet PA4AD_Ch12_Sensors/src/MyActivity.java

Your Sensor Listener should implement the `onSensorChanged` method, which will be fired when acceleration in any direction is measured.

The `onSensorChanged` method receives a `SensorEvent` that includes a `float` array containing the acceleration measured along all three axes. When a device is held in its natural orientation, the first element represents lateral acceleration; the second element represents longitudinal acceleration; and the final element represents vertical acceleration, as shown in the following extension to Listing 12-4:

```
final SensorEventListener mySensorEventListener = new SensorEventListener() {
  public void onSensorChanged(SensorEvent sensorEvent) {
    if (sensorEvent.sensor.getType() == Sensor.TYPE_ACCELEROMETER) {
      float xAxis_lateralA = sensorEvent.values[0];
      float yAxis_longitudinalA = sensorEvent.values[1];
      float zAxis_verticalA = sensorEvent.values[2];
      // TODO apply the acceleration changes to your application.
    }
  }

  public void onAccuracyChanged(Sensor sensor, int accuracy) {}
};
```

Creating a Gravitational Force Meter

You can create a simple tool to measure gravitational force (g-force) by summing the acceleration in all three directions. In the following example you'll create a simple device to measure g-force using the accelerometers to determine the current force being exerted on the device.

The acceleration force exerted on the device at rest is 9.8 m/s^2 toward the center of the Earth. In this example you'll negate the force of gravity by accounting for it using the `SensorManager.STANDARD_GRAVITY` constant. If you plan to use this application on another planet, you can use an alternative gravity constant, as appropriate.

1. Start by creating a new GForceMeter project that includes a `ForceMeter` Activity. Modify the `main.xml` layout resource to display two centered lines of large, bold text that will be used to display the current g-force and maximum observed g-force:

```xml
<?xml version="1.0" encoding="utf-8"?>
<LinearLayout xmlns:android="http://schemas.android.com/apk/res/android"
  android:orientation="vertical"
  android:layout_width="match_parent"
  android:layout_height="match_parent">
  <TextView android:id="@+id/acceleration"
    android:gravity="center"
    android:layout_width="match_parent"
    android:layout_height="wrap_content"
    android:textStyle="bold"
    android:textSize="32sp"
    android:text="Current Acceleration"
    android:editable="false"
    android:singleLine="true"
    android:layout_margin="10dp"/>
  />
  <TextView android:id="@+id/maxAcceleration"
    android:gravity="center"
    android:layout_width="match_parent"
    android:layout_height="wrap_content"
    android:textStyle="bold"
    android:textSize="40sp"
    android:text="Maximum Acceleration"
    android:editable="false"
    android:singleLine="true"
    android:layout_margin="10dp"/>
  />
</LinearLayout>
```

2. Within the `ForceMeter` Activity, create instance variables to store references to both `TextView` instances and the `SensorManager`. Also create variables to record the current and maximum detected acceleration values:

```java
private SensorManager sensorManager;
private TextView accelerationTextView;
private TextView maxAccelerationTextView;
private float currentAcceleration = 0;
private float maxAcceleration = 0;
```

3. Add a calibration constant that represents the acceleration due to gravity:

```
private final double calibration = SensorManager.STANDARD_GRAVITY;
```

4. Create a new `SensorEventListener` implementation that sums the acceleration detected along each axis and negates the acceleration due to gravity. It should update the current (and possibly maximum) acceleration whenever a change in acceleration is detected:

```
private final SensorEventListener sensorEventListener = new SensorEventListener() {

  public void onAccuracyChanged(Sensor sensor, int accuracy) { }

  public void onSensorChanged(SensorEvent event) {
    double x = event.values[0];
    double y = event.values[1];
    double z = event.values[2];

    double a = Math.round(Math.sqrt(Math.pow(x, 2) +
                                    Math.pow(y, 2) +
                                    Math.pow(z, 2)));
    currentAcceleration = Math.abs((float)(a-calibration));

    if (currentAcceleration > maxAcceleration)
      maxAcceleration = currentAcceleration;
  }
};
```

5. Update the `onCreate` method to get a reference to the two Text Views and the Sensor Manager:

```
@Override
public void onCreate(Bundle savedInstanceState) {
  super.onCreate(savedInstanceState);
  setContentView(R.layout.main);

  accelerationTextView = (TextView)findViewById(R.id.acceleration);
  maxAccelerationTextView = (TextView)findViewById(R.id.maxAcceleration);
  sensorManager = (SensorManager)getSystemService(Context.SENSOR_SERVICE);
}
```

6. Override the `onResume` handler to register your new Listener for accelerometer updates using the `SensorManager`:

```
@Override
protected void onResume() {
  super.onResume();
  Sensor accelerometer = sensorManager.getDefaultSensor(Sensor.TYPE_ACCELEROMETER);
  sensorManager.registerListener(sensorEventListener,
                                 accelerometer,
                                 SensorManager.SENSOR_DELAY_FASTEST);
}
```

7. Also override the corresponding `onPause` method to unregister the sensor listener when the Activity is no longer active:

```
@Override
protected void onPause() {
  sensorManager.unregisterListener(sensorEventListener);
  super.onPause();
}
```

8. The accelerometers can update hundreds of times a second, so updating the Text Views for every change in acceleration would quickly flood the UI event queue. Instead, create a new `updateGUI` method that synchronizes with the GUI thread and updates the Text Views:

```
private void updateGUI() {
  runOnUiThread(new Runnable() {
    public void run() {
      String currentG = currentAcceleration/SensorManager.STANDARD_GRAVITY
                        + "Gs";
      accelerationTextView.setText(currentG);
      accelerationTextView.invalidate();
      String maxG = maxAcceleration/SensorManager.STANDARD_GRAVITY + "Gs";
      maxAccelerationTextView.setText(maxG);
      maxAccelerationTextView.invalidate();
    }
  });
};
```

This will be executed regularly using a Timer introduced in the next step.

9. Update the `onCreate` method to create a timer that triggers the UI update method defined in step 8 every 100 milliseconds:

```
@Override
public void onCreate(Bundle savedInstanceState) {
  super.onCreate(savedInstanceState);
  setContentView(R.layout.main);

  accelerationTextView = (TextView)findViewById(R.id.acceleration);
  maxAccelerationTextView = (TextView)findViewById(R.id.maxAcceleration);
  sensorManager = (SensorManager)getSystemService(Context.SENSOR_SERVICE);

  Sensor accelerometer =
    sensorManager.getDefaultSensor(Sensor.TYPE_ACCELEROMETER);
  sensorManager.registerListener(sensorEventListener,
                                 accelerometer,
                                 SensorManager.SENSOR_DELAY_FASTEST);

  Timer updateTimer = new Timer("gForceUpdate");
  updateTimer.scheduleAtFixedRate(new TimerTask() {
    public void run() {
      updateGUI();
    }
  }, 0, 100);
}
```

10. Finally, because this application is functional only when the host device features an accelerometer sensor, modify the manifest to include a uses-feature node specifying the requirement for accelerometer hardware:

```
<uses-feature android:name="android.hardware.sensor.accelerometer" />
```

> 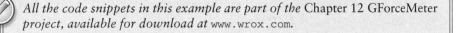 *All the code snippets in this example are part of the* Chapter 12 GForceMeter *project, available for download at* www.wrox.com.

When finished, you'll want to test this out. Ideally, you can do this in an F16 while Maverick performs high-g maneuvers over the Atlantic. That's been known to end badly, so, failing that, you can experiment with spinning around in circles while holding your phone at arms length. Remember to grip your phone tightly.

Determining a Device's Orientation

Calculating a device's orientation typically is done using the combined output of both the magnetic field Sensors (which function as an electronic compass) and the accelerometers (which are used to determine the pitch and roll).

If you've done a bit of trigonometry, you've got the skills required to calculate the device orientation based on the accelerometer and magnetometer results along all three axes. If you enjoyed trig as much as I did, you'll be happy to learn that Android does these calculations for you.

It is best practice to derive the orientation using the accelerometers and magnetic field Sensors directly, as this enables you to modify the reference frame used for orientation calculations relative to the natural orientation and current display orientation.

For legacy reasons, Android also provides an orientation sensor type that provides the rotation along all three axes directly. This approach has been deprecated, but both techniques are described in the following sections.

Understanding the Standard Reference Frame

Using the standard reference frame, the device orientation is reported along three dimensions, as illustrated in Figure 12-3. As when using the accelerometers, the standard reference frame is described relative to the device's natural orientation, as described earlier in this chapter.

Continuing the airplane analogy used early, imagining yourself perched on top of a jet fuselage during level flight, the z-axis comes out of the screen towards space; the y-axis comes out of the top of the device towards the nose of the plane; and the x-axis heads out towards the starboard wing. Relative to that, pitch, roll, and azimuth can be described as follows:

➤ **Pitch** — The angle of the device around the x-axis. During level flight, the pitch will be 0; as the nose angles upwards, the pitch increases. It will hit 90 when the jet is pointed straight up. Conversely, as you angle the nose downwards past level, the pitch will decrease until it reaches –90 as you hurtle towards imminent death. If the plane flips onto it's back the pitch will +/-180.

➤ **Roll** — The device's sideways rotation between –90 and 90 degrees around the y-axis. During level flight the roll is zero. As you execute a barrel roll towards the starboard side, the roll will increase, reaching 90 when the wings are perpendicular to the ground. As you continue, you will reach 180 when the plane is upside down. Rolling from level towards port will decrease the roll in the same way.

➤ **Azimuth** — Also heading or yaw, the azimuth is the direction the device is facing around the z-axis, where 0/360 degrees is magnetic north, 90 east, 180 south, and 270 west. Changes in the plane's heading will be reflected in changes in the azimuth value.

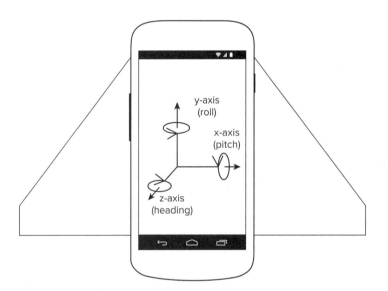

FIGURE 12-3

Calculating Orientation Using the Accelerometer and Magnetic Field Sensors

The best way to determine the current device orientation is to calculate it using the accelerometer and magnetometer results directly. In addition to providing more accurate results, this technique lets you change the orientation reference frame to remap the x-, y-, and z-axes to suit the device orientation you expect during use.

Because you're using both the accelerometer and magnetometer, you need to create and register a Sensor Event Listener to monitor each of them. Within the `onSensorChanged` methods for each Sensor Event Listener, record the `values` array property received in two separate field variables, as shown in Listing 12-5.

LISTING 12-5: Monitoring the accelerometer and magnetometer

```java
private float[] accelerometerValues;
private float[] magneticFieldValues;

final SensorEventListener myAccelerometerListener = new SensorEventListener() {
  public void onSensorChanged(SensorEvent sensorEvent) {
    if (sensorEvent.sensor.getType() == Sensor.TYPE_ACCELEROMETER)
      accelerometerValues = sensorEvent.values;
  }

  public void onAccuracyChanged(Sensor sensor, int accuracy) {}
};

final SensorEventListener myMagneticFieldListener = new SensorEventListener() {
  public void onSensorChanged(SensorEvent sensorEvent) {
    if (sensorEvent.sensor.getType() == Sensor.TYPE_MAGNETIC_FIELD)
      magneticFieldValues = sensorEvent.values;
  }

  public void onAccuracyChanged(Sensor sensor, int accuracy) {}
};
```

code snippet PA4AD_Ch12_Sensors/src/MyActivity.java

Register both Sensors with the Sensor Manager, as shown in the following code extension to Listing 12-5; this snippet uses the default hardware and UI update rate for both Sensors:

```java
SensorManager sm = (SensorManager)getSystemService(Context.SENSOR_SERVICE);
Sensor aSensor = sm.getDefaultSensor(Sensor.TYPE_ACCELEROMETER);
Sensor mfSensor = sm.getDefaultSensor(Sensor.TYPE_MAGNETIC_FIELD);

sm.registerListener(myAccelerometerListener,
                    aSensor,
                    SensorManager.SENSOR_DELAY_UI);

sm.registerListener(myMagneticFieldListener,
                    mfSensor,
                    SensorManager.SENSOR_DELAY_UI);
```

To calculate the current orientation from these Sensor values, use the `getRotationMatrix` and `getOrientation` methods from the Sensor Manager, as shown in Listing 12-6.

LISTING 12-6: Finding the current orientation using the accelerometer and magnetometer

```java
float[] values = new float[3];
float[] R = new float[9];
SensorManager.getRotationMatrix(R, null,
                                accelerometerValues,
```

continues

LISTING 12-6 *(continued)*

```
                                    magneticFieldValues);
        SensorManager.getOrientation(R, values);

        // Convert from radians to degrees if preferred.
        values[0] = (float) Math.toDegrees(values[0]); // Azimuth
        values[1] = (float) Math.toDegrees(values[1]); // Pitch
        values[2] = (float) Math.toDegrees(values[2]); // Roll
```

code snippet PA4AD_Ch12_Sensors/src/MyActivity.java

Note that `getOrientation` returns its results in radians, not degrees. The order of the returned values is also different from the axes used by the accelerometer and magnetometer Sensors. Each result is in radians, with positive values representing anticlockwise rotation around the axis:

➤ `values[0]` — The azimuth, or rotation around the z-axis, is zero when the device is heading magnetic north.

➤ `values[1]` — The pitch, or rotation around the x-axis.

➤ `values[2]` — The roll, or rotation around the y-axis.

Remapping the Orientation Reference Frame

To measure the device orientation using a reference frame other than the natural orientation, use the `remapCoordinateSystem` method from the Sensor Manager. This typically is done to simplify the calculations required to create applications that can be used on devices whose natural orientation is portrait, as well as those that are landscape.

The `remapCoordinateSystem` method accepts four parameters:

➤ The initial rotation matrix, found using `getRotationMatrix`, as described earlier

➤ A variable used to store the output (transformed) rotation matrix

➤ The remapped x-axis

➤ The remapped y-axis

The Sensor Manager provides a set of constants that let you specify the remapped x- and y-axes relative to the reference frame: `AXIS_X`, `AXIS_Y`, `AXIS_Z`, `AXIS_MINUS_X`, `AXIS_MINUS_Y`, and `AXIS_MINUS_Z`.

Listing 12-7 shows how to remap the reference frame so that the current *display* orientation (either portrait or landscape) is used as the reference frame for calculating the current *device* orientation. This is useful for games or applications that are locked to either landscape or portrait mode, as the device will report either 0 or 90 degrees based on the natural orientation of the device. By modifying the reference frame, you can ensure that the orientation values you use already take into account the orientation of the display relative to the natural orientation.

LISTING 12-7: Remapping the orientation reference frame based on the natural orientation of the device

```
// Determine the current orientation relative to the natural orientation
String windoSrvc = Context.WINDOW_SERVICE;
WindowManager wm = ((WindowManager) getSystemService(windoSrvc));
Display display = wm.getDefaultDisplay();
int rotation = display.getRotation();

int x_axis = SensorManager.AXIS_X;
int y_axis = SensorManager.AXIS_Y;

switch (rotation) {
  case (Surface.ROTATION_0): break;
  case (Surface.ROTATION_90):
    x_axis = SensorManager.AXIS_Y;
    y_axis = SensorManager.AXIS_MINUS_X;
    break;
  case (Surface.ROTATION_180):
    y_axis = SensorManager.AXIS_MINUS_Y;
    break;
  case (Surface.ROTATION_270):
    x_axis = SensorManager.AXIS_MINUS_Y;
    y_axis = SensorManager.AXIS_X;
    break;
  default: break;
}

SensorManager.remapCoordinateSystem(inR, x_axis, y_axis, outR);

// Obtain the new, remapped, orientation values.
SensorManager.getOrientation(outR, values);
```

code snippet PA4AD_Ch12_MyActivity.java

Determining Orientation Using the Deprecated Orientation Sensor

The Android framework also offers a virtual orientation Sensor.

> *The virtual orientation Sensor is available for legacy reasons, having been deprecated in favor of the technique described in the previous section. It was deprecated because it does not allow you to alter the reference frame used when calculating the current orientation.*

To use the legacy orientation sensor, create and register a Sensor Event Listener, specifying the default orientation Sensor, as shown in Listing 12-8.

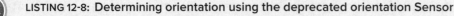

LISTING 12-8: Determining orientation using the deprecated orientation Sensor

```
SensorManager sm = (SensorManager)getSystemService(Context.SENSOR_SERVICE);
int sensorType = Sensor.TYPE_ORIENTATION;
sm.registerListener(myOrientationListener,
                    sm.getDefaultSensor(sensorType),
                    SensorManager.SENSOR_DELAY_NORMAL);
```

code snippet PA4AD_Ch12_MyActivity.java

When the device orientation changes, the `onSensorChanged` method in your `SensorEventListener` implementation is fired. The `SensorEvent` parameter includes a `values` float array that provides the device's orientation along three axes. The following extension to Listing 12-8 shows how to construct your Sensor Event Listener:

```
final SensorEventListener myOrientationListener = new SensorEventListener() {
  public void onSensorChanged(SensorEvent sensorEvent) {
    if (sensorEvent.sensor.getType() == Sensor.TYPE_ORIENTATION) {
      float headingAngle = sensorEvent.values[0];
      float pitchAngle =   sensorEvent.values[1];
      float rollAngle =    sensorEvent.values[2];
      // TODO Apply the orientation changes to your application.
    }
  }

  public void onAccuracyChanged(Sensor sensor, int accuracy) {}
};
```

The first element of the values array is the azimuth (heading), the second pitch, and the third roll.

Creating a Compass and Artificial Horizon

In Chapter 11, "Advanced User Experience," you improved the `CompassView` to display the device pitch, roll, and heading. In this example, you'll finally connect your Compass View to the hardware sensors to display the device orientation.

1. Open the Compass project you last changed in Chapter 11 and open the `CompassActivity`. Use the Sensor Manager to listen for orientation changes using the magnetic field and accelerometer Sensors. Start by adding local field variables to store the last magnetic field and accelerometer values, as well as variables to store the `CompassView`, `SensorManager`, and current screen rotation values:

```
private float[] aValues = new float[3];
private float[] mValues = new float[3];
private CompassView compassView;
private SensorManager sensorManager;
private int rotation;
```

2. Create a new `updateOrientation` method that uses new heading, pitch, and roll values to update the `CompassView`:

```
private void updateOrientation(float[] values) {
  if (compassView!= null) {
```

```
    compassView.setBearing(values[0]);
    compassView.setPitch(values[1]);
    compassView.setRoll(-values[2]);
    compassView.invalidate();
  }
}
```

3. Update the onCreate method to get references to the CompassView and SensorManager, to determine the current screen orientation relative to the natural device orientation, and to initialize the heading, pitch, and roll:

```
@Override
public void onCreate(Bundle savedInstanceState) {
  super.onCreate(savedInstanceState);
  setContentView(R.layout.main);

  compassView = (CompassView)findViewById(R.id.compassView);
  sensorManager = (SensorManager)getSystemService(Context.SENSOR_SERVICE);

  String windoSrvc = Context.WINDOW_SERVICE;
  WindowManager wm = ((WindowManager) getSystemService(windoSrvc));
  Display display = wm.getDefaultDisplay();
  rotation = display.getRotation();

  updateOrientation(new float[] {0, 0, 0});
}
```

4. Create a new calculateOrientation method to evaluate the device orientation using the last recorded accelerometer and magnetic field values. Remember to account for the natural orientation of the device by remapping the reference frame, if necessary.

```
private float[] calculateOrientation() {
  float[] values = new float[3];
  float[] inR = new float[9];
  float[] outR = new float[9];

  // Determine the rotation matrix
  SensorManager.getRotationMatrix(inR, null, aValues, mValues);

  // Remap the coordinates based on the natural device orientation.
  int x_axis = SensorManager.AXIS_X;
  int y_axis = SensorManager.AXIS_Y;

  switch (rotation) {
    case (Surface.ROTATION_90):
      x_axis = SensorManager.AXIS_Y;
      y_axis = SensorManager.AXIS_MINUS_X;
      break;
    case (Surface.ROTATION_180):
      y_axis = SensorManager.AXIS_MINUS_Y;
      break;
    case (Surface.ROTATION_270):
      x_axis = SensorManager.AXIS_MINUS_Y;
      y_axis = SensorManager.AXIS_X;
```

```
        break;
      default: break;
    }
    SensorManager.remapCoordinateSystem(inR, x_axis, y_axis, outR);

    // Obtain the current, corrected orientation.
    SensorManager.getOrientation(outR, values);

    // Convert from Radians to Degrees.
    values[0] = (float) Math.toDegrees(values[0]);
    values[1] = (float) Math.toDegrees(values[1]);
    values[2] = (float) Math.toDegrees(values[2]);

    return values;
  }
```

5. Implement a `SensorEventListener` as a field variable. Within `onSensorChanged` it should check for the calling Sensor's type and update the last accelerometer or magnetic field values, as appropriate, before making a call to `updateOrientation` using the `calculateOrientation` method.

```
private final SensorEventListener sensorEventListener = new SensorEventListener() {

  public void onSensorChanged(SensorEvent event) {
    if (event.sensor.getType() == Sensor.TYPE_ACCELEROMETER)
      aValues = event.values;
    if (event.sensor.getType() == Sensor.TYPE_MAGNETIC_FIELD)
      mValues = event.values;

    updateOrientation(calculateOrientation());
  }

  public void onAccuracyChanged(Sensor sensor, int accuracy) {}
};
```

6. Override `onResume` and `onPause` to register and unregister the `SensorEventListener` when the Activity becomes visible and hidden, respectively:

```
@Override
protected void onResume() {
  super.onResume();

  Sensor accelerometer
    = sensorManager.getDefaultSensor(Sensor.TYPE_ACCELEROMETER);
  Sensor magField = sensorManager.getDefaultSensor(Sensor.TYPE_MAGNETIC_FIELD);

  sensorManager.registerListener(sensorEventListener,
                                 accelerometer,
                                 SensorManager.SENSOR_DELAY_FASTEST);
  sensorManager.registerListener(sensorEventListener,
                                 magField,
                                 SensorManager.SENSOR_DELAY_FASTEST);
}
```

```
@Override
protected void onPause() {
  sensorManager.unregisterListener(sensorEventListener);
  super.onPause();
}
```

If you run the application now, you should see the Compass View "centered" at 0, 0, 0 when the device is lying flat on a table with the top of the device pointing North. Moving the device should result in the Compass View dynamically updating as the orientation of the device changes.

You will also find that as you rotate the device through 90 degrees, the screen will rotate and the Compass View will reorient accordingly. You can extend this project by disabling automatic screen rotation.

> *All code snippets in this example are part of the* Chapter 12 Artificial Horizon *project, available for download at* www.wrox.com.

Introducing the Gyroscope Sensor

Android devices increasingly are featuring a gyroscope sensor in addition to the traditional accelerometer and magnetometer sensors. The gyroscope sensor is used to measure angular speed around a given axis in radians per second, using the same coordinate system as described for the acceleration sensor.

Android gyroscopes return the rate of rotation around three axes, where their sensitivity and high frequency update rates provide extremely smooth and accurate updates. This makes them particularly good candidates for applications that use changes in orientation (as opposed to absolute orientation) as an input mechanism.

Because gyroscopes measure speed rather than direction, their results must be integrated over time in order to determine the current orientation, as shown in Listing 12-9. The calculated result will represent a change in orientation around a given axis, so you will need to either calibrate or use additional Sensors in order to determine the initial orientation.

LISTING 12-9: **Calculating an orientation change using the gyroscope Sensor**

```
final float nanosecondsPerSecond = 1.0f / 1000000000.0f;
private long lastTime = 0;
final float[] angle = new float[3];

SensorEventListener myGyroListener = new SensorEventListener() {
  public void onSensorChanged(SensorEvent sensorEvent) {
    if (lastTime != 0) {
      final float dT = (sensorEvent.timestamp - lastTime) *
                       nanosecondsPerSecond;
      angle[0] += sensorEvent.values[0] * dT;
      angle[1] += sensorEvent.values[1] * dT;
```

continues

LISTING 12-9 *(continued)*

```
        angle[2] += sensorEvent.values[2] * dT;
    }
    lastTime = sensorEvent.timestamp;
  }

  public void onAccuracyChanged(Sensor sensor, int accuracy) {}
};

SensorManager sm
  = (SensorManager)getSystemService(Context.SENSOR_SERVICE);
int sensorType = Sensor.TYPE_GYROSCOPE;
sm.registerListener(myGyroListener,
                    sm.getDefaultSensor(sensorType),
                    SensorManager.SENSOR_DELAY_NORMAL);
```

code snippet PA4AD_Ch12_Sensors/src/MyActivity.java

It's worth noting that orientation values derived solely from a gyroscope can become increasingly inaccurate due to calibration errors and noise. To account for this effect, gyroscopes are often used in combination with other sensors — particularly accelerometers — to provide smoother and more accurate orientation results. A virtual gyroscope was introduced in Android 4.0 (API level 14) that attempts to reduce this drift effect.

INTRODUCING THE ENVIRONMENTAL SENSORS

One of the most exciting areas of innovation in mobile hardware is the inclusion of an increasingly rich array of sensors. In addition to the orientation and movement sensors described earlier in this chapter, environmental Sensors are now becoming available in many Android devices.

Like orientation Sensors, the availability of specific environmental Sensors depends on the host hardware. Where they are available, environmental Sensors can be used by your application to:

➤ Improve location detection by determining the current altitude

➤ Track movements based on changes in altitude

➤ Alter the screen brightness or functionality based on ambient light

➤ Make weather observations and forecasts

➤ Determine on which planetary body the device is currently located

Using the Barometer Sensor

A barometer is used to measure atmospheric pressure. The inclusion of this sensor in some Android devices makes it possible for a user to determine his or her current altitude and, potentially, to forecast weather changes.

To monitor changes in atmospheric pressure, register an implementation of `SensorEventListener` with the Sensor Manager, using a Sensor object of type `Sensor.TYPE_PRESSURE`. The current atmospheric pressure is returned as the first (and only) value in the returned values array in hecto-pascals (hPa), which is an equivalent measurement to millibars (mbar).

To calculate the current altitude, you can use the static `getAltitude` method from the Sensor Manager, as shown in Listing 12-10, supplying it with the current pressure and the local pressure at sea level.

> To ensure accurate results, you should use a local value for sea-level atmospheric pressure, although the Sensor Manager provides a value for one standard atmosphere via the `PRESSURE_STANDARD_ATMOSPHERE` constant as a useful approximation.

LISTING 12-10: Finding the current altitude using the barometer Sensor

```java
final SensorEventListener myPressureListener = new SensorEventListener() {
    public void onSensorChanged(SensorEvent sensorEvent) {
        if (sensorEvent.sensor.getType() == Sensor.TYPE_PRESSURE) {
            float currentPressure = sensorEvent.values[0];

            // Calculate altitude
            float altitude = SensorManager.getAltitude(
                SensorManager.PRESSURE_STANDARD_ATMOSPHERE,
                currentPressure);
        }
    }

    public void onAccuracyChanged(Sensor sensor, int accuracy) {}
};

SensorManager sm
    = (SensorManager)getSystemService(Context.SENSOR_SERVICE);
int sensorType = Sensor.TYPE_PRESSURE;
sm.registerListener(myPressureListener,
                    sm.getDefaultSensor(sensorType),
                    SensorManager.SENSOR_DELAY_NORMAL);
```

code snippet PA4AD_Ch12_Sensors/src/MyActivity.java

It's important to note that `getAltitude` calculates altitude using the current atmospheric pressure relative to local sea-level values, not two arbitrary atmospheric pressure values. As a result, to calculate the difference in altitude between two recorded pressure values, you need to determine the altitude for each pressure and find the difference between those results, as shown in the following snippet:

```java
float altitudeChange =
    SensorManager.getAltitude(SensorManager.PRESSURE_STANDARD_ATMOSPHERE,
                              newPressure) -
    SensorManager.getAltitude(SensorManager.PRESSURE_STANDARD_ATMOSPHERE,
                              initialPressure);
```

Creating a Weather Station

To fully explore the environmental Sensors available to Android devices, the following project implements a simple weather station by monitoring the barometric pressure, ambient temperature, and ambient light levels.

1. Start by creating a new WeatherStation project that includes a `WeatherStation` Activity. Modify the `main.xml` layout resource to display three centered lines of large, bold text that will be used to display the current temperature, barometric pressure, and cloud level:

```xml
<?xml version="1.0" encoding="utf-8"?>
<LinearLayout xmlns:android="http://schemas.android.com/apk/res/android"
  android:orientation="vertical"
  android:layout_width="match_parent"
  android:layout_height="match_parent">
  <TextView android:id="@+id/temperature"
    android:gravity="center"
    android:layout_width="match_parent"
    android:layout_height="wrap_content"
    android:textStyle="bold"
    android:textSize="28sp"
    android:text="Temperature"
    android:editable="false"
    android:singleLine="true"
    android:layout_margin="10dp"/>
  />
  <TextView android:id="@+id/pressure"
    android:gravity="center"
    android:layout_width="match_parent"
    android:layout_height="wrap_content"
    android:textStyle="bold"
    android:textSize="28sp"
    android:text="Pressure"
    android:editable="false"
    android:singleLine="true"
    android:layout_margin="10dp"/>
  />
  <TextView android:id="@+id/light"
    android:gravity="center"
    android:layout_width="match_parent"
    android:layout_height="wrap_content"
    android:textStyle="bold"
    android:textSize="28sp"
    android:text="Light"
    android:editable="false"
    android:singleLine="true"
    android:layout_margin="10dp"/>
  />
</LinearLayout>
```

2. Within the `WeatherStation` Activity, create instance variables to store references to each of the `TextView` instances and the `SensorManager`. Also create variables to record the last recorded value obtained from each sensor:

```java
private SensorManager sensorManager;
private TextView temperatureTextView;
```

```
    private TextView pressureTextView;
    private TextView lightTextView;

    private float currentTemperature = Float.NaN;
    private float currentPressure = Float.NaN;
    private float currentLight = Float.NaN;
```

3. Update the onCreate method to get a reference to the three Text Views and the Sensor Manager:

```
@Override
public void onCreate(Bundle savedInstanceState) {
  super.onCreate(savedInstanceState);
  setContentView(R.layout.main);

  temperatureTextView = (TextView)findViewById(R.id.temperature);
  pressureTextView = (TextView)findViewById(R.id.pressure);
  lightTextView = (TextView)findViewById(R.id.light);
  sensorManager = (SensorManager)getSystemService(Context.SENSOR_SERVICE);
}
```

4. Create a new SensorEventListener implementation for each of the pressure, temperature, and light sensors. Each should simply record the last recorded value:

```
private final SensorEventListener tempSensorEventListener
  = new SensorEventListener() {

  public void onAccuracyChanged(Sensor sensor, int accuracy) { }

  public void onSensorChanged(SensorEvent event) {
    currentTemperature = event.values[0];
  }
};

private final SensorEventListener pressureSensorEventListener
  = new SensorEventListener() {

  public void onAccuracyChanged(Sensor sensor, int accuracy) { }

  public void onSensorChanged(SensorEvent event) {
    currentPressure = event.values[0];
  }
};

private final SensorEventListener lightSensorEventListener
  = new SensorEventListener() {

  public void onAccuracyChanged(Sensor sensor, int accuracy) { }

  public void onSensorChanged(SensorEvent event) {
    currentLight = event.values[0];
  }
};
```

5. Override the onResume handler to register your new Listeners for updates using the SensorManager. Atmospheric and environmental conditions are likely to change slowly over time, so you can choose a relatively slow update rate. You should also check to confirm a default Sensor exists for each of the conditions being monitored, notifying the user where one or more Sensors are unavailable.

```
@Override
protected void onResume() {
  super.onResume();

  Sensor lightSensor = sensorManager.getDefaultSensor(Sensor.TYPE_LIGHT);
  if (lightSensor != null)
    sensorManager.registerListener(lightSensorEventListener,
        lightSensor,
        SensorManager.SENSOR_DELAY_NORMAL);
  else
    lightTextView.setText("Light Sensor Unavailable");

  Sensor pressureSensor = sensorManager.getDefaultSensor(Sensor.TYPE_PRESSURE);
  if (pressureSensor != null)
    sensorManager.registerListener(pressureSensorEventListener,
        pressureSensor,
        SensorManager.SENSOR_DELAY_NORMAL);
  else
    pressureTextView.setText("Barometer Unavailable");

  Sensor temperatureSensor =
    sensorManager.getDefaultSensor(Sensor.TYPE_AMBIENT_TEMPERATURE);
  if (temperatureSensor != null)
    sensorManager.registerListener(tempSensorEventListener,
        temperatureSensor,
        SensorManager.SENSOR_DELAY_NORMAL);
  else
    temperatureTextView.setText("Thermometer Unavailable");
}
```

6. Override the corresponding onPause method to unregister the Sensor Listeners when the Activity is no longer active:

```
@Override
protected void onPause() {
  sensorManager.unregisterListener(pressureSensorEventListener);
  sensorManager.unregisterListener(tempSensorEventListener);
  sensorManager.unregisterListener(lightSensorEventListener);
  super.onPause();
}
```

7. Create a new updateGUI method that synchronizes with the GUI thread and updates the Text Views. This will be executed regularly using a Timer introduced in the next step.

```
private void updateGUI() {
  runOnUiThread(new Runnable() {
    public void run() {
      if (!Float.isNaN(currentPressure) {
```

```
          pressureTextView.setText(currentPressure + "hPa");
          pressureTextView.invalidate();
        }
        if (!Float.isNaN(currentLight) {
          String lightStr = "Sunny";
          if (currentLight <= SensorManager.LIGHT_CLOUDY)
            lightStr = "Night";
          else if (currentLight <= SensorManager.LIGHT_OVERCAST)
            lightStr = "Cloudy";
          else if (currentLight <= SensorManager.LIGHT_SUNLIGHT)
            lightStr = "Overcast";
          lightTextView.setText(lightStr);
          lightTextView.invalidate();
        }
        if (!Float.isNaN(currentTemperature) {
          temperatureTextView.setText(currentTemperature + "C");
          temperatureTextView.invalidate();
        }
      }
    }
  });
};
```

8. Update the onCreate method to create a Timer that triggers the UI update method defined in step 7 once every second:

```
@Override
public void onCreate(Bundle savedInstanceState) {
  super.onCreate(savedInstanceState);
  setContentView(R.layout.main);

  temperatureTextView = (TextView)findViewById(R.id.temperature);
  pressureTextView = (TextView)findViewById(R.id.pressure);
  lightTextView = (TextView)findViewById(R.id.light);
  sensorManager = (SensorManager)getSystemService(Context.SENSOR_SERVICE);

  Timer updateTimer = new Timer("weatherUpdate");
  updateTimer.scheduleAtFixedRate(new TimerTask() {
    public void run() {
      updateGUI();
    }
  }, 0, 1000);
}
```

All code snippets in this example are part of the Chapter 12 WeatherStation *project, available for download at* www.wrox.com.

13

Maps, Geocoding, and Location-Based Services

WHAT'S IN THIS CHAPTER?

➤ Understanding forward and reverse geocoding

➤ Creating interactive maps with Map Views and Map Activities

➤ Creating and adding Overlays to maps

➤ Finding your location with location-based services

➤ Using proximity alerts

One of the defining features of mobile phones is their portability, so it's not surprising that some of the most enticing APIs are those that enable you to find, contextualize, and map physical locations.

Using the external Maps library included as part of the Google API package, you can create map-based Activities using Google Maps as a user interface element. You have full access to the map, which enables you to control display settings, alter the zoom level, and pan to different locations. Using Overlays you can annotate maps and handle user input.

This chapter also covers the *location-based services* (LBS) that enable you to find the device's current location. They include technologies such as GPS and cell- or Wi-Fi-based location-sensing techniques. You can specify which technology to use explicitly by name, or you can provide a set of Criteria in terms of accuracy, cost, and other requirements and let Android select the most appropriate.

Maps and location-based services use latitude and longitude to pinpoint geographic locations, but your users are more likely to think in terms of a street address. The maps library includes a geocoder that you can use to convert back and forth between latitude/longitude values and real-world addresses.

Used together, the mapping, geocoding, and location-based services provide a powerful toolkit for incorporating your phone's native mobility into your mobile applications.

USING LOCATION-BASED SERVICES

"Location-based services" is an umbrella term that describes the different technologies you can use to find a device's current location. The two main LBS elements are:

➤ **Location Manager** — Provides hooks to the location-based services.

➤ **Location Providers** — Each of these represents a different location-finding technology used to determine the device's current location.

Using the Location Manager, you can do the following:

➤ Obtain your current location

➤ Follow movement

➤ Set proximity alerts for detecting movement into and out of a specified area

➤ Find available Location Providers

➤ Monitor the status of the GPS receiver

Access to the location-based services is provided by the Location Manager. To access the Location Manager, request an instance of the LOCATION_SERVICE using the getSystemService method, as shown in Listing 13-1.

LISTING 13-1: Accessing the Location Manager

```
String serviceString = Context.LOCATION_SERVICE;
LocationManager locationManager;
locationManager = (LocationManager)getSystemService(serviceString);
```

code snippet PA4AD_Ch13_Location/src/MyActivity.java

Before you can use the location-based services, you need to add one or more uses-permission tags to your manifest.

The following snippet shows how to request the *fine* and *coarse* permissions in your application manifest:

```
<uses-permission android:name="android.permission.ACCESS_FINE_LOCATION"/>
<uses-permission android:name="android.permission.ACCESS_COARSE_LOCATION"/>
```

Fine and coarse permissions will be described in more detail in the following sections. Generally speaking, they control the level of accuracy your application can use when determining the user's location, where fine represents high accuracy and coarse less so.

Note that an application that has been granted fine permission will have coarse permission granted implicitly.

USING THE EMULATOR WITH LOCATION-BASED SERVICES

Location-based services are dependent on device hardware used to find the current location. When you develop and test with the Emulator, your hardware is virtualized, and you're likely to stay in pretty much the same location.

To compensate, Android includes hooks that enable you to emulate Location Providers for testing location-based applications. In this section you learn how to mock the position of the supported GPS provider.

> If you plan to do location-based application development and use the Android Emulator, this section shows you how to create an environment that simulates real hardware and location changes. For the remainder of this chapter, it is assumed that you have used the examples in this section to update the location for the `LocationManager.GPS_PROVIDER` within the Emulator, or that you use a physical device.

Updating Locations in Emulator Location Providers

Use the Location Controls available from the DDMS perspective in Eclipse (Figure 13-1) to push location changes directly into the Emulator's GPS Location Provider.

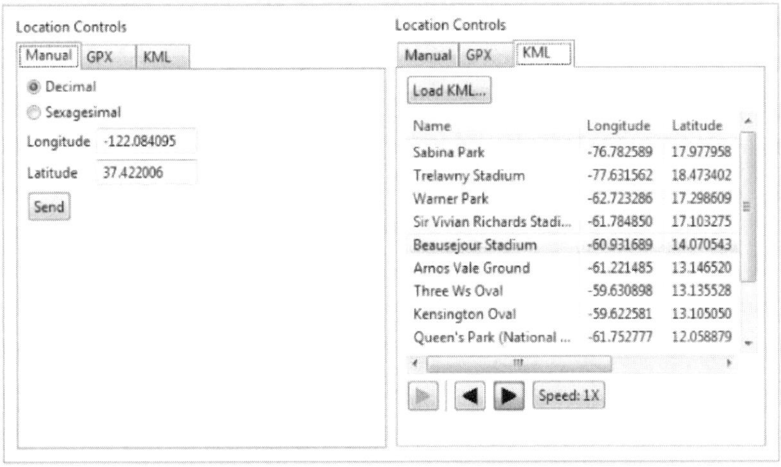

FIGURE 13-1

Figure 13-1 shows the manual and KML tabs. Using the manual tab you can specify particular latitude/longitude pairs. Alternatively, the KML and GPX tabs enable you to load Keyhole Markup Language (KML) and GPS Exchange Format (GPX) files, respectively. After these load you can jump to particular waypoints (locations) or play back each sequence of locations.

> *Most GPS systems record track-files using GPX, whereas KML is used exten-sively online to define geographic information. You can handwrite your own KML file or generate one by using Google Earth to find directions between two locations.*

All location changes applied using the DDMS location controls will be applied to the GPS receiver, which must be enabled and active.

Configuring the Emulator to Test Location-Based Services

The GPS values returned by `getLastKnownLocation` do not change unless at least one application requests location updates. As a result, when the Emulator is first started, the result returned from a call to `getLastKnownLocation` is likely to be null, as no application has made a request to receive location updates.

Further, the techniques used to update the mock location described in the previous section are effec-tive only when at least one application has requested location updates from the GPS.

Listing 13-2 shows how to enable continuous location updates on the Emulator, allowing you to use DDMS to update the mock location within the Emulator.

LISTING 13-2: Enabling the GPS provider on the Emulator

```
locationManager.requestLocationUpdates(
  LocationManager.GPS_PROVIDER, 0, 0,
  new LocationListener() {
    public void onLocationChanged(Location location) {}
    public void onProviderDisabled(String provider) {}
    public void onProviderEnabled(String provider) {}
    public void onStatusChanged(String provider, int status,
                                Bundle extras) {}
  }
);
```

code snippet PA4AD_Ch13_Location/src/MyActivity.java

Note that this code effectively locks the GPS Location Provider into an *on* state. This is considered poor practice, as it will quickly drain the battery on a real device; therefore, this technique should *only* be used when testing on the Emulator.

SELECTING A LOCATION PROVIDER

Depending on the device, you can use several technologies to determine the current location. Each technology, available as a Location Provider, offers different capabilities — including differences in power consumption, accuracy, and the ability to determine altitude, speed, or heading information.

Finding Location Providers

The `LocationManager` class includes static string constants that return the provider name for three Location Providers:

➤ `LocationManager.GPS_PROVIDER`

➤ `LocationManager.NETWORK_PROVIDER`

➤ `LocationManager.PASSIVE_PROVIDER`

> *The GPS provider requires fine permission, as does the passive provider, whereas the network (Cell ID/Wi-Fi) provider requires only coarse.*

To get a list of the names of all the providers available (based on hardware available on the device, and the permissions granted the application), call `getProviders`, using a Boolean to indicate if you want all, or only the enabled, providers to be returned:

```
boolean enabledOnly = true;
List<String> providers = locationManager.getProviders(enabledOnly);
```

Finding Location Providers by Specifying Criteria

In most scenarios it's unlikely that you want to explicitly choose a Location Provider to use. It's better practice to specify your requirements and let Android determine the best technology to use.

Use the `Criteria` class to dictate the requirements of a provider in terms of accuracy, power use (low, medium, high), financial cost, and the ability to return values for altitude, speed, and heading.

Listing 13-3 specifies Criteria requiring coarse accuracy, low power consumption, and no need for altitude, bearing, or speed. The provider is permitted to have an associated cost.

Available for download on Wrox.com

LISTING 13-3: Specifying Location Provider

```
Criteria criteria = new Criteria();
criteria.setAccuracy(Criteria.ACCURACY_COARSE);
criteria.setPowerRequirement(Criteria.POWER_LOW);
criteria.setAltitudeRequired(false);
criteria.setBearingRequired(false);
criteria.setSpeedRequired(false);
criteria.setCostAllowed(true);
```

code snippet PA4AD_Ch13_Location/src/MyActivity.java

The coarse/fine values passed in to the `setAccuracy` represent a subjective level of accuracy, where fine represents GPS or better and coarse any technology significantly less accurate than that.

Android 3.0 introduced several additional properties to the Criteria class, designed for more control over the level of accuracy you require. The following extension of Listing 13-3 specifies that a high horizontal (latitude/longitude) and medium vertical (elevation) accuracy are required. Requirements for the accuracy of returned bearing and speed are set to low.

```
criteria.setHorizontalAccuracy(Criteria.ACCURACY_HIGH);
criteria.setVerticalAccuracy(Criteria.ACCURACY_MEDIUM);

criteria.setBearingAccuracy(Criteria.ACCURACY_LOW);
criteria.setSpeedAccuracy(Criteria.ACCURACY_LOW);
```

In terms of horizontal and vertical accuracy, high accuracy represents a requirement for results correct to within 100m. Low accuracy Providers are correct to more than 500m, whereas medium accuracy Providers represent accuracy between 100 and 500 meters.

When specifying accuracy requirements for bearing and speed, only ACCURACY_LOW and ACCURACY_HIGH are valid parameters.

Having defined the required Criteria, you can use getBestProvider to return the best matching Location Provider or getProviders to return all the possible matches. The following snippet demonstrates the use of getBestProvider to return the best Provider for your Criteria where the Boolean enables you restrict the result to a currently enabled Provider:

```
String bestProvider = locationManager.getBestProvider(criteria, true);
```

If more than one Location Provider matches your Criteria, the one with the greatest accuracy is returned. If no Location Providers meet your requirements, the Criteria are loosened, in the following order, until a provider is found:

➤ Power use

➤ Accuracy of returned location

➤ Accuracy of bearing, speed, and altitude

➤ Availability of bearing, speed, and altitude

The criterion for allowing a device with monetary cost is never implicitly relaxed. If no provider is found, null is returned.

To get a list of names for all the providers matching your Criteria, use getProviders. It accepts a Criteria object and returns a String list of all Location Providers that match it. As with the getBestProvider call, if no matching providers are found, this method returns null or an empty List.

```
List<String> matchingProviders = locationManager.getProviders(criteria,
                                                               false);
```

Determining Location Provider Capabilities

To get an instance of a specific provider, call getProvider, passing in the name:

```
String providerName = LocationManager.GPS_PROVIDER;
LocationProvider gpsProvider
  = locationManager.getProvider(providerName);
```

This is useful only for obtaining the capabilities of a particular provider — specifically the accuracy and power requirements through the `getAccuracy` and `getPowerRequirement` methods.

In the following sections, most Location Manager methods require only a provider name or criteria to perform location-based functions.

FINDING YOUR CURRENT LOCATION

One of the most powerful uses of location-based services is to find the physical location of the device. The accuracy of the returned location is dependent on the hardware available and the permissions requested by your application.

Location Privacy

Privacy is an important consideration when your application uses the user's location — particularly when it is regularly updating their current position. Ensure that your application uses the device location data in a way that respects the user's privacy by:

➤   Only using and updating location when necessary for your application

➤   Notifying users of when you track their locations, and if and how that location information is used, transmitted, and stored

➤   Allowing users to disable location updates, and respecting the system settings for LBS preferences

Finding the Last Known Location

You can find the last location fix obtained by a particular Location Provider using the `getLast-KnownLocation` method, passing in the name of the Location Provider. The following example finds the last location fix taken by the GPS provider:

```
String provider = LocationManager.GPS_PROVIDER;
Location location = locationManager.getLastKnownLocation(provider);
```

> `getLastKnownLocation` *does not ask the Location Provider to update the current position. If the device has not recently updated the current position, this value may not exist or be out of date.*

The Location object returned includes all the position information available from the provider that supplied it. This can include the time it was obtained, the accuracy of the location found, and it's latitude, longitude, bearing, altitude, and speed. All these properties are available via `get` methods on the Location object.

Where Am I Example

The following example — Where Am I — features a new Activity that finds the device's last known location using the GPS Location Provider.

> *This example assumes that you have enabled the* GPS_PROVIDER *Location Provider using the techniques shown previously in this chapter, or that you're running it on a device that supports GPS and has that hardware enabled.*
>
> *In order to work, the device or Emulator must have recorded at least one location update. In the case of a device, this is most easily achieved by starting the Google Maps application; on an Emulator, enable location updates as described earlier in this chapter.*

1. Create a new Where Am I project with a `WhereAmI` Activity. This example uses the GPS provider, so you need to include the `uses-permission` tag for `ACCESS_FINE_LOCATION` in your application manifest.

```xml
<?xml version="1.0" encoding="utf-8"?>
<manifest xmlns:android="http://schemas.android.com/apk/res/android"
  package="com.paad.whereami"
  android:versionCode="1"
  android:versionName="1.0" >

  <uses-sdk android:minSdkVersion="4" />

  <uses-permission
    android:name="android.permission.ACCESS_FINE_LOCATION"
  />

  <application
    android:icon="@drawable/ic_launcher"
    android:label="@string/app_name" >
    <activity
      android:name=".WhereAmI"
      android:label="@string/app_name" >
      <intent-filter>
        <action android:name="android.intent.action.MAIN" />
        <category android:name="android.intent.category.LAUNCHER" />
      </intent-filter>
    </activity>
  </application>
</manifest>
```

2. Modify the `main.xml` layout resource to include an `android:ID` attribute for the `TextView` control so that you can access it from within the Activity.

```xml
<?xml version="1.0" encoding="utf-8"?>
<LinearLayout xmlns:android="http://schemas.android.com/apk/res/android"
  android:orientation="vertical"
  android:layout_width="match_parent"
  android:layout_height="match_parent">
  <TextView
```

```
    android:id="@+id/myLocationText"
    android:layout_width="match_parent"
    android:layout_height="wrap_content"
    android:text="@string/hello"
  />
</LinearLayout>
```

3. Override the `onCreate` method of the `WhereAmI` Activity to get a reference to the Location Manager. Call `getLastKnownLocation` to get the last known location, and pass it in to an `updateWithNewLocation` method stub.

```
@Override
public void onCreate(Bundle savedInstanceState) {
  super.onCreate(savedInstanceState);
  setContentView(R.layout.main);

  LocationManager locationManager;
  String svcName = Context.LOCATION_SERVICE;
  locationManager = (LocationManager)getSystemService(svcName);

  String provider = LocationManager.GPS_PROVIDER;
  Location l = locationManager.getLastKnownLocation(provider);

  updateWithNewLocation(l);
}

private void updateWithNewLocation(Location location) {}
```

4. Complete the `updateWithNewLocation` method to show the passed-in Location in the Text View by extracting the latitude and longitude values.

```
private void updateWithNewLocation(Location location) {
  TextView myLocationText;
  myLocationText = (TextView)findViewById(R.id.myLocationText);

  String latLongString = "No location found";
  if (location != null) {
    double lat = location.getLatitude();
    double lng = location.getLongitude();
    latLongString = "Lat:" + lat + "\nLong:" + lng;
  }

  myLocationText.setText("Your Current Position is:\n" +
                         latLongString);
}
```

> *All code snippets in this example are part of the* Chapter 13 Where Am I Part 1 *project, available for download at* www.wrox.com.

5. When running, your Activity should look like Figure 13-2.

FIGURE 13-2

Refreshing the Current Location

In most circumstances getting the last known location is unlikely to be sufficient for your applications needs. Not only is the value likely to be out of date, but most location-sensitive applications need to be reactive to user movement — and querying the Location Manager for the last known location does not force it to update.

The `requestLocationUpdates` methods are used to request regular updates of location changes using a `LocationListener`. Location Listeners also contain hooks for changes in a provider's status and availability.

The `requestLocationUpdates` method accepts either a specific Location Provider name or a set of Criteria to determine the provider to use. To optimize efficiency and minimize cost and power use, you can also specify the minimum time and the minimum distance between location change updates.

Listing 13-4 shows the skeleton code for requesting regular updates based on a minimum time and distance using a Location Listener.

LISTING 13-4: Requesting location updates Using a Location Listener

Available for
download on
Wrox.com

```
String provider = LocationManager.GPS_PROVIDER;

int t = 5000;      // milliseconds
int distance = 5; // meters

LocationListener myLocationListener = new LocationListener() {

  public void onLocationChanged(Location location) {
    // Update application based on new location.
  }

  public void onProviderDisabled(String provider){
    // Update application if provider disabled.
  }

  public void onProviderEnabled(String provider){
```

```
      // Update application if provider enabled.
    }

    public void onStatusChanged(String provider, int status,
                                 Bundle extras){
      // Update application if provider hardware status changed.
    }
  };

  locationManager.requestLocationUpdates(provider, t, distance,
                                          myLocationListener);
```

code snippet PA4AD_Ch13_Location/src/MyActivity.java

When the minimum time and distance values are exceeded, the attached Location Listener executes its `onLocationChanged` event.

> *You can request multiple location updates pointing to the same or different Location Listeners using different minimum time and distance thresholds or Location Providers.*

Android 3.0 (API level 11) introduced an alternative technique for receiving location changes. Rather than creating a Location Listener, you can specify a Pending Intent that will be broadcast whenever the location changes or the location provider status or availability changes. The new location is stored as an extra with the key KEY_LOCATION_CHANGED.

This is a particularly useful alternative if you have multiple Activities or Services that require location updates as they can listen for the same broadcast Intents.

> *To ensure your application doesn't leak sensitive location information, you need to either target a specific Broadcast Receiver, as shown in Listing 13-5, or require permissions for your location update Intents to be received. More details on applying permissions to Broadcast Intents are available in Chapter 18, "Advanced Android Development."*

Listing 13-5 shows how to broadcast a Pending Intent to announce new location updates.

LISTING 13-5: Requesting location updates using a Pending Intent

```
String provider = LocationManager.GPS_PROVIDER;

int t = 5000;       // milliseconds
int distance = 5; // meters

final int locationUpdateRC = 0;
```

continues

LISTING 13-5 *(continued)*

```
int flags = PendingIntent.FLAG_UPDATE_CURRENT;

Intent intent = new Intent(this, MyLocationUpdateReceiver.class);
PendingIntent pendingIntent = PendingIntent.getBroadcast(this,
  locationUpdateRC, intent, flags);

locationManager.requestLocationUpdates(provider, t,
                                       distance, pendingIntent);
```

code snippet PA4AD_Ch13_Location/src/MyActivity.java

Listing 13-6 shows how to create a Broadcast Receiver that listens for changes in location broadcast using a Pending Intent as shown in Listing 13-5.

LISTING 13-6: Receiving location updates using a Broadcast Receiver

```
import android.content.BroadcastReceiver;
import android.content.Context;
import android.content.Intent;
import android.location.Location;
import android.location.LocationManager;

public class MyLocationUpdateReceiver extends BroadcastReceiver {

  @Override
  public void onReceive(Context context, Intent intent) {
    String key = LocationManager.KEY_LOCATION_CHANGED;
    Location location = (Location)intent.getExtras().get(key);
      // TODO [... Do something with the new location ...]
  }

}
```

code snippet PA4AD_Ch13_Location/src/MyLocationUpdateReceiver.java

Remember that you must add your Broadcast Receiver to the application manifest before it can begin receiving the Pending Intents.

To stop location updates, call `removeUpdates`, as shown in the following code. Pass in either the Location Listener instance or Pending Intent that you no longer want to have triggered.

```
locationManager.removeUpdates(myLocationListener);
locationManager.removeUpdates(pendingIntent);
```

To minimize the cost to battery life, you should disable updates whenever possible in your application, especially in cases where your application isn't visible and location changes are used only to update an Activity's UI. You can improve performance further by making the minimum time and distance between updates as large as possible.

Where timeliness is not a significant factor, you might consider using the Passive Location Provider (introduced in Android 2.2, API level 8), as shown in the following snippet.

```
String passiveProvider = LocationManager.PASSIVE_PROVIDER;
locationManager.requestLocationUpdates(passiveProvider, 0, 0,
                                       myLocationListener);
```

The Passive Location Provider receives location updates if, and only if, another application requests them, letting your application passively receive location updates without activating any Location Provider.

Because the updates may come from any Location Provider, your application must request the ACCESS_FINE_LOCATION permission to use the Passive Location Provider. Call getProvider on the Location received by the registered Location Listener to determine which Location Provider generated each update.

Its passive nature makes this an excellent alternative for keeping location data fresh within your application while it is in the background, without draining the battery.

Tracking Your Location in Where Am I

In the following example, the Where Am I project is enhanced to update your current location by listening for location changes. Updates are restricted to one every 2 seconds, and only when movement of more than 10 meters has been detected.

Rather than explicitly selecting a provider, you update the application to use a set of Criteria and let Android find the best provider available.

1. Open the WhereAmI Activity in the Where Am I project. Update the onCreate method to use Criteria to find a Location Provider that features high accuracy and draws as little power as possible.

```
@Override
public void onCreate(Bundle savedInstanceState) {
  super.onCreate(savedInstanceState);
  setContentView(R.layout.main);

  LocationManager locationManager;
  String svcName = Context.LOCATION_SERVICE;
  locationManager = (LocationManager)getSystemService(svcName);

  Criteria criteria = new Criteria();
  criteria.setAccuracy(Criteria.ACCURACY_FINE);
  criteria.setPowerRequirement(Criteria.POWER_LOW);
  criteria.setAltitudeRequired(false);
  criteria.setBearingRequired(false);
  criteria.setSpeedRequired(false);
  criteria.setCostAllowed(true);
  String provider = locationManager.getBestProvider(criteria, true);

  Location l = locationManager.getLastKnownLocation(provider);

  updateWithNewLocation(l);
}
```

2. Create a new `LocationListener` instance variable that fires the existing `updateWithNew Location` method whenever a location change is detected.

```
private final LocationListener locationListener = new LocationListener() {
  public void onLocationChanged(Location location) {
    updateWithNewLocation(location);
  }

  public void onProviderDisabled(String provider) {}
  public void onProviderEnabled(String provider) {}
  public void onStatusChanged(String provider, int status,
                              Bundle extras) {}
};
```

3. Return to `onCreate` and call `requestLocationUpdates`, passing in the new Location Listener object. It should listen for location changes every 2 seconds but fire only when it detects movement of more than 10 meters.

```
@Override
public void onCreate(Bundle savedInstanceState) {
  super.onCreate(savedInstanceState);
  setContentView(R.layout.main);

  LocationManager locationManager;
  String svcName = Context.LOCATION_SERVICE;
  locationManager = (LocationManager)getSystemService(svcName);

  Criteria criteria = new Criteria();
  criteria.setAccuracy(Criteria.ACCURACY_FINE);
  criteria.setPowerRequirement(Criteria.POWER_LOW);
  criteria.setAltitudeRequired(false);
  criteria.setBearingRequired(false);
  criteria.setSpeedRequired(false);
  criteria.setCostAllowed(true);
  String provider = locationManager.getBestProvider(criteria, true);

  Location l = locationManager.getLastKnownLocation(provider);

  updateWithNewLocation(l);

  locationManager.requestLocationUpdates(provider, 2000, 10,
                                         locationListener);
}
```

If you run the application and start changing the device location, you see the Text View update accordingly.

All code snippets in this example are part of the Chapter 13 Where Am I Part 2 *project, available for download at* www.wrox.com.

Requesting a Single Location Update

Not every app requires regular location updates to remain useful. In many cases only a single location fix is required to provide adequate context for the functionality they provide or information they display.

Although `getLastKnownLocation` can be used to return the last known position, there's no guarantee that this location exists, or that it is still relevant. Similarly, you could use the Passive Location Provider to receive updates when other apps request them, but you have no control over when (or if) this will happen.

Introduced in Android 2.3 (API level 9), the `requestSingleUpdate` method enables you to specify a Provider or Criteria to use when requesting at least one update.

As shown in the snippet following, unlike requesting regular updates this method does not let you specify the frequency of updates because only a single update will be requested.

```
Looper looper = null;
locationManager.requestSingleUpdate(criteria, myLocationListener, looper);
```

When using a Location Listener, you can specify a Looper parameter. This allows you to schedule the callbacks on a particular thread — setting the parameter to null will force it to return on the calling thread.

Like the `requestLocationUpdates` method described earlier, you can choose to receive the single location update using either a Location Listener as previously shown, or through a Pending Intent as shown here.

```
locationManager.requestSingleUpdate(criteria, pendingIntent);
```

In either case, only one update will be received, so you need to unregister the receiver when that update occurs.

BEST PRACTICE FOR LOCATION UPDATES

When using Location within your application, consider the following factors:

➤ **Battery life versus accuracy** — The more accurate the Location Provider, the greater its drain on the battery.

➤ **Startup time** — In a mobile environment the time taken to get an initial location can have a dramatic effect on the user experience — particularly if your app requires a location to be used. GPS, for example, can have a significant startup time, which you may need to mitigate.

➤ **Update rate** — The more frequent the update rate, the more dramatic the effect on battery life. Slower updates can reduce battery drain at the price of less timely updates.

➤ **Provider availability** — Users can toggle the availability of providers, so your application needs to monitor changes in provider status to ensure the best alternative is used at all times.

Monitoring Location Provider Status and Availability

Having used Criteria to select the best provider available for receiving location updates, you need to monitor changes in the availability of Location Providers to ensure that the one selected remains available and the best alternative.

Listing 13-7 shows how to monitor the status of your selected Provider, dynamically switching to a new provider should it become unavailable and switching to a better alternative should one be enabled.

LISTING 13-7: Design pattern for switching Location Providers when a better alternative becomes available

```
package com.paad.location;

import java.util.List;

import android.app.Activity;
import android.content.Context;
import android.location.Criteria;
import android.location.Location;
import android.location.LocationListener;
import android.location.LocationManager;
import android.os.Bundle;
import android.util.Log;

public class DynamicProvidersActivity extends Activity {
  private LocationManager locationManager;
  private final Criteria criteria = new Criteria();
  private static int minUpdateTime = 0;      // 30 Seconds
  private static int minUpdateDistance = 0; // 100m

  private static final String TAG = "DYNAMIC_LOCATION_PROVIDER";

  @Override
  public void onCreate(Bundle savedInstanceState) {
    super.onCreate(savedInstanceState);
    setContentView(R.layout.main);

    // Get a reference to the Location Manager
    String svcName = Context.LOCATION_SERVICE;
    locationManager = (LocationManager)getSystemService(svcName);

    // Specify Location Provider criteria
    criteria.setAccuracy(Criteria.ACCURACY_FINE);
    criteria.setPowerRequirement(Criteria.POWER_LOW);
    criteria.setAltitudeRequired(true);
    criteria.setBearingRequired(true);
    criteria.setSpeedRequired(true);
    criteria.setCostAllowed(true);

    // Only for Android 3.0 and above
```

```
      criteria.setHorizontalAccuracy(Criteria.ACCURACY_HIGH);
      criteria.setVerticalAccuracy(Criteria.ACCURACY_MEDIUM);
      criteria.setBearingAccuracy(Criteria.ACCURACY_LOW);
      criteria.setSpeedAccuracy(Criteria.ACCURACY_LOW);
      // End of Android 3.0 and above only
  }

  @Override
  protected void onPause() {
    unregisterAllListeners();
    super.onPause();
  }

  @Override
  protected void onResume() {
    super.onResume();
    registerListener();
  }

  private void registerListener() {
    unregisterAllListeners();
    String bestProvider =
      locationManager.getBestProvider(criteria, false);
    String bestAvailableProvider =
      locationManager.getBestProvider(criteria, true);

    Log.d(TAG, bestProvider + " / " + bestAvailableProvider);

    if (bestProvider == null)
      Log.d(TAG, "No Location Providers exist on device.");
    else if (bestProvider.equals(bestAvailableProvider))
      locationManager.requestLocationUpdates(bestAvailableProvider,
        minUpdateTime, minUpdateDistance,
        bestAvailableProviderListener);
    else {
      locationManager.requestLocationUpdates(bestProvider,
        minUpdateTime, minUpdateDistance, bestProviderListener);

      if (bestAvailableProvider != null)
        locationManager.requestLocationUpdates(bestAvailableProvider,
          minUpdateTime, minUpdateDistance,
          bestAvailableProviderListener);
      else {
        List<String> allProviders = locationManager.getAllProviders();
        for (String provider : allProviders)
          locationManager.requestLocationUpdates(provider, 0, 0,
            bestProviderListener);
        Log.d(TAG, "No Location Providers currently available.");
      }
    }
  }

  private void unregisterAllListeners() {
    locationManager.removeUpdates(bestProviderListener);
```

continues

LISTING 13-7 *(continued)*

```
      locationManager.removeUpdates(bestAvailableProviderListener);
  }

  private void reactToLocationChange(Location location) {
    // TODO [ React to location change ]
  }

  private LocationListener bestProviderListener
    = new LocationListener() {

    public void onLocationChanged(Location location) {
      reactToLocationChange(location);
    }

    public void onProviderDisabled(String provider) {
    }

    public void onProviderEnabled(String provider) {
      registerListener();
    }

    public void onStatusChanged(String provider,
                                int status, Bundle extras) {}
  };

  private LocationListener bestAvailableProviderListener =
    new LocationListener() {
    public void onProviderEnabled(String provider) {
    }

    public void onProviderDisabled(String provider) {
      registerListener();
    }

    public void onLocationChanged(Location location) {
      reactToLocationChange(location);
    }

    public void onStatusChanged(String provider,
                                int status, Bundle extras) {}
  };
}
```

code snippet PA4AD_Ch13_Location/src/DynamicProvidersActivity.java

USING PROXIMITY ALERTS

Proximity alerts let your app set Pending Intents that are fired when the device moves within or beyond a set distance from a fixed location.

> *Internally, Android may use different Location Providers depending on how close you are to the outside edge of your target area. This allows the power use and cost to be minimized when the alert is unlikely to be fired based on your distance from the target area interface.*

To set a proximity alert for a given area, select the center point (using longitude and latitude values), a radius around that point, and an expiry time-out for the alert. The alert fires if the device crosses over that boundary, both when it moves from outside to within the radius, and when it moves from inside to beyond it.

To specify the Intent to fire, you use a `PendingIntent`, a class that wraps an Intent in a kind of method pointer, as described in Chapter 5, "Intents and Broadcast Receivers."

Listing 13-8 shows how to set a proximity alert that never expires and that is triggered when the device moves within 10 meters of its target.

LISTING 13-8: Setting a proximity alert

```java
private static final String TREASURE_PROXIMITY_ALERT = "com.paad.treasurealert";

private void setProximityAlert() {
    String locService = Context.LOCATION_SERVICE;
    LocationManager locationManager;
    locationManager = (LocationManager)getSystemService(locService);

    double lat = 73.147536;
    double lng = 0.510638;
    float radius = 100f; // meters
    long expiration = -1; // do not expire

    Intent intent = new Intent(TREASURE_PROXIMITY_ALERT);
    PendingIntent proximityIntent = PendingIntent.getBroadcast(this, -1,
                                                               intent,
                                                               0);

    locationManager.addProximityAlert(lat, lng, radius,
                                      expiration,
                                      proximityIntent);
}
```

code snippet PA4AD_Ch13_Location/src/MyActivity.java

When the Location Manager detects that you have crossed the radius boundary, the Pending Intent fires with an `extra` keyed as `LocationManager.KEY_PROXIMITY_ENTERING` set to `true` or `false` accordingly.

To receive proximity alerts, you need to create a `BroadcastReceiver`, such as the one shown in Listing 13-9.

LISTING 13-9: Creating a proximity alert Broadcast Receiver

```java
public class ProximityIntentReceiver extends BroadcastReceiver {

  @Override
  public void onReceive (Context context, Intent intent) {
    String key = LocationManager.KEY_PROXIMITY_ENTERING;

    Boolean entering = intent.getBooleanExtra(key, false);
    // TODO [ … perform proximity alert actions … ]
  }

}
```

code snippet PA4AD_Ch13_Location/src/ProximityIntentReceiver.java

To start listening for proximity alerts, register your receiver either by using a tag in your Manifest or in code as shown here:

```java
IntentFilter filter = new IntentFilter(TREASURE_PROXIMITY_ALERT);
registerReceiver(new ProximityIntentReceiver(), filter);
```

USING THE GEOCODER

Geocoding enables you to translate between street addresses and longitude/latitude map coordinates. This can give you a recognizable context for the locations and coordinates used in location-based services and map-based Activities.

The Geocoder classes are included as part of the Google Maps library, so to use them you need to import it into your application by adding a uses-library node within the application node as shown here:

```xml
<uses-library android:name="com.google.android.maps"/>
```

As the geocoding lookups are done on the server, your applications also requires the Internet uses-permission in your manifest:

```xml
<uses-permission android:name="android.permission.INTERNET"/>
```

The Geocoder class provides access to two geocoding functions:

➤ **Forward geocoding** — Finds the latitude and longitude of an address

➤ **Reverse geocoding** — Finds the street address for a given latitude and longitude

The results from these calls are contextualized by means of a locale (used to define your usual location and language). The following snippet shows how you set the locale when creating your Geocoder. If you don't specify a locale, it assumes the device's default.

```java
Geocoder geocoder = new Geocoder(getApplicationContext(),
                                 Locale.getDefault());
```

Both geocoding functions return a list of Address objects. Each list can contain several possible results, up to a limit you specify when making the call.

Each Address object is populated with as much detail as the Geocoder was able to resolve. This can include the latitude, longitude, phone number, and increasingly granular address details from country to street and house number.

> *Geocoder lookups are performed synchronously, so they block the calling thread. It's good practice to move these lookups into a Service or and/or background thread, as demonstrated in Chapter 9, "Working in the Background."*

The Geocoder uses a web service to implement its lookups that may not be included on all Android devices. Android 2.3 (API level 9) introduced the `isPresent` method to determine if a Geocoder implementation exists on a given device:

```
bool geocoderExists = Geocoder.isPresent();
```

If no Geocoder implementation exists on the device, the forward and reverse geocoding queries described in the following sections will return an empty list.

Reverse Geocoding

Reverse geocoding returns street addresses for physical locations specified by latitude/longitude pairs. It's a useful way to get a recognizable context for the locations returned by location-based services.

To perform a reverse lookup, pass the target latitude and longitude to a Geocoder object's `getFromLocation` method. It returns a list of possible address matches. If the Geocoder could not resolve any addresses for the specified coordinate, it returns null.

Listing 13-10 shows how to reverse-geocode a given location, limiting the number of possible addresses to the top 10.

LISTING 13-10: Reverse-geocoding a given location

Available for
download on
Wrox.com

```java
private void reverseGeocode(Location location) {

    double latitude = location.getLatitude();
    double longitude = location.getLongitude();
    List<Address> addresses = null;

    Geocoder gc = new Geocoder(this, Locale.getDefault());
    try {
        addresses = gc.getFromLocation(latitude, longitude, 10);
    } catch (IOException e) {
        Log.e(TAG, "IO Exception", e);
    }
}
```

code snippet PA4AD_Ch13_Geocoding/src/MyActivity.java

The accuracy and granularity of reverse lookups are entirely dependent on the quality of data in the geocoding database; as a result, the quality of the results may vary widely between different countries and locales.

Forward Geocoding

Forward geocoding (or just geocoding) determines map coordinates for a given location.

> *What constitutes a valid location varies depending on the locale (geographic area) within which you search. Generally, it includes regular street addresses of varying granularity (from country to street name and number), postcodes, train stations, landmarks, and hospitals. As a general guide, valid search terms are similar to the addresses and locations you can enter into the Google Maps search bar.*

To geocode an address, call `getFromLocationName` on a Geocoder object. Pass in a string that describes the address you want the coordinates for, the maximum number of results to return, and optionally provide a geographic bounding box within which to restrict your search results:

```
List<Address> result = gc.getFromLocationName(streetAddress, maxResults);
```

The returned list of Addresses may include multiple possible matches for the named location. Each Address includes latitude and longitude and any additional address information available for those coordinates. This is useful to confirm that the correct location was resolved, and for providing location specifics in searches for landmarks.

> *As with reverse geocoding, if no matches are found, null is returned. The availability, accuracy, and granularity of geocoding results depends entirely on the database available for the area you search.*

When you do forward lookups, the Locale specified when instantiating the Geocoder is particularly important. The Locale provides the geographical context for interpreting your search requests because the same location names can exist in multiple areas.

Where possible, consider selecting a regional Locale to help avoid place-name ambiguity, and try to provide as many address details as possible, as shown in Listing 13-11.

LISTING 13-11: Geocoding an address

```
Geocoder fwdGeocoder = new Geocoder(this, Locale.US);
String streetAddress = "160 Riverside Drive, New York, New York";

List<Address> locations = null;
```

```
try {
  locations = fwdGeocoder.getFromLocationName(streetAddress, 5);
} catch (IOException e) {
  Log.e(TAG, "IO Exception", e);
}
```

code snippet PA4AD_Ch13_Geocoding/src/MyActivity.java

For even more specific results, you can restrict your search to within a geographical area by specifying the lower-left and upper-right latitude and longitude as shown here:

```
List<Address> locations = null;
try {
  locations = fwdGeocoder.getFromLocationName(streetAddress, 10,
                                    llLat, llLong, urLat, urLong);
} catch (IOException e) {
  Log.e(TAG, "IO Exception", e);
}
```

This overload is particularly useful with a Map View, letting you restrict the search to the visible map area.

Geocoding Where Am I

In this example you extend the Where Am I project to include and update the current street address whenever the device moves.

1. Start by modifying the manifest to include the Internet uses-permission:

```
<uses-permission android:name="android.permission.INTERNET"/>
```

2. Then open the `WhereAmI` Activity. Modify the `updateWithNewLocation` method to instantiate a new Geocoder object and call the `getFromLocation` method, passing in the newly received location and limiting the results to a single address.

3. Extract each line in the street address and the locality, postcode, and country, and append this information to an existing Text View string.

```
private void updateWithNewLocation(Location location) {
  TextView myLocationText;
  myLocationText = (TextView)findViewById(R.id.myLocationText);

  String latLongString = "No location found";
  String addressString = "No address found";

  if (location != null) {
    double lat = location.getLatitude();
    double lng = location.getLongitude();
    latLongString = "Lat:" + lat + "\nLong:" + lng;

    double latitude = location.getLatitude();
    double longitude = location.getLongitude();
```

```
    Geocoder gc = new Geocoder(this, Locale.getDefault());

    try {
      List<Address> addresses = gc.getFromLocation(latitude, longitude, 1);
      StringBuilder sb = new StringBuilder();
      if (addresses.size() > 0) {
        Address address = addresses.get(0);

        for (int i = 0; i < address.getMaxAddressLineIndex(); i++)
          sb.append(address.getAddressLine(i)).append("\n");

        sb.append(address.getLocality()).append("\n");
        sb.append(address.getPostalCode()).append("\n");
        sb.append(address.getCountryName());
      }
      addressString = sb.toString();
    } catch (IOException e) {}
  }

  myLocationText.setText("Your Current Position is:\n" +
                         latLongString + "\n\n" + addressString);
}
```

> 🖉 *All code snippets in this example are part of the* Chapter 13 Where Am I Part 3 *project, available for download at* www.wrox.com.

If you run the example now, it should appear as shown in Figure 13-3.

FIGURE 13-3

CREATING MAP-BASED ACTIVITIES

One of the most intuitive ways to provide context for a physical location or address is to use a map. Using a `MapView`, you can create Activities that include an interactive map.

Map Views support annotation using Overlays and by pinning Views to geographical locations. Map Views offer full programmatic control of the map display, letting you control the zoom, location, and display modes — including the option to display a satellite view.

In the following sections you see how to use Overlays and the `MapController` to create dynamic map-based Activities. Unlike online mashups, your map Activities run natively on the device, giving you a more customized and personal user experience.

Introducing Map View and Map Activity

This section introduces several classes used to support Android maps:

➤ `MapView` is the user interface element that displays the map.

➤ `MapActivity` is the base class you extend to create an Activity that can include a Map View. The `MapActivity` class handles the application life cycle and background service management required for displaying maps. You can only use Map Views within `MapActivity`-derived Activities.

➤ `Overlay` is the class used to annotate your maps. Using Overlays, you can use a Canvas to draw onto any number of layers displayed on top of a Map View.

➤ `MapController` is used to control the map, enabling you to set the center location and zoom levels.

➤ `MyLocationOverlay` is a special Overlay that can be used to display the current position and orientation of the device.

➤ `ItemizedOverlays` and `OverlayItems` are used together to let you create a layer of map markers, displayed using Drawables and associated text.

Getting Your Maps API Key

To use a Map View in your application, you must first obtain an API key from the Android developer website at `http://code.google.com/android/maps-api-signup.html`.

Without an API key the Map View cannot download the tiles used to display the map.

To obtain a key, you need to specify the MD5 fingerprint of the certificate used to sign your application. Generally, you sign your application using two certificates: a default debug certificate and a production certificate. The following sections explain how to obtain the MD5 fingerprint of any signing certificate used with your application.

Getting Your Development/Debugging MD5 Fingerprint

If you use Eclipse with the ADT plug-in to debug your applications, they will be signed with the default debug certificate stored in the debug keystore.

You can find the location of your keystore in the Default Debug Keystore textbox after selecting Windows ➪ Preferences ➪ Android ➪ Build. Typically the debug keystore is stored in the following platform-specific locations:

➤ **Windows Vista** — `\users\<username>\.android\debug.keystore`

➤ **Windows XP** — `\Documents and Settings\<username>\.android\debug.keystore`

➤ **Linux or Mac** — `</.android/debug.keystore`

> *Each computer you use for development will have a different debug certificate and MD5 value. If you want to debug and develop map applications across multiple computers, you need to generate and use multiple API keys.*

To find the MD5 fingerprint of your debug certificate, use the `keytool` command from your Java installation:

```
keytool -list -alias androiddebugkey -keystore <keystore_location>.keystore
-storepass android -keypass android
```

Getting your Production/Release MD5 Fingerprint

Before you compile and sign your application for release, you need to obtain a map API key using the MD5 fingerprint for your release certificate.

Find the MD5 fingerprint using the `keytool` command and specify the `-list` parameter and the keystore and alias you will use to sign your release application.

```
keytool -list -alias my-android-alias -keystore my-android-keystore
```

You will be prompted for your keystore and alias passwords before the MD5 fingerprint is returned.

Creating a Map-Based Activity

To use maps in your applications, you need to extend `MapActivity`. The layout for the new class must then include a `MapView` to display a Google Maps interface element.

The Android maps library is not a standard Android package; as an optional API, it must be explicitly included in the application manifest before it can be used. Add the library to your manifest using a `uses-library` tag within the `application` node, as shown in the following XML snippet:

```
<uses-library android:name="com.google.android.maps"/>
```

> *The maps package as described here is not part of the standard Android open-source project (AOSP). It is provided within the Android SDK by Google and is available on most Android devices. However, be aware that because it is a nonstandard package, an Android device may not feature this particular library.*

The Map View downloads its map tiles on demand; as a result, any application that features a Map View needs to include a uses-permission for Internet access. To do this, you need to add a `uses-permission` tag to your application manifest for `INTERNET`, as shown here:

```
<uses-permission android:name="android.permission.INTERNET"/>
```

After adding the library and configuring your permission, you're ready to create your new map-based Activity.

`MapView` controls can be used only within an Activity that extends `MapActivity`. Override the `onCreate` method to lay out the screen that includes a `MapView`, and override `isRouteDisplayed` to return `true` if the Activity will be displaying routing information (such as traffic directions).

Listing 13-12 shows the framework for creating a new map-based Activity.

LISTING 13-12: A skeleton map Activity

```
import com.google.android.maps.MapActivity;
import com.google.android.maps.MapController;
import com.google.android.maps.MapView;
import android.os.Bundle;

public class MyMapActivity extends MapActivity {
  private MapView mapView;

  private MapController mapController;

  @Override
  public void onCreate(Bundle savedInstanceState) {
    super.onCreate(savedInstanceState);
    setContentView(R.layout.map_layout);
    mapView = (MapView)findViewById(R.id.map_view);
  }

  @Override
  protected boolean isRouteDisplayed() {
    // IMPORTANT: This method must return true if your Activity
    // is displaying driving directions. Otherwise return false.
    return false;
  }
}
```

code snippet PA4AD_Ch13_Mapping/src/MyMapActivity.java

The corresponding layout file used to include the `MapView` is shown in Listing 13-13. You need to include your map API key (as described earlier in this chapter) to use a Map View in your application.

LISTING 13-13: A map Activity layout resource

```
<?xml version="1.0" encoding="utf-8"?>
<LinearLayout
  xmlns:android="http://schemas.android.com/apk/res/android"
  android:orientation="vertical"
  android:layout_width="fill_parent"
  android:layout_height="fill_parent">
  <com.google.android.maps.MapView
    android:id="@+id/map_view"
    android:layout_width="fill_parent"
```

continues

LISTING 13-13 *(continued)*

```
        android:layout_height="fill_parent"
        android:enabled="true"
        android:clickable="true"
        android:apiKey="mymapapikey"
    />
</LinearLayout>
```

code snippet PA4AD_Ch13_Mapping/res/layout/map_layout.xml

Figure 13-4 shows an example of a basic map-based Activity.

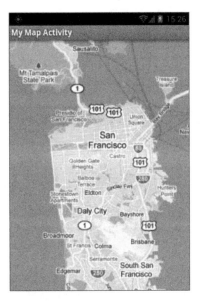

FIGURE 13-4

 Android currently supports only one MapActivity *and one* MapView *per application.*

Maps and Fragments

Map Views can be included within Fragments, provided that the Fragment is attached to a Map Activity. This can be problematic if you are using the Android Support Library to provide support for Fragments on Android platforms prior to Android 3.0.

In such scenarios, you must choose between having your Activity extend FragmentActivity in order to provide Fragment support, or MapActivity in order to include a Map View element.

At the time of writing, the support library did not include a `MapFragment` or `MapFragmentActivity` class to enable the use of Map Views within support library Fragments. As a result, it is not currently possibly to include Map Views within support library Fragments and Fragment Activities.

There are several third-party support libraries that attempt to circumvent this restriction. Alternatively, one approach is to create alternative Activity classes for pre- and post-Honeycomb devices, such that Maps within Fragments are used only where supported.

For the remainder of this chapter where Fragments are discussed, it will be assumed that they are native Fragments on devices targeting Android 3.0 (API level 11) or above.

Configuring and Using Map Views

By default the Map View shows the standard street map (refer to Figure 13-4). In addition you can choose to display a satellite view and the expected traffic overlay, as shown in the following code snippet:

```
mapView.setSatellite(true);
mapView.setTraffic(true);
```

You can also query the Map View to find the current and maximum available zoom levels:

```
int maxZoom = mapView.getMaxZoomLevel();
int currentZoom = mapView.getZoomLevel();
```

You can also obtain the center point and currently visible longitude and latitude span (in decimal degrees). This is particularly useful for performing geographically limited Geocoder lookups:

```
GeoPoint center = mapView.getMapCenter();
int latSpan = mapView.getLatitudeSpan();
int longSpan = mapView.getLongitudeSpan();
```

You can also choose to display the standard map zoom controls using the `setBuiltInZoomControls` method.

```
mapView.setBuiltInZoomControls(true);
```

To customize the zoom controls use the `getZoomButtonsController` method to obtain an instance of the Zoom Buttons Controller. You can use the controller to customize the zoom speed, enable or disable the zoom in or out controls, and add additional buttons to the zoom controls layout.

```
ZoomButtonsController zoomButtons = mapView.getZoomButtonsController();
```

Using the Map Controller

Use the Map Controller to pan and zoom a `MapView`. You can get a reference to a `MapView`'s controller using `getController`.

```
MapController mapController = mapView.getController();
```

Map locations in the Android mapping classes are represented by `GeoPoint` objects, which contain a latitude and longitude measured in microdegrees. To convert degrees to microdegrees, multiply by 1E6 (1,000,000).

Before you can use the latitude and longitude values stored in the Location objects returned by location-based services, you need to convert them to microdegrees and store them as GeoPoints.

```
Double lat = 37.422006*1E6;
Double lng = -122.084095*1E6;
GeoPoint point = new GeoPoint(lat.intValue(), lng.intValue());
```

Recenter and zoom the Map View using the `setCenter` and `setZoom` methods available on the Map View's `MapController`.

```
mapController.setCenter(point);
mapController.setZoom(1);
```

When you use `setZoom`, 1 represents the widest (or most distant) zoom and 21 the tightest (nearest) view.

The actual zoom level available for a specific location depends on the resolution of Google's maps and imagery for that area and can be found by calling `getMaxZoomLevel` on the associated Map View. You can also use `zoomIn` and `zoomOut` to change the zoom level by one step or `zoomToSpan` to specify a latitude or longitude span to zoom to.

The `setCenter` method "jumps" to a new location; to show a smooth transition, use `animateTo`.

```
mapController.animateTo(point);
```

Mapping Where Am I

The following code example extends the Where Am I project again. This time you add mapping functionality by transforming it into a Map Activity. As the device location changes, the map automatically re-centers on the new position.

   1. Start by checking your project properties to ensure your project build target is a Google APIs target rather than an Android Open Source Project target. This is necessary in order to use the Google mapping components. You can access your project's build properties by selecting it in your project hierarchy and selecting File ⇨ Properties and selecting the Android tab.

   2. Modify the application manifest to add the maps library:

```
<?xml version="1.0" encoding="utf-8"?>
<manifest xmlns:android="http://schemas.android.com/apk/res/android"
  package="com.paad.whereami"
  android:versionCode="1"
  android:versionName="1.0" >

  <uses-sdk android:minSdkVersion="4" />
  <uses-permission android:name="android.permission.INTERNET"/>

  <uses-permission
    android:name="android.permission.ACCESS_FINE_LOCATION"
  />

  <application
    android:icon="@drawable/ic_launcher"
    android:label="@string/app_name">
```

```xml
        <uses-library android:name="com.google.android.maps"/>

        <activity
          android:name=".WhereAmI"
          android:label="@string/app_name">
          <intent-filter>
            <action android:name="android.intent.action.MAIN" />
            <category android:name="android.intent.category.LAUNCHER" />
          </intent-filter>
        </activity>
      </application>
    </manifest>
```

3. Change the inheritance of the `WhereAmI` Activity to extend `MapActivity` instead of `Activity`. You also need to include an override for the `isRouteDisplayed` method. Because this Activity won't show routing directions, you can return `false`.

```java
public class WhereAmI extends MapActivity {

  @Override
  protected boolean isRouteDisplayed() {
    return false;
  }

  [ ... existing Activity code ... ]
}
```

4. Modify the `main.xml` layout resource to include a `MapView` using the fully qualified class name. You need to obtain a maps API key to include within the `android:apikey` attribute of the `com.android.MapView` node.

```xml
<?xml version="1.0" encoding="utf-8"?>
<LinearLayout
  xmlns:android="http://schemas.android.com/apk/res/android"
  android:orientation="vertical"
  android:layout_width="match_parent"
  android:layout_height="match_parent">
  <TextView
    android:id="@+id/myLocationText"
    android:layout_width="match_parent"
    android:layout_height="wrap_content"
    android:text="@string/hello"
  />
  <com.google.android.maps.MapView
    android:id="@+id/myMapView"
    android:layout_width="match_parent"
    android:layout_height="match_parent"
    android:enabled="true"
    android:clickable="true"
    android:apiKey="myMapKey"
  />
</LinearLayout>
```

5. Running the application now should display the original address text with a `MapView` beneath it, as shown in Figure 13-5.

FIGURE 13-5

6. Returning to the `WhereAmI` Activity, configure the Map View and store a reference to its `MapController` as an instance variable. Set up the Map View display options to show the satellite and zoom in for a closer look.

```
private MapController mapController;

@Override
public void onCreate(Bundle savedInstanceState) {
  super.onCreate(savedInstanceState);
  setContentView(R.layout.main);

  // Get a reference to the MapView
  MapView myMapView = (MapView)findViewById(R.id.myMapView);

  // Get the Map View's controller
  mapController = myMapView.getController();

  // Configure the map display options
  myMapView.setSatellite(true);
  myMapView.setBuiltInZoomControls(true);

  // Zoom in
  mapController.setZoom(17);

  LocationManager locationManager;
  String svcName= Context.LOCATION_SERVICE;
  locationManager = (LocationManager)getSystemService(svcName);

  Criteria criteria = new Criteria();
  criteria.setAccuracy(Criteria.ACCURACY_FINE);
```

```
criteria.setPowerRequirement(Criteria.POWER_LOW);
criteria.setAltitudeRequired(false);
criteria.setBearingRequired(false);
criteria.setSpeedRequired(false);
criteria.setCostAllowed(true);
String provider = locationManager.getBestProvider(criteria, true);

Location l = locationManager.getLastKnownLocation(provider);

updateWithNewLocation(l);

locationManager.requestLocationUpdates(provider, 2000, 10,
                                       locationListener);
}
```

7. The final step is to modify the `updateWithNewLocation` method to re-center the map on the current location using the Map Controller:

```
private void updateWithNewLocation(Location location) {
  TextView myLocationText;
  myLocationText = (TextView)findViewById(R.id.myLocationText);

  String latLongString = "No location found";
  String addressString = "No address found";

  if (location != null) {
    // Update the map location.
    Double geoLat = location.getLatitude()*1E6;
    Double geoLng = location.getLongitude()*1E6;
    GeoPoint point = new GeoPoint(geoLat.intValue(),
                                  geoLng.intValue());
    mapController.animateTo(point);

    double lat = location.getLatitude();
    double lng = location.getLongitude();
    latLongString = "Lat:" + lat + "\nLong:" + lng;

    double latitude = location.getLatitude();
    double longitude = location.getLongitude();
    Geocoder gc = new Geocoder(this, Locale.getDefault());

    if (!Geocoder.isPresent())
      addressString = "No geocoder available";
    else {
      try {
        List<Address> addresses = gc.getFromLocation(latitude, longitude, 1);
        StringBuilder sb = new StringBuilder();
        if (addresses.size() > 0) {
          Address address = addresses.get(0);

          for (int i = 0; i < address.getMaxAddressLineIndex(); i++)
            sb.append(address.getAddressLine(i)).append("\n");

          sb.append(address.getLocality()).append("\n");
```

```
            sb.append(address.getPostalCode()).append("\n");
            sb.append(address.getCountryName());
          }
          addressString = sb.toString();
        } catch (IOException e) {
          Log.d("WHEREAMI", "IO Exception", e);
        }
      }
    }

    myLocationText.setText("Your Current Position is:\n" +
      latLongString + "\n\n" + addressString);
  }
```

> All code snippets in this example are part of the Chapter 13 Where Am I Part 4, available for download at www.wrox.com.

Creating and Using Overlays

Overlays enable you to add annotations and click handling to MapViews. Each Overlay enables you to draw 2D primitives, including text, lines, images, and shapes, directly onto a canvas, which is then overlaid onto a Map View.

You can add several Overlays onto a single map. All the Overlays assigned to a Map View are added as layers, with newer layers potentially obscuring older ones. User clicks are passed through the stack until they are either handled by an Overlay or registered as clicks on the Map View itself.

Creating New Overlays

To add a new Overlay, create a class that extends Overlay. Override the draw method to draw the annotations you want to add, and override onTap to react to user clicks (generally made when the user taps an annotation added by this Overlay).

Listing 13-14 shows the framework for creating a new Overlay that can draw annotations and handle user clicks.

LISTING 13-14: Creating a new Overlay

```
import android.graphics.Canvas;
import com.google.android.maps.GeoPoint;
import com.google.android.maps.MapView;
import com.google.android.maps.Overlay;

public class MyOverlay extends Overlay {
  @Override
  public void draw(Canvas canvas, MapView mapView, boolean shadow) {
    if (shadow == false) {
      // TODO [ ... Draw annotations on main map layer ... ]
    }
```

```
      else {
        // TODO [ ... Draw annotations on the shadow layer ... ]
      }
    }

    @Override
    public boolean onTap(GeoPoint point, MapView mapView) {
      // Return true if screen tap is handled by this overlay
      return false;
    }
  }
}
```

code snippet PA4AD_Ch13_Mapping/src/MyOverlay.java

Introducing Projections

The canvas used to draw Overlay annotations is a standard `Canvas` that represents the visible display surface. To add annotations based on physical locations, you need to convert between geographical points and screen coordinates.

The `Projection` class enables you to translate between latitude/longitude coordinates (stored as `GeoPoints`) and x/y screen pixel coordinates (stored as `Points`).

A map's Projection may change between subsequent calls to draw, so it's good practice to get a new instance each time. Get a Map View's Projection by calling `getProjection`.

```
Projection projection = mapView.getProjection();
```

Use the `fromPixel` and `toPixel` methods to translate from GeoPoints to Points and vice versa.

For performance reasons, you can best use the `toPixel` Projection method by passing a Point object to be populated (rather than relying on the return value), as shown in Listing 13-15.

LISTING 13-15: Using map Projections

```
Point myPoint = new Point();
// To screen coordinates
projection.toPixels(geoPoint, myPoint);
// To GeoPoint location coordinates
GeoPoint gPoint = projection.fromPixels(myPoint.x, myPoint.y);
```

code snippet PA4AD_Ch13_Mapping/src/MyOverlay.java

Drawing on the Overlay Canvas

You handle Canvas drawing for Overlays by overriding the Overlay's `draw` handler.

The passed-in Canvas is the surface on which you draw your annotations, using the same techniques introduced in Chapter 4, "Building User Interfaces" for creating custom user interfaces for Views. The Canvas object includes the methods for drawing 2D primitives on your map (including lines, text, shapes, ellipses, images, and so on). Use `Paint` objects to define the style and color.

Listing 13-16 uses a Projection to draw text and an ellipse at a given location.

LISTING 13-16: A simple map Overlay

```java
@Override
public void draw(Canvas canvas, MapView mapView, boolean shadow) {
    Projection projection = mapView.getProjection();

    Double lat = -31.960906*1E6;
    Double lng = 115.844822*1E6;
    GeoPoint geoPoint = new GeoPoint(lat.intValue(), lng.intValue());

    if (shadow == false) {
        Point myPoint = new Point();
        projection.toPixels(geoPoint, myPoint);

        // Create and setup your paint brush
        Paint paint = new Paint();
        paint.setARGB(250, 255, 0, 0);
        paint.setAntiAlias(true);
        paint.setFakeBoldText(true);

        // Create the circle
        int rad = 5;
        RectF oval = new RectF(myPoint.x-rad, myPoint.y-rad,
                               myPoint.x+rad, myPoint.y+rad);

        // Draw on the canvas
        canvas.drawOval(oval, paint);
        canvas.drawText("Red Circle", myPoint.x+rad, myPoint.y, paint);
    }
}
```

code snippet PA4AD_Ch13_Mapping/src/MyOverlay.java

For more advanced drawing features see Chapter 11, "Advanced User Experience," that introduces gradients, strokes, and filters.

Handling Map Tap Events

To handle map taps (user clicks), override the `onTap` event handler within the Overlay extension class. The `onTap` handler receives two parameters:

➤ A `GeoPoint` that contains the latitude/longitude of the map location tapped

➤ The `MapView` that was tapped to trigger this event

When you override `onTap`, the method should return `true` if it has handled a particular tap and `false` to let another Overlay handle it, as shown in Listing 13-17.

LISTING 13-17: Handling map-tap events

```
@Override
public boolean onTap(GeoPoint point, MapView mapView) {
  // Perform hit test to see if this overlay is handling the click
  if ([ ... perform hit test ... ]) {
    // TODO [ ... execute on tap functionality ... ]
    return true;
  }

  // If not handled return false
  return false;
}
```

code snippet PA4AD_Ch13_Mapping/src/MyOverlay.java

Adding and Removing Overlays

Each `MapView` contains a list of Overlays currently displayed. You can get a reference to this list by calling `getOverlays`, as shown in the following snippet:

```
List<Overlay> overlays = mapView.getOverlays();
```

Adding and removing items from the list is thread-safe and synchronized, so you can modify and query the list safely. You should still iterate over the list within a synchronization block synchronized on the List.

To add an Overlay onto a Map View, create a new instance of the Overlay and add it to the list, as shown in the following snippet.

```
MyOverlay myOverlay = new MyOverlay();
overlays.add(myOverlay);
mapView.postInvalidate();
```

The added Overlay displays the next time the Map View is redrawn, so it's usually a good practice to call `postInvalidate` after you modify the list to update the changes on the map display.

Annotating Where Am I

This final modification to Where Am I creates and adds a new Overlay that displays a white circle at the device's current position.

1. Create a new `MyPositionOverlay` Overlay class:

```
import android.graphics.Canvas;
import android.graphics.Paint;
import android.graphics.Point;
import android.graphics.RectF;
import android.location.Location;
import com.google.android.maps.GeoPoint;
import com.google.android.maps.MapView;
```

```
import com.google.android.maps.Overlay;
import com.google.android.maps.Projection;

public class MyPositionOverlay extends Overlay {
  @Override
  public void draw(Canvas canvas, MapView mapView, boolean shadow) {
  }

  @Override
  public boolean onTap(GeoPoint point, MapView mapView) {
    return false;
  }
}
```

2.   Create a new instance variable to store the current Location, and add setter and getter methods for it.

```
Location location;

public Location getLocation() {
  return location;
}
public void setLocation(Location location) {
  this.location = location;
}
```

3.   Override the `draw` method to add a small white circle at the current location.

```
private final int mRadius = 5;

@Override
public void draw(Canvas canvas, MapView mapView, boolean shadow) {
  Projection projection = mapView.getProjection();

  if (shadow == false && location != null) {
    // Get the current location
    Double latitude = location.getLatitude()*1E6;
    Double longitude = location.getLongitude()*1E6;
    GeoPoint geoPoint;
    geoPoint = new
      GeoPoint(latitude.intValue(),longitude.intValue());

    // Convert the location to screen pixels
    Point point = new Point();
    projection.toPixels(geoPoint, point);

    RectF oval = new RectF(point.x - mRadius, point.y - mRadius,
                           point.x + mRadius, point.y + mRadius);
```

```
    // Setup the paint
    Paint paint = new Paint();
    paint.setARGB(250, 255, 255, 255);
    paint.setAntiAlias(true);
    paint.setFakeBoldText(true);

    Paint backPaint = new Paint();
    backPaint.setARGB(175, 50, 50, 50);
    backPaint.setAntiAlias(true);

    RectF backRect = new RectF(point.x + 2 + mRadius,
                               point.y - 3*mRadius,
                               point.x + 65, point.y + mRadius);

    // Draw the marker
    canvas.drawOval(oval, paint);
    canvas.drawRoundRect(backRect, 5, 5, backPaint);
    canvas.drawText("Here I Am",
                    point.x + 2*mRadius, point.y,
                    paint);
  }
  super.draw(canvas, mapView, shadow);
}
```

4. Now open the `WhereAmI` Activity class, and add the `MyPositionOverlay` to the `MapView`.

Add a new instance variable to store the `MyPositionOverlay`; then override `onCreate` to create a new instance of the class, and add it to the `MapView`'s Overlay list.

```
private MyPositionOverlay positionOverlay;

@Override
public void onCreate(Bundle savedInstanceState) {
  super.onCreate(savedInstanceState);
  setContentView(R.layout.main);

  // Get a reference to the MapView
  MapView myMapView = (MapView)findViewById(R.id.myMapView);

  // Get the Map View's controller
  mapController = myMapView.getController();

  // Configure the map display options
  myMapView.setSatellite(true);
  myMapView.setBuiltInZoomControls(true);

  // Zoom in
  mapController.setZoom(17);
```

```
// Add the MyPositionOverlay
positionOverlay = new MyPositionOverlay();
List<Overlay> overlays = myMapView.getOverlays();
overlays.add(positionOverlay);
myMapView.postInvalidate();

LocationManager locationManager;
String svcName= Context.LOCATION_SERVICE;
locationManager = (LocationManager)getSystemService(svcName);

Criteria criteria = new Criteria();
criteria.setAccuracy(Criteria.ACCURACY_FINE);
criteria.setPowerRequirement(Criteria.POWER_LOW);
criteria.setAltitudeRequired(false);
criteria.setBearingRequired(false);
criteria.setSpeedRequired(false);
criteria.setCostAllowed(true);
String provider = locationManager.getBestProvider(criteria, true);

Location l = locationManager.getLastKnownLocation(provider);

updateWithNewLocation(l);

locationManager.requestLocationUpdates(provider, 2000, 10,
                                       locationListener);

}
```

5. Modify the `updateWithNewLocation` method to update its position when a new location is received:

```
private void updateWithNewLocation(Location location) {
  TextView myLocationText;
  myLocationText = (TextView)findViewById(R.id.myLocationText);

  String latLongString = "No location found";
  String addressString = "No address found";

  if (location != null) {
    // Update the position overlay.
    positionOverlay.setLocation(location);

  [ ... Existing updateWithNewLocation method ... ]
}
```

> *All code snippets in this example are part of the* Chapter 13 Where Am I Part 5 *project, available for download at* www.wrox.com.

When run, your application displays your current device location with a white circle and supporting text, as shown in Figure 13-6.

FIGURE 13-6

> *It's worth noting that this is not the preferred technique for displaying your current location on a map. This functionality is implemented natively by Android through the* `MyLocationOverlay` *class. If you want to display and follow your current location, you should consider using (or extending) this class, as shown in the next section, instead of implementing it manually as shown here.*

Introducing My Location Overlay

The `MyLocationOverlay` class is a native Overlay designed to show your current location and orientation on a `MapView`.

To use My Location Overlay you need to create a new instance, passing in the application Context and target Map View, and add it to the `MapView`'s Overlay list, as shown here:

```
List<Overlay> overlays = mapView.getOverlays();
MyLocationOverlay myLocationOverlay = new MyLocationOverlay(this, mapView);
overlays.add(myLocationOverlay);
```

You can use My Location Overlay to display both your current location and orientation (represented as a flashing blue marker.)

The following snippet shows how to enable both the compass and marker.

```
myLocationOverlay.enableCompass();
myLocationOverlay.enableMyLocation();
```

Introducing Itemized Overlays and Overlay Items

`OverlayItems` are used to supply simple marker functionality to your Map Views via the `ItemizedOverlay` class.

`ItemizedOverlays` provide a convenient shortcut for adding markers to a map, letting you assign a marker image and associated text to a particular geographical position. The `ItemizedOverlay` instance handles the drawing, placement, click handling, focus control, and layout optimization of each `OverlayItem` marker for you.

To add an `ItemizedOverlay` marker layer to your map, create a new class that extends `ItemizedOverlay<OverlayItem>`, as shown in Listing 13-18.

 `ItemizedOverlay` is a generic class that enables you to create extensions based on any class that implements `OverlayItem`.

Within the constructor, you need to call through to the superclass after defining the bounds for your default marker. You must then call `populate` to trigger the creation of each `OverlayItem`; `populate` must be called whenever the data used to create the items changes.

Within your implementation, override `size` to return the number of markers to display and `createItem` to create a new item based on the index of each marker.

LISTING 13-18: Creating a new Itemized Overlay

```
import android.graphics.drawable.Drawable;
import com.google.android.maps.GeoPoint;
import com.google.android.maps.ItemizedOverlay;
import com.google.android.maps.OverlayItem;

public class MyItemizedOverlay extends ItemizedOverlay<OverlayItem> {

  public MyItemizedOverlay(Drawable defaultMarker) {
    super(boundCenterBottom(defaultMarker));
    populate();
  }

  @Override
  protected OverlayItem createItem(int index) {
    switch (index) {
      case 0:
        Double lat = 37.422006*1E6;
```

```
        Double lng = -122.084095*1E6;
        GeoPoint point = new GeoPoint(lat.intValue(), lng.intValue());

        OverlayItem oi;
        oi = new OverlayItem(point, "Marker", "Marker Text");
        return oi;
      }
    return null;
  }

  @Override
  public int size() {
    // Return the number of markers in the collection
    return 1;
  }
}
```

code snippet PA4AD_Ch13_Mapping/MyItemizedOverlay.java

To add an `ItemizedOverlay` implementation to your map, create a new instance (passing in the Drawable marker image to use for each marker) and add it to the map's Overlay list.

```
List<Overlay> overlays = mapView.getOverlays();
Drawable drawable = getResources().getDrawable(R.drawable.marker);
MyItemizedOverlay markers = new MyItemizedOverlay(drawable);
overlays.add(markers);
```

> *The map markers placed by the Itemized Overlay use state to indicate if they are selected. Use the `StateListDrawable` described in Chapter 11 to indicate when a marker has been selected.*

In Listing 13-18, the list of Overlay items is static and defined in code. More typically your Overlay items will be a dynamic `ArrayList` to which you want to add and remove items at run time.

Listing 13-19 shows the skeleton class for a dynamic Itemized Overlay implementation, backed by an Array List and supporting the addition and removal of items at run time.

LISTING 13-19: Skeleton code for a dynamic Itemized Overlay

```
public class MyDynamicItemizedOverlay extends
   ItemizedOverlay<OverlayItem> {

   private ArrayList<OverlayItem> items;

   public MyDynamicItemizedOverlay(Drawable defaultMarker) {
     super(boundCenterBottom(defaultMarker));
     items = new ArrayList<OverlayItem>();
     populate();
   }
```

continues

LISTING 13-19 *(continued)*

```
public void addNewItem(GeoPoint location, String markerText,
                       String snippet) {
  items.add(new OverlayItem(location, markerText, snippet));
  populate();
}

public void removeItem(int index) {
  items.remove(index);
  populate();
}

@Override
protected OverlayItem createItem(int index) {
  return items.get(index);
}

@Override
public int size() {
  return items.size();
}
}
```

code snippet PA4AD_Ch13_Mapping/src/MyDynamicItemizedOverlay.java

Pinning Views to the Map and Map Positions

You can pin any View-derived object to a Map View (including layouts and other View Groups), attaching it to either a screen position or a geographical map location.

In the latter case, the View moves to follow its pinned position on the map, effectively acting as an interactive map marker. As a more resource-intensive solution, this is usually reserved for supplying the detail "balloons" often displayed on mashups to provide further detail when a marker is clicked.

You implement both pinning mechanisms by calling `addView` on the `MapView`, usually from the `onCreate` or `onRestore` methods within the `MapActivity` containing it. Pass in the View you want to pin and the layout parameters to use.

The `MapView.LayoutParams` parameters you pass in to `addView` determine how, and where, the View is added to the map.

To add a new View to the map relative to the screen, specify a new `MapView.LayoutParams`, including arguments that set the height and width of the View, the x/y screen coordinates to pin to, and the alignment to use for positioning, as shown in Listing 13-20.

LISTING 13-20: Pinning a View to a map

```
int y = 10;
int x = 10;

EditText editText1 = new EditText(getApplicationContext());
editText1.setText("Screen Pinned");

MapView.LayoutParams screenLP;
screenLP = new MapView.LayoutParams(MapView.LayoutParams.WRAP_CONTENT,
                                    MapView.LayoutParams.WRAP_CONTENT,
                                    x, y,
                                    MapView.LayoutParams.TOP_LEFT);
mapView.addView(editText1, screenLP);
```

code snippet PA4AD_Ch13_Mapping/src/MyMapActivity.java

To pin a View relative to a physical map location, pass four parameters when constructing the new Map View LayoutParams, representing the height, width, GeoPoint to pin to, and layout alignment, as shown in Listing 13-21.

LISTING 13-21: Pinning a View to a geographical location

```
Double lat = 37.422134*1E6;
Double lng = -122.084069*1E6;
GeoPoint geoPoint = new GeoPoint(lat.intValue(), lng.intValue());

MapView.LayoutParams geoLP;
geoLP = new MapView.LayoutParams(MapView.LayoutParams.WRAP_CONTENT,
                                 MapView.LayoutParams.WRAP_CONTENT,
                                 geoPoint,
                                 MapView.LayoutParams.TOP_LEFT);

EditText editText2 = new EditText(getApplicationContext());
editText2.setText("Location Pinned");

mapView.addView(editText2, geoLP);
```

code snippet PA4AD_Ch13_Mapping/src/MyMapActivity.java

Panning the map can leave the first TextView stationary in the upper-left corner, whereas the second TextView moves to remain pinned to a particular position on the map.

To remove a View from a Map View, call removeView, passing in the View instance you want to remove, as shown here.

```
mapView.removeView(editText2);
```

MAPPING EARTHQUAKES EXAMPLE

The following step-by-step guide demonstrates how to add a map to the Earthquake project you last saw in Chapter 10. The map will be used to display a map of recent earthquakes.

> *In this example you will be adding a* MapView *to a Fragment. As a result, you will not be able to complete this example using the support library.*

1. Start by ensuring the build target in your project properties refer to an Android build that includes the Google APIs. Then modify the Earthquake Activity so that it inherits from MapActivity, and add an implementation for isRouteDisplayed that returns false:

```
public class Earthquake extends MapActivity {

  @Override
  protected boolean isRouteDisplayed() {
    return false;
  }

  [ ... Existing class code ... ]
}
```

2. You can add only one Map View to each Activity, so to ensure this is the case, you should create the Map View within the Earthquake Activity rather than the Fragment. Modify the onCreate handler to create a new MapView and store it as a public property:

```
MapView mapView;
String MyMapAPIKey = // TODO [Get Map API Key];

@Override
public void onCreate(Bundle savedInstanceState) {
  super.onCreate(savedInstanceState);

  mapView = new MapView(this, MyMapAPIKey);

  [ ... Existing onCreate handler code ... ]
}
```

3. Modify the onCreateView handler within the EarthquakeMapFragment to return the MapView from the parent Activity:

```
@Override
public View onCreateView(LayoutInflater inflater, ViewGroup container,
                         Bundle savedInstanceState) {

  MapView earthquakeMap = ((Earthquake)getActivity()).mapView;

  return earthquakeMap;
}
```

4. Update the application manifest to import the map library:

```xml
<?xml version="1.0" encoding="utf-8"?>
<manifest
  xmlns:android="http://schemas.android.com/apk/res/android"
  package="com.paad.earthquake"
  android:versionCode="1"
  android:versionName="1.0" >

  <uses-sdk android:targetSdkVersion="15"
            android:minSdkVersion="11" />

  <uses-permission android:name="android.permission.INTERNET"/>
  <uses-permission android:name="android.permission.VIBRATE"/>

  <application
    android:icon="@drawable/ic_launcher"
    android:label="@string/app_name">

    <uses-library android:name="com.google.android.maps"/>

    [ ... Existing application nodes ... ]

  </application>
</manifest>
```

At this point, starting your application should make the Map View visible either in the tablet view or when the Map tab is selected on Smartphones.

5. Create a new `EarthquakeOverlay` class that extends `Overlay`. It draws the position and magnitude of each earthquake on the Map View:

```java
import java.util.ArrayList;
import android.database.Cursor;
import android.database.DataSetObserver;
import android.graphics.Canvas;
import android.graphics.Paint;
import android.graphics.Point;
import android.graphics.RectF;
import com.google.android.maps.GeoPoint;
import com.google.android.maps.MapView;
import com.google.android.maps.Overlay;
import com.google.android.maps.Projection;

public class EarthquakeOverlay extends Overlay {
  @Override
  public void draw(Canvas canvas, MapView mapView, boolean shadow) {
    Projection projection = mapView.getProjection();

    if (shadow == false) {
     // TODO: Draw earthquakes
    }
  }
}
```

5.1 Add a new constructor that accepts a `Cursor` to the current earthquake data, and store that Cursor as an instance variable:

```
Cursor earthquakes;

public EarthquakeOverlay(Cursor cursor) {
  super();

  earthquakes = cursor;
}
```

5.2 Create a new `refreshQuakeLocations` method that iterates over the results Cursor and extracts the location of each earthquake, extracting the latitude and longitude before storing each coordinate in a List of `GeoPoints`:

```
ArrayList<GeoPoint> quakeLocations;

private void refreshQuakeLocations() {
  quakeLocations.clear();

  if (earthquakes != null && earthquakes.moveToFirst())
    do {
        int latIndex
          = earthquakes.getColumnIndexOrThrow(EarthquakeProvider.KEY_LOCATION_LAT);
        int lngIndex
          = earthquakes.getColumnIndexOrThrow(EarthquakeProvider.KEY_LOCATION_LNG);

        Double lat
          = earthquakes.getFloat(latIndex) * 1E6;
        Double lng
          = earthquakes.getFloat(lngIndex) * 1E6;

      GeoPoint geoPoint = new GeoPoint(lat.intValue(),
                                       lng.intValue());
      quakeLocations.add(geoPoint);

    } while(earthquakes.moveToNext());
}
```

5.3 Call `refreshQuakeLocations` from the Overlay's constructor:

```
public EarthquakeOverlay(Cursor cursor) {
  super();
  earthquakes = cursor;

  quakeLocations = new ArrayList<GeoPoint>();
  refreshQuakeLocations();
}
```

5.4 Create a new public `swapCursor` method that will allow you to pass in new result Cursors:

```
public void swapCursor(Cursor cursor) {
  earthquakes = cursor;
  refreshQuakeLocations();
}
```

5.5 Complete the `EarthquakeOverlay` by overriding the `draw` method to iterate over the list of `GeoPoints`, drawing a marker at each earthquake location. In this example a simple red circle is drawn, but you could easily modify it to include additional information, such as by adjusting the size of each circle based on the magnitude of the quake.

```
int rad = 5;

@Override
public void draw(Canvas canvas, MapView mapView, boolean shadow) {
  Projection projection = mapView.getProjection();

  // Create and setup your paint brush
  Paint paint = new Paint();
  paint.setARGB(250, 255, 0, 0);
  paint.setAntiAlias(true);
  paint.setFakeBoldText(true);
  if (shadow == false) {
    for (GeoPoint point : quakeLocations) {
      Point myPoint = new Point();
      projection.toPixels(point, myPoint);

      RectF oval = new RectF(myPoint.x-rad, myPoint.y-rad,
                             myPoint.x+rad, myPoint.y+rad);

      canvas.drawOval(oval, paint);
    }
  }
}
```

6. Return to the `EarthquakeMapFragment` and modify the `onCreateView` handler to create the Earthquake Overlay and add it to the Map View:

```
EarthquakeOverlay eo;

@Override
public View onCreateView(LayoutInflater inflater, ViewGroup container,
                         Bundle savedInstanceState) {

  MapView earthquakeMap = ((Earthquake)getActivity()).mapView;

  eo = new EarthquakeOverlay(null);
  earthquakeMap.getOverlays().add(eo);

  return earthquakeMap;
}
```

7. Still in the `EarthquakeMapFragment`, modify it to implement `LoaderManager.LoaderCallbacks`:

```
public class EarthquakeMapFragment extends Fragment
  implements LoaderManager.LoaderCallbacks<Cursor> {

  EarthquakeOverlay eo;
```

```
public Loader<Cursor> onCreateLoader(int id, Bundle args) {
  return null;
}

public void onLoadFinished(Loader<Cursor> loader, Cursor cursor) {
}

public void onLoaderReset(Loader<Cursor> loader) {
}

@Override
public View onCreateView(LayoutInflater inflater, ViewGroup container,
                         Bundle savedInstanceState) {

  MapView earthquakeMap = ((Earthquake)getActivity()).mapView;
  eo = new EarthquakeOverlay(null);
  earthquakeMap.getOverlays().add(eo);

  return earthquakeMap;
}
}
```

8. Implement `onCreateLoader` to create a Cursor Loader to return all the earthquakes you want to display on the map:

```
public Loader<Cursor> onCreateLoader(int id, Bundle args) {
  String[] projection = new String[] {
    EarthquakeProvider.KEY_ID,
    EarthquakeProvider.KEY_LOCATION_LAT,
    EarthquakeProvider.KEY_LOCATION_LNG,
  };

  Earthquake earthquakeActivity = (Earthquake)getActivity();
  String where = EarthquakeProvider.KEY_MAGNITUDE + " > " +
                 earthquakeActivity.minimumMagnitude;

  CursorLoader loader = new CursorLoader(getActivity(),
    EarthquakeProvider.CONTENT_URI, projection, where, null, null);

  return loader;
}
```

9. Implement the `onLoadFinished` and `onLoaderReset` methods to apply the returned Cursors to the Earthquake Overlay you created in step 5:

```
public void onLoadFinished(Loader<Cursor> loader, Cursor cursor) {
  eo.swapCursor(cursor);
}

public void onLoaderReset(Loader<Cursor> loader) {
  eo.swapCursor(null);
}
```

10. Finally, override the `onActivityCreated` handler to initiate the Loader:

```
@Override
public void onActivityCreated(Bundle savedInstanceState) {
  super.onActivityCreated(savedInstanceState);
  getLoaderManager().initLoader(0, null, this);
}
```

> *All code snippets in this example are part of the* Chapter 13 Earthquake Part 6
> project, *available for download at* www.wrox.com.

If you run the application and view the Earthquake Map, your application should appear, as shown
in Figure 13-7.

FIGURE 13-7

14

Invading the Home Screen

WHAT'S IN THIS CHAPTER?

➤ Creating home screen Widgets

➤ Creating collection-based home screen Widgets

➤ Using Content Providers to populate Widgets

➤ Surfacing search results to the Quick Search Box

➤ Creating Live Wallpaper

Widgets, Live Wallpaper, and the Quick Search Box (QSB) let you populate a piece of the user's home screen, providing either a window to your application or a stand-alone source of information directly on the home screen. They're exciting innovations for users and developers:

➤ Users get instant access to interesting information without needing to open an application.

➤ Developers get an entry point to their applications directly from the home screen.

A useful home screen Widget or Live Wallpaper increases user engagement, decreasing the chance that an application will be uninstalled and increasing the likelihood of its being used. With such power comes responsibility. Widgets run constantly as subprocesses of the home screen, so you need to be particularly careful when creating them to ensure they remain responsive and don't drain system resources.

This chapter demonstrates how to create and use App Widgets and Live Wallpaper, detailing what they are, how to use them, and some techniques for incorporating interactivity into these application components. The chapter also describes how to surface search results from your application through the QSB.

INTRODUCING HOME SCREEN WIDGETS

Home screen Widgets, more properly `AppWidgets`, are visual application components that can be added to other applications. The most notable example is the default Android home screen, where users can add Widgets to their phone-top. This functionality is typically implemented by alternative home screen replacements, although any application can become an `AppHost` and support embedding third-party Widgets.

Widgets enable your application to populate a piece of interactive screen real estate, and embed an entry point, directly on the user's home screen. A good App Widget provides useful, concise, and timely information with a minimal resource cost.

Widgets can be either stand-alone applications (such as the native clock) or compact but highly visible components of larger applications — such as the Calendar and Media Player Apps Widgets.

Figure 14-1 shows five of the standard home screen Widgets available on Android devices: the Quick Search Box, Power Control, News & Weather, Media Player, and the Photo Gallery.

FIGURE 14-1

To add an App Widget to the home screen prior to Android 3.0, long-press a piece of empty space and select Widgets. You will be presented with a list of available Widgets to add to your home screen.

In Android 3.0 and above, App Widgets are added using the application launcher. Clicking the "Widgets" tab at the top of the launcher tray presents the list of available Widgets. Click and hold a Widget, and you will be able to position it onto your home screen.

After adding a Widget, you can move it by long-pressing it and dragging it around the screen. To resize (available in Android 3.1 and above), long-press and release. You'll see small indicators along the edges of the Widget that can be dragged to resize the Widget.

Remove Widgets by dragging them into the garbage can icon or "remove" label at the top or bottom of the screen.

Widgets embedded into an application are hosted within the parent application's process. They will wake the device based on their update rates to ensure each Widget is up to date when it's visible. As a developer, you need to take extra care when creating your Widgets to ensure that the update rate is as low as possible, and that the code executed within the update method is lightweight.

The following sections show how to create Widgets and describe some best practices for performing updates and adding interactivity.

CREATING APP WIDGETS

App Widgets are implemented as `BroadcastReceivers`. They use `RemoteViews` to define and update a view hierarchy hosted within another application process; most commonly that host process is the home screen.

To create a Widget for your application, you need to create three components:

1. An XML layout resource that defines the UI
2. An XML file that describes the meta data associated with the Widget
3. A Broadcast Receiver that defines and controls the Widget

You can create as many Widgets as you want for a single application, or you can have an application that consists of a single Widget. Each Widget can use the same size, layout, refresh rate, and update logic, or it can use different ones. In many cases it can be useful to offer multiple versions of your Widgets in different sizes.

Creating the Widget XML Layout Resource

The first step in creating your Widget is to design and implement its user interface (UI).

Construct your Widget's UI as you would other visual components in Android, as described in Chapter 4, "Building User Interfaces." Best practice is to define your Widget layout using XML as an external layout resource, but it's also possible to lay out your UI programmatically within the Broadcast Receiver's `onCreate` method.

Widget Design Guidelines

Widgets are often displayed alongside other native and third-party Widgets, so it's important that yours conform to design standards — particularly because Widgets are most often used on the home screen.

There are UI design guidelines for controlling both a Widget's layout size and its visual styling. The former is enforced rigidly, whereas the latter is a guide only; both are summarized in the following sections. You can find additional detail on the Android Developers Widget Design Guidelines site, at `http://developer.android.com/guide/practices/ui_guidelines/widget_design.html`.

Widget Layout Sizes

The default Android home screen is divided into a grid of cells, varying in size and number depending on the device. It's best practice to specify a minimum height and width for your Widget that is required to ensure it is displayed in a good default state.

Where your minimum dimensions don't match the exact dimensions of the home screen cells, your Widget's size will be rounded up to fill the cells into which it extends.

To determine the approximate minimum height and width limits required to ensure your widget fits within a given number of cells, you can use the following formula:

```
Min height or width = 70dp * (cell count) - 30dp
```

Widget dimensions are specified in the Widget settings file, as described in the section "Defining Your Widget Settings."

Widget Visual Styling

The visual styling of your Widget, your application's presence on the home screen, is very important. You should ensure that its style is consistent with that of your application, as well as with those of the other home screen components.

App Widgets fully support transparent backgrounds and allow the use of NinePatches and partially transparent Drawable resources. It's beyond the scope of this book to describe the Widget style promoted by Google in detail, but note the description available at the Widget UI guidelines link provided earlier.

Also note that an App Widget Template Pack is available for download from the sample page. It provides NinePatch background graphics, XML, and source Adobe Photoshop files for multiple screen densities, OS version widget styles, and widget colors. It also includes graphics that can be used within state-list Drawables to make your entire widget or parts of your widget interactive, as described later in this chapter in the "Using Remote Views to Add Widget Interactivity" section.

Supported Widget Views and Layouts

Because of security and performance considerations, there are several restrictions on the layouts and Views available for constructing a Widget UI.

The following Views are unavailable for App Widget layouts and will result in a null pointer error (NPE) if used:

➤ All custom Views

➤ Most descendant classes of allowed Views

➤ `EditText`

Currently, the layouts available are limited to the following:

➤ `FrameLayout`

➤ `LinearLayout`

➤ `RelativeLayout`

➤ `GridLayout`

The Views they contain are restricted to the following:

➤ `AnalogClock`

➤ `Button`

➤ `Chronometer`

➤   `ImageButton`

➤   `ImageView`

➤   `ProgressBar`

➤   `TextView`

➤   `ViewFlipper`

The Text Views, Image Views, and View Flippers are particularly useful. In the section "Changing Image Views Based on Selection Focus" you'll see how to use the Image View in conjunction with the `SelectionStateDrawable` resource to create interactive Widgets with little or no code.

Android 3.0 (API level 11) introduced Collection View Widgets, a new class of Widgets designed to display collections of data in the form of a list, grid, or stack. This Widget type is described in detail in the section "Introducing Collection View Widgets."

Listing 14-1 shows an XML layout resource used to define the UI of an App Widget.

LISTING 14-1: App Widget XML layout resource

```xml
<?xml version="1.0" encoding="utf-8"?>
<LinearLayout
    xmlns:android="http://schemas.android.com/apk/res/android"
    android:orientation="horizontal"
    android:layout_width="match_parent"
    android:layout_height="match_parent"
    android:padding="5dp">
    <ImageView
        android:id="@+id/widget_image"
        android:layout_width="wrap_content"
        android:layout_height="wrap_content"
        android:src="@drawable/icon"
    />
    <TextView
        android:id="@+id/widget_text"
        android:layout_width="fill_parent"
        android:layout_height="fill_parent"
        android:text="@string/widget_text"
    />
</LinearLayout>
```

code snippet PA4AD_Ch14_MyWidget/res/layout/my_widget_layout.xml

Defining Your Widget Settings

Widget definition resources are stored as XML in the `res/xml` folder of your project. The `appwidget-provider` tag enables you to describe the Widget meta data that defines attributes including the size, layout, and update rate for your Widget using the following attributes:

➤   `initialLayout` — The layout resource to use in constructing the Widget's UI.

➤   `minWidth/minHeight` — The minimum width and minimum height of the Widget, respectively, as described in the previous section.

➤ `resizeMode` — Android 3.1 (API level 12) introduced the concept of resizable Widgets. Setting the resize mode allows you to specify the direction in which the Widget can be resized, using a combination of `horizontal` and `vertical`, or disabling resizing by setting it to `none`.

➤ `label` — The title used by your Widget in the App Widget picker.

➤ `updatePeriodMillis` — The minimum period between Widget updates in milliseconds. Android will wake the device to update your Widget at this rate, so you should specify at least an hour. The App Widget Manager won't deliver updates more frequently than once every 30 minutes. Ideally your Widget shouldn't use this update technique more than once or twice daily. More details on this and other update techniques are provided later in this chapter.

➤ `configure` — You can optionally specify a fully qualified Activity to be launched when your Widget is added to the home screen. This Activity can be used to specify Widget settings and user preferences. Using a configuration Activity is described in the section "Creating and Using a Widget Configuration Activity."

➤ `icon` — By default Android will use your application's icon when presenting your Widget within the App Widget picker. Specify a Drawable resource to use a different icon.

➤ `previewImage` — Android 3.0 (API level 11) introduced a new App Widget picker that displays a preview of Widgets rather than their icon. Specify a Drawable resource here that accurately depicts how your Widget will appear when added to the home screen.

Listing 14-2 shows the Widget resource file for a two-cell-by-two-cell Widget that updates once every hour and uses the layout resource defined in the previous section.

LISTING 14-2: App Widget Provider definition

```xml
<?xml version="1.0" encoding="utf-8"?>
<appwidget-provider
    xmlns:android="http://schemas.android.com/apk/res/android"
    android:initialLayout="@layout/my_widget_layout"
    android:minWidth="110dp"
    android:minHeight="110dp"
    android:label="@string/widget_label"
    android:updatePeriodMillis="3600000"
    android:resizeMode="horizontal|vertical"
    android:previewImage="@drawable/widget_preview"
/>
```

code snippet PA4AD_Ch14_MyWidget/res/xml/widget_provider_info.xml

Creating Your Widget Broadcast Receiver and Adding It to the Application Manifest

Widgets are implemented as Broadcast Receivers. Each Widget's Broadcast Receiver specifies Intent Filters to listen for broadcast Intents requesting Widget updates using the `AppWidget.ACTION_APPWIDGET_UPDATE`, `DELETED`, `ENABLED`, and `DISABLED` actions.

To create a Widget, extend the `BroadcastReceiver` class and implement a response to each of these broadcast Intents by overriding the `onReceive` method.

The `AppWidgetProvider` class encapsulates this Intent processing and provides you with event handlers for the update, delete, enable, and disable events.

Listing 14-3 shows a skeleton Widget implementation that extends `AppWidgetProvider`.

LISTING 14-3: App Widget implementation

```java
import android.appwidget.AppWidgetManager;
import android.appwidget.AppWidgetProvider;
import android.widget.RemoteViews;
import android.content.Context;

public class SkeletonAppWidget extends AppWidgetProvider {
  @Override
  public void onUpdate(Context context,
                       AppWidgetManager appWidgetManager,
                       int[] appWidgetIds) {
    // TODO Update the Widget UI.
  }

  @Override
  public void onDeleted(Context context, int[] appWidgetIds) {
    // TODO Handle deletion of the widget.
    super.onDeleted(context, appWidgetIds);
  }

  @Override
  public void onDisabled(Context context) {
    // TODO Widget has been disabled.
    super.onDisabled(context);
  }

  @Override
  public void onEnabled(Context context) {
    // TODO Widget has been enabled.
    super.onEnabled(context);
  }
}
```

code snippet PA4AD_Ch14_MyWidget/src/SkeletonAppWidget.java

Widgets must be added to the application manifest, using a `receiver` tag like other Broadcast Receivers. To specify a Broadcast Receiver as an App Widget, you need to add the following two tags to its manifest node, as shown in Listing 14-4.

➤ An Intent Filter for the `android.appwidget.action.APPWIDGET_UPDATE` action

➤ A reference to the `appwidget-provider` meta data XML resource, described in the previous section, that describes your Widget settings

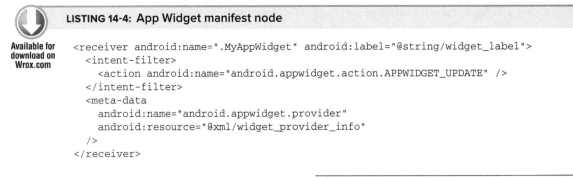

LISTING 14-4: App Widget manifest node

```xml
<receiver android:name=".MyAppWidget" android:label="@string/widget_label">
  <intent-filter>
    <action android:name="android.appwidget.action.APPWIDGET_UPDATE" />
  </intent-filter>
  <meta-data
    android:name="android.appwidget.provider"
    android:resource="@xml/widget_provider_info"
  />
</receiver>
```

code snippet PA4AD_Ch14_MyWidget/AndroidManifest.xml

Introducing the App Widget Manager and Remote Views

The AppWidgetManager class is used to update App Widgets and provide details related to them.

The RemoteViews class is used as a proxy to a View hierarchy hosted within another application's process. This lets you change a property, or run a method, on a View running within another application. For example, the UIs used by your App Widgets are hosted within their host process (typically the home screen). To modify those Views from the App Widget Provider running in your application's process, use Remote Views.

You can modify the appearance of the Views that form your App Widget UI by creating and modifying Remote Views and applying those changes using the App Widget Manager. Supported modifications include changing a Views visibility, text, or image values, and adding Click Listeners.

This section describes how to create new Remote Views and in particular how to use them within onUpdate method of an App Widget Provider. It also demonstrates how to use Remote Views to update your App Widget UI and add interactivity to your Widgets.

Creating and Manipulating Remote Views

To create a new Remote View object, pass the name of your application's package, and the layout resource you plan to manipulate, into the Remote Views constructor, as shown in Listing 14-5.

LISTING 14-5: Creating Remote Views

```java
RemoteViews views = new RemoteViews(context.getPackageName(),
                                    R.layout.my_widget_layout);
```

code Snippet PA4AD_Ch14_MyWidget/src/MyAppWidget.java

Remote Views represent a View hierarchy displayed in another process — in this instance, it will be used to define a set of changes to be applied to the UI of a running Widget.

> *The section "Applying Remote Views to Running App Widgets" describes how to use the App Widget Manager to apply the changes you made in this section to App Widgets. The modifications you apply here will not affect the running instances of your Widgets until you apply them.*

Remote Views include a series of methods that provide access to many of the properties and methods available on native Views. The most versatile of these is a collection of `set` methods that let you specify a target method name to execute on a remotely hosted View. These methods support the passing of a single-value parameter, one for each primitive type, including Boolean, integer, byte, char, and float, as well as strings, bitmaps, Bundles, and URI parameters.

Listing 14-6 shows examples of some of the method signatures supported.

LISTING 14-6: Using a Remote View to apply methods to Views within an App Widget

```
// Set the image level for an ImageView.
views.setInt(R.id.widget_image_view, "setImageLevel", 2);
// Show the cursor of a TextView.
views.setBoolean(R.id.widget_text_view, "setCursorVisible", true);
// Assign a bitmap to an ImageButton.
views.setBitmap(R.id.widget_image_button, "setImageBitmap", myBitmap);
```

code snippet PA4AD_Ch14_MyWidget/src/FullAppWidget.java

A number of methods specific to certain View classes are also available, including methods to modify Text Views, Image Views, Progress Bars, and Chronometers.

Listing 14-7 shows examples of some of these specialist methods:

LISTING 14-7: Modifying View properties within an App Widget Remote View

```
// Update a Text View
views.setTextViewText(R.id.widget_text, "Updated Text");
views.setTextColor(R.id.widget_text, Color.BLUE);
// Update an Image View
views.setImageViewResource(R.id.widget_image, R.drawable.icon);
// Update a Progress Bar
views.setProgressBar(R.id.widget_progressbar, 100, 50, false);
// Update a Chronometer
views.setChronometer(R.id.widget_chronometer,
  SystemClock.elapsedRealtime(), null, true);
```

code snippet PA4AD_Ch14_MyWidget/src/FullAppWidget.java

You can set the visibility of any View hosted within a Remote Views layout by calling `setViewVisibility`, as shown here:

```
views.setViewVisibility(R.id.widget_text, View.INVISIBLE);
```

Remember that so far you have modified the Remote Views object that represents the View hierarchy within the App Widget, but you have not you applied it. For your changes to take effect, you must use the App Widget Manager to apply your updates.

Applying Remote Views to Running App Widgets

To apply the changes you make to the Remote Views to active Widgets, use the App Widget Manager's `updateAppWidget` method, passing in the identifiers of one or more Widgets to update and the Remote View to apply.

```
appWidgetManager.updateAppWidget(appWidgetIds, remoteViews);
```

If you're updating your App Widget UI from within an App Widget Provider's update handler, the process is simple. The `onUpdate` handler receives the App Widget Manager and the array of active App Widget instance IDs as parameters, allowing you to follow the pattern shown in Listing 14-8.

LISTING 14-8: Using a Remote View within the App Widget Provider's onUpdate Handler

```java
@Override
public void onUpdate(Context context,
                     AppWidgetManager appWidgetManager,
                     int[] appWidgetIds) {
  // Iterate through each widget, creating a RemoteViews object and
  // applying the modified RemoteViews to each widget.
  final int N = appWidgetIds.length;
  for (int i = 0; i < N; i++) {
    int appWidgetId = appWidgetIds[i];

    // Create a Remote View
    RemoteViews views = new RemoteViews(context.getPackageName(),
                                        R.layout.my_widget_layout);

    // TODO Update the UI.

    // Notify the App Widget Manager to update the widget using
    // the modified remote view.
    appWidgetManager.updateAppWidget(appWidgetId, views);
  }
}
```

code snippet PA4AD_Ch14_MyWidget/src/MyAppWidget.java

It's best practice to iterate over the Widget ID array. This enables you to apply different UI values to each Widget based on its identifier and associated configuration settings.

You can also update your Widgets directly from a Service, Activity, or Broadcast Receiver. To do so, get a reference to the App Widget Manager by calling its static `getInstance` method, passing in the current context, as shown in Listing 14-9.

LISTING 14-9: Accessing the App Widget Manager

```
// Get the App Widget Manager.
AppWidgetManager appWidgetManager
    = AppWidgetManager.getInstance(context);
```

code snippet PA4AD_Ch14_MyWidget/src/MyReceiver.java

You can then use the `getAppWidgetIds` method on your App Widget Manager instance to find identifiers representing each currently running instance of the specified App Widget, as shown in this extension to Listing 14-9:

```
// Retrieve the identifiers for each instance of your chosen widget.
ComponentName thisWidget = new ComponentName(context, MyAppWidget.class);
int[] appWidgetIds = appWidgetManager.getAppWidgetIds(thisWidget);
```

To update the active Widgets, you can follow the same pattern described in Listing 14-8, as shown in Listing 14-10.

LISTING 14-10: A standard pattern for updating Widget UI

```
final int N = appWidgetIds.length;
// Iterate through each widget, creating a RemoteViews object and
// applying the modified RemoteViews to each widget.
for (int i = 0; i < N; i++) {
  int appWidgetId = appWidgetIds[i];
  // Create a Remote View
  RemoteViews views = new RemoteViews(context.getPackageName(),
                                      R.layout.my_widget_layout);

  // TODO Update the widget UI using the views object.

  // Notify the App Widget Manager to update the widget using
  // the modified remote view.
  appWidgetManager.updateAppWidget(appWidgetId, views);
}
```

code snippet PA4AD_Ch14_MyWidget/src/MyReceiver.java

Using Remote Views to Add Widget Interactivity

App Widgets inherit the permissions of the processes within which they run, and most home screen apps run with full permissions, making the potential security risks significant. As a result of these security implications, Widget interactivity is carefully controlled.

Widget interaction is generally limited to the following:

➤ Adding a Click Listener to one or more Views

➤ Changing the UI based on selection changes

➤ Transitioning between Views within a Collection View Widget

> *There is no supported technique for entering text directly into an App Widget. If you need text input from your Widget, best practice is to add a Click Listener to the Widget that displays an Activity that accepts input.*

Using a Click Listener

The simplest and most powerful way to add interactivity to your Widget is by adding a Click Listener to its Views. This is done using the `setOnClickPendingIntent` method on a Remote Views object.

Use this method to specify a Pending Intent that will be fired when the user clicks the specified View, as shown in Listing 14-11.

LISTING 14-11: Adding a Click Listener to an App Widget

```
Intent intent = new Intent(context, MyActivity.class);
PendingIntent pendingIntent =
  PendingIntent.getActivity(context, 0, intent, 0);
views.setOnClickPendingIntent(R.id.widget_text, pendingIntent);
```

code snippet PA4AD_Ch14_MyWidget/src/MyAppWidget.java

Pending Intents (described in more detail in Chapter 5, "Intents and Broadcast Receivers") can contain Intents used to start Activities or Services, or that broadcast Intents.

Using this technique you can add Click Listeners to one or more of the Views used within your Widget, potentially providing support for multiple actions.

For example, the standard Media Player Widget assigns different broadcast Intents to several buttons, providing playback control through the play, pause, and next buttons.

> *When Pending Intents are broadcast, the Intents they wrap operate under the same permissions as the application that created them. In the case of Widgets, that means your application rather than the host process.*

Changing Image Views Based on Selection Focus

Image Views are one of the most flexible Views available for your Widget UI, providing support for some basic user interactivity.

Using a `SelectionStateDrawable` resource (described in Chapter 3) you can create a Drawable resource that displays a different image based on the selection state of the View it is assigned to. By using a Selection State Drawable in your Widget design, you can create a dynamic UI that highlights the users' selection as they navigates though the Widget's controls and makes selections.

This is particularly important to ensure your Widget can be used with the trackball or D-pad in addition to a touch screen:

```xml
<selector xmlns:android="http://schemas.android.com/apk/res/android">
  <item android:state_window_focused="false"
        android:drawable="@drawable/widget_bg_normal"/>
  <item android:state_focused="true"
        android:drawable="@drawable/widget_bg_selected"/>
  <item android:state_pressed="true"
        android:drawable="@drawable/widget_bg_pressed"/>
  <item android:drawable="@drawable/widget_bg_normal"/>
</selector>
```

The referenced Drawable resources should be stored in low, medium, high, and extra high resolution in the application's `res/drawable-[ldpi/mdpi/hdpi/xhdpi]` folders, respectively. The selection state XML file should be placed in the `res/drawable` folder.

You can then use the Selection State Drawable directly as the source for an Image View or as the background image for any Widget View.

Refreshing Your Widgets

Widgets are most commonly displayed on the home screen, so it's important that they're always kept relevant and up to date. It's just as important to balance that relevance with your Widget's impact on system resources — particularly battery life.

The following sections describe several techniques for managing your Widget's refresh intervals.

Using the Minimum Update Rate

The simplest, but potentially most resource-intensive, technique is to set the minimum update rate for a Widget using the `updatePeriodMillis` attribute in the Widget's XML App Widget Provider Info definition. This is demonstrated in Listing 14-12, where the Widget is updated once every hour.

LISTING 14-12: Setting the App Widget minimum update rate

```xml
<?xml version="1.0" encoding="utf-8"?>
<appwidget-provider
  xmlns:android="http://schemas.android.com/apk/res/android"
android:initialLayout="@layout/my_widget_layout"
  android:minWidth="110dp"
  android:minHeight="110dp"
  android:label="@string/widget_label"
  android:resizeMode="horizontal|vertical"
  android:previewImage="@drawable/widget_preview"
  android:updatePeriodMillis="3600000"
/>
```

code snippet PA4AD_Ch14_MyWidget/res/xml/widget_provider_info.xml

Setting this value will cause the device to broadcast an Intent requesting an update of your Widget at the rate specified.

> *The host device will wake up to complete these updates, meaning they are completed even when the device is on standby. This has the potential to be a significant resource drain, so it's very important to consider the implications of your update rate. In most cases the system will not broadcast a minimum update broadcast more frequently than every 30 minutes.*

This technique should be used to define the absolute minimum rate at which your Widget must be updated to remain useful. Generally, the update rate should be a minimum of an hour and ideally not more than once or twice a day.

If your Widget requires more frequent updates, consider using one of the techniques described in the following sections to perform updates using either a more efficient scheduled model using Alarms or an event/Intent-driven model.

Using Intents

App Widgets are implemented as Broadcast Receivers, so you can trigger updates and UI refreshes by registering Intent Filters against them that listen for additional Broadcast Intents. This is a dynamic approach to refreshing your Widget that uses a more efficient event model rather than the potentially battery-draining method of specifying a short minimum refresh rate.

The XML snippet in Listing 14-13 assigns a new Intent Filter to the manifest entry of the Widget defined earlier.

LISTING 14-13: Listening for Broadcast Intents within App Widgets

```xml
<receiver android:name=".MyAppWidget"
    android:label="@string/widget_label">
    <intent-filter>
        <action android:name="android.appwidget.action.APPWIDGET_UPDATE" />
    </intent-filter>
    <intent-filter>
        <action android:name="com.paad.mywidget.FORCE_WIDGET_UPDATE" />
    </intent-filter>
    <meta-data
        android:name="android.appwidget.provider"
        android:resource="@xml/widget_provider_info"
    />
</receiver>
```

code snippet PA4AD_Ch14_MyWidget/AndroidManifest.xml

By updating the Widget's `onReceive` method handler, as shown in Listing 14-14, you can listen for this new Broadcast Intent and use it to update your Widget.

LISTING 14-14: Updating App Widgets based on Broadcast Intents

```java
public static String FORCE_WIDGET_UPDATE =
  "com.paad.mywidget.FORCE_WIDGET_UPDATE";

@Override
public void onReceive(Context context, Intent intent) {
  super.onReceive(context, intent);

  if (FORCE_WIDGET_UPDATE.equals(intent.getAction())) {
    // TODO Update widget
  }
}
```

code snippet PA4AD_Ch14_MyWidget/src/MyAppWidget.java

This approach is particularly useful for reacting to system, user, or application events — like a data refresh, or a user action such as clicking buttons on the Widget itself. You can also register for system event broadcasts such as changes to network connectivity, battery level, or screen brightness. By relying on existing events to trigger UI updates, you minimize the impact of Widget updates while maintaining a fresh UI.

You can also leverage this technique to trigger an update of your Widget at any time by broadcasting an Intent using the action specified in your Intent Filter, as shown in Listing 14-15.

LISTING 14-15: Broadcasting an Intent to update an App Widget

```java
sendBroadcast(new Intent(MyAppWidget.FORCE_WIDGET_UPDATE));
```

code snippet PA4AD_Ch14_MyWidget/src/MyActivity.java

Using Alarms

Alarms, covered in detail in Chapter 9, "Working in the Background," provide a flexible way to schedule regular events within your application. Using Alarms, you can poll at regular intervals using the Intent-based update technique described in the previous section to trigger regular Widget updates.

Unlike the minimum refresh rate, Alarms can be configured to trigger only when the device is already awake, providing a more efficient alternative when regular updates are required.

Using Alarms to refresh your Widgets is similar to using the Intent-driven model described previously. Add a new Intent Filter to the manifest entry for your Widget, and override its `onReceive` method to identify the Intent that triggered it. Within your application, use the Alarm Manager to create an Alarm that fires an Intent with the registered action.

Like the minimum update rate, Alarms can be set to wake the device when they trigger — making it important to minimize their use to conserve battery life.

One alternative is to use either the `RTC` or `ELAPSED_REALTIME` modes when constructing your Alarm. These modes configure an Alarm to trigger at a set time or after a specified interval has elapsed, but only if the device is awake.

Listing 14-16 shows how to schedule a repeating Alarm that broadcasts an Intent used to force a Widget update.

LISTING 14-16: Updating a Widget using a nonwaking repeating Alarm

```
PendingIntent pi = PendingIntent.getBroadcast(context, 0,
   new Intent(MyAppWidget.FORCE_WIDGET_UPDATE), 0);

alarmManager.setRepeating(AlarmManager.ELAPSED_REALTIME,
                          AlarmManager.INTERVAL_HOUR,
                          AlarmManager.INTERVAL_HOUR,
                          pi);
```

code snippet PA4AD_Ch14_MyWidget/src/MyActivity.java

Using this technique will ensure your Widget is updated regularly, without draining the battery unnecessarily by refreshing the UI when the screen is off.

A better approach is to use inexact repeating Alarms, as shown in this modification to Listing 14-16:

```
alarmManager.setInexactRepeating(AlarmManager.ELAPSED_REALTIME,
                          AlarmManager.INTERVAL_HOUR,
                          AlarmManager.INTERVAL_HOUR,
                          pi);
```

As described in Chapter 9, the inexact repeating Alarm will optimize the Alarm triggers by phase-shifting all the Alarms scheduled to occur at similar times. This ensures the device is awakened only once, rather than potentially several times within a few minutes.

Creating and Using a Widget Configuration Activity

In many cases it's useful for users to have the opportunity to configure a Widget before adding it to their home screen. Done properly, you can make it possible for users to add multiple instances of the same Widget to their home screen.

An App Widget configuration Activity is launched immediately when a Widget is added to the home screen. It can be any Activity within your application, provided it has an Intent Filter for the APPWIDGET_CONFIGURE action, as shown in Listing 14-17.

LISTING 14-17: App Widget configuration Activity manifest entry

```
<activity android:name=".MyWidgetConfigurationActivity">
  <intent-filter>
    <action android:name="android.appwidget.action.APPWIDGET_CONFIGURE"/>
  </intent-filter>
</activity>
```

code snippet PA4AD_Ch14_MyWidget/AndroidManifest.xml

To assign a configuration Activity to a Widget, you must add it to the Widget's App Widget Provider Info settings file using the `configure` tag. The activity must be specified by its fully qualified package name, as shown here:

```xml
<?xml version="1.0" encoding="utf-8"?>
<appwidget-provider
  xmlns:android="http://schemas.android.com/apk/res/android"
  android:initialLayout="@layout/my_widget_layout"
  android:minWidth="146dp"
  android:minHeight="146dp"
  android:label="My App Widget"
  android:updatePeriodMillis="3600000"
  android:configure=
    "com.paad.PA4AD_Ch14_MyWidget.MyWidgetConfigurationActivity"
/>
```

The Intent that launches the configuration Activity will include an EXTRA_APPWIDGET_ID extra that provides the ID of the App Widget being configured.

Within the Activity, provide a UI to allow the user to complete the configuration and confirm. At this stage the Activity should result to RESULT_OK and return an Intent. The returned Intent must include an extra that describes the ID of the Widget being configured using the EXTRA_APPWIDGET_ID constant. This skeleton pattern is shown in Listing 14-18.

LISTING 14-18: Skeleton App Widget configuration Activity

```java
private int appWidgetId = AppWidgetManager.INVALID_APPWIDGET_ID;

@Override
public void onCreate(Bundle savedInstanceState) {
  super.onCreate(savedInstanceState);
  setContentView(R.layout.main);

  Intent intent = getIntent();
  Bundle extras = intent.getExtras();
  if (extras != null) {
    appWidgetId = extras.getInt(
      AppWidgetManager.EXTRA_APPWIDGET_ID,
      AppWidgetManager.INVALID_APPWIDGET_ID);
  }

  // Set the result to canceled in case the user exits
  // the Activity without accepting the configuration
  // changes / settings.
  setResult(RESULT_CANCELED, null);

  // Configure the UI.
}

private void completedConfiguration() {
  // Save the configuration settings for the Widget ID
```

continues

LISTING 14-18 *(continued)*

```
    // Notify the Widget Manager that the configuration has completed.
    Intent result = new Intent();
    result.putExtra(AppWidgetManager.EXTRA_APPWIDGET_ID, appWidgetId);
    setResult(RESULT_OK, result);
    finish();
}
```

code snippet PA4AD_Ch14_MyWidget/src/ MyWidgetConfigurationActivity.java

CREATING AN EARTHQUAKE WIDGET

The following instructions, which extend the Earthquake application from Chapter 13, "Maps, Geocoding, and Location-Based Services," show you how to create a new home screen Widget to display details for the latest earthquake. The UI for this Widget is simple to the point of being inane — a side effect of keeping the example as concise as possible. It does not conform to the Widget style guidelines. When completed and added to the home screen, your Widget will appear, as shown in Figure 14-2.

FIGURE 14-2

Using a combination of the update techniques described previously, this Widget listens for Broadcast Intents that announce an update has been performed and sets the minimum update rate to ensure it is updated once per day regardless.

1. Start by creating the layout for the Widget UI as an XML resource. Save the `quake_widget` `.xml` file in the `res/layout` folder. Use a Linear Layout to configure Text Views that display the quake magnitude and location:

```
<?xml version="1.0" encoding="utf-8"?>
<LinearLayout
  xmlns:android="http://schemas.android.com/apk/res/android"
  android:orientation="horizontal"
  android:layout_width="match_parent"
  android:layout_height="match_parent"
  android:background="#F111"
  android:padding="5dp">
  <TextView
    android:id="@+id/widget_magnitude"
    android:text="---"
    android:layout_width="wrap_content"
    android:layout_height="match_parent"
    android:textSize="24sp"
    android:padding="3dp"
    android:gravity="center_vertical"
  />
  <TextView
    android:id="@+id/widget_details"
    android:text="Details Unknown"
```

```
    android:layout_width="match_parent"
    android:layout_height="match_parent"
    android:textSize="14sp"
    android:padding="3dp"
    android:gravity="center_vertical"
  />
</LinearLayout>
```

2. Create a stub for a new `EarthquakeWidget` class that extends `AppWidgetProvider`. You'll return to this class to update your Widget with the latest quake details.

```
package com.paad.earthquake;

import android.widget.RemoteViews;
import android.app.PendingIntent;
import android.appwidget.AppWidgetManager;
import android.appwidget.AppWidgetProvider;
import android.content.ComponentName;
import android.content.ContentResolver;
import android.content.Context;
import android.content.Intent;
import android.database.Cursor;

public class EarthquakeWidget extends AppWidgetProvider {
}
```

3. Create a new Widget definition file, `quake_widget_info.xml`, and place it in the `res/xml` folder. Set the minimum update rate to once a day and set the Widget dimensions to two cells wide and one cell high — 110dp × 40dp. Use the Widget layout you created in step 1 for the initial layout.

```
<?xml version="1.0" encoding="utf-8"?>
<appwidget-provider
  xmlns:android="http://schemas.android.com/apk/res/android"
  android:initialLayout="@layout/quake_widget"
  android:minWidth="110dp"
  android:minHeight="40dp"
  android:label="Earthquakes"
  android:updatePeriodMillis="86400000"
/>
```

4. Add your Widget to the application manifest, including a reference to the Widget definition resource you created in step 3, and registering an Intent Filter for the App Widget update action.

```
<receiver android:name=".EarthquakeWidget" android:label="Earthquake">
  <intent-filter>
    <action android:name="android.appwidget.action.APPWIDGET_UPDATE" />
  </intent-filter>
  <meta-data
    android:name="android.appwidget.provider"
    android:resource="@xml/quake_widget_info"
  />
</receiver>
```

5. Your Widget is now configured and will be available to add to the home screen. You need to update the `EarthquakeWidget` class from step 2 to update the Widget to display the details of the latest earthquake.

5.1 Start by creating a method stub that takes an App Widget Manager and an array of Widget IDs as well as the context. Later you'll extend this stub to update the Widget appearance using Remote Views.

```
public void updateQuake(Context context,
                        AppWidgetManager appWidgetManager,
                        int[] appWidgetIds) {

}
```

5.2 Create a second method stub that takes only the context, using that to obtain an instance of the `AppWidgetManager`. Then use the App Widget Manager to find the Widget IDs of the active Earthquake Widgets, passing both into the method you created in step 5.1.

```
public void updateQuake(Context context) {
  ComponentName thisWidget = new ComponentName(context,
                                               EarthquakeWidget.class);
  AppWidgetManager appWidgetManager =
    AppWidgetManager.getInstance(context);
  int[] appWidgetIds = appWidgetManager.getAppWidgetIds(thisWidget);
  updateQuake(context, appWidgetManager, appWidgetIds);
}
```

5.3 Within the `updateQuake` stub from step 5.1, use the Earthquake Content Provider created in Chapter 8 to retrieve the newest quake and extract its magnitude and location:

```
public void updateQuake(Context context,
                        AppWidgetManager appWidgetManager,
                        int[] appWidgetIds) {

  Cursor lastEarthquake;
  ContentResolver cr = context.getContentResolver();
  lastEarthquake = cr.query(EarthquakeProvider.CONTENT_URI,
                            null, null, null, null);

  String magnitude = "--";
  String details = "-- None --";

  if (lastEarthquake != null) {
    try {
      if (lastEarthquake.moveToFirst()) {
        int magColumn
          = lastEarthquake.getColumnIndexOrThrow(EarthquakeProvider.KEY_MAGNITUDE);
        int detailsColumn
          = lastEarthquake.getColumnIndexOrThrow(EarthquakeProvider.KEY_DETAILS);

        magnitude = lastEarthquake.getString(magColumn);
        details = lastEarthquake.getString(detailsColumn);
      }
    }
    finally {
```

```
        lastEarthquake.close();
    }
  }
}
```

5.4 Create a new `RemoteViews` object to set the text displayed by the Widget's Text View elements to show the magnitude and location of the last quake:

```
public void updateQuake(Context context,
                        AppWidgetManager appWidgetManager,
                        int[] appWidgetIds) {

  Cursor lastEarthquake;
  ContentResolver cr = context.getContentResolver();
  lastEarthquake = cr.query(EarthquakeProvider.CONTENT_URI,
                            null, null, null, null);

  String magnitude = "--";
  String details = "-- None --";

  if (lastEarthquake != null) {
    try {
      if (lastEarthquake.moveToFirst()) {
        int magColumn
          = lastEarthquake.getColumnIndexOrThrow(EarthquakeProvider.KEY_MAGNITUDE);
        int detailsColumn
          = lastEarthquake.getColumnIndexOrThrow(EarthquakeProvider.KEY_DETAILS);

        magnitude = lastEarthquake.getString(magColumn);
        details = lastEarthquake.getString(detailsColumn);
      }
    }
    finally {
      lastEarthquake.close();
    }
  }

  final int N = appWidgetIds.length;
  for (int i = 0; i < N; i++) {
    int appWidgetId = appWidgetIds[i];
    RemoteViews views = new RemoteViews(context.getPackageName(),
                                        R.layout.quake_widget);
    views.setTextViewText(R.id.widget_magnitude, magnitude);
    views.setTextViewText(R.id.widget_details, details);
    appWidgetManager.updateAppWidget(appWidgetId, views);
  }
}
```

6. Override the `onUpdate` handler to call `updateQuake`:

```
@Override
public void onUpdate(Context context,
                     AppWidgetManager appWidgetManager,
                     int[] appWidgetIds) {

  // Update the Widget UI with the latest Earthquake details.
  updateQuake(context, appWidgetManager, appWidgetIds);
}
```

Your Widget is now ready to be used and will update with new earthquake details when added to the home screen and once every 24 hours thereafter.

7. Now further enhance the Widget to update whenever the Earthquake Update Service you created in Chapter 9, has refreshed the earthquake database:

7.1 Start by updating the onHandleIntent handler in the EarthquakeUpdateService to broadcast an Intent when it has completed:

```
public static String QUAKES_REFRESHED =
  "com.paad.earthquake.QUAKES_REFRESHED";

@Override
protected void onHandleIntent(Intent intent) {
  refreshEarthquakes();
  sendBroadcast(new Intent(QUAKES_REFRESHED));
}
```

7.2 Override the onReceive method in the EarthquakeWidget class by adding a check for the QUAKES_REFRESHED action you broadcast in step 7.1 — calling updateQuakes when it's received. Be sure to call through to the superclass to ensure that the standard Widget event handlers are still triggered:

```
@Override
public void onReceive(Context context, Intent intent){
  super.onReceive(context, intent);

  if (EarthquakeUpdateService.QUAKES_REFRESHED.equals(intent.getAction()))
    updateQuake(context);
}
```

7.3 Add an Intent Filter for this Intent action to the Widget's manifest entry:

```
<receiver android:name=".EarthquakeWidget" android:label="Earthquake">
  <intent-filter>
    <action android:name="android.appwidget.action.APPWIDGET_UPDATE" />
  </intent-filter>
  <intent-filter>
    <action android:name="com.paad.earthquake.QUAKES_REFRESHED" />
  </intent-filter>
  <meta-data
    android:name="android.appwidget.provider"
    android:resource="@xml/quake_widget_info"
  />
</receiver>
```

```
    </intent-filter>
    <intent-filter>
      <action android:name="com.paad.earthquake.QUAKES_REFRESHED" />
    </intent-filter>
    <meta-data
      android:name="android.appwidget.provider"
      android:resource="@xml/quake_widget_info"
    />
  </receiver>
```

8.   As a final step, add some interactivity to the Widget. Return to the `onUpdate` handler, and add a Click Listener to both the Text Views. Clicking the Widget should open the main Activity.

```
@Override
public void onUpdate(Context context,
                     AppWidgetManager appWidgetManager,
                     int[] appWidgetIds) {

  // Create a Pending Intent that will open the main Activity.
  Intent intent = new Intent(context, Earthquake.class);
  PendingIntent pendingIntent =
    PendingIntent.getActivity(context, 0, intent, 0);

  // Apply the On Click Listener to both Text Views.
  RemoteViews views = new RemoteViews(context.getPackageName(),
                                      R.layout.quake_widget);

  views.setOnClickPendingIntent(R.id.widget_magnitude, pendingIntent);
  views.setOnClickPendingIntent(R.id.widget_details, pendingIntent);

  // Notify the App Widget Manager to update the
  appWidgetManager.updateAppWidget(appWidgetIds, views);

  // Update the Widget UI with the latest Earthquake details.
  updateQuake(context, appWidgetManager, appWidgetIds);
}
```

Your Widget will now update once per day and every time the Earthquake Update Service performs an update.

> *All code snippets in this example are part of the* Chapter 14 Earthquake Part 1 *project, available for download at* www.wrox.com.

INTRODUCING COLLECTION VIEW WIDGETS

Android 3.0 (API level 11) introduced Collection View Widgets, a new style of Widgets designed to display collections of data as lists, grids, or stacks, as shown in Figure 14-3.

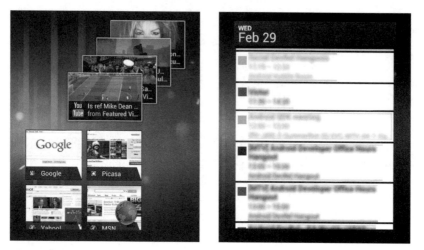

FIGURE 14-3

As the name suggests, Collection View Widgets are designed to add support for collection-based Views specifically as follows:

➤ StackView — A flip-card style View that displays its child Views as a stack. The stack will automatically rotate through its collection, moving the topmost item to the back to reveal the one beneath it. Users can manually transition between items by swiping up or down to reveal the previous or next items, respectively.

➤ ListView — The traditional List View. Each item in the bound collection is displayed as a row on a vertical list.

➤ GridView — A two-dimensional scrolling grid where each item is displayed within a cell. You can control the number of columns, their width, and relevant spacing.

> *The introduction of these dynamic collection-based App Widgets has eliminated the need for the more limited Live Folders. As a result, Live Folders have been deprecated as of Android 3.0.*

Each of these controls extends the Adapter View class. As a result, the UI used to display each item within it is defined using whatever layout you provide. Depending on the View used to display the collection, the specified layout will represent each row in a list, each card in a stack, or each cell in a grid.

The UI used to represent each item is restricted to the same Views and layouts supported by App Widgets:

➤ FrameLayout

➤ LinearLayout

➤ RelativeLayout

➤   AnalogClock

➤   Button

➤   Chronometer

➤   ImageButton

➤   ImageView

➤   ProgressBar

➤   TextView

➤   ViewFlipper

Collection View Widgets can be used to display any collection of data, but they're particularly useful for creating dynamic Widgets that surface data held within your application's Content Providers.

Collection View Widgets are implemented in much the same way as regular App Widgets — using App Widget Provider Info files to configure the Widget settings, BroadcastReceivers to define their behavior, and RemoteViews to modify the Widgets at run time.

In addition, collection-based App Widgets require the following components:

➤   An additional layout resource that defines the UI for each item displayed within the Widget.

➤   A RemoteViewsFactory that acts as a de facto Adapter for your Widget by supplying the Views that will be displayed within your collection View. It creates the Remote Views using the item layout definition and populates its elements using the underlying data you want to display.

➤   A RemoteViewsService that instantiates and manages the Remote Views Factory.

With these components complete, you can use the Remote Views Factory to create and update each of the Views that will represent the items in your collection. You can automate this process by creating a Remote View and using the setRemoteAdapter method to assign the Remote Views Service to it. When the Remote View is applied to the collection Widget, the Remote Views Service will create and update each item, as necessary. This process is described in the section "Populating Collection View Widgets Using a Remote Views Service."

Creating Collection View Widget Layouts

Collection View Widgets require two layout definitions — one that includes the Stack, List, or Grid View, and another that describes the layout to be used by each item within the stack, list, or grid.

As with regular App Widgets, it's best practice to define your layouts as external XML layout resources, as shown in Listing 14-19.

LISTING 14-19: Defining the Widget layout for a Stack Widget

```xml
<?xml version="1.0" encoding="utf-8"?>
<FrameLayout
    xmlns:android="http://schemas.android.com/apk/res/android"
```

continues

LISTING 14-19 *(continued)*

```
        android:layout_width="match_parent"
        android:layout_height="match_parent"
        android:padding="5dp">
        <StackView
          android:id="@+id/widget_stack_view"
          android:layout_width="match_parent"
          android:layout_height="match_parent"
        />
    </FrameLayout>
```

code snippet PA4AD_Ch14_MyWidget/res/layout/my_stack_widget_layout.xml

Listing 14-20 shows an example layout resource used to describe the UI of each card displayed by the Stack View Widget.

LISTING 14-20: Defining the layout for each item displayed by the Stack View Widget

```
<?xml version="1.0" encoding="utf-8"?>
<RelativeLayout
    xmlns:android="http://schemas.android.com/apk/res/android"
    android:layout_width="match_parent"
    android:layout_height="match_parent"
    android:background="#FF555555"
    android:padding="5dp">
    <TextView
      android:id="@+id/widget_text"
      android:layout_width="fill_parent"
      android:layout_height="wrap_content"
      android:layout_alignParentBottom="true"
      android:gravity="center_horizontal"
      android:text="@string/widget_text"
    />
    <TextView
      android:id="@+id/widget_title_text"
      android:layout_width="match_parent"
      android:layout_height="match_parent"
      android:layout_above="@id/widget_text"
      android:textSize="30sp"
      android:gravity="center"
     android:text="---"
    />
</RelativeLayout>
```

code snippet PA4AD_Ch14_MyWidget/res/layout/my_stack_widget_item_layout.xml

The Widget layout is used within the App Widget Provider Info resource as it would be for any App Widget. The item layout is used by a Remote Views Factory to create the Views used to represent each item in the underlying collection.

Creating the Remote Views Service

The Remote Views Service is used as a wrapper that instantiates and manages a Remote Views Factory, which, in turn, is used to supply each of the Views displayed within the Collection View Widget.

To create a Remote Views Service, extend the `RemoteViewsService` class and override the `onGetViewFactory` handler to return a new instance of a Remote Views Factory, as shown in Listing 14-21.

LISTING 14-21: Creating a Remote Views Service

```java
import java.util.ArrayList;
import android.appwidget.AppWidgetManager;
import android.content.Context;
import android.content.Intent;
import android.widget.RemoteViews;
import android.widget.RemoteViewsService;

public class MyRemoteViewsService extends RemoteViewsService {

  @Override
  public RemoteViewsFactory onGetViewFactory(Intent intent) {
    return new MyRemoteViewsFactory(getApplicationContext(), intent);
  }

}
```

code snippet PA4AD_Ch14_MyWidget/src/MyRemoteViewsService.java

As with any Service, you'll need to add your Remote Views Service to your application manifest using a `service` tag. To prevent other applications from accessing your Widgets, you must specify the `android.permission.BIND_REMOTEVIEWS` permission, as shown in Listing 14-22.

LISTING 14-22: Adding a Remote Views Service to the manifest

```xml
<service android:name=".MyRemoteViewsService"
         android:permission="android.permission.BIND_REMOTEVIEWS">
</service>
```

code snippet PA4AD_Ch14_MyWidget/AndroidManifest.xml

Creating a Remote Views Factory

The `RemoteViewsFactory` acts as a thin wrapper around the Adapter class. It is where you create and populate the Views that will be displayed in the Collection View Widget — effectively binding them to the underlying data collection.

To implement your Remote Views Factory, extend the `RemoteViewsFactory` class. This is normally done within the enclosing Remote Views Service class.

Your implementation should mirror that of a custom Adapter that will populate the Stack, List, or Grid View. Listing 14-23 shows a simple implementation of a Remote Views Factory that uses a static Array List to populate its Views. Note that the Remote Views Factory doesn't need to know what kind of Collection View Widget will be used to display each item.

LISTING 14-23: Creating a Remote Views Factory

```
class MyRemoteViewsFactory implements RemoteViewsFactory {

    private ArrayList<String> myWidgetText = new ArrayList<String>();
    private Context context;
    private Intent intent;
    private int widgetId;

    public MyRemoteViewsFactory(Context context, Intent intent) {
        // Optional constructor implementation.
        // Useful for getting references to the
        // Context of the calling widget
        this.context = context;
        this.intent = intent;

        widgetId = intent.getIntExtra(AppWidgetManager.EXTRA_APPWIDGET_ID,
            AppWidgetManager.INVALID_APPWIDGET_ID);
    }

    // Set up any connections / cursors to your data source.
    // Heavy lifting, like downloading data should be
    // deferred to onDataSetChanged()or getViewAt().
    // Taking more than 20 seconds in this call will result
    // in an ANR.
    public void onCreate() {
        myWidgetText.add("The");
        myWidgetText.add("quick");
        myWidgetText.add("brown");
        myWidgetText.add("fox");
        myWidgetText.add("jumps");
        myWidgetText.add("over");
        myWidgetText.add("the");
        myWidgetText.add("lazy");
        myWidgetText.add("droid");
    }

    // Called when the underlying data collection being displayed is
    // modified. You can use the AppWidgetManager's
    // notifyAppWidgetViewDataChanged method to trigger this handler.
    public void onDataSetChanged() {
        // TODO Processing when underlying data has changed.
    }

    // Return the number of items in the collection being displayed.
    public int getCount() {
        return myWidgetText.size();
```

```
  }

  // Return true if the unique IDs provided by each item are stable --
  // that is, they don't change at run time.
  public boolean hasStableIds() {
    return false;
  }

  // Return the unique ID associated with the item at a given index.
  public long getItemId(int index) {
    return index;
  }

  // The number of different view definitions. Usually 1.
  public int getViewTypeCount() {
    return 1;
  }

  // Optionally specify a "loading" view to display. Return null to
  // use the default.
  public RemoteViews getLoadingView() {
    return null;
  }

  // Create and populate the View to display at the given index.
  public RemoteViews getViewAt(int index) {
    // Create a view to display at the required index.
    RemoteViews rv = new RemoteViews(context.getPackageName(),
      R.layout.my_stack_widget_item_layout);

     // Populate the view from the underlying data.
    rv.setTextViewText(R.id.widget_title_text,
                      myWidgetText.get(index));
    rv.setTextViewText(R.id.widget_text, "View Number: " +
                      String.valueOf(index));

    // Create an item-specific fill-in Intent that will populate
    // the Pending Intent template created in the App Widget Provider.
    Intent fillInIntent = new Intent();
    fillInIntent.putExtra(Intent.EXTRA_TEXT, myWidgetText.get(index));
    rv.setOnClickFillInIntent(R.id.widget_title_text, fillInIntent);

    return rv;
  }

  // Close connections, cursors, or any other persistent state you
  // created in onCreate.
  public void onDestroy() {
    myWidgetText.clear();
  }
}
```

code snippet PA4AD_Ch14_MyWidget/src/MyRemoteViewsService.java

Populating Collection View Widgets Using a Remote Views Service

With your Remote Views Factory complete, all that remains is to bind the List, Grid, or Stack View within your App Widget Layout to the Remote Views Service. This is done using a Remote View, typically within the onUpdate handler of your App Widget implementation.

Create a new Remote View instance as you would when updating the UI of a standard App Widget. Use the setRemoteAdapter method to bind your Remote Views Service to the particular List, Grid, or Stack View within the Widget layout.

The Remote View Service is specified using an Intent of the following form:

```
Intent intent = new Intent(context, MyRemoteViewsService.class);
```

This Intent is received by the onGetViewFactory handler within the Remote Views Service, enabling you to pass additional parameters into the Service and the Factory it contains.

You also specify the ID of the Widget you are binding to, allowing you to specify a different Service for different Widget instances.

The setEmptyView method provides a means of specifying a View that should be displayed if (and only if) the underlying data collection is empty.

After completing the binding process, use the App Widget Manager's updateAppWidget method to apply the binding to the specified Widget. Listing 14-24 shows the standard pattern for binding a Widget to a Remote Views Service.

LISTING 14-24: Binding a Remove Views Service to a Widget

```
@Override
public void onUpdate(Context context,
                     AppWidgetManager appWidgetManager,
                     int[] appWidgetIds) {
  // Iterate through each widget, creating a RemoteViews object and
  // applying the modified RemoteViews to each widget.
  final int N = appWidgetIds.length;
  for (int i = 0; i < N; i++) {
    int appWidgetId = appWidgetIds[i];

    // Create a Remote View.
    RemoteViews views = new RemoteViews(context.getPackageName(),
      R.layout.my_stack_widget_layout);

    // Bind this widget to a Remote Views Service.
    Intent intent = new Intent(context, MyRemoteViewsService.class);
    intent.putExtra(AppWidgetManager.EXTRA_APPWIDGET_ID, appWidgetId);
    views.setRemoteAdapter(appWidgetId, R.id.widget_stack_view,
                           intent);

    // Specify a View within the Widget layout hierarchy to display
    // when the bound collection is empty.
```

```
            views.setEmptyView(R.id.widget_stack_view, R.id.widget_empty_text);

            // TODO Customize this Widgets UI based on configuration
            // settings etc.

            // Notify the App Widget Manager to update the widget using
            // the modified remote view.
            appWidgetManager.updateAppWidget(appWidgetId, views);
        }
    }
```

code snippet PA4AD_Ch14_MyWidget/src/MyStackWidget.java

Adding Interactivity to the Items Within a Collection View Widget

For efficiency reasons, it's not possible to assign a unique `onClickPendingIntent` to each item displayed as part of a Collection View Widget. Instead, use the `setPendingIntentTemplate` to assign a template Intent to your Widget, as shown in Listing 14-25.

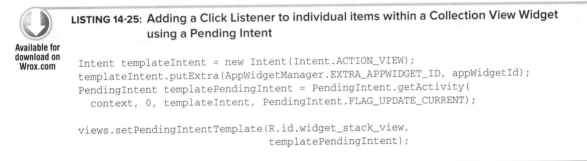

LISTING 14-25: Adding a Click Listener to individual items within a Collection View Widget using a Pending Intent

```
Intent templateIntent = new Intent(Intent.ACTION_VIEW);
templateIntent.putExtra(AppWidgetManager.EXTRA_APPWIDGET_ID, appWidgetId);
PendingIntent templatePendingIntent = PendingIntent.getActivity(
    context, 0, templateIntent, PendingIntent.FLAG_UPDATE_CURRENT);

views.setPendingIntentTemplate(R.id.widget_stack_view,
                               templatePendingIntent);
```

code snippet PA4AD_Ch14_MyWidget/src/MyStackWidget.java

This Pending Intent can then be "filled-in" within the `getViewAt` handler of your Remote Views Service implementation using the `setOnClickFillInIntent` method of your Remote Views object, as shown in Listing 14-26.

LISTING 14-26: Filling in a Pending Intent template for each item displayed in your Collection View Widget

```
// Create the item-specific fill-in Intent that will populate
// the Pending Intent template created in the App Widget Provider.
Intent fillInIntent = new Intent();
fillInIntent.putExtra(Intent.EXTRA_TEXT, myWidgetText.get(index));
rv.setOnClickFillInIntent(R.id.widget_title_text, fillInIntent);
```

code snippet PA4AD_Ch14_MyWidget/src/MyRemoteViewsService.java

The fill-in Intent is applied to the template Intent using the `Intent.fillIn` method. It copies the contents of the fill-in Intent into the template Intent, replacing any undefined fields with those defined by the fill-in Intent. Fields with existing data will *not* be overridden.

The resulting Pending Intent will be broadcast when a user clicks that particular item from within your Widget.

Binding Collection View Widgets to Content Providers

One of the most powerful uses of Collection View Widgets is to surface data from your Content Providers to the home screen. Listing 14-27 shows the skeleton code for a Remote Views Factory implementation that binds to a Content Provider — in this case, one that displays the thumbnails of images stored on the external media store.

LISTING 14-27: Creating a Content Provider–backed Remote Views Factory

```
class MyRemoteViewsFactory implements RemoteViewsFactory {

    private Context context;
    private ContentResolver cr;
    private Cursor c;

    public MyRemoteViewsFactory(Context context) {
      // Get a reference to the application context and
      // its Content Resolver.
      this.context = context;
      cr = context.getContentResolver();
    }

    public void onCreate() {
      // Execute the query that returns a Cursor over the data
      // to be displayed. Any secondary lookups or decoding should
      // be completed in the onDataSetChanged handler.
      c = cr.query(MediaStore.Images.Thumbnails.EXTERNAL_CONTENT_URI,
                  null, null, null, null);
    }

    public void onDataSetChanged() {
      // Any secondary lookups, processing, or decoding can be done
      // here synchronously. The Widget will be updated only after
      // this method has completed.
    }

    public int getCount() {
      // Return the number of items in the Cursor.
      if (c != null)
        return c.getCount();
      else
        return 0;
    }

    public long getItemId(int index) {
      // Return the unique ID associated with a particular item.
      if (c != null)
        return c.getInt(
          c.getColumnIndex(MediaStore.Images.Thumbnails._ID));
      else
```

```java
    return index;
  }

  public RemoteViews getViewAt(int index) {
    // Move the Cursor to the requested row position.
    c.moveToPosition(index);

    // Extract the data from the required columns.
    int idIdx = c.getColumnIndex(MediaStore.Images.Thumbnails._ID);
    String id = c.getString(idIdx);
    Uri uri = Uri.withAppendedPath(
        MediaStore.Images.Thumbnails.EXTERNAL_CONTENT_URI, ""
        + id);

    // Create a new Remote Views object using the appropriate
    // item layout
    RemoteViews rv = new RemoteViews(context.getPackageName(),
      R.layout.my_media_widget_item_layout);

    // Assign the values extracted from the Cursor to the Remote Views.
    rv.setImageViewUri(R.id.widget_media_thumbnail, uri);

    // Assign the item-specific fill-in Intent that will populate
    // the Pending Intent template specified in the App Widget
    // Provider. In this instance the template Intent specifies
    // an ACTION_VIEW action.
    Intent fillInIntent = new Intent();
    fillInIntent.setData(uri);
    rv.setOnClickFillInIntent(R.id.widget_media_thumbnail,
                              fillInIntent);

    return rv;
  }

  public int getViewTypeCount() {
    // The number of different view definitions to use.
    // For Content Providers, this will almost always be 1.
    return 1;
  }

  public boolean hasStableIds() {
    // Content Provider IDs should be unique and permanent.
    return true;
  }

  public void onDestroy() {
    // Close the result Cursor.
    c.close();
  }

  public RemoteViews getLoadingView() {
    // Use the default loading view.
    return null;
  }
}
```

code snippet PA4AD_Ch14_MyWidget/src/MyMediaRemoteViewsService.java

This more flexible alternative for exposing Content Provider data on the home screen is a replacement for Live Folders, which have now been deprecated.

Refreshing Your Collection View Widgets

The App Widget Manager includes the `notifyAppWidgetViewDataChanged` method, which allows you to specify a Widget ID (or array of IDs) to update, along with the resource identifier for the collection View within that Widget whose underlying data source has changed:

```
appWidgetManager.notifyAppWidgetViewDataChanged(appWidgetIds,
    R.id.widget_stack_view);
```

This will cause the `onDataSetChanged` handler within the associated Remote Views Factory to be executed, followed by the meta-data calls, including `getCount`, before each of the Views is re-created.

Alternatively, the techniques used to update App Widgets — altering the minimum refresh rate, using Intents, and setting Alarms — can also be used to update Collection View Widgets; however, they will cause the entire Widget to be re-created, meaning that refreshing the collection-based Views based on changes to the underlying data is more efficient.

Creating an Earthquake Collection View Widget

In this example you add a second Widget to the Earthquake application. This one will use a ListView-based Collection View Widget to display a list of the recent earthquakes.

1. Start by creating a layout for the Collection View Widget UI as an XML resource. Save the `quake_collection_widget.xml` file in the `res/layout` folder. Use a Frame Layout that includes the List View for displaying the earthquakes and a Text View to display when the collection is empty:

```xml
<?xml version="1.0" encoding="utf-8"?>
<FrameLayout
  xmlns:android="http://schemas.android.com/apk/res/android"
  android:layout_width="match_parent"
  android:layout_height="match_parent"
  android:padding="5dp">
  <ListView
    android:id="@+id/widget_list_view"
    android:layout_width="match_parent"
    android:layout_height="match_parent"
  />
  <TextView
    android:id="@+id/widget_empty_text"
    android:layout_width="match_parent"
    android:layout_height="match_parent"
    android:gravity="center"
    android:text="No Earthquakes!"
  />
</FrameLayout>
```

2. Create a new `EarthquakeListWidget` class that extends `AppWidgetProvider`. You'll return to this class to bind your Widget to the Remote Views Service that will provide the Views that display each earthquake.

```
package com.paad.earthquake;

import android.app.PendingIntent;
import android.appwidget.AppWidgetManager;
import android.appwidget.AppWidgetProvider;
import android.content.Context;
import android.content.Intent;
import android.widget.RemoteViews;

public class EarthquakeListWidget extends AppWidgetProvider {
}
```

3. Create a new Widget definition file, `quake_list_widget_info.xml`, in the `res/xml` folder. Set the minimum update rate to once a day, set the Widget dimensions to two cells wide and one cell high (110dp × 40dp), and make it vertically resizable. Use the Widget layout you created in step 1 for the initial layout.

```
<?xml version="1.0" encoding="utf-8"?>
<appwidget-provider
  xmlns:android="http://schemas.android.com/apk/res/android"
  android:initialLayout="@layout/quake_collection_widget"
  android:minWidth="110dp"
  android:minHeight="40dp"
  android:label="Earthquakes"
  android:updatePeriodMillis="86400000"
  android:resizeMode="vertical"
/>
```

4. Add your Widget to the application manifest, including a reference to the Widget definition resource you created in step 3. It should also include an Intent Filter for the App Widget update action.

```
<receiver android:name=".EarthquakeListWidget" android:label="Earthquake List">
  <intent-filter>
    <action android:name="android.appwidget.action.APPWIDGET_UPDATE" />
  </intent-filter>
  <meta-data
    android:name="android.appwidget.provider"
    android:resource="@xml/quake_list_widget_info"
  />
</receiver>
```

5. Create a new `EarthquakeRemoteViewsService` class that extends `RemoteViewsService`. It should include an internal `EarthquakeRemoteViewsFactory` class that extends `RemoteViewsFactory`, which should be returned from the Earthquake Remote Views Service's `onGetViewFactory` handler:

```
package com.paad.earthquake;

import android.content.ContentResolver;
```

```java
import android.content.Context;
import android.content.Intent;
import android.database.Cursor;
import android.net.Uri;
import android.provider.MediaStore;
import android.util.Log;
import android.widget.RemoteViews;
import android.widget.RemoteViewsService;

public class EarthquakeRemoteViewsService extends RemoteViewsService {

  @Override
  public RemoteViewsFactory onGetViewFactory(Intent intent) {
    return new EarthquakeRemoteViewsFactory(getApplicationContext());
  }

  class EarthquakeRemoteViewsFactory implements RemoteViewsFactory {

    private Context context;

    public EarthquakeRemoteViewsFactory(Context context) {
      this.context = context;
    }

    public void onCreate() {
    }

    public void onDataSetChanged() {
    }

    public int getCount() {
      return 0;
    }

    public long getItemId(int index) {
      return index;
    }

    public RemoteViews getViewAt(int index) {
      return null;
    }

    public int getViewTypeCount() {
      return 1;
    }

    public boolean hasStableIds() {
      return true;
    }

    public RemoteViews getLoadingView() {
      return null;
    }

    public void onDestroy() {
    }
```

```
          public void onDestroy() {
          }
      }
  }
```

6. Add a new variable to store the Service Context, and create a new Constructor that accepts the Context and stores it in this property:

```
private Context context;

public EarthquakeRemoteViewsFactory(Context context) {
  this.context = context;
}
```

7. Create a new executeCursor method to query the Earthquake Provider for the current Earthquake list. Update the onCreate handler to execute that method and store the result a new class property:

```
private Cursor c;
private Cursor executeQuery() {
  String[] projection = new String[] {
      EarthquakeProvider.KEY_ID,
      EarthquakeProvider.KEY_MAGNITUDE,
      EarthquakeProvider.KEY_DETAILS
    };

  Context appContext = getApplicationContext();
  SharedPreferences prefs =
    PreferenceManager.getDefaultSharedPreferences(appContext);
  int minimumMagnitude =
    Integer.parseInt(prefs.getString(PreferencesActivity.PREF_MIN_MAG, "3"));

  String where = EarthquakeProvider.KEY_MAGNITUDE + " > " + minimumMagnitude;

  return context.getContentResolver().query(EarthquakeProvider.CONTENT_URI,
      projection, where, null, null);
}
public void onCreate() {
  c = executeQuery();
}
```

8. Update the onDataSetChanged and onDestroy handlers to requery and destroy the Cursor, respectively:

```
public void onDataSetChanged() {
  c = executeQuery();
}

public void onDestroy() {
  c.close();
}
```

9.1 Start by updating the `getCount` and `getItemId` methods to return the number of records in the Cursor and the unique identifier associated with each record, respectively:

```
public int getCount() {
  if (c != null)
    return c.getCount();
  else
    return 0;
}

public long getItemId(int index) {
  if (c != null)
    return c.getLong(c.getColumnIndex(EarthquakeProvider.KEY_ID));
  else
    return index;
}
```

9.2 Then update the `getViewAt` method. This is where the Views used to represent each Earthquake in the List View are created and populated. Create a new Remote Views object using the layout definition you created for the previous Earthquake App Widget example, and populate it with data from the current earthquake. Also create and assign a fill-in Intent that will add the current earthquake's URI to the template Intent you'll define within the Widget provider.

```
public RemoteViews getViewAt(int index) {
  // Move the Cursor to the required index.
  c.moveToPosition(index);

  // Extract the values for the current cursor row.
  int idIdx = c.getColumnIndex(EarthquakeProvider.KEY_ID);
  int magnitudeIdx = c.getColumnIndex(EarthquakeProvider.KEY_MAGNITUDE);
  int detailsIdx = c.getColumnIndex(EarthquakeProvider.KEY_DETAILS);

  String id = c.getString(idIdx);
  String magnitude = c.getString(magnitudeIdx);
  String details = c.getString(detailsIdx);

  // Create a new Remote Views object and use it to populate the
  // layout used to represent each earthquake in the list.
  RemoteViews rv = new RemoteViews(context.getPackageName(),
                        R.layout.quake_widget);

  rv.setTextViewText(R.id.widget_magnitude, magnitude);
  rv.setTextViewText(R.id.widget_details, details);

  // Create the fill-in Intent that adds the URI for the current item
  // to the template Intent.
  Intent fillInIntent = new Intent();
  Uri uri = Uri.withAppendedPath(EarthquakeProvider.CONTENT_URI, id);
  fillInIntent.setData(uri);

  rv.setOnClickFillInIntent(R.id.widget_magnitude, fillInIntent);
  rv.setOnClickFillInIntent(R.id.widget_details, fillInIntent);
```

```
    return rv;
  }
```

10. Add the Earthquake Remote Views Service to your application manifest, including a requirement for the `BIND_REMOTEVIEWS` permission:

```
<service android:name=".EarthquakeRemoteViewsService"
  android:permission="android.permission.BIND_REMOTEVIEWS">
</service>
```

11. Return to the Earthquake List Widget class and override the `onUpdate` method. Iterate over each of the active Widgets, attaching the Earthquake Remote Views Service you created in step 5. Take this opportunity to create and assign a template Pending Intent to each item that will start a new Activity to view the URI filled in by the fill-in Intent you created in step 9.2.

```
@Override
public void onUpdate(Context context,
                     AppWidgetManager appWidgetManager,
                     int[] appWidgetIds) {

  // Iterate over the array of active widgets.
  final int N = appWidgetIds.length;
  for (int i = 0; i < N; i++) {
    int appWidgetId = appWidgetIds[i];

    // Set up the intent that starts the Earthquake
    // Remote Views Service, which will supply the views
    // shown in the List View.
    Intent intent = new Intent(context, EarthquakeRemoteViewsService.class);
    // Add the app widget ID to the intent extras.
    intent.putExtra(AppWidgetManager.EXTRA_APPWIDGET_ID, appWidgetId);

    // Instantiate the RemoteViews object for the App Widget layout.
    RemoteViews views = new RemoteViews(context.getPackageName(),
      R.layout.quake_collection_widget);

    // Set up the RemoteViews object to use a RemoteViews adapter.
    views.setRemoteAdapter(R.id.widget_list_view, intent);

    // The empty view is displayed when the collection has no items.
    views.setEmptyView(R.id.widget_list_view, R.id.widget_empty_text);

    // Create a Pending Intent template to provide interactivity to
    // each item displayed within the collection View.
    Intent templateIntent = new Intent(context, Earthquake.class);
    templateIntent.putExtra(AppWidgetManager.EXTRA_APPWIDGET_ID, appWidgetId);
    PendingIntent templatePendingIntent =
      PendingIntent.getActivity(context, 0, templateIntent,
                                PendingIntent.FLAG_UPDATE_CURRENT);

    views.setPendingIntentTemplate(R.id.widget_list_view,
                                   templatePendingIntent);

    // Notify the App Widget Manager to update the widget using
```

```
    // Create a Pending Intent template to provide interactivity to
    // each item displayed within the collection View.
    Intent templateIntent = new Intent(context, Earthquake.class);
    templateIntent.putExtra(AppWidgetManager.EXTRA_APPWIDGET_ID, appWidgetId);
    PendingIntent templatePendingIntent =
      PendingIntent.getActivity(context, 0, templateIntent,
                                PendingIntent.FLAG_UPDATE_CURRENT);

    views.setPendingIntentTemplate(R.id.widget_list_view,
                                  templatePendingIntent);

    // Notify the App Widget Manager to update the widget using
    // the modified remote view.
    appWidgetManager.updateAppWidget(appWidgetId, views);
  }
}
```

12. As a final step, enhance the Widget to update whenever the Earthquake Update Service you created in Chapter 9 has refreshed the earthquake database. Do this by updating the onHandleIntent handler in the EarthquakeUpdateService to call the App Widget Manager's notifyAppWidgetViewDataChanged method when it has completed:

```
@Override
protected void onHandleIntent(Intent intent) {
  refreshEarthquakes();
  sendBroadcast(new Intent(QUAKES_REFRESHED));

Context context = getApplicationContext();
  AppWidgetManager appWidgetManager = AppWidgetManager.getInstance(context);
  ComponentName earthquakeWidget =
    new ComponentName(context, EarthquakeListWidget.class);
  int[] appWidgetIds = appWidgetManager.getAppWidgetIds(earthquakeWidget);

  appWidgetManager.notifyAppWidgetViewDataChanged(appWidgetIds,
    R.id.widget_list_view);
}
```

> *All code snippets in this example are part of the* Chapter 14 Earthquake Part 2 *project, available for download at* www.wrox.com.

Figure 14-4 shows the Earthquake Collection View Widget added to the home screen.

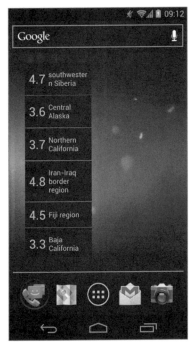

FIGURE 14-4

INTRODUCING LIVE FOLDERS

In Android 3.0 Live Folders were deprecated in favor of the richer, more customizable Collection View Widgets described in the previous section.

Live Folders provided a similar functionality for earlier versions of Android — a means by which your application can expose data from its Content Providers directly on to the home screen.

Although Collection View Widgets are the supported alternative for devices running Android 3.0 or above, you can still use Live Folders to provide dynamic home screen shortcuts to information stored in your application for devices running earlier version of Android.

When added, a Live Folder is represented on the home screen as a shortcut icon. Selecting the icon will open the Live Folder, as shown in Figure 14-5. This figure shows a Live Folder open on an Android home screen — in this case, the starred contacts list.

FIGURE 14-5

> To add a Live Folder to the home screen on Android devices prior to Android 3.0, long-press a piece of empty space and select Folders. You will be presented with a list of available Live Folders; click one to select and add it. After it is added, click to open the Live Folder, and long-press to move the shortcut. Live Folders aren't available on devices running Android 3.0 or higher.

Creating Live Folders

Live Folders are a combination of a Content Provider and an Activity. To create a new Live Folder, you need to define the following:

➤ An Activity responsible for creating and configuring the Live Folder by generating and returning a specially formatted Intent

➤ A Content Provider that provides the items to be displayed using the required column names

Unlike Collection View Widgets, each Live Folder item can display up to only three pieces of information: an icon, a title, and a description.

The Live Folder Content Provider

Any Content Provider can provide the data displayed within a Live Folder. Live Folders use a standard set of column names:

➤ `LiveFolders._ID` — A unique identifier used to indicate which item was selected if a user clicks the Live Folder list.

➤ `LiveFolders.NAME` — The primary text, displayed in a large font. *This is the only required column.*

➤ `LiveFolders.DESCRIPTION` — A longer descriptive field in a smaller font, displayed beneath the name column.

➤ `LiveFolders.ICON_BITMAP` — An image bitmap to be displayed at the left of each item. Alternatively, you can use a combination of `LiveFolders.ICON_PACKAGE` and `LiveFolder.ICON_RESOURCE` to specify a Drawable resource to use from a particular package.

Rather than renaming the columns within your Content Provider to suit the requirements of Live Folders, you should apply a projection that maps your existing column names to those required by a Live Folder, as shown in Listing 14-28.

LISTING 14-28: Creating a projection to support a Live Folder

```
private static final HashMap<String, String> LIVE_FOLDER_PROJECTION;
static {
    // Create the projection map.
    LIVE_FOLDER_PROJECTION = new HashMap<String, String>();
```

```
            // Map existing column names to those required by a Live Folder.
            LIVE_FOLDER_PROJECTION.put(LiveFolders._ID,
                                       KEY_ID + " AS " +
                                       LiveFolders._ID);
            LIVE_FOLDER_PROJECTION.put(LiveFolders.NAME,
                                       KEY_NAME + " AS " +
                                       LiveFolders.NAME);
            LIVE_FOLDER_PROJECTION.put(LiveFolders.DESCRIPTION,
                                       KEY_DESCRIPTION + " AS " +
                                       LiveFolders.DESCRIPTION);
            LIVE_FOLDER_PROJECTION.put(LiveFolders.ICON_BITMAP,
                                       KEY_IMAGE + " AS " +
                                       LiveFolders.ICON_BITMAP);
        }
```

code snippet PA4AD_Ch14_MyLiveFolder/src/MyContentProvider.java

Only the ID and name columns are required; the bitmap and description columns can be used or left unmapped, as required.

The projection typically will be applied within the query method of your Content Provider when the query request URI matches the pattern you specify for Live Folder request, as shown in Listing 14-29.

LISTING 14-29: Applying a projection to support a Live Folder

```
public static Uri LIVE_FOLDER_URI
  = Uri.parse("com.paad.provider.MyLiveFolder");

public Cursor query(Uri uri, String[] projection, String selection,
                    String[] selectionArgs, String sortOrder) {

  SQLiteQueryBuilder qb = new SQLiteQueryBuilder();

  switch (URI_MATCHER.match(uri)) {
    case LIVE_FOLDER:
      qb.setTables(MYTABLE);
      qb.setProjectionMap(LIVE_FOLDER_PROJECTION);
      break;
    default:
      throw new IllegalArgumentException("Unknown URI " + uri);
  }

  Cursor c = qb.query(null, projection, selection, selectionArgs,
                      null, null, null);

  c.setNotificationUri(getContext().getContentResolver(), uri);

  return c;
}
```

code snippet PA4AD_Ch14_MyLiveFolder/src/MyContentProvider.java

The Live Folder Activity

The Live Folder is defined using an Intent returned as the result of an Activity (typically from within the `onCreate` handler).

Use the Intent's `setData` method to specify the URI of the Content Provider supplying the data (with the appropriate projection applied), as described in the previous section.

You can configure the Intent further by using a series of extras as follows:

➤ `LiveFolders.EXTRA_LIVE_FOLDER_DISPLAY_MODE` — Specifies the display mode to use. This can be either `LiveFolders.DISPLAY_MODE_LIST` or `LiveFolders.DISPLAY_MODE_GRID` to display your Live Folder as a list or grid, respectively.

➤ `LiveFolders.EXTRA_LIVE_FOLDER_ICON` — Provides a Drawable resource that will be used as the home screen icon that represents the Live Folder when it hasn't been opened.

➤ `LiveFolders.EXTRA_LIVE_FOLDER_NAME` — Provides a descriptive name to use with the icon described above to represent the Live Folder on the home screen when it hasn't been opened.

Listing 14-30 shows the overridden `onCreate` method of an Activity used to create a Live Folder. After the Live Folder definition Intent is constructed, it is set as the Activity result using `setResult`, and the Activity is closed with a call to `finish`.

LISTING 14-30: Creating a Live Folder from within an Activity

```
@Override
public void onCreate(Bundle savedInstanceState) {
  super.onCreate(savedInstanceState);

  // Check to confirm this Activity was launched as part
  // of a request to add a new Live Folder to the home screen
  String action = getIntent().getAction();
  if (LiveFolders.ACTION_CREATE_LIVE_FOLDER.equals(action)) {
    Intent intent = new Intent();

    // Set the URI of the Content Provider that will supply the
    // data to display. The appropriate projection must already
    // be applied to the returned data.
    intent.setData(MyContentProvider.LIVE_FOLDER_URI);

    // Set the display mode to a list.
    intent.putExtra(LiveFolders.EXTRA_LIVE_FOLDER_DISPLAY_MODE,
                LiveFolders.DISPLAY_MODE_LIST);

    // Indicate the icon to be used to represent the Live Folder
    // shortcut on the home screen.
    intent.putExtra(LiveFolders.EXTRA_LIVE_FOLDER_ICON,
                Intent.ShortcutIconResource.fromContext(this,
                    R.drawable.icon));

    // Provide the name to be used to represent the Live Folder on
    // the home screen.
    intent.putExtra(LiveFolders.EXTRA_LIVE_FOLDER_NAME, "Earthquakes");
```

```
    // Return the Live Folder Intent as a result.
    setResult(RESULT_OK, intent);
  }
  else
    setResult(RESULT_CANCELED);
  finish();
}
```

code snippet PA4AD_Ch14_MyLiveFolder/src/MyLiveFolder.java

You can also provide support for selecting items in the Live Folder.

By adding a `LiveFolders.EXTRA_LIVE_FOLDER_BASE_INTENT` extra to the returned Intent, you can specify a base Intent to fire when a Live Folder item is selected. When this value is set, selecting a Live Folder item will result in `startActivity` being called with the specified base Intent used as the Intent parameter.

Best practice (as shown in Listing 14-31) is to set the data parameter of this Intent to the base URI of the Content Provider that's supplying the Live Folder's data. In such cases the Live Folder will automatically append the value stored in the selected item's `_id` column to the Intent's data value.

LISTING 14-31: Adding a base Intent for Live Folder item selection

```
@Override
public void onCreate(Bundle savedInstanceState) {
  super.onCreate(savedInstanceState);

  // Check to confirm this Activity was launched as part
  // of a request to add a new Live Folder to the home screen
  String action = getIntent().getAction();
  if (LiveFolders.ACTION_CREATE_LIVE_FOLDER.equals(action)) {
    Intent intent = new Intent();

    // Set the URI of the Content Provider that will supply the
    // data to display. The appropriate projection must already
    // be applied to the returned data.
    intent.setData(LiveFolderProvider.CONTENT_URI);

    // Set the display mode to a list.
    intent.putExtra(LiveFolders.EXTRA_LIVE_FOLDER_DISPLAY_MODE,
                    LiveFolders.DISPLAY_MODE_LIST);

    // Indicate the icon to be used to represent the Live Folder
    // shortcut on the home screen.
    intent.putExtra(LiveFolders.EXTRA_LIVE_FOLDER_ICON,
                    Intent.ShortcutIconResource.fromContext(context,
                        R.drawable.icon));

    // Provide the name to be used to represent the Live Folder on
    // the home screen.
    intent.putExtra(LiveFolders.EXTRA_LIVE_FOLDER_NAME,
                    "My Live Folder");
```

continues

LISTING 14-31 *(continued)*

```
    // Specify a base Intent that will request the responding Activity
    // View the selected item.
    intent.putExtra(LiveFolders.EXTRA_LIVE_FOLDER_BASE_INTENT,
                    new Intent(Intent.ACTION_VIEW,
                               MyContentProvider.CONTENT_URI));

    // Return the Live Folder Intent as a result.
    setResult(RESULT_OK, intent);
  }
  else
    setResult(RESULT_CANCELED);
  finish();
}
```

code snippet PA4AD_Ch14_MyLiveFolder/src/MyLiveFolder.java

In order for the system to identify an Activity as a Live Folder, you must include an Intent Filter for the CREATE_LIVE_FOLDER action when adding the Live Folder Activity to your application manifest, as shown in Listing 14-32.

LISTING 14-32: ADDING THE LIVE FOLDER ACTIVITY TO THE MANIFEST

```
<activity android:name=".MyLiveFolder"
          android:label="My Live Folder">
  <intent-filter>
    <action android:name="android.intent.action.CREATE_LIVE_FOLDER"/>
  </intent-filter>
</activity>
```

code snippet PA4AD_Ch14_MyLiveFolder/AndroidManifest.xml

Creating an Earthquake Live Folder

In the following example you extend the Earthquake application again — this time to include a Live Folder that displays the magnitude and location of each quake. The resulting Live Folder is very similar to the Collection View Widget you created earlier in this chapter, making it a useful alternative for devices running Android releases prior to Android 3.0.

1. Start by modifying the EarthquakeProvider class. Create a new static URI definition that will be used to return the Live Folder items:

```
public static final Uri LIVE_FOLDER_URI =
    Uri.parse("content://com.paad.provider.earthquake/live_folder");
```

2. Modify the uriMatcher object, and getType method to check for this new URI request:

```
private static final int QUAKES = 1;
private static final int QUAKE_ID = 2;
```

```
private static final int SEARCH = 3;
private static final int LIVE_FOLDER = 4;

private static final UriMatcher uriMatcher;

//Allocate the UriMatcher object, where a URI ending in 'earthquakes' will
//correspond to a request for all earthquakes, and 'earthquakes' with a
//trailing '/[rowID]' will represent a single earthquake row.
static {
  uriMatcher = new UriMatcher(UriMatcher.NO_MATCH);
  uriMatcher.addURI("com.paad.earthquakeprovider", "earthquakes", QUAKES);
  uriMatcher.addURI("com.paad.earthquakeprovider", "earthquakes/#", QUAKE_ID);
  uriMatcher.addURI("com.paad.provider.Earthquake", "live_folder", LIVE_FOLDER);
  uriMatcher.addURI("com.paad.earthquakeprovider",
    SearchManager.SUGGEST_URI_PATH_QUERY, SEARCH);
  uriMatcher.addURI("com.paad.earthquakeprovider",
    SearchManager.SUGGEST_URI_PATH_QUERY + "/*", SEARCH);
  uriMatcher.addURI("com.paad.earthquakeprovider",
    SearchManager.SUGGEST_URI_PATH_SHORTCUT, SEARCH);
  uriMatcher.addURI("com.paad.earthquakeprovider",
    SearchManager.SUGGEST_URI_PATH_SHORTCUT + "/*", SEARCH);
}

@Override
public String getType(Uri uri) {
  switch (uriMatcher.match(uri)) {
    case QUAKES|LIVE_FOLDER: return "vnd.android.cursor.dir/vnd.paad.earthquake";
    case QUAKE_ID: return "vnd.android.cursor.item/vnd.paad.earthquake";
    case SEARCH  : return SearchManager.SUGGEST_MIME_TYPE;
    default: throw new IllegalArgumentException("Unsupported URI: " + uri);
  }
}
```

3. Create a new hash map that defines a projection suitable for a Live Folder. It should return the magnitude and location details as the description and name columns, respectively:

```
static final HashMap<String, String> LIVE_FOLDER_PROJECTION;
static {
  LIVE_FOLDER_PROJECTION = new HashMap<String, String>();
  LIVE_FOLDER_PROJECTION.put(LiveFolders._ID,
                         KEY_ID + " AS " + LiveFolders._ID);
  LIVE_FOLDER_PROJECTION.put(LiveFolders.NAME,
                         KEY_DETAILS + " AS " + LiveFolders.NAME);
  LIVE_FOLDER_PROJECTION.put(LiveFolders.DESCRIPTION,
                         KEY_DATE + " AS " + LiveFolders.DESCRIPTION);
}
```

4. Update the query method to apply the projection map from step 3 to the returned earthquake query for Live Folder requests:

```
@Override
public Cursor query(Uri uri,
                    String[] projection,
                    String selection,
                    String[] selectionArgs,
                    String sort) {
```

```
SQLiteDatabase database = dbHelper.getWritableDatabase();

SQLiteQueryBuilder qb = new SQLiteQueryBuilder();

qb.setTables(EarthquakeDatabaseHelper.EARTHQUAKE_TABLE);

// If this is a row query, limit the result set to the passed in row.
switch (uriMatcher.match(uri)) {
  case QUAKE_ID: qb.appendWhere(KEY_ID + "=" + uri.getPathSegments().get(1));
                 break;
  case SEARCH  : qb.appendWhere(KEY_SUMMARY + " LIKE \"%" +
                     uri.getPathSegments().get(1) + "%\"");
                 qb.setProjectionMap(SEARCH_PROJECTION_MAP);
                 break;
  case LIVE_FOLDER : qb.setProjectionMap(LIVE_FOLDER_PROJECTION);
                     break;
  default      : break;
}

[ ... existing query method ... ]
}
```

5.   Create a new `EarthquakeLiveFolders` class that contains a static `EarthquakeLiveFolder` Activity:

```
package com.paad.earthquake;

import android.app.Activity;
import android.content.Context;
import android.content.Intent;
import android.os.Bundle;
import android.provider.LiveFolders;

public class EarthquakeLiveFolders extends Activity {
  public static class EarthquakeLiveFolder extends Activity {
  }
}
```

6.   Add a new method that builds the Intent used to create the Live Folder. It should use the query URI you created in step 1, set the display mode to list, and define the icon and title string to use. Also set the base Intent to the individual item query from the Earthquake Provider:

```
private static Intent createLiveFolderIntent(Context context) {
  Intent intent = new Intent();
  intent.setData(EarthquakeProvider.LIVE_FOLDER_URI);
  intent.putExtra(LiveFolders.EXTRA_LIVE_FOLDER_BASE_INTENT,
                  new Intent(Intent.ACTION_VIEW,
                             EarthquakeProvider.CONTENT_URI));
  intent.putExtra(LiveFolders.EXTRA_LIVE_FOLDER_DISPLAY_MODE,
                  LiveFolders.DISPLAY_MODE_LIST);
  intent.putExtra(LiveFolders.EXTRA_LIVE_FOLDER_ICON,
                  Intent.ShortcutIconResource.fromContext(context,
                                                          R.drawable.ic_launcher));
  intent.putExtra(LiveFolders.EXTRA_LIVE_FOLDER_NAME, "Earthquakes");
  return intent;
}
```

7. Override the `onCreate` method of the `EarthquakeLiveFolder` class to return the Intent defined in step 6:

```
@Override
public void onCreate(Bundle savedInstanceState) {
  super.onCreate(savedInstanceState);

  String action = getIntent().getAction();
  if (LiveFolders.ACTION_CREATE_LIVE_FOLDER.equals(action))
    setResult(RESULT_OK, createLiveFolderIntent(this));
  else
    setResult(RESULT_CANCELED);
  finish();
}
```

8. Add the `EarthquakeLiveFolder` Activity to the application manifest, including an Intent Filter for the action `android.intent.action.CREATE_LIVE_FOLDER`:

```
<activity android:name=".EarthquakeLiveFolders$EarthquakeLiveFolder"
        android:label="All Earthquakes">
  <intent-filter>
    <action android:name="android.intent.action.CREATE_LIVE_FOLDER"/>
  </intent-filter>
</activity>
```

Figure 14-6 shows the earthquake Live Folder open on the home screen.

FIGURE 14-6

All code snippets in this example are part of the Chapter 14 Earthquake Part 3 *project, available for download at* www.wrox.com.

SURFACING APPLICATION SEARCH RESULTS USING THE QUICK SEARCH BOX

The QSB (shown in Figure 14-7) is positioned prominently on the home screen. The user can launch it at any time by clicking it or pressing the hardware search key, where one is available.

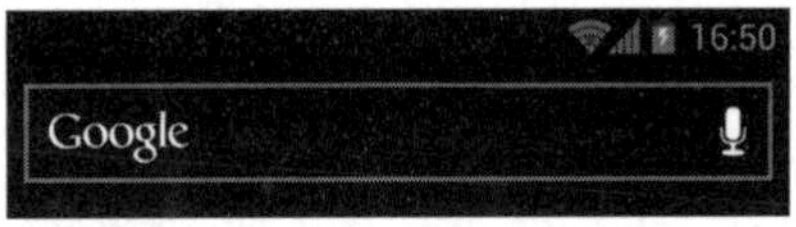

FIGURE 14-7

Android 1.6 (API level 4) introduced the ability to serve your application search results through the universal QSB. By surfacing search results from your application through this mechanism, you provide users with an additional access point to your application through live search results.

Surfacing Search Results to the Quick Search Box

To serve your search results to the QSB, you must first implement search functionality within your application, as described in Chapter 8, "Databases and Content Providers."

To make your results available globally, modify the `searchable.xml` file that describes the application search meta data and add two new attributes:

➤ `searchSettingsDescription` — Used to describe your search results in the Settings menu. This is what the users will see when browsing to include application results in their searches.

➤ `includeInGlobalSearch` — Set this to true to surface these results to the QSB.

```
<searchable xmlns:android="http://schemas.android.com/apk/res/android"
  android:label="@string/search_label"

  android:searchSuggestAuthority="com.paad.provider.mysearch"
  android:searchSuggestIntentAction="android.intent.action.VIEW"
  android:searchSettingsDescription="@string/search_description"
  android:includeInGlobalSearch="true">
</searchable>
```

To avoid the possibility of misuse, adding new search providers requires users to opt-in, so your search results will not be automatically surfaced directly to the QSB.

For users to add your application's search results to their QSB search, they must opt-in using the system settings, as shown in Figure 14-8. From the QSB Activity, they must select Menu ⇨ Settings ⇨ Searchable Items and tick the check boxes alongside each Provider they want to enable.

Because search result surfacing in the QSB is strictly opt-in, you should consider notifying your users that this additional functionality is available.

FIGURE 14-8

Adding the Earthquake Example Search Results to the Quick Search Box

To surface search results from the Earthquake project to the QSB, edit the `searchable.xml` file in your `res/xml` resources folder. Add a new attribute, setting `includeInGlobalSearch` to `true`:

```
<searchable xmlns:android="http://schemas.android.com/apk/res/android"
  android:label="@string/app_name"
  android:searchSettingsDescription="@string/search_description"
  android:searchSuggestAuthority="com.paad.earthquakeprovider"
  android:searchSuggestIntentAction="android.intent.action.VIEW"
  android:searchSuggestIntentData=
    "content://com.paad.earthquakeprovider/earthquakes"
  android:includeInGlobalSearch="true">
</searchable>
```

> *All code snippets in this example are part of the* Chapter 14 Earthquake Part 4 *project, available for download at* www.wrox.com.

CREATING LIVE WALLPAPER

Live Wallpaper was introduced in Android 2.1 (API level 7) as a way to create dynamic, interactive home screen backgrounds. They offer an exciting alternative for displaying information to your users directly on their home screen.

Live Wallpapers use a Surface View to render a dynamic display that can be interacted with in real time. Your Live Wallpaper can listen for, and reach to, screen touch events — letting users engage directly with the background of their home screen.

To create a new Live Wallpaper, you need the following three components:

➤ An XML resource that describes the metadata associated with the Live Wallpaper — specifically its author, description, and a thumbnail used to represent it from the Live Wallpaper picker.

➤ A Wallpaper Service implementation that will wrap, instantiate, and manage your Wallpaper Engine.

➤ A Wallpaper Service Engine implementation (returned through the Wallpaper Service) that defines the UI and interactive behavior of your Live Wallpaper. The Wallpaper Service Engine represents where the bulk of your Live Wallpaper implementation will live.

Creating a Live Wallpaper Definition Resource

The Live Wallpaper resource definition is an XML file stored in the `res/xml` folder. Its resource identifier is its filename without the XML extension. Use attributes within a `wallpaper` tag to define the author name, description, and thumbnail to display in the Live Wallpaper gallery.

Listing 14-33 shows a sample Live Wallpaper resource definition.

LISTING 14-33: Sample Live Wallpaper resource definition

```
<wallpaper xmlns:android="http://schemas.android.com/apk/res/android"
  android:author="@string/author"
  android:description="@string/description"
  android:thumbnail="@drawable/wallpapericon"
/>
```

code snippet PA4AD_Ch14_LiveWallpaper/res/xml/mylivewallpaper.xml

Note that you must use references to existing string resources for the `author` and `description` attribute values. String literals are not valid.

You can also use the `settingsActivity` tag to specify an Activity that should be launched to configure the Live Wallpaper's settings, much like the configuration Activity used to configure Widget settings:

```
<wallpaper xmlns:android="http://schemas.android.com/apk/res/android"
  android:author="@string/author"
```

```
    android:description="@string/description"
    android:thumbnail="@drawable/wallpapericon"
    android:settingsActivity="com.paad.mylivewallpaper.WallpaperSettings"
/>
```

This Activity will be launched immediately before the Live Wallpaper is added to the home screen, allowing the user to configure the Wallpaper.

Creating a Wallpaper Service

Extend the `WallpaperService` class to create a wrapper Service that instantiates and manages the Wallpaper Service Engine class.

All the drawing and interaction for Live Wallpaper is handled in the Wallpaper Service Engine class described in the next section. Override the `onCreateEngine` handler to return a new instance of your custom Wallpaper Service Engine, as shown in Listing 14-34.

LISTING 14-34: Creating a Wallpaper Service

Available for download on Wrox.com

```java
import android.service.wallpaper.WallpaperService;
import android.service.wallpaper.WallpaperService.Engine;

public class MyWallpaperService extends WallpaperService {
  @Override
  public Engine onCreateEngine() {
    return new MyWallpaperServiceEngine();
  }
}
```

code snippet PA4AD_Ch14_LiveWallpaper/src/MyWallpaperService.java

After creating the Wallpaper Service, add it to your application manifest using a `service` tag.

A Wallpaper Service must include an Intent Filter to listen for the `android.service.wallpaper` `.WallpaperService` action and a `meta-data` node that specifies `android.service.wallpaper` as the `name` attribute and associates it with the resource file described in the previous section using a `resource` attribute.

An application that includes a Wallpaper Service must also require the `android.permission.BIND_WALLPAPER` permission. Listing 14-35 shows how to add the Wallpaper Service from Listing 14-34 to the manifest.

LISTING 14-35: Adding a Wallpaper Service to the manifest

```xml
<application
  android:icon="@drawable/icon"
  android:label="@string/app_name"
  android.permission="android.permission.BIND_WALLPAPER">
```

continues

LISTING 14-35 *(continued)*

```xml
<service android:name=".MyWallpaperService">
  <intent-filter>
    <action android:name=
      "android.service.wallpaper.WallpaperService" />
  </intent-filter>
  <meta-data
    android:name="android.service.wallpaper"
    android:resource="@xml/mylivewallpaper"
  />
</service>
</application>
```

code snippet PA4AD_Ch14_LiveWallpaper/AndroidManifest.xml

Creating a Wallpaper Service Engine

The `WallpaperService.Engine` class is where you define the behavior of the Live Wallpaper. The Wallpaper Service Engine includes the Surface View onto which you will draw your Live Wallpaper and handlers notifying you of touch events and home screen offset changes and is where you should implement your redraw loop.

The Surface View, introduced in Chapter 11, is a specialized drawing canvas that supports updates from background threads, making it ideal for creating smooth, dynamic, and interactive graphics.

To implement your own Wallpaper Service engine, extend the `WallpaperService.Engine` class within an enclosing Wallpaper Service class, as shown in the skeleton code in Listing 14-36.

LISTING 14-36: Wallpaper Service Engine skeleton code

```java
public class MyWallpaperServiceEngine extends WallpaperService.Engine {

  private static final int FPS = 30;
  private final Handler handler = new Handler();

  @Override
  public void onCreate(SurfaceHolder surfaceHolder) {
    super.onCreate(surfaceHolder);
    // TODO Handle initialization.
  }

  @Override
  public void onOffsetsChanged(float xOffset, float yOffset,
                               float xOffsetStep, float yOffsetStep,
                               int xPixelOffset, int yPixelOffset) {
    super.onOffsetsChanged(xOffset, yOffset, xOffsetStep, yOffsetStep,
                           xPixelOffset, yPixelOffset);
    // Triggered whenever the user swipes between multiple
    // home-screen panels.
  }
```

```
    @Override
    public void onTouchEvent(MotionEvent event) {
      super.onTouchEvent(event);
      // Triggered when the Live Wallpaper receives a touch event
    }

    @Override
    public void onSurfaceCreated(SurfaceHolder holder) {
      super.onSurfaceCreated(holder);
      // TODO Surface has been created, begin the update loop that will
      // update the Live Wallpaper.
      drawFrame();
    }

    private void drawFrame() {
      final SurfaceHolder holder = getSurfaceHolder();

      Canvas canvas = null;
      try {
        canvas = holder.lockCanvas();
        if (canvas != null) {
          // Draw on the Canvas!
        }
      } finally {
        if (canvas != null)
          holder.unlockCanvasAndPost(canvas);
      }

      // Schedule the next frame
      handler.removeCallbacks(drawSurface);
      handler.postDelayed(drawSurface, 1000 / FPS);
    }

    // Runnable used to allow you to schedule frame draws.
    private final Runnable drawSurface = new Runnable() {
      public void run() {
        drawFrame();
      }
    };

  }
```

code snippet PA4AD_Ch14_LiveWallpaper/src/ MyWallpaperSkeletonService.java

You must wait for the Surface to complete its initialization — indicated by the onSurfaceCreated handler being called — before you can begin drawing on it.

After the Surface has been created, you can begin the drawing loop that updates the Live Wallpaper's UI. In Listing 14-36 this is done by scheduling a new frame to be drawn at the completion of the drawing of the previous frame. The rate of redraws in this example is determined by the desired frame rate.

You can use the onTouchEvent and the onOffsetsChanged handlers to add interactivity to your Live Wallpapers.

Audio, Video, and Using the Camera

The increasing popularity of cloud-based music players, combined with the ubiquity of modern phones with ever-increasing storage capacities, is leading to mobile devices becoming the de facto portable digital media player.

This chapter introduces you to the Android APIs for controlling audio and video playback, controlling the audio focus of the device, and reacting appropriately when other applications take focus or the output channel is changed (for example, when headphones are unplugged).

You'll also learn how to use the Remote Control Client, introduced in Android 4.0. It provides a mechanism for showing users details on the media they're playing and allows them to control the playback from the device's lock screen.

With many devices now including two high-resolution cameras, mobiles have also begun to take the place of non-SLR digital cameras. You'll learn to use the Android camera APIs to take photos and record video using any camera available to the device, as well as displaying the live camera feed. New media effects APIs provide a way to modify and enhance video images in real time from within your applications.

Android's open platform and provider-agnostic philosophy ensures that it offers a multimedia API capable of playing and recording a wide range of image, audio, and video formats, both locally and streamed.

You'll also learn how to manipulate raw audio files using the Audio Track and Audio Record classes, to create a Sound Pool, and to add newly recorded media files to the Media Store.

PLAYING AUDIO AND VIDEO

Android 4.0.3 (API level 15) supports the following multimedia formats for playback as part of the base framework. Note that some devices may support playback of additional file formats:

- ➤ **Audio**
  - ➤ AAC LC/LTP
  - ➤ HE-AACv1 (AAC+)
  - ➤ HE-AACv2 (Enhanced AAC+)
  - ➤ AMR-NB
  - ➤ AMR-WB
  - ➤ MP3
  - ➤ MIDI
  - ➤ Ogg Vorbis
  - ➤ PCM/WAVE
  - ➤ FLAC (on devices running Android 3.1 or above)
- ➤ **Image**
  - ➤ JPEG
  - ➤ PNG
  - ➤ WEBP (on devices running Android 4.0 or above)
  - ➤ GIF
  - ➤ BMP
- ➤ **Video**
  - ➤ H.263
  - ➤ H.264 AVC

➤   MPEG-4 SP

➤   VP8 (on devices running Android 2.3.3 or above)

The following network protocols are supported for streaming media:

➤   RTSP (RTP, SDP)

➤   HTTP/HTTPS progressive streaming

➤   HTTP/HTTPS live streaming (on devices running Android 3.0 or above)

> *For full details on the currently supported media formats and recommendations for video encoding and audio streaming, see the Android Dev Guide, at* `http://developer.android.com/guide/appendix/media-formats.html`.

Introducing the Media Player

The playback of audio and video within Android applications is handled primarily through the `MediaPlayer` class. Using the Media Player, you can play media stored in application resources, local files, Content Providers, or streamed from a network URL.

The Media Player's management of audio and video files and streams is handled as a state machine. In the most simplistic terms, transitions through the state machine can be described as follows:

1.   Initialize the Media Player with media to play.

2.   Prepare the Media Player for playback.

3.   Start the playback.

4.   Pause or stop the playback prior to its completing.

5.   The playback is complete.

> *A more detailed and thorough description of the Media Player state machine is provided at the Android developer site, at* `http://developer.android.com/reference/android/media/MediaPlayer.html#StateDiagram`.

To play a media resource, you need to create a new `MediaPlayer` instance, initialize it with a media source, and prepare it for playback.

The following section describes how to initialize and prepare the Media Player. After that, you'll learn to control the playback to start, pause, stop, or seek the prepared media.

To stream Internet media using the Media Player, your application must include the `INTERNET` permission:

```
<uses-permission android:name="android.permission.INTERNET"/>
```

*Android supports a limited number of simultaneous Media Player objects;
not releasing them can cause runtime exceptions when the system runs out.
When you finish playback, call* `release` *on your Media Player object to free the
associated resources:*

```
mediaPlayer.release();
```

Preparing Audio for Playback

There are a number of ways you can play audio content through the Media Player. You can include it as
an application resource, play it from local files or Content Providers, or stream it from a remote URL.

To include audio content as an application resource, add it to the `res/raw` folder of your resources
hierarchy. Raw resources are not compressed or manipulated in any way when packaged into your
application, making them an ideal way to store precompressed files such as audio files.

Initializing Audio Content for Playback

To play back audio content using a Media Player, you need to create a new Media Player object and
set the data source of the audio in question. You can do this by using the static `create` method,
passing in the Activity Context and any one of the following audio sources:

➤ A resource identifier (typically for an audio file stored in the `res/raw` resource folder)

➤ A URI to a local file (using the `file://` schema)

➤ A URI to an online audio resource (as a URL)

➤ A URI to a row within a Content Provider that returns an audio file

```
// Load an audio resource from a package resource.
MediaPlayer resourcePlayer =
  MediaPlayer.create(this, R.raw.my_audio);

// Load an audio resource from a local file.
MediaPlayer filePlayer = MediaPlayer.create(this,
  Uri.parse("file:///sdcard/localfile.mp3"));

// Load an audio resource from an online resource.
MediaPlayer urlPlayer = MediaPlayer.create(this,
  Uri.parse("http://site.com/audio/audio.mp3"));

// Load an audio resource from a Content Provider.
MediaPlayer contentPlayer = MediaPlayer.create(this,
  Settings.System.DEFAULT_RINGTONE_URI);
```

The Media Player objects returned by these `create` *methods have already had*
`prepare` *called. It's important that you do not call it again.*

Alternatively, you can use the `setDataSource` method on an existing Media Player instance, as shown in Listing 15-1. This method accepts a file path, Content Provider URI, streaming media URL path, or File Descriptor. When using the `setDataSource` method, it is vital that you call `prepare` on the Media Player before you begin playback.

LISTING 15-1: Audio playback using the Media Player

```
MediaPlayer mediaPlayer = new MediaPlayer();
mediaPlayer.setDataSource("/sdcard/mydopetunes.mp3");
mediaPlayer.prepare();
```

code snippet PA4AD_Ch15_Media_Player/src/VideoViewActivity.java

Preparing Video for Playback

Playback of video content is slightly more involved than audio. To play a video, you first must have a Surface on which to show it.

There are two alternatives for the playback of video content. The first technique, using the `VideoView` class, encapsulates the creation of a Surface and allocation and preparation of video content using a Media Player.

The second technique allows you to specify your own `Surface` and manipulate the underlying Media Player instance directly.

Playing Video Using the Video View

The simplest way to play back video is to use the Video View. The Video View includes a Surface on which the video is displayed and encapsulates and manages a Media Player instance that handles the playback.

After placing the Video View within the UI, get a reference to it within your code. You can then assign a video to play by calling its `setVideoPath` or `setVideoURI` methods to specify the path to a local file, or the URI of either a Content Provider or remote video stream:

```
final VideoView videoView = (VideoView)findViewById(R.id.videoView);

// Assign a local file to play
videoView.setVideoPath("/sdcard/mycatvideo.3gp");

// Assign a URL of a remote video stream
videoView.setVideoUri(myAwesomeStreamingSource);
```

When the video is initialized, you can control its playback using the `start`, `stopPlayback`, `pause`, and `seekTo` methods. The Video View also includes the `setKeepScreenOn` method to apply a screen Wake Lock that will prevent the screen from being dimmed while playback is in progress without requiring a special permission.

Listing 15-2 shows the skeleton code used to assign a video to a Video View. It uses a Media Controller to control playback, as described in the section "Controlling the Media Player Playback."

LISTING 15-2: Video playback using a Video View

```
// Get a reference to the Video View.
final VideoView videoView = (VideoView)findViewById(R.id.videoView);

// Configure the video view and assign a source video.
videoView.setKeepScreenOn(true);
videoView.setVideoPath("/sdcard/mycatvideo.3gp");

// Attach a Media Controller
MediaController mediaController = new MediaController(this);
videoView.setMediaController(mediaController);
```

code snippet PA4AD_Ch15_Media_Player/src/VideoViewActivity.java

Creating a Surface for Video Playback

The first step to using the Media Player directly to view video content is to prepare a Surface onto which the video will be displayed.

This is generally handled using a `SurfaceView` object. The Surface View class is a wrapper around the Surface Holder object, which, in turn, is a wrapper around the Surface that is used to support visual updates from background threads.

The Media Player uses a `SurfaceHolder` object to display video content, assigned using the `setDisplay` method. To include a Surface Holder in your UI layout, use the `SurfaceView` class, as shown in the sample layout XML in Listing 15-3.

LISTING 15-3: Sample layout using a Surface View

```xml
<?xml version="1.0" encoding="utf-8"?>
<LinearLayout
  xmlns:android="http://schemas.android.com/apk/res/android"
  android:layout_width="match_parent"
  android:layout_height="match_parent"
  android:orientation="vertical" >
  <SurfaceView
    android:id="@+id/surfaceView"
    android:layout_width="match_parent"
    android:layout_height="match_parent"
    android:layout_weight="30"
  />
  <LinearLayout
    android:id="@+id/linearLayout1"
    android:layout_width="match_parent"
    android:layout_height="wrap_content"
    android:layout_weight="1">
    <Button
      android:id="@+id/buttonPlay"
      android:layout_width="wrap_content"
      android:layout_height="wrap_content"
```

```
              android:text="Play"
            />
            <Button
              android:id="@+id/buttonPause"
              android:layout_width="wrap_content"
              android:layout_height="wrap_content"
              android:text="Pause"
            />
            <Button
              android:id="@+id/buttonSkip"
              android:layout_width="wrap_content"
              android:layout_height="wrap_content"
              android:text="Skip"
            />
          </LinearLayout>
      </LinearLayout>
```

code snippet PA4AD_Ch15_Media_Player/res/layout/surfaceviewvideoviewer.xml

Surface Holders are created asynchronously, so you must wait until the `surfaceCreated` handler has been fired before assigning the returned Surface Holder object to the Media Player by implementing the `SurfaceHolder.Callback` interface.

After creating and assigning the Surface Holder to your Media Player, use the `setDataSource` method to specify the path, URL, or Content Provider URI of the video resource to play.

After you select your media source, call `prepare` to initialize the Media Player in preparation for playback. Listing 15-4 shows the skeleton code used to initialize a Surface View within your Activity and assigns it as a display target for a Media Player.

LISTING 15-4: Initializing and assigning a Surface View to a Media Player

```
import java.io.IOException;
import android.app.Activity;
import android.media.MediaPlayer;
import android.os.Bundle;
import android.util.Log;
import android.view.SurfaceHolder;
import android.view.SurfaceView;
import android.view.View;
import android.view.View.OnClickListener;
import android.widget.Button;

public class SurfaceViewVideoViewActivity extends Activity
  implements SurfaceHolder.Callback {

  static final String TAG = "SurfaceViewVideoViewActivity";

  private MediaPlayer mediaPlayer;

  public void surfaceCreated(SurfaceHolder holder) {
    try {
```

continues

LISTING 15-4 *(continued)*

```java
      // When the surface is created, assign it as the
      // display surface and assign and prepare a data
      // source.
      mediaPlayer.setDisplay(holder);
      mediaPlayer.setDataSource("/sdcard/test2.3gp");
      mediaPlayer.prepare();
    } catch (IllegalArgumentException e) {
      Log.e(TAG, "Illegal Argument Exception", e);
    } catch (IllegalStateException e) {
      Log.e(TAG, "Illegal State Exception", e);
    } catch (SecurityException e) {
      Log.e(TAG, "Security Exception", e);
    } catch (IOException e) {
      Log.e(TAG, "IO Exception", e);
    }
  }

  public void surfaceDestroyed(SurfaceHolder holder) {
    mediaPlayer.release();
  }

  public void surfaceChanged(SurfaceHolder holder,
                             int format, int width, int height) { }


  @Override
  public void onCreate(Bundle savedInstanceState) {
    super.onCreate(savedInstanceState);

    setContentView(R.layout.surfaceviewvideoviewer);

    // Create a new Media Player.
    mediaPlayer = new MediaPlayer();

    // Get a reference to the Surface View.
    final SurfaceView surfaceView =
      (SurfaceView)findViewById(R.id.surfaceView);

    // Configure the Surface View.
    surfaceView.setKeepScreenOn(true);

    // Configure the Surface Holder and register the callback.
    SurfaceHolder holder = surfaceView.getHolder();
    holder.addCallback(this);
    holder.setType(SurfaceHolder.SURFACE_TYPE_PUSH_BUFFERS);
    holder.setFixedSize(400, 300);

    // Connect a play button.
    Button playButton = (Button)findViewById(R.id.buttonPlay);
    playButton.setOnClickListener(new OnClickListener() {
      public void onClick(View v) {
        mediaPlayer.start();
```

```
      }
    });

    // Connect a pause button.
    Button pauseButton = (Button)findViewById(R.id.buttonPause);
    pauseButton.setOnClickListener(new OnClickListener() {
      public void onClick(View v) {
        mediaPlayer.pause();
      }
    });

    // Add a skip button.
    Button skipButton = (Button)findViewById(R.id.buttonSkip);
    skipButton.setOnClickListener(new OnClickListener() {
      public void onClick(View v) {
        mediaPlayer.seekTo(mediaPlayer.getDuration()/2);
      }
    });
  }
}
```

code snippet PA4AD_Ch15_Media_Player/src/SurfaceViewVideoViewActivity.java

Controlling Media Player Playback

When a Media Player is prepared, call `start` to begin playback of the associated media:

```
mediaPlayer.start();
```

Use the `stop` and `pause` methods to stop or pause playback, respectively.

The Media Player also provides the `getDuration` method to find the length of the media being played and the `getCurrentPosition` method to find the playback position. Use the `seekTo` method to jump to a specific position in the media (refer to Listing 15-4).

To ensure a consistent media control experience, Android includes the `MediaController` — a standard control that provides the common media control buttons, as shown in Figure 15-1.

FIGURE 15-1

If you are using the Media Controller to control video playback, it's good practice to instantiate it in code and associate it with the video playback View, rather than including it within your layout. When created this way, the Media Controller will be visible only when you set it to visible, touch its host Video View, or are interacting with it.

If you're using a Video View to display your video content, you can use the Media Controller simply by the Video View's `setMediaController` method:

```
// Attach a Media Controller
MediaController mediaController = new MediaController(this);
videoView.setMediaController(mediaController);
```

You can use a Media Controller to control any Media Player and associate it with any View in your UI.

To control a Media Player, or other audio or video source directly, you need to implement a new
`MediaController.MediaPlayerControl`, as shown in Listing 15-5.

LISTING 15-5: Controlling playback using the Media Controller

```java
MediaController mediaController = new MediaController(this);
mediaController.setMediaPlayer(new MediaPlayerControl() {

  public boolean canPause() {
    return true;
  }

  public boolean canSeekBackward() {
    return true;
  }

  public boolean canSeekForward() {
    return true;
  }

  public int getBufferPercentage() {
    return 0;
  }

  public int getCurrentPosition() {
    return mediaPlayer.getCurrentPosition();
  }

  public int getDuration() {
    return mediaPlayer.getDuration();
  }

  public boolean isPlaying() {
    return mediaPlayer.isPlaying();
  }

  public void pause() {
    mediaPlayer.pause();
  }

  public void seekTo(int pos) {
    mediaPlayer.seekTo(pos);
  }

  public void start() {
    mediaPlayer.start();
  }

});
```

code snippet PA4AD_Ch15_Media_Player/src/SurfaceViewVideoViewActivity.java

Use the `setAnchorView` method to determine which view should anchor the Media Controller when it's visible, and call `show` or `hide` to show or hide the controller, respectively:

```
mediaController.setAnchorView(myView);
mediaController.show();
```

Note that you must associate a Media Player Control before attempting to display the Media Controller.

Managing Media Playback Output

The Media Player provides methods to control the volume of the output, lock the screen brightness during playback, and set the looping status.

You can control the volume for each channel during playback using the `setVolume` method. It takes a scalar float value between 0 and 1 for both the left and right channels (where 0 is silent and 1 is maximum volume).

```
mediaPlayer.setVolume(0.5f, 0.5f);
```

To force the screen to stay on during video playback, use the `setScreenOnWhilePlaying` method:

```
mediaPlayer.setScreenOnWhilePlaying(true);
```

This is preferred to using Wake Locks because it doesn't require any additional permissions. Wake Locks are described in more detail in Chapter 18, "Advanced Android Development."

Use the `isLooping` method to determine the current loop status, and the `setLooping` method to specify if the media being played should loop when it completes:

```
if (!mediaPlayer.isLooping())
  mediaPlayer.setLooping(true);
```

> *It is currently not possible to play audio into a phone conversation; the Media Player always plays audio using the standard output device — the speaker or connected headset.*

Responding to the Volume Controls

To ensure a consistent user experience, it's important that your application correctly handles users pressing the volume and any attached media playback control keys.

By default, using the volume keys, on either the device or an attached headset, changes the volume of whichever audio stream is currently playing. If no stream is active, the volume keys will alter the ringtone volume.

If your Activity is expected to play audio for a significant proportion of its visible lifetime (for example, a music player or game with a soundtrack and audio effects), it's reasonable for users to expect that the volume keys will alter the music volume even if no music is currently playing.

Using the Activity's `setVolumeControlStream` method — typically within its `onCreate` method, as shown in Listing 15-6 — allows you to specify which audio stream should be controlled by the volume keys while the current Activity is active.

You can specify any of the available audio streams, but when using the Media Player, you should specify the `STREAM_MUSIC` stream to make it the focus of the volume keys.

LISTING 15-6: Setting the volume control stream for an Activity

```java
@Override
public void onCreate(Bundle savedInstanceState) {
    super.onCreate(savedInstanceState);
    setContentView(R.layout.audioplayer);

    setVolumeControlStream(AudioManager.STREAM_MUSIC);
}
```

code snippet PA4AD_Ch15_Media_Player/src/AudioPlayerActivity.java

> *Although it's also possible to listen for volume key presses directly, this is generally considered poor practice. There are several ways a user can modify the audio volume, including the hardware buttons as well as software controls. Triggering volume changes manually based only on the hardware buttons is likely to make your application respond unexpectedly.*

Responding to the Media Playback Controls

If your application plays audio and/or video in a way users would associate with a media player, it should respond predictably to media button presses.

Some devices, as well as attached or Bluetooth headsets, feature play, stop, pause, skip, and previous media playback keys. When users press these keys, the system broadcasts an Intent with the `ACTION_MEDIA_BUTTON` action. To receive this broadcast, you must have a Broadcast Receiver declared in your manifest that listens for this action, as shown in Listing 15-7.

LISTING 15-7: Media button press Broadcast Receiver manifest declaration

```xml
<receiver android:name=".MediaControlReceiver">
  <intent-filter>
    <action android:name="android.intent.action.MEDIA_BUTTON"/>
  </intent-filter>
</receiver>
```

code snippet PA4AD_Ch15_Media_Player/AndroidManifest.xml

In Listing 15-8 this Broadcast Receiver is implemented such that when it receives the media button key presses, it simply creates a new Intent that includes the same extras and broadcasts it to the Activity playing the audio.

LISTING 15-8: A media button press Manifest Broadcast Receiver implementation

```java
public class MediaControlReceiver extends BroadcastReceiver {

  public static final String ACTION_MEDIA_BUTTON =
    "com.paad.ACTION_MEDIA_BUTTON";

  @Override
  public void onReceive(Context context, Intent intent) {
    if (Intent.ACTION_MEDIA_BUTTON.equals(intent.getAction())) {
      Intent internalIntent = new Intent(ACTION_MEDIA_BUTTON);
      internalIntent.putExtras(intent.getExtras());
      context.sendBroadcast(internalIntent);
    }
  }
}
```

code snippet PA4AD_Ch15_Media_Player/src/MediaControlReceiver.java

The key code of the media button pressed is stored within the received Intent within the EXTRA_KEY_EVENT extra, as shown in Listing 15-9.

LISTING 15-9: Media button press Broadcast Receiver implementation

```java
public class ActivityMediaControlReceiver extends BroadcastReceiver {
  @Override
  public void onReceive(Context context, Intent intent) {
    if (MediaControlReceiver.ACTION_MEDIA_BUTTON.equals(
        intent.getAction())) {
      KeyEvent event =
        (KeyEvent)intent.getParcelableExtra(Intent.EXTRA_KEY_EVENT);

      switch (event.getKeyCode()) {
        case (KeyEvent.KEYCODE_MEDIA_PLAY_PAUSE) :
          if (mediaPlayer.isPlaying())
            pause();
          else
            play();
          break;
        case (KeyEvent.KEYCODE_MEDIA_PLAY) :
          play(); break;
        case (KeyEvent.KEYCODE_MEDIA_PAUSE) :
          pause(); break;
        case (KeyEvent.KEYCODE_MEDIA_NEXT) :
          skip(); break;
        case (KeyEvent.KEYCODE_MEDIA_PREVIOUS) :
```

continues

LISTING 15-9 *(continued)*

```
        previous(); break;
      case (KeyEvent.KEYCODE_MEDIA_STOP) :
        stop(); break;
      default: break;
    }
  }
 }
}
```

code snippet PA4AD_Ch15_Media_Player/src/AudioPlayerActivity.java

If your application intends to continue playing audio in the background when the Activity isn't visible, a good approach is to keep your Media Player within a Service, controlling the media playback using Intents.

Multiple applications might be installed on a given device, each configured to receive media key presses; therefore, you must also use the Audio Manager's `registerMediaButtonEventReceiver` method to register your Receiver as the exclusive handler of media button presses, as shown in Listing 15-10, which both registers the media button event Receiver declared in your manifest and the local Broadcast Receiver that interprets the Intent when it's passed through to the Activity.

LISTING 15-10: Media button press Receiver manifest declaration

```
// Register the Media Button Event Receiver to
// listen for media button presses.
AudioManager am =
  (AudioManager)getSystemService(Context.AUDIO_SERVICE);
ComponentName component =
  new ComponentName(this, MediaControlReceiver.class);

am.registerMediaButtonEventReceiver(component);

// Register a local Intent Receiver that receives media button
// presses from the Receiver registered in the manifest.
activityMediaControlReceiver = new ActivityMediaControlReceiver();
IntentFilter filter =
  new IntentFilter(MediaControlReceiver.ACTION_MEDIA_BUTTON);

registerReceiver(activityMediaControlReceiver, filter);
```

code snippet PA4AD_Ch15_Media_Player/src/AudioPlayerActivity.java

> *Calls to* `registerMediaButtonEventReceiver` *are respected in the order in which they're received, so it's good practice to register and unregister your Receiver based on when you have (and lose) audio focus, as described in the next section.*

Requesting and Managing Audio Focus

In some cases (particularly for media players) your application should continue to respond to media buttons when it isn't visible or active. Users may have multiple media players on their devices, so it's important that your application pause playback and cede control of the media buttons when another media application takes focus.

Similarly, when your application becomes active, it should notify other audio playback applications that they should pause playback and allow it to become the focus for media button clicks. Such delegation is handled through the audio focus, a set of APIs introduced in Android 2.2 (API level 8).

To request audio focus before beginning playback, use the Audio Manager's requestAudioFocus method. When requesting the audio focus, you can specify which stream you require (typically STREAM_MUSIC), and for how long you expect to require focus — either permanently (such as when playing music) or transiently (such as when providing navigation instructions). In the latter case you can also specify if your transient interruption can be handled by the currently focused application "ducking" (lowering its volume) until your interruption is complete.

Specifying the nature of the audio focus you require allows other applications to better react to their own loss of audio focus, as described later in this section.

Listing 15-11 shows the skeleton code for an Activity that requests permanent audio focus for the music stream. You must also specify an Audio Focus Change Listener. This lets you monitor for loss of audio focus and respond accordingly (and is described in more detail later in this section).

LISTING 15-11: Requesting the audio focus

```
AudioManager am = (AudioManager)getSystemService(Context.AUDIO_SERVICE);

// Request audio focus for playback
int result = am.requestAudioFocus(focusChangeListener,
          // Use the music stream.
          AudioManager.STREAM_MUSIC,
          // Request permanent focus.
          AudioManager.AUDIOFOCUS_GAIN);

if (result == AudioManager.AUDIOFOCUS_REQUEST_GRANTED) {
  mediaPlayer.start();
}
```

code snippet PA4AD_Ch15_Media_Player/src/AudioPlayerActivity.java

Audio focus is assigned in turn to each application that requests it. This means that if another application requests audio focus, your application will lose it. You will be notified of the loss of audio focus through the onAudioFocusChange handler of the Audio Focus Change Listener you registered when requesting the audio focus, as shown in Listing 15-12.

The focusChange parameter indicates the nature of the focus loss — either transient or permanent — and whether ducking is permitted.

It's best practice to pause your media playback whenever you lose audio focus, or, in the case of a transient loss that supports ducking, to lower the volume of your audio output.

In the case of a transient focus loss, you will be notified when you have regained focus, at which point you can return to playing your audio at the previous volume.

For a permanent focus loss, you should stop playback and restart it only through a user interaction (such as pressing the play button within your UI). In such circumstances you should also take this opportunity to unregister the media button Receiver.

LISTING 15-12: Responding to the loss of audio focus

```java
private OnAudioFocusChangeListener focusChangeListener =
  new OnAudioFocusChangeListener() {

  public void onAudioFocusChange(int focusChange) {
    AudioManager am =
      (AudioManager)getSystemService(Context.AUDIO_SERVICE);

    switch (focusChange) {
      case (AudioManager.AUDIOFOCUS_LOSS_TRANSIENT_CAN_DUCK) :
        // Lower the volume while ducking.
        mediaPlayer.setVolume(0.2f, 0.2f);
        break;

      case (AudioManager.AUDIOFOCUS_LOSS_TRANSIENT) :
        pause();
        break;

      case (AudioManager.AUDIOFOCUS_LOSS) :
        stop();
        ComponentName component =
          new ComponentName(AudioPlayerActivity.this,
            MediaControlReceiver.class);
        am.unregisterMediaButtonEventReceiver(component);
        break;

      case (AudioManager.AUDIOFOCUS_GAIN) :
        // Return the volume to normal and resume if paused.
        mediaPlayer.setVolume(1f, 1f);
        mediaPlayer.start();
        break;

      default: break;
    }
  }
};
```

code snippet PA4AD_Ch15_Media_Player/src/AudioPlayerActivity.java

When you have completed your audio playback, you may choose to abandon the audio focus, as shown in Listing 15-13.

LISTING 15-13: Abandoning audio focus

```
AudioManager am =
    (AudioManager)getSystemService(Context.AUDIO_SERVICE);

am.abandonAudioFocus(focusChangeListener);
```

code snippet PA4AD_Ch15_Media_Player/src/AudioPlayerActivity.java

Typically, this is only necessary when your application takes only transient audio focus. In the case of a media player, it is reasonable to maintain the audio focus whenever the music is playing or your Activity is in the foreground.

Pausing Playback When the Output Changes

If the current output stream is an attached headset, disconnecting it will result in the system automatically switching output to the device's speakers. It's considered good practice to pause (or reduce the volume of) your audio output in these circumstances.

To do so, create a Broadcast Receiver that listens for the `AudioManager.ACTION_AUDIO_BECOMING_NOISY` broadcast and pauses your playback, as shown in Listing 15-14.

LISTING 15-14: Pausing output when the headset is disconnected

```
private class NoisyAudioStreamReceiver extends BroadcastReceiver {
  @Override
  public void onReceive(Context context, Intent intent) {
    if (AudioManager.ACTION_AUDIO_BECOMING_NOISY.equals
      (intent.getAction())) {
      pause();
    }
  }
}
```

code snippet PA4AD_Ch15_Media_Player/src/AudioPlayerActivity.java

Introducing the Remote Control Client

Android 4.0 (API level 14) introduced the Remote Control Client. Using the Remote Control Client, your application can provide data, and respond, to remote controls capable of displaying metadata, artwork, and media transport control buttons — such as the lock screen on Android 4.0 devices, as shown in Figure 15-2.

To add support for the Remote Control Client in your application, you must have a Receiver implementation that has been registered as a Media Button Event Receiver, as described earlier in the "Responding to the Media Playback Controls" section.

Create a Pending Intent containing the ACTION_MEDIA_BUTTON action that is targeted at your Receiver, and use it to create a new Remote Control Client. You register it with the Audio Manager using the registerRemoteControlClient method, as shown in Listing 15-15.

FIGURE 15-2

LISTING 15-15: Registering a Remote Control Client

```
AudioManager am =
   (AudioManager)getSystemService(Context.AUDIO_SERVICE);

// Create a Pending Intent that will broadcast the
// media button press action. Set the target component
// to your Broadcast Receiver.
Intent mediaButtonIntent = new Intent(Intent.ACTION_MEDIA_BUTTON);
ComponentName component =
  new ComponentName(this, MediaControlReceiver.class);

mediaButtonIntent.setComponent(component);
PendingIntent mediaPendingIntent =
   PendingIntent.getBroadcast(getApplicationContext(), 0,
```

```
                                        mediaButtonIntent, 0);

    // Create a new Remote Control Client using the
    // Pending Intent and register it with the
    // Audio Manager
    myRemoteControlClient =
      new RemoteControlClient(mediaPendingIntent);

    am.registerRemoteControlClient(myRemoteControlClient);
```

code snippet PA4AD_Ch15_Media_Player/src/AudioPlayerActivity.java

In this example, the Remote Control Client button presses will be received by the Media Control Receiver, which, in turn, will broadcast them to the Receiver registered within the Activity.

After registering your Remote Control Client, you can use it to modify the metadata displayed on the associated display.

Use the `setTransportControlFlags` method to define which playback controls your application supports, as shown in Listing 15-16.

LISTING 15-16: Configuring the Remote Control Client playback controls

```
myRemoteControlClient.setTransportControlFlags(
    RemoteControlClient.FLAG_KEY_MEDIA_PLAY_PAUSE|
    RemoteControlClient.FLAG_KEY_MEDIA_STOP);
```

code snippet PA4AD_Ch15_Media_Player/src/AudioPlayerActivity.java

It's also possible to use the `setPlaybackState` method to update the current state of playback by using one of the `RemoteControlClient.PLAYBACK_*` constants:

```
myRemoteControlClient.setPlaybackState(RemoteControlClient.PLAYSTATE_PLAYING);
```

You can supply a bitmap, text string, and numeric value associated with the currently playing audio — typically the album artwork, track name, and elapsed track time, respectively. To do so, use the `MetadataEditor`, accessible from the Remote Control Client's `editMetadata` method as shown in Listing 15-17.

Using the `putBitmap` on the `MetadataEditor` object, you can specify an associated bitmap using the `MetadataEditor.BITMAP_KEY_ARTWORK` key.

Using the `putLong` method you can add the track number, CD number, year of recording, and elapsed duration using the MediaMetadataRetriever.`METADATA_KEY_*` constants.

Similarly, the `putString` method lets you specify the album, album artist, track title, track title, author, compilation, composer, release data, genre, and writer of the current audio — specifying `null` where no such data is available.

To apply changes to the displayed metadata, call the `apply` method.

LISTING 15-17: Applying changes to the Remote Control Client metadata

```
MetadataEditor editor = myRemoteControlClient.editMetadata(false);

editor.putBitmap(MetadataEditor.BITMAP_KEY_ARTWORK, artwork);
editor.putString(MediaMetadataRetriever.METADATA_KEY_ALBUM, album);
editor.putString(MediaMetadataRetriever.METADATA_KEY_ARTIST, artist);
editor.putLong(MediaMetadataRetriever.METADATA_KEY_CD_TRACK_NUMBER,
               trackNumber);

editor.apply();
```

code snippet PA4AD_Ch15_Media_Player/src/AudioPlayerActivity.java

MANIPULATING RAW AUDIO

The `AudioTrack` and `AudioRecord` classes let you record audio directly from the audio input hardware and stream PCM audio buffers directly to the audio hardware for playback.

Using Audio Track streaming, you can process and play back incoming audio in near real time, letting you manipulate incoming or outgoing audio and perform signal processing on raw audio.

Although a detailed account of raw audio processing and manipulation is beyond the scope of this book, the following sections offer an introduction to recording and playing back raw PCM data.

Recording Sound with Audio Record

Use the `AudioRecord` class to record audio directly from the hardware buffers. Create a new Audio Record object, specifying the source, frequency, channel configuration, audio encoding, and buffer size:

```
int bufferSize = AudioRecord.getMinBufferSize(frequency,
                                              channelConfiguration,
                                              audioEncoding);

AudioRecord audioRecord = new AudioRecord(MediaRecorder.AudioSource.MIC,
                                          frequency, channelConfiguration,
                                          audioEncoding, bufferSize);
```

The frequency, audio encoding, and channel configuration values will affect the size and quality of the recorded audio. None of this meta data is associated with the recorded files.

For privacy reasons, Android requires that the `RECORD_AUDIO` permission be included in your manifest:

```
<uses-permission android:name="android.permission.RECORD_AUDIO"/>
```

When your Audio Record object is initialized, run the `startRecording` method to begin asynchronous recording, and use the `read` method to add raw audio data into the recording buffer:

```
audioRecord.startRecording();
while (isRecording) {
```

```
  [ ... populate the buffer ... ]
  int bufferReadResult = audioRecord.read(buffer, 0, bufferSize);
}
```

Listing 15-18 records raw audio from a microphone to a file stored on an SD card. The next section shows you how to use an Audio Track to play this audio.

LISTING 15-18: Recording raw audio with Audio Record

```java
int frequency = 11025;
int channelConfiguration = AudioFormat.CHANNEL_CONFIGURATION_MONO;
int audioEncoding = AudioFormat.ENCODING_PCM_16BIT;

File file =
  new File(Environment.getExternalStorageDirectory(), "raw.pcm");

// Create the new file.
try {
  file.createNewFile();
} catch (IOException e) {
  Log.d(TAG, "IO Exception", e);
}

try {
  OutputStream os = new FileOutputStream(file);
  BufferedOutputStream bos = new BufferedOutputStream(os);
  DataOutputStream dos = new DataOutputStream(bos);

  int bufferSize = AudioRecord.getMinBufferSize(frequency,
                                                channelConfiguration,
                                                audioEncoding);
  short[] buffer = new short[bufferSize];

  // Create a new AudioRecord object to record the audio.
  AudioRecord audioRecord =
    new AudioRecord(MediaRecorder.AudioSource.MIC,
                    frequency,
                    channelConfiguration,
                    audioEncoding, bufferSize);
  audioRecord.startRecording();

  while (isRecording) {
    int bufferReadResult = audioRecord.read(buffer, 0, bufferSize);
    for (int i = 0; i < bufferReadResult; i++)
      dos.writeShort(buffer[i]);
  }

  audioRecord.stop();
  dos.close();
} catch (Throwable t) {
  Log.d(TAG, "An error occurred during recording", t);
}
```

code snippet PA4AD_Ch15_Raw_Audio/src/RawAudioActivity.java

Playing Sound with Audio Track

Use the `AudioTrack` class to play raw audio directly into the hardware buffers. Create a new Audio Track object, specifying the streaming mode, frequency, channel configuration, and the audio encoding type and length of the audio to play back:

```
AudioTrack audioTrack = new AudioTrack(AudioManager.STREAM_MUSIC,
                                       frequency,
                                       channelConfiguration,
                                       audioEncoding,
                                       audioLength,
                                       AudioTrack.MODE_STREAM);
```

Because this is raw audio, no metadata is associated with the recorded files, so it's important to correctly set the audio data properties to the same values as those used when recording the file.

After initializing your Audio Track, run the `play` method to begin asynchronous playback, and use the `write` method to add raw audio data into the playback buffer:

```
audioTrack.play();
audioTrack.write(audio, 0, audioLength);
```

You can write audio into the Audio Track buffer either before or after `play` has been called. In the former case, playback will commence as soon as `play` is called; in the latter case, playback will begin as soon as you write data to the Audio Track buffer.

Listing 15-19 plays back the raw audio recorded in Listing 15-18 but does so at double speed by halving the expected frequency of the audio file.

LISTING 15-19: Playing raw audio with Audio Track

```
int frequency = 11025/2;
int channelConfiguration = AudioFormat.CHANNEL_CONFIGURATION_MONO;
int audioEncoding = AudioFormat.ENCODING_PCM_16BIT;

File file =
  new File(Environment.getExternalStorageDirectory(), "raw.pcm");

// Short array to store audio track (16 bit so 2 bytes per short)
int audioLength = (int)(file.length()/2);
short[] audio = new short[audioLength];

try {
  InputStream is = new FileInputStream(file);
  BufferedInputStream bis = new BufferedInputStream(is);
  DataInputStream dis = new DataInputStream(bis);

  int i = 0;
  while (dis.available() > 0) {
    audio[i] = dis.readShort();
    i++;
  }

  // Close the input streams.
  dis.close();
```

```
                // Create and play a new AudioTrack object
                AudioTrack audioTrack = new AudioTrack(AudioManager.STREAM_MUSIC,
                                                       frequency,
                                                       channelConfiguration,
                                                       audioEncoding,
                                                       audioLength,
                                                       AudioTrack.MODE_STREAM);
                audioTrack.play();
                audioTrack.write(audio, 0, audioLength);
            } catch (Throwable t) {
                Log.d(TAG, "An error occurred during playback", t);
            }
```

code snippet PA4AD_Ch15_Raw_Audio/src/RawAudioActivity.java

CREATING A SOUND POOL

You can use the SoundPool class to manage audio when your application requires low audio latency and/or will be playing multiple audio streams simultaneously (such as a game with multiple sound effects and background music).

Creating a Sound Pool preloads the audio tracks used by your application, such as each level within a game, and optimizes their resource management.

As you add each track to the Sound Pool, it is decompressed and decoded into raw 16-bit PCM streams, allowing you to package compressed audio resources without suffering from the latency and CPU effects of decompression during playback.

When creating a Sound Pool, you can specify the maximum number of concurrent streams to play, allowing it to minimize the effect of the audio mixing by automatically stopping the oldest, lowest priority stream within the pool when the limit is reached.

When creating a new Sound Pool, you specify the target stream (almost always STREAM_MUSIC) and the maximum number of simultaneous streams that should be played concurrently as shown in Listing 15-20.

The Sound Pool supports loading audio resources from an Asset File Descriptor, package resource, file path, or File Descriptor, using a series of overloaded load methods. Loading a new audio resource returns an integer that is used to uniquely identify that sample and must be used to alter its playback settings or initiate or pause playback, as shown in Listing 15-21.

LISTING 15-20: Creating a Sound Pool

```
int maxStreams = 10;
SoundPool sp = new SoundPool(maxStreams, AudioManager.STREAM_MUSIC, 0);

int track1 = sp.load(this, R.raw.track1, 0);
int track2 = sp.load(this, R.raw.track2, 0);
int track3 = sp.load(this, R.raw.track3, 0);
```

code snippet PA4AD_Ch15_Media_Player/src/SoundPoolActivity.java

Use the `play`, `pause`, `resume`, and `stop` methods to control the playback of each audio stream. When your audio samples are playing, you can use the `setLoop` method to alter the number of times the specified sample should repeat, the `setRate` method to modify the playback frequency, and the `setVolume` method to alter the playback volume. Some of these playback controls are shown in Listing 15-21.

LISTING 15-21: Controlling playback of Sound Pool audio

```
track1Button.setOnClickListener(new OnClickListener() {
  public void onClick(View v) {
    sp.play(track1, 1, 1, 0, -1, 1);
  }
});

track2Button.setOnClickListener(new OnClickListener() {
  public void onClick(View v) {
    sp.play(track2, 1, 1, 0, 0, 1);
  }
});

track3Button.setOnClickListener(new OnClickListener() {
  public void onClick(View v) {
    sp.play(track3, 1, 1, 0, 0, 0.5f);
  }
});

stopButton.setOnClickListener(new OnClickListener() {
  public void onClick(View v) {
    sp.stop(track1);
    sp.stop(track2);
    sp.stop(track3);
  }
});

chipmunkButton.setOnClickListener(new OnClickListener() {
  public void onClick(View v) {
    sp.setRate(track1, 2f);
  }
});
```

code snippet PA4AD_Ch15_Media_Player/src/SoundPoolActivity.java

Android 2.2 (API level 8) introduced two convenience methods, `autoPause` and `autoResume`, that will pause and resume, respectively, all the active audio streams.

If you are creating a game, or other application that should play audio only when visible, it's good practice to pause all the active audio unless your application is active and visible, and restart it only after the user has begun interacting with it again — typically by touching the screen.

When you no longer require the audio collected within a Sound Pool, call its `release` method to free the resources:

```
soundPool.release();
```

USING AUDIO EFFECTS

Android 2.3 (API level 9) introduced a suite of audio effects that can be applied to the audio output of any Audio Track or Media Player. After applying the effects, you can modify the effect settings and parameters to alter how they affect the audio being output within your application.

As of Android 4.0.3, the following five `AudioEffect` subclasses are available:

➤ `Equalizer` — Lets you modify the frequency response of your audio output. Use the `setBandLevel` method to assign a gain value to a specific frequency band.

➤ `Virtualizer` — Makes audio appear to be more three-dimensional. Its implementation will vary depending on the configuration of the output device. Use the `setStrength` method to set the strength of the effect between 0 and 1000.

➤ `BassBoost` — Boosts the low frequencies of your audio output. Use the `setStrength` method to set the strength of the effect between 0 and 1000.

➤ `PresetReverb` — Allows you to specify one of a number of reverb presets, designed to make your audio sound as though it were being played in one of the specified room types. Use the `setPreset` method to apply reverb equivalent to a medium or large hall, or small, medium, or large room using a `PresetReverb.PRESET_*` constant.

➤ `EnvironmentalReverb` — Like the Preset Reverb, the Environmental Reverb allows you to control the audio output to simulate the effect of a different environment. Unlike the Preset Reverb, this subclass lets you specify each of the reverb parameters yourself to create a custom effect.

To apply one of these effects to your Audio Track or Media Player, find its unique audio session ID using the `getAudioSessionId` method on either object. Use the value to construct a new instance of the Audio Effect subclass you want to use, modify its settings as desired, and enable it, as shown in Listing 15-22.

Available for download on Wrox.com

LISTING 15-22: Applying audio effects

```
int sessionId = mediaPlayer.getAudioSessionId();
short boostStrength = 500;
int priority = 0;

BassBoost bassBoost = new BassBoost (priority, sessionId);
bassBoost.setStrength(boostStrength);
bassBoost.setEnabled(true);
```

code snippet PA4AD_Ch15_Media_Player/src/AudioPlayerActivity.java

USING THE CAMERA FOR TAKING PICTURES

The T-Mobile G1 was released in 2008 with a 3.2-megapixel camera. Today, most devices feature at least a 5-megapixel camera, with some models sporting 8.1-megapixel cameras. The ubiquity of smartphones featuring increasingly high-quality cameras has made camera applications popular additions to Google Play.

The following sections demonstrate the mechanisms you can use to control the camera and take photos within your applications.

Using Intents to Take Pictures

The easiest way to take a picture from within your application is to fire an Intent using the `MediaStore.ACTION_IMAGE_CAPTURE` action:

```
startActivityForResult(
    new Intent(MediaStore.ACTION_IMAGE_CAPTURE), TAKE_PICTURE);
```

This launches a Camera application to take the photo, providing your users with the full suite of camera functionality without you having to rewrite the native Camera application.

Once users are satisfied with the image, the result is returned to your application within the Intent received by the `onActivityResult` handler.

By default, the picture taken will be returned as a thumbnail, available as a raw bitmap within the `data` extra within the returned Intent.

To obtain a full image, you must specify a target file in which to store it, encoded as a URI passed in using the `MediaStore.EXTRA_OUTPUT` extra in the launch Intent, as shown in Listing 15-23.

LISTING 15-23: Requesting a full-size picture using an Intent

```java
// Create an output file.
File file = new File(Environment.getExternalStorageDirectory(),
                    "test.jpg");
Uri outputFileUri = Uri.fromFile(file);

// Generate the Intent.
Intent intent = new Intent(MediaStore.ACTION_IMAGE_CAPTURE);
intent.putExtra(MediaStore.EXTRA_OUTPUT, outputFileUri);

// Launch the camera app.
startActivityForResult(intent, TAKE_PICTURE);
```

code snippet PA4AD_Ch15_Intent_Camera/src/CameraActivity.java

The full-size image taken by the camera will then be saved to the specified location. No thumbnail will be returned in the Activity result callback, and the received Intent's data will be null.

Listing 15-24 shows how to use `getParcelableExtra` to extract a thumbnail where one is returned, or to decode the saved file when a full-size image is taken.

LISTING 15-24: Receiving pictures from an Intent

```java
@Override
protected void onActivityResult(int requestCode,
                                int resultCode, Intent data) {
  if (requestCode == TAKE_PICTURE) {
    // Check if the result includes a thumbnail Bitmap
    if (data != null) {
      if (data.hasExtra("data")) {
        Bitmap thumbnail = data.getParcelableExtra("data");
        imageView.setImageBitmap(thumbnail);
      }
    } else {
      // If there is no thumbnail image data, the image
      // will have been stored in the target output URI.

      // Resize the full image to fit in out image view.
      int width = imageView.getWidth();
      int height = imageView.getHeight();

      BitmapFactory.Options factoryOptions = new
        BitmapFactory.Options();

      factoryOptions.inJustDecodeBounds = true;
      BitmapFactory.decodeFile(outputFileUri.getPath(),
                               factoryOptions);

      int imageWidth = factoryOptions.outWidth;
      int imageHeight = factoryOptions.outHeight;

      // Determine how much to scale down the image
      int scaleFactor = Math.min(imageWidth/width,
                                 imageHeight/height);

      // Decode the image file into a Bitmap sized to fill the View
      factoryOptions.inJustDecodeBounds = false;
      factoryOptions.inSampleSize = scaleFactor;
      factoryOptions.inPurgeable = true;

      Bitmap bitmap =
        BitmapFactory.decodeFile(outputFileUri.getPath(),
                                 factoryOptions);

      imageView.setImageBitmap(bitmap);
    }
  }
}
```

code snippet PA4AD_Ch15_Intent_Camera/src/CameraActivity.java

To make photos you save available to other applications, including the native Gallery app, it's good practice to add them Media Store — as described in the section "Adding Media to the Media Store."

Controlling the Camera Directly

To access the camera hardware directly, you need to add the CAMERA permission to your application manifest:

```
<uses-permission android:name="android.permission.CAMERA"/>
```

Use the Camera class to adjust camera settings, specify image preferences, and take pictures. To access the Camera, use the static open method on the Camera class:

```
Camera camera = Camera.open();
```

When you are finished with the Camera, remember to relinquish your hold on it by calling release:

```
camera.release();
```

> *The Camera.open method will turn on and initialize the Camera. At this point it is ready for you to modify settings, configure the preview surface, and take pictures, as shown in the following sections.*

Camera Properties

The Camera settings are stored using a Camera.Parameters object, accessible by calling the getParameters method on the Camera object:

```
Camera.Parameters parameters = camera.getParameters();
```

Using the Camera Parameters you can find many of the properties of the Camera and currently focused scene; the parameters available depend on the platform version.

You can find the focal length and related horizontal and vertical angle of view using the getFocalLength and get[Horizontal/Vertical]ViewAngle methods, respectively, introduced in Android 2.2 (API level 8).

Android 2.3 (API level 9) introduced the getFocusDistances method, which you can use to estimate the distance between the lens and the objects currently believed to be in focus. Rather than returning a value, this method populates an array of floats corresponding to the near, far, and optimal focus distances, as shown in Listing 15-25. The object most sharply focused will be at the optimal distance.

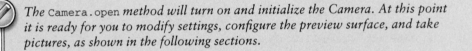

LISTING 15-25: Finding the distance to focused objects

```
float[] focusDistances = new float[3];

parameters.getFocusDistances(focusDistances);

float near =
    focusDistances[Camera.Parameters.FOCUS_DISTANCE_NEAR_INDEX];
```

```
float far =
  focusDistances[Camera.Parameters.FOCUS_DISTANCE_FAR_INDEX];
float optimal =
  focusDistances[Camera.Parameters.FOCUS_DISTANCE_OPTIMAL_INDEX];
```

code snippet PA4AD_Ch15_Camera/src/CameraActivity.java

Camera Settings and Image Parameters

To change the Camera settings, use the set* methods to modify the Parameters object. Android 2.0 (API level 5) introduced a wide range of Camera Parameters, each with a setter and getter. Before attempting to modify any camera parameter, it's important to confirm that the Camera implementation on the host device supports the change.

After modifying the Parameters, pass them back into the Camera, using its setParameters method to apply the changes:

```
camera.setParameters(parameters);
```

Most of the following parameters are useful primarily if you are replacing the native Camera application. That said, they can also be useful for customizing the way the live preview is displayed, allowing you to customize the live stream for augmented reality applications.

➤ [get/set]SceneMode — Returns/sets the type of scene being photographed using one of several SCENE_MODE_* static constants. Each scene mode optimally configures the Camera parameters (flash, white balance, focus mode, and so on) for a particular scene type (party, beach, sunset, and so on).

➤ [get/set]FlashMode — Returns/sets the current flash mode (typically one of on, off, red-eye reduction, or flashlight mode) using the FLASH_MODE_* static constants. Before attempting to set the flash mode, use the getSupportedFlashModes method to confirm which modes are available.

➤ [get/set]WhiteBalance — Returns/sets the white balance correction used to correct the scene, using one of the WHITE_BALANCE_* static constants. Before setting the white balance, use the getSupportedWhiteBalance method to confirm which settings are available.

➤ [get/set]AutoWhiteBalanceLock — Introduced in Android 4.0 (API level 14). When using automatic white balancing, enabling the auto white balance lock will pause the color correction algorithm, ensuring that multiple sequential photos use the same color balance settings. This is particularly effective when taking panoramic images or exposure bracketing for high dynamic range images. Use the isAutoWhiteBalanceLockSupported method to confirm this functionality is available on the host device.

➤ [get/set]ColorEffect — Returns/sets any special color effects to apply to the image using an EFFECT_* static constant. The color effects available (including sepia tone, posterize, and blackboard effects) vary by device and platform version. Use the getSupportedColorEffects method to find which color effects are available.

➤ [get/set]FocusMode — Returns/sets how the camera should attempt to focus using a FOCUS_MODE_* static constant. The available focus modes vary depending on the platform version. (For example, continuous autofocus was introduced in Android 4.0.) Use the getSupportedFocusModes method to find which modes are available.

➤ [get/set]Antibanding — Returns/sets the screen refresh frequency that should be used to reduce banding effects using an ANTIBANDING_* static constant. Use the getSupportedAntibanding method to find which frequencies are available.

You can also use Camera Parameters to read or specify size, quality, and format parameters for the image, thumbnail, and camera preview. The following list explains how to set some of these values:

➤ JPEG and thumbnail quality — Use the setJpegQuality and setJpegThumbnailQuality methods, respectively, passing in an integer value between 0 and 100, where 100 is the best quality.

➤ Image, preview, and thumbnail sizes — Use setPictureSize, setPreviewSize, and setJpegThumbnailSize to specify a height and width for the image, preview, and thumbnail, respectively. In each case, you should use the corresponding getSupportedPictureSizes, getSupportedPreviewSizes, and getSupportedJpegThumbnailSizes methods to determine valid values. Each method returns a List of Camera.Size objects that specify valid height/width combinations.

➤ Image and preview pixel format — Use setPictureFormat and setPreviewFormat to set the image format using a static constant from the PixelFormat class. Use the getSupportedPictureFormats and getSupportedPreviewFormats methods to return a list of the supported formats before using either of these setters.

➤ Preview frame rate — The setPreviewFpsRange method replaces the setPreviewFrameRate method that was deprecated in Android 2.3 (API level 9). Use it to specify your preferred frame rate range to use for previews. Use the getSupportedPreviewFpsRange method to find the minimum and maximum supported frame rate. Both methods represent the frame rate as an integer multiplied by 1000, so a range of 24 to 30 FPS becomes 24000 to 30000.

Checking for supported parameter values is particularly important when selecting valid preview or image sizes, as each device's camera will potentially support a different subset.

Controlling Auto Focus, Focus Areas, and Metering Areas

If the host Camera supports auto focus, you can specify the focus mode using the setFocusMode method, passing in one of the Camera.Parameters.FOCUS_MODE_* constants. The available focus modes will depend on the capabilities of the hardware and the version of the Android platform it runs. Use the getSupportedFocusModes method to find which modes are available.

To be notified when the auto focus operation has completed, initiate auto focus using the autofocus method, specifying an AutoFocusCallback implementation:

```
Camera.Parameters parameters = camera.getParameters();
if (parameters.getSupportedFocusModes().contains(
  Camera.Parameters.FOCUS_MODE_CONTINUOUS_PICTURE)) {
  parameters.setFocusMode(
```

```
        Camera.Parameters.FOCUS_MODE_CONTINUOUS_PICTURE);

    camera.autoFocus(new AutoFocusCallback() {
      public void onAutoFocus(boolean success, Camera camera) {
        Log.d(TAG, "AutoFocus: " + (success ? "Succeeded" : "Failed"));
      }
    });
}
```

Android 4.0 (API level 14) introduced two additional focus APIs that enable you to specify the focus areas and metering areas to use when focusing your pictures or determining the white balance and brightness of your scene.

Not all devices support defining focus areas. To confirm that this is available on the host device, use the Camera's `getMaxNumFocusAreas` method:

```
    int focusAreaCount = camera.getMaxNumFocusAreas()
```

This will return the maximum number of focus areas the device camera is capable of detecting. If the result is 0, focus area specification is not supported.

Specifying Focus Areas allows you to instruct the camera driver as to the relative importance of different areas of the scene when attempting to focus the image. This is typically used to focus on faces or to allow users to manually select a focal point.

To define your focus areas, use the `setFocusAreas` method, passing in a List of `Camera.Area` objects. Each Camera Area consists of a rectangle that defines the boundary of that focus area (between –1000 and 1000, measured from the upper-left corner) relative to the currently visible scene and the relative weight of that focus area. The camera driver will multiply the area of each focus area with its weight to calculate the relative weight of each area when attempting to focus the scene.

You can use the same approach to set the metering areas using `setMeteringAreas`. As with focus area support, not all devices will support multiple metering areas — use the `getMaxNumMeteringAreas` to determine if the host camera supports one or more metering areas.

Using the Camera Preview

If you are implementing your own camera, you will need to display a preview of what's being captured by the camera to allow users to compose their photos. It's not possible to take a picture using the Camera object without first displaying a preview.

Being able to display the camera's streaming video also means that you can incorporate live video into your applications, such as implementing augmented reality (the process of overlaying dynamic contextual data — such as details for landmarks or points of interest — on top of a live camera feed).

The camera preview is displayed using a `SurfaceHolder`, so to view the live camera stream within your application, you must include a Surface View within your UI hierarchy. Implement a `SurfaceHolder.Callback` to listen for the construction of a valid surface before passing it in to the `setPreviewDisplay` method of your Camera object.

A call to `startPreview` will begin the streaming, and `stopPreview` will end it, as shown in Listing 15-26.

LISTING 15-26: Previewing a real-time camera stream

```java
public class CameraActivity extends Activity implements
  SurfaceHolder.Callback {

  private static final String TAG = "CameraActivity";

  private Camera camera;

  @Override
  public void onCreate(Bundle savedInstanceState) {
    super.onCreate(savedInstanceState);
    setContentView(R.layout.main);

    SurfaceView surface = (SurfaceView)findViewById(R.id.surfaceView);
    SurfaceHolder holder = surface.getHolder();
    holder.addCallback(this);
    holder.setType(SurfaceHolder.SURFACE_TYPE_PUSH_BUFFERS);
    holder.setFixedSize(400, 300);
  }

  public void surfaceCreated(SurfaceHolder holder) {
    try {
      camera.setPreviewDisplay(holder);
      camera.startPreview();
      // TODO Draw over the preview if required.
    } catch (IOException e) {
      Log.d(TAG, "IO Exception", e);
    }
  }

  public void surfaceDestroyed(SurfaceHolder holder) {
    camera.stopPreview();
  }

  public void surfaceChanged(SurfaceHolder holder, int format,
                             int width, int height) {
  }

  @Override
  protected void onPause() {
    super.onPause();
    camera.release();
  }

  @Override
  protected void onResume() {
    super.onResume();
    camera = Camera.open();
  }
}
```

code snippet PA4AD_Ch15_Camera/src/CameraActivity.java

> The Android SDK includes an excellent example of using a `SurfaceView` to display the camera preview in real time. It can be found at `http://developer.android.com/resources/samples/ApiDemos/src/com/example/android/apis/graphics/CameraPreview.html`.

You can also assign a `PreviewCallback` to be fired for each preview frame, allowing you to manipulate or perform analysis of each preview frame in real time. Call the `setPreviewCallback` method on the `Camera` object, passing in a new `PreviewCallback` implementation overriding the `onPreviewFrame` method.

Each frame will be received by the `onPreviewFrame` event with the image passed in as a Bitmap represented as a byte array:

```
camera.setPreviewCallback(new PreviewCallback() {
  public void onPreviewFrame(byte[] data, Camera camera) {
    int quality = 60;

    Size previewSize = camera.getParameters().getPreviewSize();
    YuvImage image = new YuvImage(data, ImageFormat.NV21,
      previewSize.width, previewSize.height, null);
    ByteArrayOutputStream outputStream = new ByteArrayOutputStream();

    image.compressToJpeg(
      new Rect(0, 0,previewSize.width, previewSize.height),
        quality, outputStream);

    // TODO Do something with the preview image.
  }
});
```

Detecting Faces and Facial Features

Android 4.0 (API level 14) introduced APIs that you can use to detect faces and facial features within a scene. This feature is most useful for tweaking the focus areas, metering areas, and determining white balance when taking photos featuring people, but it can also be used creatively when applying effects.

Face detection is not necessarily available on every device, even those running Android 4.0 or above. To confirm that face detection is available on the host device, use the Camera's `getMaxNumDetectedFaces` method:

```
int facesDetectable = camera.getParameters().getMaxNumDetectedFaces()
```

This will return the maximum number of faces the device camera is capable of detecting. If the result is 0, face detection is not supported.

Before you begin monitoring a camera for faces, you need to assign a new `FaceDetectionListener`, overriding the `onFaceDetection` method. You will receive an array containing a `Face` object for each face detected within the scene (up to the maximum supported number).

Each `Face` object includes a unique identifier that can be used to track each face while it remains in the scene, a confidence score between 0 and 100 that indicates the likelihood that what's been detected is actually a face, the bounding rectangle containing the face, and the coordinates of each eye and the mouth:

```
camera.setFaceDetectionListener(new FaceDetectionListener() {
  public void onFaceDetection(Face[] faces, Camera camera) {
    if (faces.length > 0){
      Log.d("FaceDetection", "face detected: "+ faces.length +
        " Face 1 Location X: " + faces[0].rect.centerX() +
        "Y: " + faces[0].rect.centerY() );
    }
  }
});
```

To begin detecting and tracking faces, call the Camera's `startFaceDetection` method. This must be called each time you start (or restart) the Camera preview, as it will be automatically stopped whenever the preview ends.

```
public void surfaceCreated(SurfaceHolder holder) {
  try {
    camera.setPreviewDisplay(holder);
    camera.startPreview();
    camera.startFaceDetection();
    // TODO Draw over the preview if required.
  } catch (IOException e) {
    Log.d(TAG, "IO Exception", e);
  }
}
```

You can stop face detection by calling `stopFaceDetection`:

```
public void surfaceDestroyed(SurfaceHolder holder) {
  camera.stopFaceDetection();
  camera.stopPreview();
}
```

Taking a Picture

After you have configured the camera settings, and a preview is active, you can take a picture by calling `takePicture` on the `Camera` object and passing in a `ShutterCallback` and two `PictureCallback` implementations (one for the RAW and one for JPEG-encoded images). Each picture callback will receive a byte array representing the image in the appropriate format, while the shutter callback is triggered immediately after the shutter is closed.

Listing 15-27 shows the skeleton code for taking a picture and saving the JPEG image to an SD card.

LISTING 15-27: Taking a picture

```
private void takePicture() {
  camera.takePicture(shutterCallback, rawCallback, jpegCallback);
}

ShutterCallback shutterCallback = new ShutterCallback() {
```

```java
    public void onShutter() {
      // TODO Do something when the shutter closes.
    }
  };

  PictureCallback rawCallback = new PictureCallback() {
    public void onPictureTaken(byte[] data, Camera camera) {
      // TODO Do something with the image RAW data.
    }
  };

  PictureCallback jpegCallback = new PictureCallback() {
    public void onPictureTaken(byte[] data, Camera camera) {
      // Save the image JPEG data to the SD card
      FileOutputStream outStream = null;
      try {
        String path = Environment.getExternalStorageDirectory() +
                      "\test.jpg";

        outStream = new FileOutputStream(path);
        outStream.write(data);
        outStream.close();
      } catch (FileNotFoundException e) {
        Log.e(TAG, "File Note Found", e);
      } catch (IOException e) {
        Log.e(TAG, "IO Exception", e);
      }
    }
  };
```

code snippet PA4AD_Ch15_Camera/src/CameraActivity.java

Reading and Writing JPEG EXIF Image Details

The ExifInterface class provides mechanisms for you to read and modify the Exchangeable Image File Format (EXIF) meta data stored within a JPEG file. Create a new ExifInterface instance by passing the full filename of the target JPEG in to the constructor:

```java
ExifInterface exif = new ExifInterface(jpegfilename);
```

EXIF data is used to store a wide range of meta data on photographs, including date and time, camera settings (such as make and model), and image settings (such as aperture and shutter speed), as well as image descriptions and locations.

To read an EXIF attribute, call getAttribute on the ExifInterface object, passing in the name of the attribute to read. The Exifinterface class includes a number of static TAG_* constants that can be used to access common EXIF meta data. To modify an EXIF attribute, use setAttribute, passing in the name of the attribute to read and the value to set it to.

Listing 15-28 shows how to read the location coordinates and camera model from a file stored on an SD card, before modifying the camera manufacturer details.

LISTING 15-28: Reading and modifying EXIF data

```
File file = new File(Environment.getExternalStorageDirectory(),
                     "test.jpg");

try {
  ExifInterface exif = new ExifInterface(file.getCanonicalPath());
  // Read the camera model and location attributes
  String model = exif.getAttribute(ExifInterface.TAG_MODEL);
  Log.d(TAG, "Model: " + model);
  // Set the camera make
  exif.setAttribute(ExifInterface.TAG_MAKE, "My Phone");
} catch (IOException e) {
  Log.e(TAG, "IO Exception", e);
}
```

code snippet PA4AD_Ch15_Camera/src/CameraActivity.java

RECORDING VIDEO

Android offers two options for recording video within your application.

The simplest technique is to use Intents to launch the video camera application. This option lets you specify the output location and video recording quality, while letting the native video recording application handle the user experience and error handling. This is the best practice approach and should be used in most circumstances, unless you are building your own replacement video recorder.

In cases where you want to replace the native application or simply need more fine-grained control over the video capture UI or recording settings, you can use the Media Recorder class.

Using Intents to Record Video

The easiest, and best practice, way to initiate video recording is using the `MediaStore.ACTION_VIDEO_CAPTURE` action Intent.

Starting a new Activity with this Intent launches the native video recorder, allowing users to start, stop, review, and retake their video. When they're satisfied, a URI to the recorded video is provided to your Activity as the data parameter of the returned Intent:

The video capture action Intent can contain the following three optional extras:

➤ `MediaStore.EXTRA_OUTPUT` — By default, the video recorded by the video capture action will be stored in the default Media Store. If you want to record it elsewhere, you can specify an alternative URI using this extra.

➤ `MediaStore.EXTRA_VIDEO_QUALITY` — The video capture action allows you to specify an image quality using an integer value. There are currently two possible values: 0 for low (MMS) quality videos, or 1 for high (full resolution) videos. By default, the high-resolution mode is used.

➤ `MediaStore.EXTRA_DURATION_LIMIT` — The maximum length of the recorded video (in seconds).

Listing 15-29 shows how to use the video capture action to record a new video.

LISTING 15-29: Recording video using an Intent

```java
private static final int RECORD_VIDEO = 0;

private void startRecording() {
  // Generate the Intent.
  Intent intent = new Intent(MediaStore.ACTION_VIDEO_CAPTURE);

  // Launch the camera app.
  startActivityForResult(intent, RECORD_VIDEO);
}

@Override
protected void onActivityResult(int requestCode,
                                int resultCode, Intent data) {
  if (requestCode == RECORD_VIDEO) {
    VideoView videoView = (VideoView)findViewById(R.id.videoView);
    videoView.setVideoURI(data.getData());
    videoView.start()
  }
}
```

code snippet PA4AD_Ch15_Intent_Video_Camera/src/VideoCameraActivity.java

Using the Media Recorder to Record Video

You can use the `MediaRecorder` class to record audio and/or video files that can be used in your own applications or added to the Media Store.

To record any media in Android, your application needs the `CAMERA` and `RECORD_AUDIO` and/or `RECORD_VIDEO` permissions as applicable:

```xml
<uses-permission android:name="android.permission.RECORD_AUDIO"/>
<uses-permission android:name="android.permission.RECORD_VIDEO"/>
<uses-permission android:name="android.permission.CAMERA"/>
```

The Media Recorder lets you specify the audio and video source, the output file format, and the audio and video encoders to use when recording your file. Android 2.2 (API level 8) introduced the concept of profiles, which can be used to apply a predefined set of Media Recorder configurations.

Much like the Media Player, the Media Recorder manages recording as a state machine. This means that the order in which you configure and manage the Media Recorder is important. In the simplest terms, the transitions through the state machine can be described as follows:

1. Create a new Media Recorder.

2. Unlock the Camera and assign it to the Media Recorder.

3. Specify the input sources to record from.

4. Select a profile to use for Android 2.2 and above, or define the output format and specify the audio and video encoder, frame rate, and output size.

5. Select an output file.

6. Assign a preview Surface.

7. Prepare the Media Recorder for recording.

8. Record.

9. End the recording.

> *A more detailed and thorough description of the Media Recorder state machine is provided at the Android developer site, at* `http://developer.android.com/reference/android/media/MediaRecorder.html`.

When you finish recording your media, call `release` on your Media Recorder object to free the associated resources:

```
mediaRecorder.release();
```

Configuring the Video Recorder

As described in the preceding section, before recording you must allocate the camera to use, specify the input sources, choose a profile (or output format, audio, and video encoder), and assign an output file — in that order.

Start by unlocking the Camera and assigning it to the Media Recorder using the `setCamera` method.

The `setAudioSource` and `setVideoSource` methods let you specify a `MediaRecorder.AudioSource.*` and `MediaRecorder.VideoSource.*` static constant that define the audio and video source, respectively.

After selecting your input sources, you need to specify the recording profile to use. Android 2.2 (API level 8) introduced the `setProfile` method, which uses a profile created using the `CamcorderProfile` class's `get` method, specifying a quality profile using the `CamcorderProfile.QUALITY_*` constants. Not all profiles are supported on every device, so use the `CamcorderProfile.hasProfile` method to confirm the availability of profile before applying it to your Media Recorder:

```
if (CamcorderProfile.hasProfile(CamcorderProfile.QUALITY_1080P)) {
    CamcorderProfile profile = CamcorderProfile.get(CamcorderProfile.QUALITY_1080P);
    mediaRecorder.setProfile(profile);
}
```

Alternatively, you can specify the recording profile manually by selecting the output format, using the `setOutputFormat` method to specify a `MediaRecorder.OutputFormat` constant and using the `set[audio/video]Encoder` methods to specify an audio or video encoder constant from the `MediaRecorder.[Audio/Video]Encoder` class. Take this opportunity to set the frame rate or video output size, if desired.

Finally, assign a file to store the recorded media using the `setOutputFile` method before allocating a preview surface and calling `prepare`.

Listing 15-30 shows how to configure a Media Recorder to record audio and video from the microphone and camera, using the 1080p quality profile, to a file in your application's external storage folder.

LISTING 15-30: Preparing to record audio and video using the Media Recorder

```
// Unlock the Camera to allow the Media Recorder to own it.
camera.unlock();

// Assign the Camera to the Media Recorder.
mediaRecorder.setCamera(camera);

// Configure the input sources.
mediaRecorder.setAudioSource(MediaRecorder.AudioSource.CAMCORDER);
mediaRecorder.setVideoSource(MediaRecorder.VideoSource.CAMERA);

// Set the recording profile.
CamcorderProfile profile = null;

if (CamcorderProfile.hasProfile(CamcorderProfile.QUALITY_1080P))
  profile = CamcorderProfile.get(CamcorderProfile.QUALITY_1080P);
else if (CamcorderProfile.hasProfile(CamcorderProfile.QUALITY_720P))
  profile = CamcorderProfile.get(CamcorderProfile.QUALITY_720P);
else if (CamcorderProfile.hasProfile(CamcorderProfile.QUALITY_480P))
  profile = CamcorderProfile.get(CamcorderProfile.QUALITY_480P);
else if (CamcorderProfile.hasProfile(CamcorderProfile.QUALITY_HIGH))
  profile = CamcorderProfile.get(CamcorderProfile.QUALITY_HIGH);

if (profile != null)
  mediaRecorder.setProfile(profile);

// Specify the output file
mediaRecorder.setOutputFile("/sdcard/myvideorecording.mp4");

// Prepare to record
mediaRecorder.prepare();
```

code snippet PA4AD_Ch15_Intent_Video_Camera/src/VideoCameraActivity.java

The `setOutputFile` method must be called before `prepare` and after `setOutputFormat`; otherwise, it will throw an Illegal State Exception.

Android 4.0 (API level 14) introduced a technique to improve the performance of the Media Recorder by reducing startup time. When your Activity is being used only to record audio/video (rather than to take still pictures), you can use the `Camera.Parameters.setRecordingHint` method to tell the Camera you only want to record audio/video, as shown in Listing 15-31.

LISTING 15-31: Using the Camera recording hint

```
Camera.Parameters parameters = camera.getParameters();
parameters.setRecordingHint(true);
camera.setParameters(parameters);
```

code snippet PA4AD_Ch15_Intent_Video_Camera/src/VideoCameraActivity.java

Previewing the Video Stream

When recording video, it's considered good practice to display a preview of the recorded video in real time. Like the Camera preview, you can assign a `Surface` to display the video stream using the `setPreviewDisplay` method on your Media Recorder object. The preview display will be hosted within a `SurfaceView` that must be initialized within a `SurfaceHolder.Callback` interface implementation.

After creating the Surface Holder, assign it to the Media Recorder using the `setPreviewDisplay` method — after specifying the recording sources and output file but *before* calling `prepare`:

```
mediaRecorder.setPreviewDisplay(holder.getSurface());
```

The live video preview stream will begin as soon as you make a call to `prepare`:

```
mediaRecorder.prepare();
```

Controlling the Recording

After configuring the Media Recorder and setting up the preview, you can begin recording at any time by calling the `start` method:

```
mediaRecorder.start();
```

When you finish recording, call `stop` to end the playback, followed by `reset` and `release` to free the Media Recorder resources, as shown in Listing 15-32). At this point, you should also lock the camera.

LISTING 15-32: Stopping a video recording

```
mediaRecorder.stop();

// Reset and release the media recorder.
mediaRecorder.reset();
mediaRecorder.release();
camera.lock();
```

code snippet PA4AD_Ch15_Intent_Video_Camera/src/VideoCameraActivity.java

Android 4.0.3 (API level 15) introduced the ability to apply image stabilization to your video recordings. To toggle image stabilization, modify the Camera parameters using the `setVideoStabilization` method, as shown in Listing 15-33. Not all camera hardware will support image stabilization, so be sure to check that it's available using the `isVideoStabilizationSupported` method.

LISTING 15-33: Image stabilization

```
Camera.Parameters parameters = camera.getParameters();
if (parameters.isVideoStabilizationSupported())
  parameters.setVideoStabilization(true);
camera.setParameters(parameters);
```

code snippet PA4AD_Ch15_Intent_Video_Camera/src/VideoCameraActivity.java

Creating a Time-Lapse Video

Android 2.2 (API level 8) enhanced the Media Recorder to provide support for creating time-lapse videos. To configure a Media Recorder object to create a time-lapse effect, use the `setCaptureRate` to set the required frame capture rate:

```
// Capture an image every 30 seconds.
mediaRecorder.setCaptureRate(0.03);
```

The Media Recorder must also be set using one of a number of predefined profiles optimized for time-lapse video capture. Use the `setProfile` method to use one of the `QUALITY_TIME_LAPSE_*` profiles:

```
CamcorderProfile profile =
  CamcorderProfile.get(CamcorderProfile.QUALITY_TIME_LAPSE_HIGH);

mediaRecorder.setProfile(profile);
```

USING MEDIA EFFECTS

Android 4.0 (API level 14) introduced a new media effects API that can be used to apply a number of real-time visual effects to video content using the GPU via OpenGL textures.

You can apply media effects to bitmaps, videos, or the live camera previews, provided that the source images are bound to a `GL_TEXTURE_2D` texture image and contain at least one mipmap level.

Although a full examination of how to use these media effects is outside the scope of this book, generally speaking, to apply an effect to an image or video frame, you need to create a new `EffectContext`, using the `EffectContext.createWithCurrentGlContext` method from within an OpenGL ES 2.0 context.

The effects are created using an `EffectFactory`, which can be created by calling `getFactory` on the returned `EffectContext`. To create a particular effect, call `createEffect`, passing in one of the `EffectFactory.EFFECT_*` constants. Each Effect supports different parameters, which you can configure by calling `setParameter` and passing the name of the setting to change and the value to apply.

More than 25 effects are currently supported. The full list — including the parameters they support — is available at http://developer.android.com/reference/android/media/effect/ EffectFactory.html.

After configuring the effect you want to apply, use its apply method, passing in the input texture, its dimensions, and the target texture to apply it.

ADDING MEDIA TO THE MEDIA STORE

By default, media files created by your application that are stored in private application folders will be unavailable to other applications. To make them visible, you need to insert them into the Media Store. Android provides two options for this. The preferred approach is to use the Media Scanner to interpret your file and insert it automatically. Or you can manually insert a new record in the appropriate Content Provider. Using the Media Scanner is almost always the better approach.

Inserting Media Using the Media Scanner

If you have recorded new media of any kind, the MediaScannerConnection class provides the scanFile method as a simple way for you to add it to the Media Store without needing to construct the full record for the Media Store Content Provider.

Before you can use the scanFile method to initiate a content scan on your file, you must call connect and wait for the connection to the Media Scanner to complete. This call is asynchronous, so you will need to implement a MediaScannerConnectionClient to notify you when the connection has been made. You can use this same class to notify you when the scan is complete, at which point you can disconnect your Media Scanner Connection.

This sounds more complex than it is. Listing 15-34 shows the skeleton code for creating a new MediaScannerConnectionClient that defines a MediaScannerConnection, which is used to add a new file to the Media Store.

LISTING 15-34: Adding files to the Media Store using the Media Scanner

```
private void mediaScan(final String filePath) {

  MediaScannerConnectionClient mediaScannerClient = new
    MediaScannerConnectionClient() {

    private MediaScannerConnection msc = null;

    {
      msc = new MediaScannerConnection(
        VideoCameraActivity.this, this);
      msc.connect();
    }

    public void onMediaScannerConnected() {
      // Optionally specify a MIME Type, or
      // have the Media Scanner imply one based
      // on the filename.
```

```
        String mimeType = null;
        msc.scanFile(filePath, mimeType);
      }

    public void onScanCompleted(String path, Uri uri) {
      msc.disconnect();
      Log.d(TAG, "File Added at: " + uri.toString());
    }
  };
}
```

code snippet PA4AD_Ch15_Intent_Video_Camera/src/VideoCameraActivity.java

Inserting Media Manually

Rather than relying on the Media Scanner, you can add new media to the Media Store directly by creating a new `ContentValues` object and inserting it into the appropriate Media Store Content Provider yourself.

The meta data you specify here can include the title, timestamp, and geocoding information for your new media file:

```
ContentValues content = new ContentValues(3);
content.put(Audio.AudioColumns.TITLE, "TheSoundandtheFury");
content.put(Audio.AudioColumns.DATE_ADDED,
            System.currentTimeMillis() / 1000);
content.put(Audio.Media.MIME_TYPE, "audio/amr");
```

You must also specify the absolute path of the media file being added:

```
content.put(MediaStore.Audio.Media.DATA, "/sdcard/myoutputfile.mp4");
```

Get access to the application's `ContentResolver`, and use it to insert this new row into the Media Store:

```
ContentResolver resolver = getContentResolver();
Uri uri = resolver.insert(MediaStore.Video.Media.EXTERNAL_CONTENT_URI,
                          content);
```

After inserting the media file into the Media Store, you should announce its availability using a Broadcast Intent, as follows:

```
sendBroadcast(new Intent(Intent.ACTION_MEDIA_SCANNER_SCAN_FILE, uri));
```

16

Bluetooth, NFC, Networks, and Wi-Fi

This chapter begins to explore Android's hardware communications APIs by examining the Bluetooth, network, Wi-Fi, and Near Field Communication (NFC) packages.

Android offers APIs to manage and monitor your Bluetooth settings: to control discoverability, to discover nearby Bluetooth devices, and to use Bluetooth as a proximity-based, peer-to-peer transport layer for your applications.

A full network and Wi-Fi package is also available. Using these APIs, you can scan for hotspots, create and modify Wi-Fi configuration settings, monitor your Internet connectivity, and control and monitor Internet settings and preferences. The introduction of Wi-Fi Direct offers a peer-to-peer solution for communicating between devices using Wi-Fi.

Android 2.3 (API level 9) introduced support for NFC, including the support for reading smart tags, and Android 4.0 (API level 14) added the ability to communicate with other NFC-enabled Android devices using Android Beam.

USING BLUETOOTH

Bluetooth is a communications protocol designed for short-range, low-bandwidth peer-to-peer communications.

Using the Bluetooth APIs, you can search for, and connect to, other Bluetooth devices within range. By initiating a communications link using Bluetooth Sockets, you can then transmit and receive streams of data between devices from within your applications.

> *At the time of writing, only encrypted communication is supported between devices, meaning that you can form connections only between devices that have been paired.*

Managing the Local Bluetooth Device Adapter

The local Bluetooth device is controlled via the `BluetoothAdapter` class, which represents the host Android device on which your application is running.

To access the default Bluetooth Adapter, call `getDefaultAdapter`, as shown in Listing 16-1. Some Android devices feature multiple Bluetooth adapters, though it is currently only possible to access the default device.

LISTING 16-1: Accessing the default Bluetooth Adapter

```
BluetoothAdapter bluetooth = BluetoothAdapter.getDefaultAdapter();
```

code snippet PA4AD_Ch16_Bluetooth/src/BluetoothActivity.java

To read any of the local Bluetooth Adapter properties, initiate discovery, or find bonded devices, you need to include the `BLUETOOTH` permission in your application manifest. To modify any of the local device properties, the `BLUETOOTH_ADMIN` permission is also required:

```
<uses-permission android:name="android.permission.BLUETOOTH"/>
<uses-permission android:name="android.permission.BLUETOOTH_ADMIN"/>
```

The Bluetooth Adapter offers methods for reading and setting properties of the local Bluetooth hardware.

> *The Bluetooth Adapter properties can be read and changed only if the Bluetooth Adapter is currently turned on — that is, if its device state is enabled. If the device is off, these methods will return* null.

Use the isEnabled method to confirm the device is enabled, after which you can access the Bluetooth Adapter's *friendly name* (an arbitrary string that users can set to identify a particular device) and hardware address, using the getName and getAddress methods, respectively:

```
if (bluetooth.isEnabled()) {
  String address = bluetooth.getAddress();
  String name = bluetooth.getName();
}
```

If you have the BLUETOOTH_ADMIN permission, you can change the friendly name of the Bluetooth Adapter using the setName method:

```
bluetooth.setName("Blackfang");
```

To find a more detailed description of the current Bluetooth Adapter state, use the getState method, which will return one of the following BluetoothAdapter constants:

➤ STATE_TURNING_ON

➤ STATE_ON

➤ STATE_TURNING_OFF

➤ STATE_OFF

To conserve battery life and optimize security, most users will keep Bluetooth disabled until they plan to use it.

To enable the Bluetooth Adapter, you can start a system Preference Activity using the BluetoothAdapter.ACTION_REQUEST_ENABLE static constant as a startActivityForResult action string:

```
startActivityForResult(
  new Intent(BluetoothAdapter.ACTION_REQUEST_ENABLE), 0);
```

Figure 16-1 shows the resulting Preference Activity.

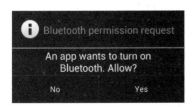

FIGURE 16-1

It prompts the user to turn on Bluetooth and asks for confirmation. If the user agrees, the sub-Activity will close and return to the calling Activity when the Bluetooth Adapter has turned on (or has encountered an error). If the user selects no, the sub-Activity will close and return immediately. Use the result code parameter returned in the `onActivityResult` handler to determine the success of this operation, as shown in Listing 16-2.

LISTING 16-2: Enabling Bluetooth

```java
private static final int ENABLE_BLUETOOTH = 1;

private void initBluetooth() {
  if (!bluetooth.isEnabled()) {
    // Bluetooth isn't enabled, prompt the user to turn it on.
    Intent intent = new Intent(BluetoothAdapter.ACTION_REQUEST_ENABLE);
    startActivityForResult(intent, ENABLE_BLUETOOTH);
  } else {
    // Bluetooth is enabled, initialize the UI.
    initBluetoothUI();
  }
}

protected void onActivityResult(int requestCode,
                                int resultCode, Intent data) {
  if (requestCode == ENABLE_BLUETOOTH)
    if (resultCode == RESULT_OK) {
      // Bluetooth has been enabled, initialize the UI.
      initBluetoothUI();
    }
}
```

code snippet PA4AD_Ch16_Bluetooth/src/BluetoothActivity.java

Enabling and disabling the Bluetooth Adapter are somewhat time-consuming, asynchronous operations. Rather than polling the Bluetooth Adapter, your application should register a Broadcast Receiver that listens for `ACTION_STATE_CHANGED`. The Broadcast Intent will include two extras, `EXTRA_STATE` and `EXTRA_PREVIOUS_STATE`, which indicate the current and previous Bluetooth Adapter states, respectively:

```java
BroadcastReceiver bluetoothState = new BroadcastReceiver() {
  @Override
  public void onReceive(Context context, Intent intent) {
    String prevStateExtra = BluetoothAdapter.EXTRA_PREVIOUS_STATE;
    String stateExtra = BluetoothAdapter.EXTRA_STATE;
    int state = intent.getIntExtra(stateExtra, -1);
    int previousState = intent.getIntExtra(prevStateExtra, -1);

    String tt = "";
    switch (state) {
      case (BluetoothAdapter.STATE_TURNING_ON) :
        tt = "Bluetooth turning on"; break;
      case (BluetoothAdapter.STATE_ON) :
```

```
        tt = "Bluetooth on"; break;
      case (BluetoothAdapter.STATE_TURNING_OFF) :
        tt = "Bluetooth turning off"; break;
      case (BluetoothAdapter.STATE_OFF) :
        tt = "Bluetooth off"; break;
      default: break;
    }
    Log.d(TAG, tt);
  }
};

String actionStateChanged = BluetoothAdapter.ACTION_STATE_CHANGED;
registerReceiver(bluetoothState,
                 new IntentFilter(actionStateChanged));
```

> *You can also turn the Bluetooth Adapter on and off directly, using the* `enable` *and* `disable` *methods, respectively, if you include the* `BLUETOOTH_ADMIN` *permission in your manifest.*
>
> *This should be done only when absolutely necessary, and the user should always be notified if you are manually changing the Bluetooth Adapter status on the user's behalf. In most cases you should use the Intent mechanism described earlier.*

Being Discoverable and Remote Device Discovery

The process of two devices finding each other to connect is called *discovery*. Before you can establish a Bluetooth Socket for communications, the local Bluetooth Adapter must bond with the remote device. Before two devices can bond and connect, they first need to discover each other.

> *Although the Bluetooth protocol supports ad-hoc connections for data transfer, this mechanism is not currently available in Android. Android Bluetooth communication is currently supported only between bonded devices.*

Managing Device Discoverability

For an Android device to find your local Bluetooth Adapter during a discovery scan, you need to ensure that it's discoverable. The Bluetooth Adapter's discoverability is indicated by its scan mode, found using the `getScanMode` method on the `BluetoothAdapter` object.

It will return one of the following `BluetoothAdapter` constants:

➤ `SCAN_MODE_CONNECTABLE_DISCOVERABLE` — Inquiry scan and page scan are both enabled, meaning that the device is discoverable from any Bluetooth device performing a discovery scan.

➤ SCAN_MODE_CONNECTABLE — Page scan is enabled but inquiry scan is not. This means that devices that have previously connected and bonded to the local device can find it during discovery, but new devices can't.

➤ SCAN_MODE_NONE — Discoverability is turned off. No remote devices can find the local Bluetooth Adapter during discovery.

For privacy reasons, Android devices will default to having discoverability disabled. To turn on discovery, you need to obtain explicit permission from the user; you do this by starting a new Activity using the ACTION_REQUEST_DISCOVERABLE action, as shown in Listing 16-3.

LISTING 16-3: Enabling discoverability

```
startActivityForResult(
    new Intent(BluetoothAdapter.ACTION_REQUEST_DISCOVERABLE),
                DISCOVERY_REQUEST);
```

code snippet PA4AD_Ch16_Bluetooth/src/BluetoothActivity.java

By default, discoverability will be enabled for 2 minutes. You can modify this setting by adding an EXTRA_DISCOVERABLE_DURATION extra to the launch Intent, specifying the number of seconds you want discoverability to last.

When the Intent is broadcast, the user will be prompted by the dialog, as shown in Figure 16-2, to turn on discoverability for the specified duration.

FIGURE 16-2

To learn if the user has allowed or rejected your discovery request, override the onActivityResult handler, as shown in Listing 16-4. The returned resultCode parameter indicates the duration of discoverability, or a negative number if the user has rejected your request.

LISTING 16-4: Monitoring discoverability request approval

```
@Override
protected void onActivityResult(int requestCode,
                                int resultCode, Intent data) {
    if (requestCode == DISCOVERY_REQUEST) {
```

```
      if (resultCode == RESULT_CANCELED) {
        Log.d(TAG, "Discovery canceled by user");
      }
    }
  }
```

code snippet PA4AD_Ch16_Bluetooth/src/BluetoothActivity.java

Alternatively, you can monitor changes in discoverability by receiving the ACTION_SCAN_MODE_CHANGED broadcast action. The Broadcast Intent includes the current and previous scan modes as extras:

```
registerReceiver(new BroadcastReceiver() {
  @Override
  public void onReceive(Context context, Intent intent) {
    String prevScanMode = BluetoothAdapter.EXTRA_PREVIOUS_SCAN_MODE;
    String scanMode = BluetoothAdapter.EXTRA_SCAN_MODE;

    int currentScanMode = intent.getIntExtra(scanMode, -1);
    int prevMode = intent.getIntExtra(prevScanMode, -1);

    Log.d(TAG, "Scan Mode: " + currentScanMode +
            ". Previous: " + prevMode);
  }
},
new IntentFilter(BluetoothAdapter.ACTION_SCAN_MODE_CHANGED));
```

Discovering Remote Devices

In this section you'll learn how to initiate discovery from your local Bluetooth Adapter to find discoverable devices nearby.

> *The discovery process can take some time to complete (up to 12 seconds). During this time, performance of your Bluetooth Adapter communications will be seriously degraded. Use the techniques in this section to check and monitor the discovery status of the Bluetooth Adapter, and avoid doing high-bandwidth operations (including connecting to a new remote Bluetooth Device) while discovery is in progress.*

You can check if the local Bluetooth Adapter is already performing a discovery scan by using the isDiscovering method.

To initiate the discovery process, call startDiscovery on the Bluetooth Adapter:

```
if (bluetooth.isEnabled())
  bluetooth.startDiscovery();
```

To cancel a discovery in progress, call cancelDiscovery.

The discovery process is asynchronous. Android uses broadcast Intents to notify you of the start and end of discovery as well as remote devices discovered during the scan.

You can monitor changes in the discovery process by creating Broadcast Receivers to listen for the `ACTION_DISCOVERY_STARTED` and `ACTION_DISCOVERY_FINISHED` Broadcast Intents:

```
BroadcastReceiver discoveryMonitor = new BroadcastReceiver() {

  String dStarted = BluetoothAdapter.ACTION_DISCOVERY_STARTED;
  String dFinished = BluetoothAdapter.ACTION_DISCOVERY_FINISHED;

  @Override
  public void onReceive(Context context, Intent intent) {
    if (dStarted.equals(intent.getAction())) {
      // Discovery has started.
      Log.d(TAG, "Discovery Started...");
    }
    else if (dFinished.equals(intent.getAction())) {
      // Discovery has completed.
      Log.d(TAG, "Discovery Complete.");
    }
  }
};

registerReceiver(discoveryMonitor,
                 new IntentFilter(dStarted));
registerReceiver(discoveryMonitor,
                 new IntentFilter(dFinished));
```

Discovered Bluetooth Devices are returned via Broadcast Intents by means of the `ACTION_FOUND` broadcast action.

As shown in Listing 16-5, each Broadcast Intent includes the name of the remote device in an extra indexed as `BluetoothDevice.EXTRA_NAME`, and an immutable representation of the remote Bluetooth device as a `BluetoothDevice` parcelable object stored under the `BluetoothDevice.EXTRA_DEVICE` extra.

LISTING 16-5: Discovering remote Bluetooth Devices

```
private ArrayList<BluetoothDevice> deviceList =
  new ArrayList<BluetoothDevice>();

private void startDiscovery() {
  registerReceiver(discoveryResult,
                   new IntentFilter(BluetoothDevice.ACTION_FOUND));

  if (bluetooth.isEnabled() && !bluetooth.isDiscovering())
    deviceList.clear();
    bluetooth.startDiscovery();
}

BroadcastReceiver discoveryResult = new BroadcastReceiver() {
  @Override
  public void onReceive(Context context, Intent intent) {
    String remoteDeviceName =
```

```
            intent.getStringExtra(BluetoothDevice.EXTRA_NAME);

        BluetoothDevice remoteDevice =
            intent.getParcelableExtra(BluetoothDevice.EXTRA_DEVICE);

        deviceList.add(remoteDevice);

        Log.d(TAG, "Discovered " + remoteDeviceName);
    }
};
```

code snippet PA4AD_Ch16_Bluetooth/src/BluetoothActivity.java

Each `BluetoothDevice` object returned through the discovery broadcasts represents a remote Bluetooth Device discovered.

In the following sections you will use Bluetooth Device objects to create a connection, bond, and ultimately transfer data between the local Bluetooth Adapter and remote Bluetooth Devices.

Bluetooth Communications

The Android Bluetooth communications APIs are wrappers around RFCOMM, the Bluetooth radio frequency communications protocol. RFCOMM supports RS232 serial communication over the Logical Link Control and Adaptation Protocol (L2CAP) layer.

In practice, this alphabet soup provides a mechanism for opening communication sockets between two paired Bluetooth devices.

> *Before your application can communicate between devices, the devices must be paired (bonded). If users attempt to connect two unpaired devices, they will be prompted to pair them before the connection is established.*

You can establish an RFCOMM communication channel for bidirectional communications using the following classes.

➤   `BluetoothServerSocket` — Used to establish a listening socket for initiating a link between devices. To establish a handshake, one device acts as a server to listen for, and accept, incoming connection requests.

➤   `BluetoothSocket` — Used to create a new client to connect to a listening Bluetooth Server Socket. Also returned by the Bluetooth Server Socket after a connection is established. Once a connection is established, Bluetooth Sockets are used by both the server and client to transfer data streams.

When creating an application that uses Bluetooth as a peer-to-peer transport layer, you'll need to implement both a Bluetooth Server Socket to listen for connections and a Bluetooth Socket to initiate a new channel and handle communications.

When connected, the Bluetooth Server Socket returns a Bluetooth Socket that's then used by the server device to send and receive data. This server-side Bluetooth Socket is used in exactly the same way as the client socket. The designations of *server* and *client* are relevant only to how the connection is established; they don't affect how data flows after that connection is made.

Opening a Bluetooth Server Socket Listener

A Bluetooth Server Socket is used to listen for incoming Bluetooth Socket connection requests from remote Bluetooth Devices. In order for two Bluetooth devices to be connected, one must act as a server (listening for and accepting incoming requests) and the other as a client (initiating the request to connect to the server). After the two are connected, the communications between the server and host device are handled through a Bluetooth Socket at both ends.

To have your Bluetooth Adapter act as a server, call its `listenUsingRfcommWithServiceRecord` method to listen for incoming connection requests. Pass in a name to identify your server and a universally unique identifier (UUID). The method will return a `BluetoothServerSocket` object — note that the client Bluetooth Socket that connects to this listener will need to know its UUID in order to connect.

Call `accept` on the Server Socket, optionally passing in a timeout duration, to have it start listening for connections. The Server Socket will now block until a remote Bluetooth Socket client with a matching UUID attempts to connect.

If a connection request is made from a remote device that is not yet paired with the local Bluetooth Adapter, the user will be prompted to accept a pairing request before the accept call returns. This prompt is made via a Notification, or a Dialog, as shown in Figure 16-3.

FIGURE 16-3

If an incoming connection request is successful, `accept` will return a Bluetooth Socket connected to the client device. You can use this socket to transfer data, as shown later in this section.

> *Note that* `accept` *is a blocking operation, so it's best practice to listen for incoming connection requests on a background thread rather than block the UI thread until a connection has been made.*

It's also important to note that your Bluetooth Adapter must be discoverable for remote Bluetooth Devices to connect to it. Listing 16-6 shows some typical skeleton code that uses the ACTION_REQUEST_DISCOVERABLE broadcast to request that the device be made discoverable, before listening for incoming connection requests for the returned discoverability duration.

LISTING 16-6: Listening for Bluetooth Socket connection requests

```
private BluetoothSocket transferSocket;

private UUID startServerSocket(BluetoothAdapter bluetooth) {
  UUID uuid = UUID.fromString("a60f35f0-b93a-11de-8a39-08002009c666");
  String name = "bluetoothserver";

  try {
    final BluetoothServerSocket btserver =
      bluetooth.listenUsingRfcommWithServiceRecord(name, uuid);

    Thread acceptThread = new Thread(new Runnable() {
      public void run() {
        try {
          // Block until client connection established.
          BluetoothSocket serverSocket = btserver.accept();
          // Start listening for messages.
          listenForMessages(serverSocket);
          // Add a reference to the socket used to send messages.
          transferSocket = serverSocket;
        } catch (IOException e) {
          Log.e("BLUETOOTH", "Server connection IO Exception", e);
        }
      }
    });
    acceptThread.start();
  } catch (IOException e) {
    Log.e("BLUETOOTH", "Socket listener IO Exception", e);
  }
  return uuid;
}
```

code snippet PA4AD_Ch16_Bluetooth/src/BluetoothActivity.java

Selecting Remote Bluetooth Devices for Communications

The BluetoothSocket class can be used on the client device to initiate a communications channel from within your application to a listening Bluetooth Server Socket. It is also returned by the Bluetooth Server Socket Listener after a connection to a client device has been established.

Create a client-side Bluetooth Socket by calling createRfcommSocketToServiceRecord on a BluetoothDevice object that represents the target remote server device. The target device should have a Bluetooth Server Socket listening for connection requests (as described in the previous section).

There are a number of ways to obtain a reference to a remote Bluetooth Device, and some important caveats regarding the devices with which you can create a communications link.

Bluetooth Device Connection Requirements

In order for a Bluetooth Socket to establish a connection to a remote Bluetooth Device, the following conditions must be true:

➤   The remote device must be discoverable.

➤   The remote device must be accepting connections through a Bluetooth Server Socket.

➤   The local and remote devices must be paired (bonded). If the devices are not paired, the users of each device will be prompted to pair them when the connection request is initiated.

Finding a Bluetooth Device to Connect To

Bluetooth Device objects are used to represents remote devices. You can query them for the properties of each remote device, and to initiate Bluetooth Socket connections.

There are several ways for you to obtain `BluetoothDevices` in code. In each case you should check to ensure that the device you intend to connect to is discoverable and (optionally) determine whether you are bonded to it. If you can't discover the remote device, you should prompt the user to enable discoverability on it.

You learned one technique for finding discoverable Bluetooth Devices earlier in this section. Using the `startDiscovery` method and monitoring `ACTION_FOUND` broadcasts allows you to receive Broadcast Intents that include a `BluetoothDevice.EXTRA_DEVICE` extra containing the discovered Bluetooth Device.

You can also use the `getRemoteDevice` method on your local Bluetooth Adapter, specifying the hardware address of the remote Bluetooth Device you want to connect to:

```
BluetoothDevice device = bluetooth.getRemoteDevice("01:23:77:35:2F:AA");
```

This is particularly useful when you know the hardware address of the target device, such as when using a technology such as Android Beam to share this information between devices.

To find the set of currently paired devices, call `getBondedDevices` on the local Bluetooth Adapter. You can query the returned set to find out if the target Bluetooth Device is already paired with the local Bluetooth Adapter.

```
final BluetoothDevice knownDevice =
  bluetooth.getRemoteDevice("01:23:77:35:2F:AA");

Set<BluetoothDevice> bondedDevices = bluetooth.getBondedDevices();

if (bondedDevices.contains(knownDevice))
  // TODO Target device is bonded / paired with the local device.
```

Opening a Client Bluetooth Socket Connection

To initiate a communications channel to a remote device, create a Bluetooth Socket using the `BluetoothDevice` object that represents it.

To create a new connection, call `createRfcommSocketToServiceRecord` on the Bluetooth Device object representing the target device. Pass in the UUID of its open Bluetooth Server Socket listener.

The returned Bluetooth Socket can then be used to initiate the connection with a call to `connect`, as shown in Listing 16-7.

> Note that `connect` is a blocking operation, so it's best practice to initiate connection requests on a background thread rather than block the UI thread until a connection has been made.

LISTING 16-7: Creating a Bluetooth client socket

```java
private void connectToServerSocket(BluetoothDevice device, UUID uuid) {
  try{
    BluetoothSocket clientSocket
      = device.createRfcommSocketToServiceRecord(uuid);

    // Block until server connection accepted.
    clientSocket.connect();

    // Start listening for messages.
    listenForMessages(clientSocket);

    // Add a reference to the socket used to send messages.
    transferSocket = clientSocket;

  } catch (IOException e) {
    Log.e("BLUETOOTH", "Bluetooth client I/O Exception", e);
  }
}
```

code snippet PA4AD_Ch16_Bluetooth/src/BluetoothActivity.java

If users attempt to connect to a Bluetooth Device that has not yet been paired (bonded) with the host device, they will be prompted to accept the pairing before the `connect` call completes. The users must accept the pairing request on both the host and remote devices for the connection to be established.

Transmitting Data Using Bluetooth Sockets

After a connection has been established, you will have a Bluetooth Socket on both the client and the server devices. From this point onward there is no significant distinction between them; you can send and receive data using the Bluetooth Socket on both devices.

Data transfer across Bluetooth Sockets is handled via standard Java `InputStream` and `OutputStream` objects, which you can obtain from a Bluetooth Socket using the appropriately named `getInputStream` and `getOutputStream` methods, respectively.

Listing 16-8 shows two simple skeleton methods — the first used to send a string to a remote device using an Output Stream, and the second to listen for incoming strings using an Input Stream. The same technique can be used to transfer any streamable data.

Data transfer across Bluetooth Sockets is handled via standard Java `InputStream` and `OutputStream` objects, which you can obtain from a Bluetooth Socket using the appropriately named `getInputStream` and `getOutputStream` methods, respectively.

Listing 16-8 shows two simple skeleton methods — the first used to send a string to a remote device using an Output Stream, and the second to listen for incoming strings using an Input Stream. The same technique can be used to transfer any streamable data.

LISTING 16-8: Sending and receiving strings using Bluetooth Sockets

```java
private void listenForMessages(BluetoothSocket socket,
                      StringBuilder incoming) {
  listening = true;
  int bufferSize = 1024;
  byte[] buffer = new byte[bufferSize];
  try {
    InputStream instream = socket.getInputStream();
    int bytesRead = -1;
    while (listening) {
     bytesRead = instream.read(buffer);
     if (bytesRead != -1) {
       String result = "";
       while ((bytesRead == bufferSize) &&
           (buffer[bufferSize-1] != 0)){
         result = result + new String(buffer, 0, bytesRead - 1);
         bytesRead = instream.read(buffer);
       }
       result = result + new String(buffer, 0, bytesRead - 1);
       incoming.append(result);
     }
     socket.close();
    }
  } catch (IOException e) {
    Log.e(TAG, "Message received failed.", e);
  }
  finally {
  }
}
```

code snippet PA4AD_Ch16_Bluetooth/src/BluetoothActivity.java

MANAGING NETWORK AND INTERNET CONNECTIVITY

With the speed, reliability, and cost of Internet connectivity being dependent on the network technology used (Wi-Fi, GPRS, 3G, LTE, and so on), letting your applications know and manage these connections can help to ensure they run efficiently and responsively.

MANAGING NETWORK AND INTERNET CONNECTIVITY

With the speed, reliability, and cost of Internet connectivity being dependent on the network technology used (Wi-Fi, GPRS, 3G, LTE, and so on), letting your applications know and manage these connections can help to ensure they run efficiently and responsively.

Android broadcasts Intents that allow you to monitor changes in network connectivity and offers APIs that provide control over network settings and connections.

Android networking is principally handled via the `ConnectivityManager`, a Service that lets you monitor the connectivity state, set your preferred network connection, and manage connectivity failover.

The section "Managing Wi-Fi" describes how to use the `WifiManager` to monitor and control the device's Wi-Fi connectivity specifically. The `WifiManager` lets you create new Wi-Fi configurations, monitor and modify the existing Wi-Fi network settings, manage the active connection, and perform access point scans.

Introducing the Connectivity Manager

The `ConnectivityManager` represents the Network Connectivity Service. It's used to monitor the state of network connections, configure failover settings, and control the network radios.

To use the Connectivity Manager, your application needs read and write network state access permissions:

```
<uses-permission android:name="android.permission.ACCESS_NETWORK_STATE"/>
<uses-permission android:name="android.permission.CHANGE_NETWORK_STATE"/>
```

To access the Connectivity Manager, use `getSystemService`, passing in `Context.CONNECTIVITY_SERVICE` as the service name, as shown in Listing 16-9.

LISTING 16-9: Accessing the Connectivity Manager

```
String service = Context.CONNECTIVITY_SERVICE;

ConnectivityManager connectivity =
  (ConnectivityManager)getSystemService(service);
```

code snippet PA4AD_Ch16_Data_Transfer/src/MyActivity.java

Supporting User Preferences for Background Data Transfers

Until Android 4.0 (API level 14), user preferences for background data transfers were enforced at the application level — meaning that for pre-Android 4.0 platforms, you are responsible for adhering to the user's preference for allowing background data transfers.

To obtain the background data setting, call the `getBackgroundDataSetting` method on the Connectivity Manager object:

```
boolean backgroundEnabled = connectivity.getBackgroundDataSetting();
```

If the background data setting is disabled, your application should transfer data only when it is active and in the foreground. By turning off this value, the user explicitly requests that your application does not transfer data when it is not visible and in the foreground.

If your application requires background data transfer to function, it's best practice to notify users of this requirement and offer to take them to the settings page to alter their preference.

If the user does change the background data preference, the system will send a Broadcast Intent with the Connectivity Manager's ACTION_BACKGROUND_DATA_SETTING_CHANGED action.

To monitor changes in the background data setting, create and register a new Broadcast Receiver that listens for this Broadcast Intent, as shown in Listing 16-10.

LISTING 16-10: Monitoring the background data setting

```
registerReceiver(
  new BroadcastReceiver() {
    @Override
    public void onReceive(Context context, Intent intent) {
      boolean backgroundEnabled =
        connectivity.getBackgroundDataSetting();
      setBackgroundData(backgroundEnabled);
    }
  },
  new IntentFilter(
      ConnectivityManager.ACTION_BACKGROUND_DATA_SETTING_CHANGED)
);
```

code snippet PA4AD_Ch16_Data_Transfer/src/MyActivity.java

In Android 4.0 and above, getBackgroundDataSetting has been deprecated and will always return true. Users now have much more control over the network data usage of applications, including setting individual data limits and restricting background data.

These preferences are now enforced at the system level, meaning that if data transfer is unavailable for your application, attempts to transfer data or check the network connectivity status will fail, with the device appearing to be offline.

The best way to prevent users from limiting or disabling your applications data transfer is to:

➤ Minimize the data you transfer

➤ Modify your data usage based on the connection type (as described in the next section)

➤ Provide user preferences for modifying your data usage (for example, background update frequency)

If you create a Preference Activity to allow users to modify your application's data usage, you can make it available from within the system settings when a user inspects your application's data usage.

Add a MANAGE_NETWORK_USAGE Intent Filter to the Preference Activity's manifest node, as shown in Listing 16-11.

LISTING 16-11: Making your application's data usage preferences available from system settings

```xml
<activity android:name=".MyPreferences"
          android:label="@string/preference_title">
  <intent-filter>
    <action
      android:name="android.intent.action.MANAGE_NETWORK_USAGE"
    />
    <category android:name="android.intent.category.DEFAULT" />
  </intent-filter>
</activity>
```

code snippet PA4AD_Ch16_Data_Transfer/AndroidManifest.xml

Once set, the View Application Settings button in the system settings will launch your Preference Activity, allowing users to refine your application's data usage rather than restricting or disabling it.

Finding and Monitoring Network Connectivity

The Connectivity Manager provides a high-level view of the available network connections. The `getActiveNetworkInfo` method returns a `NetworkInfo` object that includes details on the currently active network:

```java
// Get the active network information.
NetworkInfo activeNetwork = connectivity.getActiveNetworkInfo();
```

You can also use the `getNetworkInfo` method to find details on an inactive network of the type specified.

Use the returned `NetworkInfo` to find the connection status, network type, and detailed state information of the returned network.

Before attempting to transfer data, configure a repeating alarm, or schedule a background service that performs data transfer, use the Connectivity Manager to check that you're actually connected to the Internet, and if so, to verify which type of connection is in place, as shown in Listing 16-12.

LISTING 16-12: Determining connectivity

```java
NetworkInfo activeNetwork = connectivity.getActiveNetworkInfo();

boolean isConnected = ((activeNetwork != null) &&
                      (activeNetwork.isConnectedOrConnecting()));

boolean isWiFi = activeNetwork.getType() ==
                 ConnectivityManager.TYPE_WIFI;
```

code snippet PA4AD_Ch16_Data_Transfer/src/MyActivity.java

By querying the connectivity status and network type, you can temporarily disable downloads and updates, alter your refresh frequency, or defer large downloads based on the bandwidth available.

> *Mobile data costs, and the impact of data transfer on battery life, tend to be significantly higher than Wi-Fi, so it's good practice to lower your application's update rate on mobile connections and to defer downloads of significant size until you have a Wi-Fi connection.*

To monitor network connectivity, create a Broadcast Receiver that listens for `ConnectivityManager.CONNECTIVITY_ACTION` Broadcast Intents, as shown in Listing 16-13.

LISTING 16-13: Monitoring connectivity

```
<receiver android:name=".ConnectivityChangedReceiver" >
  <intent-filter >
    <action android:name="android.net.conn.CONNECTIVITY_CHANGE"/>
  </intent-filter>
</receiver>
```

code snippet PA4AD_Ch16_Data_Transfer/AndroidManifest.xml

These Intents include extras that provide additional details on the change to the connectivity state. You can access each extra using one of the static constants available from the `ConnectivityManager` class. Most usefully, the `EXTRA_NO_CONNECTIVITY` extra contains a Boolean that returns `true` if the device is not connected to any network. Where `EXTRA_NO_CONNECTIVITY` is `false` (meaning there is an active connection), it's good practice to use `getActiveNetworkInfo` to find further details about the new connectivity status and modify your download schedule, as appropriate.

MANAGING WI-FI

The `WifiManager`, which represents the Android Wi-Fi Connectivity Service, can be used to configure Wi-Fi network connections, manage the current Wi-Fi connection, scan for access points, and monitor changes in Wi-Fi connectivity.

To use the Wi-Fi Manager, your application must have `uses-permissions` for accessing and changing the Wi-Fi state included in its manifest:

```
<uses-permission android:name="android.permission.ACCESS_WIFI_STATE"/>
<uses-permission android:name="android.permission.CHANGE_WIFI_STATE"/>
```

Access the Wi-Fi Manager using the `getSystemService` method, passing in the `Context.WIFI_SERVICE` constant, as shown in Listing 16-14.

LISTING 16-14: Accessing the Wi-Fi Manager

```
String service = Context.WIFI_SERVICE;
WifiManager wifi = (WifiManager)getSystemService(service);
```

code snippet PA4AD_Ch16_WiFi/src/MyActivity.java

You can use the Wi-Fi Manager to enable or disable your Wi-Fi hardware using the `setWifiEnabled` method, or to request the current Wi-Fi state using the `getWifiState` or `isWifiEnabled` methods, as shown in Listing 16-15.

LISTING 16-15: Monitoring and changing Wi-Fi state

```
if (!wifi.isWifiEnabled())
  if (wifi.getWifiState() != WifiManager.WIFI_STATE_ENABLING)
    wifi.setWifiEnabled(true);
```

code snippet PA4AD_Ch16_WiFi/src/MyActivity.java

The following sections begin with tracking the current Wi-Fi connection status and monitoring changes in signal strength. Later you'll also learn how to scan for and connect to specific access points.

Monitoring Wi-Fi Connectivity

In most cases it's best practice to use the Connectivity Manager to monitor changes in Wi-Fi connectivity; however, the Wifi Manager does broadcast Intents whenever the connectivity status of the Wi-Fi network changes, using an action from one of the following constants defined in the `WifiManager` class:

➤ `WIFI_STATE_CHANGED_ACTION` — Indicates that the Wi-Fi hardware status has changed, moving between enabling, enabled, disabling, disabled, and unknown. It includes two extra values keyed on `EXTRA_WIFI_STATE` and `EXTRA_PREVIOUS_STATE` that provide the new and previous Wi-Fi states, respectively.

➤ `SUPPLICANT_CONNECTION_CHANGE_ACTION` — This Intent is broadcast whenever the connection state with the active supplicant (access point) changes. It is fired when a new connection is established or an existing connection is lost, using the `EXTRA_NEW_STATE` Boolean extra, which returns `true` in the former case.

➤ `NETWORK_STATE_CHANGED_ACTION` — Fired whenever the Wi-Fi connectivity state changes. This Intent includes two extras: the first, `EXTRA_NETWORK_INFO`, includes a `NetworkInfo` object that details the current network state, whereas the second, `EXTRA_BSSID`, includes the BSSID of the access point you're connected to.

➤ `RSSI_CHANGED_ACTION` — You can monitor the current signal strength of the connected Wi-Fi network by listening for the `RSSI_CHANGED_ACTION` Intent. This Broadcast Intent includes an integer extra, `EXTRA_NEW_RSSI`, that holds the current signal strength. To use this signal strength, you should use the `calculateSignalLevel` static method on the Wi-Fi Manager to convert it to an integer value on a scale you specify.

Monitoring Active Wi-Fi Connection Details

When an active Wi-Fi connection has been established, you can use the `getConnectionInfo` method on the Wi-Fi Manager to find information on the connection's status. The returned `WifiInfo` object includes the SSID, BSSID, MAC address, and IP address of the current access point, as well as the current link speed and signal strength, as shown in Listing 16-16.

LISTING 16-16: Querying the active network connection

```
WifiInfo info = wifi.getConnectionInfo();
if (info.getBSSID() != null) {
   int strength = WifiManager.calculateSignalLevel(info.getRssi(), 5);
   int speed = info.getLinkSpeed();
   String units = WifiInfo.LINK_SPEED_UNITS;
   String ssid = info.getSSID();

   String cSummary = String.format("Connected to %s at %s%s.
                                   Strength %s/5",
                                   ssid, speed, units, strength);
   Log.d(TAG, cSummary);
}
```

code snippet PA4AD_Ch16_WiFi/src/MyActivity.java

Scanning for Hotspots

You can also use the Wi-Fi Manager to conduct access point scans using the `startScan` method. An Intent with the `SCAN_RESULTS_AVAILABLE_ACTION` action will be broadcast to asynchronously announce that the scan is complete and results are available.

Call `getScanResults` to get those results as a list of `ScanResult` objects. Each Scan Result includes the details retrieved for each access point detected, including link speed, signal strength, SSID, and the authentication techniques supported.

Listing 16-17 shows how to initiate a scan for access points that displays a Toast indicating the total number of access points found and the name of the access point with the strongest signal.

LISTING 16-17: Conducting a scan for Wi-Fi access points

```
// Register a broadcast receiver that listens for scan results.
registerReceiver(new BroadcastReceiver() {
  @Override
  public void onReceive(Context context, Intent intent) {
    List<ScanResult> results = wifi.getScanResults();
    ScanResult bestSignal = null;
    for (ScanResult result : results) {
      if (bestSignal == null ||
          WifiManager.compareSignalLevel(
            bestSignal.level,result.level) < 0)
        bestSignal = result;
    }
```

```
String connSummary = String.format("%s networks found. %s is
                                    the strongest.",
                                    results.size(),
                                    bestSignal.SSID);

    Toast.makeText(MyActivity.this,
                   connSummary, Toast.LENGTH_LONG).show();
  }
}, new IntentFilter(WifiManager.SCAN_RESULTS_AVAILABLE_ACTION));

// Initiate a scan.
wifi.startScan();
```

code snippet PA4AD_Ch16_WiFi/src/MyActivity.java

Managing Wi-Fi Configurations

You can use the Wifi Manager to manage the configured network settings and control which networks to connect to. When connected, you can interrogate the active network connection to get additional details of its configuration and settings.

Get a list of the current network configurations using getConfiguredNetworks. The list of WifiConfiguration objects returned includes the network ID, SSID, and other details for each configuration.

To use a particular network configuration, use the enableNetwork method, passing in the network ID to use and specifying true for the disableAllOthers parameter:

```
// Get a list of available configurations
List<WifiConfiguration> configurations = wifi.getConfiguredNetworks();
// Get the network ID for the first one.
if (configurations.size() > 0) {
  int netID = configurations.get(0).networkId;
  // Enable that network.
  boolean disableAllOthers = true;
  wifi.enableNetwork(netID, disableAllOthers);
}
```

Creating Wi-Fi Network Configurations

To connect to a Wi-Fi network, you need to create and register a configuration. Normally, your users would do this using the native Wi-Fi configuration settings, but there's no reason you can't expose the same functionality within your own applications or, for that matter, replace the native Wi-Fi configuration Activity entirely.

Network configurations are stored as WifiConfiguration objects. The following is a nonexhaustive list of some of the public fields available for each Wi-Fi configuration:

➤   BSSID — The BSSID for an access point

➤   SSID — The SSID for a particular network

➤ networkId — A unique identifier used to identify this network configuration on the current device

➤ priority — The network configuration's priority to use when ordering the list of potential access points to connect to

➤ status — The current status of this network connection, which will be one of the following: WifiConfiguration.Status.ENABLED, WifiConfiguration.Status.DISABLED, or WifiConfiguration.Status.CURRENT

The Wifi Configuration object also contains the supported authentication techniques, as well as the keys used previously to authenticate with this access point.

The addNetwork method lets you specify a new configuration to add to the current list; similarly, updateNetwork lets you update a network configuration by passing in a WifiConfiguration that's sparsely populated with a network ID and the values you want to change.

You can also use removeNetwork, passing in a network ID, to remove a configuration.

To persist any changes made to the network configurations, you must call saveConfiguration.

TRANSFERRING DATA USING WI-FI DIRECT

Wi-Fi Direct is a communications protocol designed for medium-range, high-bandwidth peer-to-peer communications. Support for Wi-Fi Direct was added to Android 4.0 (API level 14). Compared to Bluetooth, Wi-Fi Direct is faster and more reliable, and works over greater distances.

Using the Wi-Fi Direct APIs, you can search for, and connect to, other Wi-Fi Direct devices within range. By initiating a communications link using sockets, you can then transmit and receive streams of data between supported devices (including some printers, scanners, cameras, and televisions) and between instances of your application running on different devices.

As a high bandwidth alternative to Bluetooth, Wi-Fi Direct is particularly suitable for operations such as media sharing and live media streaming.

Initializing the Wi-Fi Direct Framework

To use Wi-Fi Direct, your application requires the ACCESS_WIFI_STATE, CHANGE_WIFI_STATE, and INTERNET permissions:

```
<uses-permission android:name="android.permission.ACCESS_WIFI_STATE"/>
<uses-permission android:name="android.permission.CHANGE_WIFI_STATE"/>
<uses-permission android:name="android.permission.INTERNET"/>
```

Wi-Fi Direct connections are initiated and managed using the WifiP2pManager system service, which you can access using the getSystemService method, passing in the Context.WIFI_P2P_SERVICE constant:

```
wifiP2pManager =
  (WifiP2pManager)getSystemService(Context.WIFI_P2P_SERVICE);
```

Before you can use the WiFi P2P Manager, you must create a channel to the Wi-Fi Direct framework using the Wifi P2P Manager's `initialize` method. Pass in the current Context, the Looper on which to receive Wi-Fi Direct events, and a `ChannelListener` to listen for the loss of your channel connection, as shown in Listing 16-18.

LISTING 16-18: Initializing Wi-Fi Direct

```
private WifiP2pManager wifiP2pManager;
private Channel wifiDirectChannel;

private void initializeWiFiDirect() {
  wifiP2pManager =
    (WifiP2pManager)getSystemService(Context.WIFI_P2P_SERVICE);

  wifiDirectChannel = wifiP2pManager.initialize(this, getMainLooper(),
    new ChannelListener() {
      public void onChannelDisconnected() {
        initializeWiFiDirect();
      }
    }
  );
}
```

code snippet PA4AD_Ch16_WiFiDirect/src/WiFiDirectActivity.java

You will use this Channel whenever you interact with the Wi-Fi Direct framework, so initializing the WiFi P2P Manager will typically be done within the `onCreate` handler of your Activity.

Most actions performed using the WiFi P2P Manager (such as peer discovery and connection attempts) will immediately indicate their success (or failure) using an `ActionListener`, as shown in Listing 16-19. When successful, the return values associated with those actions are obtained by receiving Broadcast Intents, as described in the following sections.

LISTING 16-19: Creating a WiFi P2P Manager Action Listener

```
private ActionListener actionListener = new ActionListener() {
  public void onFailure(int reason) {
    String errorMessage = "WiFi Direct Failed: ";
    switch (reason) {
      case WifiP2pManager.BUSY :
        errorMessage += "Framework busy."; break;
      case WifiP2pManager.ERROR :
        errorMessage += "Internal error."; break;
      case WifiP2pManager.P2P_UNSUPPORTED :
        errorMessage += "Unsupported."; break;
      default:
        errorMessage += "Unknown error."; break;
    }
    Log.d(TAG, errorMessage);
  }
```

continues

LISTING 16-19 *(continued)*

```
    public void onSuccess() {
      // Success!
      // Return values will be returned using a Broadcast Intent
    }
  };
```

code snippet PA4AD_Ch16_WiFiDirect/src/WiFiDirectActivity.java

Enabling Wi-Fi Direct and Monitoring Its Status

For an Android Device to find other Wi-Fi Direct devices, or to be discoverable by them, users must first enable Wi-Fi Direct. You can launch the settings screen, for users to change this setting, by starting a new Activity using the `android.provider.Settings.ACTION_WIRELESS_SETTINGS` class, as shown in Listing 16-20.

LISTING 16-20: Enabling Wi-Fi Direct on a device

```
Intent intent = new Intent(
   android.provider.Settings.ACTION_WIRELESS_SETTINGS);

startActivity(intent);
```

code snippet PA4AD_Ch16_WiFiDirect/src/WiFiDirectActivity.java

Wi-Fi Direct will remain enabled only until you have made a connection and transferred data. It will be disabled automatically after a short period of inactivity.

You will be able to perform Wi-Fi Direct operations only while Wi-Fi Direct is enabled on the device, so it's important to listen for changes in its status, modifying your UI to disable actions that aren't available.

You can monitor the Wi-Fi Direct status by registering a Broadcast Receiver that receives the `WifiP2pManager.WIFI_P2P_STATE_CHANGED_ACTION` action:

```
IntentFilter p2pEnabledFilter = new
    IntentFilter(WifiP2pManager.WIFI_P2P_STATE_CHANGED_ACTION);

registerReceiver(p2pStatusReceiver, p2pEnabledFilter);
```

The Intent received by the associated Broadcast Receiver, as shown in Listing 16-21, will include a `WifiP2pManager.EXTRA_WIFI_STATE` extra that will be set to either `WIFI_P2P_STATE_ENABLED` or `WIFI_P2P_STATE_DISABLED`.

LISTING 16-21: Receiving a Wi-Fi Direct status change

```
BroadcastReceiver p2pStatusReceiver = new BroadcastReceiver() {
  @Override
  public void onReceive(Context context, Intent intent) {
    int state = intent.getIntExtra(
```

```
      WifiP2pManager.EXTRA_WIFI_STATE,
      WifiP2pManager.WIFI_P2P_STATE_DISABLED);

  switch (state) {
    case (WifiP2pManager.WIFI_P2P_STATE_ENABLED):
      buttonDiscover.setEnabled(true);
      break;
    default:
      buttonDiscover.setEnabled(false);
  }
  }
};
```

code snippet PA4AD_Ch16_WiFiDirect/src/WiFiDirectActivity.java

Within the onReceive handler, you can modify your UI accordingly based on the change in state.

After creating a channel to the Wi-Fi Direct framework and enabling Wi-Fi Direct on the host and its peer device(s), you can begin the process of discovering and connecting to peers.

Discovering Peers

To initiate a scan for peers, call the WiFi P2P Manager's discoverPeers method, passing in the active channel and an Action Listener. Changes to the peer list will be broadcast as an Intent using the WifiP2pManager.WIFI_P2P_PEERS_CHANGED_ACTION action. Peer discovery will remain active until a connection is established or a group is created.

When you receive an Intent notifying you of a change to the peer list, you can request the current list of discovered peers using the WifiP2pManager.requestPeers method, as shown in Listing 16-22.

LISTING 16-22: Discovering Wi-Fi Direct peers

```
private void discoverPeers() {
  wifiP2pManager.discoverPeers(wifiDirectChannel, actionListener);
}

BroadcastReceiver peerDiscoveryReceiver = new BroadcastReceiver() {
  @Override
  public void onReceive(Context context, Intent intent) {
    wifiP2pManager.requestPeers(wifiDirectChannel,
      new PeerListListener() {
        public void onPeersAvailable(WifiP2pDeviceList peers) {
          deviceList.clear();
          deviceList.addAll(peers.getDeviceList());
          aa.notifyDataSetChanged();
        }
      });
  }
};
```

code snippet PA4AD_Ch16_WiFiDirect/src/WiFiDirectActivity.java

The `requestPeers` method accepts a `PeerListListener` whose `onPeersAvailable` handler will execute when the peer list has been retrieved. The list of peers will be available as a `WifiP2pDeviceList`, which you can then query to find the name and address of all the available peer devices.

Connecting with Peers

To form a Wi-Fi Direct connection with a peer device, use the WiFi P2P Manager's `connect` method, passing in the active channel, an Action Listener, and a `WifiP2pConfig` object that specifies the address of the peer to connect to, as shown in Listing 16-23.

LISTING 16-23: Requesting a connection to a Wi-Fi Direct peer

```
private void connectTo(WifiP2pDevice device) {
    WifiP2pConfig config = new WifiP2pConfig();
    config.deviceAddress = device.deviceAddress;

    wifiP2pManager.connect(wifiDirectChannel, config, actionListener);
}
```

code snippet PA4AD_Ch16_WiFiDirect/src/WiFiDirectActivity.java

When you attempt to establish a connection, the remote device will be prompted to accept it. On Android devices this requires the user to manually accept the connection request using the dialog shown in Figure 16-4.

FIGURE 16-4

If the device accepts the connection request, the successful connection is broadcast on *both* devices using the `WifiP2pManager.WIFI_P2P_CONNECTION_CHANGED_ACTION` Intent action.

The Broadcast Intent will include a `NetworkInfo` object parceled within the `WifiP2pManager`
`.EXTRA_NETWORK_INFO` extra. You can query the Network Info to confirm whether the change in connection status represents a new connection or a disconnection:

```
boolean connected = networkInfo.isConnected();
```

In the former case, you can request further details on the connection using the `WifiP2pManager`
`.requestConnectionInfo` method, passing in the active channel and a `ConnectionInfoListener`, as shown in Listing 16-24.

LISTING 16-24: Connecting to a Wi-Fi Direct peer

```java
BroadcastReceiver connectionChangedReceiver = new BroadcastReceiver() {
  @Override
  public void onReceive(Context context, Intent intent) {

    // Extract the NetworkInfo
    String extraKey = WifiP2pManager.EXTRA_NETWORK_INFO;
    NetworkInfo networkInfo =
      (NetworkInfo)intent.getParcelableExtra(extraKey);

    // Check if we're connected
    if (networkInfo.isConnected()) {
      wifiP2pManager.requestConnectionInfo(wifiDirectChannel,
        new ConnectionInfoListener() {
          public void onConnectionInfoAvailable(WifiP2pInfo info) {
            // If the connection is established
            if (info.groupFormed) {
              // If we're the server
              if (info.isGroupOwner) {
                // TODO Initiate server socket.
              }
              // If we're the client
              else if (info.groupFormed) {
                // TODO Initiate client socket.
              }
            }
          }
      });
    } else {
      Log.d(TAG, "Wi-Fi Direct Disconnected");
    }
  }
};
```

code snippet PA4AD_Ch16_WiFiDirect/src/WiFiDirectActivity.java

The `ConnectionInfoListener` will fire its `onConnectionInfoAvailable` handler when
the connection details become available, passing in a `WifiP2pInfo` object that includes
those details.

When a collection is established, a group consisting of the peers connected is formed. The initiator
of the connection will be returned as the group owner and would typically (but not necessarily) take
on the role of server for further communications.

> *Each P2P connection is regarded as a group, even if that connection is
> exclusively between two peers. If you need to connect with legacy devices that
> don't support Wi-Fi Direct, you can manually create groups to create a virtual
> access point to which they can connect.*

Having established a connection, you can use standard TCP/IP sockets to transmit data between devices, as described later in the next section.

Transferring Data Between Peers

Although the specifics of any particular data transfer implementation is beyond the scope of this book, this section describes the basic process of transmitting data between connected devices using standard Java sockets.

To establish a socket connection, one device must create a `ServerSocket` that listens for connection requests, and the other device must create a client `Socket` that makes connection requests. This distinction is relevant only in terms of establishing the connection — after that connection is established, the data can flow in either direction.

Create a new server-side socket using the `ServerSocket` class, specifying a port on which to listen for requests. Call its `accept` method to listen for incoming requests, as shown in Listing 16-25.

LISTING 16-25: Creating a Server Socket

```
ServerSocket serverSocket = new ServerSocket(8666);
Socket serverClient = serverSocket.accept();
```

code snippet PA4AD_Ch16_WiFiDirect/src/WiFiDirectActivity.java

To request a connection from the client device, create a new `Socket` and use its `connect` method, specifying the host address of the target device, a port to connect on, and a timeout for the connection request, as shown in Listing 16-36.

LISTING 16-26: Creating a client Socket

```
int timeout = 10000;
int port = 8666;

InetSocketAddress socketAddress
  = new InetSocketAddress(hostAddress, port);


try {
  Socket socket = new Socket();
  socket.bind(null);
  socket.connect(socketAddress, timeout);
} catch (IOException e) {
  Log.e(TAG, "IO Exception.", e);
}
```

code snippet PA4AD_Ch16_WiFiDirect/src/WiFiDirectActivity.java

Like the Server Socket call to `accept`, the call to `connect` is a blocking call that will return after the Socket connection has been established.

> *Network communications such as those described here should always be handled on a background thread to avoid blocking the UI thread. This is particularly the case when establishing the network connection because both the server- and client-side logic includes blocking calls that will disrupt the UI.*

After the sockets have been established, you can create Input Streams and Output Streams on either the server- or client-side sockets to transmit and receive data bidirectionally.

NEAR FIELD COMMUNICATION

Android 2.3 (API level 9) introduced Near Field Communication (NFC) APIs. NFC is a contactless technology used to transmit small amounts of data across short distances (typically less than 4 centimeters).

NFC transfers can occur between two NFC-enabled devices, or between a device and an NFC "tag." Tags can range from passive tags that transmit a URL when scanned to complex systems such as those used in NFC payment solutions, such as Google Wallet.

NFC messages in Android are handled using the NFC Data Exchange Format (NDEF).

In order to read, write, or broadcast NFC messages, your application requires the NFC manifest permission:

```
<uses-permission android:name="android.permission.NFC" />
```

Reading NFC Tags

When an Android device is used to scan an NFC tag, the system will decode the incoming payload using its own tag dispatch system, which analyzes the tag, categorizes the data, and uses an Intent to launch an application to receive the data.

For an application to receive NFC data, you need to add an Activity Intent Filter that listens for one of the following Intent actions:

➤ `NfcAdapter.ACTION_NDEF_DISCOVERED` — The highest priority, and most specific, of the NFC messages. Intents using this action include MIME types and/or URI data. It's best practice to listen for this broadcast whenever possible because the extra data allows you to be more specific in defining which tags to respond to.

➤ `NfcAdapter.ACTION_TECH_DISCOVERED` — This action is broadcast when the NFC technology is known but the tag contains no data — or contains data that can't be mapped to a MIME type or URI.

➤ `NfcAdapter.ACTION_TAG_DISCOVERED` — If a tag is received from an unknown technology, it will be broadcast using this action.

Listing 16-27 shows how to register an Activity that will respond only to NFC tags that correspond to a URI that points to my blog.

LISTING 16-27: Listening for NFC tags

```xml
<activity android:name=".BlogViewer">
  <intent-filter>
    <action android:name="android.nfc.action.NDEF_DISCOVERED"/>
    <category android:name="android.intent.category.DEFAULT"/>
    <data android:scheme="http"
          android:host="blog.radioactiveyak.com"/>
  </intent-filter>
</activity>
```

code snippet PA4AD_Ch16_NFC/AndoridManifest.xml

It's good practice to make your NFC Intent Filters as specific as possible to minimize the number of applications available to respond to a given NFC tag and provide the best, fastest user experience.

In many cases the Intent data/URI and MIME type are sufficient for your application to respond accordingly. However, if required, the payload delivered from an NFC message is available through extras within the Intent that started your Activity.

The `NfcAdapter.EXTRA_TAG` extra includes a raw Tag object that represents the scanned tag. The `NfcAdapter.EXTRA_TNDEF_MESSAGES` extra contains an array of NDEF Messages, as shown in Listing 16-28.

LISTING 16-28: Extracting NFC tag payloads

```java
String action = getIntent().getAction();

if (NfcAdapter.ACTION_NDEF_DISCOVERED.equals(action)) {
  Parcelable[] messages =
    intent.getParcelableArrayExtra(NfcAdapter.EXTRA_NDEF_MESSAGES);

  for (int i = 0; i < messages.length; i++) {
    NdefMessage message = (NdefMessage)messages[i];
    NdefRecord[] records = message.getRecords();

    for (int j = 0; j < records.length; j++) {
      NdefRecord record = records[j];
      // TODO Process the individual records.
    }
  }
}
```

code snippet PA4AD_Ch16_NFC/src/BeamerActivity.java

Using the Foreground Dispatch System

By default, the tag dispatch system will determine which application should receive a particular tag based on the standard process of Intent resolution. In that process, the foreground Activity has no priority over other applications; so, if several applications are all registered to receive a tag of the type scanned, the user will be prompted to select which to use, even if your application is in the foreground at the time.

Using the foreground dispatch system, you can specify a particular Activity as having priority, allowing it to become the default receiver when it is in the foreground. Foreground dispatching can be toggled using the enable/disableForegroundDispatch methods on the NFC Adapter. Foreground dispatching can be used only while an Activity is in the foreground, so it should be enabled and disabled from within your onResume and onPause handlers, respectively, as shown in Listing 16-29. The parameters to enableForegroundDispatch are described following the example.

LISTING 16-29: Using the foreground dispatch system

```
public void onPause() {
  super.onPause();

    nfcAdapter.disableForegroundDispatch(this);
}

@Override
public void onResume() {
  super.onResume();
  nfcAdapter.enableForegroundDispatch(
    this,
    // Intent that will be used to package the Tag Intent.
    nfcPendingIntent,
    // Array of Intent Filters used to declare the Intents you
    // wish to intercept.
    intentFiltersArray,
    // Array of Tag technologies you wish to handle.
    techListsArray);

  String action = getIntent().getAction();
  if (NfcAdapter.ACTION_NDEF_DISCOVERED.equals(action)) {
    processIntent(getIntent());
  }
}
```

code snippet PA4AD_Ch16_NFC/src/BeamerActivity.java

The Intent Filters array should declare the URIs or MIME types you want to intercept — any received tags that don't match these criteria will be handled using the standard tag dispatching system. To ensure a good user experience, it's important that you specify only the tag content your application handles.

You can further refine the tags you receive by explicitly indicating the technologies you want to handle, typically represented by adding the `NfcF` class.

Finally, the Pending Intent will be populated by the NFC Adapter to transmit the received tag directly to your application.

Listing 16-30 shows the Pending Intent, MIME type array, and technologies array used to enable the foreground dispatching in Listing 16-29.

LISTING 16-30: Configuring foreground dispatching parameters

```
PendingIntent nfcPendingIntent;
IntentFilter[] intentFiltersArray;
String[][] techListsArray;

@Override
public void onCreate(Bundle savedInstanceState) {
  super.onCreate(savedInstanceState);
  setContentView(R.layout.main);

  [... Existing onCreate logic ...]

  // Create the Pending Intent.
  int requestCode = 0;
  int flags = 0;

  Intent nfcIntent = new Intent(this, getClass());
  nfcIntent.addFlags(Intent.FLAG_ACTIVITY_SINGLE_TOP);

  nfcPendingIntent =
    PendingIntent.getActivity(this, requestCode, nfcIntent, flags);

  // Create an Intent Filter limited to the URI or MIME type to
  // intercept TAG scans from.
  IntentFilter tagIntentFilter =
    new IntentFilter(NfcAdapter.ACTION_NDEF_DISCOVERED);
  tagIntentFilter.addDataScheme("http");
  tagIntentFilter.addDataAuthority("blog.radioactiveyak.com", null);
  intentFiltersArray = new IntentFilter[] { tagIntentFilter };

  // Create an array of technologies to handle.
  techListsArray = new String[][] {
    new String[] {
      NfcF.class.getName()
    }
  };
}
```

code snippet PA4AD_Ch16_NFC/src/BeamerActivity.java

Introducing Android Beam

Android Beam, introduced in Android 4.0 (API level 14), provides a simple API for an application to transmit data between two devices using NFC, simply by placing them back-to-back. For example, the native contacts, browser, and YouTube applications use Android Beam to share the currently viewed contact, web page, and video, respectively, with other devices.

> *To beam messages, your application must be in the foreground and the device receiving the data must not be locked.*
>
> *Android Beam is initiated by tapping two NFC-enabled Android devices together. Users are presented with a "touch to beam" UI, at which point they can choose to "beam" the foreground application to the other device.*

Android Beam uses NFC to push NDEF messages between devices when they are physically placed together.

By enabling Android Beam within your application, you can define the payload of the beamed message. If you don't customize the message, the default action for your application will be to launch it on the target device. If your application isn't installed on the target device, the Google Play Store will launch and display your application's details page.

To define the message your application beams, you need to request the NFC permission in the manifest:

```
<uses-permission android:name="android.permission.NFC"/>
```

The process to define your own custom payload is described as follows:

1. Create an `NdefMessage` object that contains an `NdefRecord` that contains your message payload.

2. Assign your Ndef Message to the NFC Adapter as your Android Beam payload.

3. Configure your application to listen for incoming Android Beam messages.

Creating Android Beam Messages

To create a new Ndef Message, create a new `NdefMessage` object that contains at least one `NdefRecord` containing the payload you want to beam to your application on the target device.

When creating a new Ndef Record, you must specify the type of record it represents, a MIME type, an ID, and a payload. There are several common types of Ndef Record that can be used to transmit data using Android Beam; note that they should always be the first record added to each beamed message.

Using the `NdefRecord.TNF_MIME_MEDIA` type, you can transmit an absolute URI:

```
NdefRecord uriRecord = new NdefRecord(
  NdefRecord.TNF_ABSOLUTE_URI,
  "http://blog.radioactiveyak.com".getBytes(Charset.forName("US-ASCII")),
  new byte[0], new byte[0]);
```

This is the most common Ndef Record transmitted using Android Beam because the received Intent will be of the same form as any Intent used to start an Activity. The Intent Filter used to decide which NFC messages a particular Activity should receive can use the `scheme`, `host`, and `path Prefix` attributes.

If you need to transmit messages that contain information that can't be easily interpreted as a URI, the `NdefRecord.TNF_MIME_MEDIA` type supports the creation of an application-specific MIME type and the inclusion of associated payload data:

```
byte[] mimeType = "application/com.paad.nfcbeam".getBytes(Charset.forName("US-ASCII"));
byte[] tagId = new byte[0];
byte[] payload = "Not a URI".getBytes(Charset.forName("US-ASCII"));

NdefRecord mimeRecord = new NdefRecord(
  NdefRecord.TNF_MIME_MEDIA,
  mimeType,
  tagId,
  payload);
```

A more complete examination of the available NDEF record types and how to use them can be found in the Android Developer Guide (`http://developer.android.com/guide/topics/nfc/nfc.html#creating-records`).

It's good practice to also include an Ndef Record in the form of an Android Application Record (AAR). This guarantees that your application will be launched on the target device, and that if your application isn't installed, the Google Play Store will be lunched for the user to install it.

To create an AAR Ndef Record, use the `createApplicationRecord` static method on the Ndef Record class, specifying the package name of your application, as shown in Listing 16-31.

LISTING 16-31: Creating an Android Beam NDEF message

```
String payload = "Two to beam across";

String mimeType = "application/com.paad.nfcbeam";
byte[] mimeBytes = mimeType.getBytes(Charset.forName("US-ASCII"));

NdefMessage nfcMessage = new NdefMessage(new NdefRecord[] {
  // Create the NFC payload.
  new NdefRecord(
    NdefRecord.TNF_MIME_MEDIA,
    mimeBytes,
    new byte[0],
    payload.getBytes()),

  // Add the AAR (Android Application Record)
```

```
        NdefRecord.createApplicationRecord("com.paad.nfcbeam")
    });
```

code snippet PA4AD_Ch16_NFCBeam/src/BeamerActivity.java

Assigning the Android Beam Payload

You specify your Android Beam payload using the NFC adapter. You can access the default NFC adapter using the static `getDefaultAdapter` method on the `NfcAdapter` class:

```
    NfcAdapter nfcAdapter = NfcAdapter.getDefaultAdapter(this);
```

There are two alternatives for specifying the NDEF Message created in Listing 16-31 as your application's Android Beam payload. The simplest way is to use the `setNdefPushMessage` method to assign a message that should *always* be sent from the current Activity if Android Beam is initiated. You would typically make this assignment once, from within your Activity's `onResume` method:

```
    nfcAdapter.setNdefPushMessage(nfcMessage, this);
```

A better alternative is to use the `setNdefPushMessageCallback` method. This handler will fire immediately before your message is beamed, allowing you to dynamically set the payload content based on the application's current context — for example, which video is being watched, which web page is being browsed, or which map coordinates are centered, as shown in Listing 16-32.

LISTING 16-32: Setting your Android Beam message dynamically

```
nfcAdapter.setNdefPushMessageCallback(new CreateNdefMessageCallback() {
    public NdefMessage createNdefMessage(NfcEvent event) {
        String payload = "Beam me up, Android!\n\n" +
            "Beam Time: " + System.currentTimeMillis();

        NdefMessage message = createMessage(payload);

        return message;
    }
}, this);
```

code snippet PA4AD_Ch16_NFCBeam/src/BeamerActivity.java

If you set both a static message and a dynamic message using the callback hander, only the latter will be transmitted.

Receiving Android Beam Messages

Android Beam messages are received much like NFC tags, as described earlier in this chapter. To receive the payload you packaged in the previous section, start by adding a new Intent Filter to your Activity, as shown in Listing 16-33.

LISTING 16-33: Android Beam Intent Filter

```
<intent-filter>
  <action android:name="android.nfc.action.NDEF_DISCOVERED"/>
  <category android:name="android.intent.category.DEFAULT"/>
  <data android:mimeType="application/com.paad.nfcbeam"/>
</intent-filter>
```

code snippet PA4AD_Ch16_NFCBeam/AndroidManifest.xml

The Activity will be launched on the recipient device when an Android Beam has been initiated, or, if your application isn't installed, the Google Play Store will be launched to allow the user to download it.

The beam data will be delivered to your Activity using an Intent with the `NfcAdapter.ACTION_NDEF_DISCOVERED` action and the payload available as an array of `NdfMessages` stored against the `NfcAdapter.EXTRA_NDEF_MESSAGES` extra, as shown in Listing 16-34.

LISTING 16-34: Extracting the Android Beam payload

```
Parcelable[] messages = intent.getParcelableArrayExtra(
  NfcAdapter.EXTRA_NDEF_MESSAGES);

NdefMessage message = (NdefMessage)messages[0];
NdefRecord record = message.getRecords()[0];

String payload = new String(record.getPayload());
```

code snippet PA4AD_Ch16_NFCBeam/src/BeamerActivity.java

Typically, the payload string will be in the form of a URI, allowing you to extract and handle it as you would the data encapsulated within an Intent to display the appropriate video, web page, or map coordinates.

Telephony and SMS

WHAT'S IN THIS CHAPTER?

- ➤ Initiating phone calls
- ➤ Reading the phone, network, data connectivity, and SIM states
- ➤ Monitoring changes to the phone, network, data connectivity, and SIM states
- ➤ Using Intents to send SMS and MMS messages
- ➤ Using the SMS Manager to send SMS messages
- ➤ Handling incoming SMS messages

In this chapter, you'll learn to use Android's telephony APIs to monitor mobile voice and data connections as well as incoming and outgoing calls, and to send and receive short messaging service (SMS) messages.

You'll take a look at the communication hardware by examining the telephony package for monitoring phone state and phone calls, as well as initiating calls and monitoring incoming call details.

Android also offers full access to SMS functionality, letting you send and receive SMS messages from within your applications. Using the Android APIs, you can create your own SMS client application to replace the native clients available as part of the software stack. Alternatively, you can incorporate the messaging functionality within your own applications.

HARDWARE SUPPORT FOR TELEPHONY

With the arrival of Wi-Fi-only Android devices, you can no longer assume that telephony will be supported on all the hardware on which your application may be available.

Marking Telephony as a Required Hardware Feature

Some applications don't make sense on devices that don't have telephony support. An application that provides reverse-number lookup for incoming calls or a replacement SMS client simply won't work on a Wi-Fi-only device.

To specify that your application requires telephony support to function, you can add a `uses-feature` node to your application manifest:

```
<uses-feature android:name="android.hardware.telephony"
              android:required="true"/>
```

> *Marking telephony as a required feature prevents your application from being found on Google Play using a device without telephony hardware. It also prevents your application from being installed on such devices from the Google Play website.*

Checking for Telephony Hardware

If you use telephony APIs but they aren't strictly necessary for your application to be used, you can check for the existence of telephony hardware before attempting to make use of the related APIs.

Use the Package Manager's `hasSystemFeature` method, specifying the `FEATURE_TELEPHONY` feature. The Package Manager also includes constants to query the existence of CDMA- and GSM-specific hardware.

```
PackageManager pm = getPackageManager();

boolean telephonySupported =
  pm.hasSystemFeature(PackageManager.FEATURE_TELEPHONY);
boolean gsmSupported =
  pm.hasSystemFeature(PackageManager.FEATURE_TELEPHONY_CDMA);
boolean cdmaSupported =
  pm.hasSystemFeature(PackageManager.FEATURE_TELEPHONY_GSM);
```

It's good practice to check for telephony support early in your application's lifecycle and adjust its UI and behavior accordingly.

USING TELEPHONY

The Android telephony APIs let your applications access the underlying telephone hardware stack, making it possible to create your own dialer — or integrate call handling and phone state monitoring into your applications.

> *Because of security concerns, the current Android SDK does not allow you to create your own in-call Activity — the screen that is displayed when an incoming call is received or an outgoing call has been placed.*

The following sections focus on how to monitor and control phone, service, and cell events in your applications to augment and manage the native phone-handling functionality. You can use the same techniques to implement a replacement dialer application.

Initiating Phone Calls

Best practice for initiating phone calls is to use an `Intent.ACTION_DIAL` Intent, specifying the number to dial by setting the Intents data using a `tel:` schema:

```
Intent whoyougonnacall = new Intent(Intent.ACTION_DIAL,
                                    Uri.parse("tel:555-2368"));
startActivity(whoyougonnacall);
```

This starts a dialer Activity that should be prepopulated with the number you specified. The default dialer Activity allows the user to change the number before explicitly initiating the call. As a result, using the `ACTION_DIAL` Intent action doesn't require any special permissions.

By using an Intent to announce your intention to dial a number, your application stays decoupled from the dialer implementation used to initiate the call. For example, if users have installed a new dialer that supports IP-based telephony, using Intents to dial a number from your application lets them use this new dialer.

Replacing the Native Dialer

Replacing the native dialer application involves two steps:

1. Intercept Intents serviced by the native dialer.

2. Initiate and manage outgoing calls.

The native dialer application responds to Intent actions corresponding to a user pressing the hardware call button, asking to view data using the `tel:` schema, or making an `ACTION_DIAL` request using the `tel:` schema, as shown in the previous section.

To intercept these requests, include `intent-filter` tags on the manifest entries for your replacement dialer Activity that listens for the following actions:

➤ `Intent.ACTION_CALL_BUTTON` — This action is broadcast when the device's hardware call button is pressed. Create an Intent Filter that listens for this action as a default action.

➤ `Intent.ACTION_DIAL` — This Intent action, described in the previous section, is used by applications that want to initiate a phone call. The Intent Filter used to capture this action should be both default and browsable (to support dial requests from the browser) and must specify the `tel:` schema to replace existing dialer functionality (though it can support additional schemes).

➤ `Intent.ACTION_VIEW` — The view action is used by applications wanting to view a piece of data. Ensure that the Intent Filter specifies the `tel:` schema to allow your new Activity to be used to view telephone numbers.

The manifest snippet in Listing 17-1 shows an Activity with Intent Filters that will capture each of these actions.

LISTING 17-1: Manifest entry for a replacement dialer Activity

```
<activity
  android:name=".MyDialerActivity"
  android:label="@string/app_name">
  <intent-filter>
    <action android:name="android.intent.action.CALL_BUTTON" />
    <category android:name="android.intent.category.DEFAULT" />
  </intent-filter>
  <intent-filter>
    <action android:name="android.intent.action.VIEW" />
    <action android:name="android.intent.action.DIAL" />
    <category android:name="android.intent.category.DEFAULT" />
    <category android:name="android.intent.category.BROWSABLE" />
    <data android:scheme="tel" />
  </intent-filter>
</activity>
```

code snippet PA3AD_Ch17_Replacement_Dialer/AndroidManifest.xml

After your Activity has been started, it should provide a UI that allows users to enter or modify the number to dial and to initiate the outgoing call. At that point you need to place the call — using either the existing telephony stack or your own alternative.

The simplest technique is to use the existing telephony stack using the Intent.ACTION_CALL action, as shown in Listing 17-2.

LISTING 17-2: Initiating a call using the system telephony stack

```
Intent whoyougonnacall = new Intent(Intent.ACTION_CALL,
                                    Uri.parse("tel:555-2368"));
startActivity(whoyougonnacall);
```

code snippet PA3AD_Ch17_Replacement_Dialer/AndroidManifest.xml

This will initiate a call using the system in-call Activity and will let the system manage the dialing, connection, and voice handling.

To use this action, your application must request the CALL_PHONE uses-permission:

```
<uses-permission android:name="android.permission.CALL_PHONE"/>
```

Alternatively, you can completely replace the outgoing telephony stack by implementing your own dialing and voice-handling framework. This is the perfect alternative if you are implementing a VOIP (voice over IP) application.

Note, also, that you can use the preceding techniques to intercept outgoing call Intents and modify outgoing numbers or to block outgoing calls as an alternative to completely replacing the dialer.

Accessing Telephony Properties and Phone State

Access to the telephony APIs is managed by the Telephony Manager, accessible using the getSystemService method:

```
String srvcName = Context.TELEPHONY_SERVICE;
TelephonyManager telephonyManager =
   (TelephonyManager)getSystemService(srvcName);
```

The Telephony Manager provides direct access to many of the phone properties, including device, network, subscriber identity module (SIM), and data state details. You can also access some connectivity status information, although this is usually done using the Connectivity Manager, as described in the previous chapter.

Reading Phone Device Details

Using the Telephony Manager, you can obtain the phone type (GSM CDMA, or SIP), unique ID (IMEI or MEID), software version, and the phone's phone number:

```
String phoneTypeStr = "unknown";

int phoneType = telephonyManager.getPhoneType();
switch (phoneType) {
  case (TelephonyManager.PHONE_TYPE_CDMA):
    phoneTypeStr = "CDMA";
    break;
  case (TelephonyManager.PHONE_TYPE_GSM) :
    phoneTypeStr = "GSM";
    break;
  case (TelephonyManager.PHONE_TYPE_SIP):
    phoneTypeStr = "SIP";
    break;
  case (TelephonyManager.PHONE_TYPE_NONE):
    phoneTypeStr = "None";
    break;
  default: break;
}

// -- These require READ_PHONE_STATE uses-permission --
// Read the IMEI for GSM or MEID for CDMA
String deviceId = telephonyManager.getDeviceId();
// Read the software version on the phone (note -- not the SDK version)
String softwareVersion = telephonyManager.getDeviceSoftwareVersion();
// Get the phone's number (if available)
String phoneNumber = telephonyManager.getLine1Number();
```

Note that, except for the phone type, reading each of these properties requires that the READ_PHONE_STATE uses-permission be included in the application manifest:

```
<uses-permission android:name="android.permission.READ_PHONE_STATE"/>
```

You can also determine the type of network you're connected to, along with the name and country of the SIM or connected carrier network.

Reading Network Details

When your device is connected to a network, you can use the Telephony Manager to read the
Mobile Country Code and Mobile Network Code (MCC+MNC), the country ISO code, the network operator name, and the type of network you're connected to using the `getNetworkOperator`,
`getNetworkCountryIso`, `getNetworkOperatorName`, and `getNetworkType` methods:

```
// Get connected network country ISO code
String networkCountry = telephonyManager.getNetworkCountryIso();
// Get the connected network operator ID (MCC + MNC)
String networkOperatorId = telephonyManager.getNetworkOperator();
// Get the connected network operator name
String networkName = telephonyManager.getNetworkOperatorName();

// Get the type of network you are connected to
int networkType = telephonyManager.getNetworkType();
switch (networkType) {
  case (TelephonyManager.NETWORK_TYPE_1xRTT)    : [… do something …]
                                                  break;
  case (TelephonyManager.NETWORK_TYPE_CDMA)     : [… do something …]
                                                  break;
  case (TelephonyManager.NETWORK_TYPE_EDGE)     : [… do something …]
                                                  break;
  case (TelephonyManager.NETWORK_TYPE_EHRPD)    : [… do something …]
                                                  break;
  case (TelephonyManager.NETWORK_TYPE_EVDO_0)   : [… do something …]
                                                  break;
  case (TelephonyManager.NETWORK_TYPE_EVDO_A)   : [… do something …]
                                                  break;
  case (TelephonyManager.NETWORK_TYPE_EVDO_B)   : [… do something …]
                                                  break;
  case (TelephonyManager.NETWORK_TYPE_GPRS)     : [… do something …]
                                                  break;
  case (TelephonyManager.NETWORK_TYPE_HSDPA)    : [… do something …]
                                                  break;
  case (TelephonyManager.NETWORK_TYPE_HSPA)     : [… do something …]
                                                  break;
  case (TelephonyManager.NETWORK_TYPE_HSPAP)    : [… do something …]
                                                  break;
  case (TelephonyManager.NETWORK_TYPE_HSUPA)    : [… do something …]
                                                  break;
  case (TelephonyManager.NETWORK_TYPE_IDEN)     : [… do something …]
                                                  break;
  case (TelephonyManager.NETWORK_TYPE_LTE)      : [… do something …]
                                                  break;
  case (TelephonyManager.NETWORK_TYPE_UMTS)     : [… do something …]
                                                  break;
  case (TelephonyManager.NETWORK_TYPE_UNKNOWN)  : [… do something …]
                                                  break;
  default: break;
}
```

These commands work only when you are connected to a mobile network and can be unreliable if
it is a CDMA network. Use the `getPhoneType` method, as shown in the preceding code snippet, to
determine which phone type is being used.

Reading SIM Details

If your application is running on a GSM device, it will usually have a SIM. You can query the SIM details from the Telephony Manager to obtain the ISO country code, operator name, and operator MCC and MNC for the SIM installed in the current device. These details can be useful if you need to provide specialized functionality for a particular carrier.

If you have included the READ_PHONE_STATE uses-permission in your application manifest, you can also obtain the serial number for the current SIM using the getSimSerialNumber method when the SIM is in a ready state.

Before you can use any of these methods, you must ensure that the SIM is in a ready state. You can determine this using the getSimState method:

```
int simState = telephonyManager.getSimState();
switch (simState) {
  case (TelephonyManager.SIM_STATE_ABSENT): break;
  case (TelephonyManager.SIM_STATE_NETWORK_LOCKED): break;
  case (TelephonyManager.SIM_STATE_PIN_REQUIRED): break;
  case (TelephonyManager.SIM_STATE_PUK_REQUIRED): break;
  case (TelephonyManager.SIM_STATE_UNKNOWN): break;
  case (TelephonyManager.SIM_STATE_READY): {
    // Get the SIM country ISO code
    String simCountry = telephonyManager.getSimCountryIso();
    // Get the operator code of the active SIM (MCC + MNC)
    String simOperatorCode = telephonyManager.getSimOperator();
    // Get the name of the SIM operator
    String simOperatorName = telephonyManager.getSimOperatorName();
    // -- Requires READ_PHONE_STATE uses-permission --
    // Get the SIM's serial number
    String simSerial = telephonyManager.getSimSerialNumber();
    break;
  }
  default: break;
}
```

Reading Data Connection and Transfer State Details

Using the getDataState and getDataActivity methods, you can find the current data connection state and data transfer activity, respectively:

```
int dataActivity = telephonyManager.getDataActivity();
int dataState = telephonyManager.getDataState();

switch (dataActivity) {
  case TelephonyManager.DATA_ACTIVITY_IN : break;
  case TelephonyManager.DATA_ACTIVITY_OUT : break;
  case TelephonyManager.DATA_ACTIVITY_INOUT : break;
  case TelephonyManager.DATA_ACTIVITY_NONE : break;
}

switch (dataState) {
  case TelephonyManager.DATA_CONNECTED : break;
  case TelephonyManager.DATA_CONNECTING : break;
```

```
        case TelephonyManager.DATA_DISCONNECTED : break;
        case TelephonyManager.DATA_SUSPENDED : break;
}
```

> *The Telephony Manager indicates only telephony-based data connectivity (mobile data as opposed to Wi-Fi). As a result, in most circumstances the Connectivity Manager is a better alternative to determine the current connectivity state.*

Monitoring Changes in Phone State Using the Phone State Listener

The Android telephony APIs lets you monitor changes to phone state and associated details such as incoming phone numbers.

Changes to the phone state are monitored using the `PhoneStateListener` class, with some state changes also broadcast as Intents. This section describes how to use the Phone State Listener, and the following section describes which Broadcast Intents are available.

To monitor and manage phone state, your application must specify the READ_PHONE_STATE uses-permission:

```
<uses-permission android:name="android.permission.READ_PHONE_STATE"/>
```

Create a new class that implements the Phone State Listener to monitor, and respond to, phone state change events, including call state (ringing, off hook, and so on), cell location changes, voice-mail and call-forwarding status, phone service changes, and changes in mobile signal strength.

Within your Phone State Listener implementation, override the event handlers of the events you want to react to. Each handler receives parameters that indicate the new phone state, such as the current cell location, call state, or signal strength.

After creating your own Phone State Listener, register it with the Telephony Manager using a bitmask to indicate the events you want to listen for:

```
telephonyManager.listen(phoneStateListener,
                    PhoneStateListener.LISTEN_CALL_FORWARDING_INDICATOR |
                    PhoneStateListener.LISTEN_CALL_STATE |
                    PhoneStateListener.LISTEN_CELL_LOCATION |
                    PhoneStateListener.LISTEN_DATA_ACTIVITY |
                    PhoneStateListener.LISTEN_DATA_CONNECTION_STATE |
                    PhoneStateListener.LISTEN_MESSAGE_WAITING_INDICATOR |
                    PhoneStateListener.LISTEN_SERVICE_STATE |
                    PhoneStateListener.LISTEN_SIGNAL_STRENGTHS);
```

To unregister a listener, call `listen` and pass in `PhoneStateListener.LISTEN_NONE` as the bitmask parameter:

```
telephonyManager.listen(phoneStateListener,
                    PhoneStateListener.LISTEN_NONE);
```

> *Your Phone State Listener will receive phone state change notifications only while your application is running.*

Monitoring Incoming Phone Calls

If your application should respond to incoming phone calls only while it is running, you can override the `onCallStateChanged` method in your Phone State Listener implementation, and register it to receive notifications when the call state changes:

```
PhoneStateListener callStateListener = new PhoneStateListener() {
  public void onCallStateChanged(int state, String incomingNumber) {
    String callStateStr = "Unknown";

    switch (state) {
      case TelephonyManager.CALL_STATE_IDLE :
        callStateStr = "idle"; break;
      case TelephonyManager.CALL_STATE_OFFHOOK :
        callStateStr = "offhook"; break;
      case TelephonyManager.CALL_STATE_RINGING :
        callStateStr = "ringing. Incoming number is: "
        + incomingNumber;
        break;
      default : break;
    }

    Toast.makeText(MyActivity.this,
      callStateStr, Toast.LENGTH_LONG).show();
  }
};

telephonyManager.listen(callStateListener,
                   PhoneStateListener.LISTEN_CALL_STATE);
```

The `onCallStateChanged` handler receives the phone number associated with incoming calls, and the `state` parameter represents the current call state as one of the following three values:

➤   `TelephonyManager.CALL_STATE_IDLE` — When the phone is neither ringing nor in a call

➤   `TelephonyManager.CALL_STATE_RINGING` — When the phone is ringing

➤   `TelephonyManager.CALL_STATE_OFFHOOK` — When the phone is currently in a call

Note that as soon as the state changes to `CALL_STATE_RINGING`, the system will display the incoming call screen, asking users if they want to answer the call.

Your application must be running to receive this callback. If your application should be started whenever the phone state changes, you can register an Intent Receiver that listens for a Broadcast Intent signifying a change in phone state. This is described in the "Using Intent Receivers to Monitor Incoming Phone Calls" section later in this chapter.

Tracking Cell Location Changes

You can get notifications whenever the current cell location changes by overriding
`onCellLocationChanged` on a Phone State Listener implementation. Before you can register
to listen for cell location changes, you need to add the `ACCESS_COARSE_LOCATION` permission to
your application manifest:

```
<uses-permission android:name="android.permission.ACCESS_COARSE_LOCATION"/>
```

The `onCellLocationChanged` handler receives a `CellLocation` object that includes methods for
extracting different location information based on the type of phone network. In the case of a
GSM network, the cell ID (`getCid`) and the current location area code (`getLac`) are available. For
CDMA networks, you can obtain the current base station ID (`getBaseStationId`) and the latitude
(`getBaseStationLatitude`) and longitude (`getBaseStationLongitude`) of that base station.

The following code snippet shows how to implement a Phone State Listener to monitor cell location
changes, displaying a Toast that includes the received network location details.

```
PhoneStateListener cellLocationListener = new PhoneStateListener() {
  public void onCellLocationChanged(CellLocation location) {
    if (location instanceof GsmCellLocation) {
      GsmCellLocation gsmLocation = (GsmCellLocation)location;
      Toast.makeText(getApplicationContext(),
                  String.valueOf(gsmLocation.getCid()),
                Toast.LENGTH_LONG).show();
    }
    else if (location instanceof CdmaCellLocation) {
      CdmaCellLocation cdmaLocation = (CdmaCellLocation)location;
      StringBuilder sb = new StringBuilder();
      sb.append(cdmaLocation.getBaseStationId());
      sb.append("\n@");
      sb.append(cdmaLocation.getBaseStationLatitude());
      sb.append(cdmaLocation.getBaseStationLongitude());

      Toast.makeText(getApplicationContext(),
                  sb.toString(),
                  Toast.LENGTH_LONG).show();
    }
  }
};
telephonyManager.listen(cellLocationListener,
                  PhoneStateListener.LISTEN_CELL_LOCATION);
```

Tracking Service Changes

The `onServiceStateChanged` handler tracks the service details for the device's cell service. Use the
`ServiceState` parameter to find details of the current service state.

The `getState` method on the Service State object returns the current service state as one of the
following `ServiceState` constants:

➤ `STATE_IN_SERVICE` — Normal phone service is available.

➤ `STATE_EMERGENCY_ONLY` — Phone service is available but only for emergency calls.

➤ `STATE_OUT_OF_SERVICE` — No cell phone service is currently available.

➤ `STATE_POWER_OFF` — The phone radio is turned off (usually when airplane mode is enabled).

A series of `getOperator*` methods is available to retrieve details on the operator supplying the cell phone service, whereas `getRoaming` tells you if the device is currently using a roaming profile:

```
PhoneStateListener serviceStateListener = new PhoneStateListener() {
  public void onServiceStateChanged(ServiceState serviceState) {
    if (serviceState.getState() == ServiceState.STATE_IN_SERVICE) {
      String toastText = "Operator: " + serviceState.getOperatorAlphaLong();
      Toast.makeText(MyActivity.this, toastText, Toast.LENGTH_SHORT);
    }
  }
};

telephonyManager.listen(serviceStateListener,
                        PhoneStateListener.LISTEN_SERVICE_STATE);
```

Monitoring Data Connectivity and Data Transfer Status Changes

You can use a Phone State Listener to monitor changes in mobile data connectivity and mobile data transfer. Note that this does not include data transferred using Wi-Fi. For more comprehensive monitoring of data connectivity and transfers, use the Connectivity Manager, as described in the previous chapter.

The Phone State Listener includes two event handlers for monitoring the device's data connection. Override `onDataActivity` to track data transfer activity, and `onDataConnectionStateChanged` to request notifications for data connection state changes:

```
PhoneStateListener dataStateListener = new PhoneStateListener() {
  public void onDataActivity(int direction) {
    String dataActivityStr = "None";

    switch (direction) {
      case TelephonyManager.DATA_ACTIVITY_IN :
        dataActivityStr = "Downloading"; break;
      case TelephonyManager.DATA_ACTIVITY_OUT :
        dataActivityStr = "Uploading"; break;
      case TelephonyManager.DATA_ACTIVITY_INOUT :
        dataActivityStr = "Uploading/Downloading"; break;
      case TelephonyManager.DATA_ACTIVITY_NONE :
        dataActivityStr = "No Activity"; break;
    }

    Toast.makeText(MyActivity.this,
      "Data Activity is " + dataActivityStr,
      Toast.LENGTH_LONG).show();
  }

  public void onDataConnectionStateChanged(int state) {
    String dataStateStr = "Unknown";

    switch (state) {
```

```
            case TelephonyManager.DATA_CONNECTED :
              dataStateStr = "Connected"; break;
            case TelephonyManager.DATA_CONNECTING :
              dataStateStr = "Connecting"; break;
            case TelephonyManager.DATA_DISCONNECTED :
              dataStateStr = "Disconnected"; break;
            case TelephonyManager.DATA_SUSPENDED :
              dataStateStr = "Suspended"; break;
          }

          Toast.makeText(MyActivity.this,
            "Data Connectivity is " + dataStateStr,
            Toast.LENGTH_LONG).show();
      }
    };

    telephonyManager.listen(dataStateListener,
                            PhoneStateListener.LISTEN_DATA_ACTIVITY |
                            PhoneStateListener.LISTEN_DATA_CONNECTION_STATE);
```

Using Intent Receivers to Monitor Incoming Phone Calls

When the phone state changes as a result of an incoming, accepted, or terminated phone call, the Telephony Manager will broadcast an ACTION_PHONE_STATE_CHANGED Intent.

By registering a manifest Intent Receiver that listens for this Broadcast Intent, as shown in the snippet below, you can listen for incoming phone calls at any time, even if your application isn't running. Note that your application needs to request the READ_PHONE_STATE permission to receive the phone state changed Broadcast Intent.

```
<receiver android:name="PhoneStateChangedReceiver">
  <intent-filter>
    <action android:name="android.intent.action.PHONE_STATE"></action>
  </intent-filter>
</receiver>
```

The Phone State Changed Broadcast Intent includes up to two extras. All such broadcasts will include the EXTRA_STATE extra, whose value will be one of the TelephonyManager.CALL_STATE_* actions described earlier to indicate the new phone state. If the state is ringing, the Broadcast Intent will also include the EXTRA_INCOMING_NUMBER extra, whose value represents the incoming call number.

The following skeleton code can be used to extract the current phone state and incoming call number where it exists:

```
public class PhoneStateChangedReceiver extends BroadcastReceiver {
  @Override
  public void onReceive(Context context, Intent intent) {
    String phoneState = intent.getStringExtra(TelephonyManager.EXTRA_STATE);
    if (phoneState.equals(TelephonyManager.EXTRA_STATE_RINGING)) {
      String phoneNumber =
        intent.getStringExtra(TelephonyManager.EXTRA_INCOMING_NUMBER);
      Toast.makeText(context,
        "Incoming Call From: " + phoneNumber,
```

```
                 Toast.LENGTH_LONG).show();
        }
    }
}
```

INTRODUCING SMS AND MMS

If you own a mobile phone that's less than two decades old, chances are you're familiar with SMS messaging. SMS is now one of the most-used communication mechanisms on mobile phones.

SMS technology is designed to send short text messages between mobile phones. It provides support for sending both text messages (designed to be read by people) and data messages (meant to be consumed by applications). Multimedia messaging service (MMS) messages allow users to send and receive messages that include multimedia attachments such as photos, videos, and audio.

Because SMS and MMS are mature mobile technologies, there's a lot of information out there that describes the technical details of how an SMS or MMS message is constructed and transmitted over the air. Rather than rehash that information here, the following sections focus on the practicalities of sending and receiving text, data, and multimedia messages from within Android applications.

Using SMS and MMS in Your Application

Android provides support for sending both SMS and MMS messages using a messaging application installed on the device with the SEND and SEND_TO Broadcast Intents.

Android also supports full SMS functionality within your applications through the SmsManager class. Using the SMS Manager, you can replace the native SMS application to send text messages, react to incoming texts, or use SMS as a data transport layer.

At this time, the Android API does not include simple support for creating MMS messages from within your applications.

This chapter demonstrates how to use both the SMS Manager and Intents to send messages from within your applications.

SMS message delivery is not timely. Compared to using an IP- or socket-based transport, using SMS to pass data messages between applications is slow, possibly expensive, and can suffer from high latency. As a result, SMS is not suitable for anything that requires real-time responsiveness. That said, the widespread adoption and resiliency of SMS networks make it a particularly good tool for delivering content to non-Android users and reducing the dependency on third-party servers.

Sending SMS and MMS from Your Application Using Intents

In most cases it's best practice to use an Intent to send SMS and MMS messages using another application — typically the native SMS application — rather than implementing a full SMS client.

To do so, call startActivity with an Intent.ACTION_SENDTO action Intent. Specify a target number using sms: schema notation as the Intent data. Include the message you want to send within the Intent payload using an sms_body extra:

```
Intent smsIntent = new Intent(Intent.ACTION_SENDTO,
                    Uri.parse("sms:55512345"));
```

```
smsIntent.putExtra("sms_body", "Press send to send me");
startActivity(smsIntent);
```

To attach files to your message (effectively creating an MMS message), add an `Intent.EXTRA_STREAM` with the URI of the resource to attach, and set the Intent `type` to the MIME type of the attached resource.

Note that the native MMS application doesn't include an Intent Receiver for `ACTION_SENDTO` with a `type` set. Instead, you need to use `ACTION_SEND` and include the target phone number as an address extra:

```
// Get the URI of a piece of media to attach.
Uri attached_Uri
  = Uri.parse("content://media/external/images/media/1");

// Create a new MMS intent
Intent mmsIntent = new Intent(Intent.ACTION_SEND, attached_Uri);
mmsIntent.putExtra("sms_body", "Please see the attached image");
mmsIntent.putExtra("address", "07912355432");
mmsIntent.putExtra(Intent.EXTRA_STREAM, attached_Uri);
mmsIntent.setType("image/jpeg");
startActivity(mmsIntent);
```

> *When running the MMS example shown in Listing 17-18, users are likely to be prompted to select one of a number of applications capable of fulfilling the send request, including the Gmail, email, and SMS applications.*

Sending SMS Messages Using the SMS Manager

SMS messaging in Android is handled by the `SmsManager` class. You can get a reference to the SMS Manager using the static `SmsManager.getDefault` method:

```
SmsManager smsManager = SmsManager.getDefault();
```

> *Prior to Android 1.6 (SDK level 4), the `SmsManager` and `SmsMessage` classes were provided by the `android.telephony.gsm` package. These have since been deprecated and the SMS classes moved to `android.telephony` to ensure generic support for GSM and CDMA devices.*

To send SMS messages, your application must specify the `SEND_SMS` uses-permission:

```
<uses-permission android:name="android.permission.SEND_SMS"/>
```

Sending Text Messages

To send a text message, use `sendTextMessage` from the SMS Manager, passing in the address (phone number) of your recipient and the text message you want to send:

```
SmsManager smsManager = SmsManager.getDefault();

String sendTo = "5551234";
String myMessage = "Android supports programmatic SMS messaging!";

smsManager.sendTextMessage(sendTo, null, myMessage, null, null);
```

The second parameter can be used to specify the SMS service center to use. If you enter `null`, the default service center for the device's carrier will be used.

The final two parameters let you specify Intents to track the transmission and successful delivery of your messages. To react to these Intents, create and register Broadcast Receivers, as shown in the section "Tracking and Confirming SMS Message Delivery."

> *The Android debugging bridge supports sending SMS messages among multiple emulator instances. To send an SMS from one emulator to another, specify the port number of the target emulator as the "to" address when sending a new message. Android will route your message to the target emulator instance, where it will be received as a normal SMS.*

Tracking and Confirming SMS Message Delivery

To track the transmission and delivery success of your outgoing SMS messages, implement and register Broadcast Receivers that listen for the actions you specify when creating the Pending Intents you pass in to the `sendTextMessage` method.

The first Pending Intent parameter is fired when the message is either successfully sent or fails to send. The result code for the Broadcast Receiver that receives this Intent will be one of the following:

➤ `Activity.RESULT_OK` — To indicate a successful transmission

➤ `SmsManager.RESULT_ERROR_GENERIC_FAILURE` — To indicate a nonspecific failure

➤ `SmsManager.RESULT_ERROR_RADIO_OFF` — To indicate the phone radio is turned off

➤ `SmsManager.RESULT_ERROR_NULL_PDU` — To indicate a PDU (protocol description unit) failure

➤ `SmsManager.RESULT_ERROR_NO_SERVICE` — To indicate that no cellular service is currently available

The second Pending Intent parameter is fired only after the recipient receives your SMS message.

The following code snippet shows the typical pattern for sending an SMS and monitoring the success of its transmission and delivery.

```
String SENT_SMS_ACTION = "com.paad.smssnippets.SENT_SMS_ACTION";
String DELIVERED_SMS_ACTION = "com.paad.smssnippets.DELIVERED_SMS_ACTION";

// Create the sentIntent parameter
Intent sentIntent = new Intent(SENT_SMS_ACTION);
PendingIntent sentPI = PendingIntent.getBroadcast(getApplicationContext(),
                                                  0,
                                                  sentIntent,
                                                  PendingIntent.FLAG_UPDATE_CURRENT);

// Create the deliveryIntent parameter
Intent deliveryIntent = new Intent(DELIVERED_SMS_ACTION);
PendingIntent deliverPI =
  PendingIntent.getBroadcast(getApplicationContext(),
                             0,
                             deliveryIntent,
                             PendingIntent.FLAG_UPDATE_CURRENT);

// Register the Broadcast Receivers
registerReceiver(new BroadcastReceiver() {
                 @Override
                 public void onReceive(Context _context, Intent _intent)
                 {
                   String resultText = "UNKNOWN";

                   switch (getResultCode()) {
                     case Activity.RESULT_OK:
                       resultText = "Transmission successful"; break;
                     case SmsManager.RESULT_ERROR_GENERIC_FAILURE:
                       resultText = "Transmission failed"; break;
                     case SmsManager.RESULT_ERROR_RADIO_OFF:
                       resultText = "Transmission failed: Radio is off";
                       break;
                     case SmsManager.RESULT_ERROR_NULL_PDU:
                       resultText = "Transmission Failed: No PDU specified";
                       break;
                     case SmsManager.RESULT_ERROR_NO_SERVICE:
                       resultText = "Transmission Failed: No service";
                       break;
                   }
                   Toast.makeText(_context, resultText,
                             Toast.LENGTH_LONG).show();
                 }
               },
               new IntentFilter(SENT_SMS_ACTION));

registerReceiver(new BroadcastReceiver() {
                 @Override
                 public void onReceive(Context _context, Intent _intent)
                 {
                   Toast.makeText(_context, "SMS Delivered",
                             Toast.LENGTH_LONG).show();
```

```
                           }
                      },
                      new IntentFilter(DELIVERED_SMS_ACTION));

// Send the message
SmsManager smsManager = SmsManager.getDefault();
String sendTo = "5551234";
String myMessage = "Android supports programmatic SMS messaging!";

smsManager.sendTextMessage(sendTo, null, myMessage, sentPI, deliverPI);
```

Conforming to the Maximum SMS Message Size

The maximum length of each SMS text message can vary by carrier, but are typically limited to 160 characters. As a result longer messages need to be broken into a series of smaller parts. The SMS Manager includes the divideMessage method, which accepts a string as an input and breaks it into an Array List of messages, wherein each is less than the maximum allowable size.

You can then use the sendMultipartTextMessage method on the SMS Manager to transmit the array of messages:

```
ArrayList<String> messageArray = smsManager.divideMessage(myMessage);
ArrayList<PendingIntent> sentIntents = new ArrayList<PendingIntent>();
for (int i = 0; i < messageArray.size(); i++)
   sentIntents.add(sentPI);

smsManager.sendMultipartTextMessage(sendTo,
                                    null,
                                    messageArray,
                                    sentIntents, null);
```

The sentIntent and deliveryIntent parameters in the sendMultipartTextMessage method are Array Lists that can be used to specify different Pending Intents to fire for each message part.

Sending Data Messages

You can send binary data via SMS using the sendDataMessage method on an SMS Manager. The sendDataMessage method works much like sendTextMessage but includes additional parameters for the destination port and an array of bytes that constitutes the data you want to send.

```
String sendTo = "5551234";
short destinationPort = 80;
byte[] data = [ … your data … ];

smsManager.sendDataMessage(sendTo, null, destinationPort,
                           data, null, null);
```

Listening for Incoming SMS Messages

When a device receives a new SMS message, a new Broadcast Intent is fired with the android.pro-vider.Telephony.SMS_RECEIVED action. Note that this is a string literal; the SDK currently doesn't include a reference to this string, so you must specify it explicitly when using it in your applications.

> ❌ *The SMS received action string is hidden — and therefore an unsupported API. As such, it is subject to change with any future platform release. It is not good practice to use unsupported APIs because doing so carries significant risk. Be cautious when using unsupported platform features because they are subject to change in future platform releases.*

For an application to listen for SMS Broadcast Intents, it needs to specify the RECEIVE_SMS manifest permission:

```
<uses-permission
 android:name="android.permission.RECEIVE_SMS"
/>
```

The SMS Broadcast Intent includes the incoming SMS details. To extract the array of SmsMessage objects packaged within the SMS Broadcast Intent bundle, use the pdu key to extract an array of SMS PDUs (protocol data units — used to encapsulate an SMS message and its metadata), each of which represents an SMS message, from the extras Bundle. To convert each PDU byte array into an SMS Message object, call SmsMessage.createFromPdu, passing in each byte array:

```
Bundle bundle = intent.getExtras();
if (bundle != null) {
  Object[] pdus = (Object[]) bundle.get("pdus");
  SmsMessage[] messages = new SmsMessage[pdus.length];
  for (int i = 0; i < pdus.length; i++)
    messages[i] = SmsMessage.createFromPdu((byte[]) pdus[i]);
}
```

Each SmsMessage contains the SMS message details, including the originating address (phone number), timestamp, and the message body, which can be extracted using the getOriginatingAddress, getTimestampMillis, and getMessageBody methods, respectively:

```
public class MySMSReceiver extends BroadcastReceiver {
  @Override
  public void onReceive(Context context, Intent intent) {
    Bundle bundle = intent.getExtras();
    if (bundle != null) {
      Object[] pdus = (Object[]) bundle.get("pdus");
      SmsMessage[] messages = new SmsMessage[pdus.length];
      for (int i = 0; i < pdus.length; i++)
        messages[i] = SmsMessage.createFromPdu((byte[]) pdus[i]);

      for (SmsMessage message : messages) {
        String msg = message.getMessageBody();
        long when = message.getTimestampMillis();
        String from = message.getOriginatingAddress();

        Toast.makeText(context, from + " : " + msg,
                 Toast.LENGTH_LONG).show();
      }
    }
  }
}
```

To listen for incoming messages, register your SMS Broadcast Receiver using an Intent Filter that listens for the android.provider.Telephony.SMS_RECEIVED action String. In most circumstances you'll want to register this in the application manifest to ensure your application can always respond to incoming SMS messages.

```
<receiver android:name="MySMSReceiver">
  <intent-filter>
    <action android:name="android.provider.Telephony.SMS_RECEIVED"/>
  </intent-filter>
</receiver>
```

Simulating Incoming SMS Messages in the Emulator

Two techniques are available for simulating incoming SMS messages in the emulator. The first was described previously in this section: you can send an SMS message from one emulator to another by using its port number as its phone number.

Alternatively, you can use the Android debug tools (introduced in Chapter 2, "Getting Started") to simulate incoming SMS messages from arbitrary numbers, as shown in Figure 17-1.

FIGURE 17-1

Handling Data SMS Messages

Data messages are received in the same way as normal SMS text messages, and are extracted in the same way as shown in the preceding section. To extract the data transmitted within a data SMS, use the getUserData method:

```
byte[] data = msg.getUserData();
```

The getUserData method returns a byte array of the data included in the message.

Emergency Responder SMS Example

In this example, you'll create an SMS application that turns an Android phone into an emergency response beacon.

When finished, the next time you're in an unfortunate proximity to an alien invasion or find yourself in a robot-uprising scenario, you can set your phone to automatically respond to your friends' and family members' pleas for a status update with a friendly message (or a desperate cry for help).

To make things easier for your would-be saviors, you can use location-based services to tell your rescuers exactly where to find you. The robustness of SMS network infrastructure makes SMS an excellent option for applications like this, for which reliability is critical.

1. Start by creating a new `EmergencyResponder` project that features an `EmergencyResponder` Activity:

```
package com.paad.emergencyresponder;

import java.io.IOException;
import java.util.ArrayList;
import java.util.List;
import java.util.Locale;
import java.util.concurrent.locks.ReentrantLock;

import android.app.Activity;
import android.app.PendingIntent;
import android.content.BroadcastReceiver;
import android.content.Context;
import android.content.Intent;
import android.content.IntentFilter;
import android.location.Address;
import android.location.Geocoder;
import android.location.Location;
import android.location.LocationManager;
import android.os.Bundle;
import android.telephony.SmsManager;
import android.telephony.SmsMessage;
import android.util.Log;
import android.view.View;
import android.widget.ArrayAdapter;
import android.widget.Button;
import android.widget.CheckBox;
import android.widget.ListView;

public class EmergencyResponder extends Activity {

  @Override
  public void onCreate(Bundle savedInstanceState) {
    super.onCreate(savedInstanceState);
    setContentView(R.layout.main);
  }

}
```

2. Add permissions for finding your location, and for sending and receiving incoming SMS messages to the manifest:

```xml
<?xml version="1.0" encoding="utf-8"?>
<manifest xmlns:android="http://schemas.android.com/apk/res/android"
  package="com.paad.emergencyresponder"
  android:versionCode="1"
  android:versionName="1.0" >

  <uses-permission android:name="android.permission.RECEIVE_SMS"/>
  <uses-permission android:name="android.permission.SEND_SMS"/>
  <uses-permission
    android:name="android.permission.ACCESS_FINE_LOCATION"/>

  <uses-sdk android:targetSdkVersion="15"/>

  <application
    android:icon="@drawable/ic_launcher"
    android:label="@string/app_name" >
    <activity
      android:name=".EmergencyResponder"
      android:label="@string/app_name" >
      <intent-filter>
        <action android:name="android.intent.action.MAIN" />
        <category android:name="android.intent.category.LAUNCHER" />
      </intent-filter>
    </activity>
  </application>

</manifest>
```

3. Update the `res/values/strings.xml` resource to include the text to display within the "all clear" and "mayday" buttons, as well as their associated default response messages. You should also define an incoming message text that the application will use to detect requests for a status response:

```xml
<?xml version="1.0" encoding="utf-8"?>
<resources>
  <string name="app_name">Emergency Responder</string>
  <string name="allClearButtonText">I am Safe and Well
  </string>
  <string name="maydayButtonText">MAYDAY! MAYDAY! MAYDAY!
  </string>
  <string name="setupautoresponderButtonText">Setup Auto Responder</string>
  <string name="allClearText">I am safe and well. Worry not!
  </string>
  <string name="maydayText">Tell my mother I love her.
  </string>
  <string name="querystring">are you OK?</string>
  <string name="querylistprompt">These people want to know if you\'re ok</string>
  <string name="includelocationprompt">Include Location in Reply</string>
</resources>
```

4. Modify the main.xml layout resource. Include a ListView to display the list of people requesting a status update and a series of buttons that will allow the user to send response SMS messages:

```xml
<?xml version="1.0" encoding="utf-8"?>
<RelativeLayout
  xmlns:android="http://schemas.android.com/apk/res/android"
  android:layout_width="match_parent"
  android:layout_height="match_parent">
  <TextView
    android:id="@+id/labelRequestList"
    android:layout_width="match_parent"
    android:layout_height="wrap_content"
    android:text="@string/querylistprompt"
    android:layout_alignParentTop="true"
  />
  <LinearLayout
    android:id="@+id/buttonLayout"
    android:orientation="vertical"
    android:layout_width="match_parent"
    android:layout_height="wrap_content"
    android:padding="5dp"
    android:layout_alignParentBottom="true">
    <CheckBox
      android:id="@+id/checkboxSendLocation"
      android:layout_width="match_parent"
      android:layout_height="wrap_content"
      android:text="@string/includelocationprompt"/>
    <Button
      android:id="@+id/okButton"
      android:layout_width="match_parent"
      android:layout_height="wrap_content"
      android:text="@string/allClearButtonText"/>
    <Button
      android:id="@+id/notOkButton"
      android:layout_width="match_parent"
      android:layout_height="wrap_content"
      android:text="@string/maydayButtonText"/>
    <Button
      android:id="@+id/autoResponder"
      android:layout_width="match_parent"
      android:layout_height="wrap_content"
      android:text="@string/setupautoresponderButtonText"/>
  </LinearLayout>
  <ListView
    android:id="@+id/myListView"
    android:layout_width="match_parent"
    android:layout_height="match_parent"
    android:layout_below="@id/labelRequestList"
    android:layout_above="@id/buttonLayout"/>
</RelativeLayout>
```

At this point, the GUI will be complete, so starting the application should show you the screen in Figure 17-2.

FIGURE 17-2

5. Now create a new Array List of Strings within the `EmergencyResponder` Activity to store the phone numbers of the incoming requests for your status. Bind the Array List to the List View using an Array Adapter in the Activity's `onCreate` method, and create a new `ReentrantLock` object to ensure thread-safe handling of the Array List. Take this opportunity to get a reference to the check box and to add Click Listeners for each response button. Each button should call the `respond` method, whereas the Setup Auto Responder button should call the `startAutoResponder` stub.

```java
ReentrantLock lock;
CheckBox locationCheckBox;
ArrayList<String> requesters;
ArrayAdapter<String> aa;

@Override
public void onCreate(Bundle savedInstanceState) {
  super.onCreate(savedInstanceState);
  setContentView(R.layout.main);

  lock = new ReentrantLock();
  requesters = new ArrayList<String>();
  wireUpControls();
}

private void wireUpControls() {
  locationCheckBox = (CheckBox)findViewById(R.id.checkboxSendLocation);
  ListView myListView = (ListView)findViewById(R.id.myListView);
```

```
    int layoutID = android.R.layout.simple_list_item_1;
    aa = new ArrayAdapter<String>(this, layoutID, requesters);
    myListView.setAdapter(aa);

    Button okButton = (Button)findViewById(R.id.okButton);
    okButton.setOnClickListener(new View.OnClickListener() {
      public void onClick(View view) {
        respond(true, locationCheckBox.isChecked());
      }
    });

    Button notOkButton = (Button)findViewById(R.id.notOkButton);
    notOkButton.setOnClickListener(new View.OnClickListener() {
      public void onClick(View view) {
        respond(false, locationCheckBox.isChecked());
      }
    });

    Button autoResponderButton =
      (Button)findViewById(R.id.autoResponder);
    autoResponderButton.setOnClickListener(new View.OnClickListener() {
      public void onClick(View view) {
        startAutoResponder();
      }
    });
  }

  public void respond(boolean ok, boolean includeLocation) {}

  private void startAutoResponder() {}
```

6. Create a Broadcast Receiver that will listen for incoming SMS messages. Start by creating a new static string variable to store the incoming SMS message intent action, and then create a new Broadcast Receiver as a variable in the EmergencyResponder Activity. The receiver should listen for incoming SMS messages and call the requestReceived method when it sees SMS messages containing the @string/querystring resource you defined in step 4.

```
public static final String SMS_RECEIVED =
  "android.provider.Telephony.SMS_RECEIVED";

BroadcastReceiver emergencyResponseRequestReceiver =
  new BroadcastReceiver() {
    @Override
    public void onReceive(Context context, Intent intent) {
      if (intent.getAction().equals(SMS_RECEIVED)) {
        String queryString = getString(R.string.querystring).toLowerCase();

        Bundle bundle = intent.getExtras();
        if (bundle != null) {
          Object[] pdus = (Object[]) bundle.get("pdus");
          SmsMessage[] messages = new SmsMessage[pdus.length];
          for (int i = 0; i < pdus.length; i++)
            messages[i] =
              SmsMessage.createFromPdu((byte[]) pdus[i]);
```

```
              for (SmsMessage message : messages) {
                if (message.getMessageBody().toLowerCase().contains
                  (queryString))
                  requestReceived(message.getOriginatingAddress());
              }
            }
          }
        }
      };

  public void requestReceived(String from) {}
```

7. Override the `onResume` and `onPause` methods to register and unregister the Broadcast Receiver created in step 6 when the Activity resumes and pauses, respectively:

```
@Override
public void onResume() {
  super.onResume();
  IntentFilter filter = new IntentFilter(SMS_RECEIVED);
  registerReceiver(emergencyResponseRequestReceiver, filter);
}

@Override
public void onPause() {
  super.onPause();
  unregisterReceiver(emergencyResponseRequestReceiver);
}
```

8. Update the `requestReceived` method stub so that it adds the originating number of each status request's SMS to the "requesters" Array List:

```
public void requestReceived(String from) {
  if (!requesters.contains(from)) {
    lock.lock();
    requesters.add(from);
    aa.notifyDataSetChanged();
    lock.unlock();
  }
}
```

9. The Emergency Responder Activity should now be listening for status request SMS messages and adding them to the List View as they arrive. Start the application and send SMS messages to the device or emulator on which it's running. When they've arrived, they should be displayed as shown in Figure 17-3.

10. Update the Activity to let users respond to these status requests. Start by completing the `respond` method stub you created in step 5. It should iterate over the Array List of status requesters and send a new SMS message to each. The SMS message text should be based on the response strings you defined as resources in step 4. Fire the SMS using an overloaded `respond` method (which you'll complete in the next step):

```
public void respond(boolean ok, boolean includeLocation) {
  String okString = getString(R.string.allClearText);
```

```
    String notOkString = getString(R.string.maydayText);
    String outString = ok ? okString : notOkString;

    ArrayList<String> requestersCopy =
      (ArrayList<String>)requesters.clone();

    for (String to : requestersCopy)
      respond(to, outString, includeLocation);
}

private void respond(String to, String response,
                     boolean includeLocation) {}
```

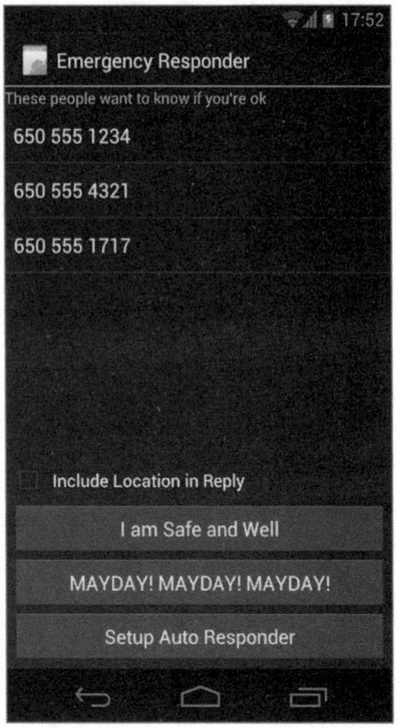

FIGURE 17-3

11. Complete the `respond` method to handle sending of each response SMS. Start by removing each potential recipient from the "requesters" Array List before sending the SMS. If you are responding with your current location, use the Location Manager to find it before sending a second SMS with your current position as both a raw longitude/latitude and a geocoded address:

```
public void respond(String to, String response,
                    boolean includeLocation) {
  // Remove the target from the list of people we
  // need to respond to.
  lock.lock();
  requesters.remove(to);
  aa.notifyDataSetChanged();
```

```
      lock.unlock();

      SmsManager sms = SmsManager.getDefault();

      // Send the message
      sms.sendTextMessage(to, null, response, null, null);

      StringBuilder sb = new StringBuilder();

      // Find the current location and send it
      // as SMS messages if required.
      if (includeLocation) {
        String ls = Context.LOCATION_SERVICE;
        LocationManager lm = (LocationManager)getSystemService(ls);
        Location l =
          lm.getLastKnownLocation(LocationManager.GPS_PROVIDER);

        if (l == null)
          sb.append("Location unknown.");
        else {
          sb.append("I'm @:\n");
          sb.append(l.toString() + "\n");

          List<Address> addresses;
          Geocoder g = new Geocoder(getApplicationContext(),
                                    Locale.getDefault());
          try {
            addresses = g.getFromLocation(l.getLatitude(),
                                          l.getLongitude(), 1);
            if (addresses != null) {
              Address currentAddress = addresses.get(0);
              if (currentAddress.getMaxAddressLineIndex() > 0) {
                for (int i = 0;
                     i < currentAddress.getMaxAddressLineIndex();
                     i++) {
                  sb.append(currentAddress.getAddressLine(i));
                  sb.append("\n");
                }
              }
              else {
                if (currentAddress.getPostalCode() != null)
                  sb.append(currentAddress.getPostalCode());
              }
            }
          } catch (IOException e) {
            Log.e("SMS_RESPONDER", "IO Exception.", e);
          }

          ArrayList<String> locationMsgs =
            sms.divideMessage(sb.toString());
          for (String locationMsg : locationMsgs)
            sms.sendTextMessage(to, null, locationMsg, null, null);
        }
      }
    }
```

12. In emergencies it's important that messages get through. Improve the robustness of the application by including auto-retry functionality. Monitor the success of your SMS transmissions so that you can rebroadcast a message if it doesn't successfully send.

12.1 Start by creating a new public static String in the Emergency Responder Activity to be used within Broadcast Intents to indicate the SMS has been sent.

```
public static final String SENT_SMS =
  "com.paad.emergencyresponder.SMS_SENT";
```

12.2 Update the `respond` method to include a new `PendingIntent` that broadcasts the action created in the previous step when the SMS transmission has completed. The packaged Intent should include the intended recipient's number as an extra.

```
Intent intent = new Intent(SENT_SMS);
  intent.putExtra("recipient", to);

  PendingIntent sentPI =
    PendingIntent.getBroadcast(getApplicationContext(),
                             0, intent, 0);

  // Send the message
  sms.sendTextMessage(to, null, response, sentPI, null);
```

12.3 Implement a new Broadcast Receiver to listen for this Broadcast Intent. Override its `onReceive` handler to confirm that the SMS was successfully delivered; if it wasn't, put the intended recipient back onto the requester Array List.

```
private BroadcastReceiver attemptedDeliveryReceiver = new
BroadcastReceiver() {
  @Override
  public void onReceive(Context _context, Intent _intent) {
    if (_intent.getAction().equals(SENT_SMS)) {
      if (getResultCode() != Activity.RESULT_OK) {
        String recipient = _intent.getStringExtra("recipient");
        requestReceived(recipient);
      }
    }
  }
};
```

12.4 Finally, register and unregister the new Broadcast Receiver by extending the `onResume` and `onPause` handlers of the Emergency Responder Activity:

```
@Override
public void onResume() {
  super.onResume();
  IntentFilter filter = new IntentFilter(SMS_RECEIVED);
  registerReceiver(emergencyResponseRequestReceiver, filter);

  IntentFilter attemptedDeliveryfilter = new IntentFilter(SENT_SMS);
  registerReceiver(attemptedDeliveryReceiver,
                attemptedDeliveryfilter);
}
```

```
@Override
public void onPause() {
  super.onPause();
  unregisterReceiver(emergencyResponseRequestReceiver);

  unregisterReceiver(attemptedDeliveryReceiver);
}
```

All code snippets in this example are part of the Chapter 12 Emergency Responder Part 1 *project, available for download at* www.wrox.com.

This example has been simplified to focus on the SMS-based functionality it is attempting to demonstrate. Keen-eyed observers should have noticed at least three areas where it could be improved:

➤ The Broadcast Receiver created and registered in steps 6 and 7 would be better registered within the manifest to allow the application to respond to incoming SMS messages even when it isn't running.

➤ The parsing of the incoming SMS messages performed by the Broadcast Receiver in steps 6 and 8 should be moved into a Service and executed on a background thread. Similarly, step 12, sending the response SMS messages, would be better executed on a background thread within a Service.

➤ The UI should be implemented using Fragments within Activities, with the UI optimized for tablet and smartphone layouts.

The implementation of these improvements is left as an exercise for the reader.

Automating the Emergency Responder

In the following example, you'll fill in the code behind the Setup Auto Responder button added in the previous example, to let the Emergency Responder automatically respond to status update requests.

1. Start by updating the application's `string.xml` resource to define a name for the `SharedPreferences` to use to save the user's auto-response preferences, and strings to use for each of its Views:

```xml
<?xml version="1.0" encoding="utf-8"?>
<resources>
  <string name="app_name">Emergency Responder</string>
  <string name="allClearButtonText">I am Safe and Well
  </string>
  <string name="maydayButtonText">MAYDAY! MAYDAY! MAYDAY!
  </string>
  <string name="setupautoresponderButtonText">Setup Auto Responder</string>
  <string name="allClearText">I am safe and well. Worry not!
  </string>
  <string name="maydayText">Tell my mother I love her.
```

```
    </string>
    <string name="querystring">are you OK?</string>
    <string name="querylistprompt">These people want to know if you\'re ok</string>
    <string name="includelocationprompt">Include Location in Reply</string>

    <string
      name="user_preferences">com.paad.emergencyresponder.preferences
    </string>
    <string name="respondWithPrompt">Respond with</string>
    <string name="transmitLocationPrompt">Transmit location</string>
    <string name="autoRespondDurationPrompt">Auto-respond for</string>
    <string name="enableButtonText">Enable</string>
    <string name="disableButtonText">Disable</string>
  </resources>
```

2. Create a new `autoresponder.xml` layout resource that will be used to lay out the automatic response configuration window. Include an `EditText` `View` for entering a status message to send, a `Spinner` View for choosing the auto-response expiry time, and a `CheckBox` View to let users decide whether they want to include their location in the automated responses:

```xml
<?xml version="1.0" encoding="utf-8"?>
<LinearLayout
  xmlns:android="http://schemas.android.com/apk/res/android"
  android:orientation="vertical"
  android:layout_width="fill_parent"
  android:layout_height="fill_parent">
  <TextView
    android:layout_width="fill_parent"
    android:layout_height="wrap_content"
    android:text="@string/respondWithPrompt"/>
  <EditText
    android:id="@+id/responseText"
    android:layout_width="fill_parent"
    android:layout_height="wrap_content"
    android:hint="@string/respondWithPrompt"/>
  <CheckBox
    android:id="@+id/checkboxLocation"
    android:layout_width="fill_parent"
    android:layout_height="wrap_content"
    android:text="@string/includelocationprompt"/>
  <TextView
    android:layout_width="fill_parent"
    android:layout_height="wrap_content"
    android:text="@string/autoRespondDurationPrompt"/>
  <Spinner
    android:id="@+id/spinnerRespondFor"
    android:layout_width="fill_parent"
    android:layout_height="wrap_content"
    android:drawSelectorOnTop="true"/>
  <LinearLayout
    xmlns:android="http://schemas.android.com/apk/res/android"
    android:orientation="horizontal"
    android:layout_width="fill_parent"
```

```
        android:layout_height="wrap_content">
        <Button
          android:id="@+id/okButton"
          android:layout_width="wrap_content"
          android:layout_height="wrap_content"
          android:text="@string/enableButtonText"/>
        <Button
          android:id="@+id/cancelButton"
          android:layout_width="wrap_content"
          android:layout_height="wrap_content"
          android:text="@string/disableButtonText"/>
      </LinearLayout>
    </LinearLayout>
```

3. Create a new `res/values/arrays.xml` resource, and create arrays to use for populating the Spinner:

```xml
<?xml version="1.0" encoding="utf-8"?>
<resources>
  <string-array name="respondForDisplayItems">
    <item>- Disabled -</item>
    <item>Next 5 minutes</item>
    <item>Next 15 minutes</item>
    <item>Next 30 minutes</item>
    <item>Next hour</item>
    <item>Next 2 hours</item>
    <item>Next 8 hours</item>
  </string-array>

  <array name="respondForValues">
    <item>0</item>
    <item>5</item>
    <item>15</item>
    <item>30</item>
    <item>60</item>
    <item>120</item>
    <item>480</item>
  </array>
</resources>
```

4. Create a new `AutoResponder` Activity, populating it with the layout you created in step 1:

```java
package com.paad.emergencyresponder;

import android.app.Activity;
import android.app.AlarmManager;
import android.app.PendingIntent;
import android.content.res.Resources;
import android.content.Context;
import android.content.Intent;
import android.content.IntentFilter;
import android.content.BroadcastReceiver;
import android.content.SharedPreferences;
import android.content.SharedPreferences.Editor;
import android.os.Bundle;
```

```
import android.view.View;
import android.widget.ArrayAdapter;
import android.widget.Button;
import android.widget.CheckBox;
import android.widget.EditText;
import android.widget.Spinner;

public class AutoResponder extends Activity {
  @Override
  public void onCreate(Bundle savedInstanceState) {
      super.onCreate(savedInstanceState);
      setContentView(R.layout.autoresponder);
  }
}
```

5. Update the onCreate method to get references to each of the controls in the layout and wire up the Spinner using the arrays defined in step 3. Create two new stub methods, save Preferences and updateUIFromPreferences, that will be updated to save the auto-responder settings to a named SharedPreferences and apply the saved SharedPreferences to the current UI, respectively.

```
Spinner respondForSpinner;
CheckBox locationCheckbox;
EditText responseTextBox;

@Override
public void onCreate(Bundle savedInstanceState) {
  super.onCreate(savedInstanceState);
  setContentView(R.layout.autoresponder);

  respondForSpinner = (Spinner)findViewById(R.id.spinnerRespondFor);
  locationCheckbox = (CheckBox)findViewById(R.id.checkboxLocation);
  responseTextBox = (EditText)findViewById(R.id.responseText);

  ArrayAdapter<CharSequence> adapter =
    ArrayAdapter.createFromResource(this,
      R.array.respondForDisplayItems,
      android.R.layout.simple_spinner_item);

  adapter.setDropDownViewResource(
    android.R.layout.simple_spinner_dropdown_item);
  respondForSpinner.setAdapter(adapter);

  Button okButton = (Button) findViewById(R.id.okButton);
  okButton.setOnClickListener(new View.OnClickListener() {
    public void onClick(View view) {
      savePreferences();
      setResult(RESULT_OK, null);
      finish();
    }
  });

  Button cancelButton = (Button) findViewById(R.id.cancelButton);
  cancelButton.setOnClickListener(new View.OnClickListener() {
```

```
    public void onClick(View view) {
      respondForSpinner.setSelection(-1);
      savePreferences();
      setResult(RESULT_CANCELED, null);
      finish();
    }
  });

  // Load the saved preferences and update the UI
  updateUIFromPreferences();
}

private void updateUIFromPreferences() {}
private void savePreferences() {}
```

6. Complete the two stub methods from step 5. Start with `updateUIFromPreferences`; it should read the current saved `AutoResponder` preferences and apply them to the UI:

```
public static final String autoResponsePref = "autoResponsePref";
public static final String responseTextPref = "responseTextPref";
public static final String includeLocPref = "includeLocPref";
public static final String respondForPref = "respondForPref";
public static final String defaultResponseText = "All clear";

private void updateUIFromPreferences() {
  // Get the saves settings
  String preferenceName = getString(R.string.user_preferences);
  SharedPreferences sp = getSharedPreferences(preferenceName, 0);

  boolean autoRespond = sp.getBoolean(autoResponsePref, false);
  String respondText = sp.getString(responseTextPref, defaultResponseText);
  boolean includeLoc = sp.getBoolean(includeLocPref, false);
  int respondForIndex = sp.getInt(respondForPref, 0);

  // Apply the saved settings to the UI
  if (autoRespond)
    respondForSpinner.setSelection(respondForIndex);
  else
    respondForSpinner.setSelection(0);

  locationCheckbox.setChecked(includeLoc);
  responseTextBox.setText(respondText);
}
```

7. Complete the `savePreferences` stub to save the current UI settings to a Shared Preferences file:

```
private void savePreferences() {
  // Get the current settings from the UI
  boolean autoRespond =
    respondForSpinner.getSelectedItemPosition() > 0;
  int respondForIndex = respondForSpinner.getSelectedItemPosition();
  boolean includeLoc = locationCheckbox.isChecked();
  String respondText = responseTextBox.getText().toString();

  // Save them to the Shared Preference file
```

```
      String preferenceName = getString(R.string.user_preferences);
      SharedPreferences sp = getSharedPreferences(preferenceName, 0);

      Editor editor = sp.edit();
      editor.putBoolean(autoResponsePref,
                        autoRespond);
      editor.putString(responseTextPref,
                       respondText);
      editor.putBoolean(includeLocPref,
                        includeLoc);
      editor.putInt(respondForPref, respondForIndex);
      editor.commit();

      // Set the alarm to turn off the autoresponder
      setAlarm(respondForIndex);
    }

    private void setAlarm(int respondForIndex) {}
```

8. The `setAlarm` stub from step 7 is used to create a new Alarm that fires an Intent when the auto responder expires, which should result in the auto responder being disabled. You'll need to create a new `Alarm` object and a `BroadcastReceiver` that listens for it before disabling the auto responder accordingly.

    8.1 Start by creating the action String that will represent the Alarm Intent:

    ```
    public static final String alarmAction =
      "com.paad.emergencyresponder.AUTO_RESPONSE_EXPIRED";
    ```

    8.2 Create a new Broadcast Receiver instance that listens for an Intent that includes the action specified in step 8.1. When this Intent is received, it should modify the auto-responder settings to disable the automatic response.

    ```
    private BroadcastReceiver stopAutoResponderReceiver
      = new BroadcastReceiver() {
      @Override
      public void onReceive(Context context, Intent intent) {
        if (intent.getAction().equals(alarmAction)) {
          String preferenceName = getString(R.string.user_preferences);
          SharedPreferences sp = getSharedPreferences(preferenceName, 0);

          Editor editor = sp.edit();
          editor.putBoolean(autoResponsePref, false);
          editor.commit();
        }
      }
    };
    ```

    8.3 Then complete the `setAlarm` method. It should cancel the existing alarm if the auto responder is turned off; otherwise, it should update the alarm with the latest expiry time.

    ```
    PendingIntent intentToFire;

    private void setAlarm(int respondForIndex) {
    ```

```
              // Create the alarm and register the alarm intent receiver.

              AlarmManager alarms =
                (AlarmManager)getSystemService(ALARM_SERVICE);

              if (intentToFire == null) {
                Intent intent = new Intent(alarmAction);
                intentToFire =
                  PendingIntent.getBroadcast(getApplicationContext(),
                                             0,intent,0);

                IntentFilter filter = new IntentFilter(alarmAction);

                registerReceiver(stopAutoResponderReceiver, filter);
              }

              if (respondForIndex < 1)
                // If "disabled" is selected, cancel the alarm.
                alarms.cancel(intentToFire);

              else {
                // Otherwise find the length of time represented
                // by the selection and set the alarm to
                // trigger after that time has passed.
                Resources r = getResources();
                int[] respondForValues =
                  r.getIntArray(R.array.respondForValues);
                int respondFor = respondForValues [respondForIndex];

                long t = System.currentTimeMillis();
                t = t + respondFor*1000*60;

                // Set the alarm.
                alarms.set(AlarmManager.RTC_WAKEUP, t, intentToFire);
              }
            }
```

9. That completes the AutoResponder. Before you can use it, however, you need to add it to your application manifest:

```
<?xml version="1.0" encoding="utf-8"?>
<manifest xmlns:android="http://schemas.android.com/apk/res/android"
  package="com.paad.emergencyresponder"
  android:versionCode="1"
  android:versionName="1.0" >

  <uses-permission android:name="android.permission.RECEIVE_SMS"/>
  <uses-permission android:name="android.permission.SEND_SMS"/>
  <uses-permission
    android:name="android.permission.ACCESS_FINE_LOCATION"/>

  <uses-sdk android:targetSdkVersion="15"/>

  <application
```

```
                android:icon="@drawable/ic_launcher"
                android:label="@string/app_name" >
                <activity
                  android:name=".EmergencyResponder"
                  android:label="@string/app_name" >
                  <intent-filter>
                    <action android:name="android.intent.action.MAIN" />
                    <category android:name="android.intent.category.LAUNCHER" />
                  </intent-filter>
                </activity>
                <activity
                  android:name=".AutoResponder"
                  android:label="Auto Responder Setup"
                />
            </application>

        </manifest>
```

10. To enable the auto-responder, return to the Emergency Responder Activity and update the `startAutoResponder` method stub that you created in the previous example. It should open the `AutoResponder` Activity you just created.

```
private void startAutoResponder() {
  startActivityForResult(new Intent(EmergencyResponder.this,
                                    AutoResponder.class), 0);
}
```

11. If you start your project, you should now be able to bring up the Auto Responder Setup window to set the auto-response settings (see Figure 17-4).

FIGURE 17-4

12. The final step is to update the `requestReceived` method in the Emergency Responder Activity to check if the auto-responder has been enabled.

If it has, the `requestReceived` method should automatically execute the `respond` method, using the message and location settings defined in the application's Shared Preferences:

```
public void requestReceived(String from) {
  if (!requesters.contains(from)) {
    lock.lock();
```

```
        lock.unlock();

        // Check for auto-responder
        String preferenceName = getString(R.string.user_preferences);
        SharedPreferences prefs
          = getSharedPreferences(preferenceName, 0);

        boolean autoRespond = prefs.getBoolean(AutoResponder.autoResponsePref, false);

        if (autoRespond) {
          String respondText = prefs.getString(AutoResponder.responseTextPref,
                                         AutoResponder.defaultResponseText);
          boolean includeLoc = prefs.getBoolean(AutoResponder.includeLocPref, false);

          respond(from, respondText, includeLoc);
        }
      }
    }
  }
```

> *All code snippets in this example are part of the* Chapter 12 Emergency
> Responder Part 2 *project, available for download at* www.wrox.com.

You should now have a fully functional interactive and automated emergency responder.

INTRODUCING SIP AND VOIP

Session Initiation Protocol (SIP) is a signaling protocol used for managing communication sessions over IP connections — typically, voice (VOIP) and video calls.

SIP APIs were introduced in Android 2.3 (API level 9), allowing you to include Internet-based telephony features in your applications without needing to manage the underling client-side media and communications stack.

Android 4.0 (API level 14) introduced the capability for applications to add voice mail entries from their underlying services to the system. If you are planning to build your own SIP client, these new voice mail APIs provide a method for integrating messages left by callers seamlessly into the device's voice mail.

> *The instructions for building your own SIP client are beyond the scope of this
> book. You can find a detailed introduction to creating SIP clients — including
> a full working example — at the Android Developer site:* http://developer
> .android.com/guide/topics/network/sip.html.

18

Advanced Android Development

WHAT'S IN THIS CHAPTER?

➤ Securing Android using permissions

➤ Sending server pushes with Cloud to Device Messaging

➤ Adding copy protection with the License Verification Library

➤ Monetizing with In-App Billing

➤ Using Wake Locks

➤ Inter-process communication (IPC) using AIDL and Parcelables

➤ Improving application performance using Strict Mode

➤ Ensuring backward and forward hardware and software compatibility

This chapter both returns to some of the possibilities touched on in previous chapters and introduces some of the more advanced options available for Android developers.

The chapter starts by taking a closer look at security — in particular, how permissions work and how to use them to secure your own applications and the data they contain.

Next, you'll be introduced to Android's Cloud to Device Messaging (C2DM) service and learn how to use it to eliminate polling within your application, replacing it with server-initiated pushes.

You'll also be introduced to the License Verification Library (LVL) and In-App Billing services. These services enable you to protect your applications from piracy and monetize them by selling virtual content.

The chapter then examines Wake Locks and the Android Interface Definition Language (AIDL). You'll use AIDL to create rich application interfaces that support full object-based inter-process communication (IPC) between Android applications running in different processes.

Finally, you'll learn how to build applications that are backward and forward compatible across a range of hardware and software platforms, and then investigate the use of Strict Mode for discovering inefficiencies within your applications.

PARANOID ANDROID

Much of Android's security is supplied by its underlying Linux kernel. Application files and resources are sandboxed to their owners, making them inaccessible by other applications. Android uses Intents, Services, and Content Providers to let you relax these strict process boundaries, using permissions to maintain application-level security.

You've already used the permission system to request access to native system services — including location-based services, native Content Providers, and the camera — using `uses-permission` manifest tags.

The following sections provide a more detailed look at the Linux security model and the Android permission system. For a comprehensive view, the Android documentation provides an excellent resource that describes the security features in depth: `developer.android.com/guide/topics/security/security.html`.

Linux Kernel Security

Each Android package has a unique Linux user ID assigned to it during installation. This has the effect of sandboxing the process and the resources it creates, so that it can't affect (or be affected by) other applications.

Because of this kernel-level security, you need to take additional steps to communicate between applications, or access the files and resources they contain. Content Providers, Intents, Services, and AIDL interfaces are designed to open tunnels through which information can flow between applications. To ensure information doesn't "leak" beyond the intended recipients, you can use Android permissions to act as border guards at either end to control the traffic flow.

Introducing Permissions

Permissions are an application-level security mechanism that lets you restrict access to application components. Permissions are used to prevent malicious applications from corrupting data, gaining access to sensitive information, or making excessive (or unauthorized) use of hardware resources or external communication channels.

As you learned in earlier chapters, many of Android's native components have permission requirements. The native permission strings used by native Android Activities and Services can be found as static constants in the `android.Manifest.permission` class.

To use permission-protected components, you need to add `uses-permission` tags to your application manifests, specifying the permission strings your application requires.

When a package is installed, the permissions requested in its manifest are analyzed and granted (or denied) by checks with trusted authorities and user feedback. All Android permission checks are done at installation. Once an application is installed, users will not be prompted to reevaluate those permissions.

Declaring and Enforcing Permissions

Before you can assign a permission to an application component, you need to define it within your manifest using the `permission` tag, as shown in the Listing 18-1.

LISTING 18-1: Declaring a new permission

```
<permission
    android:name="com.paad.DETONATE_DEVICE"
    android:protectionLevel="dangerous"
    android:label="Self Destruct"
    android:description="@string/detonate_description">
</permission>
```

code snippet PA4AD_Ch18_Permissions/AndroidManifest.xml

Within the `permission` tag, you can specify the level of access that the permission will permit (`normal`, `dangerous`, `signature`, `signatureOrSystem`), a label, and an external resource containing the description that explains the risks of granting this permission.

To define custom permissions for components within your application, use the `permission` attribute in the manifest. Permission constraints can be enforced throughout your application, most usefully at application interface boundaries — for example:

➤ **Activities** — Add a permission to limit the ability of other applications to launch a particular Activity.

➤ **Broadcast Receivers** — Add a permission to control which applications can send Broadcast Intents to your Receiver.

➤ **Intents** — Add a permission to control which Broadcast Receivers can receive a Broadcast Intent.

➤ **Content Providers** — Add a permission to limit read access and/or write operations on your Content Providers.

➤ **Services** — Add a permission to limit the ability of other applications to start or bind to a Service.

In each case, you can add a `permission` attribute to the application component in the manifest, specifying a required permission string to access each component. Listing 18-2 shows a manifest excerpt that requires the permission defined in Listing 18-1 to start an Activity, Service, and Broadcast Receiver.

LISTING 18-2: Enforcing a permission requirements

```
<activity
  android:name=".MyActivity"
  android:label="@string/app_name"
  android:permission="com.paad.DETONATE_DEVICE">
</activity>

<service
  android:name=".MyService"
  android:permission="com.paad.DETONATE_DEVICE">
</service>

<receiver
  android:name=".MyReceiver"
  android:permission="com.paad.DETONATE_DEVICE">
  <intent-filter>
    <action android:name="com.paad.ACTION_DETONATE_DEVICE"/>
  </intent-filter>
</receiver>
```

code snippet PA4AD_Ch18_Permissions/AndroidManifest.xml

Content Providers let you set `readPermission` and `writePermission` attributes to offer a more granular control over read/write access:

```
<provider
  android:name=".HitListProvider"
  android:authorities="com.paad.hitlistprovider"
  android:writePermission="com.paad.ASSIGN_KILLER"
  android:readPermission="com.paad.LICENSED_TO_KILL"
/>
```

Enforcing Permissions when Broadcasting Intents

In addition to requiring permissions for Intents to be received by your Broadcast Receivers, you can attach a permission requirement to each Intent you broadcast. This is good practice when broadcasting Intents that contain sensitive information, such as location updates that should only be used within your application.

In such cases it's best practice to require a `signature` permission to ensure that only applications signed with the same signature as the host application can receive the broadcast:

```
<permission
  android:name="com.paad.LOCATION_DATA"
  android:protectionLevel="signature"
  android:label="Location Transfer"
  android:description="@string/location_data_description">
</permission>
```

When calling `sendIntent`, you can supply the permission string required for a Broadcast Receivers to receive the Intent.

```
sendBroadcast(myIntent, "com.paad.LOCATION_DATA");
```

INTRODUCING CLOUD TO DEVICE MESSAGING

The Cloud to Device Messaging (C2DM) service provides an alternative to regularly polling a server for updates; instead, your server can "push" messages to a specific client.

The frequency of your application's background polling can have a dramatic impact on the host device's battery life, so you always need to compromise between data freshness and the resulting power drain.

Introduced in Android 2.2 (API level 8), C2DM allows you to eliminate background polling, and instead have your server notify a particular device when new data is available for it.

On the client side, C2DM is implemented using Intents and Broadcast Receivers. As a result, your application does not need to be active in order to receive C2DM messages. On the server side, C2DM messages area transmitted from your server to each target device by way of the C2DM service.

The C2DM service maintains an open TCP/IP connection with each device, allowing it to transmit information instantly whenever required. The C2DM service takes care of maintaining and restoring that connection, queuing messages, and retrying failed deliveries.

In the following sections you'll learn how to:

➤   Register each device on which your application is running with the Android C2DM server.

➤   Notify your server of the C2DM address of your application running on a particular device.

➤   Transmit messages from your server to the C2DM service.

➤   Receive your server messages within your application once they're relayed through the C2DM service.

> *C2DM is a Google service, so its documentation is available at* `http://code.google.com/android/c2dm/`.

C2DM Restrictions

C2DM is not designed as a blanket replacement for background polling. It is best used in situations where only one device (or a small, distinct group of devices) requires updates at any given time — such as email or voicemail services.

The real-time nature of each push makes C2DM an ideal alternative for situations where the updates are unlikely to be at predictable intervals; however, successful message delivery, latency, and delivery order are not guaranteed. As a result, you should not rely on C2DM for critical messages or where timeliness is important. It's also good practice to implement a traditional polling mechanism at long intervals as a fail-safe.

The transmitted messages should be lightweight and are limited to 1024 bytes. They should carry very little payload, instead containing only the information required for the client application to efficiently query your server for the data directly.

C2DM is based around existing Google services and requires Google Play to be installed on the device, and for the user to have a Google account configured.

At the time of writing, new C2DM accounts receive a development quota of up to 200,000 messages per day. If your production requirements demand more, you can request an increase — details on that process will be emailed to you after you sign up.

Signing Up to Use C2DM

The first step is to view and agree to the terms of the C2DM service at `http://code.google.com/android/c2dm/signup.html`.

As part of the registration process, you will be asked for your application's package name, an estimate of the total number of daily messages you plan to send, and the estimated peak queries per second (QPS). The C2DM team uses this information to help identify applications that may need to be granted larger quotas.

You will also be asked to supply three email addresses: your contact details, an escalation email address for urgent issues, and a role account that will be used to authenticate with the C2DM service and send messages from your server.

The role account should be a Google account used specifically for use with the C2DM service. Because you will be providing a server with authentication details for this account, it's good practice to create a new account rather than use a personal Gmail or Google Play account.

After receiving confirmation that your account has been enabled for sending C2DM messages, you can update your application to register itself, and each device it's running on, with the C2DM service.

Registering Devices with a C2DM Server

In order for your application to receive C2DM messages, it must first register each installed instance of itself with the C2DM service. Start by adding a `com.google.android.c2dm.permission.RECEIVE` uses-permission node to your manifest:

```
<uses-permission android:name="com.google.android.c2dm.permission.RECEIVE" />
```

You should also define (and request) a signature-level permission that restricts the receipt of C2DM messages targeted at your application to applications signed with the same key:

```
<permission android:name="com.example.myapp.permission.C2D_MESSAGE"
            android:protectionLevel="signature" />

<uses-permission android:name="com.example.myapp.permission.C2D_MESSAGE" />
```

Registering an application for C2DM is a three-step process, as shown in Figure 18-1.

The process of registering your application on each device with the C2DM service associates each installed instance of your application with the device on which it is installed. Once registered, the C2DM service returns a registration ID that uniquely identifies that particular installation. Your application should send that ID, along with a way to identify each installation (typically a username or anonymous UUID) to your server.

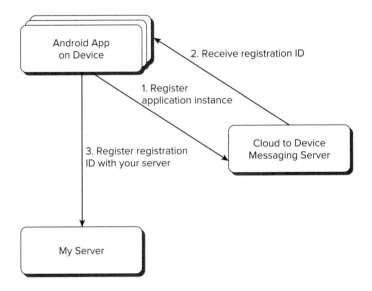

FIGURE 18-1

Begin by starting a Service using an Intent that includes the `com.google.android.c2dm.intent` `.REGISTER` action. It must include extras to identify your application and specify your sender account, as shown in Listing 18-3.

LISTING 18-3: Registering an application instance with the C2DM server

```
Intent registrationIntent =
    new Intent("com.google.android.c2dm.intent.REGISTER");

registrationIntent.putExtra("app",
    PendingIntent.getBroadcast(this, 0, new Intent(), 0));

registrationIntent.putExtra("sender",
                            "myC2DMaccount@gmail.com");

startService(registrationIntent);
```

code snippet PA4AD_Ch18_C2DM/src/MyActivity.java

Your application is identified using the `app` extra key and a Pending Broadcast Intent that will be populated by the C2DM service to send your application messages when they are received.

The `sender` extra is used to specify the role account you registered when signing up for C2DM, and will be used by your server to transmit messages.

The platform will transmit this information to the C2DM server, which will return a registration ID. To receive this, you need to register a Broadcast Receiver that listens for the `com.google.android.` `c2dm.intent.REGISTRATION` action, requires the `com.google.android.c2dm.permission.SEND` permission, and includes your application package name as a category, as shown in Listing 18-4.

LISTING 18-4: Listening for C2DM registration IDs

```xml
<receiver
    android:name=".MyC2DMReceiver"
    android:permission="com.google.android.c2dm.permission.SEND">

    <intent-filter>
      <action
        android:name="com.google.android.c2dm.intent.REGISTRATION"
      />
      <category android:name="com.mypackage.myc2dmAppName"/>
    </intent-filter>
</receiver>
```

code snippet PA4AD_Ch18_C2DM/AndroidManifest.xml

The registration ID for each application/device pair may be changed at any time, so it's important that your application continue listening for new REGISTRATION Broadcast Intents.

The registration ID itself is included in the registration_id extra, as shown in Listing 18-5. If the registration process fails, the error code will be included as an error extra, and successful deregistration requests will be signaled using the unregistered extra.

LISTING 18-5: Extracting the C2DM registration ID

```java
public void onReceive(Context context, Intent intent) {
  if (intent.getAction().equals(
    "com.google.android.c2dm.intent.REGISTRATION")) {

    String registrationId = intent.getStringExtra("registration_id");
    String error = intent.getStringExtra("error");
    String unregistered = intent.getStringExtra("unregistered");

    if (error != null) {
      // Registration failed.
      if (error.equals("SERVICE_NOT_AVAILABLE")) {
        Log.e(TAG, "Service not available.");
        // Retry using exponential back off.
      }
      else if (error.equals("ACCOUNT_MISSING")) {
        Log.e(TAG, "No Google account on device.");
        // Ask the user to create / add a Google account
      }
      else if (error.equals("AUTHENTICATION_FAILED")) {
        Log.e(TAG, "Incorrect password.");
        // Ask the user to re-enter their Google account password.
      }
      else if (error.equals("TOO_MANY_REGISTRATIONS")) {
        Log.e(TAG, "Too many applications registered.");
        // Ask the user to unregister / uninstall some applications.
      }
```

```
      else if (error.equals("INVALID_SENDER")) {
        Log.e(TAG, "Invalid sender account.");
        // The sender account specified has not been registered
        // with the C2DM server.
      }
      else if (error.equals("PHONE_REGISTRATION_ERROR")) {
        Log.e(TAG, "Phone registration failed.");
        // The phone doesn't currently support C2DM.
      }
    } else if (unregistered != null) {
      // Unregistration complete. The application should stop
      // processing any further received messages.
      Log.d(TAG, "Phone deregistration completed successfully.");
    } else if (registrationId != null) {
      Log.d(TAG, "C2DM registration ID received.");
      // Send the registration ID to your server.
    }
  }
}
```

code snippet PA4AD_Ch18_C2DM/src/MyC2DMReceiver.java

The received registration ID becomes the address your server uses to target a message at this particular device/application instance. Accordingly, you need to transmit this ID to your server, along with an identifier it can use to identify the user associated with this installation. This will allow you to look up the device address based on a particular user in order to transmit data to him or her. In the case of email, this might be the username; for voicemail, the phone number; or for a game, a generated UUID.

It's good practice to create a server-side hash to simplify the lookup. Keep in mind that a single user may have multiple devices, so you may need to include a collision algorithm that determines which device should receive the message (or if multiple devices should receive them).

Also remember that the registration ID may subsequently change, so be sure to retransmit the identifier/ID pair should that happen.

> *You can unregister a device by calling* startService, *passing in an Intent that uses the* com.google.android.c2dm.intent.UNREGISTER *action, and including an app extra that uses a Pending Intent to identify your application:*
>
> ```
> PendingIntent pi =
>   PendingIntent.getBroadcast(this, 0, new Intent(), 0);
> Intent unregister =
>   new Intent("com.google.android.c2dm.intent.UNREGISTER");
>
> unregister.putExtra("app", pi);
>
> startService(unregister);
> ```

Sending C2DM Messages to Devices

Once you've recorded a particular device's registration ID on your server, it's possible for it to transmit messages to that device. Sending messages is a two-step process, as shown in Figure 18-2.

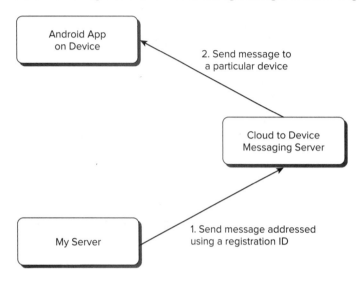

FIGURE 18-2

> *Creating the server-side implementation of C2DM is beyond the scope of this book. If your server is an AppEngine application, the Chrome 2 Phone project (http://code.google.com/p/chrometophone/) includes a server-side implementation that can be used to greatly simplify the process of authentication and message transmission to the C2DM service.*

Your server transmits a message to the C2DM service using POST requests to https://android .apis.google.com/c2dm/send that include the following parameters:

➤ registration_id — The address of the target device/application pair.

➤ collapse_key — When the target device is offline, messages transmitted to it will be queued. By specifying a collapse key, you can effectively collapse that queue, causing each message with the same key to override the previous so that only the last message gets sent to the target device.

➤ data.[key] — Payload data in the form of key/value pairs. They will be passed in to your application as extras within the C2DM message Intent, using the keys you specify. Each C2DM message is limited to 1024 bytes, so payload data should be kept to the bare minimum — typically only the information required for the client to perform an efficient lookup.

➤ `delay_while_idle` — By default, messages transmitted to a device will be sent as quickly as possible. By setting this parameter to `true`, you can delay the transmission until the device is active. This is similar to setting a non-waking alarm, and can be useful for prolonging battery life where messages don't need to be received immediately. The collapse key you specify will be used to collapse the queue of pending messages so that only one message is transmitted/received when the device becomes active.

In addition to the POST parameters, you must include a header with a Google ClientLogin auth token whose cookie must be associated with the Android C2DM service.

The auth token should be generated for the C2DM Google account that your client applications used when registering with the C2DM server.

> *Details for implementing a server-side ClientLogin process is beyond the scope of this book. You can find details on generating a Google auth token at* `http://code.google.com/apis/accounts/docs/AuthForInstalledApps.html`.

Receiving C2DM Messages

After your server transmits messages to the C2DM service, they are, in turn, sent to the device to which they are addressed. The target device then delivers each message to its recipient application as a Broadcast Intent.

To receive these Intents, you must register a Broadcast Receiver that includes the `com.google .android.c2dm.permission.SEND` permission, a filter for the `com.google.android.c2dm .intent.RECEIVE` action, and the category set to the application's package name, as shown in Listing 18-6.

LISTING 18-6: Registering to receive C2DM messages

```
<receiver
    android:name=".C2DMMessageReceiver"
    android:permission="com.google.android.c2dm.permission.SEND">

    <intent-filter>
      <action
        android:name="com.google.android.c2dm.intent.RECEIVE"
      />
      <category android:name="com.mypackage.myc2dmAppName"/>
    </intent-filter>
</receiver>
```

code snippet PA4AD_Ch18_C2DM/AndroidManifest.xml

Within the associated Broadcast Receiver implementation, you can extract any extras using the keys you specified when sending the associated server message, as shown in Listing 18-7.

LISTING 18-7: Extracting C2DM message details

```
public void onReceive(Context context, Intent intent) {
  if (intent.getAction().equals(
      "com.google.android.c2dm.intent.RECEIVE")) {
    Bundle extras = intent.getExtras();

    // Extract any extras included in the server messages.
    int newVoicemailCount = extras.getInt("VOICEMAIL_COUNT", 0);
  }
}
```

code snippet PA4AD_Ch18_C2DM/src/C2DMMessageReceiver.xml

Due to the payload data limit, it's generally considered good practice to include as little payload data as possible and to use an incoming C2DM message as a tickle to indicate that the application should perform a server update.

IMPLEMENTING COPY PROTECTION USING THE LICENSE VERIFICATION LIBRARY

Android 1.5 (API level 3) introduced a network-based solution for implementing copy protection for your applications. The License Verification Library (LVL) is a Google service that works together with Google Play to allow your application to query the license status of your application for a given user.

> Full details for implementing an LVL solution for copy protection is outside the scope of this book. This section aims to provide an introduction to the LVL, outlining its concepts and best-practice implementation patterns.
>
> The Android Developer Guide has a detailed guide to using the LVL, including a sample implementation: http://developer.android.com/guide/publishing/licensing.html.

Installing the License Verification Library

The LVL provides a series of APIs that handle the interaction with the licensing service to request licensing confirmation and return the results to your applications. It also simplifies and encapsulates the process of defining policies for caching and offline license verification. It includes the `ServerManagedPolicy` implementation that encapsulates the best-practice policy settings.

The LVL is distributed as an "extras" SDK package as the "Google Market Licensing package," and can be downloaded using the Android SDK Manager, as described in Chapter 2, "Getting Started."

After downloading the LVL, add it to Eclipse as a library project, and then import it into your existing applications. Details for creating and using Eclipse library packages using the ADT plug-in are available at `http://developer.android.com/guide/developing/projects/projects-eclipse.html`.

To use the LVL, you need to add the `com.android.vending.CHECK_LICENSE` permission to your application manifest:

```
<uses-permission android:name="com.android.vending.CHECK_LICENSE"/>
```

Finding Your License Verification Public Key

In order to perform LVL checks, you need to include a public key for validation requests. You must first create a sign-in to the Android Developer Console.

Select the Edit Profile link from `https://play.google.com/apps/publish/` and scroll down to the Licensing & In-app Billing heading, as shown in Figure 18-3.

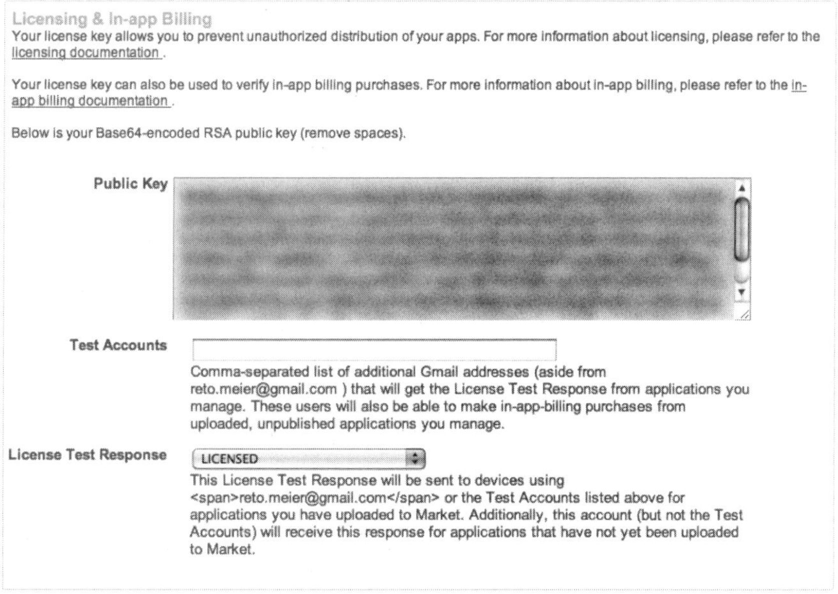

FIGURE 18-3

From here, you can also specify a number of test accounts that will receive the static response you specify.

Configuring Your License Validation Policy

The license validation Policy specifies the configuration options that will be used to execute license checks and determine their effects. It should manage caching of requests, handling of error codes, retries, and offline verification checks.

Although it's possible to create your own implementation of the `Policy` class, the LVL includes a best-practice policy whose settings are managed by the Licensing Service — the `ServerManagedPolicy`.

In order to support caching and offline validation support, the Server Managed Policy requires an obfuscator to obfuscate the cached values. The LVL includes the `AESObfuscator`, which seeds the encryption using the following:

➤ **A salt** — An array of random bytes.

➤ **A package name** — The application's full (and unique) package name.

➤ **A unique device identifier** — Typically a UUID created the first time the application is run.

Performing License Validation Checks

Start by creating a new `LicenseChecker` object in the `onCreate` handler of your Activity, specifying the Context, a Policy instance, and your public key, as shown in Listing 18-8.

LISTING 18-8: Creating a new License Checker

```
// Generate 20 random bytes, and put them here.
private static final byte[] SALT = new byte[] {
  -56, 42, 12, -18, -10, -34, 78, -75, 54, 88,
  -13, -12, 36, 17, -34, 114, 77, 12, -23, -20};

@Override
public void onCreate(Bundle savedInstanceState) {
  super.onCreate(savedInstanceState);

  // Construct the LicenseChecker with a Policy.
  licenseChecker =
    new LicenseChecker(this, new ServerManagedPolicy(this,
      new AESObfuscator(SALT, getPackageName(), deviceID)),
    PUBLIC_KEY);
}
```

code snippet PA4AD_Ch18_LVS/src/MyActivity.xml

To perform the license check, call the License Checker object's `checkAccess` method, passing in an implementation of the `LicenseCheckerCallback` interface, as shown in Listing 18-9. Successful validation will result in the `allow` handler being triggered, whereas failure will trigger `dontAllow`.

LISTING 18-9: Performing a license check

```
licenseChecker.checkAccess(new LicenseCheckerCallback(){
  public void allow() {
    // License verified.
  }
```

```
    public void dontAllow() {
      // License verification failed.
    }

    public void applicationError(ApplicationErrorCode errorCode) {
      // Handle associated error code.
    }
  });
```

code snippet PA4AD_Ch18_LVS/src/MyActivity.xml

> *Both License Checker handlers will* always *return on a background thread. If you plan to update the UI based on license verification callbacks, you will first need to synchronize with the main application thread.*

It's up to you to determine where in your application, and how frequently, you want to make license validation checks — and how to react to failure. It's generally considered best practice to be as unpredictable as possible. This makes it more difficult for hackers to determine where your application is making checks and whether their attempts at circumventing your checks have been successful.

Many developers have found it useful to only partially disable an application that fails the license checks — for example, by limiting the number of levels available, increasing the difficulty level, or otherwise providing a less complete product. As a result, they can then direct users to Google Play at a later point to encourage them to purchase the full version.

INTRODUCING IN-APP BILLING

Introduced in Android 1.6 (API level 4), In-App Billing (IAB) is a Google Play service that can be used as an alternative (or addendum) to charging up-front for an application.

Using IAB, you can charge users for digital content within your applications, including virtual in-game content, such as upgrading to the "full" version, purchasing additional levels, or buying weaponry, armor, or other in-game artifacts. You can also use IAB (though you aren't required to) when charging for downloadable content, such as music, video, books, or images.

The IAB service operates using the Google Play Store, which handles all transaction processing and operates under the same revenue-sharing model as for paid applications — specifically, requiring a 30 percent transaction fee.

IAB has proven to be a powerful new monetization option for application developers. Despite the relatively low cost of mobile games and applications, consumers are wary of paying for applications without a guarantee of their quality. By implementing an IAB solution, you provide prospective users with a risk-free way to experience the quality and usefulness of your application, along with a simple way to upgrade their experience once they're satisfied that the additional functionality is worth the cost.

Similarly, rather than charging users once for access, IAB provides an avenue for providing users with ongoing or renewable resources — particularly in games — such as the ability to skip levels or simplify their in-game experience through the purchase of virtual goods they would otherwise need to invest significant time to earn.

> *Full details for implementing an IAB solution is beyond the scope of this book. This section aims to provide an introduction to using IAB, outlining its concepts and best-practice implementation patterns.*
>
> *The Android Developer Guide has a detailed guide to integrating IAB, including a sample implementation:* `http://developer.android.com/guide/market/billing/index.html`.

In-App Billing Restrictions

IAB is a Google service implemented using the Google Play Store client. As a result, before using IAB within your applications, you must have Google Checkout Merchant account, and your IAB applications must be published on Google Play.

As a server-based solution, IAB is available only on devices that have a network connection.

IAB is only available for selling virtual goods, including in-game artifacts or downloadable digital content. It can't be used to sell physical goods or serves.

Installing the In-App Billing Library

The IAB library and sample source is distributed as an "extras" SDK package, and can be downloaded using the Android SDK Manager, as described in Chapter 2.

To use IAB, you need to specify the `com.android.vending.BILLING` permission in your application manifest:

```
<uses-permission android:name="com.android.vending.BILLING" />
```

Finding Your Public Key and Defining Your Purchasable Items

Like license verification checks, in order to perform IAB transactions, you need to include a public key.

You can find your public key from your Google Play publisher account. Once you've signed in, select the Edit Profile link from `https://play.google.com/apps/publish` and scroll down to the Licensing & In-app Billing heading (refer to Figure 18-3).

To specify the items that can be purchased within each of your applications, click the In-App Products link beneath its listing in the Android Developer Console. The link will be available if you have a Google Checkout Merchant account, and only for applications whose manifest includes the `com.android.vending.BILLING` permission.

The product list is used to store the metadata describing each product you are selling, including its unique ID and price. The content itself must be stored either within the application or on your own servers. The product ID will be used within your application when initiating an in-app purchase.

Initiating In-App Billing Transactions

To use IAB, your application sends a billing request for a specific in-app product to the IAB service; that service then handles the transaction before sending an Intent to your application containing the purchase details.

In order to execute billing requests, your application must bind to the `MarketBillingService` class. The sample application included as part of the IAB library package includes the AIDL file that defines the interface with this service, so before attempting to bind to the Market Billing Service, copy the AIDL definition into your project.

It's best practice to perform all IAB transactions within a Service, ensuring that an Activity closing or restarting does not interfere with an IAB transaction.

You can bind to the Market Billing Service from your own Service. Implement a new `ServiceConnection` to obtain a reference to the `IMarketBillingService`, as shown in Listing 18-10.

LISTING 18-10: Binding to the Market Billing Service

```
IMarketBillingService billingService;

private void bindService() {
  try {
    String bindString =
      "com.android.vending.billing.MarketBillingService.BIND";

    boolean result = context.bindService(new Intent(bindString),
      serviceConnection, Context.BIND_AUTO_CREATE);

  } catch (SecurityException e) {
    Log.e(TAG, "Security Exception.", e);
  }
}

private ServiceConnection serviceConnection = new ServiceConnection() {
  public void onServiceConnected(ComponentName className,
                                 IBinder service) {
    billingService = IMarketBillingService.Stub.asInterface(service);
  }

  public void onServiceDisconnected(ComponentName className) {
    billingService = null;
  }
};
```

code snippet PA4AD_Ch18_IAB/src/MyService.xml

You can now use this Market Billing Service reference to make billing request calls using the `send-BillingRequest` method. Note that this must be performed on the main application thread.

To make a billing request, you must pass in a `Bundle` parameter that specifies the type of transaction you want to execute, the version of the IAB API you are using, your package name, and the product ID to be purchased, as shown in Listing 18-11.

LISTING 18-11: Creating a billing request

```
protected Bundle makeRequestBundle(String transactionType,
                                    String itemId) {
    Bundle request = new Bundle();
    request.putString("BILLING_REQUEST", transactionType);
    request.putInt("API_VERSION", 1);
    request.putString("PACKAGE_NAME", getPackageName());
    if (itemId != null)
      request.putString("ITEM_ID", itemId);
    return request;
}
```

code snippet PA4AD_Ch18_IAB/src/MyService.xml

The following five billing request types are supported:

➤ `REQUEST_PURCHASE` — Initiates a purchase request.

➤ `CHECK_BILLING_SUPPORTED` — Verifies that IAB is supported on the host device.

➤ `GET_PURCHASE_INFORMATION` — Requests the transaction information for a prior purchase or a refund.

➤ `CONFIRM_NOTIFICATIONS` — Acknowledges the receipt of the transaction information related to a purchase or refund.

➤ `RESTORE_TRANSACTIONS` — Retrieves a user's transaction history for his or her managed purchases.

To initiate the billing request, call the Market Billing Service's `sendBillingRequest` method, passing in the Bundle:

```
Bundle response = billingService.sendBillingRequest(request);
```

The `sendBillingRequest` method will return a Bundle response that contains a response code, request ID, and a Pending Intent that you use to launch the checkout UI.

Handling In-App Billing Purchase Request Responses

When your billing request type is `REQUEST_PURCHASE`, your application must listen for two Broadcast Intents — one containing a response code and another containing an IAB notification — to determine the success of your attempted transaction:

```
<receiver android:name="IABReceiver">
  <intent-filter>
```

```
        <action android:name="com.android.vending.billing.IN_APP_NOTIFY" />
        <action android:name="com.android.vending.billing.RESPONSE_CODE" />
        <action android:name="com.android.vending.billing.PURCHASE_STATE_CHANGED"/>
    </intent-filter>
</receiver>
```

After the Market Billing Service successfully receives your billing request, it broadcasts a RESPONSE_CODE Intent whose result is set to RESULT_OK.

When the transaction itself has been executed, the Market Billing Service broadcasts an IN_APP_NOTIFY Intent. This Broadcast Intent contains a notification ID that, along with a nonce, is used to retrieve the purchase information for a given purchase request using the GET_PURCHASE_INFORMATION request type.

Making a purchase information request returns a Bundle containing a response code and request ID, as well as triggering two further asynchronous Broadcasts Intents. The first, a RESPONSE_CODE Intent, returns the success and error status associated with your purchase request, using the nonce you specified in the request as an identifier.

If the purchase is successful, a PURCHASE_STATE_CHANGED broadcast will also be broadcast, containing detailed transaction information as a signed JSON string.

USING WAKE LOCKS

In order to prolong battery life, when an Android device is left idle, it will first dim, then turn off the screen, and, finally, turn off the CPU.

WakeLocks are a Power Manager system Service feature that your application can use to control the power state of the host device.

Wake Locks can be used to keep the CPU running, prevent the screen from dimming, prevent the screen from turning off, and prevent the keyboard backlight from turning off.

> *Creating and holding Wake Locks can have a dramatic impact on the host device's battery life. It's good practice to use Wake Locks sparingly, creating them only when strictly necessary and holding them for as short a time as possible.*

Because of the dramatic impact Wake Locks can have on battery life, your application needs to request a WAKE_LOCK permission in order to create them:

```
<uses-permission android:name="android.permission.WAKE_LOCK"/>
```

To create a Wake Lock, call newWakeLock on the Power Manager, specifying one of the following Wake Lock types.

> ➤ FULL_WAKE_LOCK — Keeps the screen at full brightness, the keyboard backlight illuminated, and the CPU running.

> ➤ SCREEN_BRIGHT_WAKE_LOCK — Keeps the screen at full brightness and the CPU running.

➤ `SCREEN_DIM_WAKE_LOCK` — Keeps the screen on (but lets it dim) and the CPU running.

➤ `PARTIAL_WAKE_LOCK` — Keeps the CPU running.

Screen dim Wake Locks typically are used to prevent the screen from dimming during applications that are likely to involve little user interaction — for example, a video player.

Partial Wake Locks (or CPU Wake Locks) are used to prevent the device from going to sleep until an action has completed. This is most commonly used by Services started within Intent Receivers, which may receive Intents while the device is asleep. It's worth noting that in this case the system will hold a CPU Wake Lock throughout the `onReceive` handler of the Broadcast Receiver.

> *If you start a Service, or broadcast an Intent within the* `onReceive` *handler of a Broadcast Receiver, it is possible that the Wake Lock it holds will be released before your Service has started or your Intent received. To ensure the Service execution is completed, you will need to put in place a separate Wake Lock policy.*

After creating a Wake Lock, acquire it by calling `acquire`.

You can optionally specify a timeout to ensure the maximum duration the Wake Lock will be held for. When the action for which you're holding the Wake Lock completes, call `release` to let the system manage the power state.

Listing 18-12 shows the typical use pattern for creating, acquiring, and releasing a Wake Lock.

LISTING 18-12: Using a Wake Lock

```
WakeLock wakeLock;

private class MyAsyncTask extends AsyncTask<Void,  Void, Void> {
  @Override
  protected Void doInBackground(Void... parameters) {
    PowerManager pm =
      (PowerManager)getSystemService(Context.POWER_SERVICE);

    wakeLock =
      pm.newWakeLock(PowerManager.PARTIAL_WAKE_LOCK, "MyWakeLock");

    wakeLock.acquire();

    // TODO Do things in the background

    return null;
  }

  @Override
  protected void onPostExecute(Void parameters) {
    wakeLock.release();
  }
}
```

code snippet PA4AD_Ch18_Wakelocks/src/MyActivity.xml

USING AIDL TO SUPPORT INTER-PROCESS COMMUNICATION FOR SERVICES

In Chapter 9, "Working in the Background," you learned how to create Services for your applications. Here, you'll learn how to use the Android Interface Definition Language (AIDL) to support rich inter-process communication (IPC) between Services and other application components, including components running within different applications or within separate processes. This gives your Services the capability to support multiple applications across process boundaries.

To pass objects between processes, you need to deconstruct them into OS-level primitives that the underlying OS can then marshal across application boundaries. This is done by implementing them as Parcelables.

AIDL is used to simplify the code that lets your processes exchange objects. It's similar to interfaces like COM or Corba in that it lets you create public methods within your Services that can accept and return object parameters and return values between processes.

Implementing an AIDL Interface

AIDL supports the following data types:

- ➤ Java language primitives (`int`, `boolean`, `float`, `char`, etc.).

- ➤ `String` and `CharSequence` values.

- ➤ `List` objects (including generics), where each element is a supported type. The receiving class will always receive the List object instantiated as an `ArrayList`.

- ➤ `Map` objects (not including generics), where every key and element is of a supported type. The receiving class will always receive the `Map` object instantiated as a `HashMap`.

- ➤ AIDL-generated interfaces (covered later). An `import` statement is always needed for these.

- ➤ Classes that implement the `Parcelable` interface (covered next). An `import` statement is always needed for these.

The following sections demonstrate how to make your classes `Parcelable`, create an AIDL Service definition, and implement and expose that Service definition for use by other application components.

Making Classes Parcelable

In order for non-native classes to be passed between processes, they must implement the `Parcelable` interface. This lets you decompose the properties within your classes into primitive types stored within a `Parcel` that can be marshaled across process boundaries.

Implement the `writeToParcel` method to decompose your class object, using the `write*` methods to save object properties into the outgoing Parcel object:

```
public void writeToParcel(Parcel out, int flags) {
  out.writeLong(myLong);
  out.writeString(myString);
  out.writeDouble(myDouble);
}
```

To re-create an object that's been saved as a parcel, implement the public static `Creator` field (which implements a new `Parcelable.Creator` class) to create a new object based on an incoming Parcel by reading the incoming parcel using its `read*` methods:

```
private MyClass(Parcel in) {
  myLong = in.readLong();
  myString = in.readString();
  myDouble = in.readDouble();
}
```

Listing 18-13 shows a basic example of using the `Parcelable` interface for the `Quake` class you've been using in the ongoing Earthquake example.

LISTING 18-13: Making the Quake class a Parcelable

```
package com.paad.earthquake;

import java.text.SimpleDateFormat;
import java.util.Date;

import android.location.Location;
import android.os.Parcel;
import android.os.Parcelable;

public class Quake implements Parcelable {
  private Date date;
  private String details;
  private Location location;
  private double magnitude;
  private String link;
  public Date getDate() { return date; }
  public String getDetails() { return details; }
  public Location getLocation() { return location; }
  public double getMagnitude() { return magnitude; }
  public String getLink() { return link; }

  public Quake(Date _d, String _det, Location _loc,
               double _mag, String _link) {
    date = _d;
    details = _det;
    location = _loc;
    magnitude = _mag;
    link = _link;
  }

  @Override
  public String toString(){
    SimpleDateFormat sdf = new SimpleDateFormat("HH.mm");
    String dateString = sdf.format(date);
    return dateString + ":" + magnitude + " " + details;
  }
```

```
      private Quake(Parcel in) {
        date.setTime(in.readLong());
        details = in.readString();
        magnitude = in.readDouble();
        Location location = new Location("generated");
        location.setLatitude(in.readDouble());
        location.setLongitude(in.readDouble());
        link = in.readString();
      }

      public void writeToParcel(Parcel out, int flags) {
        out.writeLong(date.getTime());
        out.writeString(details);
        out.writeDouble(magnitude);
        out.writeDouble(location.getLatitude());
        out.writeDouble(location.getLongitude());
        out.writeString(link);
      }

      public static final Parcelable.Creator<Quake> CREATOR =
        new Parcelable.Creator<Quake>() {
          public Quake createFromParcel(Parcel in) {
            return new Quake(in);
          }

          public Quake[] newArray(int size) {
           return new Quake[size];
          }
        };

      public int describeContents() {
        return 0;
      }
    }
}
```

code snippet PA4AD_Ch18_Earthquake/src/Quake.java

Now that you have a Parcelable class, you need to create a corresponding AIDL definition to make it available when defining your Service's AIDL interface.

Listing 18-14 shows the contents of the `Quake.aidl` file you need to create for the `Quake` Parcelable defined in the preceding listing.

LISTING 18-14: The Quake class AIDL definition

```
package com.paad.earthquake;

parcelable Quake;
```

code snippet PA4AD_Ch18_Earthquake/src/Quake.aidl

When passing class objects between processes, remember that AIDL objects aren't self-describing, so the client process must understand the definition of the object being passed.

Creating an AIDL Service Definition

In this section you will be defining a new AIDL interface definition for a Service you'd like to use across processes.

Start by creating a new .aidl file within your project. This will define the methods and fields to include in an interface that your Service will implement.

The syntax for creating AIDL definitions is similar to that used for standard Java interface definitions.

Specify a fully qualified package name, then import all the packages required. Unlike normal Java interfaces, AIDL definitions need to import packages for any class or interface that isn't a native Java type, even if it's defined in the same project.

Define a new interface, adding the properties and methods you want to make available. Methods can take zero or more parameters and return void or a supported type. If you define a method that takes one or more parameters, you need to use a directional tag (one of in, out, and inout) to indicate whether the each parameter is a value or reference type.

> *Where possible, you should limit the direction of each parameter, as marshaling parameters is an expensive operation.*

Listing 18-15 shows a basic AIDL definition for the earthquake sample project you last modified in Listing 18-14. It should be implemented within the IEarthquakeService.aidl file.

LISTING 18-15: An Earthquake Service AIDL interface definition

```
package com.paad.earthquake;

import com.paad.earthquake.Quake;

interface IEarthquakeService {
  List<Quake> getEarthquakes();
  void refreshEarthquakes();
}
```

code snippet PA4AD_Ch18_IPC/src/IEarthquakeService.aidl

Implementing and Exposing the AIDL Service Definition

If you're using the ADT plug-in, saving the AIDL file will automatically code-generate a Java Interface file. This interface will include an inner Stub class that implements the interface as an abstract class.

Have your Service extend the `Stub` and implement the functionality required. Typically, you'll do this using a private field variable within the Service whose functionality you'll be exposing.

Listing 18-16 shows an implementation of the `IEarthquakeService` AIDL definition created in Listing 18-15.

LISTING 18-16: Implementing the AIDL Interface definition within a Service

```java
IBinder myEarthquakeServiceStub = new IEarthquakeService.Stub() {
  public void refreshEarthquakes() throws RemoteException {
    EarthquakeUpdateService.this.refreshEarthquakes();
  }

  public List<Quake> getEarthquakes() throws RemoteException {
    ArrayList<Quake> result = new ArrayList<Quake>();

    ContentResolver cr
      = EarthquakeUpdateService.this.getContentResolver();
    Cursor c = cr.query(EarthquakeProvider.CONTENT_URI,
                        null, null, null, null);

    if (c != null)
      if (c.moveToFirst()) {
        int latColumn = c.getColumnIndexOrThrow(
          EarthquakeProvider.KEY_LOCATION_LAT);
        int lngColumn = c.getColumnIndexOrThrow(
          EarthquakeProvider.KEY_LOCATION_LNG);
        int detailsColumn = c.getColumnIndexOrThrow(
          EarthquakeProvider.KEY_DETAILS);
        int dateColumn = c.getColumnIndexOrThrow(
          EarthquakeProvider.KEY_DATE);
        int linkColumn = c.getColumnIndexOrThrow(
          EarthquakeProvider.KEY_LINK);
        int magColumn = c.getColumnIndexOrThrow(
          EarthquakeProvider.KEY_MAGNITUDE);

        do {
          Double lat = c.getDouble(latColumn);
          Double lng = c.getDouble(lngColumn);
          Location location = new Location("dummy");
          location.setLatitude(lat);
          location.setLongitude(lng);

          String details =
            c.getString(detailsColumn);

          String link = c.getString(linkColumn);

          double magnitude =
            c.getDouble(magColumn);

          long datems = c.getLong(dateColumn);
          Date date = new Date(datems);
```

```
            result.add(new Quake(date, details,
                                  location, magnitude, link));
        } while(c.moveToNext());
      }
      c.close();
    return result;
  }
};
```

code snippet PA4AD_Ch18_Earthquake/src/EarthquakeUpdateService.java

When implementing these methods, be aware of the following:

➤ All exceptions will remain local to the implementing process; they will not be propagated to the calling application.

➤ All IPC calls are synchronous. If you know that the process is likely to be time-consuming, you should consider wrapping the synchronous call in an asynchronous wrapper or moving the processing on the receiver side onto a background thread.

With the functionality implemented, you need to expose this interface to client applications. Expose the IPC-enabled Service interface by overriding the onBind method within your Service implementation to return an instance of the interface. Listing 18-17 demonstrates the onBind implementation for the EarthquakeUpdateService.

LISTING 18-17: Exposing an AIDL interface implementation to Service clients

```
@Override
public IBinder onBind(Intent intent) {
    return myEarthquakeServiceStub;
}
```

code snippet PA4AD_Ch18_IPC/src/EarthquakeUpdateService.java

To use the AIDL-enabled Service from within an Activity, you must bind it, as shown in Listing 18-18.

LISTING 18-18: Binding to an AIDL Service

```
IEarthquakeService earthquakeService = null;

private void bindService() {
  bindService(new Intent(IEarthquakeService.class.getName()),
            serviceConnection, Context.BIND_AUTO_CREATE);
}

private ServiceConnection serviceConnection = new ServiceConnection() {
  public void onServiceConnected(ComponentName className,
                                 IBinder service) {
```

```
      earthquakeService = IEarthquakeService.Stub.asInterface(service);
    }

    public void onServiceDisconnected(ComponentName className) {
      earthquakeService = null;
    }
  };
```

code snippet PA4AD_Ch18_IPC/src/BoundEarthquakeActivity.java

DEALING WITH DIFFERENT HARDWARE AND SOFTWARE AVAILABILITY

From smartphones to tablets to televisions, Android is now being used on an increasingly diverse collection of hardware. Each new device potentially represents a variation in hardware configuration or software platform. This flexibility is a significant factor in Android's success, but as a result, you can't make assumptions regarding the hardware or software running on the host platform.

To mitigate this, Android platform releases are forward compatible — meaning that applications designed before a particular hardware or software innovation is available will be able to take advantage of it without requiring changes.

One example of this forward-compatibility is the location-based services described in Chapter 13, "Maps, Geocoding, and Location-Based Services." Rather than specifying a particular hardware provider, you choose a set of conditions and allow the system to select the best alternative using a generic interface. Should future hardware and software provide a better alternative, your application can take advantage without requiring an update.

Android platform releases are also backward compatible, meaning your application will continue to work on new hardware and platform releases — again without you needing to upgrade it each time.

By combining forward and backward compatibility, your Android application will continue to work, and even take advantage of new hardware and software features, as the platform evolves without requiring updates.

That said, each platform release includes new APIs and platform features. Similarly, new hardware may become available (such as NFC technology). Either advance could provide features that might improve the features and user experience of your application.

Attempting to use APIs that aren't available on a given host platform will cause a runtime exception. To take advantage of these new features without losing support for hardware running earlier platforms, you need to ensure your *application* is also backward compatible.

Similarly, the wide range of different Android device hardware platforms means that you can't make assumptions over what hardware might be available.

The following sections explain how to specify certain hardware as required, check for hardware availability at run time, and build applications that are backward compatible.

Specifying Hardware as Required

Application hardware requirements generally fall into two categories: hardware that is required for your application to have utility, and hardware that is useful if it is available but isn't strictly necessary. The former accounts for applications built around a particular piece of hardware — for example, a replacement camera application isn't useful on a device without a camera.

To specify a particular hardware feature as a requirement to install your application, add a uses-feature node to its manifest:

```
<uses-feature android:name="android.hardware.sensor.compass"/>
<uses-feature android:name="android.hardware.camera"/>
```

This can also be used for applications that don't necessarily require a particular piece of hardware, but which haven't been designed to support certain hardware configurations — for example, a game that requires tilt sensors or a touch screen to control.

> *The more hardware restrictions you place on your applications, the smaller the potential target audience becomes, so it's good practice to limit your hardware restrictions to those required to support core functionality.*

Confirming Hardware Availability

For hardware that would be useful but isn't necessary, you need to query the host hardware platform at run time to determine what hardware is available. The Package Manager includes a `hasSystemFeature` method that accepts `FEATURE_*` static constants.

```
PackageManager pm = getPackageManager();
pm.hasSystemFeature(PackageManager.FEATURE_SENSOR_COMPASS);
```

The Package Manager includes a constant for every piece of optional hardware, making it possible to customize your UI and functionality based on the hardware available.

Building Backward-Compatible Applications

Each new Android SDK release brings with it a raft of new hardware support, APIs, bug fixes, and performance improvements. It's best practice to update your applications as soon as possible following a new SDK release in order to take advantage of these new features and ensure the best possible user experience for new Android owners.

At the same time, ensuring your applications are backward compatible is critical to ensure users of devices running earlier Android platform versions can continue to use them — particularly as this is likely to be a significantly larger share of the market than that held by new devices.

Many of the convenience classes and UI improvements (such as Cursors and Fragments) are distributed as a stand-alone support library. Where features aren't available as part of the support library, this means incorporating new features and using the techniques described here to support multiple platform versions within the same package.

> ⊗ *Importing a class or attempting to call a method not available in the underlying platform will cause a runtime exception when the enclosing class is instantiated or the method is called.*

For each technique described, it's important to know the API level associated with the underlying platform. To find this at run time, you can use the `android.os.Build.VERSION.SDK_INT` constant:

```
private static boolean nfc_beam_supported =
  android.os.Build.VERSION.SDK_INT > 14;
```

This can then be used within the techniques described below to decide which components to start or interfaces to implement.

Alternatively, you can use reflection or use exceptions — as shown in the following snippet — to check if a particular class or method is supported on the current device:

```
private static boolean fragmentsSupported = true;

private static void checkFragmentsSupported()throws NoClassDefFoundError {
  fragmentsSupported = android.app.Fragment.class != null;
}

static {
  try {
    checkFragmentsSupported();
  } catch (NoClassDefFoundError e) {
    fragmentsSupported = false;
  }
}
```

Both reflection and exceptions are particularly slow operations on Android, so it's best practice to use the SDK version to determine which classes are available.

The easiest way to determine which API level is required for a given class or method is to progressively lower your project's build target and note which classes break the build.

Parallel Activities

The simplest, though least efficient, alternative is to create separate sets of parallel Activities, Services, and Broadcast Receivers, based on a base class compatible with the minimum Android platform version you support.

When using explicit Intents to start Services or Activities, you can select the right set of components at run time by checking the platform version and targeting the appropriate Services and Activities accordingly:

```
private static boolean nfc_beam_supported =
  android.os.Build.VERSION.SDK_INT > 14;

Intent startActivityIntent = null;

if (nfc_beam_supported)
  startActivityIntent = new Intent(this, NFCBeamActivity.class);
else
  startActivityIntent = new Intent(this, NonNFCBeamActivity.class);

startActivity(startActivityIntent);
```

In the case of implicit Intents and Broadcast Receivers, you can add an `android:enabled` tag to their manifest entries that refers to a Boolean resource:

```
<receiver
  android:name=".MediaControlReceiver"
  android:enabled="@bool/supports_remote_media_controller">
  <intent-filter>
    <action android:name="android.intent.action.MEDIA_BUTTON"/>
  </intent-filter>
</receiver>
```

You can then create alternative resource entries based on API level:

```
res/values/bool.xml
  <bool name="supports_remote_media_controller">false</bool>

res/values-v14/bool.xml
  <bool name="supports_remote_media_controller">true</bool>
```

Interfaces and Fragments

Interfaces are the traditional way to support multiple implementations of the same functionality. For functionality that you want to implement differently based on newly available APIs, create an interface that defines the action to be performed, and then create API level-specific implementations.

At run time, check the current platform version and instantiate the appropriate class and use its methods:

```
IP2PDataXfer dataTransfer;

if (android.os.Build.VERSION.SDK_INT > 14)
  dataTransfer = new NFCBeamP2PDataXfer();
else
  dataTransfer = new NonNFCBeamP2PDataXfer();

dataTransfer.initiateP2PDataXfer();
```

With Fragments now available as part of the Android support library, they provide a more encapsulated alternative to parallelized components.

Rather than duplicating Activities, use Fragments — combined with the resource hierarchy — to create a consistent UI that's optimized for different platform releases and hardware configurations.

Most of the UI logic for your Activities should be contained within individual Fragments rather than the Activity itself. As a result, you need only create alternative Fragments to expose and utilize different functionality and inflate different versions of the same layout stored within their respective `res/layout-v[API level]` folders.

Interaction between and within Fragments is usually maintained within each Fragment, so only code related to missing APIs will need to be changed within the Activity. If each variation of a Fragment implements the same interface definition and ID, you shouldn't need to create multiple Activities to support multiple layouts and Fragment definitions.

OPTIMIZING UI PERFORMANCE WITH STRICT MODE

The resource-constrained nature of mobile devices amplifies the effect of performing time-consuming operations on the main application thread. Accessing network resources, reading or writing files, or accessing databases while blocking the UI thread can have a dramatic impact on the user experience, causing your application to become less smooth, more laggy, and, in the most extreme case, unresponsive.

You learned how to move such time-consuming operations onto background threads in Chapter 9. Strict Mode (introduced in Android 2.3 (API level 9) is a tool that helps you identify cases you may have missed.

Using the Strict Mode APIs, you can assign a set of policies that monitor actions within your application and define how you should be alerted. You can define policies related to either the current application thread or to your application's virtual machine (VM) process. The former is perfect for detecting slow operations being performed on the UI thread, whereas the latter helps you detect memory and Context leaks.

To use Strict Mode, create a new `ThreadPolicy` class and a new `VmPolicy` class, using their static builder classes with the `detect*` methods to define the actions to monitor. The corresponding `penalty*` methods control how the system should react to detecting those actions.

The Thread Policy can be used to detect disk reads/writes and network access, whereas the Vm Policy can monitor your application for Activity, SQLite, and closeable object leaks.

The penalties available to both policies include logging or application death, while the Thread Policy also supports displaying an on-screen dialog or flashing screen border.

Both builder classes also include a `detectAll` method that includes all the possible monitoring options supported by the host platform. You can also use the `StrictMode.enableDefaults` method to apply the default monitoring and penalty options.

To enable Strict Mode across your entire application, you should extend the Application class, as shown in Listing 18-19.

LISTING 18-19: Enabling Strict Mode for an application

```java
public class MyApplication extends Application {

    public static final boolean DEVELOPER_MODE = true;

    @Override
    public final void onCreate() {
      super.onCreate();

      if (DEVELOPER_MODE) {
        StrictMode.enableDefaults();
      }
    }
  }
```

code snippet PA4AD_Ch18_StrictMode/src/MyApplication.java

To enable Strict Mode (or customize its settings) for a particular Activity, Service, or other application component, simply use the same pattern within that component's onCreate method.

19

Monetizing, Promoting, and Distributing Applications

WHAT'S IN THIS CHAPTER?

➤ Creating a signing certificate

➤ Signing your applications for distribution

➤ Publishing on Google Play

➤ Monetization strategies

➤ Application promotion strategies

➤ Using Google Analytics

Having created a compelling new Android application, the next step is to share it with the world. In this final chapter you'll learn how to create and use a signing certificate to sign your applications and distribute them.

You'll be introduced to the application launch process and gain some insight into your options for monetizing and promoting your application, and how to ensure you have a successful launch.

You'll also be introduced to Google Play (which expands and replaces the Android Market), learn how to create a developer profile, and how to create your application listing. You'll then be shown how to access the distribution reporting statistics, user comments, and error reports in the Android Developer Console.

After a look at some of the best practices for launch and promotion, you'll learn how to use Google Analytics to gain critical insight into the demographics of your users and how they use your application.

SIGNING AND PUBLISHING APPLICATIONS

Android applications are distributed as Android package files (.APK). In order to be installed on a device or emulator, Android packages need to be signed.

During development, your applications will be signed using a debug key that is automatically generated by the ADT tools. Before distributing your application beyond your testing environment, you must compile it as a release build and sign it using a private release key — typically using a self-signed certificate.

The JDK includes the Keytool and Jarsigner command-line tools necessary to create a new keystore/signing certificate, and to sign your APK, respectively. Alternatively, you can use the Export Android Application wizard, as described in the next section.

> *The importance of maintaining the security of your signing certificate can't be overstated. Android uses this certificate as the means of identifying the authenticity of application updates, and applying inter-process security boundaries between installed applications.*
>
> *Using a stolen key, a third party could sign and distribute applications that maliciously replace your authentic applications.*
>
> *Similarly, your certificate is the only way you can upgrade your applications. If you lose your certificate, it is impossible to perform a seamless update on a device or from within Google Play. In the latter case, you would need to create a new listing, losing all the reviews, ratings, and comments associated with your previous package, as well as making it impossible to provide updates to the existing users of your application.*

Signing Applications Using the Export Android Application Wizard

The Export Android Application wizard simplifies the process of creating and signing a release build of your application package. Once the wizard is complete, your signed package will be ready for distribution.

To launch the wizard, open the Package Explorer and select File ⇨ Export, open the Android folder, select Export Android Application, and then click Next. Alternatively, select Use the Export Wizard from the manifest GUI, as shown in Figure 19-1. The wizard will prompt you to either select a new keystore or create one, as shown in Figure 19-2.

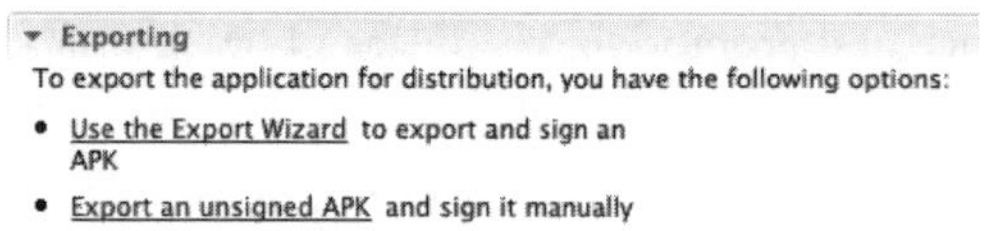

FIGURE 19-1

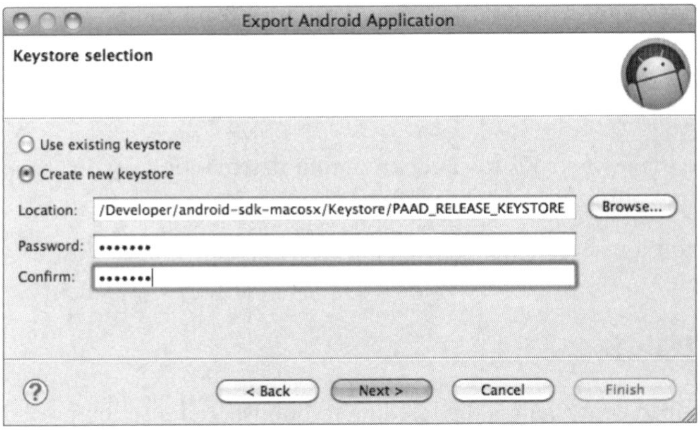

FIGURE 19-2

To apply an upgrade to an installed application, it must be signed with the same key, so you must always sign an application using the same release key.

The Android guidelines further suggest that you sign all your application packages using the same certificate, as applications signed with the same certificate can be configured to run in the same process, and signature-based permissions can be used to expose functionality between trusted applications signed with the same certificate.

As described earlier, the security of your keystore is extremely important, so be sure to use a strong password to secure it.

After creating or selecting your keystore, you'll be asked to create or select a signing certificate. If you've created a new keystore, you'll need to create a new signing certificate, as shown in Figure 19-3.

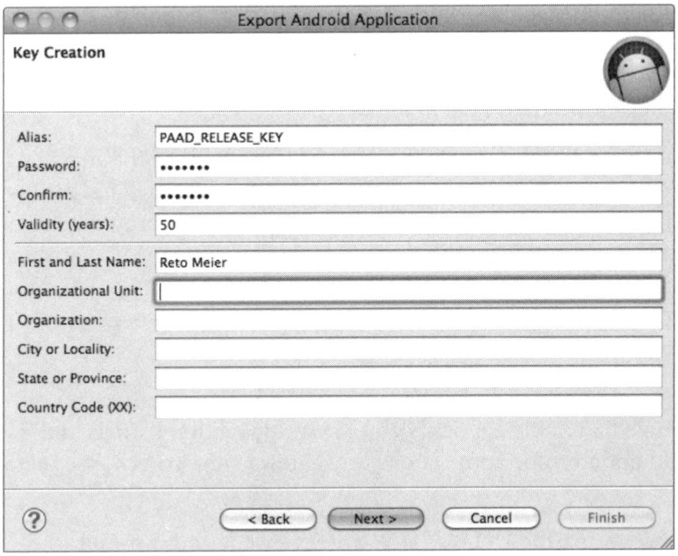

FIGURE 19-3

Applications published on Google Play require a certificate with a validity period ending after October 22, 2033. More generally, your certificate will be used through the lifetime of your application and is necessary to perform upgrades, so you should ensure your signing certificate will outlast your application.

Having selected a signing certificate, the next step is to select an output destination for your package. The wizard will then compile, sign, and zip-align the package.

Your package is now ready for distribution. Before doing anything else, *back up your keystore*.

DISTRIBUTING APPLICATIONS

One of the advantages of Android's open ecosystem is the freedom to publish and distribute your applications however, and wherever, you choose. The most common and popular distribution channel is Google Play; however, you are free to distribute your applications using alternative markets, your own website, social media, or any other distribution channel.

In addition to Google Play, there are several alternatives of varying reach, including OEM and carrier pre-installs, the Amazon App Store, and carrier-specific stores.

When distributing your application, it's important to note that application package names are used as unique identifiers for each application. As a result, each application — including variations that you plan to distribute separately — must each have a unique package name. Note that the filename of your APK does not have to be unique — it will be discarded during the installation process (only the package name is used).

Introducing Google Play

The Google Play Store is the largest and most popular Android application distribution point. At the time of writing this book, it has been reported that there are in excess of 450,000 applications in Google Play, with more than 10 billion application downloads from users in 130 countries — and with a growth rate of more than a billion new downloads each month.

The Google Play Store is a marketplace — that is, Google Play acts as a mechanism for you to sell and distribute your application rather than as a merchant reselling it on your behalf. That means there are far fewer controls restricting what you distribute and how you choose to promote, monetize, and distribute it. Those restrictions are detailed within the Google Play Developer Distribution Agreement (DDA) (www.android.com/us/developer-distribution-agreement.html) and the Google Play Developer Program Policies (DPP) (www.android.com/us/developer-content-policy.html).

Unlike the Apple App Store and Windows Phone Marketplace, there is no review process for applications before they are listed in Google Play. This applies both to new application listings and updates, allowing you to publish and update your applications at whatever time you choose, without needing to wait for approval.

Applications that are suspected of breaching the DDA or DPP are reviewed, and if found to have breached those agreements and policies, are suspended and the developer notified. In extreme cases of malware, the Google Play Store can remotely uninstall malicious applications from devices.

> *A lack of a review and approval process does not imply a carte blanche for applications distributed in Google Play. Before publishing your applications, it's important to carefully review the DDA and DPP to ensure your application is compliant. Applications that are in breach of these policies will be suspended, and multiple infringements can result in the suspension or banning of your developer account.*
>
> *If your application can't be distributed through Google Play, you can still distribute it using an alternative distribution platform.*

Google Play provides all the tools and mechanisms required to handle application distribution, updates, sales (domestic and international), and promotion. Once listed, your application will begin to appear in search results and category lists, as well as potentially within promotional categories described later in this chapter.

Getting Started with Google Play

To publish on Google Play, create a developer account at `https://play.google.com/apps/publish/signup`, as shown in Figure 19-4.

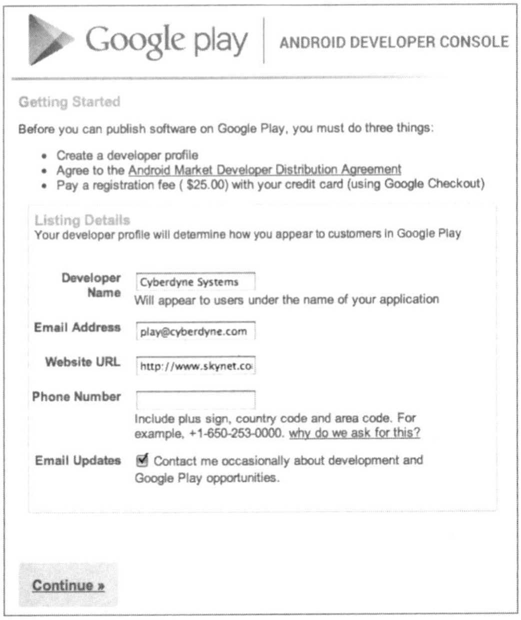

FIGURE 19-4

> *Your Android Developer Profile will be associated with whichever Google account (if any) you are currently signed in to. It's common that multiple people will need access to this account, particularly if you're distributing applications on behalf of a company.*
>
> *It's good practice to create a new Google account specifically for your Android Developer Profile.*

You will be asked to provide a "Developer Name" — typically your company name — that will be used within Google Play to identify the developer of your applications. Note that it is not a requirement that the developer name used here represents the company or individual who actually wrote the code — it simply identifies the company or individual distributing it.

Completing the registration includes paying a US $25.00 fee and agreeing to the terms of the Android DDA.

Publishing Applications

After creating your Android Developer Profile, you are ready to upload your application. Select the Upload Application button on the Android Developer Console. You'll be prompted to upload your signed release package

> *The package name (not the file name) must be unique. Google Play uses application package names as unique identifiers and will not allow you to upload a duplicate package name.*

After the application is uploaded, you'll be asked to enter your application's assets and listing details, as shown in Figures 19-5 and 19-6.

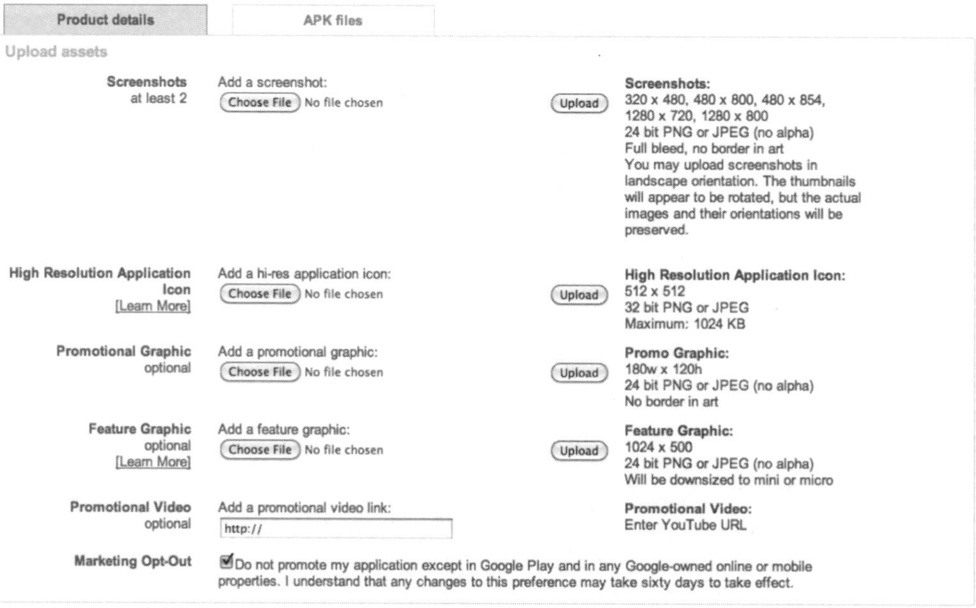

| Product details | APK files |

Upload assets

| Screenshots at least 2 | Add a screenshot: (Choose File) No file chosen (Upload) | Screenshots: 320 x 480, 480 x 800, 480 x 854, 1280 x 720, 1280 x 800 24 bit PNG or JPEG (no alpha) Full bleed, no border in art You may upload screenshots in landscape orientation. The thumbnails will appear to be rotated, but the actual images and their orientations will be preserved. |

High Resolution Application Icon [Learn More] — Add a hi-res application icon: (Choose File) No file chosen (Upload) — High Resolution Application Icon: 512 x 512 / 32 bit PNG or JPEG / Maximum: 1024 KB

Promotional Graphic optional — Add a promotional graphic: (Choose File) No file chosen (Upload) — Promo Graphic: 180w x 120h / 24 bit PNG or JPEG (no alpha) / No border in art

Feature Graphic optional [Learn More] — Add a feature graphic: (Choose File) No file chosen (Upload) — Feature Graphic: 1024 x 500 / 24 bit PNG or JPEG (no alpha) / Will be downsized to mini or micro

Promotional Video optional — Add a promotional video link: [http://] — Promotional Video: Enter YouTube URL

Marketing Opt-Out — ☑ Do not promote my application except in Google Play and in any Google-owned online or mobile properties. I understand that any changes to this preference may take sixty days to take effect.

FIGURE 19-5

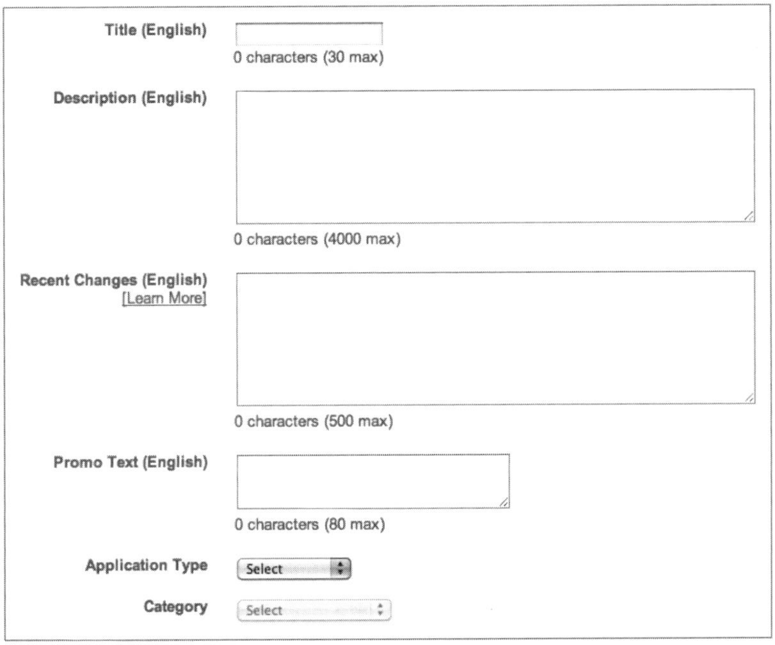

FIGURE 19-6

It's important that you supply all the assets available — even those that may be listed as optional. Each asset is used throughout Google Play, including the website, Google Play Store clients, and promotional campaigns. Not including some assets may prevent your application from being featured or promoted.

The title, description, and category determine how and where your application will be displayed within Google Play. It's important to provide high quality, descriptive titles and application descriptions in this section to make it easier for users to discover your application and make an informed choice on its suitability.

Do not engage in keyword stuffing or other SEO spam in your title or description, as doing so will likely result in your application being suspended.

It's also possible to supply the title and description in multiple languages.

The listing page also lets you specify the availability of your application, providing mechanisms to set its maturity level and the countries in which you want it to be available.

Finally, you can supply application-specific contact details for users of your applications, as shown in Figure 19-7.

These details will be published alongside your application's listing in Google Play, so the email and phone number provided should point to a managed support queue rather than to your personal email address.

When your listing details are complete, click the Publish button. Your application will be live and available for download almost immediately.

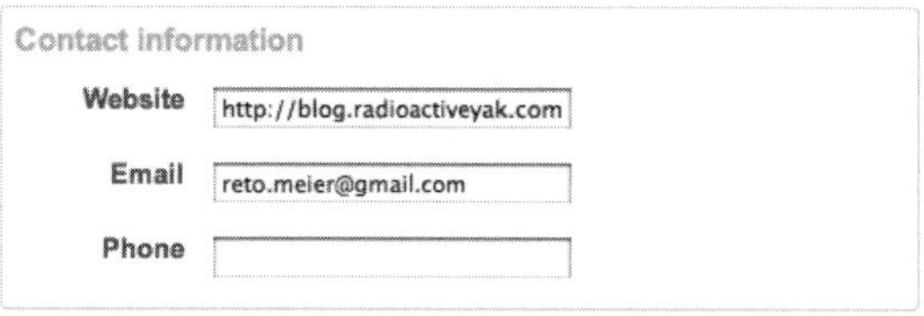

Contact information

Website   http://blog.radioactiveyak.com

Email   reto.meier@gmail.com

Phone

FIGURE 19-7

Application Reports Within the Developer Console

Once your applications are listed, your publisher page will list each application, along with the number of users and installs, average rating, and total number of ratings, as shown in Figure 19-8.

FIGURE 19-8

Your publisher page also provides a link to reader comments. Direct feedback from users is invaluable, but such feedback can be unreliable and contradictory. It's good practice to use analytics (as described later in this chapter) to reconcile user comments with statistical analysis.

The Statistics link provides access to a more detailed breakdown of your application's installation statistics, including a graph-based timeline of the application's active installs.

The statistics page also provides some analytical insight into your users, and how they compare to the average for all applications in the same category. This includes the percentage of users running on or in each:

➤ Platform release

➤ Hardware device

➤ Country and language

This information can be extremely useful for deciding where to allocate your resources, which versions of the Android platform you want to support, and in which areas your application is underperforming. For example, you might find that despite Japan being a top 3 country for applications in your category, it doesn't feature in your top 5. This would suggest that a Japanese translation might be a worthwhile investment.

Accessing Application Error Reports

The Android Developer Console provides anonymous error reports and stack traces received from users who experience crashes and freezes while running your application.

When the Android system detects a freeze or crash, users have the option to anonymously upload the error and the associated stack trace. New errors are shown on your applications listing on your publisher site list.

Clicking the Errors link will show you a summary of the errors received, as shown in Figure 19-9, indicating the number of new freezes and crashes, along with rate at which new reports are received each week.

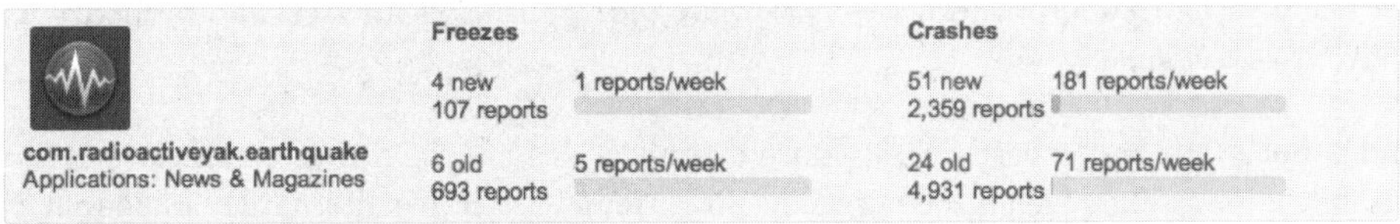

	Freezes		Crashes	
com.radioactiveyak.earthquake Applications: News & Magazines	4 new 107 reports	1 reports/week	51 new 2,359 reports	181 reports/week
	6 old 693 reports	5 reports/week	24 old 4,931 reports	71 reports/week

FIGURE 19-9

You can drill down into new or old freezes/crashes to get further details on each error, as shown in Figure 19-10. Each error is described in terms of the exception at the head of the stack, along with the class that threw it and the number/frequency of reports that match those criteria.

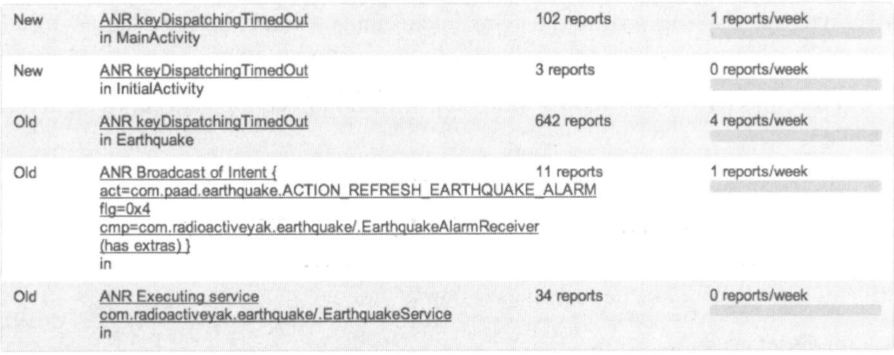

New	ANR keyDispatchingTimedOut in MainActivity	102 reports	1 reports/week
New	ANR keyDispatchingTimedOut in InitialActivity	3 reports	0 reports/week
Old	ANR keyDispatchingTimedOut in Earthquake	642 reports	4 reports/week
Old	ANR Broadcast of Intent { act=com.paad.earthquake.ACTION_REFRESH_EARTHQUAKE_ALARM flg=0x4 cmp=com.radioactiveyak.earthquake/.EarthquakeAlarmReceiver (has extras) } in	11 reports	1 reports/week
Old	ANR Executing service com.radioactiveyak.earthquake/.EarthquakeService in	34 reports	0 reports/week

FIGURE 19-10

Drilling down further into each error will provide access to any user messages submitted along with the error, the distribution of devices on which the errors occurred, and the full stack trace for each error.

These error reports are invaluable for debugging your application in the wild. With hundreds of different Android devices being used in dozens of countries and languages, it's impossible to test every variation. These error reports make it possible for you to determine which edge cases you've missed and rectify them as quickly as possible.

AN INTRODUCTION TO MONETIZING YOUR APPLICATIONS

As an open ecosystem, Android enables you to monetize your applications using whatever mechanism you choose. If you choose to distribute and monetize your applications using Google Play, three options typically are available:

➤ **Paid applications** — Charge users an upfront fee before they download and install your application.

➤   **Free applications with In-App Billing (IAB)** — Make the download and installation of the application free, but charge within the application for virtual goods, upgrades, and other value-adds.

➤   **Advertising-supported applications** — Distribute the application for free, and monetize it by displaying advertising.

Although paid applications and advertising-supported applications are the traditional mechanisms for monetizing mobile applications, IAB has emerged as an extremely effective alternative. In March 2012, 19 of the top 20 Google Play applications in terms of revenue were free downloads with IAB.

If you choose to charge for your applications on Google Play, either through upfront charges or IAB, the revenue is split between you and Google Play in the form of a transaction fee. At the time of writing this book, that revenue split is set at 70 percent for the developer.

In order to use either approach, you must first create a Google Checkout Merchant Account — you can do this from your Android publisher account. Your application listings will then include the option to set a price for the application and the items sold using IAB (described in Chapter 18).

In each case you are the application distributor and merchant of record, so you are responsible for any legal or taxation obligations associated with the sale of your application, subject to the terms described in the DDA.

You can also monetize your application using in-app advertising. The specific process required to set up advertising within your application will vary depending on the ads provider you choose.

It's beyond the scope of this book to describe the setup process for any particular advertising API; however, the general process could be described as follows:

1. Create a publisher account.

2. Download and install the associated ads SDK.

3. Update your Fragment or Activity layouts to include an add banner.

It's important to ensure that any ads included within your application are as unobtrusive as possible and don't detract significantly from the user experience of your application. It's also important to ensure that your user interaction model doesn't encourage accidental clicks on the ad banner.

In many cases, developers have chosen to offer a paid alternative (either using up-front payment or IAB) to allow users to eliminate ad banners from their applications.

APPLICATION MARKETING, PROMOTION, AND DISTRIBUTION STRATEGIES

The first step in effectively marketing and promoting your application is ensuring that you provide the full set of high quality assets for your Google Play listing.

Several promotional opportunities are available within Google Play (described in the next section). However, with more than 450,000 other applications available, it's important that you consider alternative avenues for marketing and promotion rather than simply launching your application.

While your marketing and promotion strategies will vary widely depending on your goals and budget, the following list details some of the most effective techniques to consider:

➤ **Offline cross promotion** — If you have a significant offline presence (such as a stores or branches), or a large media presence (such as within newspapers, magazines, or on TV), cross promoting your application through those channels can be a particularly effective way to increase awareness and help to ensure users trust the download. Traditional advertising techniques such as TV and newspaper advertisements can be extremely effective in raising awareness of your application.

➤ **Online cross promotion** — If you have a significant web presence, promoting your application through direct links to Google Play can be an effective way to drive downloads. If your application provides a better user experience than your mobile website, you can detect browser visitors from Android devices and direct them to Google Play to download your native app.

➤ **Third-party promotion** — Distributing a promotional video on YouTube and leveraging social networks, blogs, press releases, and online review sites can help provide positive word of mouth.

➤ **Online advertising** — Online advertising using in-app ad networks (such as AdMob) or traditional search-based advertising (such as Google AdWords) can drive significant impressions and downloads for your application.

Application Launch Strategies

Ratings and reviews can have a significant impact on your application's ranking in category lists and within Google Play search results. As a result, it can be difficult to recover from a poor launch. The following list describes some of the strategies you can use to ensure a successful launch:

➤ **Iterate on features not quality** — A poorly implemented but feature-rich application will receive worse reviews than a well-polished application that doesn't do everything. If you are using an agile approach of releasing early and often, ensure each release is of the same high quality, adding new features as part of each release. Similarly, each release should be more polished and stable than the last.

➤ **Create high quality Google Play assets** — The first impression your application makes is through its appearance in Google Play. Maximize the likelihood of that impression resulting in an installation by creating assets that represent the quality of your application.

➤ **Be honest and descriptive** — Disappointed users who find your application is not as it was described are likely to uninstall it, rate it poorly, and leave negative comments.

Promotion Within Google Play

In addition to the effect of reviews, downloads, and installs will have on your Google Play listing, there are several automated and curated lists that are used by the Google Play editorial team to highlight high quality applications.

Additionally, a small number of applications are chosen as "featured" applications, receiving priority placement in Google Play. Featured applications typically receive a significant boost in download numbers, making featuring highly prized goal.

While the criteria used to determine which applications become featured is not publicly available, there are certain criteria that have generally become associated with featured applications, including:

> ➤ **High quality and innovative** — The featured applications in Google Play act as a showcase for the platform. As a result, the easiest way to be featured is by creating a high quality application that is useful and innovative.

> ➤ **A high degree of fit-and-finish** — The listings for featured applications include all the requisite promotional assets, while the applications themselves have few bugs and a high quality user interface.

> ➤ **Broad device and platform support** — Featured applications typically support a broad range of device types and platform versions, including both handsets and tablets.

> ➤ **Use of newly released features** — Applications that leverage hardware features and software APIs from new Android platform releases offer an opportunity for the Google Play team to highlight those new features to reviewers and early adopters.

> ➤ **Consistency with the platform user experience** — Featured applications provide a compelling user experience that is consistent with the UI and interaction models offered by the Android platform.

Internationalization

At the time of writing, Google Play was available in more than 190 countries. While the exact breakdown varies by application category, in most cases more than 50 percent of application installations are downloaded from countries outside the United States on devices whose language is set to non-English.

Japan and South Korea represent the two largest consumers of applications outside the United States, while on a per capita basis South Korea, Taiwan, and Hong Kong represent the most voracious consumers of Android applications.

Externalizing all your application's string (and where appropriate, image) resources, as described in Chapter 2, makes it easy to localize your applications by providing alternative translated resources.

In addition to the application itself, Google Play provides support for adding local language titles and descriptions for your applications, as shown in Figure 19-11.

While non-native speakers may be able to use your applications, there is a very good chance that they'll search and browse Google Play using *their* native language. To maximize the discoverability of your application, it's good practice to invest in creating translations for at least the title and description of your application.

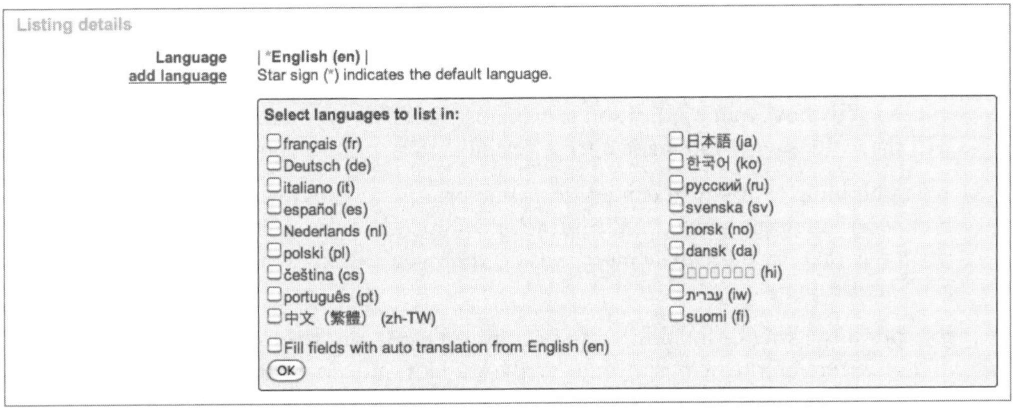

Listing details

Language add language	| *English (en) | Star sign (*) indicates the default language.

Select languages to list in:

- ☐ français (fr)
- ☐ Deutsch (de)
- ☐ italiano (it)
- ☐ español (es)
- ☐ Nederlands (nl)
- ☐ polski (pl)
- ☐ čeština (cs)
- ☐ português (pt)
- ☐ 中文（繁體）(zh-TW)
- ☐ 日本語 (ja)
- ☐ 한국어 (ko)
- ☐ русский (ru)
- ☐ svenska (sv)
- ☐ norsk (no)
- ☐ dansk (da)
- ☐ ◻◻◻◻◻◻ (hi)
- ☐ עברית (iw)
- ☐ suomi (fi)

☐ Fill fields with auto translation from English (en)

(OK)

FIGURE 19-11

> *The process of providing fully localized translations for your application can be expensive and time-consuming, so it's often useful to use the Android Developer Console statistics to prioritize the languages to localize for.*
>
> *Anecdotally, it has been found by many developers that bad translations are considered worse than no translation.*

ANALYTICS AND REFERRAL TRACKING

Mobile application analytics packages, such as Google Analytics and Flurry, can be effective tools for you to better understand who is using your application and how they are using it. Understanding this information can help you make objective decisions on where to focus your development resources.

While the statistics provided by the Android Developer Console (described earlier in this chapter) offer valuable insight into your users' language, country, and handsets, using detailed analytics can provide a much richer source of information, from which you can discover bugs, prioritize your feature list, and decide where best to allocate your development resources.

Broadly speaking, you can track three types of data within your application:

➤ **User analytics** — Understand the geographic locations (and language settings) of your users, as well as the speed of their Internet connections, their screen sizes and resolutions, and the orientation of their displays. Use this information to prioritize your translation efforts and optimize your layout and assets for different screen sizes and resolutions.

➤ **Application usage patterns** — The first step in integrating analytics is to record each Activity as you would a web site. This will help you understand the way your application is being used, and will help you to optimize your workflows in the same way you would a web site.

Taken one step further, you can record any action — which options were changed, which menu items or Action Bar actions were selected, which popup menus were displayed, if a Widget was added, and which buttons were pressed. Using this information, you can determine exactly how your application is being used, allowing you to better understand how well the assumptions you made during design match actual usage.

When building games, you can use the same process to gain insight into players' progress though the game. You can track how far people progress before quitting, identify levels that are more difficult (or easier) than you expected, and then modify your game accordingly.

➤ **Exception tracking** — In addition to printing an error into the log output, post each unique exception thrown using your analytics. Not only does this alert you to which exceptions are being thrown, you will also gain insight into their context. Specifically, you'll be able to see if there are particular devices, locations, or usage patterns that lead to particular exceptions.

While it's important to track as much analytic information as possible, care must be taken when transmitting that data back to the analytics server. Every time a new data connection is created, the wireless radio may be activated — and it will continue to draw power for up to 20 seconds on a typical 3G wireless radio. As a result it's important to bundle the analytics information you collect and queue it for transfer the next time your application transfers data, rather than transmitting it as it's collected.

Using Google Analytics for Mobile Applications

Google provides an SDK for using Google Analytics on mobile devices. You can download the Google Analytics for Mobile Apps SDK from `http://code.google.com/apis/analytics/docs/mobile/download.html#Google_Analytics_SDK_for_Android`.

> *There are no restrictions on which analytics packages you can use within your Android applications. Although this section describes the process for configuring and using Google Analytics specifically, the same general process is applicable for most alternatives.*

After downloading the SDK, you need to copy the `libGoogleAnalytics.jar` into your application's `/lib` folder and add it to the project's build path.

The Google Analytics library requires access to the Internet and the network state, so add the `INTERNET` and `ACCESS_NETWORK_STATE` permissions to your manifest:

```
<uses-permission android:name="android.permission.INTERNET" />
<uses-permission android:name="android.permission.ACCESS_NETWORK_STATE" />
```

> ⓧ *The use of Google Analytics is governed by its Terms of Service, available at* www.google.com/analytics/tos.html. *Also note that you must indicate to your users — either within the application or in your Terms of Service — that you reserve the right to anonymously track and report their activity within your application.*

Each application uses a web property ID (a *UA number*) for tracking within Google Analytics. It's generally good practice to use the Google account used to maintain your Google Play listing to control the related Google Analytics account.

To create a new UA number for your application, create a new web property at google.com/analytics, using a dummy web site URL that represents your application. It's good practice to use your reversed package name (for example, http://earthquake.paad.com). Once you've created the new property, note the UA number.

The use of Google Analytics within your application is handled by the GoogleAnalyticsTracker class. You can get an instance of this service using its getInstance method:

```
GoogleAnalyticsTracker tracker = GoogleAnalyticsTracker.getInstance();
```

To begin tracking, use the start method, passing in the UA number in the form UA-MY_CODE-[UA Code] (without the brackets) and the current context:

```
tracker.start("UA-MY_CODE-XX", this);
```

For every action you want to track, use the trackPageView method, passing in a descriptive text string alias to represent it:

```
tracker.trackPageView("/list_activity");
```

Note that the page names you're tracking are totally arbitrary, letting you create a new page for every action you want to track.

Each update is recorded in a private SQLite database, so to minimize the battery impact of activating the wireless radio to transmit analytics data, it's best practice to batch the updates and dispatch them the next time your application accesses the Internet. To send your updates to the Google Analytics server, use the dispatch method:

```
tracker.dispatch();
```

Google Analytics also supports tracking events and ecommerce transactions. Further details on their use are available at http://code.google.com/apis/analytics/docs/mobile/android.html#trackingModes.

Referral Tracking with Google Analytics

It's possible to use Google Analytics for Android to track application installation referrals using the referrer URL parameter in links to Google Play. You can track the source of each installation and associate future actions with it. This is particularly useful for evaluating the effectiveness of a particular marketing technique.

To add referral tracking to your applications, create a new `receiver` tag in your manifest:

```
<receiver
  android:name="com.google.android.apps.analytics.AnalyticsReceiver"
  android:exported="true">
  <intent-filter>
    <action android:name="com.android.vending.INSTALL_REFERRER" />
  </intent-filter>
</receiver>
```

You can generate a referral link for Google Analytics campaign tracking at `http://code.google` `.com/apis/analytics/docs/mobile/android.html#android-market-tracking`.

INDEX